WORLD TRADE ORGANIZATION

Dispute Settlement Reports

2008
Volume XI

Pages 3889-4370

CAMBRIDGE
UNIVERSITY PRESS

CAMBRIDGE UNIVERSITY PRESS
Cambridge, New York, Melbourne, Madrid, Cape Town, Singapore, São Paulo,
Delhi, Dubai, Tokyo

Cambridge University Press
The Edinburgh Building, Cambridge CB2 8RU, UK

Published in the United States of America by Cambridge University Press, New York

www.cambridge.org
Information on this title: www.cambridge.org/9780521196628

First published 2010

Printed in the United Kingdom at the University Press, Cambridge

A catalogue record for this publication is available from the British Library

Library of Congress Cataloguing in Publication data

ISBN 978-0-521-19662-8 hardback

THE WTO DISPUTE SETTLEMENT REPORTS

The *Dispute Settlement Reports* of the World Trade Organization (the "WTO") include panel and Appellate Body reports, as well as arbitration awards, in disputes concerning the rights and obligations of WTO Members under the provisions of the *Marrakesh Agreement Establishing the World Trade Organization*. The *Dispute Settlement Reports* are available in English. Volumes comprising one or more complete cases contain a cumulative list of published disputes. The cumulative list for cases that cover more than one volume is to be found in the first volume for that case.

This volume may be cited as DSR 2008:XI

TABLE OF CONTENTS

UNITED STATES – CONTINUED SUSPENSION OF OBLIGATIONS IN THE EC – HORMONES DISPUTE

Report of the Panel
WT/DS320/R

Adopted by the Dispute Settlement Body
on 14 November 2008
as Modified by the Appellate Body Report

TABLE OF CONTENTS

LIST OF ANNEXES

ANNEX A

CORRESPONDENCE FROM THE PANEL TO THE PARTIES AND WORKING PROCEDURES

Contents	
Annex A-1	Letter to the Parties dated 1 August 2005 on the Panel Decision on Open Hearings for Public Observation
Annex A-2	Working Procedures for the Panel
Annex A-3	Letter to the Parties dated 20 October 2005 on the Panel Decision on Consulting Scientific and Technical Experts
Annex A-4	Letter to the Parties dated 25 November 2005 on the Panel Decision on Certain Issues concerning the Experts' Working Procedures
Annex A-5	Working Procedures for Consultations with Scientific and/or Technical Experts

ANNEX B

REPLIES OF THE PARTIES TO QUESTIONS POSED BY THE PANEL AND OTHER PARTIES AFTER THE FIRST SUBSTANTIVE MEETING

Contents	
Annex B-1	Replies of the European Communities to questions posed by the Panel after the first substantive meeting (3 October 2005)
Annex B-2	Replies of the European Communities to questions posed by the United States after the first substantive meeting (3 October 2005)
Annex B-3	Replies of the United States to questions posed by the Panel after the first substantive meeting (3 October 2005)
Annex B-4	Replies of the United States to questions posed by the European Communities after the first substantive meeting (3 October 2005)

ANNEX C

REPLIES OF THE PARTIES TO QUESTIONS POSED BY THE PANEL AND OTHER PARTIES AFTER THE SECOND SUBSTANTIVE MEETING AND COMMENTS BY THE PARTIES ON THE OTHER PARTIES' REPLIES

ANNEX D

REPLIES OF THE SCIENTIFIC EXPERTS TO QUESTIONS POSED BY THE PANEL

ANNEX E

REPLIES OF THE CODEX ALIMENTARIUS COMMISSION, THE JOINT FAO/WHO JECFA SECRETARIAT AND THE INTERNATIONAL AGENCY FOR RESEARCH ON CANCER TO CERTAIN QUESTIONS POSED BY THE PANEL TO INTERNATIONAL ORGANIZATIONS

Contents
Annex E-1 Replies of the Codex Alimentarius Commission to certain questions posed by the Panel to international organizations
Annex E-2 Replies of the joint FAO/WHO JECFA Secretariat to certain questions posed by the Panel to international organizations
Annex E-3 Replies of the International Agency for Research on Cancer to certain questions posed by the Panel to international organizations

ANNEX F

COMMENTS BY THE PARTIES ON THE REPLIES OF THE SCIENTIFIC EXPERTS, CODEX, JECFA AND IARC TO QUESTIONS POSED BY THE PANEL AND COMMENTS BY THE PARTIES ON THE OTHER PARTIES' COMMENTS

Contents
Annex F-1 Comments by the European Communities on the replies of the scientific experts to the questions posed by the Panel (30 June 2006)
Annex F-2 Comments by the European Communities on the replies of Codex, JECFA and IARC to questions posed by the Panel (30 June 2006)
Annex F-3 Comments by the European Communities to the comments by the United States and Canada on the replies of the scientific experts to questions posed by the Panel (12 July 2006)
Annex F-4 Comments by the United States on the replies of the scientific experts, Codex, JECFA and IARC to questions posed by the Panel (30 June 2006)
Annex F-5 Comments by the United States to the comments by the European Communities on the replies of the scientific experts, Codex, JECFA and IARC to questions posed by the Panel (12 July 2006)

ANNEX G

TRANSCRIPT OF THE PANEL'S JOINT MEETING
WITH SCIENTIFIC EXPERTS ON
27-28 SEPTEMBER 2006

TABLE OF WTO CASES CITED IN THIS REPORT

Short Title	Full Case Title and Citation
Argentina – Footwear (EC)	Appellate Body Report, *Argentina – Safeguard Measures on Imports of Footwear*, WT/DS121/AB/R, adopted 12 January 2000, DSR 2000:I, 515
Argentina – Footwear (EC)	Panel Report, *Argentina – Safeguard Measures on Imports of Footwear*, WT/DS121/R, adopted 12 January 2000, as modified by Appellate Body Report, WT/DS121/AB/R, DSR 2000:II, 575
Australia – Salmon	Appellate Body Report, *Australia – Measures Affecting Importation of Salmon*, WT/DS18/AB/R, adopted 6 November 1998, DSR 1998:VIII, 3327
Australia – Salmon	Panel Report, *Australia – Measures Affecting Importation of Salmon*, WT/DS18/R and Corr.1, adopted 6 November 1998, as modified by Appellate Body Report, WT/DS18/AB/R, DSR 1998:VIII, 3407
Australia – Salmon (Article 21.5 – Canada)	Panel Report, *Australia – Measures Affecting Importation of Salmon – Recourse to Article 21.5 of the DSU by Canada*, WT/DS18/RW, adopted 20 March 2000, DSR 2000:IV, 2031
Brazil – Desiccated Coconut	Appellate Body Report, *Brazil – Measures Affecting Desiccated Coconut*, WT/DS22/AB/R, adopted 20 March 1997, DSR 1997:I, 167

Short Title	Full Case Title and Citation
Brazil – Desiccated Coconut	Panel Report, *Brazil – Measures Affecting Desiccated Coconut*, WT/DS22/R, adopted 20 March 1997, upheld by Appellate Body Report, WT/DS22/AB/R, DSR 1997:I, 189
Canada – Aircraft (Article 21.5 – Brazil)	Appellate Body Report, *Canada – Measures Affecting the Export of Civilian Aircraft – Recourse by Brazil to Article 21.5 of the DSU*, WT/DS70/AB/RW, adopted 4 August 2000, DSR 2000:IX, 4299
Canada – Aircraft (Article 21.5 – Brazil)	Panel Report, *Canada – Measures Affecting the Export of Civilian Aircraft – Recourse by Brazil to Article 21.5 of the DSU*, WT/DS70/RW, adopted 4 August 2000, as modified by Appellate Body Report, WT/DS70/AB/RW, DSR 2000:IX, 4315
Canada – Aircraft Credits and Guarantees	Panel Report, *Canada – Export Credits and Loan Guarantees for Regional Aircraft*, WT/DS222/R and Corr.1, adopted 19 February 2002, DSR 2002:III, 849
Canada – Dairy (Article 21.5 – New Zealand and US II)	Appellate Body Report, *Canada – Measures Affecting the Importation of Milk and the Exportation of Dairy Products – Second Recourse to Article 21.5 of the DSU by New Zealand and the United States*, WT/DS103/AB/RW2, WT/DS113/AB/RW2, adopted 17 January 2003, DSR 2003:I, 213
Canada – Dairy (Article 21.5 – New Zealand and US II)	Panel Report, *Canada – Measures Affecting the Importation of Milk and the Exportation of Dairy Products – Second Recourse to Article 21.5 of the DSU by New Zealand and the United States*, WT/DS103/RW2, WT/DS113/RW2, adopted 17 January 2003, as modified by Appellate Body Report, WT/DS103/AB/RW2, WT/DS113/AB/RW2, DSR 2003:I, 255
Canada – Periodicals	Appellate Body Report, *Canada – Certain Measures Concerning Periodicals*, WT/DS31/AB/R, adopted 30 July 1997, DSR 1997:I, 449
Canada – Periodicals	Panel Report, *Canada – Certain Measures Concerning Periodicals*, WT/DS31/R and Corr.1, adopted 30 July 1997, as modified by Appellate Body Report, WT/DS31/AB/R, DSR 1997:I, 481
Canada – Wheat Exports and Grain Imports	Appellate Body Report, *Canada – Measures Relating to Exports of Wheat and Treatment of Imported Grain*, WT/DS276/AB/R, adopted 27 September 2004, DSR 2004:VI, 2739

Short Title	Full Case Title and Citation
Canada – Wheat Exports and Grain Imports	Panel Report, *Canada – Measures Relating to Exports of Wheat and Treatment of Imported Grain*, WT/DS276/R, adopted 27 September 2004, upheld by Appellate Body Report, WT/DS276/AB/R, DSR 2004:VI, 2817
Chile – Alcoholic Beverages	Appellate Body Report, *Chile – Taxes on Alcoholic Beverages*, WT/DS87/AB/R, WT/DS110/AB/R, adopted 12 January 2000, DSR 2000:I, 281
Chile – Alcoholic Beverages	Panel Report, *Chile – Taxes on Alcoholic Beverages*, WT/DS87/R, WT/DS110/R, adopted 12 January 2000, as modified by Appellate Body Report, WT/DS87/AB/R, WT/DS110/AB/R, DSR 2000:I, 303
EC – Approval and Marketing of Biotech Products	Panel Report, *European Communities – Measures Affecting the Approval and Marketing of Biotech Products*, WT/DS291/R, WT/DS292/R, WT/DS293/R, Corr.1 and Add.1, 2, 3, 4, 5, 6, 7, 8 and 9, adopted 21 November 2006
EC – Asbestos	Appellate Body Report, *European Communities – Measures Affecting Asbestos and Asbestos-Containing Products*, WT/DS135/AB/R, adopted 5 April 2001, DSR 2001:VII, 3243
EC – Asbestos	Panel Report, *European Communities – Measures Affecting Asbestos and Asbestos-Containing Products*, WT/DS135/R and Add.1, adopted 5 April 2001, as modified by Appellate Body Report, WT/DS135/AB/R, DSR 2001:VIII, 3305
EC – Bananas III	Appellate Body Report, *European Communities – Regime for the Importation, Sale and Distribution of Bananas*, WT/DS27/AB/R, adopted 25 September 1997, DSR 1997:II, 591
EC – Bananas III (Article 21.5 – EC)	Panel Report, *European Communities – Regime for the Importation, Sale and Distribution of Bananas – Recourse to Article 21.5 of the DSU by the European Communities*, WT/DS27/RW/EEC and Corr.1, 12 April 1999, unadopted, DSR 1999:II, 783
EC – Bananas III (US) (Article 22.6 – EC)	Decision by the Arbitrators, *European Communities – Regime for the Importation, Sale and Distribution of Bananas – Recourse to Arbitration by the European Communities under Article 22.6 of the DSU*, WT/DS27/ARB, 9 April 1999, DSR 1999:II, 725

Short Title	Full Case Title and Citation
EC – Bed Linen (Article 21.5 – India)	Appellate Body Report, *European Communities – Anti-Dumping Duties on Imports of Cotton-Type Bed Linen from India – Recourse to Article 21.5 of the DSU by India*, WT/DS141/AB/RW, adopted 24 April 2003, DSR 2003:III, 965
EC – Bed Linen (Article 21.5 – India)	Panel Report, *European Communities – Anti-Dumping Duties on Imports of Cotton-Type Bed Linen from India – Recourse to Article 21.5 of the DSU by India*, WT/DS141/RW, adopted 24 April 2003, as modified by Appellate Body Report, WT/DS141/AB/RW, DSR 2003:IV, 1269
EC – Commercial Vessels	Panel Report, *European Communities – Measures Affecting Trade in Commercial Vessels*, WT/DS301/R, adopted 20 June 2005
EC – Hormones	Appellate Body Report, *EC Measures Concerning Meat and Meat Products (Hormones)*, WT/DS26/AB/R, WT/DS48/AB/R, adopted 13 February 1998, DSR 1998:I, 135
EC – Hormones (Canada)	Panel Report, *EC Measures Concerning Meat and Meat Products (Hormones), Complaint by Canada*, WT/DS48/R/CAN, adopted 13 February 1998, as modified by Appellate Body Report, WT/DS26/AB/R, WT/DS48/AB/R, DSR 1998:II, 235
EC – Hormones (US)	Panel Report, *EC Measures Concerning Meat and Meat Products (Hormones), Complaint by the United States*, WT/DS26/R/USA, adopted 13 February 1998, as modified by Appellate Body Report, WT/DS26/AB/R, WT/DS48/AB/R, DSR 1998:III, 699
EC – Hormones	Award of the Arbitrator, *EC Measures Concerning Meat and Meat Products (Hormones) – Arbitration under Article 21.3(c) of the DSU*, WT/DS26/15, WT/DS48/13, 29 May 1998, DSR 1998:V, 1833
EC – Hormones (Canada) (Article 22.6 – EC)	Decision by the Arbitrators, *European Communities – Measures Concerning Meat and Meat Products (Hormones), Original Complaint by Canada – Recourse to Arbitration by the European Communities under Article 22.6 of the DSU*, WT/DS48/ARB, 12 July 1999, DSR 1999:III, 1135

Short Title	Full Case Title and Citation
EC – Hormones (US) (Article 22.6 – EC)	Decision by the Arbitrators, *European Communities – Measures Concerning Meat and Meat Products (Hormones), Original Complaint by the United States – Recourse to Arbitration by the European Communities under Article 22.6 of the DSU*, WT/DS26/ARB, 12 July 1999, DSR 1999:III, 1105
EC – Tube or Pipe Fittings	Appellate Body Report, *European Communities – Anti-Dumping Duties on Malleable Cast Iron Tube or Pipe Fittings from Brazil*, WT/DS219/AB/R, adopted 18 August 2003, DSR 2003:VI, 2613
EC – Tube or Pipe Fittings	Panel Report, *European Communities – Anti-Dumping Duties on Malleable Cast Iron Tube or Pipe Fittings from Brazil*, WT/DS219/R, adopted 18 August 2003, as modified by Appellate Body Report, WT/DS219/AB/R, DSR 2003:VII, 2701
India – Patents (US)	Appellate Body Report, *India – Patent Protection for Pharmaceutical and Agricultural Chemical Products*, WT/DS50/AB/R, adopted 16 January 1998, DSR 1998:I, 9
India – Patents (US)	Panel Report, *India – Patent Protection for Pharmaceutical and Agricultural Chemical Products, Complaint by the United States*, WT/DS50/R, adopted 16 January 1998, as modified by Appellate Body Report, WT/DS50/AB/R, DSR 1998:I, 41
Japan – Agricultural Products II	Appellate Body Report, *Japan – Measures Affecting Agricultural Products*, WT/DS76/AB/R, adopted 19 March 1999, DSR 1999:I, 277
Japan – Agricultural Products II	Panel Report, *Japan – Measures Affecting Agricultural Products*, WT/DS76/R, adopted 19 March 1999, as modified by Appellate Body Report, WT/DS76/AB/R, DSR 1999:I, 315
Japan – Alcoholic Beverages II	Appellate Body Report, *Japan – Taxes on Alcoholic Beverages*, WT/DS8/AB/R, WT/DS10/AB/R, WT/DS11/AB/R, adopted 1 November 1996, DSR 1996:I, 97
Japan – Apples	Appellate Body Report, *Japan - Measures Affecting the Importation of Apples*, WT/DS245/AB/R, adopted 10 December 2003, DSR 2003:IX, 4391

Short Title	Full Case Title and Citation
Japan – Apples	Panel Report, *Japan – Measures Affecting the Importation of Apples*, WT/DS245/R, adopted 10 December 2003, upheld by Appellate Body Report, WT/DS245/AB/R, DSR 2003:IX, 4481
Japan – Apples (Article 21.5 – US)	Panel Report, *Japan – Measures Affecting the Importation of Apples – Recourse to Article 21.5 of the DSU by the United States*, WT/DS245/RW, adopted 20 July 2005
Korea – Dairy	Appellate Body Report, *Korea – Definitive Safeguard Measure on Imports of Certain Dairy Products*, WT/DS98/AB/R, adopted 12 January 2000, DSR 2000:I, 3
Korea – Dairy	Panel Report, *Korea – Definitive Safeguard Measure on Imports of Certain Dairy Products*, WT/DS98/R and Corr.1, adopted 12 January 2000, as modified by Appellate Body Report, WT/DS98/AB/R, DSR 2000:I, 49
Korea – Procurement	Panel Report, *Korea – Measures Affecting Government Procurement*, WT/DS163/R, adopted 19 June 2000, DSR 2000:VIII, 3541
US – Carbon Steel	Appellate Body Report, *United States – Countervailing Duties on Certain Corrosion-Resistant Carbon Steel Flat Products from Germany*, WT/DS213/AB/R and Corr.1, adopted 19 December 2002, DSR 2002:IX, 3779
US – Carbon Steel	Panel Report, *United States – Countervailing Duties on Certain Corrosion-Resistant Carbon Steel Flat Products from Germany*, WT/DS213/R and Corr.1, adopted 19 December 2002, as modified by Appellate Body Report, WT/DS213/AB/R and Corr.1, DSR 2002:IX, 3833
US – Certain EC Products	Appellate Body Report, *United States – Import Measures on Certain Products from the European Communities*, WT/DS165/AB/R, adopted 10 January 2001, DSR 2001:I, 373
US – Certain EC Products	Panel Report, *United States – Import Measures on Certain Products from the European Communities*, WT/DS165/R and Add.1, adopted 10 January 2001, as modified by Appellate Body Report, WT/DS165/AB/R, DSR 2001:II, 413
US – FSC	Appellate Body Report, *United States – Tax Treatment for "Foreign Sales Corporations"*, WT/DS108/AB/R, adopted 20 March 2000, DSR 2000:III, 1619

Short Title	Full Case Title and Citation
US – FSC	Panel Report, *United States – Tax Treatment for "Foreign Sales Corporations"*, WT/DS108/R, adopted 20 March 2000, as modified by Appellate Body Report, WT/DS108/AB/R, DSR 2000:IV, 1675
US – Gambling	Appellate Body Report, *United States – Measures Affecting the Cross-Border Supply of Gambling and Betting Services*, WT/DS285/AB/R and Corr.1, adopted 20 April 2005, DSR 2005:XII, 5663
US – Gambling	Panel Report, *United States – Measures Affecting the Cross-Border Supply of Gambling and Betting Services*, WT/DS285/R, adopted 20 April 2005, as modified by Appellate Body Report, WT/DS285/AB/R, DSR 2005:XII, 5797
US – Hot-Rolled Steel	Appellate Body Report, *United States – Anti-Dumping Measures on Certain Hot-Rolled Steel Products from Japan*, WT/DS184/AB/R, adopted 23 August 2001, DSR 2001:X, 4697
US – Hot-Rolled Steel	Panel Report, *United States – Anti-Dumping Measures on Certain Hot-Rolled Steel Products from Japan*, WT/DS184/R, adopted 23 August 2001 modified by Appellate Body Report, WT/DS184/AB/R, DSR 2001:X, 4769
US – Line Pipe	Appellate Body Report, *United States – Definitive Safeguard Measures on Imports of Circular Welded Carbon Quality Line Pipe from Korea*, WT/DS202/AB/R, adopted 8 March 2002, DSR 2002:IV, 1403
US – Line Pipe	Panel Report, *United States – Definitive Safeguard Measures on Imports of Circular Welded Carbon Quality Line Pipe from Korea*, WT/DS202/R, adopted 8 March 2002, as modified by Appellate Body Report, WT/DS202/AB/R, DSR 2002:IV, 1473
US – Offset Act (Byrd Amendment)	Appellate Body Report, *United States – Continued Dumping and Subsidy Offset Act of 2000*, WT/DS217/AB/R, WT/DS234/AB/R, adopted 27 January 2003, DSR 2003:I, 375
US – Offset Act (Byrd Amendment)	Panel Report, *United States – Continued Dumping and Subsidy Offset Act of 2000*, WT/DS217/R, WT/DS234/R, adopted 27 January 2003, as modified by Appellate Body Report, WT/DS217/AB/R, WT/DS234/AB/R, DSR 2003:II, 489

Short Title	Full Case Title and Citation
US – Section 211 Appropriations Act	Appellate Body Report, *United States – Section 211 Omnibus Appropriations Act of 1998*, WT/DS176/AB/R, adopted 1 February 2002, DSR 2002:II, 589
US – Section 211 Appropriations Act	Panel Report, *United States – Section 211 Omnibus Appropriations Act of 1998*, WT/DS176/R, adopted 1 February 2002, as modified by Appellate Body Report, WT/DS176/AB/R, DSR 2002:II, 683
US – Section 301 Trade Act	Panel Report, *United States – Sections 301-310 of the Trade Act of 1974*, WT/DS152/R, adopted 27 January 2000, DSR 2000:II, 815
US – Shrimp	Appellate Body Report, *United States – Import Prohibition of Certain Shrimp and Shrimp Products*, WT/DS58/AB/R, adopted 6 November 1998, DSR 1998:VII, 2755
US – Shrimp	Panel Report, *United States – Import Prohibition of Certain Shrimp and Shrimp Products*, WT/DS58/R and Corr.1, adopted 6 November 1998, as modified by Appellate Body Report, WT/DS58/AB/R, DSR 1998:VII, 2821
US – Softwood Lumber VI	Panel Report, *United States – Investigation of the International Trade Commission in Softwood Lumber from Canada*, WT/DS277/R, adopted 26 April 2004, DSR 2004:VI, 2485
US – Upland Cotton	Appellate Body Report, *United States – Subsidies on Upland Cotton*, WT/DS267/AB/R, adopted 21 March 2005
US – Upland Cotton	Panel Report, *United States – Subsidies on Upland Cotton*, WT/DS267/R, and Corr.1, adopted 21 March 2005, as modified by Appellate Body Report, WT/DS267/AB/R
US – Wool Shirts and Blouses	Appellate Body Report, *United States – Measure Affecting Imports of Woven Wool Shirts and Blouses from India*, WT/DS33/AB/R and Corr.1, adopted 23 May 1997, DSR 1997:I, 323
US – Wool Shirts and Blouses	Panel Report, *United States – Measure Affecting Imports of Woven Wool Shirts and Blouses from India*, WT/DS33/R, adopted 23 May 1997, upheld by Appellate Body Report, WT/DS33/AB/R, DSR 1997:I, 343

I. INTRODUCTION

A. *Request for Consultations and Request for the Establishment of a Panel*

1.1   On 8 November 2004, the European Communities requested consultations with the United States pursuant to Article XXII:1 of the General Agreement on Tariffs and Trade 1994 ("GATT 1994") and Article 4 of the Understanding on Rules and Procedures Governing the Settlement of Disputes ("DSU") regarding the United States' continued suspension of concessions and other obligations under the covered agreements, after the European Communities' adoption of Directive 2003/74/EC on 22 September 2003 and its notification to the Dispute Settlement Body (DSB) that it has fully implemented the recommendations and rulings of the DSB in the dispute *European Communities – Measures Concerning Meat and Meat Products (Hormones)* (*EC – Hormones*). The consultation request was circulated in document WT/DS320/1 dated 10 November 2004. The consultations were held on 16 December 2004 but the parties failed to reach a mutually satisfactory resolution of the dispute.

1.2   On 14 January 2005, the European Communities requested the establishment of a Panel pursuant to Articles 4.7 and 6 of the DSU, as well as Article XXIII of the GATT 1994.[1]

B. *Establishment and Composition of the Panel*

1.3   At its meeting on 17 February 2005, the DSB established a Panel pursuant to the request of the European Communities in document WT/DS320/6, in accordance with Article 6 of the DSU (WT/DSB/M/183), with standard terms of reference as below:

> "To examine, in the light of the relevant provisions of the covered agreements cited by the European Communities in document WT/DS320/6, the matter referred to the DSB by the European Communities in that document, and to make such findings as will assist the DSB in making the recommendations or in giving the rulings provided for in those agreements."[2]

---

[1]   WT/DS320/6.
[2]   WT/DS320/7.

1.4   On 27 May 2005, the European Communities requested the Director-General to determine the composition of the Panel, pursuant to paragraph 7 of Article 8 of the DSU. On 6 June 2005, the Director-General accordingly composed the Panel as follows:

> Chairman: Mr. Tae-yul Cho
> Members: Mr. William Ehlers
>   Ms. Claudia Orozco

1.5   Australia, Brazil, Canada, China, India, Mexico, New Zealand, Norway and Chinese Taipei, have reserved their rights to participate in the Panel proceedings as a third party.

C.   Panel Proceedings

1.6   At the joint request of the parties, on 1 August 2005, the Panel decided that its meetings at which the parties were invited to appear, would be open for public observation through closed-circuit broadcast, provided the Secretariat could maintain satisfactory logistical arrangements. The Panel, however, after consulting the third parties, also decided that the session with the third parties would remain closed.[3] The Panel notified the DSB Chairman of this decision on the same day.[4] The Panel held its first joint substantive meeting with the parties to this dispute and the parties to the dispue on *Canada – Continued Suspension of Obligations to the EC – Hormones Dispute* (WT/DS321) on 12-15 September 2005. The meeting with the parties was opened for public observation through closed-circuit broadcast. The Panel also met with the third parties in a closed special session on 14 September 2005.

1.7   The Panel in this dispute also decided to seek advice from scientific and technical experts after consultation with the parties on 20 October 2005.[5] After consulting the parties, it finalized its Working Procedures for Consultations with Scientific and/or Technical Experts on 25 November 2005.[6] It selected six scientific and technical experts in consultation with parties, sought their advice as well as advice from Codex Alimentarius Commission (Codex), the Joint FAO/WHO Expert Committee on Food Additives (JECFA), and the International Agency for Research on Cancer (IARC) on scientific and technical ques-

---

[3]   See Annex A-1, Letter to the Parties dated 1 August 2005 on the Panel Decision on Open Hearings for Public Observation. Annex A-2, Working Procedures for the Panel.
[4]   WT/DS320/8.
[5]   Annex A-3, Letter to the Parties dated 20 October 2005 on the Panel Decision on Consulting Scientific and Technical Experts.
[6]   Annex A-4, Letter to the Parties dated 25 November 2005 on the Panel Decision on Certain Issues concerning the Experts' Working Procedures; Annex A-5, Working Procedures for Consultations with Scientific and/or Technical Experts.

tions in writing. The Panel also met with the six experts and four representatives from Codex, JECFA and IARC in the presence of the parties to this dispute and the parties to the dispute on *Canada – Continued Suspension of Obligations to the EC – Hormones Dispute* (WT/DS321) on 27-28 September 2006. The expert from IARC served both as an individual scientific expert and as the representative of the IARC. The Panel held its joint second substantive meeting with the parties on 2-3 October 2006. These meetings were also open for public observation through a closed-circuit broadcast.

1.8   On 31 July 2007, the Panel issued its interim report to the parties. On 28 September and 19 October 2007, the Panel received comments from the parties on the interim report. Neither of the parties requested an interim review meeting. On 21 December 2007, the Panel issued its final report to the parties.

II.   FACTUAL ASPECTS

A.   History of the Dispute

2.1   On 13 February 1998, the Dispute Settlement Body ("DSB") adopted the Panel and Appellate Body reports in *EC – Hormones*. In doing so, the DSB recommended that the European Communities bring the measures at issue into conformity with WTO rules. The Arbitrator appointed pursuant to Article 21.3(c) of the DSU determined that the European Communities should have a "reasonable period of time" up to 13 May 1999 to comply with the recommendations. On 26 July 1999, the United States obtained from the DSB the authorization to suspend obligations up to the level of 116.8 million US Dollars per year. The arbitrators acting pursuant to Article 22.6 of the DSU had previously determined this level to be equivalent to the level of nullification or impairment (Article 22.4 of the DSU) suffered by the United States at the time of its recourse to arbitration in May 1999. On 29 July 1999 and pursuant to the DSB's authorization, the United States introduced import duties in excess of bound rates on imports from the European Communities by imposing a 100 % *ad valorem* rate of duty on a list of articles that are the products of certain EC Member States.[7]

2.2   The original measures in the *EC – Hormones (US)* dispute were provided in Directive 96/22/EC, which prohibited the administering to farm animals of substances having a *thyrostatic* action or substances having an *oestrogenic, androgenic,* or *gestagenic* action as well as the placing on market of meat from such animals.[8] On 22 September 2003, the European Communities adopted Di-

---

[7]   These measures were published in the Federal Register Notice in Vol. 64, No. 143 of 27 July 1999.
[8]   WT/DS26/R/USA, paras. 2.1-2.5.

rective 2003/74/EC of the European Parliament and of the Council amending
Council Directive 96/22/EC concerning the prohibition on the use in stockfarming of certain substances having a hormonal or thyrostatic action and of beta-
agonists. The Directive was published and entered into force on 14 October
2003. It provides for a permanent prohibition on oestradiol-17β and a provisional prohibition on testosterone, progesterone, trenbolone acetate, zeranol and
melengestrol acetate.

2.3   Prior to the adoption of the Directive 2003/74/EC, and in order to comply
with the recommendations and rulings of the DSB and the covered agreements,
the European Communities initiated and funded a number of specific scientific
studies and research projects for the purpose of conducting risk assessment (17
in total). The Scientific Committee on Veterinary Measures relating to Public
Health (SCVPH), an independent experts committee established under EC legislation, reviewed the results of these studies and other publicly available information as well as the data it collected from various sources including
CODEX/JECFA, and published its opinion entitled "Assessment of Potential
Risks to Human Health from Hormones Residues in Bovine meat and Meat
Products" ("the 1999 SCVPH Opinion") on 30 April 1999. The SCVPH subse-
quently reviewed this Opinion on two occasions and adopted review reports on 3
May 2000 (" the 2000 SCVPH Opinion") and on 10 April 2002 (the 2002
SCVPH Opinion"). The SCVPH Opinions address six hormonal substances:
*oestradiol-17β, testosterone, progesterone, trenbolone acetate, zeranol and
melengestrol acetate.* [9]

2.4   In light of these Opinions, which the European Communities contends are
risk assessments, the European Communities prohibited the placing on the market of meat and meat products from animals that have been treated with oestra-
diol-17β for growth promotion purposes on the grounds that there was a substantial body of evidence showing that its residues are both carcinogenic and
genotoxic. With respect to testosterone, progesterone, trenbolone acetate,
zeranol and melengestrol acetate, the European Communities introduced the
same measure on a provisional basis on the grounds that the available pertinent
scientific information reflected in the above-mentioned Opinions, showed the
existence of risks but all the information and data necessary to conduct a more
objective and complete risk assessment were insufficient or missing. [10]

2.5   On 27 October 2003, the European Communities notified to the DSB the
adoption, publication and entry into force of the Directive as well as the preceding scientific Opinions. In the same communication, the European Communities
explained that it considered itself to have fully implemented the recommenda-

---

[9]   See Request for the Establishment of a Panel by the European Communities, WT/DS320/6.
[10]   *Ibid. See also*, EC's second written submission, para. 139.

tions and rulings of the DSB in the *EC – Hormones* dispute, and as a consequence, it considers the United States' suspension of concessions vis-à-vis the European Communities to be no longer justified.[11]

2.6   The United States raised doubt in the DSB meeting held on 7 November 2003 on whether the new Directive was based on science and on whether the European Communities implemented the DSB's recommendations and rulings as well as the European Communities' obligations under the *SPS Agreement*.[12] The United States continued to impose retaliatory duties on certain products from the European Communities.

B.   Measure at Issue

2.7   The measure challenged by the European Communities is the suspension of concessions and other obligations under the covered agreements, continued without recourse to the procedures under the DSU, after the European Communities' adoption of Directive 2003/74/EC on 22 September 2003 amending Council Directive 96/22/EC concerning the prohibition on the use in stock-farming of certain substances having a hormonal or thyrostatic action and of beta-agonists. The measure is provided in the Federal Register Notice in Vol. 64, No. 143 of 27 July 1999 and is enforced as of 29 July 1999. The EC's Directive 2003/74/EC was published and entered into force on 14 October 2003. The EC stated in its notification to the Dispute Settlement Body (DSB) that it had fully implemented the recommendations and rulings of the DSB in the dispute *European Communities – Measures concerning Meat and Meat Products (Hormones)* (WT/DS26/AB/R, WT/DS26/R/USA).[13]

III.   PARTIES' REQUESTS FOR FINDINGS AND RECOMMENDATIONS

3.1   The European Communities requests that the Panel find that the United States continued suspension of concessions and related obligations under the covered agreements:

(a)   violates Article 23.2(a), read together with Article 21.5 and Article 23.1 of the DSU;

---

[11]   *European Communities – Measures Concerning Meat and Meat Products (Hormones)*, Communication from the European Communities, WT/DS26/22, WT/DS48/20, 28 October 2003.
[12]   DSB, *Minutes of Meeting held on 7 November 2003*, WT/DSB/M/157, 18 December 2003, paras. 29-30.
[13]   WT/DS320/6. WT/DS26/22.

(b)   violates Article 23.1 of the DSU read in conjunction with Articles 22.8 and 3.7 of the DSU; and

(c)   violates Articles I and II of the GATT 1994.[14]

3.2   In the alternative, should the Panel find no violation of Article 23 of the DSU, the European Communities requests the Panel to find that the United States measure violates Article 22.8 of the DSU and Articles I and II of the GATT 1994.[15]

3.3   The United States requests the Panel to find that:

(a)   the European Communities has failed to demonstrate that the United States has breached Article 22.8 of the DSU, and that the United States continued suspension of concessions to the European Communities is consistent with the requirements of that provision;

(b)   the United States has not breached Articles 3.7, 21.5, 23.1 or 23.2(a) of the DSU; and

(c)   the United States has not breached Articles I or II of the GATT 1994.[16]

IV.   ARGUMENTS OF THE PARTIES

A.   Introduction

4.1   The arguments of the parties are set out in their written submissions to the Panel and in their oral statements made during Panel meetings, as well as in their written replies to questions from the Panel. This Section presents a summary of the arguments of the parties based on the executive summaries prepared by the parties where such summaries were made available to the Panel.

B.   Parties' Requests and Arguments on Opening the Panel Meeting for Public Observation

4.2   At the Panel's organizational meeting with parties on 13 June 2005, the parties requested that the Panel hold open meetings with the parties in this dispute. The Panel posed written questions to the parties and the third parties regarding this joint request after its organizational meeting. The parties answered these questions in writing on 20 June 2005 and 7 July 2005.

---

[14]   EC's first written submission, para. 149.
[15]   EC's first written submission, para. 150.
[16]   US's first written submission, para. 210.

1.   Arguments of the European Communities

(a)   Whether panels are permitted to open hearings under Article 12 (including Appendix 3), Articles 14.1 and 17.10 of the DSU

4.3   The European Communities argues that open hearings are permissible at the panel level. The European Communities submits that Appendix 3, second paragraph, first sentence of the DSU excludes public access to the panel hearings, but this rule is not obligatory, as Article 12.1 of the DSU states: "Panels shall follow the Working Procedures in Appendix 3 unless the panel decides otherwise after consulting the parties to the dispute." In the European Communities' view, it is therefore permissible for a panel to adopt, under the procedure of Article 12.1 of the DSU, working procedures that foresee open hearings.

4.4   The European Communities also argues that this conclusion is not affected by Article 14.1 of the DSU. The term "deliberations" under Article 14.1 of the DSU designates the part of the panel's work where it internally discusses the case, including the decision it intends to pronounce in its report and the supporting reasoning. This is the ordinary meaning of this term, in which it is also used in other systems of adjudication, and the French ("délibérations") and Spanish versions ("deliberaciones") fully coincide with this meaning. These deliberations take place in the presence of the Secretariat team working on the dispute, but without the parties. The term "deliberations" does not cover the meetings with the parties, for which different terminology is used in Appendix 3 of the DSU. The context supports this reading because everything that is addressed in the three paragraphs of Article 14 of the DSU relates to the independent work which the panel conducts alone, in the absence of the parties. Had the drafters of the DSU wanted to exclude open panel hearings, they would have used different language in Article 14.1 of the DSU. They would not have addressed this question solely in the Appendix 3 working procedures from which a panel may depart, as Article 12.1 expressly stipulates.

4.5   In the European Communities' view, this interpretation is also corroborated by the use of the term "proceedings" in Article 17.10 of the DSU which appears to be broader. Meaning must therefore be given to the DSU negotiators' deliberate choice of the term "deliberations" in Article 14.1 of the DSU.

4.6   The European Communities argues that such interpretation is the long-standing position of several Members and has never been rejected by any WTO Member in any dispute. WTO Members have repeatedly stated that the DSU rules on panel procedures are flexible and allow the provision of open hearings (Articles 14.1, 12.1, Appendix 3). Obviously, since a panel is obliged to consult the parties before departing from the working procedures suggested in Appendix 3, the parties' position carries significant weight for the panel's decision. The EC considers that in the present case where all the parties have agreed to open hearings, the Panel should accommodate the parties' request. Article 18.2 of the DSU also provides context and supports this position as it implies that parties are entitled to "waive" the confidentiality of their positions.

(b) Legal implications of open hearings on covered persons under the Rules of Conduct

4.7   The European Communities considers that no legal issues arise under the Rules of Conduct. These Rules state in Section II, paragraph 1 that each covered person "shall respect the confidentiality of proceedings" (see also Section VII, paragraph 1), and also that "[t]hese Rules shall in no way modify the rights and obligations of Members under the DSU nor the rules and procedures therein." In the European Communities view, the Rules of Conduct are and remain fully binding on all covered persons in this dispute, even if the hearings are opened to the public. Simultaneously, the Rules of Conduct do not prevent the panel from fulfilling its task under the DSU and in accordance with the procedural rules contained therein, which permit public hearings. The Rules of Conduct expressly state that they do not modify these DSU rules.

4.8   The European Communities also considers that Article 18.2 of the DSU again provides context in that it shows that the parties are entitled to "waive" the confidentiality of their positions. The Panel's deliberations will in any event not be affected by the opening and remain confidential, as required by Article 14.1 of the DSU.

(c) Systemic and political impact of opening hearings

4.9   The European Communities is of the view that there are no implications for WTO Members who are not parties to this dispute, notably the parties to another dispute remain able to adhere to their preference, if any, not to open the hearings in their dispute. Opening a hearing for observers who will remain completely passive during the session would not change anything about the intergovernmental character of the WTO, nor would it impair the chances to reach a mutually agreed solution, as preferred by the DSU (Article 3.7), if the parties jointly request the hearings to be open, in line with their general policy to apply transparency where the DSU rules allow (for instance by making public their submissions). Also, there are no implications for third parties and accordingly there is no need to consult them before the Panel adopts its working procedures because the parties have jointly requested that the public be excluded from the third parties' session during the presentation by a third party who prefers this. Thus, opening hearings to public observation will not affect third parties beyond the extent to which they themselves agree. The DSU is clear in that the panel must consult the parties, not the third parties, before adopting Working Procedures in departing from Appendix 3.

4.10   The European Communities also states that consulting the DSB and General Council Chairs or the Director-General before opening the hearing for public observation does not seem necessary because under the DSU the Panel has the power to take decisions regarding its Working Procedures and is required to fulfil its task in full independence. If all parties are in agreement on this question of working procedures, the Panel should accommodate their request if the parties consider that this is part of the best way to "secure a positive solution to the dispute", which is the aim of the dispute settlement mechanism (Article 3.7 of the DSU).

(d)   What procedures can be adopted to protect confidential information in an open hearing

4.11   The European Communities indicates that it does not expect that confidential information will be submitted in this dispute. Should this nevertheless happen, one could easily apply appropriate means to close the portion of any meeting where confidential information is discussed.

4.12   The European Communities does not consider that there is any issue of confidentiality in relation to information submitted by other Members or non-Members (under Article 13 of the DSU), unless the confidentiality requirement of the last sentence of Article 13.1 of the DSU applies, in which case the corresponding portion of any meeting where this information is discussed could be closed.

4.13   With respect to the third party session, the European Communities considers that each third party should decide whether to open the part of the third party session dealing with that third party's statement.

2.   Arguments of the United States

(a)   Whether panels are permitted to open hearings under Article 12 (including the Appendix 3), Articles 14.1 and 17.10 of the DSU

4.14   The United States notes that in the Panel's organizational meeting held on June 13, 2005, the United States, Canada and the European Communities agreed that the panel meetings in these disputes should be opened to interested Members and the public. In the view of the United States, open panel meetings are permissible under the DSU, including under Appendix 3 thereto.

4.15   The United States argues that whether substantive meetings of the Panel are open is not affected by Article 14.1 of the DSU, which provides that the deliberations of a panel shall be confidential. The United States agrees that any deliberations among the three panel members must be confidential. However,

Article 14.1 of the DSU does not apply to the meetings of the panel with the parties. Therefore, DSU Article 14.1 does not prohibit opening panel meetings to the public.

4.16   The United States also argues that although Paragraph 2 of Appendix 3 states that a panel "shall meet in closed session", Article 12.1 of the DSU states that a panel may depart from the working procedures in Appendix 3 after consulting with the parties. In other words, the Panel has the ability to remove any provision of Appendix 3 that might be perceived as an impediment to accommodating the parties' decision to make their statements public by allowing the public to observe them as they are delivered. Second, Article 18.2 of the DSU, which is echoed in Paragraph 3 of Appendix 3, explicitly provides that "[n]othing in this Understanding shall preclude a party to a dispute from disclosing statements of its own positions to the public." Appendix 3 is part of the DSU and so, per Article 18.2, nothing in Appendix 3 prevents a party from disclosing statements of its own position to the public. Since each of the parties to this dispute agrees to the opening of panel meetings to the public, the United States considers that the parties should not be prevented from allowing the public to view the meetings at which the parties present their positions. The United States believes that the best way for the United States to disclose its statements to the public is to allow the public to observe those statements as they are being made.

4.17   The United States also argues that Article 17 of the DSU pertains to the Appellate Review process. As such, its provisions, including Article 17.10, do not apply to a determination of whether a panel can or will open its meetings to the public. A decision to open a panel meeting to the public would not have any bearing on any subsequent decision to open the Appellate Body proceedings to the public. Therefore, Article 17.10 of the DSU should not act as a bar to open panel meetings. The United States also believes that this dispute will have a substantial public interest, and permitting the public to observe the proceedings and be able to see first-hand the professional, impartial and objective manner in which they are conducted can only further enhance the credibility of the result.

(b)   Legal implications of open hearings on covered persons under the Rules of Conduct

4.18   The United States argues that the provisions in the Rules of Conduct that require panelists to maintain confidentiality apply only to information that is in fact confidential. For information that is not confidential in the first place, there is no confidentiality to be "maintained." However, the parties to this dispute are affirmatively exercising their rights under Article 18.2 of the DSU to make their written and oral statements public. The parties have also agreed to open to the public the panel meetings in which these oral statements will be read and written submissions discussed. The parties believe that they have the ability under the DSU to have open proceedings and that nothing prevents the Panel from adapting its working procedures to reflect that ability. The United States considers that the opening of Panel meetings would not include the deliberations of the Panel, which would remain confidential under Article 14.1 of the DSU.

4.19 The United States further argues that while the Rules of Conduct state that covered persons "shall respect the confidentiality of proceedings,"[17] they also clarify that "[t]hese Rules shall in no way modify the rights and obligations of Members under the DSU nor the rules and procedures therein."[18] As already noted by the United States in its response to the Panel's question, the procedural rules of the DSU permit public hearings. Therefore, the confidentiality provisions of the Rules of Conduct do not prevent the opening of panel meetings to the public.

(c)   Systemic and political impact of opening hearings

4.20 The United States argues that opening the panel meetings to the public is a natural extension of the discretion provided to the parties in Article 18.2 of the DSU for a party to disclose its statements to the public. In this dispute, the parties have agreed to waive their rights to keep written and oral statements confidential, and to open the meetings in which these submissions will be discussed to the public. It is not necessary or appropriate to consult the chairpersons of the Dispute Settlement Body ("DSB"), the General Council or the DSB Special Session, or the WTO Director-General, on whether or not panel meetings in this dispute will or can be opened to the public. In the view of the United States, Article 12.1 of the DSU provides for panels to adapt their working procedures after consulting the parties. Article 12.1 nowhere refers to consulting other WTO bodies and such consultation could be viewed as setting an unfortunate precedent since panels routinely adopt working procedures beyond or different from those in Appendix 3.

4.21 The United States believes that the third parties should be consulted, but only to determine if they would also choose to open portions of the third party session with the Panel to the public. The third parties need not be consulted regarding the opening of panel meetings with the parties.

4.22 The United States considers that opening panel meetings to the public will have a positive impact on the perception of the WTO dispute settlement system, but does not foresee a decision in this dispute to open panel meetings as having a political or systemic impact. For example, the opening of panel meet-

---

[17]   *Rules of Conduct for the Understanding on the Rules and Procedures Governing the Settlement of Disputes* ("Rules of Conduct"), II.1; *see* Rules of Conduct, VII.1 ("Each covered person shall at all times maintain the confidentiality of dispute settlement deliberations and proceedings.").
[18]   Rules of Conduct, II.1.

ings in this dispute would not prejudice the ability of parties to other disputes to choose to open, or keep confidential, their respective panel meetings.

(d) What procedures can be adopted to protect confidential information in an open hearing

4.23 The United States believes that any portions of the Panel meetings dealing with confidential information would not be open to the public. Additional safeguards to provide against the disclosure of confidential information could be included in the working procedures. The United States notes that the issue of access to confidential information is not limited to the question of open panel meetings, but is one that panels have had to deal with in a number of disputes. For example, if meetings are broadcast electronically, it may be possible to include a delay in the broadcast to ensure that there would be no inadvertent disclosure of confidential information.

4.24 The United States argues that the third parties would retain their ability to decide whether their submissions and statements are public. Any confidential statements would not be broadcast. It also considers that it is uncertain what information would come from a Member that is not a party or a third party to the dispute, but any such information that is confidential would be respected in the same manner as any other confidential information.

C. First Written Submission of the European Communities

1. Introduction

4.25 This case is about procedural obligations under the DSU of Members that continue to apply the suspension of concessions or other obligations after almost two years despite the proper notification by the responding party that it has adopted the necessary measures to implement the DSB recommendations and rulings. In the alternative, the European Communities makes conditional substantive claims under Article 22.8 of the DSU and Articles I:1 and II of the GATT 1994.

2. Factual aspects

4.26 Following an authorization by the DSB, the United States suspended tariff concessions and other related obligations up to the level of US$ 116.8 million. Subsequently, the European Communities implemented the original DSB recommendations and rulings by adopting Council Directive 2003/74/EC. However, the United States continues to suspend concessions and related obligations against certain products originating in the European Communities based on a unilateral determination that the EC's implementation measure is insufficient to comply with the DSB recommendations and rulings.

3.   *Legal arguments: Part I – Violation of Articles 23, 21.5, 22.8 and 3.7 of the DSU and Articles I and II of the GATT*

(a)   The structure of Article 23 of the DSU

4.27   Article 23 of the DSU lays down the fundamental principle that the dispute settlement system of the WTO is the exclusive means to redress any violation of any provision of the WTO Agreement. Any attempt to seek "redress" can take place only in the institutional framework of the WTO and pursuant to the rules and procedures of the DSU. This has been confirmed in *US – Section 301 Trade Act* and *US – Certain EC Products*.

4.28   Article 23.1 of the DSU contains a general obligation to follow the rules and procedures of the DSU whereas Article 23.2 of the DSU lists a number of "specific and clearly-defined forms of prohibited unilateral action". The relationship between the two paragraphs has two distinguishing features: One, Article 23.2 of the DSU has to be read in the context of the first paragraph ("in such cases"), that is, it has to be established that the Member's action is performed with a view to redressing a WTO violation. Two, the specific forms described in paragraph 2 do not exhaust the list of prohibited unilateral action. There is a relationship of *lex specialis* and *lex generalis* which implies, on the one hand, that whenever there is a violation of a specific case in Paragraph 2 of Article 23, there always is also a violation of Paragraph 1 of that provision; and on the other hand, that a particular conduct that may not come under the specific cases listed in Paragraph 2 of Article 23, may still constitute a violation under Paragraph 1.

(b)   Applicability of Article 23 – Article 23.1 of the DSU: Seeking the redress of a WTO violation

4.29   The meaning of "seeking the redress of a violation" under Article 23.1 of the DSU has been extensively discussed by previous panels, i.e. *US – Section 301 Trade Act* and *US – Certain EC Products*. The "violation" with regard to which redress is sought need not be one that has been identified as such by the relevant WTO bodies. It suffices if it is perceived as being one by the Member in question. The suspension of concessions or other obligations is a means of "redress." Indeed it is the very means the WTO system envisages as a last resort remedy to WTO violations according to Articles 3.7 and 22.1 of the DSU.

4.30   It is obvious that when it suspended concessions in July 1999, the United States was seeking to redress a (WTO-determined) violation. Back then, the United States reacted to the European Communities' failure to implement, within the reasonable period of time, the DSB recommendations in the *EC – Hormones* case. It requested and obtained a DSB authorisation under Article 22.2 (respectively 22.7) of the DSU, following which the United States decided on the imposition of additional duties at a rate of 100% *ad valorem* for the listed imports. The United States' way of proceeding back then is the very example of a "seeking to redress a WTO violation" in line with the rules and procedures of the DSU.

4.31   There can equally be no doubt that, if the United States is continuing the suspension of concessions to this day despite the European Communities' adoption of an implementation measure, it does so because it is still seeking to redress a WTO violation. This can be deduced from the fact that the July 1999 measure of applying duties in excess of bound rates is being continued without any modification. Because that measure was imposed as "a result of the EC's failure to implement the recommendations and rulings of the WTO," and since the United States has neither abolished nor changed the measure, nor modified its reasons for the imposition, the United States is obviously of the view that the EC's failure to implement the recommendations and rulings of the WTO still persists. Indeed, the continuation of the suspension of concessions is an unequivocal indication that the United States believes that there continues to be a violation. Otherwise it would have ended the suspension of concessions in accordance with its obligations under Article 22.8 of the DSU. Moreover, this is the explicit view the United States has formally taken in the DSB and in various official statements.

(c)   Violation of Articles 23.2(a) and 21.5 and of Article 23.1 of the DSU

4.32   This conduct of the United States is contrary to the specific prohibition of unilateral conduct set out in Article 23.2(a) of the DSU. Instead of seeking redress of the perceived continued failure of the European Communities to implement the DSB's recommendations and rulings through the continued suspension of concessions, the United States should have introduced a compliance procedure under Article 21.5 of the DSU. Because it has not done so, it has violated the specific prohibition of unilateral conduct set out in Article 23.2(a) of the DSU. This violation of Article 23.2(a) and 21.5 constitutes at the same time a violation of Article 23.1 of the DSU.

4.33   As the Panel in *US – Section 301 Trade Act* has noted, the following conditions need to be fulfilled in order to find a violation of Article 23.2(a) of the DSU. First, given the "chapeau" of Article 23.2, it needs to be established that there is "such a case", namely that a Member is seeking to redress a WTO violation. This is the case here.

4.34   Second, Article 23.2(a) of the DSU requires that a Member has made a "determination to the effect that a WTO violation has occurred." The ordinary meaning of the term "determination," has been noted by the Panels in *US – Section 301 Trade Act* and *US – Certain EC Products.* Such a decision need not have a specific form, and can be inferred from action. The suspension of concessions or other obligations is the very means (albeit of last resort) to react to a violation and therefore necessarily implies a decision that there is a violation. That such a decision bears consequences in WTO trade relations hardly requires any explanation. The present case is similar to the situation in *US – Certain EC Products*. Again, the action in question is the suspension of concessions and related obligations. In contrast to the above case, nevertheless, the suspension here had initially been authorised by the DSB based on a multilateral determination that there was a violation. This multilateral determination, however, was made with respect to the measures applied by the European Communities at the time. Logically, it could not and did not apply to the measures subsequently adopted and properly notified to the WTO by the European Communities. With regard to the current legislative situation in the European Communities, no multilateral determination has been made by the time at which this Panel was established. If the United States nevertheless continues to apply the suspension of concessions and related obligations, it necessarily implies that it has unilaterally determined that there continues to be a violation. It has, in addition, explicitly said so.

4.35   Third, Article 23.2(a) of the DSU is violated if the determination to suspend concessions is not made in accordance with the rules and procedures of the DSU, or is not consistent with the findings of a dispute settlement organ. The DSU provides for a specific procedure, namely Article 21.5 of the DSU, to address the situation that Members disagree over the existence or consistency of measures taken to comply with the recommendations and rulings of the DSB.

4.36   There exists obviously a disagreement as to whether, by adopting Directive 2003/74/EC, the European Communities has implemented the recommendations and rulings from the DSB in the *Hormones* case. Article 21.5 of the DSU requires that such a disagreement *shall* be decided through recourse to dispute settlement. The European Communities has invited the United States several times to initiate a compliance procedure under Article 21.5 (or, for that matter, any other dispute settlement procedure under the DSU), but to this date the United States refuses to do so. Instead, it simply continues to apply the suspension of concessions and related obligations as if no "measure to comply" had been taken or the non-compliance of the new directive of the European Communities had already been established.

4.37   As the determination in the present case has been made *before* the commencement, let alone the exhaustion of the Article 21.5 procedure, it is necessarily not one that has been made consistent with the findings contained in an adopted panel or Appellate Body report.

(d)   The United States' continued suspension of
        concessions and related obligations is in violation
        of Article 23.1, read together with Articles 22.8
        and 3.7 of the DSU

4.38   Under Article 23.1 of the DSU, the United States is obliged to have recourse to, and abide by, the rules and procedures of this Understanding. This
encompasses, *inter alia*, Articles 22.8 and 3.7 of the DSU. In this respect, the
following should be noted:

4.39   The suspension of concessions or other obligations is limited in time.
This temporal limitation is the very foundation of the retaliation system under
the DSU. The importance of this principle is already demonstrated by the fact
that the "temporary nature" of countermeasures appears contextually at two
places in Article 22 of the DSU, in Paragraph 8 and in Paragraph 1. The temporal limitation is a practical consequence of the fact that suspension of concessions should only be applied as "a last resort", Article 3.7 of the DSU. This
means that the suspension of concessions should only apply where justified and
necessary.

4.40   The temporary nature of the suspension of concessions or other obligations has been recurrently interpreted by arbitrators to indicate that one of the
main objects and purposes of sanctions is to induce the violating WTO member
to comply with its obligations. Indeed, in reaching this conclusion the arbitrators
followed a suggestion by the United States (see *EC - Bananas III (US) (Article 22.6 – EC)*). The objective of inducing compliance entails, however, that
once a Member has adopted compliance measures which are not properly challenged by the complaining Member, the suspension of concessions or other obligations can no longer be applied. Indeed, in such a scenario the suspension of
concessions or other obligations would be deprived of one of its main objectives,
i.e. to achieve implementation of a DSB decision, for the simple reason that the
WTO Member has already taken measures to implement the DSB recommendation. In this case, the objective to induce compliance can only revive after it has
been properly established that the implementing measure has been insufficient to
remedy a WTO violation.

4.41   Article 22.8 of the DSU prohibits the continued unilateral application of
the suspension of concessions or other obligations when the measure which has
been found inconsistent is removed. The term "removed" thereby refers to the
compliance by a WTO Member because this provision is based on the respect of
the WTO obligations by the Member concerned (see Article XVI:4 of the WTO
Agreement and Article 19.1 of the DSU). The scope of the compliance obligation is determined by the DSB recommendations and rulings following the adoption of the Panel and/or Appellate Body report (Articles 21.5, 22.2 of the DSU).

4.42   Article 22.8 of the DSU does not specify how the removal of the WTO inconsistency is determined. However, in the light of its context, i.e. Articles 21.5 and 23.2(a) of the DSU, and given the exceptional nature of countermeasures, i.e. their temporal limitation, it is clear that a Member can not unilaterally determine that the WTO inconsistency persists despite the notification of a compliance measure. In very much the same vein, a Member can not decide to continue to suspend concessions or other obligations unilaterally. The WTO inconsistency of the implementing measure can only be determined in accordance with the appropriate procedure, namely Article 21.5 of the DSU. Unless such a procedure concludes that the compliance measure does not fully implement the DSB recommendations and rulings, it cannot be presumed that this is the case.

4.43   This also follows from the general principle of good faith as it applies in international State relations, under which States are normally considered to act in conformity with their obligations. This principle has been widely confirmed in the international (trade) jurisprudence (see ICJ *Corfu Channel, EC – Hormones (Article 22.6), Chile – Alcoholic Beverages, Canada – Aircraft (Article 21.5 – Brazil)* and it also applies for implementing measures (*Canada – Dairy (Article 21.5 – New Zealand and US II), EC – Bed Linen (Article 21.5 –India)*).

4.44   Therefore, it is clear that the United States could not unilaterally determine that the European Communities implemented the DSB recommendations and rulings in a WTO inconsistent way. To the contrary, the European Communities must be presumed to have complied with its WTO obligations, if the United States refuses to establish the contrary.

4.45   Once the inconsistency of the measure has been removed, Article 22.8 of the DSU provides that "the suspension of concessions or other obligations shall be temporary, and shall only be applied until such time as the measure found to be inconsistent with a covered agreement has been removed." This provision is mandatory. It does not leave any margin of discretion to the retaliating Member, thereby corroborating the exceptional nature of the imposition of countermeasures. As explained above, a Member which contests the removal of the inconsistency of the measure has to abide by the rules and procedures under the DSU, i.e. Article 21.5 of the DSU. Only if it is established in such a procedure that the WTO inconsistency persists is the application of the suspension of concessions or other obligations permissible under Article 22.8 of the DSU.

4.46   Under the same logic, Article 22.8 of the DSU does not allow for the application of countermeasures on the basis of a *unilateral* determination regarding the WTO inconsistency of a measure. Rather, Article 22.8 of the DSU, read in its context with Articles 21.5 and 23.2(a) of the DSU, requires that in the absence of an adverse finding, the suspension of concessions or other obligations shall not "be applied" any longer. This language is open in, at least, three directions:

4.47   Firstly, it indicates that the suspension of concessions or other obligations must be terminated in case a compliance measure is not challenged, the measure thus being accepted as being in full accordance with the WTO agreements.

4.48   Secondly, Article 22.8 of the DSU shows that the suspension of concessions or other obligations must not be applied any longer if the complaining Member delays, postpones or refuses the initiation of an Article 21.5 proceeding. As a WTO Member is presumed to act in conformity with its obligations, it follows necessarily that through the compliance measure it is presumed to have removed the WTO inconsistency of the measure at least when the following three conditions are fulfilled: (1) the Member has followed its internal decision-making procedures that are normally applied for the purpose of adopting compliance measures of that kind; (2) the elaboration, deliberation and adoption of the compliance measure is done in an open and transparent manner, and (3) the compliance measure is notified properly to the WTO. Therefore, the suspension of concessions or other obligations should not apply any longer. This case is particularly relevant in the present dispute where the United States has been refusing for almost two years to initiate the compliance procedure under Article 21.5 and to cease the suspension of concessions and related obligations against the European Communities. Thus, the United States continues the suspension of concessions and related obligations on the basis of a unilateral determination regarding the WTO-inconsistency of the notified compliance measure.

4.49   In the light of the two first conclusions, it would also be appropriate to infer from Article 22.8 read together with Article 23.1 of the DSU that the suspension of concessions or other obligations should not continue to be applied until the WTO inconsistency of the properly notified measure has been positively determined by the DSB.

4.50   This result is also corroborated by the system and overall thrust of Article 23 of the DSU, which is to strengthen the multilateral system. If a WTO Member were allowed to continue the application of suspension of concessions without challenging the implementing measure, it would necessarily have to base its assessment on a unilateral determination of the WTO inconsistency of the new measure. This would be in plain contradiction of Article 23.2(a), in conjunction with Article 21.5 of the DSU, as explained above.

4.51   The scenario described above follows the same *ratio legis* that applies for the initial imposition of suspension of concessions or other obligations. Thus, whether a Member suspends concessions for the first time or other obligations or wishes to maintain the suspension despite an implementation act does not make a difference. In both cases, a Member must not substitute unilaterally its assessment of a WTO inconsistency of an implementation measure to the procedures under the DSU.

4.52   In the case of the initial imposition of suspension of concessions or other obligations, the DSU implies first a determination that the Member concerned has not implemented the DSB recommendations and rulings. The DSB would not authorize the suspension of concessions or other obligations, if a WTO Member has taken implementing measures. If a WTO Member has taken implementing measures, it is established practice that the Member which intends to suspend concessions or other obligations first obtains a DSB decision regarding the insufficiency of the implementing measure following an Article 21.5 of the DSU proceeding. This normal course of events and legal steps in the case of the imposition of suspension of concessions or other obligations is in full accordance with the overarching principle set out in Article 23 of the DSU prohibiting Members from making unilateral determinations that another Member has violated its obligations.

4.53   Regarding the question of the conditions under which the suspension of concessions or other obligations could be *maintained,* there is no reason to assume that this fundamental logic should change in any way whatsoever. In fact, the legal situation is identical where the implementing Member has taken the necessary measures to comply with its WTO obligations in accordance with its internal rules and procedures and notified the measures in question to the WTO.

4.54   This comparability is even more striking if one focuses on the timing of an implementation measure. In the case of the initial *imposition* of the suspension of concessions or other obligations, a WTO Member has not implemented its obligations *before* the DSB's authorization to suspend concessions or other obligations. In the case of the *maintenance* of suspension of concessions or other obligations, a WTO Member implements its obligations *after* the DSB's authorization to suspend concessions or other obligations. This difference in timing, however, does not alter the normal legal sequencing between the multilateral review of the compliance measure and the application of suspension of concessions or other obligations. Indeed, the sole difference in timing does not give the retaliating Member all of a sudden the substantive right to make *unilateral* decisions as to whether or not the implementing measure is appropriate and sufficient and, if it is not considered sufficient, to continue applying the countermeasures as if nothing had happened.

4.55   In light of the above, there is an absolute need to refrain from continuing to apply the suspension of concessions or other obligations in cases where the retaliating Member has not properly challenged the compliance measure in an Article 21.5 proceeding. In fact, if a Member were allowed to maintain the suspension of concessions or other obligations even in such a new legal situation, it could make the kind of unilateral determinations which Article 23 specifically outlaws. Also, it could continue to apply the suspension of concessions or other obligations even if the WTO violation has been objectively removed. The implementing Member would then have to suffer from the suspension of concessions or other obligations even though it has fully abided by its obligations. It goes without saying that such a result would be in plain contradiction to the DSU provisions governing the suspension of concessions or other obligations, in particular Articles 3.7 and 22.

4.56   These fundamental principles are not altered by the fact that there exists a DSB authorization under Article 22.7 of the DSU to suspend concessions or other obligations. The DSB authorization cannot change the fundamental rules under the DSU. Rather, the DSB implements these rules. Thus, as the DSU provides that the suspension of concessions or other obligations should not be applied unless it has been properly established that a Member's measure violates its WTO obligations, the DSB authorization cannot be interpreted to justify such a suspension if a WTO violation of a Member's (new) measures has not been properly determined.

4.57   The basis for a DSB authorization to suspend concessions or other obligations is a prior *multilateral* determination that the implementing WTO Member has failed to comply with its obligations. This is the case if an Article 21.5 proceeding concludes that the implementing measure was insufficient. This is also implicitly the case if a Member has not adopted any implementing measure at all at the time of the DSB decision under Article 22.7 of the DSU. On the contrary, if a WTO Member implements properly its obligations after the DSB has authorized the suspension of concessions or other obligations, the basis for this decision changes fundamentally. As the original DSB authorization was taken in view of the original measure, it cannot logically encompass the new implementing measure. Hence, the DSB authorization cannot cover the continued application of the suspension of concessions or other obligations, if a WTO Member subsequently implements its obligations in the absence of a multilateral review regarding the compliance (or not) of this new measure.

4.58   Regarding this DSB authorization it is once again useful to compare the two situations of the *imposition* and the *maintenance* of the suspension of concessions or other obligations. The DSB could not authorize the imposition of retaliatory measures under Article 22.7 of the DSU, if the implementing Member had undertaken measures to comply with its obligations and if those had not been found WTO inconsistent following an Article 21.5 proceeding. In the very same vein, the DSB authorization cannot justify the maintenance of suspension of concessions or other obligations if a Member properly complies with its obligations after the imposition of these measures and if its compliance measure is not challenged in an Article 21.5 proceeding. Again, the mere temporal difference of the new implementing measure does not mean that the DSB authorization, once received, serves as a blank authorization for a Member to continue the application of the suspension of concessions or other obligations indefinitely in the future and on the basis of unilateral determinations.

4.59   Furthermore, the European Communities would note, that from a systemic point of view, Article 22.8 of the DSU is subsequent to Article 22.7 of the DSU. This indicates that once the situation under Paragraph 8 occurs it overtakes the authorization granted under Paragraph 7. Paragraph 8 conditions Paragraph 7. As it must be assumed that the DSU negotiators followed a logical sequencing in the way they drafted Article 22, it is clear that Article 22.8 of the DSU was supposed to impact on the authorization under Article 22.7 of the DSU. Indeed, to assume that the removal of the inconsistency of the measure under Paragraph 8 has no impact on the DSB authorization under Paragraph 7 is not legally coherent or reasonable.

4.60   Moreover, this reading of the DSB authorization is corroborated if one takes a closer look at the substance of this authorization. The level of nullification or impairment has to be determined in relation to the violation determined for the existing measure (Article 3.8 of the DSU). Thus, assuming that a WTO Member has not undertaken any implementation steps, the level of nullification should be determined in relation to the original violation. But assuming, in a second scenario, that a Member has implemented partly or fully its WTO obligations, the level of nullification or impairment would have to be determined accordingly. Obviously, in the area where the Member implemented properly its obligations there would be no nullification or impairment. This logic had also been recognized by the arbitrators in *EC – Bananas III (US) (Article 22.6 – EC)*.

4.61   Applying the same reasoning in the present case, it is clear that the level of suspension of concessions or other obligations as authorized by the DSB was based on a non-implementation by the European Communities. However, this level and, therefore, the scope of the authorization may not be justified any longer once the European Communities has properly implemented its obligations.

4.62   Finally, following the jurisprudence by the Appellate Body, once a Member violates Article 23.1 read in conjunction with Article 22.8 of the DSU it necessarily also acts contrary to Article 3.7 of the DSU.

(e)   The United States is in violation of Article I:1 of the GATT 1994 because of the continued suspension of concessions and related obligations

4.63   The United States is acting inconsistently with Article I:1 of the GATT 1994 by imposing import duties in excess of bound rates on products originating in certain EC Member States.

(f)   The United States is acting inconsistently with
        Article II of the GATT by the continued
        application of countermeasures on products
        originating in the European Communities.

4.64   The United States is violating its obligations under Article II:1(a) and
Article II:1(b) of the GATT by suspending concessions and related obligations
against the European Communities.

4.   *Legal Arguments: Part II – Conditional claim in the
        event that the Panel does not find any violation of
        Article 23 of the DSU as set out in Part I*

(a)   The United States is violating Article 22.8 of the
        DSU because the measure found to be
        inconsistent has been removed by the European
        Communities

4.65   The United States is violating Article 22.8 of the DSU by continuing to
suspend concessions and related obligations even though the measure found to
be inconsistent has been removed. Consequently, the United States is under an
obligation not to apply the suspension of concessions any longer. In the following, the European Communities will set out in more detail why the new measure
is not only in presumed compliance as argued above but in actual compliance
with the recommendations and rulings of the DSB.

4.66   The rulings of both the Panel and the Appellate Body essentially turned
on the reading of Article 5.1 of the *SPS Agreement,* and in particular, the requirement that a measure be based on a risk assessment. The Appellate Body
upheld the Panel's finding that the EC measures at issue were inconsistent with
the requirements of Article 5.1 of the *SPS Agreement.* At the same time, the report contains an important clarification as to how the European Communities
could bring its regime for hormones-treated meat into accordance with its obligations under the covered agreements. As seen above in relation to Part I, the
Appellate Body held "that Article 5.1, read in conjunction with Article 2.2, requires that the results of the risk assessment must sufficiently warrant the SPS
measure at stake."

4.67   On the basis of the scientific data presented by the European Communities, the Appellate Body found that that data did not sufficiently warrant or reasonably support the import prohibition. The Appellate Body found, in particular,
that the scientific reports and studies submitted by the European Communities
did not rationally support the EC's import prohibition or were too general, i.e.
relevant but not sufficiently specific to the case. It is important to understand,
therefore, that the Appellate Body did not find that an import prohibition for
beef from hormone treated cattle was *per se* in violation of the *SPS Agreement.*

Rather it found that the EC's import prohibition was not sufficiently warranted, that is to say reasonably supported, by the specific risk assessment relied upon at that time by the European Communities.

4.68   In order to comply with the above findings the European Communities conducted a comprehensive risk assessment. The risk assessment focussed on potential risks to human health from hormone residues in bovine meat and meat products, in particular such risks arising from residues of the six hormonal substances (oestradiol-17β, testosterone, progesterone, trenbolone acetate, zeranol and melengestrol acetate). In carrying out the risk assessment, the European Communities initiated and during 1998-1999 funded altogether 17 specific scientific studies and research projects in order to obtain as much as possible of the missing scientific information as identified in the above rulings. Moreover, the European Communities addressed in 1998 specific requests for the submission of scientific data to the United States, Canada, Australia and New Zealand which all authorise the use of these six hormones for animal growth promotion. It also published an open call for documentation requesting any interested party, including the industry, to provide any relevant and recent scientific data and information in their possession to be taken into account in the complementary risk assessment.

4.69   The data collected was submitted to the *Scientific Committee on Veterinary Measures relating to Public Health* (SCVPH), an independent expert Committee established under EC legislation to evaluate these kind of substances in the EC legal system. This scientific body was the one responsible for scientific and technical questions concerning consumer health and food safety related to production, processing and supply of food of animal origin. The SCVPH reviewed all the old and new data and issued its opinion on 30 April 1999, which it reviewed and confirmed again in 2000 and once more in 2002 on the basis of additional and new information submitted subsequently.

4.70   Based on this comprehensive risk assessment, the European Communities adopted Directive 2003/74/EC. In accordance with the above scientific conclusions the Directive provides for a definite import prohibition on meat and meat products from animals treated for growth promotion purposes with oestradiol-17β. Furthermore, on the basis of the available but still incomplete data, the Directive provides for a provisional ban on meat and meat products from animals treated for growth promotion purposes with testosterone, progesterone, trenbolone acetate, zeranol and melengestrol acetate. The Directive places an obligation on the Commission to seek more complete scientific information from any source which could shed light and clarify gaps in the present state of knowledge on these substances.

4.71   Article 22.8 of the DSU obliges the United States to cease applying the suspension of concessions, once an inconsistent measure has been removed.

However, even though the inconsistent measure has been removed, the United States continues to apply the suspension of concessions. The United States, therefore, is in violation of Article 22.8 of the DSU.

(b)   The United States is in violation of Articles I and II of the GATT 1994 following the continued application of suspension of concessions

4.72   As explained above, the illegal continued suspension of concessions and related obligations automatically entails a violation of Articles I and II of the GATT.

D.   *First Written Submission of the United States*

1.   Introduction

4.73   On 26 July 1999, the Dispute Settlement Body ("DSB") authorized the United States to suspend concessions to the European Communities ("EC") in the amount of $116.8 million because the EC failed to implement the DSB's recommendations and rulings in *European Communities – Measures Concerning Meat and Meat Products (Hormones)* (WT/DS26).

4.74   That authorization has never been revoked. In this proceeding, the EC claims that multilateral decisions of the DSB can be overridden by implication when the Member who has been determined not to have complied merely asserts that it has complied. However, there is no basis in the text of the DSU for the EC's claim. Instead, the EC approach would unsustainably create an endless loop of litigation and nullify the right of complaining parties to suspend concessions for non-compliance following DSB-authorization by negative consensus.

4.75   The EC has strenuously tried to avoid any multilateral examination of its claim of compliance, claiming that this proceeding "is about procedural violations" and "is not about the European Communities' compliance in the previous case *EC – Hormones*". The EC consequently strongly urges this Panel not to examine whether the EC has complied, but rather to take at face value the EC's assertion and to find that this assertion not only overrides the DSB's multilateral authorization, but also would revoke US rights under the covered agreements.

4.76   However, the EC, having made an Article 22.8 claim, bears the burden of establishing its claim of an inconsistency with Article 22.8 of the DSU. Accordingly, the issue presented to the Panel in this proceeding can be reduced to the simple question of whether the EC has established that it has come into compliance.

4.77   The EC has failed to even attempt to establish that it has come into compliance, and the EC's DSU Article 22.8 claim should be rejected on this basis
alone. The EC's Article 21.5 of the DSU claim should likewise be rejected.

4.78   The EC's claims under Articles 23.1 and 23.2(a) of the DSU also fail. In
compliance with Article 23.1 of the DSU, the United States has already sought
and received multilateral authorization in relation to the EC's failure to comply
with DSB recommendations and rulings. The United States has made no determination concerning whether the EC has come into compliance. Accordingly
there is no basis for the EC's claims under these provisions.

2.   *Factual background*

4.79   At the core of the matter described in the EC's panel request, and squarely
within the Panel's terms of reference, lies the EC's assertion that it has removed
the measure found to be inconsistent with its WTO obligations in the original
Hormones dispute. In its panel request, the EC states: "The European Communities subsequently removed the measure found to be inconsistent with a covered
agreement," and that "it considers itself to have fully implemented the recommendations and rulings of the DSB in the *EC – Hormones* dispute." The latter
statement was confirming the EC's statement at the DSB meeting held on November 7, 2003, that the EC "consider[s] that with the entry into force of [Direc-
tive 2003/74, amending Directive 96/22], it [is] in conformity with the recommendations and rulings made by the DSB."

4.80   The EC alleges that its amended import ban, which continues to prohibit
the importation of animals and meat from animals to which any of six growth
promoting hormones have been administered, according to good veterinary practices, is "fully compliant" with its WTO obligations and the DSB's recommendations and rulings. According to the EC, the amended import ban is "based on
comprehensive risk assessments, in particular on the opinions of the EC independent Scientific Committee on Veterinary Measures relating to Public Health"
(the "Opinions").

4.81   The EC complains of the "continued" US suspension of concessions to
the EC "after the European Communities has removed the measure found to be
inconsistent with WTO law in [the *EC – Hormones* dispute]." It suggests, in the
wake of a declaration of its own compliance with DSB recommendations and
rulings, that the United States' authorization to suspend concessions to the EC is
no longer in effect or valid.

4.82   However, US suspension of concessions to the EC was, and remains,
multilaterally authorized by the DSB. On 26 July1999, the DSB authorized the
United States to suspend concessions or other obligations to the EC in the
amount of $116.8 million as a consequence of the EC's failure to comply with its

recommendations and rulings in the *EC – Hormones* dispute. To date, this authorization has not been revoked by the DSB, and the United States continues to act pursuant to that authority.

(a)   The six hormones used for growth promotion purposes

4.83   The EC's hormone ban prohibits the importation and marketing of meat and meat products from cattle to which the hormones have been administered for growth promotion purposes, according to good veterinary practices. The United States permits the administering of these hormones to cattle for that very purpose, *i.e.*, in order to increase the growth, feed conversion efficiency and leanness of carcass.

4.84   For purposes of growth promotion, five of the six hormones (oestradiol-17β, progesterone, testosterone, zeranol, and trenbolone acetate) are administered to cattle as subcutaneous implants in the animals' ears. The ears are then discarded at slaughter. The sixth hormone, melengestrol acetate, a synthetic progestogen, is administered as a feed additive.

4.85   International standards exist regarding the use of five of the six hormones for growth promotion purposes. Upon review of safety assessments conducted by JECFA and recommendations by CCRVDF, the Codex Alimentarius Commission ("Codex"), specified as the relevant international standards-setting body in the *SPS Agreement*, adopted recommended maximum residue limits ("MRLs"), where appropriate, for oestradiol-17β, progesterone, testosterone, trenbolone acetate and zeranol. Codex adopted these recommended MRLs to ensure that consumption of animal tissue containing residues of these substances does not pose a risk to consumers and to facilitate fair trading practices in international commerce.

4.86   Scientific reviews of the six hormones, international standards pertaining to their use, and a longstanding history of administering the six hormones to cattle for growth promotion purposes point to a single conclusion – that the use of the six hormones as growth promoters, according to good veterinary practices, is safe. This conclusion remains valid, and is supported by all relevant risk assessments.

4.87   The EC's 1999 and 2002 Opinions purport to offer a contrary view. However, as will be discussed below, the EC has not demonstrated how its Opinions indeed constitute risk assessments and the conclusions reached in the Opinions have been summarily dismissed by numerous regulatory bodies (including review bodies within the EC).

4.88   As in the original *EC – Hormones* panel proceeding, the EC has neglected to present any new scientific evidence of a risk, or a risk assessment drawn from that evidence, which would contradict the reams of scientific evidence demonstrating that residues in meat from cattle treated with the six hormones for growth promotion according to good veterinary practice, are safe for consumers.

3.   Legal arguments

4.89   The core of the EC case in this proceeding is that the United States is not authorized to suspend concessions and related obligations as a result of the EC's failure to comply with the DSB's recommendations and rulings. However, the simple response to the EC is that the DSB granted multilateral authorization to the United States to suspend concessions and related obligations. The EC cannot deny that the DSB's authorization has never been revoked. Because the EC cannot claim that the DSB has ever decided to revoke the authorization, the EC instead attempts to construct a new legal theory under which the EC's unsupported assertion of its own compliance has somehow invalidated the DSB's authorization.

4.90   The EC's theory is not contemplated by the text of the DSU and should be rejected. The EC's argument that an implementing Member may, through a unilateral declaration of compliance, invalidate the DSB's multilateral authorization would undermine the right of Members to obtain that authorization through operation of the negative consensus rule. According to the EC's logic, a Member could effectively invalidate another Member's authority to suspend concessions and force further litigation through a unilateral declaration of compliance the very day after the DSB grants that authority. According to the EC's approach, that implementing Member could then continuously force successive new rounds of litigation at will simply by asserting that it has complied. The EC's approach would create the very endless loop of litigation the DSU operates to prevent.

4.91   The EC's argument simply assumes a key element it must establish to prevail in this proceeding – that it has, in fact, "removed" its WTO-inconsistent measure. The EC's various claims based on this assumption must therefore fail.

4.92   Before addressing the EC's claims, it is worthwhile to review the applicable burden of proof in this proceeding. It is well-established that the complaining Member in WTO dispute settlement bears the burden of proof. This means, as an initial matter, that the EC, as the complaining party, bears the burden of coming forward with evidence and argument that establish a prima facie case of a violation. In establishing its prima facie case, the complaining party must set forth sufficient facts and arguments to establish each element of its case. Mere assertions are not sufficient. The EC has failed to meet this burden in these proceedings.

(a)   The EC has failed to demonstrate that the United
       States has breached DSU Article 22.8 because the
       EC has neither demonstrated that it has
       "removed" the WTO-inconsistencies of the
       original hormones ban, nor demonstrated how the
       amended ban has provided a solution to the
       nullification or impairment of benefits to the
       United States

4.93   Article 22.8 states, in relevant part, that:

> [t]he suspension of concessions or other obligations shall be tem-
> porary and shall only be applied until such time as the measure
> found to be inconsistent with a covered agreement has been *re-*
> *moved*, or the Member that must implement recommendations or
> rulings *provides a solution* to the nullification or impairment of
> benefits, or a *mutually satisfactory solution is reached*. (Emphasis
> added)

Article 22.8 thus establishes three conditions under which a DSB-authorized
suspension of concessions may no longer be applied: (1) the Member imposing
the WTO-inconsistent measure "removes" the measure; (2) that Member "provides a solution to the nullification or impairment of benefits"; or (3) the parties
to the dispute reach a "mutually satisfactory solution." In order to prevail in its
claim that the United States is breaching Article 22.8, the EC must establish that
one of these conditions has been met.

4.94   The EC's assertion that it has removed its measure or provided a solution
is not supported by any demonstration that it actually has done either. Instead, it
relies on an already rejected legal theory that a Member found to have breached
its WTO obligations is to be excused from its burden of proof in dispute settlement if it invokes the phrase "good faith." This argument is no more valid today
than when a WTO panel last rejected it, and the EC's failure to meet its burden
on the critical element of its case under Article 22.8 means that the EC's claim
must likewise fail. The United States continues to apply the suspension of concessions to the EC in a WTO-consistent manner, fully in accordance with the
authorization of the DSB.

4.95   The EC fails to demonstrate that it has in fact removed its WTO-
inconsistent measure, the import ban on meat and meat products from cattle
treated with hormones for growth promotion purposes or that it has "provide[d] a
solution" to the nullification or impairment of benefits to the United States
caused by the ban.

4.96   Article 22.8 nowhere provides that the issue of removal of a measure or
providing a solution can be decided by a Member's simple assertion that it has
developed a new, WTO-consistent measure, or that it alone has deemed that it

has provided a "solution" to WTO nullification or impairment, without a DSB determination. Indeed the EC's proposed interpretation is directly at odds with the last sentence of Article 22.8 which makes it clear that these are questions for ongoing *DSB* surveillance. Article 22.8 stresses that "the DSB shall continue to keep under surveillance the implementation of adopted recommendations or rulings", in situations where "concessions or other obligations have been suspended but the [DSB] recommendations ... have not been implemented." This statement that the DSB's role is to monitor an implementing Member's compliance with DSB recommendations as well as the complaining Member's suspension of concessions further emphasizes that Article 22.8 is concerned with multilateral review of compliance. The EC simply errs in claiming that under Article 22.8 the US authorization to suspend concessions could be withdrawn in the absence of a DSB determination to that effect. Furthermore, the EC's approach would fundamentally undermine the operation of several critical DSU provisions, most notably the right of complaining parties to seek authorization to suspend concessions through a DSB decision taken by negative consensus under Article 22.6 or Article 22.7 of the DSU.

4.97   The EC argues that the Panel should find that it has "removed" its WTO-inconsistent measure within the meaning of Article 22.8 analysis because it "must be presumed to have complied with its WTO obligations, if the United States refuses to establish to the contrary." However, the *EC – Bananas* compliance panel highlighted that there is simply no basis in the WTO Agreement for the EC's argument that it is presumed compliant with its obligations absent a finding against its measures. Similarly, there is no presumption of compliance for the EC's amended ban in this proceeding. Because compliance of the EC's amended ban is a condition precedent to several of the claims raised by the EC as a complaining party, the EC bears the burden in this proceeding of demonstrating its compliance.

(b)   The EC has failed to demonstrate that its amended import ban on meat and meat products treated with hormones for growth promotion purposes is WTO-consistent

4.98   Whereas the EC claims in its Opinions and Directive 2003/74 to have developed a risk assessment and scientific evidence supporting its import ban on oestradiol-17β, it qualifies the ban on the other five hormones as "provisional." Consistent with this characterization, the EC invokes Article 5.7 of the *SPS Agreement* in its first written submission, alleging that the results of its Opinions provide "'the available pertinent information' on the basis of which the provisional prohibition regarding the other five hormones has been enacted." However, the EC fails to demonstrate how its ban satisfies Article 5.7's four cumulative elements, and it thereby fails to demonstrate how its ban is a legitimate provisional measure within the meaning of that Article.

4.99   Specifically, the EC: (1) fails to demonstrate that its "provisional" ban on meat and meat products from cattle treated with five of the hormones for growth promotion purposes is maintained in a situation where "relevant scientific evidence is insufficient"; (2) fails to demonstrate how its "provisional" ban has been adopted on the "basis of available pertinent information"; (3) has not sought "to obtain the additional information necessary for a more objective assessment of risk"; and (4) has not "reviewed [its] ... measure accordingly within a reasonable period of time" within the meaning of Article 5.7.

4.100   In addition, the EC fails to demonstrate that its amended ban is "based on" a risk assessment within the meaning of Article 5.1 since: (1) the EC's Opinions do not appear to be risk assessments within the meaning of Article 5.1, and (2) the results of the EC's Opinions do not rationally relate to or reasonably support its import ban.

4.101   The EC fails to demonstrate how its Opinions are indeed "risk assessments" within the meaning of Article 5.1 and Annex A of the *SPS Agreement*. By failing to examine relevant pathways, explore the fate of the relevant risk (that posed by meat products to consumers) or to support their conclusions with scientific evidence, the Opinions neither "identify the adverse effects on human health" arising from the consumption of meat from cattle treated with hormones for growth promotion purposes according to good veterinary practice nor "evaluat[e] the potential for adverse effects on human or animal health" arising from consumption of meat products from cattle treated with hormones for growth promotion purposes.

4.102   Furthermore, the EC's Opinions and their underlying studies identify theoretical risks from oestradiol-17β generally, but fail to address the relevant risk – that arising from the presence in meat of residues resulting from the administration to animals, according to good veterinary practice, of any of the six hormones for growth promotion purposes. Therefore, the EC's Opinions fail to sufficiently warrant or reasonably support the EC's ban on meat from cattle treated with hormones for growth promotion purposes according to good veterinary practice. As a result, the EC's ban is not based on a risk assessment within the meaning of Article 5.1 of the *SPS Agreement*.

4.103   Finally, the EC fails to demonstrate that its amended ban, which is not based on international standards, satisfies the conditions of Article 3.3 of the *SPS Agreement*. Specifically, the EC maintains its amended ban in breach of Article 3.3 because it fails to base its amended ban on a risk assessment within the meaning of Article 5.1 of the *SPS Agreement*.

> (c) The United States has not breached any other
> WTO obligations by continuing to suspend
> concessions to the EC

4.104 The EC argues that the United States has breached Articles 3.7, 21.5, 22.8, 23.1 and 23.2(a) of the DSU. There are two cornerstones to this argument, through which the EC seeks to avoid having to demonstrate how its amended ban in fact cures the WTO-inconsistencies of the original ban. First, the EC argues that the original complaining party, in this case the United States, is obligated to seek recourse to dispute settlement in order to continue to suspend properly-authorized concessions. In particular the EC cites to the United States' failure "to initiate dispute settlement proceedings pursuant to Article 21.5 of the DSU." The EC links this failure to initiate a compliance proceeding to breaches of Articles 23.2(a) and 23.1 of the DSU, and asserts that a US failure to initiate an Article 21.5 proceeding equates to a presumption of EC compliance. As discussed below, Article 21.5 does not, among other things, obligate the original complaining party to seek immediate recourse to dispute settlement to evaluate a Member's unilateral declaration that it has taken a measure to comply.

4.105 Second, the EC asserts that it has "removed" its measure within the meaning of Article 22.8 of the DSU, and that as a result the United States now violates the provisions of that Article by suspending concessions to the EC. The EC links its "removal" of the offending measure and alleged US breach of Article 22.8 to breaches of Articles 23.1 and 3.7 of the DSU.

> (i) The United States continues to satisfy its
> obligations under Article 23 of the DSU

4.106 Prior to addressing the EC's intertwined claims alleging breaches of several DSU provisions, it is first necessary to examine an alleged DSU breach common to each of those claims – that the United States has breached its obligations under DSU Article 23. Notwithstanding the EC's claim that by continuing to suspend concessions the United States seeks redress of a perceived violation on the part of the EC, the United States does not now, and did not at the time of the EC's unilateral declaration of compliance, "seek" anything within the meaning of Article 23.1 with respect to the EC's declaration. The United States did not make a determination that the EC's amended hormone ban is in violation of a covered agreement (the current proceeding provides an opportunity for the WTO to resolve that question), nor did the United States try to obtain or bring about compensation or remedy for some new wrong or alleged WTO violation.

4.107 In fact, the United States, at the appropriate time, adhered to the letter of Article 23.1 by seeking redress of the nullification or impairment caused by the EC's import ban on hormone-treated meat and meat products through recourse to the provisions of the DSU. The multilaterally-authorized suspension of concessions stemming from the US recourse to dispute settlement remains valid to this day, and is unaffected by the EC's unilateral declaration of compliance. In other words, the United States has already sought and obtained redress through the multilateral dispute settlement system for a violation found by the DSB. There is no provision in the WTO Agreement that provides that a single Member can unilaterally invalidate the multilateral decision of the DSB to authorize suspension of concessions.

4.108 While Article 22.8 does set forth conditions under which that authorization may no longer be applied, as discussed above, the EC has offered no meaningful argumentation as to how those conditions have been fulfilled. Absent such a demonstration, the EC has quite simply failed to meet its burden in this proceeding that the US suspension of concessions is in any way inconsistent with the DSB's authorization and US WTO obligations. The United States is not seeking redress for anything but the import ban which the DSB ruled inconsistent with EC obligations, regarding which the EC has presented no evidence of having removed or provided a solution to the resulting nullification or impairment.

      (ii)   The US suspension of concessions does not breach Articles 23.2(a), 21.5 and 23.1 of the DSU

4.109 The EC argues that the United States "should have introduced a compliance procedure under Article 21.5 of the DSU," and in failing to do so "violated the specific prohibition of unilateral conduct set out in Article 23.2(a) of the DSU." The EC argues that the alleged breach of Articles 23.2(a) and 21.5 further constitutes a breach of Article 23.1 of the DSU. To the contrary, the United States continues to satisfy its obligations under each of these Articles, and the EC has failed to demonstrate the contrary.

4.110 As discussed above, the United States has not, through its continued application of the DSB's authorization to suspend concessions, sought redress for another Member's violation, in breach of Article 23.1. This also means the United States is not breaching Article 23.2(a). Likewise, the United States is not breaching Article 23.2(a) because it did not make a "determination" within the meaning of Article 23.2(a).

4.111 Since it received authorization to suspend concessions to the EC, the United States has simply continued to act according to its DSB authorization to suspend concessions to the EC. Contrary to the EC's claims in this panel proceeding, the United States made no determinations concerning the EC's import ban, amended or not. The United States did not need to make any further determinations to continue to apply that suspension of concessions, and it did not. Further, as noted above, the conditions under which a Member may no longer apply a DSB-authorized suspension of concessions are set forth in Article 22.8, and the EC has made no effort to demonstrate that those conditions have been met.

4.112 Further, the EC alleges that, contrary to the requirements of Article 23.2(a) of the DSU, the United States made a determination not "in accordance with the rules and procedures of the DSU," and in a manner "not consistent with the findings of a dispute settlement organ." Specifically, the EC alleges that the United States made a determination that the EC had not implemented the recommendations and rulings of the DSB in breach of Article 21.5 of the DSU. As demonstrated below, the United States has not breached its obligations under Article 21.5 of the DSU.

4.113 The EC's Article 21.5 claim fails for four reasons: (1) the EC has not established that there is a "disagreement as to the existence or consistency with a covered agreement of measures taken to comply;" (2) Article 21.5 sets no deadline by which such a proceeding must be brought; (3) nothing in the text of Article 21.5 places the onus of initiating a compliance proceeding on the original complaining party (in this case, the United States); and (4) the phrase "these dispute settlement proceedings" in Article 21.5 is not restricted to proceedings under Article 21.5, but rather could include proceedings under the DSU such as Article 22.6 arbitration proceedings, Article 25 proceedings, or the proceedings of a *de novo* panel, as the EC has sought in this instance.

4.114 First, the United States has continued to evaluate the EC's claim, and at the time of panel establishment had been awaiting the EC's response to the US request under Article 5.8 of the *SPS Agreement*. The United States has continued to evaluate the EC's claim, including its 19 May 2005 response to the US request. The US evaluation depends to a large extent on the EC's response to questions such as those posed in this submission, including why the EC believes that scientific evidence has now become insufficient to perform a risk assessment for five of the six hormones. To date the EC has been less than thorough in its responses. Article 21.5 only applies "[w]here there is disagreement."

4.115 Next, the EC interpretation of Article 21.5 as requiring immediate resort to litigation by a complaining party would definitively prevent that complaining party from exercising any judgment as to the fruitfulness of dispute settlement, and would preclude Members from seeking mutually agreeable solutions through negotiations. The aim of the dispute settlement system is to secure a positive solution by whatever means possible, and not simply through litigation. In the absence of any obligation in Article 21.5 to immediately resort to litigation, the fact that the United States had not done so by the time the EC initiated this proceeding cannot constitute a breach of Article 21.5.

4.116 Thirdly, contrary to the EC's argument, the text of Article 21.5 assigns no obligation to the *complaining* party to seek recourse to "these dispute settlement

procedures" in the event that there is a disagreement "as to the existence or consistency with a covered agreement of measures taken to comply." The text does
not require that the original complaining Member, in this case the United States,
initiate dispute settlement proceedings in the event of a disagreement. Thus, the
mere fact that the United States had not yet decided to invoke Article 21.5 proceedings before the EC undertook the present challenge is not in itself grounds
for concluding that the United States breached Article 21.5, any more than the
EC's failure to do so was.

4.117 Finally, it is important to recognize that the text of Article 21.5 refers to
"these dispute settlement procedures," without specifying any particular subset
of WTO dispute settlement procedures. The panel in the *US – Certain EC Products* dispute recognized that the ordinary meaning of this phrase covers any dispute settlement procedure provided in the DSU "that could be used to assess the
compatibility of the new implementing measure, including Article 25 or Article 22 of the DSU". In other words, there is no basis in Article 21.5 for excluding any WTO dispute settlement procedure that could be used to assess the
WTO-compatibility of a new implementing measure. In bringing these proceedings, the EC availed itself of one such means, though, as discussed above, it has
failed to meet its required burden to prevail. Also, in bringing these proceedings,
the EC has conceded that an Article 21.5 compliance panel is not the exclusive
means to resolve a "disagreement" even if one existed. If it were the exclusive
means, then the EC itself would have invoked Article 21.5, as it has done in the
past. However, it did not, nor did it seek to have the matter that is the subject of
this proceeding referred to the "original panel" as provided in Article 21.5. None
of the original panelists are serving on this Panel. Thus the EC's approach in this
proceeding itself refutes the EC's Article 21.5 claim.

(iii)   The United States has not violated
        Article 23.1 of the DSU, read together with
        Articles 22.8 and 3.7 of the DSU

4.118 The EC claims that the United States violates Article 23.1 of the DSU,
when read together with Articles 22.8 and 3.7 of the DSU. The EC asserts that
these three Articles, together, demonstrate "that a WTO Member shall not apply
the suspension of concessions or other obligations in the presence of an implementation act, which has not been found to be inconsistent following an Article 21.5 proceeding." Contrary to this claim, the United States continues to satisfy its obligations under each of these Articles.

4.119 As discussed above, the United States does not seek to redress a WTO
violation within the meaning of Article 23.1 of the DSU, and it continues to act
pursuant to its multilateral authorization to suspend concessions to the EC.
Therefore, the EC's claim that the United States has violated DSU Article 23.1,
read together with Articles 22.8 and 3.7 of the DSU fails.

(iv)   The United States has not breached its
        obligations under Article I or II of the
        GATT 1994

4.120 Finally, the EC claims that the United States acts in breach of Articles I and II of the GATT 1994. However, the DSB has specifically authorized the United States to suspend concessions under Articles I and II of the GATT 1994. Until the DSB withdraws its authorization or the conditions of Article 22.8 have been found to have been met, the United States cannot be found in breach of GATT 1994 Articles I or II.

4.   Conclusion

4.121 In light of the foregoing, the United States asks the Panel to find that: (1) the EC has failed to demonstrate that the United States has breached Article 22.8 of the DSU, and that the United States continues to suspend concessions to the EC consistent with the requirements of that provision; (2) The United States has not breached Articles 3.7, 21.5, 23.1 or 23.2(a) of the DSU; and (3) The United States has not breached Articles I or II of the GATT 1994.

E.   Oral Statement of the European Communities During the First Substantive Meeting

1.   Introduction

4.122 The central provision on which the European Communities bases its claims is Article 23 of the DSU. Article 23 requires WTO Members to have recourse to the procedures set out in the *DSU* instead of resorting to any kind of "self-help." Article 23, in other words, prohibits a WTO Member from making itself the judge over other WTO Members. What is and what is not a violation of the covered agreements and what one can do to remedy it, are to be determined multilaterally, not unilaterally.

2.   Seeking redress – Article 23.1

4.123 As to Article 23.1 all parties seem to agree that when, in 1999, the US and Canada requested, obtained and started using a DSB authorization to suspend concessions, they were seeking to redress a violation established at that time. The parties differ on what the US and Canada are doing right now. One should think that they are still seeking redress. After all, they are still applying their suspension of concessions stating explicitly that they fail to see how the European Communities' implementation measure achieves compliance. This can only mean that they still see a violation, especially given that Article 22.8 of the DSU would prohibit the continuation of sanctions in the opposite case.

4.124 The defending parties, however, flatly deny that what they are doing right now is seeking redress of a violation against an alleged WTO-inconsistency of the implementing measure. The United States states that it "has already sought and obtained redress through the multilateral dispute settlement system for a violation found by the DSB". Canada not only uses the same terms – "sought and obtained" – but also takes the trouble of underlining those words in its submission in order for everyone to understand the difference between the present tense ("seeking"), in Article 23.1 of the DSU, and the past tense of "sought and obtained". That difference seems obvious enough. What is much less obvious, however, is how, by referring to the past, the defending parties want to explain what they are doing right now. Applying sanctions is a form of seeking redress as the defending parties have admitted themselves. They are currently applying sanctions – present tense, not past tense – so how could they not be seeking redress?

4.125 They are not seeking redress, so the defending parties say, because they are acting under an authorization. An authorization, however, can neither deny facts nor derogate from a Member's obligations outside its scope. Thus, as regards specifically Article 23 of the DSU, it is clear that the mere existence of an authorization cannot simply do away with the obligation to abide by the rules and procedures of the DSU, when a Member is seeking redress of a violation.

3.   *Article 23.2(a) of the DSU in conjunction with Article 21.5 of the DSU*

4.126 As regards specifically the EC's claim under Article 23.2(a) in conjunction with Article 21.5 the defending parties put forward a number of reasons as to why there is no determination by them. Interestingly enough, they hardly deal with one of the main points the European Communities has raised, namely that their "unilateral determination" can be inferred from the fact that they continue to apply sanctions unilaterally. And how could it not be inferred from it? It is inconceivable – and indeed would be even worse than what we are discussing now – if they did so without any good reason. On the other hand, both spend considerable time in their first written submissions explaining - in a rather defensive manner - that their public statements do not constitute determinations, that they never alluded to a violation, that they have not yet concluded on non-compliance, etc. And finally, elsewhere in their submissions, they spend even more time explaining why the European Communities' implementing measure actually falls short of compliance.

4.127 Whether or not a specific statement reaches – as Canada puts it – the "threshold" of a determination is one thing. Yet, another thing is if that statement is accompanied by conduct that severely affects the EC's trade. We are not looking at statements made *in abstracto* here. A "determination" need not be pinned down to a specific statement in a specific form, it is the whole conduct a WTO Member is displaying that needs to be looked at.

4.128 The defending parties further claim that they do not have an obligation under Article 21.5 of the DSU to launch compliance proceedings. This Panel, however, is asked to find whether, under Article 23 of the DSU, in conjunction with Article 21.5, a Member has an obligation to launch a compliance procedure if and because it continues to apply sanctions against another Member, even though there is a new implementing measure. It is not relevant for this dispute what obligations can be found directly in 21.5 in the absence of such unilateral conduct.

4.129 Finally, the United States claims that there is no obligation for the retaliating complainants to *immediately* launch a compliance review. In the present context and circumstances, with almost one and a half years that have passed after the adoption of the European Communities' implementing measure at the moment when this Panel was established and with all the discussions that took place between the parties to this dispute regarding this implementing measure, both before and after it was adopted, the question of how quickly a retaliating complainant must react to an implementing measure does not pose itself. If anything, one could discuss the defendants' bad faith and their contradictory behaviour (*venire contra factum proprium*).

4. Article 23.1 in conjunction with Articles 22.8 and 3.7

4.130 As regards the EC' claim under Article 23.1 in conjunction with Article 22.8, 3.7, the defending parties submit that the conditions of Article 22.8 are not fulfilled because the European Communities did not prove that it has "removed" the inconsistency of the measure. This argumentation overlooks the fact that dispute settlement proceedings are about a non-compliance review not a compliance review. Indeed, in all dispute settlement proceedings that have ever been adopted by the DSB it was for a complaining Member to prove the WTO *in*consistency of a measure by another Member. This is explicitly confirmed by Article 6 of the DSU, the provision under which panels are established.

4.131 The defending parties ignore that the European Communities makes its systemic claim under *Article 22.8, in conjunction with Article 23.1*. Thus, the Panel is called upon to decide whether or not the conditions under Article 22.8 are fulfilled *in view of* the prohibition under Article 23 to make unilateral determinations of non compliance. It is not possible for the defending parties to contest the removal by the EC of the inconsistency of our old measure (Article 22.8), without making a unilateral determination under Article 23.

4.132 Further, both defending parties submit that the European Communities cannot base itself on a presumption of good faith compliance. The European

Communities bases itself on the same *rationale* as the Appellate Body in the *Byrd Amendment* case. Thus, even though the defending parties allege that the European Communities is still in violation of the *SPS Agreement*, this does not in any event affect the presumption of good faith. As the Appellate Body has made clear, these are two completely different questions.

4.133 The defending parties claim that there is a reversed burden of proof in a compliance case. Contrary to what Canada believes, a reversal of presumption can also not be deduced from the DSB authorization granted in 1999. The DSB authorization is limited to giving a Member the right to apply sanctions. However, it does not go further than that. The DSB authorization cannot reverse the normal rules which apply for subsequent implementing measures.

4.134 If Canada's criterion of a "day-to-day business" conduct for the presumption of good faith should bear any relevance at all, the European Communities considers that in the present case it even supports the EC' reliance on good faith. Indeed, the European Communities prepared the implementation of the DSB recommendations and rulings with extraordinary carefulness. During the compliance process, the European Communities has made every effort to analyse the relevant scientific evidence in full transparency and with an open mind. All stakeholders – whether inside or outside the European Communities - had at every moment in time the opportunity to submit relevant information and to intervene in the whole process.

4.135 It is therefore also absurd, and indeed turns reality on its head, to maintain that the European Communities in this case seeks to end the sanctions on the basis of a "mere declaration of compliance", and that this could be done also just "a week after" the DSB authorization. It insinuates that the European Communities abused its rights and it just waives its hand to claim compliance. In the light of the whole process, as just described, it is instead fully legitimate for the European Communities to rely on the presumption of good faith for its compliance.

4.136 As to the relevance of the DSB authorization for the continued application of sanctions in the context of Article 22.8, obviously, the defending parties and the European Communities have different views about the scope of the DSB authorization. For the United States and Canada, the DSB authorization operates like a sort of "absolute justification" which makes every behaviour *per se* WTO consistent, irrespective of any subsequent events and compliance acts. On the other hand, the European Communities considers that it is necessary to put the DSB authorization in its proper context under the DSU.

4.137 In this case, the DSB authorization has been granted under Article 22.7 following an arbitration procedure under Article 22.6 of the DSU. The subject-matter of this Article 22.6 arbitration was the level of nullification or impairment caused by the original EC's Hormones legislation. Thus, it is crucial to note that the very basis of the DSB authorization has been the WTO-inconsistency of the Member *before* the authorization was granted. On the other hand, the DSB authorization is not based on any (alleged) WTO inconsistency of a compliance measure that has been adopted *afterwards*.

4.138 What follows from this important and undisputable fact is that, first of all, in case of a subsequent compliance that is properly adopted and duly notified to the WTO, the basis on which the DSB has granted its authorization has fundamentally changed. The DSB only granted the authorization to suspend concessions precisely because a WTO Member had been found to be WTO inconsistent in the past and no implementation measure was taken within the reasonable period of time. The DSB's authorization was to induce compliance by the other Member and to rebalance temporarily the rights and obligations until the other Member has complied.

4.139 Second, the DSB authorization is even more fundamentally changed in the case of a subsequent compliance measure which has never been found WTO-inconsistent, because the defending parties do not dare to challenge it under Article 21.5. In its first written submission, the European Communities has referred to the "sequencing" discussion and practice of WTO Members in case of a compliance act before the DSB authorization is granted. Quite remarkably, in the "Bananas" dispute the DSB Chairman explicitly stated that the sequencing of a determination of (non-)compliance and the suspension of concessions should be treated in a "logical way forward".

4.140 As it happened, the logical way forward at the time was to assess first whether the compliance measure was sufficient before determining the nullification or impairment caused by the WTO-inconsistent measure. In stark contrast to this sequencing, the defending parties consider now that the logical way forward is to continue to apply sanctions even though the EC' compliance measure has not been challenged by them and not been found WTO-inconsistent. And what is more, they even refuse to challenge the EC's compliance measure, pretending that this is not necessary becuase they have a DSB authorization.

4.141 But how can Canada and the United States know that the European Communities is still not in compliance with its obligations? They do so solely on the basis of a unilateral determination of the EC's compliance measure which is in obvious contradiction to Article 23 and Article 21.5 of the DSU.

4.142 One might argue that the DSU is not explicit on this question. However, the DSU contains several elements which indicate that the DSB authorization can not serve as a blank cheque for the continuous application of the sanctions even after a subsequent compliance measure has been adopted and notified properly to the DSB.

4.143 First, let us consider the wording of Article 22.8 of the DSU and what it does *not* say. Even in case of a removal of the inconsistency of the measure, Article 22.8 does *not* say that the "DSB authorization ceases to apply". Instead, it states that the suspension of concessions or other obligations shall not "be applied" any longer. Thus, Article 22.8 does not formally address the fate of the DSB authorization. In an Article 22.8 situation it is, therefore, perfectly conceivable that although the DSB authorization is not *formally* terminated or withdrawn, a WTO Member is not entitled to continue the application of suspension of concessions. Furthermore, Article 22.8 does *not* say that the removal of the inconsistency or the termination of the application of suspension requires whatever kind of DSB decision. Rather, Article 22.8 is self-executing. The use of the word "shall" supports this interpretation, which does not give any margin of manoeuvre and requires no additional acts.

4.144 Second, contextually, Article 22.8 describes the next procedural step in the course of a dispute after an authorization has been granted. Article 22.8, therefore, provides for the next logical step. Consequently, once the inconsistency of the measure has been removed, the application of suspension of concessions or other obligations is no longer permitted.

4.145 In addition, Article 22.8 should be interpreted in the context of Article 23 of the DSU, which prohibits WTO Members from judging unilaterally the properly adopted and notified compliance measures of other WTO members. According to the text, object, purpose and context of Articles 22.8 and 23, the defending parties must seek a determination of non-compliance under the normal DSU procedures. This general principle is not altered in whatever way under Article 22.8.

4.146 Another contextual element which should be taken into account is Articles 3.7 and 22.1 of the DSU, which underline the exceptional and temporal nature of the application of suspension of concessions or other obligations. Their exceptional and temporal nature effectively complements the principle of good faith. In case of a properly adopted and notified compliance measure, the exceptional and temporal justification of countermeasures is put into question. In the presence of a subsequent compliance measure, the "normal" situation revives and sanctions can no longer be applied as if nothing has changed.

4.147 Canada tries to draw contextual support for its position from Article 3.2, emphasizing the security and predictability given by the DSB authorization. The "security and predictability" under Article 3.2, also applies to the WTO Member who properly implements its obligations. Once this Member has removed the inconsistency of the measure it should have the reassurance that sanctions are no longer applied. At a minimum, the implementing Member must have the reassurance that its measure is properly challenged under the DSU by the retaliating Member, which does not agree with the compliance measure. But even this,

Canada and the United States refuse to do despite the repeated requests by the European Communities to do so.

4.148 The European Communities would also recall the object and purpose of the trade sanctions, which is to induce compliance and to rebalance the rights and obligations under the WTO agreements. However, both objectives require that a Member's measure has been found first to be WTO-inconsistent in accordance with the DSU rules. And such a determination concerns logically not just any measure, but the measure that is currently in force in the Member concerned. Transposed in the present context, it means that Canada and the United States cannot simply argue that the "old" measure has been found to be WTO-inconsistent in 1998. This measure is not any longer in force, since the European Communities adopted and notified its compliance measure in 2003. It is simply not rational and credible to argue that the object and purpose of the suspension of concessions continues to exist, if its basic reason, i.e. the old WTO-inconsistency, has disappeared.

5. Concluding statement of the European Communities

4.149 The EC believes that allowing public observation of the debate during this hearing has been very beneficial for the public's understanding of the dispute settlement process as well as this particular dispute. The public observation has in no way hindered an efficient conduct of this hearing. On the contrary, the third parties have clearly benefited from their observation of this hearing during the first two days for the purpose of their participation in this dispute.

4.150 What we have heard from the defendants in the last few days is essentially that a retaliating Member has no obligation whatsoever under the DSU. Instead, the retaliating Member may continue to apply sanctions until the authorization is "revoked" by the DSB. The United States and Canada argue that by virtue of this authorization they can simply lean back and see what the complying Member comes up with. If eventually the complying Member adopts an implementation measure they do not even see a need to review it in due time. Let me remind that in this case the United States and Canada claim that they have even after two years (and I should add after an additional three years of preparation) not made up their mind whether the EC's measure is WTO consistent. Indeed there seems to be no prospect that the United States and Canada will ever make up their minds. Canada has stated that it would never make a determination about the EC's new measures and the United States gave even less cause for reassurance stubbornly refusing even to agree that there is a disagreement.

4.151 Whatever the defendants may mean by these statements, it is clear that the United States and Canada do not accept a responsibility to submit the EC's legislation to a multilateral review as has been done in any other case by WTO Members which ended in an adopted WTO decision. And although they do not contest that the EC has acted in good faith, they do not even concede that the EC's measure can benefit from a presumption of good faith compliance.

4.152 This is a very easy going way for the United States and Canada. But it cannot be the correct one under the DSU.

4.153 The EC would recall some essential points which have been discussed by the parties:

4.154 First, the EC has advanced what would be the logical solution to this dispute, i.e. to follow its example in the *US – FSC* case (launching Article 21.5 compliance procedure by original complaining party, suspension of sanctions in the meantime). Quite remarkably, the United States fully agreed with the EC's approach and considered it as "the appropriate solution" in the *US – FSC* dispute. Yet, the EC struggles to understand why in a reverse situation where the United States is retaliating, the United States does not follow this example if it considers it as "appropriate".

4.155 Second, there has been a lot of discussion about the presumption of good faith and the presumption of compliance, which is important for the EC's claim under Article 22.8 and Article 23.1 of the DSU. Neither the United States nor Canada nor any of the Third Parties have contested that the EC has adopted its compliance measure in good faith. Yet, the United States and Canada refuse to accept that the EC may rely on this principle in a "post-implementation" scenario. The United States even wants to go so far as to say that the principle of good faith is not part of the DSU. Obviously, this view is contrary to what the Appellate Body has consistently ruled but also irreconcilable with general principles of public international law. Moreover, when we asked Canada about the basis in the DSU of its assumption that an implementing Member faced with retaliation is not entitled to this presumption, it could not provide any answer. Indeed, this is so because there is no basis for Canada's theory.

4.156 Third, during the proceeding we have heard a lot about the risks of an "endless loop of litigation" by a "mere declaration of compliance". Yet, as everybody agrees that the EC has adopted its compliance measure in good faith, it is clear that this "endless loop of litigation" does not arise in this dispute. Indeed, such an endless loop scenario presupposes a sort of scam measure notified by a WTO Member in bad faith. This is not the case before us. Indeed, even the EC would not consider that a "mere declaration of compliance" is sufficient but what matters is that a Member complies with its obligations. This is what the EC has actually done in this case after a most thorough review of its measure involving a comprehensive review and assessment of the available scientific evidence.

4.157 There is a paradox about the approach of the defendants to the principle of good faith. They do not contest that the EC has acted in good faith but they argue that WTO Members in general cannot be expected to act in good faith. They argue, Members with a duty to implement will adopt sham or scam measures to escape retaliation, it is argued that implementing Members must have the burden of proving their compliance. The EC does not believe that WTO Members act in bad faith. No Member wants to lose WTO disputes – and to do so repeatedly and ignominiously. There would be a high political cost. Also, WTO Members are not excessively litigious and do not gaily engage in endless loops of litigation. This fear is unfounded. But if this argument about bad faith is allowed, it can also be used the other way around – to argue that the United States' and Canada's approach will lead to Members seeking and exploiting retaliation rights for improper purposes. Seeking redress of WTO violations must not be too difficult; and implementation and removal of retaliation must not be made subject to the often impossible task of proving a negative. Retaliation rights should not become a new means of advancing unilateralist agendas.

4.158 Fourth, when it comes to the DSB authorization, the United States and Canada argue that this may be revoked if the EC would launch a proceeding under the DSU, be it Article 21.5, 22.8 or Article 25 etc. However, both defending parties cannot explain how this would even result in revocation of the DSB authorization. Well, Canada argues that the DSB could probably eventually make a recommendation to itself to revoke the DSB authorization but there is absolutely no basis for this in the DSU. And I am not talking about the procedural implications which this could entail. For instance – according to Canada – in an Article 21.5 proceeding brought by the EC against itself the burden of proof would be partly on the EC for the implementation of the original DSB recommendations and ruling. On the other hand, Canada could bring in its "defence" (in which they would complain about the WTO consistency of the measure) new claims for which it would bear the burden of proof. And of course, Canada's theory cannot even address the question on how these new claims could be reconciled with the more limited Panel request.

4.159 Finally, let me once stress again that the EC is not seeking to avoid a proper examination of its compliance measures in the Hormones dispute. We would be delighted if the United States and Canada would initiate an Article 21.5 dispute tomorrow and would do all we can to facilitate and accelerate its conclusion. However the United States and Canada stubbornly refuse to take this logical – indeed appropriate – step. It is they who have sought to avoid having to confront the new EC measures and set out their objections to it in a manner in which the EC can properly respond. They have, it is true, started to set out – for the first time – their objections in their first written submissions. The EC does not understand why they did not want to do this in a proper Article 21.5 proceeding.

4.160 We hope that we have assisted you in your important task and look forward to helping you in any further way that we can in coming weeks.

F.   *Oral Statement of the United States During the First Substantive Meeting*

1.   *Introduction*

4.161 There are two central facts in this dispute. The first is that the WTO's Dispute Settlement Body authorized the United States to suspend concessions against the European Communities in the *EC – Hormones* dispute over five years ago because the DSB found that the EC lacked a scientific risk assessment to justify its ban on imports of meat in connection with hormones and that the EC then failed to implement the DSB's recommendations and rulings. The second is that the EC has made no effort to demonstrate that the conditions in the WTO's DSU for ending that DSB-authorized suspension have been met. Those conditions are set forth in DSU Article 22.8. While the EC has alleged that the United States is breaching this provision, the EC apparently considers that it can simply assert that those conditions have been met, that it can unilaterally declare itself to be in compliance and that it can thereby invalidate the multilateral authorization of the DSB.

4.162 This position is not sustainable. The EC is alleging that the United States is breaching its WTO obligations, and there can be no dispute that the EC bears the burden of demonstrating this – including demonstrating that it has removed the measure or provided a solution to the nullification or impairment suffered by the Member suspending concessions.

4.163 Despite this burden, the EC has insisted that this proceeding should not reach the question of whether it has actually complied with its WTO obligations in the *EC – Hormones* dispute. We can understand the EC's reluctance to deal with this issue, since we do not see how the EC can credibly claim it is in compliance with those obligations. Nevertheless, the EC's failure to make any effort at all to demonstrate its compliance is by itself grounds for rejecting the EC's claims, since this question goes to the heart of those claims.

2.   *The European Communities' amended ban*

4.164 It is notable what the EC has not argued in these proceedings – how and why it has come into compliance with the DSB's recommendations and rulings. The absence of this argument is odd since the majority of its claims are premised on the assertion that its ban is now WTO-consistent. Let us look for a moment at what, exactly, the EC has done. As far as the United States can tell in the absence of any explanation by the EC, the EC's "amended" ban simply preserves the *status quo* of its original ban found by a WTO panel and the WTO Appellate Body to violate the *SPS Agreement* in 1997 and 1998, respectively. Under the ban, found in Directives 96/22/EC and 2003/74/EC, the same products that were prohibited entry into the EC almost ten years ago when we first challenged the measure still may not enter the EC today.

3. The six hormones used for growth promotion purposes according to good veterinary practices

4.165 The six hormones at issue are oestradiol-17β, testosterone, progesterone, zeranol, trenbolone acetate and melengestrol acetate (or "MGA"). These hormones have been used for growth promotion purposes in cattle for decades in several countries, and meat from treated animals has been consumed by millions of people, without any evidence of risk or harm to human health.

4.166 In terms of human food safety, the six hormones have been studied extensively, by national authorities and by Codex, the relevant international standard-setting body with scientific expertise in this area. In fact, the study of these hormones dates back over twenty years. The consensus throughout the course of this study is that meat from cattle treated with these six hormones for growth promotion purposes according to good veterinary practices is safe.

4.167 In stark contrast to the several reviews finding the use of these hormones to be safe, there is one view that the EC portrays as dissenting – that of its Scientific Committee on Veterinary Measures Relating to Public Health ("SCVPH"), contained in the SCVPH's 1999 and 2002 Opinions and 2000 Review, ostensibly supported by several (17) studies commissioned by the EC. It is this view which the EC now asks the Panel to accept wholesale without any explanation or analysis.

4.168 It is therefore not surprising that the EC has been unable to convince several of its own agencies of the conclusions set out in its Opinions and studies. For example, in 1999, a sub-group of the United Kingdom's Veterinary Products Committee dismissed the methodology and conclusions of the EC's 1999 Opinion. Recently, in a May 2005 draft report reviewing the EC's 2002 Opinion and the 17 studies, the Veterinary Products Committee ("UK Group") again concluded that it was "unable to support the conclusion reached by the SCVPH that risks associated with the consumption of meat from hormone-treated cattle may be greater than previously thought." The UK Group also stated that, regarding estradiol 17β, "there is ample information to show that zoo-technical and therapeutic uses of oestradiol-17β do not pose any risk to humans unless an active implant site is ingested."

4.169 Regarding the other five hormones, the majority of the U.K. Group determined that the "available evidence on genotoxicity, tumorigenicity, hormonal activity and endocrine disrupting effects was supportive of the view that eating meat from animals treated with these five hormones was unlikely to be harmful to human health."

4.170 In addition, the EC's own Committee for Veterinary Medicinal Products ("CVMP"), which in 1999 evaluated the conclusions of the 1999 Opinion and the new EC studies on oestradiol and progesterone, determined that the EC had not presented sufficient new evidence to cause the CVMP to conduct a new risk assessment on either hormone or alter its previous conclusions on their safety.

4.171 Let me reiterate: these are internal criticisms of the work produced by the EC and of the very documents it now asserts bring its measure into compliance with DSB recommendations and rulings. Despite these criticisms, and despite the extensive history of study of these hormones finding their use to be safe, the EC would have this Panel endorse its assertion that its new measure is WTO-consistent without a demonstration of why this is so. A determination of an Article 22.8 breach absent a thorough evaluation of these documents would not only ignore the rules of burden of proof in WTO dispute settlement, it would cast aside the substantial history of review of these hormones – a history that has, time and again, demonstrated that their use for growth promotion purposes according to good veterinary practices, is safe for consumers.

4. The EC's assertion of its own compliance

4.172 Contrary to the EC's argument, a WTO Member may not, in effect, revoke DSB authorization to suspend concessions, and consequently establish a breach of Article 22.8 of the DSU, by simply asserting that it has brought its measure into compliance. This interpretation ignores the rules of burden of proof in WTO dispute settlement as well as the Article's text and context.

5. Burden of proof

4.173 As a threshold matter, the EC fails to meet its burden of proving that the United States has breached Article 22.8 of the DSU. As the complaining party, it shoulders the burden of proving each element of its claims against the United States. Article 22.8 requires that a Member either remove its WTO-inconsistent measure or provide a solution to the nullification or impairment suffered by the Member suspending concessions in order to demonstrate a breach. In other words, for purposes of its Article 22.8 claim, the EC must demonstrate how it has in fact accomplished either of these two conditions.

4.174 The EC's bald assertion of compliance in the context of this scientific and factual landscape highlights the fact that it has made no effort to demonstrate how its new import ban satisfies the conditions of a "provisional" ban under Article 5.7 of the *SPS Agreement* or "rationally relates" to or is "reasonably supported" by a risk assessment for purposes of Article 5.1 of the *SPS Agreement*. Its mere assertion that it can invoke Article 5.7 for the five hormones, and that it has developed a proper risk assessment for the sixth and that its ban is now based on such an assessment is not sufficient to demonstrate that it has removed its WTO-inconsistent measure or provided a solution to the EC's nullification or impairment of benefits, and thereby does not satisfy its burden of proof and make its prima facie case.

6. *"Presumption of good faith"*

4.175 In lieu of an attempt to satisfy its burden of proof, the EC argues the existence of a presumption or principle of good faith. Or, at least such a presumption applied selectively on the EC's terms. For the EC, the presumption applies to its unilateral declaration of compliance, but apparently does not apply to a Member's suspension of concessions in accordance with a DSB authorization.

4.176 In support of its argument, the EC cites dicta from WTO disputes in which panels, arbitrators, and the Appellate Body are simply elaborating on the appropriate burdens of proof in WTO dispute settlement. It is unexceptional and uncontested that, in a dispute, the complaining party bears the initial burden of proof to establish its claims of a WTO violation, and that there is no presumption of bad faith with respect to the responding party. Were it otherwise, complaining Members would not have to mount any case whatsoever to demonstrate a WTO violation. They could simply allege that it was so and prevail.

7. *The EC's interpretation of the DSU*

4.177 The EC claims that the United States has breached Articles 21.5 and 23 of the DSU by continuing to suspend concessions to the EC despite its claim of compliance. However, the EC's analysis of these provisions is not consistent with their terms, nor does it reflect the fact that the United States' DSB authorization remains valid.

(a) Article 21.5

4.178 For instance, the EC reads into Article 21.5 of the DSU an obligation that a Member duly authorized to suspend concessions must request an Article 21.5 panel the moment that another Member declares its own compliance with DSB recommendations and rulings. However, nothing in Article 21.5's text hints at such an obligation. Indeed, the DSU simply does not prescribe the particular procedures to follow in a situation where the DSB has granted authorization to suspend concessions to a Member, and the implementing Member later claims to have complied. Rather, it leaves open to the parties to choose one of various means to proceed, including bilateral consultations, use of good offices, conciliation and mediation under Article 5 of the DSU, recourse to DSU Article 21.5, arbitration under Article 25 of the DSU, and recourse to normal panel proceedings such as we are party to here.

4.179 Despite this fact, the EC would instead remove all alternatives except an Article 21.5 compliance proceeding and would read into that Article a deadline that is not there. The EC would also read into Article 21.5 an obligation for the complaining Member, and only that Member, to invoke Article 21.5. The EC does not base its proposed approach on the actual text of the Article, but rather constructs a series of policy arguments as to why the DSU should be re-written in the manner it desires.

4.180 There are three basic shortcomings in the EC's Article 21.5 analysis. First, Article 21.5 only applies in situations where there is a disagreement regarding the WTO-consistency of a measure taken to comply. Prior to the EC's request for the establishment of this Panel (and so by definition prior to the EC's request for consultations), the United States had not formulated an opinion as to the WTO-consistency of the EC's ban.

4.181 Second, Article 21.5 does not contain any time limitation or deadline by which a Member must initiate dispute settlement proceedings – a point emphasized by the fact that there is often substantial delay between claims of compliance and the initiation of Article 21.5 proceedings (presumably responding Members normally welcome such delays since they would not be in a hurry to have their claims of compliance questioned before a panel). The EC's interpretation of Article 21.5 would prevent Members such as the United States from exercising any judgment as to the fruitfulness of dispute settlement prior to finding themselves obligated to do so and would similarly preclude Members from seeking mutually agreeable solutions through negotiations.

4.182 Third, and finally, the EC argues that the United States was obligated to seek recourse to an Article 21.5 compliance panel, and only such a panel, upon hearing the EC's declaration. However, the text of Article 21.5 simply refers to "these dispute settlement procedures," without specifying any particular subset of procedures. Therefore, the EC's argument that the United States was specifically obligated to initiate a compliance proceeding under Article 21.5 is groundless.

(b)   Article 23

4.183 In addition to its claim of a US breach of Article 21.5, the EC also contends that the United States has breached Article 23.1 by seeking redress of a perceived WTO violation without recourse to dispute settlement and made a "determination" of the WTO-consistency of the EC's ban in breach of Article 23.2(a). We have done neither.

4.184 The United States was not obligated to seek recourse to dispute settlement pursuant to the general rule set out in Article 23.1 once the EC declared its own compliance at the DSB. The United States adhered to the letter of Article 23.1 by seeking redress of the nullification or impairment caused by the EC's import ban through recourse to the provisions of the DSU. The multilaterally-authorized suspension of concessions stemming from US recourse to dispute settlement remains valid to this day. It is unaffected by the EC's unilateral declaration of compliance, and the EC has failed to demonstrate to the contrary.

4.185 Similarly, the United States has made no Article 23.2(a) determination as to the WTO-consistency of the EC's amended ban. Since receiving authorization to suspend concessions to the EC, we have simply continued to act according to that authorization. Contrary to the EC's claims in this panel proceeding, we have made no determinations regarding the WTO-consistency of its import ban, amended or not. We did not have to make any further determinations in order to continue to suspend concessions. Article 22.8, discussed earlier, sets the parameters for when we would no longer have been authorized to do so. The EC has made no effort to demonstrate that any of the conditions of that Article have been met.

8.   Conclusion

4.186 For all the reasons discussed above and in its first written submission, the United States respectfully requests the Panel to reject the EC's claims in their entirety.

9.   Concluding Statement of the United States

4.187 The United States has actively engaged in this week's debate, examined in detail provisions of the DSU and the facts of this dispute. Taking into account all of these discussions and facts, it becomes clear that we find ourselves here today for a simple reason: the EC, a WTO Member who claimed to have come into conformity with DSB recommendations in the *EC – Hormones* dispute, did not want to undertake the effort of explaining why this was indeed the case. It chose not to attempt to satisfy its burden despite its eagerness to have the suspension of concessions lifted, and despite its possession of new Opinions and studies it so confidently alleged to support its ongoing ban. It has chosen not to make this attempt despite several avenues available to it in the current text of the DSU, including Article 22.8 (as well as Articles 5 and 25).

4.188 Instead, it chose to seek a suspension of sanctions in the most roundabout way possible – by alleging that the United States, by not lifting its suspension of concessions, breached its obligations under elaborate, intertwining interpretations of the DSU. This choice is remarkable given the fanfare that the EC attached to its ban and Opinions. One would have thought that an Article 22.8 finding that it had removed the ban or provided a solution to nullification or impairment would have been a logical and simple approach.

4.189 Yet, the EC did not pursue this straightforward course. Instead, it alleged that the United States had made a unilateral determination that the EC's new ban was not WTO-consistent. In this, it ignored the fact that the United States has been suspending concessions to the EC pursuant to DSB authorization. Moreover, having eschewed Article 22.8, the EC could not identify a standalone provision in the DSU regarding which it could allege a US breach. So, rather than looking to Members' obligations as they currently exist in the text of the DSU, the EC concocted two claims, melding and rewriting provisions of the DSU, and contending that it has demonstrated that the US suspension of concessions can no longer be applied.

4.190 The EC asserts that these claims are a "refinement" of the individual claims described in its panel request. However, rather than becoming more clear or "refined", the EC's claims blending multiple DSU provisions have become more and more muddled. I would like to take a moment to discuss a few of these "in conjunction with" claims.

4.191 I would first reiterate a question raised in Tuesday's session, and add one additional question for future consideration. In that meeting, the United States asked the EC whether it still alleged a US breach of Article 21.5 of the DSU *per se*. I would now ask a further question: does the EC still allege that the United States has breached Article 22.8 of the DSU? Why do I ask if there is a violation of these provisions *per se*? Because the EC has failed to identify, anywhere in the text of either Article, an obligation breached by the United States, and those are the only breaches possible under the DSU as currently written. Instead, the EC cloaks its alleged claims of breach "in conjunction" with claims of breach of other DSU provisions, ranging from Article 3.7 to Article 23.

4.192 The EC's repeated invocation of the phrase "in conjunction with" does not make the EC's interpretive approach any more credible. To the contrary, the phrase should be viewed as a signal that the argument which follows is based not on the text of the DSU, but on how the EC would like to see the DSU rewritten. Or, at least, how it would like to see the DSU rewritten for purposes of this dispute.

4.193 From our standpoint, it is impossible to tell if, through these "in conjunction with" claims, the EC still alleges an actual US breach of these provisions (Articles 21.5 and 22.8). Ironically, the EC refers to our attempts to respond to their jumbled claims on an individual, article-by-article basis as "obfuscat[ion]", yet it has told us all that, if the Panel makes a finding in its favour on one of these "in conjunction" claims, it expects very real, individual, un-conjoined breaches of Articles 21.5 and 22.8 to be an integral part of those findings.

4.194 According to the EC, an analysis of the black-and-white text of Articles 22.8 and 21.5 is "obfuscation," since these can only be analysed "in conjunction with" other provisions. In particular, I would highlight the following quotes from the EC's oral statement:

> "This Panel is asked to find whether, under Article 23, in conjunction with Article 21.5, a Member has an obligation ..." but that *"[i]t is not relevant for this dispute what obligations can be found directly in 21.5* in the absence of such unilateral conduct."

> "The defending parties ... ignore that the European Communities makes its systemic claim under *Article 22.8, in conjunction with Article 23.1.* Thus, the Panel is called upon to decide whether or not the conditions under Article 22.8 are fulfilled *in view of* the prohibition under Article 23 ..."

4.195 The EC's non-textual approach appears to be an attempt to distract from the fact that it does not wish to attempt to make its prima facie case of an Article 22.8 breach by demonstrating, pursuant to the actual, current, text of that provision that it has either removed its WTO-inconsistent measure or provided a solution to the nullification or impairment. Likewise, it seeks to avoid any analysis of what obligations are actually found in the text of Article 21.5, since that provision does not in fact obligate the United States to bring an Article 21.5 proceeding, nor does it contain a time limitation for doing so.

4.196 Rather than a "refinement" of the EC's case, these "in conjunction" arguments only make the EC's case all the more obtuse – creating in essence a moving target for responding parties. We are forced to defend ourselves against accusations that we are in breach of provisions that do not, in fact, exist. We have exposed in the question and answer session the potentially confusing outcome of recommendations and rulings on some of the EC's claims – an outcome that would result from the EC's inability to demonstrate a US breach of any of these provisions standing alone. Fortunately, there is a simple way to avoid this confusing outcome – to look instead to the text of the DSU as it is currently written, not as a single Member's policy would have it rewritten.

4.197 We have demonstrated in our submissions that Article 21.5 does not contain any obligations that the United States could theoretically have breached. For example, there is no obligation that the United States bring a compliance proceeding upon learning of the EC's declaration of compliance. Further, there is no time period, whether that period is immediate or is unspecified, indefinable and unwritten "reasonable delay" championed by the EC. Pursuant to this fictional new Article 21.5 requirement developed by the EC, if a Member requests an Article 21.5 panel "a month or two – rather than two years – into implementation" it has satisfied its imaginary deadline to do so. Maybe I have not been looking hard enough at the text of Article 21.5, but I have not been able to locate the "reasonable delay" deadline yet. This is not surprising, because the EC makes every effort to avoid the actual text of Article 21.5. According to the EC, the fact that we can demonstrate that we have not breached the provisions of Article 21.5 is not the point – because "[i]t is not relevant for this dispute what obligations can be found directly in 21.5."

4.198 We have demonstrated in our submissions that we have not breached Article 22.8, which requires that the suspension of concessions "only be applied until such time as the measure found to be inconsistent with a covered agreement has been removed, or the Member that must implement recommendations or rulings provides a solution to the nullification or impairment of benefits, or a mutually satisfactory solution is reached." We have shown that the EC has failed to demonstrate that any of these three conditions have been met. There is no satisfactory solution, no removal of the measure, and no provision of a solution to US nullification or impairment. Indeed, the EC does not engage in a discussion of whether or not it has satisfied these conditions whatsoever. In the eyes of the EC any substantive analysis of Article 22.8 would involve analysis of a "(direct) violation" of Article 22.8. Evidently, a direct analysis of a direct violation of the actual text of Article 22.8 is not relevant to this proceeding. This is the case because, for the EC, its reference to Article 22.8 in Part I of its submission is only to be read "in conjunction with" Article 23. As a result, the United States is evidently left to rebut an "indirect" claim. Indirect, that is, in that it evidently does not involve analysis of the obligations specifically set out in Article 22.8. Not so indirect in that, through this Article 22.8 "in conjunction with" Article 23 claim, the EC seeks a finding of a very full-fledged, very direct US violation of Article 22.8.

4.199 So, finally, we come to the "central provision" of the EC's claims against the United States – Article 23. Like it did for Articles 21.5 and 22.8, the United States set out clear arguments, based on the text of this provision as it is currently set out in the DSU. We demonstrated that, at the appropriate time, we sought recourse to dispute settlement and obtained the proper DSB authorization. We continued to suspend those concessions pursuant to this authorization.

4.200 It is critical to note that, just because the DSU does not set out an explicit path for Members to pursue in this "post-suspension" scenario, it provides several options by which, pursuant to its text as currently written, the EC may have sought review of its measure. The EC, contrary to what it would apparently have this Panel believe, was not without avenues for obtaining a multilateral determination that its measure was or was not WTO-consistent. For example, I should reiterate that, as we have indicated on several occasions, we find ourselves in a perfectly suitable panel proceeding to examine the EC's compliance pursuant to DSU Article 22.8. While the EC would argue that an Article 22.8 claim against the United States, and a need to make a prima facie case that it has either removed its offending measure or provided a solution to nullification or impairment is only raised in its Part II claim, we would note that it is also squarely before this Panel in the Part I claims set out in the EC's first written submission, only in the form of the opaque "23 in conjunction with 22.8" claim, which evidently sets out an "indirect" Article 22.8 claim.

4.201 We have also commented that an Article 21.5 compliance panel could be a possible avenue for determining whether or not the EC has brought its measure into compliance with DSB recommendations and rulings. The EC has raised various issues concerning a Member bringing a compliance proceeding against itself. Among these, it has argued that the *EC – Bananas (Article 21.5)* proceeding does not demonstrate that a Member may do so. In the third party session, it responded to another party's comment that, by the very fact that the EC composed an Article 21.5 panel, it demonstrated that this is a possible avenue. However, the EC's dismissal of this comment because the report was not adopted ignored the point being made. Apart from the fact that the report was not adopted for the simple reason that the EC never requested its adoption, it is unclear why adoption or lack of adoption of the report has any bearing on the simple fact that the EC was indeed able to request the Article 21.5 panel.

4.202 I would now like to turn to Part II of the EC's argument.

4.203 Part II of the EC's argument, its "direct" Article 22.8 claim against the United States, is the embodiment of what this case would look like if the EC chose to put its amended measure forward for multilateral review. That the EC has brought this claim is testament to the fact that it is possible to do so, that it is possible for an implementing Member to put its measure squarely before an Article 6 panel and to seek multilateral review and findings of the WTO-consistency of that measure.

4.204 The issue of burden of proof came up in yesterday's meetings, and I think that we should touch upon it at this point. Yesterday, the EC expressed its concern regarding what would be involved in setting out a prima facie case of removal of its measure or providing a solution to nullification or impairment for purposes of an Article 22.8 claim against the United States. I think that everyone here would agree that this is not exactly an insurmountable task, in particular, for a Member like the EC who has just spent the last six years producing studies on these hormones and developing Opinions evaluating those risks. The EC believes its ongoing ban is tied neatly to these studies and Opinions, and one would think it of little consequence for the EC to explain why it felt justified in declaring itself to be in compliance with the DSB's recommendations and rulings, why it believes that its ban on oestradiol-17β is based on a risk assessment within the meaning of Article 5.1 of the *SPS Agreement*, and whether its provisional ban on the five other hormones satisfied the conditions of Article 5.7. The EC could, for example, have addressed its alleged compliance with specific panel and Appellate Body findings. But the EC did not do so, and instead relies on unsupported assertions.

4.205 It is worth noting that the question of the precise level of evidence and argumentation necessary to establish a prima facie case is rarely at issue in WTO dispute settlement, for the simple reason that both sides typically engage on the merits, allowing the panel to evaluate the totality of the evidence presented to determine whether the responding party has adequately rebutted the complaining party's arguments. Indeed, the United States in this proceeding has engaged on the substance of the EC's new studies as if the EC had attempted to make its prima facie case. The EC's failure to actually do so, and its reliance in this dispute on creative redrafting of the DSU, says more about the EC's lack of confidence in its own scientific evidence than it does about the supposed difficulty of understanding how to establish a prima facie case.

G.   Second Written Submission of the European Communities

1.   Introduction

4.206 The European Communities' case is straightforward. WTO Members that apply sanctions against another WTO Member cannot adopt a lean-back-and-wait-attitude over years and continue to suspend concessions in the presence of a subsequent compliance measure. Just as WTO Members who have been found to be in violation of the covered agreements have a positive obligation to implement, so have retaliating Members a positive obligation under Article 22.8 not to apply sanctions any more and/or, if they disagree with the compliance measure, to initiate WTO proceedings under Article 21.5. This has always been the practice in WTO proceedings. If a retaliating WTO Member fails to respect these rules and procedures under the DSU, it will be in violation of Articles 23.1 and 23.2(a).

2.   PART 1: Violation of Articles 23.1, 23.2(a), 21.5 and 22.8 of the DSU (systemic issues)

(a)   The United States is in violation of Article 23.1 and 23.2(a) read together with Article 21.5

4.207 The existence of a DSB authorization does not exclude that a WTO Member is still seeking the redress of a violation within the meaning of Article 23.1. The very fact of applying sanctions implies that a Member is seeking to redress a violation. Such an application of sanctions may be justified if a measure by a WTO-Member has been properly found to be WTO-inconsistent and, if on that basis, the DSB authorizes the suspension of concessions. However, the situation is different regarding the *continuation* of sanctions in the presence of a compliance measure which the DSB has never found to be WTO-inconsistent or which has not even been challenged. In such case, a DSB authorization which has been granted in view of an original WTO-inconsistent measure can not justify the continued application of sanctions against a different measure. Rather, since the application of sanctions requires a causal relationship to a WTO-inconsistent measure, any *present* application of sanctions must be linked to a *present* measure, i.e. violation. Conversely, the *present* application of sanctions to a *past*, no longer existing measure is not justified just as it would be unjustified to link the *present* application of sanctions to a *future*, not yet existing measure.

4.208 The US counter-argument would lead to the absurd result that the United States could continue to apply sanctions irrespective of any events occurring after the DSB authorization and thus ignoring the object and purpose of sanctions, i.e. to induce compliance and to rebalance rights and obligations in case of a WTO violation. If the United States applies sanctions merely because of the existence of a DSB authorization and irrespective of a subsequent compliance measure, they are neither inducing nor rebalancing anything. The United States fails to acknowledge that the situation has changed by the adoption of the EC implementing measure. Yet, since the United States has adopted a negative position on the EC compliance measure and since the United States has been under no obligation to continue the suspension of concessions, the very fact that it nevertheless continues the application of sanctions proves that despite its claim to the contrary the United States is indeed drawing a causal link between the continuation of the suspension and the determination of inconsistency of the EC compliance measure.

4.209 The opposite US view would lead to the conclusion that the United States is currently applying sanctions against a no longer existing measure, because it is uncontested that the original measure which the DSB found inconsistent has been removed by the EC. However, the true reason for the US application of sanctions is that it considers the existence of an "import ban" as such as a violation. The United States does so on the basis of a unilateral determination since the current import ban is a totally new measure which has never been found WTO-inconsistent. Thus, in the presence of a compliance measure the United States assumes a right to determine unilaterally whether this measure is sufficient or not. Furthermore, the fact that the United States seeks redress is also evidenced for instance by its statement in the 2005 Trade Policy Agenda whereby the United States openly links the continued application of sanctions to the EC compliance measure. Conversely, the United States did *not* state that it continues to apply sanctions because of the DSB authorization.

4.210 The United States has also made a unilateral "determination" that a violation has occurred. The term "determination" is defined, *inter alia*, as an "authoritative opinion"; "a conclusion reached"; "the action of coming to a decision"; "the result of this"; "a fixed intention". This term has been further elaborated by the Panel in *US – Section 301*. Thus, even an implicit determination by the appropriate behaviour, such as the continuation of sanctions, would be covered by a "broad reading" of this requirement, in particular if the continuation occurs deliberately and is accompanied by respective statements.

4.211 Moreover, the interpretation of the word "determination" should be guided by the context of Article 23.2(a), which is Article 23.1, and the object and purpose of this provision. This provision as a whole aims at preventing that a Member takes "the law in its hands" and seeks the redress of a violation on the basis of a unilateral determination. The importance of this general principle is also confirmed by the title of this provision. The crucial importance of Article 23 has also been acknowledged by the Panel in *US – Section 301*. It is therefore necessary to look at a Member's behaviour as a whole when confronted with a respective situation. If a WTO Member repeatedly and consistently states that a violation by another Member exists and, in this context, this Member applies concrete measures against the other Member, it can be concluded that this Member is seeking a redress against a violation on the basis of a unilateral determination. Applying these principles to the present case, there can be no doubt that the United States has made a unilateral "determination" of non-compliance of the EC measure. This is demonstrated by the 2005 Trade Policy Agenda and, for instance, the US statement in the DSB meeting of December 2003. In addition, it deliberately *continues* to apply sanctions against the European Communities. Contrary to what the US purports, this continuation is also a positive action and not just some "inaction".

4.212 The European Communities adopted and notified its compliance measure over two years ago. To these two years one could add another three years since the European Communities notified its legislative proposal to the SPS Committee in November 2000. Against this time lag it is not credible for the United States to argue that it has still not made a determination. Rather the US attitude is explained by the attempt to declare its rights sacrosanct and to refuse any responsibility for a prompt resolution (see Article 3.3) of the dispute.

4.213 Finally, Article 23 in conjunction with Article 22.8 obliges a retaliating Member to take note of a compliance measure and to decide if the continued application of sanctions is still justified. Furthermore, Article 23 prohibits making a unilateral determination of *non-compliance*. Conversely, nothing prevents the United States under Article 23 to make a unilateral determination of *compliance*. Thus, unlike what the United States pretends Article 23 does not prohibit any "determination".

4.214 The European Communities considers that, by refusing to initiate a compliance proceeding in this situation, the United States is in breach of Article 21.5. Contrary to what the United States purports, there exists a "disagreement" between the European Communities and the United States. The term "disagreement" is defined as "a refusal to accord or agree, difference of opinion, quarrel". The US attitude towards the EC compliance measure cannot escape this basic definition in the light of its statements and the continuation of sanctions. There is no contradiction between Articles 21.5 and 23. Article 23 does not apply to any sort of "disagreement' but only in case of a "determination" of a violation which a Member is "seeking to redress". This is exactly what the United States is currently doing. In any event Article 23 contains an explicit reference to dispute settlement proceedings, which includes Article 21.5 of the DSU. Thus, had the United States invoked a procedure under Article 21.5 of the DSU, it would have fully satisfied Article 23.2(a) of the DSU.

4.215 Finally, it is appropriate to read into Article 21.5 a reasonable timeframe until which a retaliating Member can be expected to decide whether an implementing member is WTO consistent and whether to launch a compliance proceeding. This is not to be confused with a "deadline" as the United States asserts. According to Article 3.3, disputes should be settled "promptly". Also, every treaty must be performed in good faith, according to Article 26 of the Vienna Convention. Moreover, Article 21.5 provides that a Panel has 90 days to determine whether an implementing measure is WTO-consistent. If a Panel can be asked to decide in 90 days whether there is compliance, it is not acceptable that a retaliating Member argues eight times as long that it cannot determine the consistency of the measure. This is even more relevant in a case like this one which involves the continued application of sanctions.

4.216 Regarding the US argument about alternative procedures other than Article 21.5 the US conceptual approach is not clear. In any case, Article 21.5 literally provides for a specific panel proceeding in case there is a disagreement about the WTO consistency of a compliance measure. This is consistent with Article 3.3. Contrary to what the United States asserts, Article 21.5 is therefore not purely a matter of political opportunity in particular if at the same time it assumes the right to continue to sanction the implementing WTO Member. As explained in detail in its second written submission, the European Communities considers that the US examples in this respect demonstrate an extraordinary denial of any responsibility for the well-functioning of the dispute settlement system and the prompt settlement of disputes. This is also corroborated by the US reply to Questions 46 and 42 of the Panel where the United States first mischaracterizes the correct implementation in this case and, second, where the United States contradicts itself regarding its alleged interest for a quick resolution of the dispute. Finally, the special procedure under Article 21.5 is also not overridden by any alternative means such as good offices, conciliation, mediation or arbitration under Articles 5 and 25 which are neither enforceable nor legally binding.

4.217 Regarding the self-initiation of an Article 21.5 proceeding the European Communities demonstrated that also in the light of the *Bananas* case, the whole approach does not work and it would be inconsistent to the logic of the DSU as well as specific provisions such as Article 6 or 1.1.

(b)   The United States' continued suspension of
       concessions and related obligations is in violation
       of Article 23.1, read together with Articles 22.8
       and 3.7

4.218 The European Communities disagrees with the US assertion that the continued application of the sanctions is unrelated to the EC compliance measure. Since the original EC measure has been removed, the US argument would mean that the US is currently applying sanctions against a non-existing measure. Such a conclusion would not only be illogical it would also be in plain contradiction with the purpose of sanctions, namely to rebalance rights and obligations and to induce compliance in the light of a *current* WTO violation. As explained several times, it is obvious that the United States continues to apply the sanctions because it considers the EC compliance measure as WTO inconsistent. However, the continued application of an "old" DSB authorization cannot be justified against a "new" measure on which the DSB authorization is not based and if this new measure has never properly been found to be WTO-inconsistent.

4.219 Contrary to what the United States asserts the prohibition to continue the application of sanctions under Article 22.8 does not depend on whether the DSB authorization has been formally removed. Article 22.8 is unequivocal in the sense that the suspension of concessions and related obligations may only be "applied" until the inconsistency of the measure has been removed. In addition, Article 22.8 subjects the application of sanctions to a measure which has been found inconsistent. Yet, this can only occur through a proper proceeding under WTO but not through a unilateral determination. Article 22.8 is also of self-executing nature and the termination of the application of sanctions under this provision does not depend on a specific finding of the DSB or a withdrawal of the DSB authorization. Rather, once the conditions under Article 22.8 of the DSU are met – including in the presence of an unchallenged compliance measure – the application of suspension "shall" automatically stop.

4.220 Finally, the European Communities does not agree with the US that the principle of good faith is not relevant for WTO proceedings in general or only relevant for the issue of burden of proof. This radical position is not supported by the general public international law, which also applies to the WTO, as for instance expressed in Article 26 of the Vienna Convention. In this context, the European Communities also considers that due to the specific circumstances for the adoption of its compliance measure as explained in detail in its various submissions and in the absence of a concrete challenge by the United States and in the light of the time that has passed since the measure was prepared and adopted, it is fully entitled to invoke the principle of good faith and the presumption of compliance.

3. *PART 2: The WTO-consistency of the EC compliance measure*

4.221 The European Communities, in its Oral Statement at the first substantive hearing as well as in a number of replies to the Panel's questions, has explained the various steps undertaken to carry out the comprehensive risk assessment which led to the adoption of its implementation measure, i.e. the revised Hormones Directive 2003/74/EC. As the Appellate Body found that the studies and other evidence presented by the European Communities was relevant but not sufficiently specific, the objective of the compliance effort undertaken was to re-assess all existing and most recent data from any relevant source for the six hormones and to complement these data in particular in three respects, namely: (a) on certain issues regarding specific health risks from residues in meat treated with hormones for growth promotion purposes, (b) on risks arising from possible abusive use and difficulties of control, and (c) on an appropriate risk assessment for melengestrol acetate (MGA), which had not been carried out so far. To this effect the European Communities launched 17 specific studies and tried to collect information from all relevant sources, including from third countries, international scientific bodies (such as JECFA) and industry. All these steps were undertaken in full transparency and after consulting the relevant scientific committees and bodies that are responsible under Community law to conduct this kind of assessment.

4.222 In November 1998, the European Communities mandated its Scientific Committee on Veterinary measures relating to Public Health (SCVPH), to address the potential risks to human health from hormone residues in bovine meat and meat products treated with the six hormones for growth promotion. The SCVPH adopted its opinion unanimously taking into account all pertinent scientific information available at the time, including JECFA's revised assessment of the three natural hormones oestradiol-17β, testosterone and progesterone that had been issued in February 1999. The 1999 Opinion concluded that a risk to the consumer had been identified with different levels of conclusive evidence for the six hormones evaluated. Subsequently, the SCVPH was twice requested to review its opinion in light of new assessments carried out by other bodies or institutions and new evidence. The SCVPH did so in 2000 and 2002. The SCVPH concluded both times that the new evidence did not provide convincing data and arguments demanding revision of its previous conclusions. On the basis of the above scientific risk assessments provided by the SCVPH, the competent European regulatory authorities carried out an analysis of risk management options in light of the appropriate level of protection it had chosen. This lead to the adoption of the EC compliance measure 2003/74/EC.

4.223 As explained in detail in the second written submission, JECFA's assessment proved insufficient in various respects and where the SCVPH conducted a more thorough analysis. These areas concern *carcinogenicity* of the three natural hormones and the outdated *residues data* as well as for data concerning the dose-response relationship. In respect of the latter, JECFA also neglected the endogenous production in the case of *pre-pubertal children*. Furthermore, the 1999 JECFA report has been seriously undermined by recent developments concerning the *bioavailability* of residues of these hormones. JECFA also failed to address the possibilities for *misuse or abuse* when the administration of these hormones is freely authorised "over the counter", as is the situation in the United States.

4.224 Turning to the legal arguments, the European Communities disagrees with the US arguments regarding the burden of proof. The European Communities, at the oral hearing and in reply to the Panel's questions, has demonstrated a violation of Articles I:1 and II of the GATT 1994 by the US and that the measure found to be inconsistent has been "removed" in the context of a direct claim under Article 22.8. In particular, the European Communities has pointed out that it cannot be required to prove a negative, namely that there is no violation of WTO obligations. In line with the established case law of the Appellate Body, it is for the United States, in this case, to set out a prima facie case of violation, and not for the European Communities to set out a case of non-violation.

(a)   Article 5.7 of the *SPS Agreement*

4.225 In respect of the provisional prohibition of the relevant hormones under Article 5.7 SPS the European Communities considers that the compliance measure fully respects the respective standard. As regards the "insufficiency" of the scientific evidence for conducting a risk assessment the European Communities recalls that: (1) what the European Communities had considered to be sufficient evidence had been found to be insufficient by the Appellate Body and proved indeed to be insufficient also in the light of risk assessment standards that were developed in the years after the *Hormones* decision; and (2) the body of evidence, in the meantime, has developed and, while still not providing enough knowledge to carry out a complete and definitive risk assessment, supports the conclusion that precautionary measures are required in order to achieve its chosen level of protection.

4.226 As further detailed in its Written and Oral Submissions the European Communities considers, on the basis of the 1999 – 2002 SCVPH opinions, that the current evidence is full of gaps in pertinent information and important contradictions that render the conclusions reached by JECFA in 1988, 1999 and 2000 no longer valid. Thus, it does not allow, in qualitative or quantitative terms, the performance of an adequate assessment of risks as required under Article 5.1 and as defined in Annex A to the *SPS Agreement*. Furthermore, since the latest risk assessment by the SCVPH in 2002, there appeared internationally a number of further scientific developments all of which converge toward, and provide further support to, the conclusions reached by the relevant scientific committee of the European Communities, such as a study supported by the Ohio State University, the US National Cancer Institute and the US Department of Defence Breast Cancer Research program concerning zeranol (and oestradiol-17β) or a large scale epidemiological study in Europe suggesting that high red meat intake is associated with (statistically significant) increased colorectal cancer risk, confirming results from previous smaller studies. Additionally, in 2002 results were published from the women's health Initiative Randomised Controlled Trial findings indicating that the risks outweigh the benefits from the use of oestrogen plus progestin in healthy postmenopausal women, thus reinforcing the previous findings made by the IARC in this respect. All this evidence and most recent scientific developments have now clearly tipped the balance against the previously held assumption (by the US and Codex/JECFA) that residues of these hormones in meat from animals treated for growth promotion pose no risk to human health.

4.227 Consequently, the evidence which served as the basis in the 1988 and 1999-2000 JECFA evaluations of these hormones is not sufficient to perform a definitive risk assessment, in particular by the WTO Members applying a high level of health protection of no risk from exposure to unnecessary additional residues in meat of animals treated with hormones for growth promotion. To deny the existence of this new scientific reality would deprive the European Communities and other WTO Members of their autonomous right to choose their appropriate level of protection, because it would in effect impose on them a requirement to demonstrate positively the existence of clear harm, which they may not always be able to fulfil in case of cancer because of the long latency period and the numerous confounding factors that play a role. This will render the application of Article 5.7 impossible in a situation where the body of the pertinent scientific evidence is in the process of moving from a state of presumed "sufficiency" into a state of pertinent "insufficiency". The text and preparatory history of the *SPS Agreement* do not support such a (restrictive) construction of Article 5.7, which would moreover be against the principle of effective treaty interpretation.

4.228 In its second written submission the European Communities has set out in detail the state of insufficient evidence as determined by the SCVPH for each of the hormones which have been provisionally (progesterone, testosterone, trenbolone, zeranol, MGA) prohibited by the Directive 2003/74/EC.

4.229 As regards progesterone, the US has not pointed to relevant evidence to rebut the SCVPH conclusions. The US instead merely relies on old JECFA conclusions which have been overtaken by more recent studies in 2002. Equally erroneous is the US' reference to the CVMP's opinion which is irrelevant for the purposes of this dispute as it concerns an assessment of progesterone for zootechnical and therapeutic purposes. In any case, even the CVMP's assessment pointed out that only few recent data were available for re-evaluation of the carcinogenic and/or genotoxic properties of progesterone and had concluded that the compound (1) is not genotoxic in most of the tests performed and (2) increases tumor incidences in animals at exposure levels clearly above the physiological levels.

4.230 As regards testosterone, the US other than referring to the 1999 JECFA assessment, does not put forward any specific argument. However, the JECFA assessment had been addressed by the SCVPH in 1999. As pointed out above with regard to progesterone, the US' reference to the epidemiological studies on the effects of the hormones on post-menopausal women, in the context of an assessment of testosterone, is equally erroneous. Furthermore, as regards the US' comparison between bulls and steers and which have different endogenous testosterone levels very much depends on the age at slaughter, the breed used, and the type of husbandry employed in rearing these animals. The US argument is therefore at best irrelevant in deciding the central issues of the present dispute.

4.231 As regards trenbolone, the US does not put forward any specific argument as to why the evidence assessed by the SCVPH would not be insufficient. As a matter of fact, the only assessment on trenbolone publicly available is that of JECFA 1988. The SCVPH took into account this assessment but disagreed with a number of its basic findings on the bases of more recent scientific evidence, some of which was generated by the 17 EC studies.

4.232 As regards zeranol, the US does not put forward any specific argument as to why the evidence assessed by the SCVPH would not be insufficient. The only assessment on zeranol publicly available is that of JECFA which dates back to 1988. The SCVPH took into account this assessment but disagreed with a number of its basic findings on the bases of more recent scientific evidence, some of which was generated by the 17 EC studies. Moreover, the most recent study on zeranol and the risks associated with its administration to meat producing animals is done by independent US scientists mentioned above and it clearly invalidates the findings of the 1988 JECFA opinion.

4.233 As regards MGA, there is currently no international standard or recommendation on MGA, as Codex has not adopted one. JECFA assessed MGA for the first time in 2000 (and in 2004 as regards the calculation of the MRL only), but this has not yet led to the adoption of a standard. If one examines the evidence that served as the basis of the 2000 JECFA report it can be seen that nearly all the studies referred to therein date from the 1960s and 1970s. These very old studies constitute in fact the evidence which the defending parties have refused to provide to the European Communities, despite its repeated requests on the grounds that they are confidential. In the absence of a Codex standard, the opinion of JECFA becomes irrelevant, for the additional reason that it failed to take into account the more recent data generated by the 17 EC studies and the 2002 SCVPH assessment. The US does not put forward any specific argument as to why the evidence assessed by the SCVPH would not be insufficient. It does not even refer, in this context, to the fact that MGA, in the meantime (2000), has been assessed (for the first time) by the JECFA and which subsequently has been taken into account by the SCVPH in its 2002 Opinion. Moreover, the US referred to a draft 2005 report from the UK CVP in support of its arguments. However, even this draft report confirms the insufficiency of the currently available evidence.

4.234 Contrary to what the US asserts, the EC's compliance measure has been adopted on the basis of available pertinent information. In this context, the European Communities would reject the US assumption that a risk has to be demonstrated in order to justify a measure adopted on the basis of Article 5.7 of the *SPS Agreement*. The whole point of evidence being "insufficient" is that it does not allow the clear demonstration of a risk. If a risk can be demonstrated, it means that there is sufficient evidence to carry out a proper risk assessment. In its reply to the Panel Question 68 the European Communities explained the difference between the objective or rational relationship between sufficient scientific evidence and a measure within the meaning of Article 5.1, on the one hand, and insufficient evidence and a measure within the meaning of Article 5.7, on the other. Under Article 5.1, an objective or rational relationship is required between the evidence and the measure. Under Article 5.7 a scientifically established doubt must be sufficient. As explained for each of the five hormones, the available pertinent information while being inconclusive in terms of demonstrating a risk, nevertheless points to the possible occurrence of certain adverse effects, which invalidate or put into serious doubts previously held assumptions about the safety of these hormones by the defending parties and Codex/JECFA.

4.235 Furthermore, in contrast to the US, the European Communities does see itself under an obligation, under Article 5.7 of the *SPS Agreement*, to seek additional information. It has specifically laid down that obligation in Directive 2003/74/EC and the European Communities has already undertaken initiatives to seek additional information. In particular, it has issued a new call for scientific data and research from 2002 onwards, on substances with hormonal activity which may be used for growth promotion purposes in bovine meat.

4.236 Finally, the European Communities has not violated its obligation to review the provisional measure within a reasonable period of time as argued by the US. First, it is erroneous for the US to apply a review requirement to a measure before that measure has even come into existence. That shortcoming becomes even more apparent as it raises the question how the US explains what it is the European Communities has actually done between 1998 and 2003 if not to review the measure in question. In the view of the European Communities a requirement to review a measure "within a reasonable period of time" can only apply after the provisional measure has come into effect. In the light of the time it took to review the original measure (1998-2002) it can hardly be argued that a reasonable period of time has actually already elapsed. Furthermore, the only new information that has come to the knowledge of the European Communities until now is the recent draft assessment of the UK Group. That draft report has already been forwarded to European Food Safety Authority (EFSA) for review. Equally, should the recent call for new scientific information yield any new evidence, such evidence would also be assessed by EFSA without any undue delay.

(b)   Article 5.1 of the *SPS Agreement*

4.237 The European Communities has based the permanent prohibition of oestradiol-17β on an appropriate risk assessment. The European Communities has already pointed out in its reply to Question 24 of the Panel, the difference between a scientific risk assessment in the narrow sense clearly referred to here by the United States and the risk assessment within the meaning of Article 5.1 and Annex A Point 4 of the *SPS Agreement.* The latter, as has been stated by the Appellate Body, also comprises a risk management stage which is the responsibility of the regulator to carry out and not of the scientific bodies. Furthermore, the SCVPH has explicitly based its assessment on the three elements of hazard identification, hazard characterization and exposure assessment recommended and applied by the Codex. A few qualifications, however, apply. First, risk assessment criteria as they have been developed by the dispute settlement bodies are clearly more relevant to the application of the *SPS Agreement* than those developed by international scientific bodies. This follows naturally from the fact that it is the former's duty and privilege to interpret the provisions of the *SPS Agreement*. Second, there is no Codex standard specifically on the risk assessment of effects of residues of veterinary drugs. There only exists a general standard on microbiological assessment. Third, Codex techniques or standards exclusively apply to risk assessments on food safety and not to other risk assessments such as those for animal health and environmental risks. This is of relevance here insofar as the SCVPH Opinions also discuss environmental risks of the hormonal substances in question and some of the 17 EC studies have generated for the first time pioneering results in these areas.

4.238 Regarding the various steps of the risk assessment, the US does not criticize the hazard identification by the SCVPH but its hazard characterization because no or no adequate dose response assessment would have been carried out. However, the US' equation of hazard characterization and dose-response assessment is clearly erroneous. As defined by Codex, hazard characterization refers to the possibility of either a *quantitative* or a *qualitative* evaluation. While a dose-response assessment is a quantitative evaluation, a qualitative evaluation may equally be done, in particular in the absence of available data on dose-response. That is confirmed by the last sentence of the definition which recognises that data may not be available on biological or physical agents. More generally, it is confirmed by the Appellate Body which stressed that a risk assessment within the meaning of Article 5.1 does not necessarily require a quantitative evaluation. Moreover, it should be further clarified that it is generally recognised that for substances which have genotoxic potential (as is the case with oestradiol-17β) a threshold cannot be identified. Therefore it cannot be said that there exists a level below which intakes from residue should be considered to be safe. Therefore the fact the doses used in growth promotion are low is not of relevance. Thus, the argument of the United States that there is no hazard characterization is incorrect.

4.239 Regarding the exposure assessment, the US argument concerning pathway/residue analysis, no risks of abuse and low bioavailability do not demonstrate that the Opinions of the SCVPH fail to complete an exposure assessment as defined by Codex. Moreover, what the US does also not explain is that its own responsible health authorities have, for the first time since 2002, declared that oestradiol-17β is proven to be a human carcinogen and it is now listed as such, since 2002, in the USA Annual Report on Carcinogens.

4.240 The European Communities' ban on oestradiol-17β is also based on a risk assessment. Contrary to what the United States asserts, the SCVPH's assessment supports the ban on oestradiol-17β, but more recent research as referred to in detail in the EC second written submission equally confirms that that measure is warranted.

(c)   Article 3.3 of the *SPS Agreement*

4.241 The US argues that a violation of Article 3.3 exists because the ban would not be in conformity with Article 5.1 of the *SPS Agreement*. The European Communities does not contest that the ban on oestradiol-17β is not based on international standards. The only relevant standard is the Codex recommendation on MRLs for oestradiol-17β. The European Communities, however, has decided not to set MRLs as recommended by Codex, but instead to prohibit the use of oestradiol-17β for growth promotion purposes altogether. That decision is based on a comprehensive risk assessment which, as has been demonstrated above is in full conformity with Article 5.1 of the *SPS Agreement*.

H.   Second Written Submission of the United States

1.   Introduction

4.242 The United States maintains the measures at issue in this dispute in accordance with express authority from the Dispute Settlement Body. At this point in this dispute, it is clear that the European Communities has not, and cannot, demonstrate that these measures breach US obligations under the DSU or the GATT 1994, nor has nor can the EC demonstrate that other so-called "measures" that it challenges in fact existed as of the time this Panel was established.

4.243 As the United States has already pointed out, the EC's arguments relating to its DSU claims underscore its inability to meet its burden in this dispute, that is, to demonstrate that it has satisfied the Article 22.8 condition of removing the WTO-inconsistencies of its measures or providing a solution to US nullification or impairment. Moreover, for the reasons already set forth in previous submissions and discussed further below, the EC's arguments that various DSU provisions can create obligations "in conjunction with" each other cannot change the fact that whether a provision is read on its own or "in conjunction with" another provision does not alter the substance of the provision. Nor can unilateral declarations by a Member concerned create a "presumption of good faith."

4.244 The United States has not breached Article 23 of the DSU. The United States was authorized to suspend concessions by the DSB, and the EC's declaration of compliance did not cause this authorization to lapse, to be revoked or to be suspended. The EC's declaration did not mean that the United States could no longer apply the suspension of concessions without breaching its obligations under the DSU. Nor did the EC's declaration and development of a "new" measure create a scenario whereby US application of the suspension of concessions could be considered a "determination" as to the WTO-consistency or inconsistency of the amended ban.

4.245 Regarding the EC's purported demonstration of how it has come into compliance, the EC merely asserted in its first submission that it had come into compliance. Notwithstanding the EC's failure to even undertake the required demonstration, the United States responded in its first written submission by explaining in detail that the EC's import bans, despite DSB recommendations and rulings, continue not to be based on a risk assessment within the meaning of Article 5.1 of the *SPS Agreement*. Neither are they legitimate "provisional" bans within the meaning of Article 5.7 of the *SPS Agreement*. The materials put forward by the EC in its replies to questions from the Panel do little to change these conclusions. In fact, in several of its replies, the EC appears to have completely shifted its focus from theoretical risks posed by the six hormones themselves to a perceived "risk" of failure to satisfy good veterinary practices in administering the hormones to cattle in the United States.

2.   *Legal arguments*

(a)   The EC has failed to demonstrate a US breach of DSU Articles 21.5, 22.8 or 23

4.246 The EC has failed to demonstrate that the United States has breached its obligations under Article 21.5 of the DSU. In fact, the EC has failed to link US action or inaction to any obligation contained in Article 21.5's text whatsoever. Instead, it claims that the United States has breached Article 21.5 by acting in contravention of Article 23 of the DSU. The United States has not acted in breach of Article 23, and therefore, even under the EC's theory, the United States can not have breached any obligations under Article 21.5 of the DSU.

4.247 Rather than pointing the Panel to a particular obligation in Article 21.5 of the DSU that it alleges the United States breached, the EC instead persists in its argument that a violation of Article 21.5 can only be found "in conjunction with" or when that Article is "read together" with DSU Article 23. In support of this claim, the EC notes that "there is nothing unusual to cite various provisions to substantiate a claim. This follows actually the same approach the Panel took in the dispute *US - Certain Measures*."

4.248 The EC is simply wrong about the approach that the Panel took, however. When the Appellate Body examined the findings to which the EC is referring, the Appellate Body pointed out that "[o]ur reading of the Panel Report does not lead us to conclude that the Panel based its finding of the inconsistency of the 3 March Measure with Article 21.5 on its conclusion that the measure was inconsistent with Article 23.2(a) ... The Panel's *references to Article 23.2(a) cannot be construed as the basis upon which the Panel reached its conclusions under Article 21.5*."

4.249 As the United States has demonstrated, nowhere in Article 21.5 of the DSU is there an obligation for the United States to have sought recourse to an Article 21.5 compliance panel, and only such a panel, upon hearing the EC's declaration of compliance. Nor does Article 21.5 contain any time limitation or deadline by which a Member must initiate dispute settlement proceedings. Indeed, the EC does not claim that such obligations can be found in the text of Article 21.5. Yet, it seeks a specific finding of a US breach of Article 21.5 just the same. Taking into account the Appellate Body's guidance in *India – Patent* and *US – Shrimp*, the EC's theory in this dispute (*i.e.*, a violation of Article 21.5 read "in conjunction with" Article 23) has no textual basis and must therefore be rejected. Any analysis of whether US actions have breached Article 21.5 of the DSU must be based on the text of that provision.

4.250 In addition to its attempt to impute obligations into the text of Article 21.5, the EC provides other non-textual arguments in support of its claim of a US Article 21.5 breach. Primary among these is the EC's reference to a presumption or principle of good faith. The EC considers that referring to such a presumption justifies imputing into Article 21.5 an unspecified and unwritten obligation that "[a] retaliating Member has at a minimum a *good faith obligation* to assess within a reasonable delay the compliance measure". As noted above, the key to interpretation of the DSU, and Members' obligations under its provisions, lies in the actual text of the provisions. The text of Article 21.5 does not contain a time limitation, let alone what would amount to a case-by-case-determined "reasonable time period". Neither does it contain an obligation that, in the post-suspension setting, the suspending Member initiate dispute settlement proceedings upon a declaration of compliance by the Member concerned. "Good faith" applies to implementing the obligations that are agreed upon by Members, evidenced in the text; "good faith" cannot serve to create new obligations that were never agreed by Members.

4.251 Similarly, the EC has failed to make a prima facie case of a US violation of Article 22.8 of the DSU. Rather than presenting any evidence of how it has satisfied the conditions of Article 22.8 (removal of WTO-inconsistent measure; provision of solution to nullification or impairment of benefits; mutually satisfactory solution), it posits its claim "in conjunction with" Article 23 and asserts that the "presumption of good faith" or compliance satisfies its burden of proof. Even were one to presume that the EC implemented its amended bans in good faith, this fact would not in turn demonstrate that the EC's bans actually satisfy the elements of Article 22.8, *e.g.*, the EC could be acting in good faith, but still be wrong about the WTO-consistency or compliance of its amended measure.

4.252 The United States notes that the EC's interpretation of Article 23, and specifically Article 23.2(a), is complicated by a lack of clarity regarding when, exactly, a determination on the part of the suspending Member would be inferred. Regardless of whether this fictional deadline is a "reasonable period" or immediate, the EC's interpretation establishing such a deadline is not sustainable. Not only would it beg litigation to determine on a case-by-case basis whether a Member has unreasonably delayed in making a determination, it would convert Article 23.2(a) from a prohibition on making determinations into an obligation to make them – ironically, a Member would in effect be required to make a determination upon learning of another Member's declaration of compliance, and to do so within some unspecified time frame.

4.253 Furthermore, as the United States has noted on several occasions, the United States was in the course of reviewing the EC's materials at the outset of this dispute. In light of this fact, it is difficult to comprehend how the United States could have made a "determination" as to the WTO-consistency of the EC's amended bans. A critical element of this US evaluation is the review of the studies and Opinions ostensibly underpinning the EC's bans. Specifically, the EC refers to a number of studies which it commissioned after the Appellate Body proceedings in the *EC – Hormones* dispute, referring to them as the "17 Studies". The EC invokes these studies throughout its 2000 Review and 2002 Opinion, and a review of their methodology and results are therefore critical to an analysis of the EC's measure. However, as noted at the first substantive meeting with the Panel, the United States has not had the opportunity to review all of these documents, and referred to this fact in explaining why it had not yet been able to reach a determination of the EC's Opinions or its bans. Indeed, the EC has only recently informed us of a number of studies – which it contends comprise the basis for its claim of compliance with the DSB's recommendations and rulings – that were not referenced in the EC's response to the US request for information under Article 5.8 of the *SPS Agreement*, through which the United States sought all relevant scientific information on which the EC premised its bans.

4.254 Because the EC has failed to demonstrate a US breach of its obligations under the DSU, there can be no "in conjunction with" breach of the objectives set out in Article 3.7 of the DSU, even were such a claim possible.

4.255 Because the United States has not breached its obligations under the DSU and continues to suspend concessions pursuant to DSB authorization, there can be no US breach of Articles I or II of the GATT 1994. Any finding of a breach of these provisions would be premised on a finding that the United States did not have authorization to suspend concessions to the EC.

(b)   The EC has neither removed its WTO-
        inconsistent bans nor provided a solution to US
        nullification or impairment within the meaning of
        Article 22.8 of the DSU

4.256 A determination of whether or not the EC has complied with the DSB's recommendations and rulings in the *EC – Hormones* dispute is central to an analysis of whether or not it has satisfied the conditions of Article 22.8 by either removing its WTO-inconsistent measure or providing a solution to US nullification or impairment. The EC has failed to make its prima facie case of a US breach of Article 22.8 of the DSU because it has not demonstrated, other than by simple assertions that it deems its own measure to satisfy DSB recommendations and rulings, how its import bans are now WTO-consistent.

(i)   The EC has failed to demonstrate that its
        import ban is a provisional measure within
        the meaning of SPS Article 5.7

4.257 Despite several opportunities to present evidence as to why its ban on five of the hormones (testosterone, progesterone, trenbolone acetate, zeranol and MGA) is a legitimate provisional measure, the EC fails to demonstrate how its ban on meat and meat products from cattle treated with these five hormones in fact satisfies the criteria of Article 5.7 of the *SPS Agreement*. Because the EC's ban fails to meet the requirements of Article 5.7, the EC is therefore not exempt from satisfying its obligations under Article 2.2 (measures not to be maintained without sufficient scientific evidence) and Article 5.1 (measures to be based on a risk assessment) of the *SPS Agreement*.

4.258 The simple fact regarding the five hormones at issue is that international standards and a significant body of scientific studies exist on the risks posed by each hormone. The Joint FAO/WHO Expert Committee on Food Additives

("JECFA") and several national regulatory bodies have determined that the scientific evidence regarding these hormones is adequate or sufficient to conduct a risk assessment. The EC alone alleges that this body of information is not "sufficient" to conduct a risk assessment, as required by Article 5.1 of the *SPS Agreement*, and the EC has only taken this position after firmly stating to the WTO several times that the information is sufficient and only after the WTO finding that the EC had breached its SPS obligations. In so doing, however, the EC does little more than assert that this is the case, failing to cite to any scientific evidence demonstrating risks to consumers from the five hormones when used for growth promotion purposes in meat according to good veterinary practices. Indeed, our review of the available materials comprising the 17 Studies has failed to uncover any new evidence of risk from the five provisionally banned hormones, further casting doubt on the EC's conclusion that evidence relating to these hormones is now somehow insufficient.

4.259 In the case of the five hormones "provisionally" banned by the EC, there is no "pertinent information" upon which the EC's import ban can be based because none of the information presented by the EC in its Opinions suggests that meat and meat products from cattle treated with the five hormones for growth promotion purposes according to good veterinary practice pose a risk to consumers. The EC does not consider information pertaining to the specific risk in question (*i.e.*, that to consumers ingesting hormones in meat from cattle treated according to good veterinary practices), including relevant international standards for the five hormones and their underpinning studies, which indicates that hormone residues in such meat are safe. Instead, the EC restricts its consideration to general information or evidence on the hormones – evidence that was considered by Codex and JECFA in determining that the hormones do not pose a risk to consumers.

4.260 Finally, the EC has failed to demonstrate that it has reviewed its ban within a reasonable period of time. As noted by the Appellate Body, the "reasonable period of time" is not a fixed period, but rather reflects circumstances on a case-by-case basis. Furthermore, in determining whether a reasonable time has elapsed, one of the factors that should be taken into account is the "difficulty of obtaining the additional information necessary for the review and the characteristics of the provisional SPS measure." In the case of the five hormones banned by the EC, as noted above, there is already a substantial body of evidence available for completing a risk assessment, contradicting the suggestion that any "additional information" whatsoever might be required to review the amended ban. In addition, the "provisional" ban simply prolongs the original ban, marking over fifteen years that the import ban, the most trade-restrictive measure possible, has been in place. Taking into account the severity of the measure, and the ready availability of information on the five hormones, the EC has not reviewed its measure within a reasonable period of time within the meaning of Article 5.7.

(ii)   The EC has failed to base its import ban on meat from cattle treated with oestradiol-17β for growth promotion purposes according to good veterinary practices on a risk assessment within the meaning of SPS Article 5.1

4.261   The EC has failed to base its import ban on meat from cattle treated with oestradiol-17β on a risk assessment within the meaning of SPS Article 5.1. Indeed, the EC's Opinions and underpinning studies fail to demonstrate a risk from residues in meat from cattle treated with oestradiol-17β for growth promotion purposes according to good veterinary practices. Instead, the studies on which the Opinions rely only succeed in demonstrating theoretical risks when the hormones are administered at doses or levels well-above those present in residues from hormone-treated meat; when good veterinary practices are not met; or in ways not germane to the relevant risk pathway.

4.262   The EC's assumption that oestradiol is genotoxic is essential to its overall conclusions regarding this hormone. Nevertheless, despite reaching the conclusion that oestradiol-17β is genotoxic in its Opinions, the EC does not in fact demonstrate through scientific evidence that this is the case. It fails to provide evidence demonstrating that oestradiol has carcinogenic effects other than through the receptor mediated, cell division stimulating activity of the hormone – in other words, at levels exerting a hormonal effect on consumers, and not at the exponentially smaller levels that would be found in meat residues. The fact that effects may be observed at exposure levels above the hormonal effect level or threshold is well established, and is one of the reasons that groups such as Codex set acceptable daily intakes ("ADIs") and maximum residue levels ("MRLs") at levels exponentially lower than this threshold.

4.263   The EC seeks support for its argument that oestradiol-17β is genotoxic in a JECFA conclusion that "oestradiol-17β has genotoxic potential", yet fails to cite to the rest of the relevant paragraph, in which JECFA notes, "[t]he Committee reviewed studies of the genotoxic potential of oestradiol-17β. Estradiol-17β *did not cause gene mutations in vitro*. In some other assays, sporadic but unconfirmed positive results were obtained." Furthermore, the EC's citation to the JECFA safety assessment ignores its ultimate conclusion, *i.e.*, that a maximum residue level for oestradiol-17β in meat need not be specified because there is a "wide margin of safety for consumption of residues in food when the drug is administered according to good practice in the use of veterinary drugs." JECFA's conclusion corresponds to that of the EC's own Center for Veterinary Medicinal Products ("CVMP").

4.264   The EC's CVMP, upon review of the 1999 IARC monograph cited in the US Report on Carcinogens, as well as the scientific materials comprising the EC's 1999 Opinion, concluded that oestradiol-17β "belong[s] to the group of non-genotoxic carcinogens" and "exogenous exposure to hormones would need to be substantial (*i.e.*, in the order of post-menopausal therapy levels) before carcinogenic effects would be detectable in humans." These conclusions do not ignore the fact that, at physiological, hormonal-effect concentrations, there are carcinogenic risks from oestrogens. However, they do not support a theory that oestradiol-17β is either genotoxic, or will have carcinogenic effects, at concentrations present in meat from cattle treated with the hormone for growth promotion purposes according to good veterinary practices.

4.265 The severe limitations of the alleged "evidence" for genotoxicity of oestradiol-17β was also noted in the recent 2005 U.K. Report. In that Report, the Veterinary Products Committee ("VPC") concluded that only limited evidence was available to indicate that oestradiol-17β is capable of inducing gene mutations, and cautioned that even this "evidence" has been obtained using non-standard assays, some of which suffer from flawed experimental design.

4.266 The EC also asserts that the US argument that oestradiol-17β is generally inactive when given orally, while "well known", is "still controversial and not consensually accepted by the scientific community." To the contrary, oestradiol's low oral bioavailability has found international support in Codex and JECFA ("[i]n general, oestradiol-17β is inactive when given orally because it is inactivated in the gastrointestinal tract and liver"), as well as support within the EC from the CVMP, which noted that "the *bioavailability of 17β-oestradiol* esters after oral administration *is low (3% as unchanged oestradiol)*, but might be higher if estron, an oestrogenic metabolite, is included." The EC's assertion is also surprising in light of unpublished, EC-generated data which the EC only recently provided to the US which confirmed the internationally-accepted principle that bioavailability of oestradiol-17β is low in humans.

4.267 In an attempt to bolster its argument on the bioavailability of estradiol 17β, the EC cites to data it has developed on estrogen levels in young children. While it is unclear how this comparison relates in any way to a discussion on bioavailability, we can only assume that the EC makes this argument in an attempt to cast doubt on previously established standards for estradiol 17β and the other hormones at issue, *i.e.*, that the relevant standard setting groups were not taking into account populations identified as more sensitive than previously thought. The EC's argument fails for two fundamental reasons: (1) populations such as young children were indeed taken into account in establishing international standards and domestic requirements for the six hormones; and (2) the studies cited by the EC by which it attempts to cast such groups as even more susceptible than previously thought are flawed.

4.268 As to the first point, JECFA, in its safety assessment for the hormones, including oestradiol-17β, took into account data on most sensitive populations. The CVMP, in determining that oestradiol-17β is safe within certain concentrations also took into account data on prepubertal boys. As to the second point, the EC's own CVMP and the U.K. Group raised serious doubts relating to the methodology of the Klein assay, and determined that these concerns were sufficient to cast doubt on the conclusions drawn in the EC's Opinions.

4.269 The EC's Opinions also conclude that meat from cattle treated with oestrogens may accelerate the onset of puberty in children. The EC attempts to support this conclusion with a publication describing an outbreak of breast enlargement (gynecomastia) in school children in Milan in 1977. The study's authors state that oestrogenic contamination of meat served in the school canteen was the "suspected" cause of breast enlargement. However, the presence of oestrogen in meat consumed by the students was never confirmed and a causal link between oestrogen in meat and gynecomastia was never demonstrated. Indeed, in a retrospective study conducted some twenty years later, the original study's author questions his own earlier conclusions and recognizes the likelihood that some other factor caused the early onset of puberty. The results of this unpublished, and previously unavailable study clearly demonstrate that the conclusion that hormones in meat are causative factors for early onset of puberty is unfounded.

4.270 In addition, the EC's Opinions ignore the scientific evidence relating to human *in vivo* DNA repair mechanisms, specifically that genotoxic effects of relevant residue levels of growth promoting hormones would not be expressed *in vivo* based in part on the existence of the efficient DNA repair mechanisms that exist in all mammalian cells. The efficacy of these repair mechanisms is exemplified in one of the unpublished reports recently provided by the EC. In this study, it was suggested that the lack of genotoxic effects of oestradiol-17β on human intestinal cells was due to a very efficient and rapid repair system. Despite these relevant findings, however, the EC's Opinions completely ignore the influence of endogenous DNA repair mechanisms, and instead attempt to implicate genotoxicity as a basis for the purported human health risk associated with oestradiol-17β residues in meat and meat products at any concentration.

> (iii) The EC fails to demonstrate that there is a risk of failure of controls or failure to satisfy good veterinary practices

4.271 The EC's replies to the Panel's questions were enlightening regarding what, exactly, is the perceived "risk" against which the EC has imposed its import bans on US meat and meat products. From the outset, the United States has argued that the scientific evidence, and the EC's Opinions and 17 Studies, do not demonstrate a risk from the six growth promoting hormones when used for growth promotion purposes according to good veterinary practices. Our focus on this specific risk and exposure pathway seemed obvious because this is the legally permitted use of growth promoting hormones in the United States. This focus also seemed obvious since, if a WTO Member were concerned about a failure of controls, or a failure to satisfy good veterinary practices, there are countless less trade restrictive methods for mitigating against this perceived risk than an absolute ban on another Member's goods, and Article 5.6 of the *SPS Agreement* requires Members to ensure that their SPS measures are not more trade-restrictive than required. Furthermore, a logical extension of the EC's argument is that since the EC cannot be confident its own controls will never fail (indeed, as discussed below, there is evidence that these controls have failed), the EC should ban all EC meat and meat products. Nevertheless, the EC's replies consistently invoke the "risk" of a failure to satisfy good veterinary practices. Indeed, it is as a result of this additional perceived "risk" that the EC appears to discount the conclusions reached in previous JECFA risk assessments and set out in Codex standards as MRLs and ADIs.

4.272   In its replies to the Panel's questions, the EC frequently cites to the processes of "risk analysis" and "risk management", neither of which are explicitly referred to in the text of the *SPS Agreement*. This is not to say that concepts such as "risk management" and "risk analysis" find no expression in the *SPS Agreement* whatsoever. Rather, they may be found in, *e.g.*, Article 5.2 of the *SPS Agreement*. Whether or not the EC engaged in a proper evaluation of the factors set out in SPS Article 5.2 would inform a decision on whether or not they have indeed properly assessed the risk of failure to satisfy good veterinary practices within the meaning of Article 5.1 and Annex A of the *SPS Agreement*. As discussed below, the EC has not engaged in the necessary evaluation of these factors as required by Articles 5.1, 5.2 and Annex A of the *SPS Agreement*.

4.273   The United States has rigorous controls in place, which include the establishment of tolerances (maximum allowable levels) for hormone residues in food by the Food and Drug Administration, and USDA/Food Safety and Inspection Service ("FSIS") enforcement of these tolerances through (1) residue control programs; and (2) ante mortem, post mortem, and processing inspection, to which all cattle entering the human food supply are subjected. This system provides extremely efficient safeguards against a hypothetical failure of controls in the United States, while at the same time being significantly less trade restrictive than an outright ban on US meat and meat products. A review of these relevant factors in its Opinions would have assisted the EC in making its ultimate determination of whether a ban on US meat and meat products is "not maintained without sufficient scientific evidence" and is not "significantly more trade restrictive than required to achieve the appropriate level of sanitary or phytosanitary protection" as required by the *SPS Agreement*.

4.274   Instead, the EC's Opinions focus on several hypothetical "failure of control" scenarios that ignore actual regulatory processes in the United States, and for which it presents no support. It asserts that these scenarios "clearly identify a risk for excessive exposure of consumers to residues from misplaced or off-label used implants and incorrect dose regimes." Yet, the EC fails to produce any evidence identifying a real risk of failure of controls or failure to satisfy good veterinary practices in the United States.

4.275   The EC's 1999 Opinion alleges that "from 6% to 30% of the original dose [of a hormone implant] remained in the ears from 65 to 150 days after implantation ... These data indicate that consumption of tissue from implantation sites would result in substantial exposure." This hypothetical assumes that ears containing implants will enter the human food chain, but provides no evidence in support of this scenario. Contrary to the EC's assumption, very clear instructions are provided on manufacturers' labels on all FDA-approved growth promoting implants, indicating that implants must be placed beneath the skin of the middle third of ears of cattle. Because ears are then discarded at slaughter, excess dietary exposure to hormone residues via consumption of implant sites does not occur. USDA inspectors confirm through ante- and post-mortem inspections that ears are discarded and that no hypothetical misplaced implants enter the human food chain. Therefore, the EC's conclusion that cattle ears containing hormone implants will enter the human food chain is unsupported by relevant scientific evidence and real world conditions.

4.276   The EC's Opinions also contemplate a scenario whereby growth promoting hormone implants are placed in parts of cattle other than the ear. In support of its claim that this is a realistic scenario, the EC asserts that "correct implantation can neither be guaranteed nor expected." However, the EC provides no evidence in support of this claim. In the real world, the likelihood that a US beef producer would intentionally misplace hormone implants in muscle is negligible given the economic and enforcement considerations at stake. First, the implants are specifically designed to achieve maximum effect when inserted into the animal's ear. There is therefore no economic benefit for injecting cattle in other parts of the body. Second, misplaced implants would ruin surrounding muscle tissue, thereby decreasing the value of the carcass. Third, discovery of any intramuscular (non-ear) implants at slaughter by a federal inspector would cause the entire carcass to be condemned, resulting in not only zero profit, but significant economic loss to the producer.

4.277   In another portion of the failure of controls discussion, the EC's Opinions allege that overdosing cattle with hormone implants is commonplace in the United States. The EC fails to provide evidence to support its conclusion that off-label use actually occurs in the United States. The EC Opinion cites to one publication from which it extrapolates its conclusion that off-label use of hormones occurs, but it appears to misinterpret the data and information provided in that document. Furthermore, there is no economic incentive for the off-label implant use alleged by the EC; to the contrary, such use would have negative economic effects on cattle producers. Therefore, the Opinions' conclusion that off-label use of hormone implants occurs in cattle for export to the EC in the United States is unsupported by available scientific evidence and real world conditions. Indeed, the conclusion that multiple implanting poses a hypothetical health risk to consumers appears to ignore the findings of some of the very laboratory studies commissioned by the EC ostensibly in support of its claim that multiple implanting actually occurs and poses a risk to consumers in the real world. Accordingly, the EC fails to take into account available scientific evidence related to this "risk" within the meaning of SPS Article 5.2.

4.278 The EC's Opinions also cite to the existence of "black market" drugs, other non-authorized pharmaceutical formulations, or hormone "cocktails" as contributing to the risk of a failure of controls. However, the EC again provides no evidence of such a black market actually existing in the United States. Indeed, the analysis set out in the EC's Opinions ignores available evidence relating to black markets, as well as relevant processes and production methods and relevant inspection, sampling and testing methods as they exist in the United States. Available materials focusing on the black market use of growth promoting hormones only discuss evidence of such a market for their use within the EC (and thus would indicate that the EC, under its own approach in this dispute, should ban the sale of EC meat and meat products). EC inspection missions appear to confirm this fact. The presence of this market emphasizes that a total ban is not necessarily the most effective (and certainly not the least trade restrictive) means of preventing a theoretical failure of good veterinary practices. The *Hormones* panel reiterated this concern, noting that "the banning of a substance does not necessarily offer better protection of human health than other means of regulating its use."

3. Conclusion

4.279 In light of the foregoing, the United States asks the Panel to find that: (1) the EC has failed to demonstrate that the United States has breached Article 22.8 of the DSU, and that the United States continues to suspend concessions to the EC consistent with the requirements of that provision; (2) the United States has not breached Articles 3.7, 21.5, 23.1 or 23.2(a) of the DSU; and (3) the United States has not breached Articles I or II of the GATT 1994.

I. Oral Statement of the European Communities on Experts Opinions During the Second Substantive Meeting

4.280 There are certain "procedural" aspects to this expert meeting which the European Communities would like to comment on before turning to the substantive results of this meeting. As you are well aware, the European Communities, during the selection process last year, had objected to the selection of Drs. Boobis and Boisseau as experts to this Panel. This mainly, because both have been involved in drafting and adopting the very same risk assessments which the European Communities has not accepted as valid basis for its measures regarding hormone treated beef, that is JECFA's risk assessments. The European Communities' concern was that Drs. Boobis and Boisseau would lack the objectivity required to give the Panel the advice needed to make an objective assessment of the facts in this dispute. Last week's meeting has confirmed that this concern was more than justified. It is unavoidable what Drs. Boobis and Boisseau have done, namely to defend the conclusions of the risk assessment they were involved in against any alternative conclusions which the EC's risk assessment has come to. We do not blame them for doing so. However, we do believe that their obvious partiality was not only unacceptable for the purpose of the role of experts in this dispute, it also made it necessary, at times, to enter into technical scientific discussions that we would probably all have rather avoided.

4.281 The European Communities does not wish to discredit in general the work which is done by JECFA and Codex, nor does it believe that these latter would wish to put into question in any way the EC's sovereign choices on the desired level of health protection. This is not a case "EC against JECFA". This is a case between Members of the WTO and it currently turns on the question whether a WTO Member has legitimately relied on its right under the *SPS Agreement* to base its measures on its own assessment of scientific evidence and available pertinent information, assessment which may deviate from that performed (but not necessarily adopted) by an international standard setting body. Objective expert advice of the kind that came from Drs. Guttenplan, Cogliano, Sippell and De Brabander, can explain what the scientific positions on either side are. It is not helpful, therefore, to have had (not only one but even two) scientific experts at this meeting who considered themselves to be representatives of JECFA.

4.282 It is not helpful either to have had JECFA representatives at this meeting who considered themselves to be scientific experts. Both Dr. Tritscher's and Dr. Wennberg 's role would have been to provide, in their capacity as secretaries to JECFA, factual information on how JECFA works, the way Dr. Miyagishima did for Codex. Instead, both have repeatedly overstepped their role and ventured into statements on the substance of the scientific issues. Although we are, for example, quite grateful for Dr. Tritscher's indiscretion on the origin of JECFA's reference to "potential genotoxicity" (she stated that it was because JECFA felt there was scientific uncertainty), we do not think that it was appropriate for her to provide information on the substance of the science or to assume the role of defending the substance of JECFA's work. And we certainly feel that Dr. Wennberg would have done better not to intervene on the issue of residue data used in the 1999 evaluation (on which she was obviously not informed) or to keep her opinion, for example on Radio Immuno Assays, to herself.

4.283 Let me end my comments on the procedural aspects of this expert meeting here by inviting the Panel to take them into account when it assesses all the different advice it has been given at this meeting.

4.284 I will now turn to the substantive results of this meeting and place them in the legal context. For the sake of this discussion, the European Communities accepts for a moment the assumption that your task in this dispute is indeed to assess whether measures taken to comply with DSB rulings and recommendations are consistent or not with Articles 5.1 and 5.7 of the *SPS Agreement*. However, we will come back to this at a later stage.

4.285 The United States and Canada claim that the European Communities has violated Article 5.1 of the *SPS Agreement* in re-adopting its ban on oestradiol-17β for growth promotion purposes. (I'll open a parenthesis here: this is not quite the way they put it as they believe the burden of proof is on the EC to demonstrate compliance. However, the EC strongly rejects this point, and I will also come back to that later. Fact is that they have raised a number of arguments as to why the EC allegedly violated Articles 5.1 and also 5.7 and therefore is not in compliance).

4.286 They argue essentially on two levels. First, that there is no risk assessment, supposedly because the EC Opinions of 1999, 2000 and 2002 failed to perform the second and third of the four steps usually done in a risk assessment on substances of this kind by the members of Codex. Second, that the evidence put forward by the EC allegedly does not support the ban.

4.287 Last week's expert meeting has yielded a wealth of information which is crucial to dealing with these two levels of argument. Rather than repeating all the legal arguments as set out in our submissions, I will concentrate on where the scientific advice you got helps to clarify the issues.

4.288 On the first level of argument, we learned from the rather *unisono* statements of the experts. We have learned that while everyone (including the European Communities) accepts that in a risk assessment you may proceed in the four steps of hazard identification, hazard characterization, exposure assessment and risk characterization, you only do that to the extent possible and necessary. In other words, how you proceed exactly is a function of the data you have available and of how your risk assessment is framed, namely by the mandate you have received from the risk manager. Thus, we learned from Drs. Boobis and Cogliano that data are never complete, but are or are not sufficient for the purpose of completing a risk assessment. We learned that this is a matter of judgment involving considerations on what sort of possible gap/uncertainty/insufficiency we are dealing with and whether that can be dealt with through interpretation or bridging tools such as safety factors and assumptions, or not. Most importantly, however, we learned that this judgment is informed – indeed, is framed – by the risk *manager*. It is the risk manager, as Dr. Miyagishima pointed out, who decides whether or not to carry out an evaluation and who factors into that decision the question of whether there are sufficient data. I draw your attention in this context to paragraph 19 of the Codex draft Risk Analysis Principles for the CCRVDF, which are about to be adopted. Paragraph 19 specifies that it is for the CCRVDF to provide "a qualitative preliminary risk profile as well as specific guidance [to JECFA] on the CCRVDF risk assessment request."

4.289 Finally, it is the risk manager, as several experts repeatedly confirmed, who decides on the acceptable level of risk, in other words on the level of protection. This informs for example concepts such as that of "appreciable risk", as Dr. Guttenplan explained in reply to your question. Let us not go into the whole concept of risk communication, but it is important for you to understand that risk assessors and risk managers – as two different instances of a risk analysis process – do not make decisions in isolation from each other. This has already been confirmed by the Appellate Body in the 1998 *Hormones* report.

4.290 This brings us back to the famous four steps of the risk assessment. If there is a risk management decision that the intended acceptable level of risk is "additional risk to the extent such a risk is judged 'insignificant' or 'non appreciable,'" here is what you do as a risk assessor: once you have identified that there is the possibility of an adverse effect, you go on and calculate whether and at what threshold the risk becomes "non appreciable" using safety factors and whatever other tools you have available to bridge possible gaps of knowledge. This is what JECFA has done.

4.291 If, on the other hand, there is a risk management decision that the intended acceptable level of risk is "no additional risk," the situation is different: as a risk assessor, once you have identified the possibility of an adverse effect and the possibility of its occurrence in real life, there is no point in going on and calculating a threshold, as no additional risk, however minimal, would be accepted. As a risk assessor you have done enough for the purposes of the risk assessment that the risk manager has asked from you. Essentially (I am saying essentially because the European Communities, as even Dr. Boobis had to confirm, has actually quantified exposure to the extent possible) this is what the EC risk assessors have done. Your experts have confirmed this, not least Dr. Boobis, who first advised you that the European Communities had not carried out a proper risk assessment and then qualified his reply by stating that it was based on the assumption that a threshold would apply. Where this is not the case, so he explained last week and in his written replies to Questions 11, 19 and 37, the remaining steps after hazard identification look quite different. In particular, a dose response assessment is unnecessary (see in particular reply to Question 37). However, as to what exactly the remaining steps are supposed to look like in a non-threshold scenario, neither Dr. Boobis nor the other experts gave you clear advice on that question. You heard statements that the European Communities failed to present new residue data or failed to refer to the problem of endocrine effects in its risk assessment or failed to present evidence on *in vivo* genotoxicity, all of which the European Communities proved to be wrong by pointing the

Panel to the exact page where this issue was discussed or a study was referred to in the EC Opinions. Frankly, Chairman, one might choose to disagree with the conclusions the EC has come to, but to claim that the EC has not carried out a proper risk assessment is a bit of a joke, obvious to anyone who has actually taken pains to read the EC risk assessments (and, if I may add, to compare them to other relevant risk assessments).

4.292 So let me turn to the second level of argument, which turns on whether the evidence presented by the European Communities supports - or, as the Appellate Body would put it – sufficiently warrants a prohibition on oestradiol-17β. Chairman, I could go back to the details of all the adverse effects that the EC risk assessment has identified and that were at least in part discussed at last week's meeting. I could now launch into discussing everything that was said about old and new residue data, old and new detection methods, good veterinary practice and abuse, hormonal development of children and the value of epidemiological studies. But I think there is probably no better way of putting in a nutshell the controversy at the heart of this debate than the way Dr. Cogliano has done it. He said essentially "at the heart of the scientific disagreement here is the interpretation of data. JECFA's assessment felt that a threshold could be assumed even if there was some evidence on genotoxicity. Therefore they assumed there was a threshold. It seems to me that the EC is unwilling to assume a threshold, because of genotoxicity and because of low dose response and the fact that the shape of the curve cannot be defined with certainty. Those are the scientific arguments on both sides – depending on how you phrase the question, you will get a response of yes or no." Dr. Cogliano answered your question of whether this disagreement is arbitrary or unreasonable by stating "this is a longstanding area of disagreement for scientists since many years, the reason for the controversy being the assumptions that scientists bring to the risk assessment. It is an area of legitimate disagreement."

4.293 Even Dr. Boobis, who may have wanted to make you believe that JECFA's - that is: his - interpretation of the data is the only reasonable interpretation, had to concede that both genotoxicity and low dose response are issues that are a long way from being resolved. What better way to demonstrate this than the vivid debate between Dr. Guttenplan and Dr. Boobis on proof of *in vivo* genotoxicity? What better way to say it than Dr. Boobis' reply to the EC expert's intervention on low dose response, when he stated "this is a major issue of scientific controversy. Dr. Vom Saal can point to so many papers which support his argument, but currently this is not resolved in the scientific community."

4.294 I could add to this now an account of the many things that were said last week about pre-pubertal children, where the advice you received from the Panel's experts ranges all the way from warning you not to feed your children broccoli (Dr. De Brabander) to stating that there is no problem whatsoever for hormonal substances despite evidence demonstrating that JECFA's calculations on endogenous production of hormones are actually wrong (Dr. Boobis).

4.295 But the point can already be made: what you should take away from last week's meeting is the following: First, the European Communities bases itself on evidence which well respected scientists, including some of your own experts (Drs. Guttenplan and Cogliano) understand to demonstrate direct genotoxicity of Oestradiol 17 β. Direct genotoxicity, not only for the EC risk manager but actually for most risk managers in this world (see Dr. Boobis' reply to Question 11) is a reason not to accept any added risk and therefore to decline setting a threshold. Second, the European Communities bases itself on evidence which is read by respected scientists – and, apart from Drs. Cogliano and Sippell this may well include most endocrinologists in the world – to mean that one actually knows precious little about what hormonal substances do at low doses, and in particular, what they do to especially sensitive populations such as pre-pubertal children. For the EC risk manager, and this may well be a position not shared by the risk managers in the US and Canada, this is a reason to decline setting any threshold.

4.296 The European Communities considers that it is not for this Panel to enter into the deep scientific theories and try to resolve the scientific controversies, to which you became witnesses last week. The scientists have not managed to resolve it and you will not be able to do it with the legal provisions and tools you are supposed to apply here. Indeed, you are not asked to now come down on either side of the debate, apply your own – as Dr. Boobis would put it – "weight of evidence" approach, provide your own interpretation of how the data should be read. It is sufficient for you to ascertain that there is a genuine divergence of scientific opinions here, which may indeed – as the Appellate Body has put it – "indicate a state of scientific uncertainty"[19] and that the European Communities has relied on – and I quote the Appellate Body again – "divergent opinion[s] coming from qualified and respected sources"[20] as your own experts have confirmed. The US and Canada may think that this source may not (yet) represent "mainstream" scientific opinion (although one may well argue that there is at least equal balance between the different opinions) but this, as the Appellate Body teaches us, "does not necessarily indicate the absence of a reasonable relationship between the SPS measure and the risk assessment, especially where the risk involved is life-threatening in character and is perceived to constitute a clear and imminent threat to public health and safety."[21] There is no other indication that the European Communities may not have acted in good faith (may those who cherish protectionist theories go back to reading what the Appellate Body

---

[19] Appellate Body Report, *EC – Hormones*, at para. 194.
[20] *Ibid.*
[21] *Ibid.*

had to say about that).[22] Therefore, Chairman and Members of the Panel, your conclusion must be that the EC's risk assessment sufficiently warrants – that is to say reasonably supports – its ban on oestradiol-17β.

4.297 This concludes my comments on the United States' and Canada's claim that there is a violation of Article 5.1 of the *SPS Agreement* as regards the EC's implementation measure on Oestradiol 17β. I should add that this also deals with the rather vague claim made by the United States and Canada that there would also be a violation of Article 3.3 of the *SPS Agreement*. "Vague" because it is not clear what they would be relying on with regard to oestradiol-17β. The standard adopted by Codex on this substance dates back to 1988 and is outdated, not only in the EC's view but also in the view of Codex' own scientific committee JECFA, which has re-evaluated the substance since. However, JECFA's updated assessment of 1999 has never been adopted as a standard. In any event, as is clear from the above, the European Communities who has a scientific justification not to base itself on the Codex standard, and also (not "or")[23] has a higher level of protection than that implied in the Codex standard, acted consistently with Article 5.1. of the *SPS Agreement*. Therefore, there is no violation of Article 3.3.

4.298 Let me turn to the European Communities provisional ban on the other five substances, progesterone, testosterone, zeranol, trenbolone acetate and melengestrol acetate (MGA). With regard to that measure the United States and Canada claim that there is a violation of Article 5.7 of the *SPS Agreement*. I will not go back to all legal arguments that have been exchanged between the parties on the four conditions that Article 5.7 of the *SPS Agreement* requires, but will instead concentrate on what the expert meeting has yielded in this regard, which mainly relates to the issue of sufficiency.

4.299 Obviously, you as the Panel wonder what to make of the fact that an international body such as Codex and its scientific committee JECFA, with regard at least to four of these substances, has considered that there is sufficient evidence to come to a conclusion on them, while the EC claims that this is not the case.

4.300 This brings us back to the debate touched upon earlier about completeness of data, sufficiency, gaps and scientific uncertainty. For all of those among us lawyers who love to think in clear cut-categories, this is a bit of a disappointment. The world of science clearly does not think in terms of definitive and provisional measures, of sufficiency and insufficiency of evidence. Data are never

---

[22]   Appellate Body Report,*EC – Hormones* at para. 245.
[23]   As the Appellate Body has put it so delicately, "Article 3.3. is evidently not a model of clarity in drafting and communication", see Appellate Body Report, *EC – Hormones*, para. 175.

complete, as we learned; whether you can come to definitive conclusions on a risk assessment is a function of what data you have and how your risk assessment has been framed by the risk manager. Dr. Boobis, who emphasised several times how careful he was about choosing his words, certainly was careful when replying to the question of whether it was possible to complete a risk assessment on the five substances. He agreed with the European Communities that this was a question of risk management and then stated: "I can only speak for JECFA, not for the EC, we considered the data to be sufficient." Indeed, he speaks for a different set of data and against the background of a different decision on acceptable level of risk/intended level of protection! The EC's scientific committee worked on the basis of the most up to date research on these substances and against the background of the risk manager's decision not to accept any additional risk from residues in hormone treated-meat. Under these circumstances, the EC scientific committee, in the face of evidence indicating that there may be risks with regard to genotoxicity and in light of the scientific uncertainty regarding the low-dose response problem, was careful to conclude only provisionally on the existence of a risk, and to recommend further research. Chairman, members of the Panel, would you have preferred a bold conclusion based on all sorts of gap-bridging assumptions, that these substances present a risk, and on the basis of that a definitive ban adopted by the EC regulator?

4.301 This concludes my remarks on the Article 5.7 claim, which has been shown to be unfounded. Let me add a brief remark, once again on the Article 3.3 claim made by the United States and Canada. The United States and Canada are relying on standards for zeranol and trenbolone acetate adopted in 1988, which are as outdated as the standards for progesterone and testosterone also dating back to 1988. Again, as is clear from the above, the European Communities, who has a scientific justification not to base itself on the Codex standard, and also a higher level of protection than that implied in the Codex standard, acted consistently with Article 5.7 of the *SPS Agreement*. Therefore, there is no violation of Article 3.3.

4.302 These remarks of the European Communities attempted to help you place the results of last week's experts' meeting in the context of your analysis on the relevant provisions of the *SPS Agreement*. Before turning to my reservation on that exercise, which I stated in the beginning, let me make one final remark. It seems fashionable, in the debate on the *SPS Agreement*, to raise the spectre of regulators who close off their markets by putting never ending demands for more evidence on scientists on the basis of a declared need to prove safety. There is a danger for abuse of the *SPS Agreement* in this respect, no doubt. But there is another spectre out there, which is equally haunting: that the *SPS Agreement* would be abused by those who value market profit over safety. That those who do not bother to look into possible health concerns, referring, at best, to industry data that no member of the public has ever seen, would benefit from some sort of presumption of being right under the *SPS Agreement*.

4.303 With this, I have ended my opening remarks on the outcome of the expert hearing. Now, with regard to my earlier reservation: Chairman, we want to raise the question with you, why it is we are going through this exercise of looking into a violation of the *SPS Agreement*. As suggested in your e-mail we will come back to this issue in the second part of our opening statement when we discuss legal issues.

J. Oral Statement of the United States on Experts Opinions During the Second Substantive Meeting

4.304 The United States has repeatedly argued throughout these proceedings that the European Communities' ("EC") permanent ban on oestradiol-17β ("estradiol") is not based on a risk assessment within the meaning of Article 5.1 of the *Agreement on the Application of Sanitary and Phytosanitary Measures* ("*SPS Agreement*"). We have also argued that the EC's provisional bans on progesterone, testosterone, zeranol, trenbolone acetate ("TBA"), and melengestrol acetate ("MGA") do not satisfy the necessary conditions for a provisional measure within the meaning of Article 5.7 of the *SPS Agreement*. Indeed, the very conclusions underpinning the EC's decision-making are unsupported by the scientific evidence relating to these hormones. The experts' written responses and oral testimony support these US arguments.

4.305 At the outset of this meeting, it is essential to recall the purpose of last week's meetings and today's discussions. The World Trade Organization ("WTO") and this Panel are not being called upon to conduct a risk assessment for the EC. You have not been requested to provide or complete a *de novo* review of the numerous scientific materials relating to the six hormones at issue. The pertinent analysis, as discussed a moment ago, is what the EC has done. Not what the EC could have done, or may still do. Not what this Panel can do for the EC. To conduct an analysis of what the EC has actually done, we may ask much less complex questions such as: has the EC presented scientific evidence of a risk from these hormones when consumed as residues in meat and assessed this risk in the proper fashion?

4.306 As I will highlight this morning, the experts' responses confirm that the EC has not based its ban on meat from cattle treated with oestradiol for growth promotion purposes on a risk assessment. It has not satisfied the four necessary steps for a risk assessment, and several of the conclusions set out in the EC's Opinions are not supported by scientific evidence. A measure banning meat from cattle treated with oestradiol cannot be "sufficiently warranted" or "reasonably supported" by this absence of a risk or assessment of the risk.

4.307 Likewise, the experts' responses confirm that there is sufficient scientific evidence to complete a risk assessment for each of the five "provisionally banned" hormones and that the EC has not based its provisional bans on available pertinent information. In other words, the EC's measures and "risk assessment" do not satisfy its obligations under the *SPS Agreement*.

4.308 I think that a brief discussion of the term zero risk provides a good starting point for today's discussions. It is an important principle and one to which the EC referred several times in the meeting with the experts. Indeed, the EC at several points asked the experts whether they could ensure that there was "zero risk" of a certain event occurring. The EC used this same tactic in its written comments on the experts' answers. For example, it demanded that *Dr. Boobis* "provide the necessary assurance" to the EC that residues in meat will never be shown to pose a risk to consumers. (*See, e.g.*, EC Comments on Question 20).

4.309 The analysis must refocus on the question of whether the EC has provided any evidence of a risk. The relevant discussion is one of whether the EC, in support of its ban, has adduced sufficient evidence to demonstrate a risk from meat from cattle treated with oestradiol for growth promotion purposes. Included in this discussion is an analysis of whether the EC has provided scientific evidence that oestradiol is genotoxic, mutagenic or carcinogenic (at levels found in residues in meat from treated cattle). Whether a scientist refuses to commit to a stance that there will never be a risk from meat treated with oestradiol at some point in the future is not pertinent to this analysis because it is not scientific evidence of a risk. It is simply theoretical uncertainty and cannot be the basis for a risk assessment or an SPS measure.

4.310 Regarding what, exactly, makes up a risk assessment, the experts and international organizations reiterated the four steps of risk assessment. In addition, the Codex representative stressed that a risk assessment must be based on all available data.

4.311 As to whether and when a risk assessment must satisfy each of the four steps, there was clear agreement among *Drs. Boobis and Boisseau* and JECFA that an evaluation of the human food safety of a drug should include all four steps of risk assessment. JECFA noted that a hazard identification does not qualify as a risk assessment and that the assessment should continue through each of the four steps unless there is "clear cut" evidence, both *in vitro* and *in vivo*, of genotoxicity. *Dr. Boobis* commented that the only instance in which such an assessment would stop at the hazard identification stage would be if the compound were identified as a DNA-reactive mutagen. *Dr. Boisseau* confirmed *Dr. Boobis'* opinion.

4.312 Recalling that, as we learned last week, genotoxicity and mutagenicity are not synonymous. Genotoxic substances damage DNA but the damage may be repaired. If the damage results in a mutation and the cell divides, then the substance is a "mutagen." As will be discussed in a moment, the experts did not identify any scientific evidence in the EC's Opinions that confirms, *in vivo*, the effects of oestradiol at levels below those causing a hormonal response, let alone any evidence that effects at that level are those of a DNA-reactive mutagen.

4.313 There are four steps for a risk assessment that have been clearly defined by the experts and the original *Hormones* panel. And the EC accepts that these four steps are required. As just mentioned, a risk assessment for oestradiol may not stop at the first step of hazard identification unless there is *in vivo*-confirmed evidence that oestradiol is either a genotoxin or a DNA-reactive mutagen. The EC has failed to present any evidence that oestradiol is genotoxic at levels below those eliciting a hormonal response, nor has it provided evidence that oestradiol is mutagenic at relevant levels *in vivo*. The EC was therefore not justified in failing to complete the three remaining steps.

4.314 The experts confirmed that the EC did *not* complete the remaining steps. *Dr. Boobis* noted, and *Dr. Boisseau* agreed, that the EC's Opinions are focused on the first step of risk assessment, hazard identification. As noted by JECFA, a hazard identification does not equal a risk assessment. An assessor must finish all four steps. Although he did not speak on this subject in last week's meetings, *Dr. Guttenplan* has described the EC materials as deserving at best a "mixed rating" in terms of the four steps of risk assessment(Question 14). He noted particular deficiencies in the hazard characterization and risk characterization sections (Questions 13 and 14).

4.315 Another avenue for finding that the EC has not completed a risk assessment for oestradiol is by determining that the conclusions set out in its assessment are not supported by scientific evidence. For example, the experts agree that the EC has not presented any scientific evidence that oestradiol is genotoxic *in vitro* or *in vivo* at physiological levels. The normal action of oestradiol on a cell is mediated through the oestrogen receptor. The genotoxic effects, which are abnormal, are not mediated through the estrogen receptor but instead involve direct damage to DNA. To date, concentrations of oestradiol required to cause genotoxic effects have been well above those required to elicit normal physiological effects.

4.316 As noted by *Dr. Boobis*, positive *in vitro* tests require positive *in vivo* confirmation, as toxicity is not always expressed *in vivo*. For *Dr. Boobis*, *in vivo* confirmation is critical because, among other things, it takes into account DNA repair mechanisms. He commented that he was "not persuaded" that oestradiol is genotoxic at levels below the normal hormonal concentrations present *in vivo*. In other words, that the genotoxicity has a threshold that requires overwhelming the DNA repair mechanisms – an event that will only occur at concentrations well beyond physiological levels.

4.317 The experts could not identify any studies providing evidence of the *in vivo* confirmation of genotoxicity of oestradiol at levels below those required to elicit a hormonal response. When put on the spot at last week's meetings with a new study produced by the EC in a last minute attempt to provide evidence of *in vivo* effects, *Dr. Boobis* quickly dismissed the study as irrelevant. The study's authors had treated the subject rats with so much oestradiol that the sheer level of the dose itself killed fifty percent of them, precluding any interpretation of oestradiol-specific effects.

4.318 Another example of an unsupported conclusion in the EC's Opinions is that oestradiol residues in meat from treated cattle are carcinogenic. The EC has failed to present any scientific evidence that oestradiol will have carcinogenic effects at levels found in residues in meat from treated cattle. Their failure to provide any evidence makes abundant sense. We consume oestradiol residues from numerous sources every day at levels much greater than those found in meat residues, whether from cattle treated for growth promotion or not. Milk, butter, eggs and, as noted by *Dr. Boobis*, a great number of phytoestrogens in plant products are all sources of oestrogen in our diets.

4.319 The EC has failed to support either of these major conclusions on genotoxicity or carcinogenicity with scientific evidence. The *SPS Agreement* does not permit the EC to do so. An assessment that fails to adduce scientific evidence in support of its underlying conclusions is not a risk assessment, as appropriate to the circumstances, under SPS Article 5.1.

4.320 There is a similarly uncomplicated analysis by which it can be determined that the EC's "provisional bans" do not satisfy the requirements of SPS Article 5.7. The first of Article 5.7's requirements for a provisional ban is that the evidence be insufficient to conduct a risk assessment. None of the experts believes that this is the case for testosterone, progesterone, zeranol, TBA or MGA.

4.321 Because the experts have confirmed that the evidence for each of the five hormones is sufficient to complete a risk assessment, discussion of the "provisional" bans may stop here in light of the cumulative nature of Article 5.7's requirements. The EC's ban is not a provisional measure for purposes of the *SPS Agreement*.

4.322 The second of Article 5.7's requirements is that a provisional measure be maintained on the basis of available pertinent information. The EC's "provisional" bans do not satisfy this requirement because there is no available pertinent information indicating that any of the five hormones poses a risk to consumers when used as a growth promoter in cattle.

4.323 The views of the experts are evidence of a lack of available pertinent information indicating that the five hormones pose a risk when consumed as residues in meat. Indeed, all available pertinent information indicates that consumption of these residues is safe. The EC has therefore not based its "provisional" bans on available pertinent information within the meaning of SPS Article 5.7.

4.324 In light of the experts' responses, it is clear that the EC has neither based its permanent ban on oestradiol on a risk assessment nor developed legitimate provisional bans. An analysis of these points would not entail the type of *de novo* review to which I alluded earlier. As noted, none of us are equipped for such a review and the *SPS Agreement* does not require or condone such a review.

4.325 While the Panel's analysis need not extend to this issue, I will now take a moment to discuss the EC's arguments relating to pre-pubertal children. The EC claims that oestradiol residues in meat from treated cattle pose a risk to this sub-population. However, the EC fails to provide scientific evidence of this risk.

4.326 In particular, the EC relies on an assay that, to date, remains unvalidated; the EC has failed to produce any scientific evidence demonstrating that JECFA's ADIs do not sufficiently protect children; and the EC has failed to complete the necessary steps of a risk assessment for this population.

4.327 This does not mean that the doubts and theoretical uncertainty on circulating oestradiol levels in pre-pubertal children identified in last week's meetings are unimportant. They are important. Indeed, JECFA reaffirmed that ensuring the safety of children is a "basic principle" of risk assessment and a fundamental focus of its work. As such, it is a safe guess that JECFA would be interested in any new evidence relating to this sub-population. As we have learned from the JECFA and Codex representatives, however, the EC has not shared any information with them. If the EC believes that the information it possesses has been properly validated and that the evidence is sound, then every Codex member around the world would benefit from its conclusions. The EC is not alone in its desire to protect the health of pre-pubertal children and other sensitive sub-populations.

4.328 Finally, we come to the issue of misuse of growth promoting hormones in the United States. I have left this subject for last because, quite frankly, it is unclear what role misuse plays in the EC's Opinions and arguments. The EC apparently considers potential misuse to be a risk, but has failed to provide any evidence or argument as to how it has actually assessed this risk. It provides no evaluation of the actual system of controls in place in the United States. We have described these controls at length in our previous submissions to the Panel. *Dr. De Brabander* claimed to have examined the US system of controls when he opined that the US system is nothing but "audits and paper work." However, he provided no analysis of the actual US system. Neither did the EC. In fact, when asked in last week's meetings whether he was familiar with the US and Canadian meat safety systems, *Dr. De Brabander* noted that he was not a meat inspector and was not qualified to make judgments on these systems.

4.329 Even if one were to assume the unrealistic and hypothetical misuse scenarios developed by the EC, the EC has failed to present convincing evidence that misuse leads to violative residue levels.

4.330 Finally, the EC fails to assess the risk of misuse. While the experts did not have a chance to turn to this point last week, the necessary evidence of the EC's failure may be found in their written responses. (*See, e.g.,* the responses of *Drs. Boobis and Boisseau* to Question 48).

4.331 When you take a step back from the EC's Opinions, it becomes more and more clear that they are flawed in larger ways than the EC would like us to see or focus on. In light of its line of questioning to the experts last week, the EC apparently hopes to make this dispute one about getting lost in the weeds of several scientific dead-ends. The spectres of misuse, risks to sensitive populations and the unwillingness of the experts to commit to a position that there will never be evidence of a risk from any of these hormones in the future are examples of these scientifically unfounded pitfalls. We could go on *ad nauseam* in a debate as to whether science in these areas is evolving. As we know from our discussions with the experts last week, science is continually evolving. This evolution cannot be equated with evidence of a risk, however. We are not scientists, and an attempt to thrust ourselves into the debates on these issues would be nothing more than a misguided *de novo* review of the science by us, laypersons.

4.332 If we follow the paths laid out by the EC, we will lose sight of the larger problems of the EC's Opinions and the fundamental obligations and requirements against which they are to be measured – those set out in the *SPS Agreement*. When we view the EC's measures in this context – in which we have the necessary knowledge and can perform the necessary analysis – it is clear that there are several avenues by which we can conclude that the EC has not based its permanent ban on oestradiol on a risk assessment within the meaning of SPS Article 5.1, nor has it implemented a provisional ban on the other five hormones within the meaning of SPS Article 5.7. I have discussed these avenues and the appropriate conclusions that can be reached for each based on the scientific record in this dispute this morning.

K.   *Oral Statement of the European Communities on Legal Issues During the Second Substantive Meeting*

1.   *Introduction*

4.333 The European Communities made a reservation in its statement yesterday when it questioned the point of going through this exercise of looking at the possible violation of provisions under the *SPS Agreement*. I am afraid that we have to postpone our discussion of that issue once again, to the end of this meeting, as it seems more important at this stage to respond to the Panel's request to clarify a few issues about the *SPS Agreement* and its application to the facts of this case. This is without prejudice to our position on the provisions of the *SPS Agreement* which, if any, might be invoked against our measures.

2.   Article 5.1 of the SPS Agreement

4.334 Let us start with the main violation found by the Appellate Body in the original *EC –Hormones* case, Article 5.1. The first point to make is that the situation today is very different from that which confronted the Appellate Body in 1998.

4.335 The Appellate Body had found that the old risk assessment performed by the European Communities was not specific enough to address residues in meat treated with hormonal growth promoters.

4.336 The optimal way to remedy that would be to establish a quantitative dose response relationship. However, the scientists last week have agreed (even though we did not need them to tell us) that this is not possible to perform because the necessary studies would entail, as the 2002 US Carcinogenesis Report says, conducting studies of long term human exposure and cancer incidence in very restricted environments which will be able to eliminate with confidence confounding factors in the initiation and promotion of cancer over a long latent period.

4.337 Visualize the study: a perfect place would seem a prison where you have a sufficient number of very long term prisoners living in identical conditions, half of whom would eat non-hormone treated beef and the other would eat hormone treated beef. Chairman, even under these circumstances, which can not possibly be more restricted, the results of the study would be rebuttable due to differences in the past exposure history of those in custody. You may visualize another situation where you have a sufficient number of newly born children with whom you perform a similar experiment for about 30 years. Do I need to go on?

4.338 In the absence of such studies we had to follow an alternative approach which is also acceptable under the *SPS Agreement*. Let's review what we have done and some important knowledge that we have acquired:

4.339 First, we now have sufficient scientific evidence that oestradiol-17β is genotoxic. This is not a theoretical risk, it is not negligible and definitely not "zero", it is a real risk however minimal.

4.340 Second, we have sufficient evidence that endogenous production of natural hormones by pre-pubertal children is many times less than what was originally thought to be the case.

4.341 Third, most of the scientists have agreed that the dose-response curve cannot be defined with certainty for low exposure to these substances.

4.342 Fourth, there is sufficient evidence, which is consistent with the observation that already exposure from background endogenous production can lead to cancer;

4.343 Fifth, we know today that the old data used by the defending parties and JECFA and the method by which they have been collected, are questionable or no longer valid (*e.g.* depletion data produced with method of analysis not apt to detect metabolites);

4.344 Sixth, there is a sufficient body of evidence indicating increased rates of cancer in the US and Canada which is consistent with the argument that residues of meat treated with these hormones can contribute to these higher rates.

4.345 Seventh, we know that under realistic conditions of use, good veterinary practice cannot be respected in the administration of hormones in the US and Canada and this invalidates the ADIs and MRLs (as Dr. Boisseau confirmed last week).

4.346 These things we did not know back then in the 1990s, but do know them now. Last week we have heard that there is a difference of scientific views and of interpretation of data about some of these issues, but that this difference is not arbitrary and indeed reflects genuine scientific uncertainty. In light of this, it is not indispensable that the third step of the risk assessment, the exposure assessment, is performed in a quantitative manner.

4.347 With these data the European Communities has conducted a qualitative dose-response assessment and has come to the conclusion that residues of hormone-treated meat will constitute an added risk to human health. As the Appellate Body has explained in 1998, risk is not measured in the laboratories but in the real world where people live, work and die.

4.348 In conclusion on this point, we believe that the European Communities performed a risk assessment as appropriate to the circumstances and the very nature of these substances, and therefore the ban on oestradiol-17β is based thereon – that is: sufficiently warranted by that risk assessment.

4.349 Before turning to some comments on other SPS provisions, I would like to stress the important point that we have made. A proper risk assessment can come to the legitimate conclusion that there are gaps in knowledge. This is expressly recognized in point 11 of the General Working Principles for Risk Analysis of Codex Alimentarius Commission. JECFA's risk assessment bridges all knowledge gaps and scientific uncertainty by assumptions in favor of allowing the use of hormones in growth promoters.

4.350 It seems that the US and Canada do not accept that a proper risk assessment can conclude that there are gaps and scientific uncertainty. For example, the US relies on a contention, at para 56 of its statement of yesterday, that a risk assessment must fully address the four "mandatory" steps (and it claims that the European Communities has not done so).

4.351 There is no basis for this. Article 5.1 of the *SPS Agreement* states that a risk assessment must be "appropriate to the circumstances" and *take into account* techniques developed by international organizations. As the European Communities has so often explained, and the experts have confirmed, the four steps of the Codex guidelines only need to be taken where possible and necessary. A qualitative assessment of the exposure of the kind performed by the EC must be acceptable. Our exposure assessment is not worse than that performed by the defending parties and JECFA, because both are based on assumptions and extrapolations from data on animal experiments to human beings.

4.352 It seems that the US and Canada would like to make it almost impossible for the European Communities to conduct a risk assessment they would ever accept. If they were to succeed with this tactic, however, the result would not be more authorizations but more provisional measures under Article 5.7 SPS.

3.   Article 3.3 of the SPS Agreement

4.353 There has also been mention of Article 3.3 of the *SPS Agreement*. The argument is not clear but the European Communities would like to make a couple of important points. First, WTO Members have a sovereign right to set a higher level of protection than reflected in international standards. Article 3.3 only requires Members to have a scientific justification for their measures reflecting this higher level of protection, not for the higher level of protection itself.

4.354 Another point that needs to be made is that Article 3 of the *SPS Agreement* applies to standards and measures, and does not require Members to accept risk assessments by organizations such as JECFA. Accordingly, the fact that JECFA may have made a different risk assessment, which is outdated by today's standards and reflects a lower level of protection is not a basis for holding the EC risk assessment to be inadequate. In any event, the European Communities has shown that its measure has the necessary scientific justification and aims to achieve a higher level of protection. For this reason we fail to see the relevance of Article 3 of the *SPS Agreement* as a basis for the claims of US and Canada in this case.

4. Article 5.7 of the SPS Agreement

4.355 Similarly, the fact that JECFA could carry out risk assessments on the 5 other hormones, is not a reason for holding that the European Communities cannot adopt provisional measures based on Article 5.7 of the *SPS Agreement*. For JECFA, the information is apparently sufficient to conduct risk assessments; for the European Communities it is not. Even Dr. Boobis agreed (and the US misrepresents his position at paragraph 35 of its statement yesterday morning).

4.356 The United States is also wrong to say (in para 6 of its statement) that the European Communities has failed to review the provisional bans within a reasonable time. The European Communities is in fact now conducting such a review once again.

5. Article 5.5 of the SPS Agreement

4.357 There have also been suggestions that the EC ban on oestradiol-17β (and the provisional prohibition of the other five hormones) are unreasonable or arbitrary in view of the large amounts of hormones that human beings are already exposed to from many different sources. Here again, we are not sure what the argument is. We cannot see how compatibility with Article 5.5 of the *SPS Agreement* is relevant to this case because no violation of this provision has been invoked by the Defendants. But even if it were, we would remind you of the interpretation of the Appellate Body of this provision. You cannot compare natural presence of these substances in a great many products with added risk from hormone-treated meat.[24]

6. Conclusion on the SPS Agreement

4.358 Chairman, Members of the Panel, our review of the possible relevance of the *SPS Agreement* has been somewhat cursory. Our problem is that we do not know what we are accused of. The US and Canada have not set out their claims in a Panel Request and their arguments criticizing our measures are varied and wide-ranging. We would be happy to discuss these issues in more detail if only we would be told exactly what it is we are doing wrong, because it is scientifically unsound and arbitrary.

---

[24] See para.221 of the Appellate Body Report in *EC – Hormones*.

7.   Concluding statement of the European Communities

(a)   Introduction

4.359 The European Communities would first of all thank you again for the professionalism and objectivity with which you have conducted these proceedings. Let me just recall that it was more than a year ago that we met for the first time to discuss the main claims of the European Communities against the US and Canada's illegal unilateral determination of the alleged inconsistency of the EC's implementing measure and, based thereupon, their illegal continuation of the sanctions against the European Communities.

4.360 The European Communities has explained in detail why in order to resolve these disputes it is not necessary for you to address the scientific issues related to the use of hormones as animal growth promoters. The Panel has nevertheless decided to look at these scientific issues. And we are the first to acknowledge that the scientific debate has not facilitated your life. As we have learned, the questions related to the use of these hormones are subject to a longstanding legitimate scientific debate amongst scientists with respected and reasonable arguments on both side.

4.361 However, one bottom line with which probably everybody will agree is that these hormones do not improve your health. These hormones are animal growth promoters but not health promoters. Instead we discuss scientific issues such as genotoxocity, mutagenicity, carcinogenesis, DNA repair mechanism, the risks of early puberty to our children, obesity, cancer as well as abuse and misuse of these hormones. Whatever one may think about this, it does certainly not increase our appetite for meat.

4.362 Another bottom line, which can be safely drawn, is that these hormones present a hazard and potentially a risk. Now, I agree that this is where the controversy starts. But whatever one may think about it as lawyers or consumers, neither of the scientists nor of the respondents can reasonably argue that there is no potential risk related to the use of these hormones as growth promoters in cattle. Instead, we have heard a lot of talk about "thresholds", "appreciable risk" or "acceptable risk". But whether a risk is appreciable or not, whether a risk is acceptable or not, it still remains a risk. And contrary to what the responding parties have argued yesterday this is not a theoretical risk. No, the risk is real, however minimal it may be.

4.363 Why should we accept such a risk? Why should we expose our public to an additional risk to human health? Indeed, Chairman, Members of the Panel, we have heard repeatedly that we should not care about the addition of the natural hormones since they are also present in natural food, such as broccoli, milk, eggs or butter or produced endogenously. But the question persists why we should add on top of this an additional burden on the consumer without any health benefit in return. It is true that we all take risks in life whether we drive with a car, or when we take a plane or if we drink a glass of milk. However, we take these risks because we also see the benefit. Driving a car is comfortable, taking the plane is fast and milk contains a lot of vitamins. Yet, the story is different with hormones used as growth promoters in cattle. Here the risk is on the consumer. He has to face an additional health risk by being exposed to higher hormone levels, but he has no additional health benefit. Thus, from the perspective of a public health regulator, the risk/benefit calculation does not speak in favour of the use of these hormones either.

4.364 If at all, one may argue that the issue of not allowing hormones as growth promoters in cattle while we allow our children to drink milk is a matter of consistency. However, that would also be a very superficial view of the issues at stake. As we have explained yesterday and as the Appellate Body has already decided, one cannot compare these two things. On the one hand, we talk about natural food products that are part of our daily life over centuries and where there is a concrete risk/benefit for the consumer. On the other hand, the use of hormones in beef is an unavoidable risk which does not bring any advantages to public health.

4.365 How can this be better exemplified than by looking at our children. Children are the most sensitive part of the population and we must protect them wherever we can. There is a lot of uncertainty about how the mechanism of hormones in these children work but one can be sure that doubling the oestradiol doses - as would be the case by allowing hormones in beef - will have an effect. One of your experts, Dr. Sippell, has confirmed this pointing to the examples of early puberty or obesity. We should take his judgment very seriously when he drew the conclusion of the scientific hearing that he is "very concerned". Whatever toxicologists or veterinarian may have to say we should take this testimony of a paediatrician very, very seriously.

4.366 This brings me to one last point in this introduction which is about misuse and abuse of hormones as growth promoters. It is already striking that we always refer to "Good Veterinary Practices" even though no veterinarian or other trained health professionals is involved in the use of these hormones in the United States and Canada. As they are sold freely over the counter to farmers you will admit that controlling the correct use of these substances is difficult under these circumstances. It should strike us all that one implant contains the amount of hormones contained to up to 10,000 carcasses of animals. The European Communities has assessed what happens if these implants are misused and, indeed, there exists concrete evidence on this in the United States and Canada.

(b)   The scientific debate

4.367 Let me now turn briefly to the outcome of the scientific debate regarding the use of these hormones as growth promoters in cattle. The European Communities is still puzzled by the United States' and Canada's attempts to present this debate as if there were only one single monolithic opinion in the scientific world on the safety of these hormones. This serves the US' and Canada's purpose but it is not objective.

4.368 It is true that we are all sometimes tempted to provide easy answers to difficult questions. And, certainly, this natural reflex is made even easier in the face of scientists who are able to "quickly dismiss" scientific evidence that they have not taken into account in the first place.

4.369 What is important for your decision, however, is to look at the differences and to see whether these differences are scientifically legitimate. The European Communities has never claimed that its scientific findings are the only valid ones, unlike what the United States and Canada have done. However, what the European Communities has repeatedly insisted upon is that its scientific views and its risk assessment are appropriate to the circumstances and that they come from respected and legitimate sources. One may not like the EC' conclusions but one cannot ignore or discredit them either.

4.370 It also appears sometimes ironic to present the EC' risk assessment in opposition to the JECFA's assessment. There is no doubt that the JECFA 's assessments have been based on outdated data since despite its assessment in 1999 this does not mean that the data also come from the 90's. Rather the JECFA representative admitted that they only review data as they receive them and in this particular case they had only received data from the FDA some of which date back to the 1960s. Despite the general acknowledgement that science is constantly moving forward and reveals new evidence this is an astonishing procedure itself which, again, we leave to your discretion on how you take this into account. A second undisputable issue is that JECFA's (and indeed the United States and Canada's) approach to risk is different to the one by the European Communities. JECFA has set thresholds in order to minimize the risk, the European Communities has prohibited the use of these hormones in order to exclude avoidable risks.

4.371 These are two completely different risk management decisions. Both are legitimate and we are, therefore, not criticizing JECFA for what it has done. However, we also cannot be blamed for deviating from JECFA's approach. It is ultimately the responsibility of the regulator or risk manager to decide what level of risk he wants to accept, and as I have indicated earlier, this is a very complex decision to which no easy answer can be given.

4.372 Let me then turn to our puzzlement by the United States and Canada's characterization of the scientific debate. We mentioned already yesterday that they very selectively refer to the scientific evidence in order to make their case.

Chairman, Members of the Panel, we trust that you have a better recollection of what was actually said.

4.373 Let me just give a few examples. The United States has stated that "the experts agree that the EC has not presented any scientific evidence that oestradiol is genotoxic *in vitro* or *in vivo* at physiological levels". However, may I remind you about the lively debate between Dr. Boobis and Dr. Guttenplan on this particular issue where Dr. Boobis "quickly dismissed" a study that was co-authored by one of his expert colleagues. Isn't it simply disingenuous to present this debate as if "all experts agree" that there is no evidence? And I'm not even talking about the experts that have not expressed an opinion on this issue.

4.374 Another example is the US' statement that "the experts have confirmed that the evidence for each of the five hormones is sufficient to complete a risk assessment". This is again incorrect. First, some of the experts have not even expressed a view on this. And even Dr. Boobis, who the United States often likes to rely on has merely stated that JECFA had enough information for completing a risk assessment whereas he could not say this for the European Communities. Again, as we have just explained, we all know the difference in these perceptions which is based on the fundamentally different approach by JECFA and the European Communities on how to deal with risks and whether or not it is appropriate to set a threshold in light of the possible direct and indirect genotoxicity of these substances.

4.375 A third and last example is Canada's statement today that "nothing in what the Experts have written, nothing in what we have heard from the Experts (…) or the Experts have said demonstrates that there is any risk to human health, adult or child, old or young, man or woman, boy or girl, arising out of the correct use of these growth-promoting agents in cattle". It suffices to contrast this simplistic summary by Canada with Dr. Sippell's conclusion of last week that he is "very concerned" about the health of children if they were exposed to these hormones in beef. Again, we trust the Panel Members that they take into account what has actually been said by the scientists in their variety and not what the United States or Canada make out of it.

4.376 In this context, let me also refer to the closing statements by some of the experts during last week's hearing and which summarizes adequately the level of differences in the scientific world. Dr. Guttenplan stated that as regards young girls and boys we have to worry about the developmental effects of oestradiol on them and that hormones sensitive cancer might be increased by raising the level of oestradiol. Dr. Sippell stated that we do not know enough about children and that the data are insufficient to be confident that the additional exposure from hormones treated beef poses no risk. Dr. Cogliano himself referred to the messiness of science and to the split within the scientific community. He also stated that these issues are not likely to be resolved any time soon. Finally, Dr. De Brabander even referred to other aspects related to the use of hormones as growth promoters such as animal welfare or environmental concern.

4.377 There is a bottom line which one cannot ignore. The scientific issues on which the European Communities and the United States and Canada disagree are not arbitrary but they are the result of a legitimate and genuine disagreement amongst scientists. This was the main result of the Panel' experts hearing. We do not believe that this Panel is in a position, or required, to resolve these long-standing scientific issues. Instead we would urge you to acknowledge the legitimate scientific controversy and to draw the respective conclusions from it in resolving these two disputes.

(c) The context of the scientific debate

4.378 With these remarks, let me come back to where we ended last year after our discussion on the systemic issues under the DSU.

4.379 The European Communities would recall that these two disputes are still not about the *SPS Agreement*, despite the extensive scientific debate that has taken place on the public health risk related to hormones in animal treated beef. Chairman, Members of the Panel, the panel requests by the European Communities which provide the legal basis for these two disputes do not refer to any single provision under the *SPS Agreement*. Rather, as we discussed extensively last year, the European Communities has based its case against the illegal continuation of sanctions by the United States and Canada on systemic violations of the DSU, in particular Article 23, paragraphs 1 and 2(a), Article 21.5 and Article 22.8.

4.380 As repeatedly stated, in order to resolve these disputes it is not necessary for you to make a substantive finding on the scientific issues. We have already set out that in our view the proper forum and the right procedural way to deal with these would be a compliance Panel under Article 21.5 of the DSU initiated by the United States or Canada.

4.381 This said, it is true that the European Communities has also made an alternative claim which requires you to address the substantive scientific aspects in order to determine that the original inconsistent measure has been removed and that the European Communities has addressed all the rulings and recommendations of the DSB.

4.382 However, this alternative claim has been only made "if, and only if" the Panel were to disagree with the European Communities on its systemic arguments under the DSU. Up until now, the Panel has not decided that this is the case. Therefore, the main claims and arguments as set out by the European

Communities in its submissions are still valid and you are still called upon to take a decision.

4.383 Our discussion of the scientific issues may nevertheless be useful in respect of the main systemic claims made by the European Communities. I would just like to recall that one of the claims is that the US and Canada's continued suspension of obligations is in violation of Article 23.1 and Article 22.8 of the DSU. This is so because by continuing to apply sanctions against the European Communities, the United States and Canada are unilaterally seeking to redress an alleged WTO inconsistency of the EC compliance measure with the WTO obligations. Furthermore, as you recall, in view of the requirements of Article 22.8 of the DSU, the European Communities has explained in great detail that its implementing measure must be presumed to be WTO-consistent since there is no multilateral finding to the contrary. This presumption is derived from the general principle of good faith whereby WTO Members are presumed to act in conformity with their obligations.

4.384 In this particular context, the European Communities considers that the scientific debate fully supports its proposition of a presumed compliance of its implementing measure. Indeed, since the scientific evidence demonstrates that the EC compliance measure is in actual compliance, it follows *a fortiori* that the lower standard of presumed compliance is also fulfilled.

4.385 Let me explain this aspect in more detail.

4.386 From the beginning of these two proceedings, the United States and Canada have tried to discredit the European Communities' compliance measure and its scientific foundations. Arguably, by this criticism the defendants have tried to undermine the European Communities' reliance on the principle of good faith (or in this case the presumption of compliance) under Article 22.8 of the DSU. And one has to admit that this litigation tactic by the United States and Canada was not completely unsuccessful because you felt the need to address the scientific issues related to the use of these six hormones as growth promoters in cattle notwithstanding the applicability of the general principle of good faith.

4.387 However, following the extensive discussion of the scientific issues, it is clear that this approach by the United States and Canada is no longer sustainable. As we have seen last week, there can be no doubt that there exists a real and actual risk to public health related to the use of the six hormones as growth promoters. The European Communities was therefore fully entitled to ban the use of these hormones in beef. And in legal terms, the European Communities was therefore also right in invoking the principle of presumed compliance within the context of its systemic claim under Article 23.1, 22.8 of the DSU.

4.388 The logic of this argument may also be further elucidated when the invocation of good faith is linked to the issue of burden of proof. The United States and Canada have attempted to make a prima facie case against the EC compliance measure. Yet, following the scientific debate the European Communities has refuted this prima facie case. The burden of proof is therefore still on the United States and Canada for questioning the European Communities' conclusion that the use of these six hormones for animal growth promotion is a risk to public health. The United States and Canada have failed to meet this burden of proof and they could not support their conclusions that the EC's ban on hormones treated beef was scientifically unsound.

4.389 We would like to recall that the European Communities also made violation claims under Articles 23 and 21.5 of the DSU that do not depend on the WTO-consistency of the EC's compliance measure. Rather these claims are directly linked to the US' and Canada's unilateral determination of the alleged inconsistency of the EC' compliance measure.

4.390 Finally, we have heard again this morning that the United States maintains that it could not have possibly made a "determination" that the EC's new ban is in fact WTO-consistent by the time the EC initiated these proceedings because the European Communities failed to provide all the necessary materials relevant to its measure.

4.391 This is a rather disingenuous characterization of the real facts and I will, at this stage not recall all our arguments that we have submitted to you. Let me just first point out that the United States erroneously keeps referring to a determination of WTO-consistency which it claims it could not make. The DSU neither requires nor forbids such "consistency determination". What the DSU prohibits, however, is the unilateral determination of a WTO violation by another Member.

4.392 Let me also recall, that while the United States in its view struggled to come up with a "determination" as early as November 2003 they dismissed the EC compliance measure and explicitly stated in its Trade Policy Review of 2005 that "they failed to see how the revised measure could be considered to implement the recommendations and rulings of the DSB". And in addition to that, since then the United States simply continued to apply its sanctions against the European Communities. There is no other way than to qualify this behaviour as an illegal determination of non-compliance. And, finally, it is also simply not true that the United States had been confronted with the evidence for the first time in 2003. All the underlying studies have been peer-reviewed and been published in journals and the European Communities undertook even an effort to discuss with the United States in Washington the scientific evidence. All this is on the record. The European Communities, therefore, cannot express again its puzzlement by the way the United States represents the facts in this dispute.

(d)   Conclusion

4.393 For all these reasons, the European Communities would ask the Panel to find:

(a)   First, that the United States' and Canada's continued suspension of concessions against the European Communities was inconsistent with the provisions referred to under Part I of the EC's first written submission.

(b)   In the alternative, the United States' and Canada's continued suspension of concessions against the European Communities is inconsistent with the provisions set out under Part II of the EC's first written submission.

L.   *Oral Statement of the United States on Legal Issues During the Second Substantive Meeting*

1.   *Oral statement*

4.394 The United States considers that last week's meeting with the scientific experts reinforced a fundamental point – that the European Communities ("EC") has failed to demonstrate that the conditions of Article 22.8 of the WTO's *Understanding on Rules and Procedures Governing the Settlement of Disputes* (the "DSU") for ending the Dispute Settlement Body ("DSB") - authorized suspension of concessions in the *Hormones* dispute have been met. To prevail on its claim that the United States has breached Article 22.8, the EC must demonstrate that it has either removed its WTO-inconsistent measures or provided a solution to the nullification or impairment suffered by the United States as a result of its ongoing bans on US meat and meat products. The EC has done neither.

4.395 The EC could have satisfied its burden by demonstrating that its "amended" ban brought it into conformity with its obligations under the WTO *Agreement on the Application of Sanitary and Phytosanitary Measures* ("*SPS Agreement*"). But it did not. The experts have provided valuable scientific and technical advice that confirms this fact. Their written and verbal responses demonstrate that the EC has failed to complete a risk assessment for oestradiol or base its ban on a risk assessment within the meaning of SPS Article 5.1.

4.396 Similarly, the experts' responses confirm that the EC has not imposed provisional bans within the meaning of SPS Article 5.7. Before discussing the EC's failure to bring its measures into conformity with the *SPS Agreement* and DSB recommendations and rulings, and thereby satisfy the conditions of DSU Article 22.8, however, I would like to briefly touch on the other DSU claims raised by the EC in the course of these proceedings.

4.397 The Panel will recall that the EC initially alleged that the United States was breaching its WTO obligations by failing to meet the requirements of several provisions of the DSU – namely Articles 21.5, 22.8, 3.7 and several provisions of Article 23 read "in conjunction" with each other. The United States has demonstrated that the EC's DSU claims are merely a reflection of how the EC would like to see the DSU rewritten rather than based in the actual text of the DSU as written and agreed to by WTO Members. As noted by the Appellate Body, "[d]etermining what the rules and procedures of the DSU ought to be is not our responsibility nor the responsibility of panels; it is clearly the responsibility solely of the Members of the WTO."

4.398 The EC alleges that its "provisional bans" on meat and meat products from cattle treated with the five other hormones (testosterone; progesterone; zeranol; trenbolone acetate; and melengestrol acetate) satisfy its obligations under SPS Article 5.7 and thereby bring it into conformity with the DSB recommendations and rulings that it must base its measures for these hormones on a risk assessment, as appropriate to the circumstances, within the meaning of Article 5.1 of the *SPS Agreement*.

4.399 Article 5.7 is a qualified exemption from Article 2.2 of the *SPS Agreement* which stipulates, among other things, that Members shall not maintain sanitary measures without sufficient scientific evidence "except as provided for in paragraph 7 of Article 5". In light of the fact that "Article 5.1 may be viewed as a specific application of the basic obligations contained in Article 2.2" and that "Articles 2.2 and 5.1 should constantly be read together," it is clear that Article 5.7 is also a temporary exception from a Member's obligation to base its measure on a risk assessment within the meaning of Article 5.1. In order to qualify for this exception, however, the EC must demonstrate that it has satisfied the four cumulative conditions of Article 5.7.

4.400 The experts' written and oral comments confirm that the EC has failed to do so and thereby failed to demonstrate that it has brought its measures into conformity with DSB recommendations and rulings. As a result, the EC has not removed the WTO-inconsistencies of its measures or provided a solution of the nullification or impairment suffered by the United States within the meaning of DSU Article 22.8.

4.401 For example, the EC's bans on the other five hormones are not imposed in a situation where relevant scientific information relating to the hormones is insufficient within the meaning of SPS Article 5.7. As demonstrated by the United States and confirmed by the written and oral responses of the experts, there is more than sufficient scientific evidence to permit "performance of an adequate assessment of risks as required under Article 5.1" for the five hormones.

4.402 In addition, the EC's bans on the other five hormones are not based on available pertinent information within the meaning of SPS Article 5.7. Its bans cannot be based on available pertinent information, because none of that information suggests that meat and meat products from cattle treated with the five hormones for growth promotion purposes according to good veterinary practices pose a risk to consumers.

4.403 The EC alleges that its permanent ban on meat and meat products from cattle treated with oestradiol for growth promotion purposes is based on a risk assessment within the meaning of Article 5.1 of the *SPS Agreement*. In these proceedings we have examined what, exactly, constitutes a risk assessment for Article 5.1 purposes from several angles and have confirmed a few basic concepts regarding the necessary components of a risk assessment for oestradiol. A risk assessment must identify adverse effects from the consumption of meat from cattle treated with oestradiol and evaluate the potential occurrence of such effects, and it must engage in four fundamental steps: hazard identification; hazard characterization; exposure assessment; and risk characterization.

4.404 Rather than concluding that the EC's Opinions constitute a complete risk assessment, the experts' responses indicate that the EC has failed to progress beyond the first step of risk assessment, hazard identification. As noted by the United States, this stage of risk assessment addresses the simple question of what can possibly go wrong, not the likelihood of something going wrong.

4.405 The EC has also failed to base its permanent ban on meat and meat products from cattle treated with oestradiol for growth promotion purposes on a risk assessment, as appropriate to the circumstances, within the meaning of SPS Article 5.1. In order for the EC's measure to be "based" on a risk assessment, its assessment (the Opinions) must sufficiently warrant or reasonably support its measure, a ban on meat and meat products from cattle treated with oestradiol for growth promotion purposes. Yet, the EC's Opinions and their underlying studies simply identify theoretical risks from oestradiol generally rather than the specific risk ostensibly addressed by the EC's measure.

4.406 The materials relied on by the EC focus on potential adverse effects from exposure to oestradiol or estrogens generally rather than providing evidence of the specific risk from residues in meat from cattle treated with oestradiol for growth promotion purposes. In its most recent set of exhibits, the EC has failed yet again to provide evidence of the specific risk allegedly posed by residues in meat from treated cattle.

4.407 While the sort of scientific evidence of a general risk presented by the EC, of which the US *Report on Carcinogens* it has referred to is a good example, may be handy for completing the hazard identification (first) component of a risk assessment, it is not evidence of the specific risk against which the EC purports to mitigate with its bans.

4.408 A measure banning the import of meat treated with oestradiol for growth promotion purposes cannot be premised on the EC's failure to produce evidence of a risk from this product. This failure represents the very type of theoretical uncertainty that is "not the kind of risk which, under Article 5.1, is to be assessed." As a result, the EC's Opinions fail to sufficiently warrant or reasonably support its measure.

4.409 This point is highlighted by the fact that so many of the studies relied on by the EC in its Opinions do not actually support the conclusions it has drawn from them. For instance, as discussed yesterday morning, the EC's Opinions reach conclusions on the genotoxicity, carcinogenicity and mutagenicity of oestradiol that simply are unsupported by scientific evidence. The experts have confirmed this point. The experts looked at the materials put forward by the EC in its attempt to produce evidence of the specific risk, yet have disagreed with the fundamental conclusions the EC draws from those materials. For example, the experts agreed that the scientific evidence did not support the conclusion that residue levels found in meat would be carcinogenic.

4.410 This is why, in yesterday's meeting, the United States made the point in the discussion of Appellate Body guidance from the original *Hormones* dispute that the Appellate Body's language on appropriate levels of protection was not necessarily relevant to the debate at hand. The point the United States made is that if there is no evidence of a risk from meat treated with oestradiol for growth promotion purposes, it does not matter what level of protection the EC has set for itself. Its level of protection could be zero risk, no additional risk, negligible risk, or some risk – if the product in question is safe, all of these levels of protection are satisfied and there is no need to parse distinctions between them. Despite this fact, if the Panel wishes to delve deeper into this Appellate Body discussion, the United States would note that the Appellate Body provided additional guidance on the matter of appropriate levels of protection and existence of distinctions in those levels in its Report in the *Australia – Salmon* dispute beginning at page 42.

4.411 For these reasons, those set out in the US submissions, and in light of the responses of the Panel's scientific experts, the EC has failed to conduct a risk assessment for oestradiol and has failed to base its permanent import ban on meat and meat products from cattle treated with oestradiol for growth promotion purposes on a risk assessment, as appropriate to the circumstances, within the meaning of Article 5.1 of the *SPS Agreement*.

4.412 Finally, by failing to base its permanent ban on meat from cattle treated with oestradiol on a risk assessment within the meaning of SPS Article 5.1 or to satisfy the conditions of SPS Article 5.7 for its provisional bans on meat from cattle treated with the other five hormones, the EC has not brought its measures into conformity with its obligations under SPS Article 3.3. As a consequence, the EC has again failed to satisfy the conditions of DSU Article 22.8 because it has not removed the WTO-inconsistencies of its measure.

4.413 The EC's measures are not based on international standards, and must therefore be premised on a "scientific justification" or maintained "as a consequence of the level of ... protection [the EC] determined to be appropriate in accordance with the relevant provisions of [Article 5 of the *SPS Agreement*]."[25] Because the EC's measures are neither based on a risk assessment nor satisfy the necessary conditions for a provisional ban as required by Article 5 of the *SPS Agreement*, they fail to satisfy its obligations under SPS Article 3.3.

4.414 In conclusion, the EC has failed to base its permanent ban on oestradiol on a risk assessment within the meaning of Article 5.1 of the *SPS Agreement* or to satisfy the conditions of SPS Article 5.7 with its provisional ban on the other five hormones. As a consequence, the EC also fails to satisfy its obligations under Article 3.3 of the *SPS Agreement*. The experts' responses and comments provide the necessary scientific underpinning for these conclusions, as well as the corresponding conclusion that the EC has not satisfied the conditions of DSU Article 22.8, the conditions by which the United States would have been obligated to cease to apply the suspension of concessions in the *Hormones* dispute to the EC.

4.415 For all the reasons discussed above and in its various submissions to the Panel, as well as the arguments raised by Canada in these proceedings, the United States respectfully requests the Panel to reject the EC's claims in their entirety.

2.   *Concluding statement by the United States*

4.416 The United Stated considers that we have had a very productive debate over the last week-and-a-half. In the course of our discussions, which included meetings with the panel of scientific experts, a few central issues have come to light.

4.417 First, as I noted yesterday, the task at hand is not one of conducting a risk assessment for the European Communities. It is not one of conducting a review for the EC of the numerous materials it has put forward since completion of its Opinions. Rather, the relevant analysis is one of what the EC has actually accomplished in its Opinions.

---

[25]   SPS Article 3.3.

4.418 Second, the Panel has consulted scientific experts to sift through the EC's Opinions and related materials in an attempt to determine whether any of these materials actually addressed the specific risk at issue in these proceedings – that from oestradiol residues in meat from animals treated with growth promoting hormones. The experts also looked at information put forward by the EC in support of its provisional bans on the other five hormones. The experts noted, as discussed in the US statement yesterday, that the EC had not completed the necessary steps of a risk assessment for oestradiol. Nor had the EC presented evidence that oestradiol residues in meat from treated cattle are carcinogenic. The United States described how these major conclusions factor into an analysis of the EC's permanent ban on oestradiol. They demonstrate that it is not based on risk assessment for purposes of SPS Article 5.1.

4.419 As to the other five hormones, the experts indicated that there was sufficient scientific evidence to conduct a risk assessment for each one and that the scientific evidence did not demonstrate a risk at levels found in residues in meat from treated cattle. This means that the EC failed to demonstrate that scientific evidence was insufficient to conduct a risk assessment for these hormones or that it had based its ban on available pertinent information. Therefore, the EC's bans do not satisfy the conditions of Article 5.7 of the *SPS Agreement*.

4.420 Third, the EC has claimed a US breach of Article 22.8 of the DSU. To demonstrate this breach, it must show that it has removed the WTO-inconsistencies of its measures or provided a solution to the nullification or impairment of benefits suffered by the United States. These conditions could theoretically be met if the EC's measures satisfy its obligations under the *SPS Agreement*. However, they do not. The experts' comments inform this analysis.

4.421 Fourth, and finally, the EC's various other DSU claims reflect the EC's hopes for how the DSU should be rewritten rather than finding a basis in the text of the DSU as it currently reads. Through a string of provisions read "in conjunction" with each other, it seeks very specific findings of specific provisions of the DSU. As the Appellate Body cautioned, "[d]etermining what the rules and procedures of the DSU ought to be is not our responsibility nor the responsibility of panels; it is clearly the responsibility solely of the Member of the WTO. Disregarding this guidance, the EC seeks to insert new obligations into the text of the DSU through the vehicle of dispute settlement. It may not do this. The EC, like the rest of the Membership of the WTO, is left with the text of the DSU as it reads today, and the EC has failed to demonstrate any US violation of the specific provisions of that text.

4.422 In closing, I would like to thank you for the professional manner in which you have conducted these proceedings. Thank you very much.

V.   ARGUMENTS OF THE THIRD PARTIES

A.   *Australia*

1.   *Introduction*

5.1   According to Australia, this dispute is about one fundamental question; whether the DSU provides that a Member's announcement of its compliance with DSB recommendations and rulings triggers an obligation on a retaliating Member to either (i) cease retaliation or (ii) initiate a new process for a multilateral determination of compliance.[26]

2.   *Opening Panel meetings for public observation*

5.2   Australia contends that when parties agree not to follow the Working Procedures in Appendix 3, or parts thereof, it would be difficult for the Panel to justify a decision that goes against the wishes of the parties. In Australia's view, to do so would undermine a basic principle of dispute settlement whereby parties consult with each other and with the Panel and seek mutual agreement on the conduct of disputes, according to Article 12.1 of the DSU.[27]

5.3   Australia submits that the decision to open the meetings with the parties to the public would not pose a problem, in principle, to Australia. Australia was however concerned about the modalities of organising the meetings, equity of access and logistic issues. Australia was of the view that the opening of the Panel's meetings to the public should be subject to the provisions that allow for protection of confidential information.[28]

3.   *Whether the DSB authorization remains in effect*

5.4   Australia argues that a Member's announcement of its compliance with DSB recommendations and rulings triggers an obligation on a retaliating Member to either cease retaliation or initiate a new process for a multilateral determination of compliance. Australia claims that as seen in Articles 22.1 and 22.8 of the DSU, the right to suspend concessions authorised by the DSB is temporary and conditional upon the respondent continuing to be in non compliance or upon a solution not being reached. According to Australia, by continuing retaliation in the face of a respondent's notification of compliance, a complainant is effectively challenging the measure(s) taken to comply. According to Australia therefore, in

---

[26]   Third party submission of Australia, para. 4.
[27]   Replies to Panel questions concerning an open hearing by Australia, question 1.
[28]   Replies to Panel questions concerning an open hearing by Australia, question 2.

such a case it is for the complainant to invoke a compliance panel pursuant to Article 21.5 of the DSU.[29]

5.5   Australia contends that the suspension of concessions or other obligations is the "last resort" for Members invoking the dispute settlement procedures, as stated in Article 3.7 of the DSU.[30]

4.   Article 21.5 of the DSU

5.6   Australia acknowledges that Article 21.5 of the DSU does not explicitly place the obligation to invoke a compliance panel on a complaining party. The text simply provides that in cases of disagreement over compliance such dispute shall be decided through recourse to the dispute settlement procedure. Australia however argues that requiring a respondent to invoke a compliance panel against its own measure(s) constitutes an implicit unilateral determination of inconsistency by the complainant and undermines the presumption that Members act in good faith in taking action to comply with DSB recommendations and rulings.[31]

5.7   Australia further submits that this position is consistent with Appellate Body findings on the presumption of good faith in *Chile – Alcoholic Beverages*,[32] where the Appellate Body stated that Members of the WTO should not be assumed, in any way, to have *continued* previous protection or discrimination through the adoption of a new measure, as this would come close to a presumption of bad faith.[33] Australia also noted observations on good faith made by the Appellate Body in *US – Hot- Rolled Steel*[34] and *US – Line Pipe*.[35]

5.8   Australia thus points out that the fact that a complainant may have been granted temporary authorisation to retaliate against a Member found to be in non-compliance does not change the fundamental application of the presumption of good faith. Australia stresses that disregarding the presumption in the specific circumstances of a Member announcing that it has taken action which it consid-

---

[29]   Third party submission of Australia, para. 5.
[30]   Replies to Panel questions by Australia, question 5.
[31]   Third party submission of Australia, para. 6.
[32]   *Chile – Taxes on Alcoholic Beverages*, (WT/DS87/AB/R and WT/DS110/AB/R), para. 74, (emphasis in original, footnote omitted).
[33]   Third party submission of Australia, para. 7.
[34]   *US – Anti-Dumping Measures on Certain Hot-Rolled Steel Products from Japan* (WT/DS184/AB/R), para. 101.
[35]   *US – Definitive Safeguard Measures on Imports of Circular Welded Carbon Quality Line Pipe from Korea* (WT/DS202/AB/R), para. 110.

ers brings it into compliance would go against the design and underlying logic of the DSU.[36]

5.9   Australia posits that the DSU is explicit on the following points, which provide context for the interpretation of Article 21.5:[37]

- Members must not take unilateral action to seek redress for alleged violations of obligations or other nullification or impairment of benefits (Article 23).

- Instead, Members must have recourse to the DSU and abide with its rules and procedures (Article 23).

- DSU procedures, including those provided for in Article 21, must be used to resolve disagreements over compliance (Article 23.1).

- The suspension of concessions or other obligations is a "last resort" by Members and is temporary. That is, it is only authorised until compliance is achieved (Articles 3.7 and 22).

5.10   Australia contends that by refusing to invoke a "compliance panel", a complainant who disagrees with the respondent's announcement of its compliance allows the dispute to continue unresolved.[38] Australia argues that the longer the time period in which the United States did not take action under Article 21.5, the greater the firmness or immutability the United States made of its determination. Australia emphasizes that this is because a determination within the meaning of Article 23.2(a) of the DSU may be inferred once a certain amount of time has passed after communication by a responding party that it has complied and in which a complaining party continues to retaliate. According to Australia therefore, the longer the period of time that a complaining party continues its retaliation in the face of this communication, the greater degree of certainty there is for the inference that the retaliating party has determined that a violation has occurred, that benefits have been nullified or impaired or that the attainment of any objective of the covered agreements has been impeded.[39]

5.11   Australia argues that there is no procedure that a Member claiming compliance can invoke in order to obtain a multilateral determination of actual compliance. According to Australia, the possibility of a new dispute whereby the original respondent complains against the continued retaliating measures on the basis of actual compliance assumes that there is no obligation upon the retaliating Member to either initiate an Article 21.5 panel or cease retaliation after

---

[36]   Third party submission of Australia, para. 8.
[37]   Third party submission of Australia, para. 9.
[38]   Third party submission of Australia, para. 10.
[39]   *Ibid.*

communication of compliance by a respondent, which is an incorrect interpretation of the DSU.[40]

B.   Brazil

1.   Introduction

5.12   Brazil claims that it files the present submission in light of its interests in the interpretation to be developed by the parties and the Panel in these proceedings. Brazil states that it will address what it considers to be the fundamental objective of the European Communities in the current dispute, namely to obtain multilateral recognition that it has fully implemented the recommendations of the DSB without having to bear the burden of proving how it would have effectively implemented those rulings.[41]

2.   Opening Panel meetings for public observation

5.13   Brazil questioned the specific grounds and the DSU provisions on which the Panel based its decision to accept the parties' request to open the panel meetings for public observation. According to Brazil, transparency is one of the key issues in the DSU review process and constitutes an important element in the debate carried out by Members in the DSB meetings. As such, Brazil notes that the debate on transparency will largely benefit from any further clarification by the Panel as to the legal reasons which motivated its decision to open the meetings to the public.[42]

5.14   Brazil argues that a decision on whether or not to open panels' proceedings to the public relies solely on the WTO membership, in particular the DSU review process which is the appropriate *locus* to deal with issues regarding the Dispute Settlement Mechanism. According to Brazil, if panels were to decide on this issue, they would go beyond their mandate, playing a role that is exclusive to the WTO membership.[43]

5.15   Brazil further submits that the right to be present at or to watch a panel meeting should be granted first to WTO Members subject to the rules for third party participation set forth in Article 10 of the DSU. Brazil also contends that opening the meetings to the public would represent a reinterpretation of Arti-

---

[40]   Replies by Australia to Panel questions, question 4.
[41]   Third party submission of Brazil, paras. 1 and 2.
[42]   Oral statement of Brazil, para. 2.
[43]   Replies by Brazil to Panel questions concerning open hearings, question 1.

cle 14 of the DSU, signaling that there are cases to which confidentiality is not applied, such as Panel and Appellate Body meetings.[44]

3. Whether the DSB authorization remains in effect

5.16   In Brazil's point of view, the European Communities must prove that the new measure is in full compliance with the DSB recommendations. Brazil stresses that the European Communities' claim is based only on a unilateral sole assertion of compliance. However, a mere assertion is insufficient to prove compliance. Brazil submits that the European Communities may modify its legislation over and over and notify changes to the WTO without actually bringing the measures into conformity with WTO rules.[45]

5.17   Brazil considers that if the European Communities argument were accepted, it would give the implementing Member the power to unilaterally dispel a previous multilateral determination authorizing suspension of concessions. Brazil contends that such Member would therefore be allowed to act as arbitrator, making use of a procedural artifice that could go on *ad infinitum*. Brazil notes that it would be absurd to have that practice accepted as the common practice in the implementation of WTO disputes. It would mean that a mere assertion that a Member has changed a measure found to be inconsistent automatically revokes a DSB authorization to suspend concessions, while exempting the Member from proving why and how the new measure complies with the DSB recommendations and rulings.[46]

5.18   Brazil submits that only in the case of a multilateral determination confirming that the EC has fully complied could there be grounds for consideration of whether the United States is in breach of Articles 23, 21.5, 3.7 and 22.8 of the DSU and Articles I:1 and II of the GATT 1994, as claimed.[47]

5.19   Brazil argues that just as the initial imposition of suspension of concessions must be preceded by a DSB determination of non-compliance, the authorization for a Member to discontinue the suspension of those concessions can only be made by a DSB determination of compliance, be it for the initial suspension of concessions, or at a later stage for the lifting of the authorized suspension of concessions.[48]

---

[44]   *Ibid.*
[45]   Third party submission of Brazil, paras. 5 and 6.
[46]   Third party submission of Brazil, para. 8.
[47]   Third party submission of Brazil, para. 9.
[48]   Third party submission of Brazil, para. 20.

5.20   Brazil posits that the right to suspend concessions is temporary and conditional because it can only be applied based on a multilateral authorization (Article 23.2 (c) of the DSU) and until the party in violation complies with the recommendations of the DSB or a mutually satisfied solution is agreed between the parties in the dispute (Article 22.1 and 22.8 of the DSU).[49]

4.   Article 21.5 of the DSU

5.21   Brazil contends that the present situation is different from the one resulting from the relationship between Articles 21.5 and 22.6 of the DSU and it does not consider examples referred to by the European Communities regarding the *US – Upland Cotton* dispute[50], and *Softwood Lumber*[51] disputes, to be applicable to the present proceedings. Brazil argues that the proceedings under Article 21.5 in those disputes had already established at the time the implementing party requested the arbitration to determine the level of the suspension of concessions. Brazil stresses that in the current dispute, Article 21.5 proceedings and Article 22.6 arbitration are not "simultaneously ongoing", since no request for a compliance panel has been presented.[52]

5.22   Brazil submits that in the post-retaliation phase, one should bear in mind that there is a multilateral authorization in effect. According to Brazil, a presumption of good faith in carrying out the implementing measure cannot by itself override a DSB authorization. That authorization should be revoked by a multilateral determination of compliance not by a unilateral declaration of implementation or a presumption of compliance.[53]

5.   Burden of proof

5.23   Brazil posits that the party who makes a particular claim bears the burden of proof. Brazil further contends that by merely asserting that it has removed the inconsistency found by the DSB, the European Communities is not supporting its claim.[54]

5.24   Brazil also argues that the European Communities professes that no Member shall be 'judged' except through multilateral judicial proceedings.[55] However, Brazil notes that this notwithstanding, the European Communities

---

[49]   Replies by Brazil to questions from the European Communities, question 3.
[50]   *US –Upland Cotton*, WT/DS267/22.
[51]   *US – Softwood Lumber VI*, WT/DS277/11.
[52]   Third party submission of Brazil, paras. 22-24.
[53]   Replies by Brazil to Panel questions, question 3.
[54]   Third party submission of Brazil, paras. 10 and 11.
[55]   See EC's first written submission, para. 1.

serves itself with a "blank authorization" to determine unilaterally its compliance with WTO obligations and the inconsistency of the continued suspension of concessions granted by the DSB to the United States. Brazil states that had the European Communities wanted to follow multilateral rules, it should have requested an Article 21.5 compliance panel, as it did in *EC – Bananas III (Article 21.5 – EC).*[56]

5.25   Brazil argues that Article 21.5 of the DSU does not specify which Member is to initiate an Article 21.5 proceeding. Therefore, in Brazil's point of view, when disagreement exists as to the consistency of the measures taken to comply with the DSB recommendations, any party to a dispute may have recourse to the Article 21.5 proceedings. Brazil asserts that nothing in the DSU precludes an implementing Member from resorting to an Article 21.5 panel review. Brazil further argues that Article 6 of the DSU provides a rule for the development of special terms of reference, which could be applied in those cases where the implementing Member requests a panel to analyse its own measure.[57]

C.   Canada

1.   Introduction

5.26   Canada submits that for the reasons set out in its first written submission in *Canada – Continued Suspension of Obligations in the EC – Hormones Dispute* (WT/DS321)[58], the continued suspension by the United States of concessions to the European Communities is fully consistent with the obligations of the United States under the Marrakesh Agreement Establishing the World Trade Organization. Consequently, Canada agrees with the United States that the claims of the European Communities have no basis in the DSU or GATT 1994.[59]

2.   Opening Panel meetings for public observation

5.27   Canada submits that its views on this matter have been expressed in the relevant portion of the Panel's Report (Section IV.B.2) in *Canada – Continued Suspension of Obligations in the EC – Hormones Dispute* (WT/DS321). The arguments that Canada expressed in that dispute as the defendant equally apply to the present case as Canada's third party arguments.[60]

---

[56]   Third party submission of Brazil, paras. 13 and 14.
[57]   Replies by Brazil to Panel questions, questions 2 and 5.
[58]   WT/DS321/06.
[59]   Letter of 19 August 2005 to the Panel explaining Canada's third party submission.
[60]   Letter of 30 June 2005 from Canada to the Panel.

D.   China

1.   Introduction

5.28   China submits that the disputes raised in this case are derived from loopholes embedded in the DSU. China states that this brings to attention the importance of amending those loopholes in the new round of negotiation. According to China, in absence of any revision of the DSU, it is a challenge for this Panel to find suitable dispute settlement solution according to the current DSU.[61]

2.   Opening Panel meetings for public observation

5.29   China did not provide a reply on the potential legal constraint that would exclude the Panel from opening the Panel meeting for public observation. China however preferred the Panel to meet the third parties in closed session. It argues that based on Article 18.2 of the DSU, panels do not have the right to unilaterally disclose the third party submissions and oral presentations.[62]

3.   The current status of the DSB authorized suspension of concessions

5.30   China submits that under Article 22.8, a DSB authorized suspension of concessions shall not be applied, if one of three of the following conditions has been met:[63]

(a)   The measure found to be inconsistent with a covered agreement has been removed;

(b)   The Member that must implement the recommendations or rulings provides a solution to the nullification or impairment of benefits;

(c)   A mutually satisfactory solution is reached.

5.31   China contends that if a mutually satisfactory solution is reached by the parties on (a) or (b) above, it will fall into condition (c) and then a DSB authorized suspension of concessions shall not be applied. China posits that if there is no mutually satisfactory solution reached by the parties on whether condition (a) and/or (b) above has been met, the parties have to invoke the dispute settlement procedures to let the Panel make such determination. China posits that in case the responding party declares any of the above conditions has been satisfied,

---

[61]   Third party submission of China, paras. 1 and 2.
[62]   Replies by China to Panel questions concerning open hearings, questions 1 and 2.
[63]   Third party submission of China, para. 6.

there are only two options for the complaining party: (a) to admit the compliance of new measures; or (b) to deny it.[64]

5.32   In China's view, in case the original complaining party denies the compliance of new measures, that is, if no agreement is reached between the parties as to whether the conditions under Article 22.8 of the DSU have been met, under Article 23 of the DSU, the parties shall have recourse to the DSB's determination to avoid unilateral determination.[65]

5.33   China thus considers that there are only two ways to terminate a DSB authorized suspension of concessions: (i) to reach a mutually satisfactory solution; (ii) to get a final determination from the DSB. According to China, this is the case, even when the original complaining party needs a reasonable period of time to evaluate the WTO consistency of the implementation measure.[66]

5.34   China argues that the European Communities' allegation that it has removed the measure at issue in itself could not give the European Communities ground to terminate the authorization of suspension of concessions. China asserts that Article 23 of the DSU lays down the fundamental principle that the dispute settlement system of the WTO is the exclusive means to redress any violation of any provision of the WTO Agreement. It argues that since there is no mutually satisfactory solution between the European Communities and the United States, the DSB authorized suspension of concessions shall be applied until the DSB makes a new determination on the authorization of suspension of concessions. China notes that the suspension of concessions pursuant to a DSB authorization is temporary and conditional, with the condition being that the original responding party fully implements the rulings and recommendations of the DSB. China emphasizes that no party can make a unilateral determination on whether condition (i) and/or (ii) has been met.[67]

5.35   China emphasizes that if this Panel allows the original responding party to terminate a DSB authorized suspension of concessions by introducing an implementing measure, there is a risk that it could be abused by an original responding party who, instead of bringing its measures into full conformity with the recommendations and rulings of the DSB, may implement legislation which does not cure all the defects in its earlier inconsistent legislation. China argues that if this Panel finds a DSB authorized suspension of concessions to remain in

---

[64]   Third party submission of China, paras. 7 and 8.
[65]   Replies by China to Panel questions, question 7.
[66]   Third party submission of China, para. 9.
[67]   Third party submission of China, para. 10.

effect after the original responding party introduced an implementing measure, it can help enforcing WTO rules by inducing actual compliance.[68]

5.36   China is of the view that the suspension of concessions has at least two functions: (i) to rebalance the interests among parties; (ii) to force the responding party to bring its measure into compliance with the covered agreement. China posits that if this Panel allows the original responding party to introduce an implementing measure to override the DSB-authorized suspension of concessions, it invalidates the second function of suspension of concessions.[69]

4.   Article 21.5 of the DSU and burden of proof

5.37   China states that Article 21.5 of the DSU does not preclude the original responding party from having recourse to the dispute settlement procedures in the event that there is disagreement as to the existence or consistency with a covered agreement of measures taken to comply with the recommendations and rulings. China advances the following reasons for this argument.[70]

5.38   First, according to China, it would be natural and logical only for the original complaining party to initiate an Article 21.5 proceeding. China quotes *Chile – Alcoholic Beverages*[71] and *Canada – Aircraft (Article 21.5 – Brazil)*[72] and argues that the original responding party when adopting measures to implement recommendations and rulings of the DSB shall be presumed to have fulfilled its WTO obligations, and therefore, shall not bear the burden to demonstrate compliance. China notes that this is further justified because the European Communities' implementation measure requires conducting extensive scientific studies and performing a comprehensive risk assessment in a transparent and objective manner. According to China therefore, after the European Communities notifies the DSB of its measure to implement the recommendation and rulings of the DSB, it has fulfilled the procedure obligation under the DSU, and should not be required to bear the burden of proof.[73]

5.39   Secondly, China refers to the practice of treaty interpretation as elucidated in Article 31.3 of the *Vienna Convention on the Law of Treaties* and *Japan – Alcoholic Beverages II*[74], and points out that the statistics of panel proceedings on compliance under Article 21.5 of the DSU show that in most cases, it is the

---

[68]   Third party submission of China, paras. 11 and 12.
[69]   Replies by China to Panel questions, question 3.
[70]   Third party submission of China, para. 15.
[71]   Third party submission of China, para. 17.
[72]   Third party submission of China, para. 18.
[73]   Third party submission of China, paras. 19 and 20.
[74]   See Appellate Body Report, *Japan – Alcoholic Beverages II* (WT/DS8/AB/R, WT/DS10/AB/R, WT/DS11/AB/R) p. 13

original complaining party that initiates the dispute settlement procedure under Article 21.5 of the DSU. China stresses that the only precedent for an original responding party to initiate the dispute settlement procedure under Article 21.5 of the DSU is in the *EC – Bananas*[75] dispute where the European Communities as an original responding party sought the establishment of a compliance panel under Article 21.5 of the DSU with the hope of preventing the United States from having recourse to Article 22.6 of the DSU directly. China asserts that this subsequent practice in the application of Article 21.5 of the DSU establishes the agreement of the parties regarding their interpretation that the original complaining party should initiate the Article 21.5 proceeding.[76]

5.40   Thirdly, China argues, the balance of hardship to initiate an Article 21.5 proceeding does not favour the original complaining party. China believes that the original complaining party will suffer no cognizable harm if it initiates an Article 21.5 proceeding, because the DSB authorized suspension of concessions is still in effect. China asserts that it is not proper to let the European Communities initiate an Article 21.5 proceeding simply because the original complaining party is reluctant or has no incentive to do so.[77]

5.41   China stresses that it should be presumed that when the original responding party introduces an implementation measure, it has fulfilled its WTO obligation, and it should be the duty of the original complaining party to demonstrate that the implementation measure is still inconsistent with the covered agreement. China believes if this Panel rules that the European Communities, as an original responding party, should initiate an Article 21.5 proceeding, it will unduly shift the heavy burden onto the shoulders of the European Communities to establish compliance, which is against the nature and logic of the Article 21.5 proceeding.[78]

5.42   China contends that it is usually the case that the responding party has more information on its implementation measure, therefore it is better positioned to demonstrate the WTO consistency of the measure. However, according to China, the nature and logic of Article 21.5 proceedings stands against this approach. China stresses that subsequent practice in the application of Article 21.5 confirms this conclusion. China is therefore of the opinion that the United States

---

[75]   *European Communities – Regime for the Importation, Sale and Distribution of Bananas – Recourse to Article 21.5 by the European Communities*, Report by the Panel (WT/DS27/RW/EEC), 12 April 1999 – report never adopted.
[76]   Third party submission of China, paras. 21-24.
[77]   Third party submission of China, para. 25.
[78]   Third party submission of China, para. 26.

as an original complaining party should bear the burden to institute the Article 21.5 proceeding.[79]

5.43   China continues that the unique part of this case is that the original complaining party has a DSB authorized suspension of concessions. According to China, in addition to the function of inducing compliance, this authorized suspension of concessions can rebalance the trading relationship between the complaining and the original responding party in order to restore the economic equilibrium embodied in the original WTO deal. China submits that if after the original panel proceeding, an original complaining party finds that the original responding party does not implement the recommendations and rulings of the DSB, it has incentive to initiate an Article 21.5 proceeding, because it still suffers from a WTO inconsistent measure. However, in this case, China submits that due to the rebalance by the authorized suspension of concessions, the original complaining party may not have the same incentive, therefore it may be necessary to set up a time limit for it to initiate an Article 21.5 proceeding.[80]

5.44   China argues that the proceedings under Article 21.5 of the DSU shall be initiated in a reasonable period of time. China points out that it is in line with the good faith requirement established by Article 26 of the *Vienna Convention on the Law of Treaties* and it is also consistent with the requirement of "prompt settlement of situations" in Article 3.3 and the "temporary nature" of the retaliation system of the DSU.[81]

5.45   China stresses that it wants to bring to the Panel's attention that both Article 22.8 and Article 21.5 of the DSU do not preclude this Panel from setting a time limit to initiate the dispute settlement proceedings. If this Panel holds that it should be the original complaining party to invoke Article 21.5 of the DSU, to facilitate the implementation of this recommendation and ruling, it may be necessary to set up a time limit for the original complaining party to initiate an Article 21.5 proceeding.[82]

5.   Article 23.2 of the DSU

5.46   China argues that to establish a violation of Article 23.2 (a), the Panel shall firstly assess whether the act of "determination" is made "in such cases", where a Member seeks the redress of a WTO violation.[83]

---

[79]   Third party submission of China, paras. 27 and 28.
[80]   Third party submission of China, para. 29.
[81]   Third party submission of China, para. 31.
[82]   Third party submission of China, para. 32.
[83]   Third party submission of China, para. 35.

5.47   China analyses the different interpretations of the term "seek the redress of violation" in *US – Section 301 Trade Act,*[84] in *US – Certain EC Products*"[85] and in *European Communities – Measures Affecting Trade in Commercial Vessels,*[86] and states that the term "seek the redress of a violation" should be read broadly to cover any act as long as it seeks to obtain unilateral results that can be achieved through means other than recourse to the DSU. China states that in this case, the original complaining party's continued suspension of concessions could be considered as a measure seeking the redress of a WTO violation, if it had a chance to challenge the European Communities' WTO violation but held back, allowing the DSB authorized suspension of concessions to apply continuously.[87]

5.48   China argues that after the European Communities provided notice of the Directive to the DSB in October 2003, the original complaining party raised doubt on the WTO consistency of this European Communities' implementation measure. Since then it has had a reasonable period of time to review the European Communities measure and to initiate Article 21.5 proceedings. China argues that it is the lack of action under Article 21.5 of the DSU by the original complaining party, rather than the DSB authorized suspension of concessions itself, that may be considered as seeking the redress of a violation.[88]

5.49   With respect to the meaning of the term "determination", China refers to the panel in *US – Section 301 Trade Act*[89] and argues that the term "determination" in Article 23.2(a) of the DSU needs to be read broadly and it does not require that a measure clearly sets out in its text that a WTO violation has occurred. China argues that such a determination may be inferred from actions. According to China, the longer the time period in which the original complaining party took no action under Article 21.5 of the DSU, the greater the firmness or immutability that it made such a determination.[90]

5.50   China argues that where there is no official determination, the Panel has to find a way to evaluate the firmness and immutability of the alleged determination. China notes that before the decision becomes final, there could be a gradual change process in which a time lapse can be a parameter. According to China, in the post-retaliation phase, the clock starts ticking when the original responding party introduces a new measure. China argues that the amount of time needed to constitute a final determination by the original complaining party under Article 23 of the DSU depends on several factors, including but not limited to (1) the

---

[84]   See Panel Report, *US – Section 301 Trade Act*, para. 7.50, footnote 657.
[85]   See Panel Report, *US – Certain EC Products*, paras. 6.22 and 6.23.
[86]   See Panel Report, *EC – Commercial Vessels*, WT/DS301/R, para. 7.196.
[87]   Third party submission of China, paras. 36-39.
[88]   Third party submission of China, para. 41.
[89]   See Panel Report, *US – Section 301 Trade Act*, para. 7.50, footnote 657.
[90]   Third party submission of China, paras. 41 and 42.

complexity of the compliance measure; (2) sufficiency of information related to the compliance measure; and (3) the ability of the original complaining party to evaluate such new measure.[91]

E.   India

1.   Introduction

5.51   India submits that it takes no position on the respective assertions of the parties in this dispute. India notes however that the treaty text is not clear on the respective rights and obligations of the party taking a compliance measure and the party applying sanctions. India contends that this is evidenced by the fact that this is one of the major issues on which the WTO Membership is currently engaged in negotiation with a view to improve or clarify the legal text. India states that it has views on how the lacunae in the DSU on this issue can be improved or clarified, but that is a matter for the Membership to decide through future negotiations.[92]

2.   Opening Panel meetings for public observation

5.52   India submits that the issue of external transparency is being discussed in the ongoing negotiations in the Special Session of the Dispute Settlement Body. India states that the negotiations have not yet been completed, and there is no consensus on whether and which form of external transparency is acceptable to the WTO Members. Until that happens, India believes that the Panel proceedings have to be in closed session,[93] and its deliberations have to remain confidential[94] as provided in the DSU.[95]

5.53   India posits that it is not a function of a panel to respond to any requests from the parties that do not assist in resolution of the matter before it, and which are not in the terms of reference of the panel.[96]

5.54   India contends that the possibility of a panel to decide to deviate from the Working Procedures in Appendix 3 has been provided with a view to have panel procedures with sufficient flexibilities so as to ensure high-quality panel reports.[97] In India's view, deviation from the Working Procedures, therefore,

---

[91]   Replies by China to Panel questions, question 1.
[92]   Oral statement by India, para. 3.
[93]   Paragraph 2 of the Working Procedures in Appendix 3 of the DSU.
[94]   Paragraph 3 of the Working Procedures in Appendix 3 of the DSU.
[95]   Replies by India to Panel questions concerning open hearings, question 1.
[96]   Oral statement of India, para. 5.
[97]   Article 12.2, DSU.

should meet this qualitative objective. India quotes Article 12.1 of the DSU and the Panel in *India – Patents (US)*[98] *and argues that although p*anels are *given* some discretion in establishing their own working procedures, they do not have the discretion to modify the substantive provisions of the DSU. India argues that the confidentiality requirements for panel proceedings are a substantive provision of the DSU, and the Panel cannot use its discretion to modify them in order to cater to a request by the parties on a matter that does not serve to improve the quality of the Panel's Report.[99]

5.55 India argues that Article VII of the Rules of Conduct[100] requires each 'covered person' to maintain the confidentiality of dispute settlement deliberations and proceedings at all times. India questions how the Panel is going to ensure that these requirements are met after opening the proceedings to the public for observation.[101]

5.56 India submits that the decision of the Panel to open its proceedings to the public necessarily involves some issues on which consultation and decisions with WTO Members, and not just the parties and third parties, would have been necessary. For example, India questions how the Panel, at its own level, addressed issues relating to the implications on the functioning of the WTO Secretariat, budgetary implications and implications relating to the use of the official languages of the WTO, for which rules and practices have been established by other bodies of the WTO. India also questions how the Panel could take a view on the additional costs arising out of the opening up of the proceedings to public without the Budget Committee having considered the matter.[102]

5.57 According to India, the WTO is a Member driven organization and it is solely for the WTO Members to decide whether or not to change the WTO rules and open up panel proceedings to the public; a Panel cannot take upon itself that function, even at the request of parties to the dispute.[103]

5.58 India posits that the meeting of the Panel's session with the third parties should be in closed session as required under paragraph 2 of the Working Procedures contained in Appendix 3 of the DSU.[104]

---

[98] *India – Patent Protection for Pharmaceutical and Agricultural Chemical Products – Complaint by the United States,* Panel Report, WT/DS50/R.
[99] Oral statement of India, para. 6.
[100] Rules of conduct for the understanding on rules and procedures governing the settlement of disputes adopted by the DSB on 3 December 1996 (WT/DSB/RC/1).
[101] Oral statement of India, para. 7.
[102] Oral statement of India, para. 8.
[103] Oral statement of India, para. 9.
[104] Replies by India to Panel questions concerning open hearings, question 2.

F.   Mexico

1.   Introduction

5.59   Mexico submits that the systemic implications of this dispute are of great importance in terms of the functioning of the DSU and in particular of defining a way of proceeding when there is an authorization to suspend benefits and then further disagreement as to whether or not the DSB's recommendations and rulings have been implemented. In Mexico's view, the most important issue in this case is whether the adoption of implementation measures "require" immediate termination of retaliatory measures and if not, who should require termination and how. According to Mexico, the role of the Panel in this case is to give precise answers to these questions and to ensure that they fulfil not only the letter of the DSU, but also the objectives of security, predictability and prompt settlement of the dispute.[105]

2.   Opening Panel meetings for public observation

5.60   Mexico disagreed with the opening of the panel meetings to the public on the grounds that panel meetings constitute panel "deliberations" and as such should be confidential, as per Article 14.1 DSU. Mexico also argues that transparency is a sensitive issue that is currently under discussion in the negotiations to amend the DSU thus to force one or another negotiating position by taking such a decision is inappropriate. Mexico argues that the DSU rules require that the meetings be confidential and therefore, bilateral agreement among parties is not suffice to bend the rules. In its view, the decision of the two parties should only prevail to the extent that it does not affect the right of other DSB Members including third parties. Mexico contends that if the Panel is to depart from the Working Procedures of Appendix 3, the Panel must do so with caution as such deviation is meant to grant flexibility so as to ensure high quality panel reports, as seen in Article 12.2 DSU.[106]

5.61   Mexico emphasizes that public hearings are a cross-cutting issue that should be addressed in all the discussions conducted in the WTO, and should not be imposed by a panel at the request of three Members. Mexico regrets that the decision will set a precedent that may affect the outcome of the negotiations and will in all likelihood end up complicating the preparation of working procedures of future panels.[107]

5.62   Mexico notes that if the Panel is to open the meetings to the public observation, as a policy perspective, it poses systemic questions as to the necessity to

---

[105]   Replies by Mexico to Panel questions concerning open hearings, question 1, paras. 2, 3 and 9.
[106]   Oral statement of Mexico, para. 2; Replies by Mexico to Panel questions, paras. 9 and 3.
[107]   Oral statement of Mexico, para. 3.

open negotiation meetings and ordinary sessions of the WTO to the public.[108] Mexico suggests that third party sessions follow the established WTO practice of being in closed session.[109]

3. Whether the DSB authorization remains in effect

5.63   According to Mexico, the Panel should reject the argument that a simple unilateral notification is enough to reduce multilateral effort to nothing. Mexico contends that the Panel should bear in mind the lengthy procedure and high political costs to Members of obtaining a multilateral authorization to suspend concessions.[110]

5.64   Mexico stresses that it can not allow a dispute settlement system to deprive all effect of the authority to suspend benefits when a Member has failed to implement the DSB's recommendations and rulings within the reasonable period. In its view, in such a case, if the parties fail to agree, the matter must be resolved by a multilateral decision.[111]

5.65   Mexico argues in its reply to the questions posed by the European Communities that a DSB decision may be affected only by another DSB decision taking away the effect of the first decision.[112]

4. Article 21.5 of the DSU

5.66   Mexico claims that Article 21.5 DSU affords the most suitable procedure for resolving this dispute and it could be initiated by any party. Mexico however submits that the dispute could be dealt with either by an ordinary panel, or through arbitration under Article 25 DSU or indeed by any of the proceedings provided for in Article 5 DSU. Mexico however points out that it takes a constructive approach and good will by the parties to make Article 21.5 DSU function and be able to resolve any disagreements.[113]

---

[108]   Replies by Mexico to Panel questions concerning open hearings, question 1, para. 7.
[109]   Replies by Mexico to Panel questions concerning open hearings, question 2.
[110]   Oral statement of Mexico, para. 5.
[111]   Oral statement of Mexico, para. 4.
[112]   Replies by Mexico to questions from the European Communities, question 4.
[113]   Oral statement of Mexico, para. 6.

G.   New Zealand

1.   Introduction

5.67   New Zealand submits that this case raises important issues about the integrity and effectiveness of the WTO dispute settlement system, as it is principally about issues of compliance and the proper interpretation and application of the rules of the DSU as they relate to the post-retaliation phase. In New Zealand's view, the case taken by the European Communities is for all intents and purposes a compliance case and is thus akin to an Article 21.5 case. According to New Zealand, the same determinations are required to resolve the case at hand, as would be required had it been commenced under Article 21.5. In New Zealand's view, the Panel's terms of reference[114] are sufficiently broad to encompass this question and in doing so, the Panel should focus on actual compliance and not presumed compliance.[115]

2.   Opening Panel meetings for public observation

5.68   According to New Zealand, there are no legal constraints that would prevent the Panel from opening the Panel hearings to the public. New Zealand quotes Article 12.1 which allows panels to follow Working Procedures unless the panel decides otherwise after consulting the parties. New Zealand argues that while Appendix 3 provides for closed session hearings, the Working Procedure can be amended on the consent of the panel and the parties. New Zealand further stipulates that the reference in Article 14.1 of the DSU to panel deliberations being confidential refers to the internal deliberations of the panel, not the hearings with the parties. New Zealand submits that this is in line with the practice of other international tribunals which have open hearings but whose deliberations are nonetheless confidential. According to New Zealand, Article 18.2 of the DSU allows parties to waive confidentiality. New Zealand did not object to its third party hearings being public.[116]

3.   Whether the DSB authorization remains in effect

5.69   New Zealand submits that there is no obligation on the United States to take an Article 21.5 case, and that in the absence of a determination of compli-

---

[114]   WT/DS320/6 of 14 January 2005 and WT/DS/320/7. The Request for the Establishment of a Panel by the European Communities states, *inter alia*, that:

The United States has acted inconsistently with Article 22.8 of the DSU by failing to apply the suspension of concessions or other obligations *only until such time as the measure found to be inconsistent with a covered agreement has been removed,* or the implementing Member has provided a solution to the nullification or impairment of benefits previously caused to the United States. (emphasis added).

[115]   Third party submission of New Zealand, paras. 1.06 and 2.19.

[116]   Replies by New Zealand to Panel questions concerning open hearings, questions 1 and 2.

ance from the DSB, the DSB's authorisation of suspension of concessions remains valid.[117]

5.70   New Zealand argues that underlying the European Communities' arguments is the assumption that it should benefit in these circumstances from a presumption of compliance on the basis of the principle of good faith.[118] New Zealand however does not agree that the said principle applies in the current circumstances, to require the United States to cease the suspension of concessions and commence Article 21.5 proceedings simply because the European Communities has notified that it now considers itself to be in compliance. According to New Zealand, a presumption of good faith cannot override an explicit multilateral authorisation from the DSB to impose a retaliatory suspension of concessions.[119]

5.71   In New Zealand's view, the cases cited by the European Communities in support of the application of a presumption of compliance involve measures that were implemented within the reasonable period of time and where there was no authorisation to suspend concessions, which is not the situation at present. New Zealand opines that even if it can be said that a presumption of compliance operates in the pre-retaliation period while the reasonable period of time is still pending, in the current circumstances any presumed compliance on the part of the European Communities has given way to the actual compliance of the suspension of concessions which has been duly authorised by the DSB.[120]

4.   Articles 21.5, 22.8 and 23 of the DSU

5.72   New Zealand argues that while it would be open to the respondent to initiate compliance review under Article 21.5, the argument that Article 23 read with Articles 21.5, 22.8 and 3.7 imposes a requirement to do so cannot be sustained. New Zealand insists that Article 21.5 merely states that the disagreement shall be dealt with through recourse to the dispute settlement procedures, but does not place any particular onus on any one to commence proceedings.[121]

5.73   New Zealand contends that Article 23 is the framework provision setting up the requirement to have recourse to dispute settlement when seeking redress of a violation of obligations. New Zealand however argues that Article 23 does not address the specific situation in this case, where the United States has had

---

[117]   Third party submission of New Zealand, para. 2.09.
[118]   The European Communities sets out its arguments on the 'presumption of compliance' in paras. 81-94 of its first written submission in addressing its argument that the United States is in violation of Article 23.1 read together with Articles 22.8 and 3.7 of the DSU.
[119]   Third party submission of New Zealand, paras. 2.10 and 2.11.
[120]   Third party submission of New Zealand, para. 2.12.
[121]   Third party submission of New Zealand, para 2.14.

recourse to dispute settlement in accordance with this Article and has taken all the steps there identified. New Zealand submits that Article 23 does not impose an obligation on the United States to cease the application of the suspension of concessions or to take a compliance review case where it does not accept that the measure has been removed. Nor does it do so when "read together" with Articles 3.7 and 22.8. New Zealand argues that it cannot see how these provisions can be read to displace the specific authorisation under Article 22.6, which has never been revoked.[122]

5.74   New Zealand posits that if the Panel were to adopt the European Communities' approach, it would give rise to a situation where an implementing Member could continually impose successive rounds of litigation at will, by a mere assertion of compliance. In New Zealand's view this could render useless the mechanism of suspension of concessions. According to New Zealand, this approach is inconsistent with the aims and objectives of the dispute settlement system given the fundamental importance of suspension of concessions as the 'last resort' of the dispute settlement system, as per Article 3.7 of the DSU.[123]

5.75   New Zealand points out that the suspension of concessions may not be maintained indefinitely in circumstances where the violation has been addressed as stipulated in Article 22.8 of the DSU. According to New Zealand, if the respondent maintains the suspension notwithstanding, then there is a "disagreement as to the existence or consistency ... of measures taken to comply" with the recommendations within the terms of Article 21.5. As a consequence it is open to the party concerned about this to have recourse to the dispute settlement procedures to resolve the disagreement.[124]

5.76   New Zealand notes that this does not mean however, that sanctions may go on forever even in cases where there is full compliance but the new measure has not been challenged. New Zealand considers that if a measure taken to comply does indeed remove the inconsistency with the recommendations and rulings of the DSB, the suspension of concessions should be ceased. In its view, the justification for continuing to suspend concessions would be the combination of the continuing DSB authorisation and the absence of any agreement that the original respondent has brought its measures into compliance.[125]

5.77   In New Zealand's view, it is possible for an implementing Member to initiate an Article 21.5 proceeding in any case "where there is disagreement as to

---

[122]   Third party submission of New Zealand, paras. 2.14-2.16.
[123]   Third party submission of New Zealand, para. 2.17.
[124]   Third party submission of New Zealand, para. 2.18.
[125]   Replies by New Zealand to questions from the European Communities, questions 4 and 5.

the existence or consistency with a covered agreement of measures taken to comply with the recommendations and rulings" of the DSB.[126]

5.78 New Zealand states that Article 21.5 does not specify the procedures to be applied, beyond stipulating that the matter be referred to the original panel and that there be an accelerated timeframe for circulation of the report. It further contends that the consequence is that it is up to the Panel to establish the Panel procedures in accordance with Article 12 of the DSU.[127]

5.79 New Zealand submits that there is no textual basis in the DSU for concluding that an original complainant that maintains a multilaterally authorized suspension of concessions after notification of a compliance measure by the original respondent and does not initiate Article 21.5 proceedings, is in violation of its obligations under the DSU.[128]

5. Burden of proof

5.80 New Zealand submits that the European Communities bears the burden of proving a prima facie inconsistency with Article 22.8 of the DSU. New Zealand refers to the Appellate Body decision in US – Wool Shirts and Blouses[129], and contends that the European Communities must adduce evidence sufficient to raise a presumption that the suspension of concessions continues to apply and that: (a) it has removed the measure found to be inconsistent with the SPS Agreement; or (b) it has provided a solution to the nullification or impairment of benefits; or (c) a mutually satisfactory solution has been reached. The EC does not argue (b), and (c) is clearly not the case, but it instead relies on (a).[130]

5.81 New Zealand submits that the European Communities has not demonstrated in its first written submission that it has removed the inconsistent measure. According to New Zealand, 'removal' of an inconsistent measure for the purposes of Article 22.8 of the DSU may be interpreted as compliance with the recommendations and rulings of the DSB. 'Removal' of the measure in this case could involve the removal of the import prohibition and/or establishing a justification for the prohibition through a risk assessment consistent with the

---

[126] Replies by New Zealand to questions from the European Communities, question 6.
[127] Replies by New Zealand to Panel questions, question 2.
[128] Replies by New Zealand to Panel questions, question 5.
[129] United States – Measure Affecting Imports of Woven Wool Shirts and Blouses from India (US – Wool Shirts and Blouses), WT/DS33/AB/R, 25 April 1997, p. 14.
[130] Third party submission of New Zealand, paras. 2.21-2.22.

SPS Agreement, taking into account the particular requirements which the Panel and Appellate Body reports identified.[131]

6. Article 5.7 of the SPS Agreement

5.82   New Zealand posits that as the Member seeking to have recourse to Article 5.7, the burden of proof rests on the European Communities to demonstrate that the four requirements of that provision have been met.[132] New Zealand is of the view that while not explicitly stated by the European Communities, the provisional import ban on the five hormones other than oestradiol-17β appears to be an attempt to bring those measures within the qualified exemption provided of Article 5.7 of the *SPS Agreement*. According to New Zealand, as seen in *Japan – Agricultural Products II*[133], the European Communities must demonstrate that: (a) its measure was imposed in a situation where 'relevant scientific evidence is insufficient'; and that (b) its measure was adopted "on the basis of available pertinent information, including that from relevant international organisations as well as from sanitary or phytosanitary measures applied by other Members."[134]

5.83   New Zealand claims that pursuant to the second sentence of Article 5.7, the European Communities may not maintain its measure unless it also: (a) 'seek[s] to obtain the additional information necessary for a more objective assessment of risk'; and (b) 'review[s] the measure accordingly within a reasonable period of time'. New Zealand posits further that the Appellate Body added that "[w]herever *one* of these four requirements is not met, the measure at issue is inconsistent with Article 5.7."[135] New Zealand argues that the European Communities states that its provisional ban on five of the six hormones was adopted "on the basis of the available but still incomplete data".[136] However, according to New Zealand, the European Communities is not required under Article 5.7 to show that the relevant scientific evidence was 'incomplete', but rather that it was 'insufficient'. New Zealand quotes the Appellate Body in the *Japan – Apples* case, which analysed the meaning of this expression that:[137]

> " '[R]elevant scientific evidence' will be 'insufficient' within the meaning of Article 5.7 if the body of available scientific evidence

---

[131]   Third party submission of New Zealand, para. 2.26.

[132]   The Panel in *Japan – Measures Affecting the Importation of Apples* (*Japan – Apples*), WT/DS245/R, 15 July 2003, discussed at para. 8.212 the burden of proof under Article 5.7.

[133]   Appellate Body Report on *Japan – Measures Affecting Agricultural Products (Japan – Agricultural Products II)*, WT/DS76/AB/R, 22 February 1999, para. 89.

[134]   Third party submission of New Zealand, paras. 2.28 and 2.29.

[135]   Appellate Body Report on *Japan – Agricultural Products II*, para. 89. Emphasis original.

[136]   First written submission of the European Communities, para. 145.

[137]   Third party submission of New Zealand, paras. 2.30-2.32.

does not allow, in quantitative or qualitative terms, the performance of an adequate assessment of risks as required under Article 5.1 and as defined in Annex A to the *SPS Agreement*."[138]

5.84   New Zealand is of the opinion that the European Communities in its first
written submission does not establish a prima facie case that relevant scientific
evidence does not allow an adequate risk assessment to be carried out. New Zealand argues that the European Communities fails in its first written submission to
explain how the current state of scientific knowledge has prevented it from conducting an adequate risk assessment with respect to the five hormones. According to New Zealand, this is even more difficult to understand when the same
measure, an import ban, which the European Communities previously maintained was based on sufficient scientific evidence to be definitive, is now held
out as a merely 'provisional' measure.[139]

5.85   New Zealand submits that on the other hand, the respondent in its first
written submissions shows that a considerable body of relevant scientific evidence exists as to the use of hormones for growth promotion purposes.[140] New
Zealand argues that the United States points out that the hormones at issue have
been "intensively studied over the last twenty-five years"[141] and that the five
particular hormones subject to the provisional ban have been "studied in greater
detail in the intervening period (since the original *Hormones* case)".[142] According to New Zealand, the inference to be taken is that the relevant scientific evidence is both quantitatively and qualitatively sufficient to have enabled the
European Communities to conduct an adequate risk assessment, and avoid the
need for recourse to provisional measures.[143]

5.86   New Zealand further opines that even if the Panel were to accept that
there was insufficient scientific evidence for the European Communities to conduct an adequate risk assessment, the European Communities must also show
that its new measure was adopted 'on the basis of available pertinent information'. New Zealand stresses that in order to satisfy the burden of proof, the European Communities must present the 'available pertinent information' it evaluated
and the factors that led it to conclude that a provisional import ban on the five
hormones could reasonably be based on this information. New Zealand states
that the European Communities failed in its first written submission to establish
any connection between its provisional import ban and: (a) the available pertinent information; (b) information from relevant international organisations; and

---

[138]   Appellate Body Report on *Japan – Apples*, para. 179.
[139]   Third party submission of New Zealand, para. 2.34.
[140]   See US's first written submission, paras. 55-91.
[141]   US's first written submission, para. 122.
[142]   US's first written submission, para. 123.
[143]   Third party submission of New Zealand, para. 2.35.

(c) information from sanitary or phytosanitary measures applied by other Members.[144]

5.87   According to New Zealand, by contrast, the United States claims that a large body of 'available pertinent information'[145] indicates that proper use of the hormones in question poses no risk to consumers.[146]

5.88   New Zealand submits that under the third prong of Article 5.7, in a situation where the relevant scientific evidence is insufficient to conduct an adequate risk assessment, the European Communities is required to 'seek to obtain the additional information necessary for a more objective assessment of risk'. New Zealand contends that the European Communities implies that this requirement is reflected in Directive 2003/74/EC, which obliges the Commission "to seek more complete scientific information from any source which could shed light and clarify gaps in the present state of knowledge on [the hormones]."[147] New Zealand however submits that the European Communities offers no evidence in its first written submission to explain how the Commission is fulfilling this obligation.[148]

5.89   New Zealand further opines that the final element of Article 5.7 requires the European Communities to 'review' its provisional measures 'within a reasonable period of time'. New Zealand notes that while a competent WTO body has yet to analyse what constitutes a 'reasonable period of time,' Directive 2003/74/EC has been in force for nearly two years, but the European Communities makes no suggestion in its first written submission that a review of the provisional import ban is contemplated at all, let alone within a 'reasonable period of time'. New Zealand submits that the European Communities has failed to discharge its burden of proof with respect to the four elements of Article 5.7 in its first written submission.[149]

7.   Article 5.1 of the SPS Agreement

5.90   New Zealand alleges that the European Communities has not demonstrated in its first written submission that its new measures meet the requirements of Article 5.1 *SPS Agreement*. New Zealand contends that the Appellate Body in *EC – Hormones* established that the obligation in Article 5.1 contains two elements: (a) an assessment of risks; and (b) that Members ensure that their SPS

---

[144]   Third party submission of New Zealand, para. 2.36.
[145]   See US's first written submission at paras. 127-128.
[146]   Third party submission of New Zealand, para. 2.37.
[147]   EC's first written submission, para. 145.
[148]   Third party submission of New Zealand, para. 2.38.
[149]   Third party submission of New Zealand, paras. 2.38 and 2.39.

measures are "based on" such an assessment. New Zealand argues that concerning the first element of Article 5.1, paragraph 4 of Annex A of the *SPS Agreement* sets out the definition of a "risk assessment". New Zealand quotes the Appellate Body[150] that recalled Article 5.2 of the *SPS Agreement*, which provides an indicative list of factors that must be taken into account in a risk assessment.[151]

5.91   New Zealand further argues that the panel in the *Japan – Apples* case summarized its consideration of the elements of Article 5.1 by recalling that a risk assessment would also involve an evaluation of whether the risk assessment was 'as appropriate to the circumstances', and whether it took into account 'risk assessment techniques developed by the relevant international organizations'.[152] New Zealand posits that the panel in that case added that these two factors would "pervade the entire assessment of the risk".[153]

5.92   New Zealand stresses that while the European Communities claims to have conducted "a comprehensive risk assessment" since the Appellate Body decision in 1998[154], it devotes only three paragraphs of its first written submission to attempting to establish what constitutes a valid risk assessment for the purposes of Article 5.1. New Zealand submits that the European Communities notes that it has initiated 17 scientific studies and research projects, but enters into no discussion of the substance, conduct or conclusions of these studies.[155] According to New Zealand, the European Communities observes that it addressed specific requests for scientific data to several countries and published an open call for relevant and recent scientific data and information from any interested party, but makes no comment on the information received.[156]

5.93   New Zealand further opines that in its first written submission, the European Communities simply refers to the SCVPH Opinions and presents a three-paragraph excerpt from Directive 2003/74/EC[157] which provide, on the face of it, a rather limited and constrained justification for the European Communities' import ban. Further, New Zealand posits that the European Communities articulates no clear link between "excess intake of hormone residues" (which is not defined

---

[150]   Appellate Body Report on *EC – Hormones*, para. 187.
[151]   Third party submission of New Zealand, paras. 2.42-2.44.
[152]   Panel Report on *Japan – Apples*, para. 8.236.
[153]   Panel Report on *Japan – Apples*, para. 8.237.
[154]   EC's first written submission, para. 142.
[155]   *Ibid.*
[156]   Third party submission of New Zealand, para. 2.48.
[157]   EC's first written submission, para. 144.

in relation to use as a growth-promoting hormone) and "a risk" that has been identified.[158]

5.94   In New Zealand's view, the European Communities' recital and its bare conclusion fall well short of demonstrating that the European Communities has met the threshold required under the *SPS Agreement* for the existence of a valid risk assessment. New Zealand notes that in particular, the European Communities fails in its first written submission to adduce sufficient evidence that its risk assessment: (a) adequately identifies any adverse effects on human health arising from the presence of the hormones in question when used as growth promoters in meat;[159] (b) evaluates the potential or possibility of occurrence of such adverse effects;[160] (c) is 'as appropriate to the circumstances';[161] (d) takes into account risk assessment techniques developed by the relevant international organisations;[162] and (e) takes into account the available scientific evidence as matters specified in Article 5.2 of the *SPS Agreement*.[163]

5.95   New Zealand argues that none of these criteria is optional in the performance of a risk assessment, and therefore the European Communities is required to demonstrate that all of them have been satisfied in the development of its opinions. New Zealand submits that the European Communities has failed to adduce sufficient evidence to discharge this burden.[164]

5.96   New Zealand contends that in contrast, the United States outlines some of the scientific evidence that exists on the use of growth-promoting hormones,[165] and evokes long-standing practice on the proper assessment of risks related to veterinary drug residues.[166] According to New Zealand, this casts doubt on both the process and the substance of the European Communities' risk assessment.[167]

5.97   New Zealand states that in the event that the Panel decides that the European Communities' opinions constitute a valid risk assessment for the purposes of Article 5.1, the European Communities is also required to demonstrate that the measures in question are 'based on' a risk assessment. According to New

---

[158]   Third party submission of New Zealand, para. 2.49.
[159]   *SPS Agreement*, Annex A, para. 4. Extrapolated from the Panel Report in *EC – Hormones*, para. 8.101, as considered in the Appellate Body Report at paras. 183-184.
[160]   *SPS Agreement*, Annex A, para. 4. Extrapolated from the Panel Report in *EC – Hormones*, para. 8.101, as considered and modified in the Appellate Body Report at paras. 183-184.
[161]   *SPS Agreement*, Article 5.1.
[162]   *Ibid.*
[163]   Third party submission of New Zealand, para. 2.51.
[164]   Third party submission of New Zealand, para. 2.52.
[165]   See, for example, US's first written submission, paras. 55–91.
[166]   US's first written submission, para. 136.
[167]   Third party submission of New Zealand, para. 2.53.

Zealand, the Appellate Body analysed this relationship in *EC – Hormones*,[168] and states that the term 'based on' required a certain objective relationship between the risk assessment and the measure in question.[169]

5.98   New Zealand argues that the European Communities does not attempt to explain in what way or to what extent its new measures are considered to be 'in accordance' with the scientific conclusions of the SCVPH. New Zealand further stipulates that the European Communities offers no basis at all for concluding that its risk assessment 'reasonably supports' its new measures. New Zealand argues that in this case, the European Communities bears the burden of establishing that its risk assessment 'sufficiently warrants' the new measures it adopted. In New Zealand's view it was not open to the European Communities to leave the existence of a 'rational relationship' to be inferred from a brief summary of the conclusions of the European Communities' opinions.[170]

H.   Norway

1.   Opening Panel meetings for observation by the public

5.99   Norway considers that Article 12.1 of the DSU gives the Panel the discretion to follow other working procedures than the ones provided in Appendix 3 after consulting the parties. It sees no legal constraints in granting the request to the parties to open the hearings to the public. Norway also agrees to have the third party session of the hearing open to the public.[171]

2.   Whether the DSB authorization remains in effect

5.100   Norway considers that the right to apply the suspension of concessions pursuant to a DBS authorization is temporary and conditional. According to Norway, the application of the right rests on two basic conditions. First; that there be an authorization pursuant to Article 22.6 DSU and that the conditions set out in Article 22.6 DSU and 22.7 DSU, are respected and secondly, that the temporal condition of Article 22.8 is met.[172]

5.101   Norway opines that the temporal condition in Article 22.8 has three alternative elements: (a) the measure found to be inconsistent with a covered agreement has been removed; or (b) the Member that must implement recommenda-

---

[168]   Appellate Body Report on *EC – Hormones*, para. 193.
[169]   Third party submission of New Zealand, para. 2.55.
[170]   Third party submission of New Zealand, para. 2.58.
[171]   Replies by Norway to Panel questions concerning open hearings, questions 1 and 2.
[172]   Replies by Norway to questions from the European Communities, questions 3, 4 and 5, para. 2.

tions or rulings provides a solution to the nullification or impairment of benefits; or (c) a mutually satisfactory solution is reached.[173]

5.102 Norway contends that the common concept in all three elements is that continued suspension is related to continued non-compliance or lack of any other mutually satisfactory solution to the inconsistency. According to Norway therefore, the temporal condition is intrinsically linked to the substance of compliance. Norway posits that out of the three elements, the third one, "a mutually satisfactory solution", can in principle be achieved at any point in time and once achieved, would resolve the matter and no suspension may continue. Norway adds that this is even so if the original measure found to be inconsistent with a covered agreement is still in place.[174]

5.103 Norway considers that the first two elements are in reference to compliance, which can be achieved through the removal of the original measure or through another solution to the nullification or impairment of benefits, and the second element is the normal situation where one measure is replaced by another measure.[175]

5.104 Norway submits that once compliance is achieved, be it through a simple revocation of the inconsistent measure or its replacement with another measure that ensures compliance, the right to suspend obligations automatically lapses. Norway is of the view that similarly, once compliance has been established by a panel pursuant to Article 21.5 of the DSU, the previous authorization lapses *ipso facto* once the report is adopted, without there being a need for the DSB to revoke it formally as the temporal condition no longer exists.[176]

5.105 Norway contends that once a measure taken to comply is notified by the original respondent, the question arises whether this amounts to full compliance or not. Norway submits that if the original complainant considers that the measure taken to comply falls short of what is required by the adopted rulings and recommendations, then the obligation to refer a "compliance dispute" to a panel according to Article 21.5 is incumbent upon them.[177]

---

[173] Replies by Norway to questions from the European Communities, questions 3, 4 and 5, para. 3.
[174] Replies by Norway to questions from the European Communities, questions 3, 4 and 5, paras. 4 and 5.
[175] Replies by Norway to questions from the European Communities, questions 3, 4 and 5, para. 6.
[176] Replies by Norway to questions from the European Communities, questions 3, 4 and 5, para. 7.
[177] Replies by Norway to Panel questions, question 5 para. 10.

3.   Article 21.5 of the DSU

5.106 Norway argues that the situation addressed by Article 21.5 DSU occurs when the original respondent claims to have complied with the recommendation and ruling of the DSB, but the original complainant disagrees. According to Norway, Article 21.5 is competent both where the parties disagree as to the very existence of measures taken to comply, and where they disagree as to whether the measures taken to comply actually achieve compliance. Norway is of the view that the case at hand is typical in this respect, and falls squarely within the ambit of Article 21.5. Norway notes that neither Article 22.8 nor Article 21.5 sets forth time lines in this respect.[178]

5.107 According to Norway, the original complainant must be accorded a certain amount of time to assess the measure before going to a compliance panel. Norway posits that the length of time needed will vary from case to case, and it is hard to set a fixed dead-line. In Norway's view, the DSU does not include such a fixed dead-line, however, this does not mean that the original complainant can refuse to take action according to Article 21.5 within a reasonable time. Norway thus contends that in order to avoid such unreasonable delay, Article 21.5 allows the original respondent to have recourse to a compliance panel.[179]

5.108 Norway contends that the obligation to refer a "compliance dispute" to a panel according to Article 21.5 rests on both parties in the dispute. According to Norway, Article 21.5 does not specify that it must be the original complainant to refer the matter to a "compliance panel". Norway submits that Article 21.5 is written in the passive form, concentrating on the result, specifically to place this obligation on all parties to the original dispute.[180]

5.109 Norway submits that the standard practice has been that the original complainant refers the matter to the panel. It argues that the one exception so far has been the referral to a compliance panel by the European Communities in *EC – Bananas III (Article 21.5 – EC)*.[181] According to Norway, the fact that the report remains unadopted and that the panel in that case refused to make any recommendations or rulings in the case, does not in itself prove that an original respondent may not invoke Article 21.5.[182] Rather, the position of the Panel in that

---

[178] Replies by Norway to questions from the European Communities, questions 3, 4 and 5, para. 8.
[179] Replies by Norway to Panel questions, question 5, paras. 11 and 12.
[180] Joint reply by Norway to question 2 from the Panel and question 6 from the European Communities, para. 13.
[181] *European Communities – Regime for the Importation, Sale and Distribution of Bananas – Recourse to Article 21.5 by the European Communities*, Report by the Panel (WT/DS27/RW/EEC), 12 April 1999 – report never adopted.
[182] Joint reply by Norway to question 2 from the Panel and question 6 from the European Communities, para. 14.

case must be seen in the light of the fact that Ecuador also requested a separate compliance panel[183], and that the United States had submitted a request for retaliation that led to arbitration.[184] Norway submits that the panel in that particular case could thus justify not making any recommendations or rulings by pointing to these other proceedings.[185]

5.110 In Norway's view, a panel launched by the respondent cannot just make a declaratory judgment based on the presentation of the original respondent, but must make an objective assessment of the matter before it. The scope of the "terms of reference" would be to examine whether the measures taken to comply imply that there is now compliance with the rulings and recommendations of the original panel, *i.e.*, that the original violation has been removed. Only the violations specifically addressed in the original report will be addressed by the compliance panel, not any other violations that the new measure may cause.[186]

5.111 Norway argues that where the original complainants refuse to participate, then any claim that the new measure is inconsistent with other provisions of the covered agreements will not be heard (will be outside of the "terms of the reference" for the compliance panel), and the original complainants risk a finding of compliance that does not take into account all the arguments that they would otherwise have presented. By not launching the Article 21.5 panel in a timely manner, the original complainants thus lose certain rights to present new claims that they would have had, had they themselves launched the panel request first. Such claims will thus have to await another panel. As such, the incentive structure that is created by allowing the original respondent to launch an Article 21.5 panel proceeding works to provide the original complainants with the incentive to go ahead themselves and launch the Article 21.5 panel first.[187]

5.112 In case a compliance panel is requested by the original respondent, the reference in Article 6.2 to "provide a brief summary of the legal basis of the complaint sufficient to present the problem clearly" can be fulfilled by referring to the original panel report, together with the identification of the specific measure taken to comply and how it ensures compliance.[188] Where the original re-

---

[183] *European Communities – Regime for the Importation, Sale and Distribution of Bananas – Recourse to Article 21.5 by the Ecuador*, Report by the Panel (WT/DS27/RW/ECU), 12 April 1999.

[184] *European Communities – Regime for the Importation, Sale and Distribution of Bananas – Recourse to Arbitration by the European Communities under Article 22.6 of the DSU*, (WT/DS27/ARB), Report of the arbitrators dated 9 April 1999.

[185] See paras. 4.15 and 4.16 of the Panel Report in WT/DS27/RW/EEC.

[186] Joint reply by Norway to question 2 from the Panel and question 6 from the European Communities, paras. 16 and 18.

[187] Joint reply by Norway to question 2 from the Panel and question 6 from the European Communities, para. 16.

[188] Joint reply by Norway to question 2 from the Panel and question 6 from the European Communities, para. 18.

spondent has to request an Article 21.5 panel because the original complainants refused to do so, the original respondent may be considered as "complainant" for the purpose of Article 6.1 and "applicant" for the purpose of Article 6.2. The question who is "complainant" and who is "respondent" does not matter for the rest of the proceedings.[189]

I.   Separate Customs Territory of Taiwan, Penghu, Kinmen and Matsu

1.   Introduction

5.113 The Separate Customs Territory of Taiwan, Penghu, Kinmen and Matsu (Chinese Taipei) submits that it presents its views in this dispute because of the important systemic issues involved, in particular, the DSU provisions that are under negotiations in the Special Session of the Dispute Settlement Body. In its view, the resolution of certain issues in this case could significantly impact these negotiations.[190]

2.   Opening Panel meetings for public observation

5.114 Chinese Taipei argues that in accordance with the procedures and customary practices developed over more than half a century under GATT, which are reflected in Articles 14.1, 18.2 and Appendix 3 of the DSU, panel proceedings are to be kept confidential. It argues that only Members by consensus can change the rules of confidentiality. According to Chinese Taipei, a panel, even with the consent of the parties does not have the legal authority to open the proceedings to the public.[191]

5.115 Chinese Taipei refers to Article VII of the Rules of Conduct which requires that each covered person shall at all times maintain the confidentiality of the dispute settlement deliberations and proceedings. According to it, the only exception to this confidentiality obligation is Article 18.2 of the DSU which states that nothing in the DSU shall preclude a party to a dispute from disclosing statements of its own positions to the public. Chinese Taipei is therefore of the

---

[189] Joint reply by Norway to question 2 from the Panel and question 6 from the European Communities, paras. 17 and 19.
[190] Third party submission of Chinese Taipei, para. 1.
[191] Replies by Chinese Taipei to Panel questions concerning open hearings, question 1, paras. 1 and 2.

opinion that this exception does not extend to the possibility of allowing parties to decide whether to open panel meetings to the public.[192]

5.116 According to Chinese Taipei, "panel deliberations" implies more than one form of deliberation, thus includes not only internal consideration among panelists, but also the entire process of the panel's consideration of the dispute.[193]

5.117 Chinese Taipei argues that the flexibility from Article 12.1 of the DSU to change Working Procedures in Appendix 3 cannot be extended to cover provisions in the Working Procedures that directly elaborate on the obligations of the DSU. It further argues that if the drafters had contemplated that the confidentiality requirement can be changed, they would have said so, just like in Article 18.2 of the DSU. In the absence of such language, only an amendment to the DSU by the Members through negotiations can change the requirement of confidential deliberations.[194]

5.118 Chinese Taipei is of the opinion that the third party sessions be in closed session.[195]

3. Whether the DSB authorization remains in effect

5.119 Chinese Taipei contends that the new implementing measure is required to be confirmed by a multilateral determination that the measure is compliant with the DSB's recommendations and rulings. According to it, a unilateral claim of compliance together with the principle of good faith does not overturn the DSB authorization of suspension of concessions, and that suspension of concessions can continue until the conditions in Article 22.8 have been met.[196]

5.120 According to Chinese Taipei, the suspension of concessions can only be lifted after a multilateral determination of compliance, which involves an examination of the implementing measure against the recommendations and rulings of the DSB, or by mutual agreement of the parties. In its view, until then, the DSB authorization remains valid and the suspension of concessions may continue. Chinese Taipei further states that if none of the parties brings the implementing measure to the panel, whether through Article 21.5 or Article 22.8, the suspension of concessions may continue. It contends that without the initiation of a

---

[192] Replies by Chinese Taipei to Panel questions concerning open hearings, question 1, paras. 4 and 5.
[193] Replies by Chinese Taipei to Panel questions concerning open hearings, question 1, para. 3.
[194] Replies by Chinese Taipei to Panel questions concerning open hearings, question 1, paras. 6 and 7.
[195] Replies by Chinese Taipei to Panel questions concerning open hearings, question 2, para. 12.
[196] Replies by Chinese Taipei to questions from the European Communities, question 1.

dispute that results in the examination of the implementing measure, the *status quo* would be considered as maintaining the existing balance of rights and obligations among WTO Members.[197]

5.121 Chinese Taipei does not consider that there is a need to justify the continuing suspension of concessions after the implementing Member's claim that it has complied with the DSB's recommendations and rulings.[198]

5.122 Chinese Taipei rejects the view that the lack of action for any period of time on the part of the United States and Canada constitutes an expression of the US and Canada's determination. According to Chinese Taipei, the existence of the determination by the United States and Canada cannot depend on such an indeterminate criteria as the length of time it takes for the United States and Canada to take action under Article 21.5 of the DSU. Therefore, in its view, Article 22.8 of the DSU allows the United States and Canada to continue its suspension of concessions until one of the three conditions therein have been met.[199]

4. *Article 21.5 of the DSU*

5.123 Chinese Taipei considers that one of the ways to arrive at a multilateral determination in the current situation is through Article 21.5 of the DSU. With respect to the European Communities' argument that in the absence of the initiation by the United States of an Article 21.5 compliance panel, the European Communities' implementing measure must be presumed to be consistent with WTO rules and the continuation of the suspension of concessions by the United States would amount to a unilateral determination of a violation of WTO rules[200], it argues that Article 23.2(a) is valid only if two requirements are present in the text of Article 21.5, namely, (a) a deadline by which a 21.5 panel must be initiated, and (b) an obligation only on the original complaining party to initiate the proceeding.[201]

5.124 Chinese Taipei considers that neither one of these requirements currently exists in the text, nor is it reasonable to interpret their existence. It submits that it is up to the Member involved to choose whether and when to initiate the Article 21.5 proceeding. It opines that while it recognizes that the party suffering the suspension of concessions has an interest to lift such suspension as early as possible, that interest has to be balanced with the fact that the same party had origi-

---

[197] Replies by Chinese Taipei to questions from the European Communities, question 4.
[198] Replies by Chinese Taipei to questions from the European Communities, question 5.
[199] Replies by Chinese Taipei to Panel questions, question 1.
[200] EC's first written submission para. 61.
[201] Oral statement of Chinese Taipei, para. 2.

nally been determined, through a lengthy WTO process, to be in violation of its obligations, and had a chance to implement, but failed to do so, within a reasonable period of time. Further, it argues that consistent with the text of Article 21.5, if the original respondent considers the conditions for the suspension of concessions to be no longer valid, the respondent may initiate the Article 21.5 proceeding at any time.[202]

5.125 Chinese Taipei stresses that as the DSU currently stands, there is no deadline and no designated party to initiate the Article 21.5 proceeding. Chinese Taipei agrees with the United States that just because the United States has not initiated the Article 21.5 proceeding does not mean that the European Communities automatically enjoys the presumption of compliance. According to Chinese Taipei, at this stage, only a multilateral procedure can reach that conclusion, and one of the ways the European Communities can obtain such a multilateral determination is through its initiation of an Article 21.5 panel.

5.126 Chinese Taipei to remind the Panel that the procedural issues involved in this case are currently under discussion in the negotiations on the improvement and clarification of the DSU. It argues that several competing proposals are on the table, including one from the European Communities. Chinese Taipei notes that it is a view widely shared by Members that the DSU procedures in this so-called "post-retaliation stage" are imperfect. In its view, it is not the task of the Panel, or indeed any Member, through litigation, to make up for such imperfection. Therefore, Chinese Taipei urges the Panel to avoid interpreting the current provisions in a way that would impose rules or requirements that are not written in the text.[203]

5.   *The relationship between DSU Article 22.8 and Article 23*

5.127 Chinese Taipei argues that Articles 23 and 22.8 apply to different situations and therefore should not be read together, as this would lead to a weakening of the WTO dispute settlement system. It contends that Article 22.8 differs from Article 23 in that it deals with the specific post-retaliation situation, outlining the conditions under which the suspension of the concessions pursuant to authorization from the DSB can be lifted. Chinese Taipei states that the general principle of resolving disputes under the multilateral system in Article 23 has been specifically modified by Article 22.8. Article 22.8 thus has its own inde-

---

[202] Oral statement of Chinese Taipei, para. 3.
[203] Oral statement of Chinese Taipei, para. 4.

pendent set of requirements applicable specifically to the post-retaliation situation, apart from the general principles in Article 23.[204]

5.128 Chinese Taipei opines that the basis upon which European Communities builds its arguments for its interpretation of DSU Articles 23 and 22.8 is the general principle of good faith under which States are normally considered to act in conformity with their obligations.[205] Chinese Taipei agrees that Article 23.2(a) embodies that principle in prohibiting Members from making any unilateral determination to the effect that a violation has occurred.[206]

5.129 Chinese Taipei argues that by its title, Article 23 applies to the normal situations when the Member is responding to a perceived violation, nullification, impairment, or impediment, to which the Member is seeking remedy. It argues that this is the normal situation under which most cases begin and are first brought to the attention of the Dispute Settlement Body.[207]

5.130 According to Chinese Taipei, Article 23.2 prescribes the actions Members may take in the normal situation described in Article 23.1. According to it, specifically, 23.2(a) prevents a Member from acting upon the unilateral perception of violation until it is validated under multilateral procedures. Chinese Taipei considers that this amounts to the presumption that a Member is normally considered to be acting in conformity with its obligations until a multilateral determination under the WTO says otherwise.[208]

5.131 Chinese Taipei posits that Article 22.8 on the other hand describes situations that depart from the norm. It submits that the general principle in Article 23 relating to normal situations therefore has limited application and must be modified by the specific requirements spelt out in Article 22.8. In its view, the situation at hand is one where the redress of violation has already been determined at least once through multilateral procedures and where suspension of concessions has been authorized. Chinese Taipei argues that the requirement is not that the suspension of concessions must be lifted in the absence of an adverse finding, but rather that the suspension shall be applied until the violation has been removed or any of the other two conditions in the provision have been met.[209]

5.132 According to Chinese Taipei, it therefore follows from this difference in situation and requirement that the normal presumption that a Member is considered to be in conformity with its obligations until proven otherwise in a multilat-

---

[204] Third party submission of Chinese Taipei, paras. 2 and 7.
[205] EC's first written submission para. 87.
[206] Third party submission of Chinese Taipei, paras. 2-4.
[207] Third party submission of Chinese Taipei, para. 5.
[208] Third party submission of Chinese Taipei, para. 6.
[209] Third party submission of Chinese Taipei, para. 7.

eral determination does not apply. It contends that since Article 22.8 provides that the suspension of concessions can continue until the removal of the violation, the presumption here is that there is no removal of the violation until a multilateral determination says otherwise.[210]

5.133 Chinese Taipei contends that if the normal presumption were to apply to Article 22.8, despite the existence of a multilateral determination and authorization for retaliation, any offending Member can simply declare itself to have removed the violation. It submits that this would create the incentive for Members to implement partially or not at all, and drag the Member suspending concessions into an endless loop of Article 21.5 litigations.[211]

5.134 Chinese Taipei is of the view that under both normal and Article 22.8 situations, a multilateral determination is the prerequisite to any action that changes the existing balance of rights and obligations. It further notes that normally, a Member cannot seek redress of a violation without a multilateral determination because a balance is presumed to exist. Similarly, Chinese Taipei argues that under the Article 22.8 situation where suspension of concessions is in place, that situation is the presumed balance, and that existing balance cannot be changed without another multilateral determination.[212]

5.135 Chinese Taipei thus argues that the suspension of concessions by the United States does not fall into the normal situation described in Article 23 and until a multilateral determination deems the European Communities' implementing measure to have removed the previously multilaterally determined inconsistency, the continuation of suspension of concessions by the United States does not violate the existing provisions of the DSU.[213]

VI. INTERIM REVIEW

A.   Introduction

6.1   Pursuant to Article 15.3 of the DSU, the findings of the final panel report shall include a discussion of the arguments made by the parties at the interim review stage. This section of the Panel report provides such a discussion. As is clear from Article 15.3, this Section is part of the Panel's findings.

6.2   The European Communities and the United States separately requested an interim review by the Panel of certain aspects of the interim report issued to the

---

[210] Third party submission of Chinese Taipei, para. 8.
[211] Third party submission of Chinese Taipei, para. 9.
[212] Third party submission of Chinese Taipei, para. 10.
[213] Third party submission of Chinese Taipei, para. 11.

Parties on 31 July 2007.[214] The European Communities stated that it stood ready to attend an interim review hearing to discuss the issues raised in its letter, "should the Panel consider it useful". The Panel notes that it is not for it to decide whether holding an interim review hearing would be useful. Article 15.2 of the DSU provides that it is "[a]t the request of a party [that] the panel shall hold a further meeting with the parties on the issues identified in the written comments." The Panel does not understand the EC statement above as a request by the European Communities for the Panel to hold an additional meeting with the parties. Furthermore, the Panel notes that the United States did not request such a meeting. As a result, the Panel did not hold an interim review meeting.

6.3   In accordance with the Panel working procedures and timetable, the parties had, and used, the opportunity to submit further written comments on each other's requests for review of specific aspects of the interim report.[215] These comments are discussed, where relevant, together with the requests to which they relate.

6.4   The Panel issued its final report to the parties on a confidential basis on 21 December 2007.

6.5   The Panel has structured its treatment of the Parties' requests below in the following manner:

(a)   first, it addresses a number of the comments made in relation to the descriptive part of the report (Section IV) that the Panel could not address at an earlier stage of the proceedings;

(b)   second, it discusses the comments of the parties relating to the findings of the Panel and, more particularly:

(i)   the aspects of the report regarding procedural issues (Section VII.A);

(ii)   the comments of the parties regarding the Panels findings of violation of Article 23.2(a) read together with Articles 21.5 and 23.1 of the DSU (Section VII.B); and

(iii)   the comments of the parties regarding the compliance of the EC ban on meat and meat products treated with the six hormones at issue for growth promotion purposes with the *SPS Agreement* in relation to the Panel's findings on the EC claims on Article 23.1, read together with Articles 22.8 and 3.7 of the DSU (Section VII.C).

---

[214]   Letters of the parties dated 28 September 2007.
[215]   Letters of the parties dated 19 October 2007.

6.6   In addition, minor editing changes where made, which the Panel did not deem necessary to list in this section.

B.   Parties' Comments on the Descriptive Part

6.7   The Panel considered and incorporated in its revised descriptive part the majority of the parties' comments. In two instances, however, the Panel partly rejected the modifications requested by the European Communities and deems it appropriate to provide its reasons in this section.

6.8   The first instance relates to the EC request that the Panel incorporate in the descriptive part the parties' arguments on logistical issues relating to the opening to public observation of the Panel's substantive meetings with the parties and with the experts.

6.9   In its comments on paragraph 4.2 and following of the descriptive part of this report, the European Communities notes that, while the parties' answers of 20 June 2005 to a number of questions of the Panel have been reported in full, there is no reference to the parties' replies of 7 July 2005 to the additional questions of the Panel. This, in the opinion of the European Communities, raises a question of the completeness of the record of the parties' arguments. Inserting the replies of the parties of 7 July 2005 is also important according to the European Communities since the comments of the third parties on logistical matters have been reported in the descriptive part. Thus, the European Communities requested the Panel to reflect the parties' responses to these additional questions in its report.

6.10   The Panel notes that the parties' replies of 7 July 2005 essentially addressed technical questions of a logistical nature. The Panel did not deem it necessary to insert in its report any account of the logistical aspects of the opening of the hearings to public observation. The Panel notes in this respect that it did not include in the descriptive part of the report extracts from the replies of the parties of 20 June 2005 that related to logistical issues. Given that among the third parties, only India and Mexico mentioned, in a general manner, the logistical implications of opening hearings to public observation, the discussion on logistical issues essentially took place between the parties themselves, or between the parties and the Secretariat. The Panel did not address the details of the logistical issues in its decision on opening meetings for public observation. This matter is, in the opinion of the Panel, purely administrative. It is neither procedurally nor factually relevant for the resolution of the dispute before us. The Panel is mindful that such an account might be useful from a practical point of view for future panels. However, it considers that the technical solutions found in this case may not necessarily be extended to other panel procedures, if only because the parties' expectations and constraints, e.g. in terms of confidentiality, may be different in future cases.[216] Whereas the Panel provided a detailed account of the legal issues related to the opening of the Panel's hearings for public observation, for the reasons mentioned above, it decided not to follow the suggestion of the European Communities.

6.11   The Panel nonetheless wishes to confirm that the technical options available were extensively discussed with the parties and that the solutions finally selected, more particularly the broadcast of the hearings into a separate room through closed-circuit television, were adopted in accordance with the positions expressed by the parties.

6.12   The second instance where a request for modification of the descriptive part was at least partly rejected by the Panel relates to paragraph 4.234. In its second written submission to the Panel, the European Communities stated that, "[u]nder Article 5.1 of the *SPS Agreement*, a *convincing* link is required between the evidence and the measure. Under Article 5.7 a *mere* doubt must be sufficient."[217] In its comments on the descriptive part of the report and in its comments of 19 October 2007[218] in response to a request by the United States for review of a precise aspect of the interim report[219], the European Communities requested us to replace the term "convincing link" with "rational relationship", and to replace "mere doubt" with "reasonable doubt". We recall that in its reply to question 9 of the Panel, after the second substantive meeting, the European Communities had clarified that what it meant by "mere doubt" was "doubt that has been scientifically established". In light of that request, we replaced "mere" with "scientifically established". The Panel also notes that the EC reply to question 68 of the questions of the Panel after the first substantive meeting qualified the relationship addressed by Article 5.1 of the *SPS Agreement* as an "objective or rational relationship". As a result, the Panel replaced the term "convincing link" with "objective or rational relationship."

---

[216]   In the present dispute, after comparing different alternatives, the Secretariat was able to arrange open hearings through closed-circuit broadcast from one room to another utilizing the existing facilities of the Secretariat. The cost of open hearings was covered by the regular budget under the Secretariat arrangement. There may be different cost implications for future disputes in different circumstances but that consideration would fall outside of the remit of this Panel.

[217]   See EC's second written submission, para. 181, and second executive summary, para. 29 (emphasis added).

[218]   EC's comments of 19 October 2007, para. 24.

[219]   US's written request of 28 September 2007, p. 9.

C. Parties' Comments Regarding the Findings of the Panel

1. Preliminary remarks

6.13   As a preliminary remark, the Panel notes that the European Communities mentions in the introduction to its written request for the Panel to review precise aspects of the interim report that it:

> "[W]ill try to provide *some examples* of the numerous and serious errors in the reasoning of the Panel on the scientific issues underpinning this dispute. *However, it is not possible in the time available to provide a detailed and complete list of all omissions and errors of the two interim reports* as it would in reality require rewriting substantial parts of the Panel's report in order to rectify its analysis and reasoning ... Therefore, the European Communities *reserves the right to make all its comments at the appeal stage*, if the Panel's findings on the issue were to be maintained."[220] (emphasis added)

6.14   This statement suggests that the European Communities did not identify all the precise aspects of the interim report with which it disagrees due to lack of time and because this would require rewriting substantial parts of the Panel report. It would, however, be able to make all its comments at the appeal stage. The Panel wishes first to make it clear that parties were free to request an extension if they needed more time to review the interim report and identify precise aspects that should be addressed by the Panel. The Panel notes in this respect that it is at the request of the European Communities that parties were granted several additional weeks to review the interim report. The Panel also notes that the European Communities gave as a justification for its request the expected length and complexity of the report. The Panel therefore regrets that the European Communities is now alleging lack of time as a justification for providing only "some examples" of errors in the reasoning of the Panel on the scientific issues underpinning this dispute.

6.15   In contrast, the European Communities mentions that it may make "all its comments" at the appeal stage. The Panel is surprised by the apparent choice of the European Communities to "make all its comments" before the Appellate Body rather than before the Panel, at the procedural stage expressly designed for the purpose of considering any and all comments on the interim report. This is because the decision of the European Communities to provide only "some examples" of errors of the Panel suggests that it has already decided to appeal the Panel report unless the Panel makes changes which the European Communities will not specify. It is also not clear whether the "examples" given by the Euro-

---

[220]   EC's written request of 28 September 2007, para. 5.

pean Communities exhaust all its factual comments or whether it intends to make further comments on factual issues before the Appellate Body. Having regard to Article 17.6 of the DSU, we consider this to be equivalent to depriving the interim review stage of its purpose.

6.16   The Panel therefore regrets that the European Communities did not request an extension so as to ensure that all the comments it deemed necessary on precise aspects of the interim report be made at the procedural stage of the dispute settlement process intended for that very purpose.

6.17   The Panel also notes that some of the EC comments are general statements on whole sections of the report, not a written request for the Panel to review *precise aspects* of the interim report. We recall that the panel in *Australia – Salmon*[221] stated as follows:

> "According to Canada, it is not open to the Panel to consider anything other than comments dealing with 'precise aspects' of the interim report. We agree with Canada and have therefore only reviewed our interim report in light of the comments made by the parties which relate to 'precise aspects' of the interim report."

6.18   We agree with the reasoning of the above-mentioned panel and therefore consider that the general comments by the European Communities did not require a specific reply from the Panel. We limited our replies to the portions of the report on which specific comments, in the form of precise requests for reconsideration on specific paragraphs, had been made by the European Communities. We addressed the EC general comments as part of our review of specific paragraphs.

2.   *Parties' requests for review related to aspects of the report on procedural issues*

(a)   Comments by the European Communities

6.19   The European Communities considers the Panel's reference to Article 17.10 of the DSU in paragraph 7.50 of the interim report unnecessary and potentially detrimental as implicitly suggesting that the Appellate Body could be legally barred by Article 17.10 of the DSU from opening its own hearings to public observation. The European Communities requests that we remove that paragraph from our findings. We note that a similar request was made by the United States. Since this reference was only an additional argument, we accepted

---

[221]   Panel Report on *Australia – Salmon*, para. 7.3.

the parties' requests and removed our discussion of the term "proceedings" in Article 17.10 of the DSU.

6.20   The European Communities considers that the description of IARC contained in paragraph 7.78 footnote 378 is incomplete. It refers to Dr. Cogliano's statement in Annex G, paragraph 541. In paragraph 541, Dr. Cogliano essentially says that IARC monographs simply indicate which substances are carcinogenic or are probably not carcinogenic to humans. Monographs identify occurrence (i.e. exposure to a chemical through some particular pathway), but not the specific level of exposure for a particular population. Dr. Cogliano also says in paragraph 541 that different decision-making authorities will decide whether the evidence contained in IARC monographs sufficiently supports an SPS decision or whether they need to conduct further analysis. Thus it seems that IARC monographs provide information and serve in risk assessment. This said, as also pointed out by the United States in its comments on comments of 19 October 2007[222], the text in the footnote is a verbatim quote from the IARC website, describing what IARC does. Thus the Panel did not deem it necessary to augment the footnote.

6.21   The European Communities argues that the second sentence of paragraph 7.85 does not reflect reality, since the European Communities did not agree with the final decision on Working Procedures for Consultation with Scientific and/or Technical Experts adopted by the Panel. The Panel notes that, in a letter of 3 November 2005, the European Communities commented on the draft expert working procedures. One of the comments was that the experts should act as a single expert review group in order to provide a consistent advice on the issues concerned. The European Communities also suggested that the experts should be independent from the industry or regulatory bodies which had a vested interest in the issue on which they would be consulted. The Panel rejected the EC request that experts should act as a single review group in its letter sent to the parties on 25 November 2005, together with its finalized Working Procedures for Consultation with Scientific and/or Technical Experts. We therefore modified paragraph 7.85 to reflect the absence of full agreement of the European Communities on the Panel's Working Procedures for Consultation with Scientific and/or Technical Experts.

6.22   The European Communities further requests us to redraft the fourth sentence of paragraph 7.85 to reflect better its concerns that two of the experts selected by the Panel participated in the preparation and drafting of the JECFA risk assessment of the hormonal substances at issue in this case, with which the EC risk assessment disagrees. The Panel sees no problem in clarifying the nature of the work of these two experts with JECFA It remains however puzzled by the

---

[222]   Para. 3.

EC suggestions that a scientist who worked with JECFA could be deemed to be biased in assessing the scientific evidence on which EC Directive 2003/74/EC relies and could be assumed to defend JECFA's work. First, scientists would readily admit that science is constantly evolving and the fact that new studies are peer reviewed is evidence that assessing new ideas and findings is part of scientific work. Assuming that scientists may lack objectivity because they participated in the preparation and drafting of JECFA's risk assessments on the hormones at issue would call into question the whole principle of peer review. The Panel also notes that JECFA is the body that provides the independent scientific advice on which the work of Codex is based and Codex is expressly recognized by the *SPS Agreement* as having responsibilities for the establishment of "international standards, guidelines and recommendations". The Panel also recalls the role given to international standards, guidelines and recommendations by Article 3.1 and 3.2 of the *SPS Agreement*. It is therefore consistent with this role for the Panel to rely on experts who contributed in the preparation and drafting of JECFA's risk assessments of the substances at issue.

6.23   The Panel does not agree either with the EC arguments according to which the two experts at issue should not be described as "internationally recognized specialists". The Panel recalls that they have been selected by the FAO and WHO as part of the JECFA selection process. The selection procedure has been described in JECFA's reply to question 14 to JECFA.[223] The Panel fails to understand why the JECFA selection would not be evidence of the international reputation of the scientists at issue.[224] The EC concerns about JECFA's work and the selection of experts to participate in that work are in contradiction with the role attributed by the *SPS Agreement* to Codex and to international standards, guidelines and recommendations. The Panel was fully aware of the area of expertise of the two scientists at issue, and believed that they would be more at liberty to comment on the content of JECFA's work than officials of the JECFA Secretariat. It also specified the reasons why those experts were selected in spite of not having carried out experiments with the substances at issue and does not see any need for further substantial elaboration. The Panel notes that the United States, in its comments of 19 October 2007, considered that any new objection on the experts by the European Communities would be untimely. The Panel has nevertheless deemed it necessary to make some clarifications, in response to the EC request, to paragraph 7.85.

6.24   The European Communities requests that we modify the first sentence of paragraph 7.87 to better reflect the content of its letter of 28 March 2006. We consider that the letter largely reiterated points which the Panel already ad-

---

[223]   Annex E-2, pp. 115-116.
[224]   See also Dr. Boobis, Annex G, para. 511; Dr. Tritscher, Annex G, para. 515; Dr. Wennberg, Annex G, para. 517.

dressed in paragraph 7.85 i.e. the involvement of experts in the preparation and drafting of JECFA's risk assessments and their alleged lack of scientific expertise. Besides this, the EC letter of 28 March deals exclusively with conflict of interest, which is the subject addressed by the Panel in paragraph 7.87. While the Panel has modified the paragraph to reflect the fact that the EC letter addressed other issues already discussed in this report, it did not deem it necessary to modify the rest of the paragraph, except to clarify the elements on the basis of which the Panel considered that the experts concerned should be deemed to be the best among the very few individuals available.

6.25   Having reviewed the EC comments on paragraph 7.89 of the interim report, the Panel agrees that this paragraph did not directly relate to the issue of the alleged conflict of interest of two of the experts consulted by the Panel and has deleted it.

6.26   The European Communities argues that the statements in paragraph 7.123 and footnote 396 are not accurate as some of the subsequent evidence did expand and confirm the scientific basis of Directive 2003/74/EC. The European Communities refers to the replies of Dr. Guttenplan and Dr. Sippell. The Panel also notes the US comments of 19 October 2007 on this request for review from the European Communities. In paragraph 7.123 and footnote 396, the Panel states that nothing new was submitted after the adoption of Directive 2003/74/EC that differed *in any fundamental way* from previous evidence. This is not contradicted by the EC comment that subsequent evidence expanded and confirmed the scientific basis of its Directive, including the EC reply to question 5 of the Panel after the second substantive meeting.[225] The statements of Dr. Guttenplan referred to by the European Communities[226] do not support the EC argument. Dr. Sippell mentions in paragraph 611 of Annex G that he changed his opinion on exposure to exogenous oestrogens and precocious puberty because the acceptance of the significance of the ultrasensitive assays within paediatric endocrinology increased tremendously after he published his review article in 1999. However, the ultrasensitive assays he is referring to were not carried out or published after the adoption of Directive 2003/74/EC. In his written replies[227], where he discusses the ultrasensitive assay techniques, Dr. Sippell refers to *Klein et al (1994)* and *Larmore et al (2002)* and other studies dated 1999 or 2001. As a result, in the opinion of the Panel, the statement of Dr. Sippell cited by the European Communities is not about evidence that became available after the adoption of the Directive. Consequently the Panel did not modify paragraph 7.123 and footnote 396.

---

[225]   Annex C, pp. 5-7.
[226]   Annex G, paras. 709 and 713.
[227]   Annex D, para. 319.

6.27   The European Communities also argues with respect to paragraph 7.124 that it had reserved its right to submit the finally published version of the study contained in Exhibit EC-107. According to the European Communities, this study was submitted in time and should have been accepted. The Panel notes that, when it submitted Exhibit EC-107 on 21 December 2005, the European Communities specified that it "reserve[d] its right to submit further evidence, if and to the extent this appears necessary for the purpose of commenting on any further submissions by the other parties as well as on replies of the panel's experts". The Panel does not read this reservation as reserving the EC right to submit the finally published version of the study. Moreover, the Panel recalls that the European Communities stated that it left it to the discretion of the Panel whether to forward the published version to the experts.[228] The Panel, having regard to the comments of the United States of 19 October 2007, considers that it sufficiently explained in its report the reasons why the published version of this study had not been sent to the experts. In particular, it considered that submitting a modified study to experts at a relatively late stage of the expert consultation proceedings could generate confusion.

6.28   The European Communities also considers with respect to paragraph 7.133 that the Panel should accept that the European Communities submit the comments it wished to make in relation to some factual errors made by the United States in its replies to the Panel questions posed after the second substantive meeting. The Panel considers that its decision was clear. If inaccuracies resulting from US factual arguments had been reflected in the interim report, the European Communities could have identified them in its comments or in its comments on comments. There does not seem to be any need for the Panel to reverse its decision of 20 November 2006.

6.29   The European Communities also alleges, with respect to paragraphs 7.135 *et seq.,* that one paragraph was added to the transcript of the experts' hearing annexed to this report compared with the version sent to the parties in January 2007. There are, indeed, more paragraph numbers. However, there is no additional text in Annex G as compared to the version sent to the parties in January 2007. In fact, the difference results from a correction to the paragraph numbers of the transcript. In the version sent to the parties for comments, there was a paragraph between paragraphs 29 and 30 that did not have a number. This paragraph became the new paragraph 30 in the final version of the transcript, and as a consequence, all the other paragraph numbers shifted by one. On the same subject, two more changes were made in paragraph numbers: paragraph 827 of the draft transcript was divided into two paragraphs, following a comment by the United States[229], and became paragraphs 828 and 829 in the final version of the

---

[228]   See EC's letter to the Panel dated 29 May 2006.
[229]   See US letter dated 14 February 2007.

transcript. Finally, another paragraph lacked a number, between paragraphs 926 and 927. This paragraph corresponded to a short statement by Dr. Boisseau clarifying that he had asked a question to Dr. Boobis, not to the European Communities. This unnumbered paragraph became paragraph 929. In conclusion, three additional paragraph numbers were added in the final version of the transcript compared to the draft version sent for comments to the parties. The draft version had 1069 numbered paragraphs; the final version has 1072 numbered paragraphs.

6.30   The European Communities also seems to request, with respect to paragraph 7.148 that the Panel specify the nature of the "editorial adjustments" made in the transcript. The Panel deems it appropriate to recall that the tapes of the meeting of the Panel with the experts were given to a typist who transcribed them. Two types of editorial adjustments were made to the transcript. First, the Secretariat proofread the transcript, identifying any words or passages the typist had misunderstood and checking these passages against the tapes. The type of errors identified were limited to confusions regarding technical terms (e.g. "N-point" instead of "endpoint"; "safe defactual" instead of "safety factor"[230] or "defactual threshold" instead of "de facto threshold"[231]). Other corrections involved minimal adjustments to sentences, for example to remove repeated words and occasionally adding punctuation marks. Once these corrections were made, the transcript was sent to the experts and subsequently to the parties in order to give each speaker the chance to verify that his or her own interventions had been accurately reflected. The experts' comments consisted of further corrections of technical words which had been improperly transcribed, or corrections of word order or colloquial expressions to make the transcript more legible. This is the reason why the Panel considered that these corrections did not go beyond "minimal editorial adjustments".

(b)   Comments by the United States

6.31   With respect to the discussion of the procedural question of the opening of the Panel meetings with parties and experts for public observation, the United States requests that we remove our discussion of the term "proceedings" as it appears in Article 17.10 of the DSU. We note that the same request was made by the European Communities. Since this reference was only an additional argument, we accepted the parties' requests and removed our discussion of the term "proceedings" in Article 17.10 of the DSU.

6.32   The United States also requests that we modify paragraphs 7.151 and 2.7. We see no reason not to adjust the description of the measure since it is actually

---

[230]   Annex G, para. 422.
[231]   Annex G, para. 707.

the absence of recourse to the DSU by the United States which seems to be at the origin of the EC complaint. However, under the circumstances, we also deem in necessary to specify that the issue stems from the fact that the United States maintained the measure after the notification of Directive 2003/74/EC to the DSB and we modified paragraphs 2.7 and 7.151 accordingly.

6.33   The United States contests the conclusion of the Panel in paragraphs 7.162-7.164 that the European Communities narrowed the terms of reference of the Panel through the approach it followed in its first written submission. For the United States, the EC approach is a "choice of legal strategy" which is not binding on the Panel. The European Communities cannot constrain the terms of reference of the Panel by adopting a specific approach to its claims in its first written submission.

6.34   The Panel agrees that it is well established that a complainant cannot change the terms of reference of a panel in its first submission or subsequently. As stated by the Appellate Body in *EC – Bananas III*:

> "If a *claim* is not specified in the request for the establishment of a panel, then a faulty request cannot be subsequently 'cured' by a complaining party's argumentation in its first written submission to the panel or in any other submission or statement made later in the panel proceeding."[232]

6.35   However, the Panel does not believe that this is the issue in the present case. The European Communities did not try to cure a faulty request. It made its claims more specific. As the Panel itself noted[233], there could be several ways to find a violation of Article 23 of the DSU. The European Communities has clarified how it considered that this violation should be approached by the Panel. As stated by the Panel on *EC – Tube or Pipe Fittings*[234]:

> "In our view, it is in the nature of the Panel process that the claims made by a party may be progressively clarified and refined throughout the proceedings."

6.36   The Panel also quotes the Appellate Body in *US – Carbon Steel*.[235] It seems to be accepted that complainants can clarify their claims throughout the proceedings. In this instance however, it appears that the United States is con-

---

[232]   Appellate Body Report on *EC – Bananas III*, paras. 141-143; Appellate Body Report on *US – Lead and Bismuth II*, paras. 72 and 73.
[233]   See para. 7.176.
[234]   Panel Report on *EC – Tubes and Pipes Fittings*, para. 7.10.
[235]   See para. 7.161.

cerned by the conclusion of the Panel that it is *bound* by these clarifications or that they are part of the Panel's terms of reference.

6.37   Panels are free to address claims in the order that they deem appropriate.[236] However, if a party specifies in its first written submission that a claim is raised in the alternative, can a panel disregard this clarification? To a lesser extent, can a panel disregard the fact that the complainant addressed the violation of a given provision in a particular way? Regarding the first question, it seems that panels should be bound by a claim made "in the alternative" as acknowledged by the Appellate Body.[237] Regarding the second question, the reply might be less clear and depend on the type of "clarification" made by the complainant. In this case, the clarification had serious consequences on how the Panel could address the claims listed in the terms of reference. It was not a violation of Article 23 in general, but a violation of Article 23 as a consequence of a breach of Article 22.8 of the DSU. The Panel also notes the arguments of the European Communities in its comments of 19 October 2007. The Panel recalls, in particular, that the rights of the respondent or its ability to defend itself were in no way affected by the "narrowing" of its claims by the European Communities. The Panel remains of the view that it is bound by the EC approach to its claims and, accordingly, has not modified paragraphs 7.162-7.164.

3.   *Comments of the parties regarding the Panel's findings of violation of Article 23.2(a) read together with Articles 21.5 and 23.1 of the DSU and on the EC claims on Article 23.1, read together with Articles 22.8 and 3.7 of the DSU*

(a)   Comments by the European Communities

6.38   The European Communities disagrees with the interpretation the Panel makes, in paragraphs 7.174 *et seq.*, as well as in paragraph 7.272 of the EC claims as set out in its first written submission. The European Communities insists in its comments that "it did not argue [in its main claims] that there was a violation of Article 22.8 itself, but rather one of Article 23.1". In other words, the European Communities seems to suggest that the Panel should not have addressed the conformity of the US measure under Article 22.8 of the DSU – even though this article was listed in the EC request for establishment of a panel – but only under Article 23.1. Yet, the European Communities alleges a violation of Article 22.8 in various parts of its first submission and subsequently.[238]

---

[236]   Appellate Body Report in *Canada – Wheat Exports and Grain Imports*, para. 126.
[237]   See, e.g., Appellate Body Report on *EC – Selected Customs Matters*, para. 308.
[238]   See, for instance:

6.39   In the opinion of the Panel, the use of the term "in conjunction with" or "read together with" is not indicative that the European Communities only claims a violation of Article 23. In Section III.E.3 of its first written submission, the European Communities alleges a violation of Article 3.7 even though in its conclusions it states that the United States' and Canada's unilateral conduct "violates Article 23.1 of the DSU read in conjunction with Articles 22.8 and 3.7 of the DSU". One cannot conclude either that the European Communities draws a conclusion of violation of Article 22.8 from the violation of Article 23.1 since its allegation of violation of Article 23.1 stems from the obligation to withdraw the measure if the violation has been removed. Rather, one must conclude the opposite, i.e. that the European Communities draws a conclusion of violation of Article 23.1 from a violation of Article 22.8. For those reasons, the Panel does not agree with the argument made by the European Communities at the interim review stage that it never made a claim of violation of Article 22.8 of the DSU, and that its claims related only to violations of Article 23.

6.40   The European Communities also contests the qualifications made by the Panel of its second series of main claims (i.e. its claims of violation of Article 23.1 of the DSU in conjunction with Article 22.8 and Article 3.7 of the DSU) as claims "premised on compliance by the European Communities with the DSB recommendations and rulings in the *EC – Hormones* case" in paragraph 7.181. The Panel notes that it has clearly explained in paragraphs 7.277-7.278 why it believes that this claim was premised on compliance with the DSB recommendations and rulings in the *EC – Hormones* case.

6.41   Consequently, the Panel will not delete the section of its report considering the allegedly non-existent EC claim under Article 22.8 of the DSU.

6.42   The Panel, however, deems it appropriate to clarify paragraph 7.181, and to make the modification suggested by the United States in its comments of 19

-   EC's first written submission, para. 73: "Under Article 23.1 of the DSU, the United States is obliged to have recourse to, and abide by, the rules and procedures of this Understanding. This encompasses, *inter alia*, Articles 22.8 and 3.7 of the DSU";
-   EC's first written submission, section III.E.2, title: "The obligation not to apply suspension of concessions or other obligations under Article 22.8 of the DSU";
-   EC's first written submission, Section III:E.3, title "Violation of Article 23.1 and Article 22.8 of the DSU necessary entails a violation of Article 3.7";
-   EC's first written submission, para. 122: "For these reasons, the United States, by violating Articles 23.1, 22.8 of the DSU, also acted contrary to Article 3.7 of the DSU";
-   EC's oral statement at first meeting, para. 56: a "systemic claim under Article 22.8, *in conjunction with Article 23.1*";
-   EC's reply to questions of the United States after the first substantive meeting, para. 8: "More specifically, the European Communities considers that the continued application of sanctions despite the unchallenged EC compliance measure is in violation of Articles 23.1 and 22.8 read together."
-   EC's second written submission, para. 217.

October 2007 with respect to paragraph 7.359 in order to make clear that it is not reviewing the EC claim of violation of Article 22.8 in isolation.

6.43   The European Communities also argues that, even though the obligation of the respondent clearly emerges from the Panel's reasoning, the Panel should clarify its recommendations. This could be done either by removing from the findings any consideration of the second series of main EC claims (i.e. its claim of violation of Article 23.1 of the DSU in conjunction with Articles 22.8 and 3.7 of the DSU) or, if necessary, through suggestions under Article 19.1 of the DSU, or through clarifications in the Panel's reasoning. A somewhat similar request has been made by the respondent in its request for review of precise aspects of the interim report. However, the European Communities suggests that the Panel should clarify that the United States must remove its suspension of concessions, whereas the United States requests that we note that, once our findings are adopted by the DSB, recourse to dispute settlement in accordance with the rules and procedures of the DSU for the purpose of Article 23.2(a) read together with Articles 21.5 and 23.1 of the DSU will have been achieved in respect of this matter.

6.44   The Panel is mindful of its duty to assist the DSB in making recommendations or rulings aimed at achieving a satisfactory settlement of the matter. The Panel notes that the parties have both requested that the Panel make suggestions or concluding remarks aimed at clarifying what is expected from the United States. The Panel notes, however, that their proposed suggestions or concluding remarks are divergent. The Panel wishes to recall its conclusion in paragraph 7.251. This conclusion is based on the terms of Article 23.1 and 23.2(a). Those provisions require that recourse should be had to "the rules and procedures of the [DSU]" (Article 23.1) or, in the case of Article 23.2(a), that recourse be had to "dispute settlement in accordance with the rules and procedures of this Understanding". Moreover, for reasons explained in this report, the Panel does not believe that recourse by the European Communities to dispute settlement exempts the United States from its obligations under Article 23.1 and 23.2(a) of the DSU. The Panel has clarified this point in paragraph 8.3.

(b)   Comments by the United States

6.45   The United States requests the Panel to harmonize the lists of means of dispute settlement which appear in paragraphs 7.247 and 7.350. While the Panel sees no reason not to expressly refer to panel proceedings in paragraph 7.247, it notes that paragraph 7.247 uses the word "including" before listing means of dispute settlement. Its list is, thus, not exhaustive. The Panel also believes that this would be more necessary for the sake of completeness than for the sake of consistency. Indeed, the two lists relate to different matters. In paragraph 7.247, the Panel listed the means of dispute settlement available *to the United States* to comply with the requirements of Article 23.2(a) of the DSU to have "recourse to dispute settlement in accordance with the rules and procedures of [the DSU". Comparatively, paragraph 7.350, addresses the means available *to the European Communities* to obtain the termination of the suspension of concessions or other obligations. The addition of recourse to a "normal" panel in paragraph 7.247 should not be taken to imply that the United States would satisfy its obligation under Article 23.2(a) if any party to the dispute such as, for instance, the European Communities had recourse to dispute settlement. The Panel reads Article 23.2(a) and 23.1 as requiring that the dispute settlement procedure be initiated by the United States. Having also regard to the EC comments of 19 October 2007[239], the Panel does not deem it necessary to modify paragraph 7.247.

6.46   The Panel also accepted the US request to harmonize certain terms of paragraph 7.270 with the terms of paragraph 7.251.

6.47   In its comments on paragraphs 7.308 through 7.359, the United States argues that, whereas it is the case that a complaining party in WTO dispute settlement bears the burden of proof to make out a prima facie case of the WTO-inconsistency of the defending Member's measure, that concept does not equate to, nor does it imply that, there exists a presumption that the responding Member is in good faith compliance with its WTO obligations. The United States argues that questions of good faith or bad faith do not form a basis for a presumption of consistency or inconsistency.

6.48   The Panel agrees with the United States that good faith in the performance of treaties and the question of consistency are ultimately to be distinguished in the panel proceedings. A finding of violation of a Member's obligations will ultimately be based on an objective assessment of the conformity of the measure at issue. However, the Panel considers that, whereas a party to a dispute may ultimately be found in breach of its obligation irrespective of whether it is acting in good faith or not, good faith remains the premise on which the presumption of compliance is based. In other words, it is because a Member is supposed to comply with its obligations in good faith that it can be presumed to be in conformity with its obligations and that it is for the complaining Member in a dispute to make a prima facie case of violation.

6.49   The United States argues, on the contrary, that the burden of proof is testament solely to the fact that there is no presumption of bad faith that attaches to measures taken by a WTO Member. The Panel disagrees. The Panel note that the United States does not cite to any report in support of its position. Comparatively, the Panel notes that the Appellate Body, in *EC – Sardines*, stated that:

---

[239]   Paras. 14-16.

"We must assume that Members of the WTO will abide by their treaty obligations in good faith, as required by the principle of *pacta sunt servanda* articulated in Article 26 of the *Vienna Convention*. And, always in dispute settlement, every Member of the WTO must assume the good faith of every other Member."[240]

6.50   In that context, the Panel fails to see why burden of proof should be based on an absence of presumption of bad faith.

6.51   Likewise, the Panel does not understand why good faith should not form the basis for a presumption of consistency because it is ultimately irrelevant for purposes of finding whether a measure is consistent or not with the WTO. Since WTO Members are to be assumed to abide by their treaty obligations in good faith, it is normal that, until a prima facie case has been made by the complaining Member, the responding Member enjoy this presumption of compliance in good faith. Whereas this presumption goes to the substance or the "merits" of the measures at issue, it does not affect the ultimate finding of the Panel, which will be ultimately based on an objective assessment of the matter, including all the relevant evidence submitted by the parties. For these reasons, the Panel sees no reason to modify its findings in paragraphs 7.308 through 7.359.

6.52   The United States also requests that we modify paragraph 7.360. According to the United States, the fact that the Panel's terms of reference do not include provisions of the *SPS Agreement* does not necessarily mean that the conformity of the EC Directive 2003/74/EC with the *SPS Agreement* lies outside the Panel's mandate. The United States refers to the Appellate Body report in *Argentina – Footwear (EC)*[241] to conclude that the Panel would not exceed its terms of reference by examining provisions not cited in the Panel request and would comply with its obligations under Article 11 of the DSU.

6.53   The European Communities, in its comments of 19 October 2007[242], disagrees with the comments of the United States to the extent that, unlike in the case referred to by the United States where there was an express reference to another provision in the article allegedly breached, there is no reference in the term "removed" in Article 22.8 to any other provision. The European Communities considers that if the US interpretation prevailed, the responding party would effectively be free to refer to any provision of the covered agreements and the terms of reference would become meaningless.

6.54   The Panel considers that it has extensively explained why it believes that, while making actual findings regarding the compatibility of the EC Directive

---

[240]   Appellate Body Report in *EC – Sardines*, para. 278.
[241]   Appellate Body Report on *Argentina – Footwear (EC)*, paras. 74-75.
[242]   Para. 21.

2003/74/EC with the *SPS Agreement* is not part of its mandate, it has jurisdiction to address the compatibility of the Directive with the *SPS Agreement* to the extent necessary to make findings in relation to Article 22.8 of the DSU, which is part of its mandate. The Panel agrees with the United States that this is part of its duty to make an objective assessment of the matter pursuant to Article 11 of the DSU and a sentence has been added to that effect in paragraph 7.377. The Panel also believes that its approach is consistent with the scope of a panel mandate as confirmed by the Appellate Body.

6.55   The United States also requests that we modify the second sentence of paragraph 7.366 to take into account the terms of Article 7.2 of the DSU which provides that "Panels shall address the relevant provisions of any covered agreement cited *by the parties to the dispute*" (emphasis added). The Panel agrees with the United States that provisions invoked by the responding party, for instance, as affirmative defence must be addressed by a panel. The Panel notes, however, that the "matter" before it is defined by the request for establishment of the Panel. The matter before this Panel is whether the United States' measure has breached, *inter alia*, Article 22.8 of the DSU, not whether EC Directive 2003/74/EC complies with the *SPS Agreement*. As a result, the US references to provisions of the *SPS Agreement* are not claims. The Panel may address them, however, as part of its findings on Article 22.8 of the DSU. The Panel has nevertheless clarified paragraphs 7.366 and 7.367.

6.56   Finally, the United States requests a modification to paragraph 8.2 and the addition of concluding observations. Regarding paragraph 8.2, having duly considered the EC comments on comments, we nonetheless decided to replace the term "legislation" with the term "measure", consistent with Article 19.1 of the DSU.

6.57   Regarding the addition of concluding observations, we do not agree with the United States that, "once [our findings are] adopted by the Dispute Settlement Body, recourse to dispute settlement in accordance with the rules and procedures of the DSU for the purpose of Article 23.2(a) read together with Articles 21.5 and 23.1 of the DSU will have been achieved in respect of this matter." For reasons explained in this report, the Panel does not believe that recourse by the European Communities to dispute settlement exempts the United States from its obligations under Article 23.1 and 23.2(a) of the DSU. The Panel has clarified this point in paragraph 8.3.

4.   *Comments of the parties on the compliance of the EC ban on meat and meat products treated with the six hormones at issue for growth promotion purposes with the SPS Agreement in relation to the Panel's findings on*

the EC claims on Article 23.1, read together with Articles 22.8 and 3.7 of the DSU

(a) Comments by the European Communities

(i) Introductory comments

6.58 In an introduction to its specific comments, the European Communities alleges:

(a) that the Panel has dismissed the 1999, 2000 and 2002 Opinions as not constituting a proper risk assessment based on an alleged absence of specific evidence which, the European Communities claims, is impossible to provide;

(b) that the Panel dismissed the Opinions as not having presented sufficient evidence to call into question the conclusions of JECFA;

(c) that the Panel should have scrutinized JECFA's evaluations, which are based on old studies which were not publicly available and were not communicated to the Panel or the Panel's experts for review;

(d) that the Panel has reached its conclusions on the EC implementing measure (Directive 2003/74/EC) by relying selectively, for a number of important issues, on the statements of two experts in a group of six. The European Communities recalls that those two experts had participated in the drafting of the JECFA's assessments contradicted by the EC Opinions and were obviously defending their own work and the methodology applied by JECFA and Codex. Comparatively, the other four experts had overall validated and supported the conclusions of the EC Opinions; and, finally,

(e) that the Panel's methodology and reasoning are contrary to established principles on burden of proof and standards of review of genuine scientific questions by WTO panels and ordinary courts of law.

6.59 Regarding the argument under (a) above, the Panel will address this question when it addresses the EC comments on the Panel's findings under Article 5.1 of the *SPS Agreement.* As a preliminary remark, however, the Panel wishes to clarify that it did not "dismiss the opinion of a relevant committee constituted of highly regarded, independent scientific experts". The Panel concluded that the European Communities had not evaluated specifically the possibility that the adverse effects related to the association between excess hormones and neurobiological, developmental, reproductive and immunological effects, as well as immunotoxicity, genotoxicity and carcinogenicity coming into being, originating or resulting from the consumption of meat or meat products which contain veterinary residues of oestradiol-17β as a result of the cattle being treated with oestradiol-17β for growth promotion purposes. The Panel also found that the scientific evidence referred to in the Opinions does not support the EC con-clusions on genotoxicity, or the conclusion that the presence of residues of oestradiol-17β in meat and meat products as a result of a cattle being treated with this hormone for growth promotion purposes leads to increase cancer risk. Nor does the scientific evidence support the EC conclusions about the adverse im-munological and developmental effects of consuming meat and meat products from cattle treated with oestradiol-17β for growth promotion purposes. This does not put into question the results of the studies and research relied upon by the SCVPH, nor the conclusions reached by the scientists, but simply the conclu-sions drawn by the European Communities on the basis of the science.

6.60   Regarding the argument under (b) above, it is correct that the Panel con-sidered that, in order to determine whether relevant scientific evidence was in-sufficient within the meaning of Article 5.7 of the *SPS Agreement*, it had to take the results of the risk assessments made by JECFA as a "benchmark" of the exis-tence of sufficient scientific evidence. This is in line with the findings of the Appellate Body in *Japan – Apples* that the relevant scientific evidence will be insufficient within the meaning of Article 5.7 if the body of available scientific evidence does not allow, in quantitative or qualitative terms, the performance of an adequate assessment of risks as required under Article 5.1 and as defined in Annex A to the *SPS Agreement*[243], as well as with the presumption of compli-ance under Article 3.2 of the *SPS Agreement*.

6.61   As far as the argument under (c) is concerned, the Panel explained in its findings why it relied on JECFA's work without questioning it.[244] First, using JECFA's risk assessments as "benchmarks" did not mean that the Panel had to examine the scientific evidence supporting JECFA's conclusions. Second, none of the parties contested that JECFA and Codex work on the hormones at issue (with the exception of MGA) constitute international standards, guidelines and recommendations within the meaning of Article 3.2. Because sanitary measures which conform to international standards, guidelines or recommendations are deemed to be consistent with the provisions of the *SPS Agreement*, the Panel had no reason to scrutinize the evaluation made by JECFA. The only benefit of such an evaluation would have been to determine whether JECFA's risk assessment met the conditions of Article 5.1. However, the question before the Panel is not to review the validity of international standards: the Panel has no mandate to do that. It is not to review whether JECFA's risk assessments are compatible with Article 5.1, but whether the EC implementing measure is compatible with Arti-cle 5.1 as far as oestradiol-17β is concerned or justified under Article 5.7 for the other five hormones at issue. The Panel also notes in this respect that, whereas Members have, pursuant to Article 3.3, a right to introduce or maintain sanitary

---

[243]   Appellate Body Report on *Japan - Apples*, para. 179.
[244]   Paras. 7.643-7.647.

measures which result in a higher level of sanitary protection than would be achieved by measures based on the relevant international standards, guidelines and recommendations, the way to do this is not by seeking to demonstrate that those standards, guidelines and recommendations are flawed or outdated, which would simply show that they have become insufficient and would not justify the EC measure, but by providing positive evidence or information supporting the conformity of the measure at issue with Article 5.1 and/or Article 5.7. It was, thus, for the European Communities to provide convincing evidence, in line with the requirements of Article 3.3 of the *SPS Agreement*, to justify its definitive ban on oestradiol and that relevant scientific evidence was insufficient for the other five hormones.

6.62   Regarding the argument according to which the two experts involved in the drafting of JECFA's risk assessments were defending their own work and the methodology applied by JECFA and Codex, the Panel wishes to add to what it has already said above that, since JECFA's risk assessments were used as the reference risk assessments for purposes of the analysis under Article 5.7 of the *SPS Agreement*, it was necessary for the Panel to be able to rely on the advice of experts intimately knowledgeable about the substance of JECFA's risk assessments.[245] The purpose was not to check whether JECFA's risk assessments were supported by sufficient scientific evidence or carried out in accordance with Article 5 of the *SPS Agreement*, but to identify to what extent the concerns raised by the European Communities in its submissions had been considered in the development of its risk assessments by JECFA (e.g. how the risk to prepubertal children had been taken into account by JECFA). Second, the Panel recalls that JECFA is an international, independent entity composed of highly qualified experts selected by the WHO or FAO according to strict procedures.[246] JECFA also regularly reassesses its risk assessments, normally at the request of Members of Codex, and evidence before the Panel suggest that the European Communities did not request JECFA to reassess the hormones at issue on the basis of the new evidence it had gathered. Instead, the European Communities relied on its own risk assessment. Moreover, JECFA reaches its conclusions by consensus. So the opinions expressed by the two experts were given with regard to the consensual view of JECFA on this matter, not just their own personal positions in the past. This does not mean, however, that JECFA's work is these particular experts' own work: it is a joint work by several experts. The experts that the European Communities claims were defending their work acknowledge that the state of knowledge can evolve. For instance, Dr. Boobis stated that:

---

[245]   In order to assess the appropriateness for the Panel to seek advice from experts involved in the preparation of JECFA's risk assessment, it is also important to recall that the experts are being consulted in the context of an assessment of the EC implementing measure under Articles 5.1, 5.2, 5.7 and 3.3 of the *SPS Agreement*, and of the presumption of conformity with the *SPS Agreement*.

[246]   JECFA's reply to question 14 of the Panel. See also Dr. Boobis, Annex G, para. 511; Dr. Tritscher, Annex G, para. 515; Dr. Wennberg, Annex G, para. 517.

"[S]cience moves on, and it would be complacent for a risk assessment body to assume that it knew everything about a substance at a particular point in time. We have to work within the available information, and the question we ask is: do we have sufficient information at this point to conduct a risk assessment? – not: is the data complete and are there no scientific questions remaining to be answered."[247]

6.63   The experts consulted by the Panel are used to considering and peer reviewing studies that go beyond what they have published themselves or perhaps even contradict them. In other words, they are not likely to feel any need to defend their own previous work results in the light of new, convincing evidence or techniques that put such previous work into doubt. The Panel also notes that other experts referred to JECFA's work in their replies, just as they also referred to studies commissioned by the European Communities.[248]

6.64   The European Communities also argues that the remaining four experts "overall validated and supported the conclusions of the [SCVPH] Opinion[s]". The Panel does not share this point of view. First, not all experts expressed their views on all the issues. The experts who expressed their views often agreed with each other. Second, the impression that a majority of experts overall validated and supported the conclusions of the SCVPH Opinions is incorrect. With respect to the five provisionally banned hormones, to different degrees, the experts agreed that new studies would be useful. This does not mean, however, that they considered them useful for the reasons advocated by the European Communities. The four experts agreed regarding the hazard related to hormones, or the risk attached to high doses. But so did the two experts with JECFA experience.

6.65   As to the argument that the Panel's methodology and reasoning are contrary to established principles on burden of proof and standards of review of genuine scientific questions by WTO panels and ordinary courts of law, the Panel wishes to recall its findings at paragraphs 7.380-7.386 and 7.412-7.427 on the standard of review and burden of proof. The Panel has also explained why it gave particular relevance to JECFA's risk assessments and why, to the extent that the European Communities disagreed with JECFA, it had to prove that its measure was based on a risk assessment consistent with Article 5.1 and Annex A(4) of the *SPS Agreement,* or that the relevant scientific evidence was insufficient.

6.66   The European Communities argues that the statement originally found in paragraph 7.371 was not accurate as the European Communities was allegedly

---

[247]   See Annex G, para. 346.
[248]   See, e.g., Dr. Guttenplan, Annex D, para. 145.

replying to a hypothetical question and stated that it was not necessary to look into the scientific issues. The Panel notes that the European Communities stated in its reply to question 74 of the Panel[249] that "it did not believe that it [was] necessary to look into the scientific issues". The European Communities did not formally *object* to the Panel seeking scientific opinion even if the Panel proceeded with reviewing the *SPS Agreement*. Indeed, the European Communities added in its reply to the same question 74:[250]

> "However, the European Communities does not believe that the Panel would have the expertise to decide on such issues itself, should the Panel decide to go down [the road] of deciding the scientific issues at stake. In such a scenario, the European Communities believes that the consultation of scientific and technical advice would be absolutely necessary."

6.67   The European Communities argues that it was replying to an hypothetical question. Yet, the European Communities uses the affirmative and not the conditional in its reply when it states that "New experts will have to be consulted".[251] The Panel concludes that, whereas the European Communities was not of the view that it was necessary to look into the scientific issues, it was nevertheless in favour of the consultation of scientific experts if the Panel decided to address the scientific issues at stake. Paragraph 7.371 was modified accordingly.

6.68   The European Communities suggests that the Panel contradicted itself in paragraph 7.377 of the interim report when it stated, on the one hand, that parties had had sufficient opportunity to comment on the other party's allegations and, on the other hand, in paragraph 7.133, refused to allow the European Communities clarify the nature of a number of factual errors allegedly made by the United States and Canada. In paragraph 7.133, the Panel took the view that the European Communities should not be allowed to make further comments, lest the other parties would also comment and this would launch an endless exchange of arguments. The Panel notes that parties were allowed to comment on the experts' responses and to comment on the comments of the other party. In addition, the parties were allowed to comment on each other's replies to the questions of the Panel after the second substantive meeting. This is fully consistent with usual panel procedures. Moreover, the European Communities could correct any factual error appearing in the interim report by requesting the Panel to review precise aspects of the interim report, if the allegedly erroneous information provided

---

[249]   EC's replies to Panel questions after the first substantive meeting, Annex B, para. 274.

[250]   EC's replies to Panel questions after the first substantive meeting, Annex B, para. 275.

[251]   The Panel also notes that the European Communities made an alternative claim of violation of Article 22.8 of the DSU and Articles I and II of the GATT 1994, in isolation from its claim under Articles 23.1 and 3.7 of the DSU which was based on an allegation of actual compliance with the recommendations and rulings of the DSB in the *EC – Hormones* case.

by the United States and Canada had been used in the findings. The Panel notes that the EC request to correct some factual statements made by the other parties was limited to factual aspects, not to legal issues such as allegations of inconsistency with the *SPS Agreement*, which was the subject of this paragraph. The Panel nonetheless decided to clarify paragraph 7.374.

6.69   The European Communities argues that, in paragraphs 7.376-7.377, the Panel states that its approach was a "pragmatic solution" and the "most logical way forward" without further explanation. The European Communities considers that the approach of the Panel is arbitrary and negatively affects the interests of the parties and reverses existing case law and established practice. The Panel first notes that the European Communities does not specify which "existing case law" and "established practice" it refers to, and that it does not make any reference to its previous submissions. Second, the Panel notes that these paragraphs contain only additional arguments. The Panel has amply justified its decision to address the compatibility of the EC implementing measure with the *SPS Agreement* throughout the preceding paragraphs. The Panel also explains the reason why it follows this approach in paragraph 7.377, emphasizing the need to assist the parties and the DSB in solving this dispute and the need to determine whether there is a violation of Article 23.1 in conjunction with Article 22.8 and Article 3.7 of the DSU. The Panel's choice was directed by the requirement to make an objective assessment of the matter before it, in accordance with Article 11 of the DSU, having regard to the particular circumstances of this case, as recalled in section VII.C.2.(a) of this report.

6.70   The European Communities states that paragraph 7.404 and footnote 516 are factually inaccurate. This comment can only relate to and be limited to the refusal of the Panel to let the European Communities correct alleged *factual* errors in the comments of Canada and the United States on the EC replies to the questions of the Panel after the second substantive meeting. First, the European Communities never identified the factual errors at issue. Second, the Panel explained its position in its letter of 20 November 2006. The Panel recalls that it followed the standard practice of panels in terms of procedure, allowing comments on replies to the questions of the Panel. The Panel felt justified in not allowing further comments. The Panel stressed that the European Communities could address these factual errors at the interim review stage, if they were reflected in the findings of the Panel. It appears that the European Communities did not take advantage of this opportunity as no such factual corrections were made. Thus, the Panel sees no reason to correct paragraph 7.404 and footnote 516.

6.71   With respect to paragraph 7.410, the European Communities argues that the statement of the Panel is unsupported and is an error of law. We do not share the European Communities' opinion. First, the Panel did not base its decision to include Article 5.2 of the *SPS Agreement* in its review of the conformity of Directive 2003/74/EC exclusively on the comment of the European Communities quoted in paragraph 7.409. In paragraph 7.404, the Panel mentioned that it would "consider all allegations and arguments raised by each party". Since the United States had alleged a violation of Article 5.2, the Panel could look at it irrespective of the EC position on this matter. In paragraph 7.410, the Panel simply notes the absence of objection of the European Communities. It was, therefore, not deemed necessary to modify paragraph 7.410.

6.72   The European Communities argues, with respect to paragraph 7.420, that the Panel misconstrued its role by engaging in settling a scientific debate and arbitrating the opinions expressed by the scientific community by "picking and choosing" from individual replies of experts without any valid explanation. The Panel explained in its findings in paragraph 7.71 why it deemed it preferable to consult experts individually. The Panel had also explained in its letter to the parties of 25 November 2005 how it understood its role in terms of assessment of scientific opinions. The Panel believes that weighing the scientific evidence before it was necessary to reply to the two main legal questions in relation to the *SPS Agreement*, i.e. whether the European Communities had performed a risk assessment within the meaning of Article 5.1 for oestradiol-17β and if the relevant scientific evidence was sufficient within the meaning of Article 5.7 as far as the other hormones were concerned. In fact, the Appellate Body confirmed the discretion of Panels in weighing evidence in *EC – Asbestos*.[252] This is also part of the role of panels under Articles 11 and 13 of the DSU. The Panel also considers that the role of the experts was to act as an "interface" between the scientific evidence and the Panel, so as to allow it to perform its task as the trier of fact. If panels were not to weigh the scientific evidence before them, then the DSU would have mandated the recourse to experts review groups. The Panel also notes that the Appellate Body took the view in *EC – Hormones*, that both the *SPS Agreement* and the DSU leave to the discretion of a panel the determination of whether the establishment of an expert review group is necessary or appropriate.[253] The Panel explained its approach in detail in paragraph 7.420 and thus does not believe that it engaged into "picking and choosing" without any valid explanation. The Panel notes that some replies to its questions were more detailed than others and supported by bibliographical references. The Panel believes that, in case of divergence of opinions between the experts, and having due regard to the comments of the parties and the clarifications provided by the experts at the meeting with the Panel, it was a sound approach to take into account, in forming its own opinion, the opinions that were the most precise and elaborate. Therefore, having also considered the comments of the respondent of 19 October 2007, the Panel did not deem it necessary to revise paragraph 7.420.

---

[252]   Appellate Body Report on *EC – Asbestos*, para. 161.
[253]   See para. 7.74.

6.73   The European Communities considers that, in paragraphs 7.423-7.427, the Panel missed the point made by the European Communities, namely that neither the United States, Canada nor JECFA have provided conclusive proof that the methods used to generate the outdated evidence on which they based and continue to base their risk assessment were validated. The Panel first notes that the paragraphs at issue are part of an introductory section, not one where the validity of the evidence actually relied upon by JECFA is being discussed. Second, the purpose of the discussion contained in the paragraphs at issue is clearly stated in paragraph 7.427. The point made by the Panel is that a study is not *ipso facto* irrelevant because it is old. The Panel makes two points in paragraph 7.427: (i) that accuracy is a problem when one is at the limits of detection of the older methods and (ii) that in any event an essential question is whether a given method has been validated.

6.74   Second, the European Communities' comment raises the question whether there is a need for the United States and Canada to prove that JECFA's risk assessments were based on validated studies. In the opinion of the Panel, this is not a question that needs to be addressed in order to resolve this dispute. JECFA's risk assessments were used as the bases for Codex recommendations which are, pursuant to Article 3.1 and Annex A(3) of the *SPS Agreement*, "international standards, guidelines or recommendations". Pursuant to Article 3.3, it is for the WTO Member wishing to introduce or maintain sanitary measures which result in a higher level of sanitary protection than would be achieved by measures based on the relevant international standards, guidelines and recommendations to provide scientific justification in support of such measures. In that context, the question before the Panel is not whether JECFA's risk assessments were based on validated studies[254], but whether the European Communities' permanent ban

---

[254]   The Panel did not use the quotation from Dr. Wennberg in paragraph 7.426 to argue that JECFA's studies were actually validated, but to stress that if a study used a validated method, there is no reason to reject it simply because it is old. The problem with some of the more recent studies on which the European Communities relies is that they have not been validated. The European Communities also refers to statements of Dr. De Brabander (Annex G, paras. 670, 675, 681 and 687) and Dr. Sippell (Annex G, para. 689). The Panel understands from Dr. De Brabander's comments that there would be reasons to re-do certain assessments, *inter alia* because the separation power of components has increased considerably since the 1980s (see para. 681). However, the Panel notes that Dr. De Brabander insists on the fact that one cannot say that the "old" data are not correct on not valid until they are checked with modern analytical methods, which, according to him, has not been done. Dr. Sippell states that, for infant and young children, a standard commercially available radio-immunoassay is not able to pick up the real concentrations, because there are numerous other cross-reacting steroids. Dr. Sippell concludes that "one should really look at the new data". Whereas this statement suggests that old data are not valid, Dr. Sippel stops short of formally concluding that they are not valid. We also note Dr. Boobis' comment following Dr. Sippell's intervention (Annex G, para. 691):

> "I would make the point that a method that is used to measure low levels of oestrogens in infants is a different question from a method that is being used to measure residues in food. The analytical challenges are quite different and the methods that were developed in the 1980s for the residues were fit for that purpose, and that is

on meat and meat products containing veterinary residues of oestradiol-17β derived from cattle treated with this hormone for growth promotion purposes is based on a risk assessment within the meaning of Article 5.1 and, for the five provisionally banned hormones, whether there exists *validated* studies that sufficiently put into question the evidence on which JECFA's risk assessments are based, so as to support a conclusion that the relevant scientific evidence is insufficient to permit the assessment of risk.

(ii)   General comments on the Panel's analysis regarding oestradiol-17β

6.75   The European Communities argues that the use of the term "measure" in paragraphs 7.443 and 7.518 to describe the Panel's function is unfortunate because "it is clear that a panel does not measure anything (which implies that there is something quantitative to measure), but simply examines the conformity of the measure with the relevant provisions."[255] The Panel notes that it used the term "measure" in the sense, as defined by the Oxford English Dictionary, to "judge or estimate the greatness or value of (a person, a quality, etc.) by a certain standard or rule; appraise by comparison with something else."[256] The Panel believes that judging or appraising something, in this case the SCVPH Opinions, against a certain standard or rule, in this case Articles 5.1 (including an examination of Article 5.2) and Annex A(4) of the *SPS Agreement*, is precisely examining the conformity of the measure with the relevant provisions. Therefore, the Panel will not change the term. However, the Panel wishes to clarify here that it did not intend to use the term "measure" to imply any sort of quantitative analysis.

6.76   The European Communities also states that it did not understand the Panel's use of the term "objective measures" in the paragraph of the interim report corresponding to paragraph 7.443. The European Communities correctly points out an error in the paragraph. The fourth sentence should read "The Panel must objectively measure the Opinions against the relevant standard for whether a risk assessment has been conducted, which can be found in the texts of Articles 5.1 (including an examination of Article 5.2) as well as Annex A(4) of the *SPS Agreement*." Again, the Panel notes that it is using the term "measure" in the sense of a qualitative appraisal of the SCVPH Opinions against a standard or rule, namely the *SPS Agreement*.

---

what they were used for. If you ask the question about the circulating concentrations, that is a different issue. So in terms of residues the methods were suitable."

[255]   EC's comments on interim report, para. 50.
[256]   *Shorter Oxford English Dictionary*, 5th edition (1993), p.1730.

(iii) Comments on "risk assessment techniques"

6.77 The European Communities argues that the discussion by the Panel of risk assessment techniques in paragraphs 7.446 to 7.469 is irrelevant and unnecessary given that no relevant international risk assessment techniques for veterinary drug residues have been agreed upon.[257]

6.78 The Panel notes that Article 5.1 requires that Members take into account the risk assessment techniques of the relevant international organizations when ensuring that their sanitary and phytosanitary measures are based on a risk assessment. Therefore, the Panel believes that an analysis of whether such techniques exist and whether the European Communities took them into account is necessary and appropriate to an analysis of whether the European Communities has removed the previously found inconsistency of its ban on the importation of meat and meat products treated with oestradiol-17β for growth promotion purposes with Article 5.1 of the *SPS Agreement*.

6.79 The Panel notes in paragraph 7.449 that no specific techniques or guidelines had thus far been formally adopted by Codex for use by national governments in conducting risk assessments of veterinary drug residues. However, there are relevant definitions of the phases of a risk assessment as well as guidelines and practices for conducting a risk assessment in the general sense and the Panel, therefore, analyses whether the European Communities took these into account when it adopted Directive 2003/74/EC.

6.80 The European Communities also argues that these passages convey the erroneous message that the concept of risk assessment as defined in the *SPS Agreement* is the same as in Codex Alimentarius.[258]

6.81 The Panel is surprised by this comment, because it states in paragraph 7.467:

"[T]he Panel must concur with the reasoning of the panel in *Japan – Apples*, that the requirement to 'take into account' the risk assessment techniques of international organizations:

'[D]oes not impose that a risk assessment under Article 5.1 be 'based on' or 'in conformity with' such risk assessment techniques. This suggests that such techniques should be considered relevant, but that a failure to respect each and every aspect of them

---

[257] EC's comments on interim report, para. 51.
[258] *Ibid.*

would not necessarily, *per se*, signal that the risk assessment on which the measure is based is not in conformity with the requirements of Article 5.1.'"[259]

6.82   The Panel finds that this quotation adequately conveys the Panel's opinion that although the risk assessment techniques of the relevant international organizations must be considered by the Members, they are not binding on Members and that not following them would not necessarily lead to the conclusion that the risk assessment did not conform with Article 5.1 and Annex A(4) of the *SPS Agreement*. However, to avoid confusion, the Panel clarified paragraph 7.467 and added paragraph 7.468.

6.83   The European Communities also takes issue with paragraph 7.455. In that paragraph the Panel summarizes the arguments of the European Communities as follows:

> "The **European Communities** agrees that the risk assessment techniques developed by Codex are relevant and contemplated in Article 5.1's requirement to take into account the risk assessment techniques developed by relevant international organizations. However, the European Communities maintains that the risk assessment criteria as developed by the WTO dispute settlement bodies are clearly more relevant to the application of the *SPS Agreement*."

6.84   The European Communities argues that this paragraph is misleading because the European Communities has followed the four steps of risk assessment described by Codex. The European Communities asserts that it has followed the four steps because its legislation so provides, not because it is required to do so under the *SPS Agreement*, since such techniques do not exist.

6.85   The arguments summarized in this paragraph are contained in paragraph 192 of the European Communities' second written submission.

6.86   Paragraph 192 of the European Communities' second written submission states:

> "[A]ll parties to this dispute agree on the relevance of the risk assessment techniques developed by Codex recently. Indeed, Article 5.1 itself points to the relevance of risk assessment techniques developed by relevant international organisations. Furthermore, the SCVHP has explicitly based its assessment on the three ele-

---

[259]   Panel Report on *Japan – Apples*, para. 8.241.

ments of risk identification, risk characterization and exposure assessment recommended and applied by the Codex.[260] A few qualifications, however, apply. First, risk assessment criteria as they have been developed by the dispute settlement bodies are clearly more relevant to the application of the *SPS Agreement* than those developed by international scientific bodies. This follows naturally from the fact that it is the former's duty and privilege to interpret the provisions of the *SPS Agreement*."

6.87   The Panel believes that the sentiment of the European Communities' argument is adequately summarized in paragraph 7.455 and will not alter the paragraph.

6.88   As to the European Communities' argument that paragraph 7.455 is misleading because the European Communities has followed the four steps of risk assessment as defined by Codex, the Panel notes that it does not discuss in any way in paragraph 7.455 whether the European Communities' has complied with the four steps. In addition, the Panel notes in paragraph 7.458 that "the European Communities argues that the risk assessment at the basis of Directive 2003/74/EC precisely follows the four steps of risk assessment as defined by Codex ..."

6.89   It is irrelevant for the Panel whether the EC internal legislation mandates that the European Communities follow the four steps or whether the European Communities complied with its own legislation. The Panel's analysis focuses on whether the European Communities "took into account" the relevant risk assessment techniques of the relevant international organizations as required by Article 5.1 of the *SPS Agreement* and, in paragraph 7.469, the Panel finds that it has.

---

[260]   In response to a question from the Panel, the European Communities clarified the following: "As regards the statement in para. 192 of its Rebuttal Submission, the European Communities is grateful to the Panel for pointing out the error and oversight. The error is double because: first, the steps of a risk assessment as defined by Codex are four (not three) and, second, the terminology used in para. 192 to describe the first three of them is not correct either (see following para. 193 where the proper terminology is used for the first three steps). The words used in para. 192 is an isolated oversight and does not reflect the position which the European Communities has expressed in so many other places in its written submissions and the oral hearing. Indeed, with its reply of 3 October 2005 to Written Question No. 24 from the Panel, in particular paragraphs 140-143, the European Communities has properly described the four steps of a risk assessment and the reasons for which it thinks it has complied with them in this case. See also paragraphs 145-152 of its reply of 3 October to Written Question No. 25 from the Panel. Moreover, a careful examination of the 1999 Opinion shows beyond doubt that the European Communities has completed the four steps, albeit it made a qualitative exposure assessment for the reasons explained therein." (EC's replies to Panel questions after the second substantive meeting, question 8, para. 34, Annex C-1)

6.90   The European Communities asks the Panel to more fully summarize its arguments in paragraphs 7.502 and 7.503.[261] The Panel has, therefore, modified those paragraphs.

(iv)   Assessment of the scientific arguments

6.91   The European Communities, argues that paragraphs 7.504 through 7.573 are incoherent and confused. Specifically, the European Communities believes that they do not adequately present the debate on the "threshold approach" which it believes is the central scientific debate.[262] The Panel notes that the content of paragraphs 7.504 through 7.573 contains the reasoning of the Panel on whether the Opinions satisfy the definition of a risk assessment set forth in Annex A(4) of the *SPS Agreement*. This section of the Panel's reasoning is not the appropriate place to present a debate between the parties about a particular scientific issue.

6.92   The Panel, however, is mindful that the parties did expend a significant amount of argument on the relevance of "thresholds" to the risk assessment process and that perhaps it would provide further clarity to include more explanation of the various arguments. Therefore, the Panel made modifications to the summaries of the parties' arguments. The Panel believes that the debate over the "threshold" issue can be divided into two main components. First, whether all four of the risk assessment steps as defined by Codex should be followed when the substance under review exhibits no threshold. Second, whether oestradiol-17β is such a substance that exhibits no threshold because it is genotoxic *in vivo* and therefore would lead to adverse effects even at the doses found in meat as a result of treatment of cattle with oestradiol-17β for growth promotion purposes.

6.93   The Panel also feels that it would be helpful to include some additional information provided by the experts with respect to this matter. Therefore, the Panel inserted a new paragraph after paragraph 7.464. The Panel also changed the first sentence of paragraph 7.467.

6.94   With respect to whether oestradiol-17β, in particular, is genotoxic *in vivo* and has no threshold, the Panel finds that the issue arises in two different contexts: first, in the context of what such a conclusion means for evaluating whether the SCVPH Opinions constitute a risk assessment within the meaning of the *SPS Agreement;* second, in the context of the analysis of whether the science supports the conclusions reached by the European Communities with respect to the genotoxic properties of oestradiol-17β. To address both of these issues the Panel edited paragraph 7.497.

---

[261]   EC's comments on interim report, para. 52.
[262]   EC's comments on interim report, para. 53.

6.95   The Panel also feels that it would be helpful to include some additional information provided by the experts with respect to this matter. Therefore, the Panel inserted a new paragraph after paragraph 7.529.

6.96   With respect to whether the science supports the conclusion that oestra-diol-17β is a substance that exhibits no threshold, the Panel has added Dr. Cogliano's response to question 19 from the Panel[263] as paragraph 7.559.

6.97   The European Communities argues that paragraphs 7.518 and 7.519 of the interim report are a misinterpretation of what the Appellate Body found in the original *EC – Hormones* case about the concept of risk assessment and its significance in the *SPS Agreement*.[264] The European Communities does not provide any specific parts of the analysis that it feels are a misinterpretation, neither does it provide what it believes is the correct interpretation. The Panel can only assume that the European Communities maintains its position as summarized in paragraph 7.517.

6.98   The Panel based its reasoning in paragraphs 7.518 and 7.519 of the interim report on several passages in the Appellate Body Report on *EC – Hormones*. Paragraph 181 of the Appellate Body Report reads as follows:

> "The second preliminary consideration relates to the Panel's effort to distinguish between 'risk assessment' and 'risk management'. The Panel observed that an assessment of risk is, at least with respect to risks to human life and health, a 'scientific' examination of data and factual studies; it is not, in the view of the Panel, a 'policy' exercise involving social value judgments made by political bodies.[265] The Panel describes the latter as 'non-scientific' and as pertaining to 'risk management' rather than to 'risk assessment'.[266] We must stress, in this connection, that Article 5 and Annex A of the *SPS Agreement* speak of 'risk assessment' only and that the term 'risk management' is not to be found either in Article 5 or in

---

[263] Panel question 19, Annex D, p. 34 ("The European Communities states that '... it is generally recognized that for substances which have genotoxic potential (as is the case with oestradiol-17β) a threshold can not be identified. Therefore it cannot be said that there exist a safe level below which intakes from residue should be considered to be safe. Therefore the fact that doses used in growth promotion are low is not of relevance'. Does the scientific evidence referred to by the European Communities support these conclusions? Would your reply have been different at the time of adoption of the EC Directive in September 2003? If so, why? [see para. 201 of EC Rebuttal Submission (US case), paras. 120-122 of EC Rebuttal Submission (Canada case), paras. 73 and 86-98 of Canada Rebuttal Submission, paras. 87-91 and 153-156 of US First Submission and paras. 35-40 and 46 of US Rebuttal Submission]").

[264] EC's comments on interim report, para. 55.

[265] (*footnote original*) US Panel Report, para. 8.94; Canada Panel Report, para. 8.97.

[266] (*footnote original*) US Panel Report, para. 8.95; Canada Panel Report, para. 8.98.

any other provision of the *SPS Agreement*. Thus, the Panel's distinction, which it apparently employs to achieve or support what appears to be a restrictive notion of risk assessment, has no textual basis. The fundamental rule of treaty interpretation requires a treaty interpreter to read and interpret the words actually used by the agreement under examination, and not words which the interpreter may feel should have been used."

6.99   The Appellate Body disapproved of the panel's use in the original *EC – Hormones* dispute of the distinction between "risk assessment" and "risk management" because it had no textual basis. However, this did not mean that the Appellate Body endorsed an interpretation of Article 5.1 or Annex A(4) of the *SPS Agreement* that included a risk management stage. In fact, it emphatically stated that the term "risk management" is not to be found in Article 5 or any other provision of the *SPS Agreement*. The Panel, therefore, finds no basis for the European Communities' assertion that the Appellate Body "confirmed that a risk assessment within the meaning of Article 5.1 includes a risk management stage which is the responsibility of the regulator to carry out and not of the scientific bodies."[267]

6.100   This Panel, following the advice of the Appellate Body, has adhered strictly to the text of Article 5.1 and Annex A(4) of the *SPS Agreement* in its interpretation. In analysing the European Communities' compliance with Article 5.1 and Annex A(4) of the *SPS Agreement*, the Panel is also cognisant of the Appellate Body's finding that:

> "The listing in Article 5.2 begins with 'available scientific evidence'; this, however, is only the beginning. We note in this connection that the Panel states that, for purposes of the EC measures in dispute, a risk assessment required by Article 5.1 is 'a *scientific* process aimed at establishing the *scientific* basis for the sanitary measure a Member intends to take'.[268] To the extent that the Panel intended to refer to a process characterized by systematic, disciplined and objective enquiry and analysis, that is, a mode of studying and sorting out facts and opinions, the Panel's statement is unexceptionable.[269] However, to the extent that the Panel purports to

---

[267]   EC's second written submission, para. 191.

[268]   (*footnote original*) US Panel Report, para. 8.107; Canada Panel Report, para. 8.110.

[269]   (*footnote original*) "The ordinary meaning of 'scientific', as provided by dictionary definitions, includes of, relating to, or used in science', broadly, having or appearing to have an exact, objective, factual, systematic or methodological basis', of, relating to, or exhibiting the methods or principles of science' and of, pertaining to, using, or based on the methodology of science'. Dictionary definitions of science' include the observation, identification, description, experimental investigation, and theoretical explanation of natural phenomena', any methodological activity, discipline, or study', and knowledge attained through

---

exclude from the scope of a risk assessment in the sense of Article 5.1, all matters not susceptible of quantitative analysis by the empirical or experimental laboratory methods commonly associated with the physical sciences, we believe that the Panel is in error. Some of the kinds of factors listed in Article 5.2 such as 'relevant processes and production methods' and 'relevant inspection, sampling and testing methods' are not necessarily or wholly susceptible of investigation according to laboratory methods of, for example, biochemistry or pharmacology. Furthermore, there is nothing to indicate that the listing of factors that may be taken into account in a risk assessment of Article 5.2 was intended to be a closed list. It is essential to bear in mind that the risk that is to be evaluated in a risk assessment under Article 5.1 is not only risk ascertainable in a science laboratory operating under strictly controlled conditions, but also risk in human societies as they actually exist, in other words, the actual potential for adverse effects on human health in the real world where people live and work and die."[270]

6.101 Therefore, the Panel finds that a risk assessment consistent with Article 5.1 need not be limited to empirical or experimental laboratory methods commonly associated with the physical sciences. However, the Panel also agrees with the Appellate Body's statement that a requirement that a risk assessment be "a process characterized by systematic, disciplined and objective enquiry and analysis, that is, a mode of studying and sorting out facts and opinions" is unexceptionable.

6.102 Nowhere in the texts of Article 5.1 and Annex A(4) does the Panel find support for the European Communities' contention that a risk assessment within the meaning of the *SPS Agreement* includes "weighing policy alternatives in light of the results of risk assessment and, if required, selecting and implementing appropriate control options, including regulatory measures."[271] What the European Communities seems to be describing is how a government chooses an appropriate SPS measure based on a risk assessment. The Panel does not find that this is contemplated by the texts of Article 5.1 and Annex A(4) of the *SPS Agreement*.

6.103 To avoid any confusion or misunderstanding the Panel modified paragraphs 7.518 through 7.521.

---

study or practice'". (footnotes omitted) *United States' Statement of Administrative Action, Uruguay Round Agreements Act*, 203d Congress, 2d Session, House Document 103-316, Vol. 1, 27 September 1994, p. 90.

[270] Appellate Body Report on *EC – Hormones*, para. 187.

[271] EC's reply to question 24 of the Panel after the first substantive meeting, Annex B-1, para. 137.

6.104 The Panel is aware that the experts responded to the Panel's questions with respect to what the European Communities had evaluated in its Opinions by using a terminology that is standard for risk assessments conducted according to the process outlined in the Codex Procedural Manual. Although the scientific experts' responses may include terms such as "hazard characterization" or "exposure assessment", the Panel is at all times aware that the relevant standard against which it is assessing the European Communities' measure is that of the *SPS Agreement*. In order to emphasize this point, the Panel added a new paragraph before paragraph 7.522.

6.105 The European Communities takes issue with the reliance of the Panel on certain statements by the experts in paragraphs 7.522 to 7.528 and cites to various other statements by the same experts which it claims stand for the opposite proposition.[272] The Panel takes note that Annex D, which contains the replies of the experts to the Panel's questions is 116 pages long and Annex G which contains the transcript of the Panel's meeting with the experts is 170 pages long. This does not include the various comments and comments on comments of the parties on the experts' responses and on the transcripts. With this volume of information, every comment by the experts could not be included in the Panel findings and, for that matter, did not have to be.[273] Therefore, the Panel made a decision to select quotations that are representative of a particular expert's opinion on a given topic. The Panel has reviewed the specific paragraphs referred to by the European Communities in an attempt to determine if it misunderstood or misrepresented a particular expert's opinion. It also considered the comments of the United States of 19 October 2007.

6.106 With respect to Dr. Guttenplan, the European Communities objects to the Panel's reliance on paragraph 145 of the experts replies to the Panel's questions and refers the Panel to paragraphs 366, 393, 713 and 716-718 of Annex G as well as his written reply to Panel question 17 which is at paragraph 176 of Annex D.[274]

6.107 With respect to the Panel's reliance on paragraph 145 of Annex D, which is Dr. Guttenplan's response to Panel question 13, cited in paragraph 7.523, the Panel amended the paragraph to better reflect Dr. Guttenplan's complete response to the question.

6.108 Additionally, to more fully reflect Dr. Guttenplan's written answer to question 52 of the Panel, the Panel modified paragraph 7.528.

---

[272] EC's comments on interim report, para. 56.
[273] Appellate Body Report on *EC – Hormones*, para. 138; see also section VII.C.3.(d)(iii) of this report.
[274] EC's comments on interim report, para. 56.

6.109 With respect to Dr. Guttenplan's other interventions cited by the European Communities, the Panel did not deem it necessary to make any additional changes in this section.

6.110 Paragraph 366 of Annex G refers to Dr. Guttenplan's opinion that oestrogen is genotoxic, but that it may not be possible to "really estimate the risk at this point from such low levels of genotoxic effects."[275] Paragraph 393 of Annex G refers generally to the issue of conducting risk assessments of genotoxic substances with no threshold.[276] The Panel believes it has dealt with these issues in the amendments mentioned above.

6.111 Paragraphs 713 and 716-718 of Annex G reflect Dr. Guttenplan's opinion that although, because anything is possible, there may be a risk from consumption of meat derived from cattle treated with oestradiol-17β for growth promotion purposes, it is so low that it is not susceptible to calculation. It also reflects an interjection by the European Communities asking Dr. Guttenplan to confirm his statement that, although the risk is small and cannot be evaluated or calculated, it is not zero.

6.112 The Panel does not believe that these statements are directly relevant to the Panel's reasoning on whether the European Communities conducted a risk assessment consistent with the definition set forth in Annex A(4) of the *SPS Agreement*. As the Panel has noted, the purpose of the risk assessment is to evaluate the possibility that an identified adverse effect comes into being, originates, or results from the presence of the identified additives, contaminants, toxins or disease-causing organisms in food, beverages or feedstuffs. It is not to guarantee that said possibility will be below the Member's appropriate level of protection or indeed will be zero.

6.113 Finally, the European Communities cites Dr. Guttenplan's written response to question 17 of the Panel. In that paragraph, Dr. Guttenplan states that the absence of catechol metabolites in meat from treated animals does not imply that the meat is without risk for genotoxicity. Dr. Guttenplan was being asked to evaluate a particular argument by Canada. The Panel does not read this statement as implying that the residues of oestradiol-17β in meat from treated cattle are definitely genotoxic. However, even if this were the case, the issue of genotoxicity is only relevant to the issue of whether a threshold could be determined for this substance. Again, the Panel believes it has addressed this point with the additions and edits suggested above.

---

[275] Transcript of the Panel meeting with the experts, Annex G, para. 366.
[276] Transcript of the Panel meeting with the experts, Annex G, para. 393.

6.114 The European Communities also refers the Panel to various interventions by Dr. Cogliano at the Panel meeting with the experts, namely, paragraphs 400, 404, 406, 409, 870, and 1021-1025 of Annex G.[277] In paragraphs 400, 404, and 406 of Annex G, Dr. Cogliano provides the Panel with general background information on the issue of thresholds and linear dose response curves. The comments are not specific to the Opinions of the European Communities and therefore are not relevant to the analysis the Panel is undertaking in this particular section. Paragraph 409 of Annex G contains a question from the Chairman. The Panel is unsure whether the European Communities meant to refer to paragraph 408 or paragraph 410.[278] In any event, in both those paragraphs Dr. Cogliano provides general background information on what is meant by a linear dose response curve.

6.115 Dr. Cogliano, in paragraph 871 of Annex G[279], states that the data are not sufficient to conduct a "JECFA-style" risk assessment if oestradiol-17β has no threshold. The Panel finds this statement unremarkable for two reasons. First, the Panel is not evaluating whether the European Communities has done a "JECFA-style" risk assessment, but whether it has done a risk assessment consistent with the definition set forth in Annex A(4) of the *SPS Agreement*. Second, the European Communities has not argued that there is insufficient data to conduct a risk assessment of oestradiol-17β, it has argued that it has conducted a risk assessment of oestradiol-17β that is consistent with the *SPS Agreement*, that its measure is based on that risk assessment and that, consequently, it has acted consistently with Article 5.1 of the *SPS Agreement*. Dr. Cogliano's statement, in the paragraph cited by the European Communities, is not directly relevant in this context.

6.116 Paragraphs 1021 through 1025 of the transcript of the panel meeting with the experts report a discussion where both Drs. Boobis and Cogliano confirm that the fundamental difference between the JECFA study and the SCVPH Opinions is the willingness to assume a threshold and interpret the data from that standpoint. The Panel has now cited these interventions in the new paragraphs 7.465, 7.466 and 7.530.

6.117 In its comments on the interim report, the European Communities argues that if the Panel had properly looked at Dr. Cogliano's interventions in these

---

[277] EC's comments on interim report, paras. 56-58.

[278] Because the specific paragraph references by the European Communities in its comments on the interim report frequently tend to differ from the version in Annex G, the Panel believes that the European Communities must have prepared its interim comments with a different version of the transcript than the one contained in Annex G. In each instance of mistaken citation, the Panel has read the paragraphs in the transcript surrounding those cited by the European Communities to ensure that it has correctly identified and is responding to the concerns expressed by the European Communities.

[279] Paragraph 870 is the Chairman giving the floor to Dr. Cogliano.

paragraphs of the transcript the Panel would have had to conclude that the European Communities' risk assessment has followed one side of a legitimate debate while JECFA has followed another.[280] The European Communities seems to imply that if the Panel recognizes this it would also conclude that the European Communities' ban on the importation of meat and meat products from cattle treated with oestradiol-17β for growth promotion purposes was based on a risk assessment within the meaning of Article 5.1 and Annex A(4) of the *SPS Agreement*. The Panel does not see the issue in quite the same manner as the European Communities. The issue is not whether a risk assessment following the four steps as defined by Codex could or should have been completed. The issue is whether the European Communities has conducted a risk assessment within the meaning of Article 5.1 and Annex A(4) of the *SPS Agreement*.

6.118 The Panel does not take a position on the science or on how to evaluate data when a particular substance exhibits no threshold.[281] However, whatever approach the European Communities adopts in its assessment of the risks, it is obligated to conduct a risk assessment that is consistent with the definition set forth in Annex A(4) of the *SPS Agreement*. The Panel finds that the *SPS Agreement* requires an analysis that goes beyond the identification of a potential adverse effect. The analysis must include an examination of the potential for that adverse affect to come into being, originate, or result from the presence of the specific substance under review in food, beverages, or feedstuffs, in this case oestradiol-17β in meat and meat products derived from cattle treated with the hormone for growth promotion purposes. The Panel will not prescribe a particular manner or approach for how the analysis should be conducted, but the analysis must be conducted.

6.119 The intervention by Dr. Sippell in paragraph 576 of Annex G cited by the European Communities mentions a scientific study cited in the 1999 Opinion which posits that the radioimmuno assays originally used to calculate daily endogenous production levels of the hormones may have overestimated these levels. The Panel addressed this issue, by inserting in paragraph 7.535 quotations from the 1999 SCVPH Opinion on this issue directly, and a new paragraph 7.536.

6.120 Additionally, the Panel felt that more direct quotation from the Opinions with respect to the other identified potential adverse effects would provide greater clarity. Therefore, the Panel modified paragraphs 7.534 and 7.535.

---

[280] EC's comments on interim report, paras. 57-64.

[281] EC's comments on interim report, para. 78. Contrary to the assertion of the European Communities, the Panel does not endorse any one particular way to approach risk assessment.

6.121 The European Communities also refers to a statement by Dr. Boobis at paragraph 725 of Annex G.[282] The Panel has reviewed the surrounding paragraphs and found that, like Dr. Guttenplan, Dr. Boobis had engaged in an exchange with the European Communities about the concept of zero risk. Again, Dr. Boobis confirms that science cannot provide absolute assurance of the absence of risk or an absolute guarantee of safety. Dr. Boobis also states "it is not clear to me how you would ever conduct a risk assessment and guarantee that, without ensuring zero exposure, and of course that would cease all use of all compounds where there is any risk whatsoever, and they all have some risk."[283]

6.122 As with the citations to Dr. Guttenplan's statements at the meeting with the Panel, the Panel is unclear what the European Communities believes this reference to certain statements by Dr. Boobis will add to the Panel's reasoning on whether it conducted a risk assessment consistent with the definition set forth in Annex A(4) of the *SPS Agreement*. The Panel notes again that the purpose of a risk assessment is to evaluate the possibility that an identified adverse effect comes into being, originates, or results from the presence of the identified additives, contaminants, toxins or disease-causing organisms in food, beverages or feedstuffs, not to guarantee that said possibility will be below a Member's appropriate level of protection or indeed will be zero.[284]

6.123 The European Communities argues that in paragraphs 7.557 to 7.566 the Panel relies solely on the responses of Drs. Boobis and Boisseau and does not reflect the opinions of the other experts.[285]

6.124 The Panel notes that the relevant section is from paragraphs 7.552 to 7.572 and that the Panel cites Dr. Cogliano and Dr. Guttenplan in paragraph 7.568, and Dr. Guttenplan again in paragraph 7.569. Nevertheless, the Panel has examined the written answers of the other experts to the same questions of the Panel as well as the transcript of the Panel meeting with the experts and made additional references to experts' statements.

6.125 The European Communities argues that the Panel is in error in paragraph 7.570 when it states that the only study cited with respect to susceptible populations was one having to do with *in utero* exposure to DES, which is banned in the United States.[286] The Panel has reviewed the paragraphs in the 1999 Opinion referenced by the European Communities. Although the European Communities

---

[282] Paragraph 725 is an interjection by Canada. See transcript of the Panel meeting with the experts, Annex G, para. 725.
[283] Transcript of the Panel meeting with the experts, Annex G, paras. 723 and 729.
[284] The Panel notes that the Appellate Body in para 186 of its report on *EC – Hormones*, asked "if a risk is not ascertainable, how does a Member ever know or demonstrate that it exists?"
[285] EC's comments on interim report, footnote 11.
[286] *Ibid.*

is correct that other studies regarding susceptible populations are referenced in section 2.2.2.4 entitled "Potential adverse effects of exogenous sex hormones on growth and puberty upon exposure of prepubertal children," the Panel, in paragraph 7.570, was specifically referring to the link between *cancer* and consumption of hormone treated meat. With respect to that specific identified potential adverse effect, the only study mentioned in section 2.3.2.4 under susceptible populations with respect to oestrogen is one involving *in utero* exposure to DES. The Panel modified the third sentence of paragraph 7.570.

6.126 Additionally, based on the European Communities' comment, the Panel also reviewed the paragraphs in the interim report which dealt with Section 2.2.2.4 of the 1999 Opinion. In order to ensure that the Panel fully reflects the science the European Communities relied upon in this section, the Panel amended paragraph 7.533.

6.127 The European Communities argues with respect to paragraph 7.572 that because the Panel based its findings on the views expressed by the "most convincing" experts, the Panel has failed to make an objective assessment of the matter, failed to take properly into account the totality of the available evidence and failed to give proper weight to different scientific views which are based on genuine and legitimate scientific grounds. The European Communities also argues that the Panel's "most convincing" experts are the ones it had alleged had a conflict of interest.

6.128 The Panel bases its analysis in this section on its own reading of the plain language in the Opinions which was corroborated by the views expressed by the experts and this combination leads the Panel to its conclusions. Additionally, the Panel disagrees with the European Communities that it fails to examine the totality of the evidence or to give proper weight to particular scientific views. As the Panel notes, it does not disregard any of the statements by the experts. However, the Panel could not possibly provide full quotations of every answer or statement of every expert. The fact that the Panel may have cited specific passages from specific experts does not mean that the Panel did not consider and weigh all of the responses.

6.129 The Panel, after reading the Opinions, the experts' answers to questions, the transcript of the meeting with the experts, and the parties submissions and comments, made a determination about which experts had provided the Panel with answers that responded to the questions asked in a clear and consistent manner supported by expertise and evidence. This determination is the essence of weighing the evidence. As the Panel noted in paragraphs 7.552-7.572, the section to which paragraph 7.572 belongs, the Panel cited Dr. Boisseau, Dr. Boobis, Dr. Cogliano and Dr. Guttenplan. These are the experts who answered the relevant questions and who had identified expertise in risk assessment, toxicology, studies of carcinogens, and biochemistry.[287] The Panel regrets if it caused any confusion by using the phrase "most convincing" and accordingly clarified paragraph 7.572.

6.130 The European Communities fails to see why the Panel, after having concluded that there is no risk assessment, goes on to examine whether the science supports the conclusions in the Opinions and asks for more explanation than previously provided for. The Panel modified paragraph 7.538 in order to provide additional explanation.

(v) Comments on the Panel analysis regarding the other five hormonal substances

6.131 The European Communities argues that paragraph 7.605 is unclear and seems irrelevant for the further analysis of the Panel. The European Communities first argues that, in its oral statement, it spoke about whether a risk assessment can reach a definitive conclusion, not whether or not it is possible to perform a definitive risk assessment. First, the Panel recalls that the EC reference to a "definitive risk assessment" is found in the EC second written submission.[288] Second, the Panel does not see any real difference between "reach[ing] a definitive conclusion" and making a "definitive risk assessment". Its reasoning in paragraph 7.605 thus applies equally to both statements.

6.132 Second, the European Communities considers that the Panel should have referred to what the experts said at the hearing about the issue of whether scientific data can ever allow for a definitive conclusion to be reached. This seems to suggest that the European Communities no longer argues that what matters in order to justify the application of Article 5.7 is whether a definitive conclusion can be reached or whether a definitive risk assessment can be made. If this is correct, the Panel does not believe that it is entitled to address new arguments at the interim review stage. The Panel nevertheless reviewed the comments of Dr. Cogliano referred to by the European Communities. In paragraph 776 of Annex G, Dr. Cogliano suggests that there can be different types of risk assessments, depending on the specificity of the risk one wishes to identify. The Panel fails to see in what respect this statement affects its finding in paragraph 7.605. As recalled by the Panel in its findings[289], the type of risk assessment requested under Article 5.1 is a risk assessment within the meaning of Annex A(4) of the *SPS Agreement*, which is not one of the types of risk assessment identified by Dr. Cogliano. It is in the context of the completion of a risk assessment within

---

[287] Transcript of the Panel meeting with the experts, Annex G, paras. 54-72.
[288] *Inter alia* in paras. 137, 143, 149, 153, 176 and 183.
[289] See paras. 7.443-7.444.

the meaning of Article 5.1 and Annex A(4) of the *SPS Agreement* that the Panel discussed the EC argument regarding a "definitive risk assessment" or a "risk assessment reach[ing] a definitive conclusion". The other comment of Dr. Cogliano referred to by the European Communities[290] suggests that data may be sufficient to do one type of risk assessment (e.g. "the JECFA-style ADI") but not one based on a theory according to which it is not possible to identify a dose below which there is no risk, because there is a risk at any dose level, even the low doses one might find in hormone-treated meat. The Panel notes in this regard that this is different from arguing that one should be able to invoke Article 5.7 because one cannot make a "definitive risk assessment". As mentioned by the Panel, the Appellate Body in *Japan – Apples* did not say that relevant scientific evidence would become insufficient if a Member could not perform a particular type of risk assessment, but only if it would be unable to perform a risk assessment within the meaning of Article 5.1 and Annex A(4) of the *SPS Agreement*.

6.133 Having also regard to the comments of the United States of 19 October 2007, the Panel did not deem it necessary to delete or modify paragraph 7.605.

6.134 The European Communities makes a general reference to its second written submission and takes issue with the assessment of the Panel in paragraphs 7.649 to 7.721 by stating that the Panel did not properly and fully examine the reasons contained in the Opinions and relied exclusively on certain statements of a minority of the experts it had chosen to advise it, while ignoring pertinent statements of the other experts. The Panel notes that it addressed the EC comments on its findings where they were directed at precise aspects of the interim report. This was the case regarding comments on the Panel's reliance on the views expressed by some of the experts it consulted and for comments regarding the existence of sufficient relevant scientific evidence. The Panel does not deem it necessary to address those issues in general terms here.

6.135 The European Communities finds the Panel reference to a risk assessment "in substance" in paragraph 7.628 to be "entirely unclear". In the opinion of the Panel, one can always follow each of the Codex steps provided for the gathering and analysis of scientific evidence. However, in order to be a risk assessment within the meaning of Article 5.1, that exercise must reach scientific conclusions that are supported by the scientific evidence therein.[291] Thus, the possibility to complete a risk assessment depends on whether the relevant scientific evidence is sufficient to support a conclusion on whether the identified adverse effect arises from, comes into being, or occurs as a result of the presence of the substance at issue in food, beverages, or feedstuffs.

---

[290] Annex G, para. 871.
[291] Panel Report on *Japan – Apples (Article 21.5 – US)*, para. 8.136.

6.136 The European Communities seems to suggest, in substance, that whether a risk assessment can be completed depends on the level of protection chosen by a given Member. The European Communities seems to link the conduct of the risk assessment with the desired outcome of a given SPS measure; i.e., to ensure zero risk. The Panel believes that this is not what the *SPS Agreement* requires. The Panel considers that the European Communities' interpretation is not supported by the text of Article 5.7, which only refers to the insufficiency of relevant scientific evidence. There is no indication that this insufficiency is to be assessed in relation to the Member's level of protection. Otherwise the negotiators would have stated "in cases where relevant scientific evidence is insufficient in the light of the level of protection chosen by the Member adopting of maintaining a sanitary measure". Nothing in the context of Article 5.7 suggests this interpretation either. Articles 2.2, 3.3 and 5.1 provide relevant contextual support for the proposition that the purpose of the *SPS Agreement* was to ensure that Member's SPS measures are "objectively justified"[292] by science. This purpose would be defeated if a Member could invoke Article 5.7 whenever relevant scientific evidence is insufficient to objectively justify the type of measure that would achieve a particular desired level of protection. The Panel modified paragraph 7.628 in order to clarify what it meant.

6.137 Regarding paragraphs 7.630 to 7.637, the European Communities argues that the Panel's discussion does not do justice to the role genuine scientific uncertainty plays in risk assessment. It contests the Panel's exclusive reliance on the opinions of Dr. Boisseau and Dr. Boobis and refers to statements by experts other than those quoted by the Panel. As far as the Panel's reliance on Dr. Boisseau and Dr. Boobis is concerned, it should be recalled that this is a risk assessment issue and these two scientists were selected by the Panel *inter alia* because of their expertise on risk assessment. Yet, Dr. Boisseau and Dr. Boobis were not the only ones with the same view. Dr. Tritscher's remarks on the subject also support the Panel's conclusion.[293]

6.138 None of the interventions of experts cited by the European Communities in its comments contradicts the conclusions reached by the Panel in its interim report, which are clearly spelled out in paragraph 7.637. More particularly, none of Dr. Cogliano's statements cited by the European Communities contradicts the Panel. In the paragraphs cited by the European Communities, Dr. Cogliano mainly explains the role of IARC and whether there is uncertainly about genotoxicity. Similarly, in the paragraphs cited by the European Communities, Dr. Guttenplan says that there is uncertainty about certain scientific issues, but he does not address the role of uncertainty in risk assessment. Dr. Sippell addresses an issue unrelated to risk assessment. Dr. De Brabander addresses the

---

[292] Appellate Body Report on *EC – Hormones*, para. 190.
[293] Annex G, para. 348.

quality of data and improved methods. Regarding the alleged misinterpretation of some of the statements of Dr. Boobis on the existence or not of genuine scientific uncertainty, it seems that the paragraph referred to by the European Communities (Annex G, paragraph 1049) deals with a different issue: that of scientific uncertainty in relation to U-shaped dose-response curves, not how scientific uncertainty is treated in risk assessment.

6.139 The European Communities argues, with respect to paragraph 7.644, that the risk assessments performed by JECFA do not contain the specific evidence that the Panel allegedly found to be missing in the EC Opinions and, therefore, cannot constitute proper risk assessments. The Panel notes that there is no reference to the JECFA risk assessment of oestradiol-17β in the Panel's analysis of the consistency of the European Communities' permanent ban on meat and meat products derived from cattle treated with oestradiol-17β for growth promotion purposes, because the European Communities claimed that it completed its own risk assessment for oestradiol-17β. The Panel thus conducted an analysis of the SCVPH Opinions and sought to determine whether they complied with the definition of a risk assessment in Annex A(4) and whether the science contained therein supported the European Communities' decision to institute a total ban. Unlike the analysis under Article 5.7, with respect to oestradiol-17β the Panel was not trying to determine whether there was sufficient scientific information to conduct a risk assessment. The Panel recalls that the fault it found with the Opinions was not that any particular piece of evidence was missing, but rather that the Opinions did not specifically analyse the risk of the identified adverse effects *arising from* the presence of oestradiol-17β in food, beverages, or feedstuffs. Therefore, whether JECFA relied on the same evidence as the European Communities in its analysis of oestradiol-17β is irrelevant. The Panel notes that JECFA did take into account the dose levels in meat and meat products and attempted to calculate the risk to humans from consuming typical amounts of meat. JECFA used a series of assumptions regarding meat consumption, circulating levels of oestrogen in the blood for various sub-groups of the population, etc. The European Communities may very well be right that there are other ways to analyse the risk than those JECFA utilized. The Panel does not take a position on that issue. What the Panel has said, is that such an analysis is required by Article 5.1 and Annex A(4) of the *SPS Agreement*.

6.140 With respect to the Panel's reference to the concept of "critical mass" in paragraph 7.648, the European Communities request that we provide an explanation of where this criterion comes from and whether it is in conformity with the findings of the Appellate Body in *EC – Hormones*.

6.141 The Panel used the term "critical mass" in full knowledge of its meaning.[294] It used it in the sense of a situation where evidence becomes quantitatively and qualitatively sufficient to call into question the fundamental precepts of previous knowledge and evidence. The Panel does not mean that there must be sufficient evidence to perform a new risk assessment. Otherwise, Article 5.7 of the *SPS Agreement* would become meaningless. It used the term "critical mass" very much in its common scientific usage, i.e. the new scientific information and evidence must be such that they are *at the origin* of a change in the understanding of a scientific issue. We do not see in what respect this approach by the Panel, which applies to the specific situation in this case (i.e. one where a party alleges that previously sufficient scientific evidence has become insufficient) would be contrary to the findings of the Appellate Body in *EC – Hormones*.

6.142 The United States suggests in its counter-comments[295] that the Panel consider using the term "weight of evidence" to explain its use of the "critical mass" criterion in conducting its analysis and reaching its conclusions. The United States adds that the weight of evidence approach is standard in science. Weight of evidence is explained by the experts primarily in paragraphs 487, 489, 493, 501 of Annex G. At the experts' hearing, Dr. Boobis defined weight of evidence as:

> "[T]he evaluation of the available information about a particular toxicological endpoint taking into account factors such as the adequacy and number of available studies and the consistency of results across studies. It is not an issue of seeking to weigh one person's opinion against another." (para. 487)

and:

> "This is not a question of what people think and minority opinions, it is a question of looking at the data ... There is an element of interpretation of the quality of the study, I accept, but that is why you have experts on the evaluation committee." (para. 501)

6.143 From the above it may be concluded that weight of evidence is in the first instance concerned with the quality of studies. "Badly done" studies are ex-

---

[294] In mathematics and physics "critical" is defined as "constituting or relating to a point of transition from one state, etc. to another". "Critical size" or "critical mass" are defined as the minimum size or mass of a body of a given fissile material which is capable of sustaining a nuclear chain reaction (Shorter Oxford English Dictionary, 5th edition (1993), p. 558). In other words, the Panel assessed whether it had been provided with the minimum evidence necessary to conclude that knowledge has become quantitatively and qualitatively sufficient to call into question the fundamental precepts of previous knowledge and evidence.
[295] At para. 28.

cluded so that the evaluation is based only on studies that are "well done" i.e. studies carefully carried out using validated methods. In a second stage, an assessor taking a weight of the evidence approach looks at the number of studies and the consistency of results across studies. If one follows Dr. Boobis, in particular his comment in paragraph 501 of the transcript (Annex G), the weight of the evidence approach may contradict the views of the Appellate Body in paragraph 194 of its report in *EC – Hormones* because it would favour the "mainstream" scientific opinion, whereas the Appellate Body accepted that an SPS measure may be based on a "divergent opinion coming from qualified and respected sources" and still be in compliance with the substantive obligations of the *SPS Agreement*. This is why we do not wish to replace the terms "critical mass" used in our report with "weight of evidence". In our view, a "critical mass" of scientific evidence and information could be small and may include situations where the weight of the evidence has not shifted away from the existing prevailing knowledge, but where the new knowledge is qualitatively and quantitatively sufficient to create a situation where a Member can legitimately decide that the pre-existing scientific evidence is no longer sufficient to complete a risk assessment within the meaning of Article 5.1 and Annex A(4) of the *SPS Agreement*.

6.144 The European Communities takes issue with paragraph 7.662. The European Communities contests the Panel's approach in defining a list of general issues common to all five hormones. The European Communities argues that it has identified exactly, for each hormonal substance, the sections in the 1999 Opinion that deals individually with that substance and suggests that the Panel's list of "general issues" common to all five hormones is arbitrary.

6.145 The Panel first recalls that, as a general principle, panels are free to structure the order of their analysis as they see fit.[296] The Panel does not deny that the EC Opinions addressed each hormone individually. However, as explained in paragraphs 7.660 to 7.662, some issues were common to all five hormones and the evidence provided was not always sufficiently specific to address a particular issue in relation to each hormone individually. The Panel modified paragraph 7.652 to 7.663 and the title to Section VII.C.3.(f)(vi) to reflect the fact that what is discussed are issues common to all hormones for which hormone-specific evidence was not provided.

6.146 The Panel also clarified that certain insufficiencies identified in the EC Opinions had not as such been discussed by the European Communities in its submissions. The Panel concluded that the European Communities was not arguing that these particular insufficiencies were what made it impossible to complete a risk assessment. Therefore, the Panel decided not to address these insuffi-

---

[296] Appellate Body Report on *Canada – Wheat Exports and Grain Imports*, para. 126.

ciencies. This may have prompted the EC comment that the Panel analysis on the individual hormonal substances in paragraphs 7.722 to 7.830 was incomplete. The clarification brought by the Panel demonstrates that it did not draw a random list of issues common to all hormones and explains the reasons why a more limited number of issues was discussed compared with what had been identified in the Opinions. The Panel has also clarified this point in the sections relating to each hormone individually and did not follow the request of the European Communities that it address each and every issue of insufficiency raised in the Opinions.[297]

6.147 The European Communities contests the conclusions of the Panel in paragraph 7.665, footnote 792 as inaccurate, but without specifying why. In that footnote, the Panel refers to a new method and new assays to detect small amounts of hormones in meat, mentioned in the 2002 Opinion. From what is mentioned in the 2002 Opinion, the studies were on the subject of hormone levels in meat, not in people. Whereas it might be possible to apply these method and assays to detect endogenous levels of hormones in humans, the European Communities does not argue this in its comments, and this is not what the method and assays are about. It also appears that, according to the 2002 Opinion, the method and assays mentioned were not exactly successful or trustworthy. The conclusion in section 4.1.1 of the 2002 Opinion, where the new method is discussed, reads: "[D]espite a number of positive analytical results in this study, the low number of samples does not allow a qualified validation of typical characteristics such as sensitivity, specificity, accuracy and reproductibility." (2002 Opinion, page 9). The conclusion of section 4.1.2, where the bioassays are discussed, is that: "[T]he obtained results suggest that the use of recombinant yeast and rainbow trout hepatocytes to detect oestrogenic compounds is not justified in view of their lack of sensitivity". (2002 Opinion, page 9). It seems that, even if they were relevant in the context of paragraph 7.665, this new method and assays do not contribute to a critical mass of evidence that would put into question existing knowledge. The Panel, therefore, did not modify footnote 792.

6.148 With respect to paragraphs 7.667 to 7.670, the European Communities argues that the Panel reduces the discussion to only two quotations and draws a conclusion that is not based on the debate with the experts at the hearing. The European Communities argues that "much more was said about this issue" at that hearing.[298] The Panel notes, however, that the discussion related to the sensitivity of children to hormones in general, without drawing any direct link with any of the five hormones at issue in this section, and to the validation of methods, particularly of the new ultrasensitive assay (the "Klein" methodology). The only hormone expressly discussed in relation to this assay was oestradiol-17β. The

---

[297] EC's comments on Sections VII.C.3(f)(vii), (viii), (ix), (x), (xi).
[298] Annex G, para. 561 *et seq.*

Panel notes that it concludes in this section that (a) the studies using the new ultrasensitive assay were limited to oestradiol-17β; and (b) that the ultrasensitive assay had not been validated. Thus, the Panel does not agree with the European Communities that its conclusions are not based on the debate referred to above.

6.149 The European Communities requests that we clarify the first sentence in paragraph 7.670. More particularly, the European Communities requests that we specify whether this is a legal argument or a scientific argument. The Panel considers that the finding that the evidence relates only to oestradiol is not an argument but a factual consideration. The Panel considers that, since the new detection method measured oestradiol only[299] and since no evidence was provided that suggested that extrapolation had been made or could be made to other hormones, the evidence is insufficient to conclude, with respect to the five hormones subject to a provisional ban under Article 5.7 of the *SPS Agreement*, that existing knowledge has been put into question.

6.150 With respect to the EC comment on the second sentence of paragraph 7.670, the Panel confirms that, indeed, its understanding is that the ultrasensitive detection method used by Klein and subsequently relates only to oestradiol and has not been validated. This has been confirmed by Dr. Boobis at the hearing.[300] As a result, the Panel cannot conclude that existing knowledge and evidence have been put into question by the results of the ultrasensitive assay with regard to the impact of the five hormones on prepubertal children if the available evidence relates only to oestradiol.

6.151 Even if the ultrasensitive assay had been validated and had demonstrated lower levels of the five hormones at issue in this section – and not only oestradiol – in sensitive populations, the Panel notes that the 1999 Opinion itself states that "[A] corollary is that perhaps the hormones residues in beef, which are also low and which have also been determined by RIA are equally variable and over representative of the actual hormone concentrations."[301]

6.152 In its comments regarding paragraphs 7.672-7.675 the European Communities considers that the Panel's approach to the issue of dose response is flawed and circular.

6.153 The European Communities bases its contention that the Panel's reasoning is circular on the assumption that the Panel rejected the EC approach based on an absence of a dose response analysis. Even though it rejected that approach in this particular case for oestradiol-17β, the Panel did not exclude that there

---

[299] See para. 7.668 quoting Dr. Sippell. See, also, Dr. Sippell's statement in Annex G, para. 588.
[300] Annex G, para. 572.
[301] 1999 Opinion, section 3.2, p. 30.

could be situations where dose response would not apply. The Panel believes, on the contrary, that it is the European Communities that is making contradictory arguments. The European Communities cannot argue that "the Appellate Body clearly judged that a risk assessment [could] be either qualitative or quantitative"[302] and that a dose response is not *required* in order to complete a risk assessment and, at the same time, argue for the five hormones at issue that relevant scientific evidence is insufficient to perform a risk assessment because the data available do not allow a dose response assessment. Yet, this is what appears to be concluded in the 1999 Opinion as far as the five hormones are concerned. The Panel nonetheless clarified the paragraphs at issue.

6.154 The European Communities argues that, in paragraph 7.677, the Panel declines to discuss bioavailability on the basis that the studies relied upon by the European Communities do not relate to the five hormones in question, but only to oestradiol and that there is no indication that the conclusions can be applied to hormones other than oestrogens. The European Communities considers that this assertion by the Panel is without foundation.

6.155 In order to reach its conclusion, the Panel examined most particularly the portions of the 1999 and 2002 Opinions quoted by the European Communities in its reply to question 28 of the questions of the Panel after the first substantive meeting[303] and in its second written submission.[304] The two extracts quoted by the European Communities address only oestradiol, while making references to oestrogens. Furthermore, the extract of the 1999 Opinion quoted by the European Communities is part of the section of the Opinion regarding oestradiol. The Panel notes that the European Communities argued that "similar findings [had been] made for all the other five hormones".[305] However, the European Communities did not specify where such findings had been made. This allegation has to be considered in relation to the comments of the experts. The Panel nonetheless deemed it necessary to clarify the section on bioavailability.

6.156 In its comments on the interim report, the European Communities also refers to the experts' replies to question 43. The Panel first notes that this question concerns bioavailability in general, not the sufficiency of evidence regarding bioavailability. The Panel has included quotations of the relevant passages of the experts' replies in its findings. The European Communities also refers to paragraphs 132 *et seq.* of the transcript of the hearing (Annex G). The Panel reviewed the comments of the experts on bioavailability and found that those

---

[302] See EC reply to question 26 of the first series of questions of the Panel, para. 153, Annex B; see also EC's second written submission, paras. 196-200.
[303] Annex B-1, paras. 155-159.
[304] Paras. 133-176.
[305] EC reply to question 28 of the questions of the Panel after the first substantive meeting, Annex B-1, para. 158.

comments address neither the bioavailability of the five hormones at issue, nor the sufficiency or insufficiency of evidence on it.

6.157 With respect to paragraphs 7.685 to 7.700, the European Communities argues first that the discussion on long latency of cancer and confounding factors should have been in the Panel's analysis under Article 5.1 of the *SPS Agreement*. We note that the Panel addressed this question to the extent this was necessary for its analysis under Article 5.1. The question of the latency period of cancer and of the epidemiological survey of the occurrence of cancer in various populations was addressed in paragraphs 7.567 *et seq.* The Panel also deemed it necessary to address the latency of cancer in its section under Article 5.7 because the European Communities argued that the long latency period of cancer made it impossible to demonstrate positively the existence of clear harm in relation to the hormones at issue. The Panel first determined whether long latency of cancer was relevant for the performance of a risk assessment for the hormones at issue. It then proceeded to determine whether relevant scientific evidence in relation to the latency of cancer was insufficient to the point of making it impossible to perform a risk assessment within the meaning of Article 5.1 and Annex A(4) of the *SPS Agreement*. In order to do this, it assessed whether it could be considered that a "critical mass" of new information or evidence was now available which could unsettle the way long latency of cancer has been taken into account in risk assessment so far. The Panel clarified the part of Section VII.C.3.(f)(vi) dealing with long latency of cancer and confounding factors in order to better present its analysis.

6.158 The European Communities also argues that the section on long latency of cancer and confounding factors is evidence that we applied a "double standard" of evidence for the removal as compared to the approval of the hormones at issue. We did not argue that JECFA or the respondent performed the epidemiological studies necessary to demonstrate an absence of long term effect of the hormones at issue in terms of cancer. We note that the long latency of cancer has been acknowledged. We also note that confounding factors make it difficult to assign a particular cancer to specific circumstances of ingestion of hormone residues. We recall that JECFA's risk assessments take into account the long latency of cancer through the ADI. To the extent that the European Communities disagrees with the approach followed by JECFA, it is for the European Communities to provide a "critical mass" of evidence – not a "positive evidence" – that this approach is no longer valid.[306] We conclude that, in these proceedings, the European Communities has not pointed at evidence suggesting that long latency of cancer has not been appropriately taken into account in existing risk assessments.

---

[306] In this respect, the Panel inserted a footnote in para. 7.648 to address the EC argument on standard of proof.

6.159 The European Communities also takes issue with the Panel's discussion on the immunological effect of the five hormones in paragraphs 7.701 to 7.708. The European Communities seems to raise two issues in its comments. The first one is related to the question of whether a threshold approach must be followed. The second one is whether the Panel dismissed the EC arguments on the basis that the scientific evidence relates to oestrogens only.

6.160 Regarding the first issue, the Panel notes that all three experts who answered question 59[307] stated that there is no evidence of effects on the immune system from doses such as those resulting from consumption of meat from treated animals. If the point the European Communities wishes to make in its comments is that the approach based on a "threshold" is not required to assess the effect of the five hormones at issue on the immune system, then the Panel fails to understand why, under those circumstances, the relevant scientific evidence on the effect of the five hormones on the immune system is insufficient for the European Communities to perform a risk assessment for those hormones.

6.161 With respect to the second issue, the Panel notes that Dr. Boobis and Dr. Guttenplan address the effect of oestrogen/oestradiol on the immune system (Dr. Boobis refers to "hormones such as oestradiol"). As the Panel mentions in paragraph 7.704, the main reason for dismissing the EC arguments on insufficiency of evidence regarding the effect of hormones on the immune system is the fact that the evidence made available to the Panel relates exclusively to the effect of oestrogens. The European Communities has not identified any evidence that specifically addresses any of the five hormones at issue in this section. The European Communities has not explained either to the Panel why it thinks the evidence on oestrogens would be relevant for the other hormones. The Panel notes in this respect that the Opinions do not identify any evidence with respect to the five hormones that residue levels in meat might have an effect on the immune system. The Panel nonetheless clarified paragraphs 7.706-7.707.

6.162 Regarding paragraphs 7.709 to 7.721, the European Communities argues that the Panel quotes Dr. Sippell as identifying adverse effects, but does not discuss his statement. The European Communities adds that there is also no discussion of the other experts' views put forward at the hearing.

6.163 Regarding Dr. Sippell's statement in paragraph 7.714, the Panel has further discussed the points raised by the experts on this matter in paragraphs 7.715 through 7.721.

6.164 With respect to paragraphs 7.700 to 7.713 of the interim report, the European Communities argues that the Panel's discussion of the potential misuse and

---

[307] Annex D, paras. 443-448.

abuse in the administration of hormones is in the wrong place, to the extent that this is an aspect of risk assessment, in the sense of Article 5.1 to 5.3 of the *SPS Agreement*, that is applicable across all identified potential risks and for all six hormones. The Panel agrees with the European Communities that the question of misuse and abuse in the administration of hormones may apply to all six hormones at issue and is an element that can be taken into account in risk assessment, as set forth in Article 5.2 of the *SPS Agreement* and confirmed by the Appellate Body in *EC – Hormones*. However, the Panel did not deem it necessary to address this question in the section regarding the conformity with Article 5.1 of the definitive ban on oestradiol-17β, to the extent that the question whether misuse or abuse exists in the administration of hormones did not have an impact on the issues addressed by the Panel under Article 5.1.[308] Indeed, the question of misuse or abuse in the administration of hormones is relevant to the extent that it can lead to higher concentrations of hormone residues in meat and meat products than would occur if good veterinary practices were applied. As stated by the 1999 Opinion, it is an aspect of exposure assessment. In this case, the Panel found that the European Communities had not evaluated specifically the possibility that the adverse effect that it had identified in its risk assessment come into being, originate, or result from the consumption of meat or meat products which contain veterinary residues of oestradiol-17β as a result of the cattle being treated with this hormone for growth promotion purposes. Therefore, whether the concentrations of hormone residues in meat and meat products could be higher as a result of misuse or abuse did not have to be addressed. The Panel does not deem it necessary to move this section to another part of its findings.

6.165 Having regard to the point made by the European Communities that misuse and abuse in the administration of hormones is an aspect of risk assessment within the meaning of Article 5.1 to 5.3, the Panel reflected further on whether this issue related at all to the question of insufficiency of relevant scientific evidence under Article 5.7. In the view of the Panel, the question of whether JECFA properly took into account misuse and abuse in its risk assessments is irrelevant to the question whether the European Communities can take this matter into account in its own risk assessment, since it has full discretion to do so pursuant Article 5.2 and to the Appellate Body finding in *EC – Hormones*. In that context, whether evidence exists of misuse or abuse in the administration of hormones is not as such a scientific issue likely to make a risk assessment within the meaning of Article 5.1 and Annex A(4) of the *SPS Agreement* impossible.

6.166 For these reasons, the Panel decided to delete the section regarding misuse or abuse in the administration of hormones from its final report and modified paragraph 7.603.

---

[308] It is nonetheless discussed in para. 7.483, in relation to Article 5.2 of the *SPS Agreement*.

6.167   The European Communities argues that the Panel's analysis on the issue of carcinogenicity of progesterone in Section VII.C.3(f)(vii) is flawed. However, the European Communities does not explain specifically in what respect it is flawed. The Panel therefore did not modify its reasoning.

6.168   The European Communities argues that the Panel's analysis on the issue of carcinogenicity and genotoxicity of testosterone in Section VII.C.3(f)(viii) is clearly incorrect and flawed. The European Communities refers to a statement by Dr. Tritscher allegedly admitting that JECFA found that there was scientific uncertainty about genotoxicity of testosterone.[309] The Panel consulted the transcript and noted that Dr. Tritcher discussed the genotoxicity of oestradiol, not that of testosterone. She did say that "all information is being looked at, in particular with compounds that have a genotoxic potential", but she did not mention that progesterone had a genotoxic potential.

6.169   The European Communities argues that the approach and analysis of the Panel on the issue of metabolism and carcinogenicity of trenbolone acetate in Section VII.C.3(f)(ix) is flawed, *inter alia*, because JECFA's assessment defended by Dr. Boobis and Dr. Boisseau dates back to 1988 and is clearly outdated. The Panel has already discussed this argument and considers that a risk assessment does not become invalid merely because it is "old". The Panel believes that, in order to demonstrate that a risk assessment is "outdated", a party must provide studies showing that the data on which the risk assessment is based are no longer valid.

6.170   The European Communities argues that the reasoning of the Panel regarding carcinogenicity of zeranol is flawed, *inter alia*, because if the extrapolation to meat consumption mentioned by Dr. Guttenplan was necessary, as the Panel seems to require in paragraph 7.799, this would have amounted to a complete risk assessment in the sense of Article 5.1 of the *SPS Agreement*. The European Communities argues that this is not the relevant standard in the context of Article 5.7. We agree with the European Communities that being able to perform a risk assessment compatible with Article 5.1 is not the standard applicable in the context of Article 5.7 and we do not consider that we applied any such standard in this case. Indeed, the reason why the Panel paraphrased Dr. Guttenplan's statement was not to say that the European Communities could demonstrate that relevant scientific evidence was insufficient only if it were able to extrapolate some genotoxic effect of zeranol to meat consumption. The point that the Panel wanted to make was that the extrapolation of the study commented by Dr. Guttenplan would have entailed, according to Dr. Guttenplan, a "myriad of uncertainties". As a result, this study could hardly serve as a basis to put in question existing knowledge. We clarified this in paragraph 7.799.

---

[309]   Statement of Dr. Tritcher, Annex G, para. 463.

6.171 As regards the alleged application of a similar standard in paragraphs 7.803-7.804, the Panel recalls that what has to be demonstrated for Article 5.7 to apply is that no risk assessment within the meaning of Article 5.1 and Annex A(4) of the *SPS Agreement* can be performed. Our reference to Dr. Guttenplan means that we consider, as mentioned in paragraph 7.637, that not just any form of scientific uncertainty can justify a recourse to Article 5.7. As previously noted, we consider that when scientific evidence has been sufficient, it may only be considered as insufficient if a critical mass of scientific information and evidence exists, in terms of quantity and quality, to put into question existing knowledge and evidence. We therefore did not consider it necessary to modify our reasoning.

6.172 In paragraph 7.812, the European Communities expresses its disagreement with the Panel's approach consisting of applying a presumption of conformity with the *SPS Agreement* to JECFA's risk assessment on melengestrol acetate (MGA), even though that risk assessment has not yet been endorsed by Codex. The Panel has explained in paragraph 7.813 why some degree of relevance should be given to JECFA's work, even though it is not formally a "standard, guideline or recommendation" within the meaning of Article 3.2 of the *SPS Agreement*. The Panel also notes that the European Communities does not specify in which respect the Panel's analysis of the issue of the residue data used by JECFA on carcinogenicity is flawed, except for suggesting that the residue data is "outdated", a question already addressed by the Panel in paragraphs 7.814 to 7.817.

6.173 Finally, the European Communities requests the Panel to clarify the meaning and extent of its conclusion in paragraph 7.837. This paragraph simply states that, because relevant scientific evidence is not insufficient, the European Communities cannot invoke Article 5.7. The corollary is that the European Communities should be able to complete a risk assessment under Article 5.1. The European Communities argues that the Panel should clarify further how the risk assessment could be completed in the presence of the gaps identified in the EC Opinions with respect to oestradiol-17β. The gaps identified in the EC Opinions for oestradiol-17β are:

    (a)   that the European Communities has not evaluated specifically the possibility of the adverse effects related to the association between excess hormones and neurobiological, developmental, reproductive and immunological effects, as well as immunotoxicity, genotoxicity and carcinogenicity coming into being, originating or resulting from the consumption of meat or meat products which contain veterinary residues of oestradiol-17β as a result of the cattle being treated with this hormone for growth promotion purposes;

(b)   The scientific evidence referred to in the Opinions does not support the European Communities' conclusions on genotoxicity, or the conclusion that the presence of residues of oestradiol-17β in meat and meat products as a result of cattle being treated with the hormone for growth promotion purposes leads to increased cancer risk. The scientific evidence does not support the EC conclusions on the adverse immunological and developmental effects of consuming meat and meat products from cattle treated with oestradiol-17β for growth promotion purposes.

6.174 Thus, the problems identified by the Panel are not related to the the fact that a risk assessment cannot be performed, but rather that the European Communities did not conduct a risk assessment pursuant to Article 5.1 and Annex A(4) and that the scientific evidence did not support the conclusions which the European Communities reached. The European Communities' comment apparently underlines an approach to risk assessment that seems to consist of identifying a risk from a particular substance and if there is any possibility, no matter how remote, of that risk occurring because of that substance, deciding that there is no need to further study whether the risk could arise from the levels of that substance found in food, beverages, or feedstuffs. As discussed in paragraph 6.112 above, the purpose of a risk assessment under Article 5.1 and Annex A(4) is not to provide guarantees that risks will be below a particular appropriate level of protection or even zero, but to objectively determine the possibility for the risk to arise from the presence of the substance under review in food, beverages, or feedstuffs. The Panel therefore, does not believe that the European Communities' approach to risk assessment, whereby the desired level of protection informs the risk assessment rather than the risk assessment providing objective data to be utilized by a government in determining how to achieve its appropriate level of protection, is consistent with the object and purpose of Article 5 of the *SPS Agreement.*

(b)   Comments by the United States

6.175 The United States observes that the EC Opinions to which the Panel refers in the first sentence of paragraph 7.482 address bioavailability and susceptibility of sensitive populations, but not *in vivo* repair mechanisms. The United States refers the Panel to paragraph 46 of its second written submission, where it noted that the Opinions ignore the scientific evidence relating to human *in vivo* DNA repair mechanisms. Therefore, the United States requests that the Panel strike the phrase "and *in vivo* repair mechanisms" from the first sentence of paragraph 7.482.[310]

---

[310]   US's comments on interim report, p. 7.

6.176 The Panel has reviewed paragraph 46 of the US second written submission as well as the Opinions themselves and has found that the United States is correct that the SCVPH Opinions do not mention the phrase "*in vivo* repair mechanisms". However, as also noted by the European Communities in its comments of 19 October 2007, they do contain reviews of data on DNA adducts and DNA damage and the Panel maintains its conclusion that the European Communities did not ignore the scientific evidence with respect to the effects of oestradiol-17β on DNA. Therefore, the Panel clarified paragraph 7.482 accordingly.

6.177 The United States also suggests that the Panel change the phrase "general risk" in paragraph 7.537 as it may be confusing to the reader, because the Panel has carefully defined "risk", but has not defined "general risk".[311] The European Communities, in its comments of 19 October 2007[312], argues that the Appellate Body has already found, in *EC – Hormones*, that the EC risk assessment at that time had indeed shown the "existence of a general risk of cancer".[313]

6.178 The United States' point about avoiding confusion in terminology is well taken. The Panel accordingly modified paragraph 7.537. However, the Panel will not use the term "identified the hazard" as this too has very specific meanings as set forth in the Codex Procedural Manual and cited in paragraph 7.448. Instead, it will modify paragraph 7.537 to read:

> "All of the statements of the experts, and indeed statements from the Opinions, indicate that the European Communities has evaluated the potential for the identified adverse effects to be associated with oestrogens in general, but has not provided analysis of the potential for these effects to arise from consumption of meat and meat products which contain residues of oestradiol-17β as a result of the cattle they are derived from being treated with the hormone for growth promotion purposes."

6.179 The Panel also considers this correction to be in line with the finding of the Appellate Body in paragraph 200 of its report on *EC – Hormones* referred to above by the European Communities.

6.180 When necessary, the Panel also made a number of minor editorial or typographical corrections suggested by the United States. However, the Panel refrained from making the changes suggested in two instances. With respect to the correction suggested in paragraph 4.234, the Panel refers to paragraph 6.12

---

[311] US's comments on interim report, p. 8.
[312] Para. 23.
[313] Appellate Body Report on *EC – Hormones*, para. 200.

above. With respect to another correction suggested by the United States but opposed by the European Communities (in paragraph 7.566), the Panel decided not to modify the existing sentence to the extent that it paraphrased a statement of Dr. Boobis. The European Communities objected to any change by arguing that it did not know what Dr. Boobis had actually said since it did not have access to the tape recording of the hearing with the experts. The Panel notes, however, that the statement at issue comes from the written reply of Dr. Boobis to question 22 of the Panel, Annex D, paragraph 202.

VII.   FINDINGS

A.   Procedural Issues

1.   Opening of the Panel meetings with the parties and experts for public observation

(a)   Introduction

7.1   On 13 June 2005, at the first organizational meeting of the Panel, the parties jointly requested that the Panel's substantive meetings with parties be open for public observation. Through written questions, the Panel requested the parties to specify the legal basis in the DSU for such a request. Parties replied on 20 June 2005. On 30 June 2005, the Panel posed additional questions to the parties on the logistical implications of a hearing that was open to the public. The parties replied on 7 July 2005. The Panel held a second organizational meeting with the parties to discuss this issue on 8 July 2005.[314]

(b)   Summary of the main arguments of the parties[315]

7.2   With reference to the Panel's question whether panels are permitted to open hearings to public observation under Articles 12 (including Appendix 3), 14.1 and 17.10 of the DSU, the **European Communities** argues that a panel may adopt working procedures that foresee open hearings, as Article 12.1 of the DSU provides that panels may depart from the working procedures in Appendix 3 after consulting the parties to the dispute.

7.3   The European Communities also argues that this conclusion is not affected by Article 14.1 of the DSU on confidentiality of panel deliberations. The term "deliberations" does not cover the meetings with the parties, for which a different terminology is used in Appendix 3 of the DSU.

---

[314]   The parties agreed to hold joint panel meetings in this case and that against Canada (WT/DS321) and to harmonize the Panels' timetables.
[315]   A more detailed account of the parties' arguments can be found in Section IV of the descriptive part of this Report.

7.4   The European Communities considers that in the present case where all the parties have agreed to open hearings, the Panel should accommodate the parties' request. Article 18.2 of the DSU also supports the position that parties are entitled to "waive" the confidentiality of their positions.

7.5   Regarding the legal implications of open hearings on covered persons under the Rules of Conduct, the European Communities considers that no legal issues arise under the Rules of Conduct. In the European Communities view, the Rules of Conduct are and remain fully binding on all covered persons in this dispute, even if the hearings are opened to the public. The Panel's deliberations will in any event not be affected by the opening and remain confidential, as required by Article 14.1 of the DSU.

7.6   With respect to the systemic and political impact of opening hearings, the European Communities is of the view that there are no implications for WTO Members who are not parties to this dispute, or on the intergovernmental character of the WTO, nor would it impair the chances to reach a mutually agreed solution, as preferred by the DSU (Article 3.7). Also, there are no implications for third parties because the parties have jointly requested that the public be excluded from the third parties' session during the presentation by a third party, unless that third party agreed to make its presentation open for observation by the public.

7.7   Regarding the procedures that may be adopted to protect confidential information in an open hearing, the European Communities indicates that it does not expect that confidential information will be submitted in this dispute. The European Communities does not consider that there is any issue of confidentiality in relation to information submitted by other Members or non-Members (under Article 13 of the DSU), unless the confidentiality requirement of the last sentence of Article 13.1 of the DSU applies, in which case the corresponding portion of any meeting where this information is discussed could be closed.

7.8   With respect to the third-party session, the European Communities considers that each third party should decide whether to open the part of the third-party session dealing with that third-party's statement.

7.9   Regarding the question whether panels are permitted to open hearings under Articles 12 (including Appendix 3), 14.1 and 17.10 of the DSU, the **United States** notes that the parties agreed that the panel meetings in this dispute should be opened to interested Members and the public. In the view of the United States, open panel meetings are permissible under the DSU, including under Appendix 3 thereto.

7.10   The United States agrees that any deliberations among the three panel members must be confidential. However, Article 14.1 of the DSU does not apply to the meetings of the panel with the parties and does not prohibit opening panel meetings to the public.

7.11   The United States also argues that the Panel has the ability to remove any provision of Appendix 3 that might be perceived as an impediment to accommodating the parties' decision to make their statements public by allowing the public to observe them as they are delivered. Second, Article 18.2 of the DSU, which is echoed in Paragraph 3 of Appendix 3, explicitly provides that "[n]othing in this Understanding shall preclude a party to a dispute from disclosing statements of its own positions to the public." Appendix 3 is part of the DSU and so, per Article 18.2, nothing in Appendix 3 prevents a party from disclosing statements of its own position to the public.

7.12   Concerning the legal implications of open hearings on covered persons under the Rules of Conduct, the United States argues that the provisions in the Rules of Conduct that require panelists to maintain confidentiality apply only to information that is in fact confidential.

7.13   The United States further argues that since the procedural rules of the DSU permit public hearings, the confidentiality provisions of the Rules of Conduct do not prevent the opening of panel meetings to the public.

7.14   Regarding the systemic and political impact of opening hearings, the United States argues that opening the Panel meetings to the public is a natural extension of the discretion provided to the parties in Article 18.2 of the DSU for a party to disclose its statements to the public.

7.15   The United States believes that the third parties should be consulted, but only to determine if they would also choose to open portions of the third-party session with the Panel to the public.

7.16   The United States does not foresee a decision in this dispute to open panel meetings as having a political or systemic impact. For example, the opening of panel meetings in this dispute would not prejudice the ability of parties to other disputes to choose to open, or keep confidential, their respective panel meetings.

7.17   Regarding the procedures to be adopted to protect confidential information in an open hearing, the United States believes that any portions of the Panel meetings dealing with confidential information would not be open to the public. Additional safeguards to provide against the disclosure of confidential information could be included in the working procedures.

7.18   Finally, the United States argues that the third parties would retain their ability to decide whether their submissions and statements are public. Any confidential statements would not be broadcast.

(c)   Summary of the arguments of the third parties[316]

7.19   **Australia** contends that when parties agree not to follow the Working Procedures in Appendix 3, or parts thereof, it would be difficult for the Panel to justify a decision that goes against the wishes of the parties. In Australia's view, to do so would undermine a basic principle of dispute settlement whereby parties consult with each other and with the Panel and seek mutual agreement on the conduct of disputes, according to Article 12.1 of the DSU.[317]

7.20   While not objecting to the opening of the Panel's hearing for public observation, Australia is however concerned about the modalities of organizing the meetings, equity of access and logistic issues and believes that the opening of the Panel's meetings to the public should be subject to the provisions that allow for protection of confidential information.[318]

7.21   **Brazil** questions the specific grounds and the DSU provisions on which the Panel based its decision to accept the parties' request to open the Panel meetings for public observation. According to Brazil, transparency constitutes an important element in the debate carried out by Members in DSB meetings, which will largely benefit from any further clarification by the Panel as to the legal reasons which motivated its decision to open the meetings to the public.[319]

7.22   Brazil argues that a decision on whether or not to open panels' proceedings to the public relies solely on the WTO membership, in particular the DSU review process which is the appropriate *locus* to deal with issues regarding the dispute settlement mechanism. According to Brazil, if panels were to decide on this issue, they would go beyond their mandate, playing a role that is exclusive to the WTO membership.[320]

7.23   Brazil also contends that opening the meetings to the public would represent a reinterpretation of Article 14 of the DSU, signalling that there are cases to

---

[316]   A more detailed account of the third parties' arguments can be found in Section V of the descriptive part of this Report.
[317]   Replies by Australia to Panel questions concerning open hearings, question 1.
[318]   Replies by Australia to Panel questions concerning open hearings, question 2.
[319]   Oral statement of Brazil, para. 2.
[320]   Replies by Brazil to Panel questions concerning open hearings, question 1.

which confidentiality is not applied, such as Panel and Appellate Body meetings.[321]

7.24   **China** prefers the Panel to meet the third parties in closed session. It argues that based on Article 18.2 of the DSU, panels do not have the right to unilaterally disclose the third-party submissions and oral presentations.[322]

7.25   **India** submits that the issue of external transparency is being discussed in the ongoing negotiations in the Special Session of the DSB. Until there is a consensus on the opening of panel meetings to public observation and the modalities therefor, India believes that the Panel proceedings have to be in closed session[323], and its deliberations have to remain confidential[324] as provided in the DSU.[325]

7.26   India contends that the possibility of a panel to decide to deviate from the Working Procedures in Appendix 3 has been provided with the view of having panel procedures with sufficient flexibility so as to ensure high-quality panel reports.[326] In India's view, although panels are given some discretion in establishing their own working procedures, they do not have the discretion to modify the substantive provisions of the DSU, such as confidentiality requirements.[327]

7.27   India argues that Article VII of the Rules of Conduct[328] requires each "covered person" to maintain the confidentiality of dispute settlement deliberations and proceedings at all times. India questions how the Panel is going to ensure that these requirements are met after opening the proceedings to the public for observation.[329]

7.28   India submits that the decision of the Panel to open its proceedings to the public necessarily involves some issues on which consultation and decisions with WTO Members, and not just the parties and third parties, would have been necessary. For example, India questions how the Panel, at its own level, addressed issues relating to the implications on the functioning of the WTO Secretariat, budgetary implications and implications relating to the use of the official languages of the WTO, for which rules and practices have been established by

---

[321]   *Ibid.*
[322]   Replies by China to Panel questions concerning open hearings, question 1 and 2.
[323]   Paragraph 2 of the working procedures in Appendix 3 of the DSU.
[324]   Paragraph 3 of the working procedures in Appendix 3 of the DSU.
[325]   Replies by India to Panel questions concerning open hearings, question 1.
[326]   Article 12.2 of the DSU
[327]   Oral statement of India, para. 6.
[328]   Rules of Conduct for the Understanding on Rules and Procedures Governing the Settlement of Disputes, adopted by the DSB on 3 December 1996 (WT/DSB/RC/1).
[329]   Oral statement of India, para. 7.

other bodies of the WTO. India also questions how the Panel could take a view on the additional costs arising out of the opening up of the proceedings to public without the Budget Committee having considered the matter.[330]

7.29   According to India, the WTO is a Member-driven organization and it is solely for the WTO Members to decide whether or not to change the WTO rules and open up panel proceedings to the public; a Panel cannot take upon itself that function, even at the request of parties to the dispute.[331]

7.30   India posits that the meeting of the Panel with the third parties should be in closed session as required under paragraph 2 of the Working Procedures contained in Appendix 3 of the DSU.[332]

7.31   **Mexico** disagrees with the opening of the Panel meetings to the public on the grounds that panel meetings constitute panel "deliberations" and as such should be confidential, as per Article 14.1 of the DSU. Mexico also argues that transparency is a sensitive issue that is currently under discussion in the negotiations to amend the DSU. Mexico argues that the DSU rules require that the meetings be confidential and, therefore, the decision of the two parties should only prevail to the extent that it does not affect the right of other Members including third parties.[333]

7.32   Mexico emphasizes that public hearings are a cross-cutting issue that should be addressed in general by the WTO, and should not be imposed by a panel at the request of two Members. Mexico regrets that the decision will set a precedent that may affect the outcome of the negotiations and will in all likelihood end up complicating the preparation of working procedures of future panels.[334] Mexico suggests that the third-party session follow the established WTO practice of being held in closed session.[335]

7.33   According to **New Zealand**, there are no legal constraints that would prevent the Panel from opening its hearings to the public. New Zealand quotes Article 12.1 of the DSU which allows panels to follow the working procedures in the DSU unless the panel decides otherwise after consulting the parties. New Zealand argues that while Appendix 3 provides for closed session hearings, the working procedures can be amended with the consent of the Panel and the parties. New Zealand further notes that the reference in Article 14.1 of the DSU to

---

[330] Oral statement of India, para. 8.
[331] Oral statement of India, para. 9.
[332] Replies by India to Panel questions concerning open hearings, question 2.
[333] Oral statement of Mexico, para. 2; Mexico replies to Panel questions following the first meeting, paras. 3 and 9.
[334] Oral statement of Mexico, para. 3.
[335] Replies by Mexico to Panel questions concerning open hearings, question 2.

panel deliberations being confidential refers to the internal deliberations of the panel, not the hearings with the parties. New Zealand submits that this is in line with the practice of other international tribunals which have open hearings but whose deliberations are nonetheless confidential. According to New Zealand, Article 18.2 of the DSU allows parties to waive confidentiality. New Zealand did not object to its third party hearings being public.[336]

7.34   **Norway** considers that Article 12.1 of the DSU gives the Panel the discretion to follow other working procedures than the ones provided in Appendix 3 after consulting the parties. It sees no legal constraints in granting the parties' request to open the hearings to the public. Norway also agrees to having the third party session of the hearing open to the public.[337]

7.35   The **Separate Customs Territory of Taiwan, Penghu, Kinmen and Matsu** (Chinese Taipei) argues that, in accordance with the procedures and customary practices developed over more than half a century under GATT, which are reflected in Articles 14.1, 18.2 and Appendix 3 of the DSU, panel proceedings are to be kept confidential. It argues that only Members by consensus can change the rules of confidentiality. According to Chinese Taipei, a panel, even with the consent of the parties does not have the legal authority to open the proceedings to the public.[338]

7.36   Chinese Taipei refers to Article VII of the Rules of Conduct which requires that each covered person shall at all times maintain the confidentiality of the dispute settlement deliberations and proceedings. According to it, the only exception to this confidentiality obligation is Article 18.2 of the DSU. Chinese Taipei is therefore of the opinion that this exception does not extend to the possibility of allowing parties to decide whether to open panel meetings to the public.[339]

7.37   According Chinese Taipei, "panel deliberations" implies more than one form of deliberation, thus including not only internal consideration among panelists, but also the entire process of the panel's consideration of the dispute.[340]

7.38   Chinese Taipei argues that the flexibility arising from Article 12.1 of the DSU to change working procedures in Appendix 3 cannot be extended to cover provisions in the working procedures that directly elaborate on the obligations of

---

[336]   Replies by New Zealand to Panel questions concerning open hearings, questions 1 and 2.
[337]   Replies by Norway to Panel questions concerning open hearings, questions 1 and 2.
[338]   Replies by Chinese Taipei to Panel questions concerning open hearing, question 1, paras. 1 and 2.
[339]   Replies by Chinese Taipei to Panel questions concerning open hearing, question 1, paras. 4 and 5.
[340]   Replies by Chinese Taipei to Panel questions concerning open hearing, question 1, para. 3.

the DSU. It further argues that if the drafters had contemplated that the confidentiality requirement could be changed, they would have said so, just like in Article 18.2 of the DSU. In the absence of such language, only an amendment to the DSU by the Members through negotiations can change the requirement of confidential deliberations.[341]

7.39   Chinese Taipei is of the opinion that the third-party sessions should be held in closed session.[342]

(d)   Decision of the Panel

7.40   On 1 August 2005, the Panel decided to accept the parties' joint request to open the Panel hearings for public observation. The Panel also decided that the meetings at which the parties are invited to appear, as referred to in paragraph 2 of Appendix 3 to the DSU, would be open for observation by the public through a closed-circuit broadcast, keeping in mind the Panel's obligation to ensure that its Working Procedures are objective, impartial and non-discriminatory, and after careful consideration of the existing provisions of the DSU and its Appendix 3. In addition, since not all third parties had agreed that their session with the Panel be open for observation by the public, the Panel decided that that session would remain closed. As provided in paragraph 3 of the Panel's Working Procedures[343], the parties retain the right to request at any time, including during panel meetings at which they are invited to appear, that their specific statements not be broadcast so as to remain confidential. The Panel also reserved its right to decide on its own to suspend broadcasting at any time, including during such meetings.[344] The Panel sent its revised Working Procedures and timetable to the parties and third parties on 1 August 2005.

7.41   The Chairman of the Panel also sent letters to the Chairman of the DSB[345] and the Director-General of the WTO[346], informing them of the Panel decision

---

[341] Replies by Chinese Taipei to Panel questions concerning open hearing, question 1, paras. 6 and 7.

[342] Replies by Chinese Taipei to Panel questions concerning open hearing, question 2, para. 12.

[343] The Panel's working procedures are contained in Annex A-2 to this Report.

[344] The letter of the Panel to the Parties of 1 August 2005 is reproduced in Annex A-1 to this Report.

[345] See WT/DS320/8, 2 August 2005.

[346] Letter of the Chairman of the Panel to the Director-General of the WTO of 2 August 2005. The letter reads as follows:

"On behalf of the Panels in the two cases referred to above, I would like to request your assistance concerning the implementation of a procedural decision taken by the Panels.

Following a common request made by the parties on 13 June 2005, we have decided that the panel meetings to which the parties are invited to appear will be open for observation by the public through a closed-circuit TV broadcast. We informed the parties of our decision on 1 August 2005. The session with the third parties will remain closed as not all the third parties have agreed to have it open for observation

on this matter and requesting the assistance of the WTO Secretariat in making appropriate logistical arrangements for the open hearings.

7.42   After the Panel decided to consult scientific experts[347], the opinion of the parties was sought on whether they wished that any meeting with the parties and the scientific experts also be open for public observation. The parties replied affirmatively.

7.43   Since this was the first time in GATT/WTO history that a panel has held hearings open for public observation, the Panel deems it appropriate to elaborate further on the reasons why it agreed to open its substantive meetings for public observation.

7.44   The Panel first wishes to recall that it acted at the joint request of the parties. Some third parties, however, objected to the holding of a hearing that would be observable by the public. As a result, the hearing with third parties was not opened to public observation.

7.45   The Panel considers that the DSU does not expressly contemplate the possibility for meetings of panels to be open for public observation. On the contrary, Paragraph 2 of Appendix 3 to the DSU provides that "the panel shall meet in closed session" and that "The parties to the dispute, and interested parties, shall be present at the meeting only when invited by the panel to appear before it." The Panel understands this to mean that it shall always meet *in camera*, whether or not the parties and/or interested parties have been invited to appear

---

by the public. The third parties were advised of our decision on 1 August 2005. Finally, the Chairman of the DSB has also been advised of our decision, with a request that he informs the entire DSB membership of the possibility to observe the hearings.

The Panels appreciate the assistance of the Secretariat on these cases to date and would like to request continued Secretariat assistance with respect to the logistical arrangements needed to implement our decision. In this regard, we would like to ensure transparency and non-discriminatory access by all, in particular by all WTO Members, to the closed-circuit TV broadcast. For that purpose, we would request the Secretariat to guarantee that each WTO Member delegation has *at least* two seats available in the room where the closed-circuit broadcast will be shown. We would also ask the Secretariat through its website to make all Members and the public aware that they are allowed to attend the closed-circuit broadcast and to provide details on pre-registration and seating arrangements.

We have scheduled the first substantive meeting of the Panels with the parties for 12-15 September 2005 and understand that this meeting could take place in Room W with a closed-circuit TV broadcast of the meeting in the General Council Room.

I would greatly appreciate your assistance in ensuring that the logistical arrangements to which I have referred in this letter can be finalized by the Secretariat."

[347]   See Section VII.A.2 below.

before it. No reference is made in that provision to other Members or to the general public.

7.46   However, Article 12.1 of the DSU provides that "[p]anels shall follow the Working Procedures in Appendix 3 unless the panel decides otherwise after consulting the parties to the dispute." In other words, the Panel has the possibility to depart from any provision of Appendix 3, its only obligation being to consult the parties to the dispute first.

7.47   This discretion, however, applies only to the provisions of the Working Procedures in Appendix 3, not to any other provision of the DSU. The Panel thus is of the view that Article 12.1 entitles it to proceed with any adaptation of the working procedures contained in Appendix 3, as long as such an adaptation is not expressly prohibited by any provision of the DSU. Therefore, we need to examine whether there is any DSU provision that would explicitly prohibit the opening of panel meetings to public observation.

7.48   The Panel notes in this respect the confidentiality requirements contained in Articles 14.1, 18.2 and Appendix 3, paragraph 3 to the DSU. It also recalls the obligations of its members pursuant to the Rules of Conduct for the Understanding on Rules and Procedures Governing the Settlement of Disputes.[348]

7.49   Regarding the requirement in Article 14.1 of the DSU that "[p]anel deliberations shall be confidential", the Panel first notes that one of the ordinary meanings of the word "deliberations" is "careful consideration, weighing up with a view to decision". The term "deliberations" also applies to "[c]onsideration and discussion of a question by a legislative assembly, a committee, etc.; debate".[349] However, the Panel is not of the view that a panel hearing is similar to a consideration by a legislative body or a committee. Even though exchanges of points of view take place in both instances, the nature of the exchange of arguments by parties to a dispute before an adjudicating body remains different from that of an assembly or a committee. This suggests that the term "deliberation" was not intended to cover the exchange of arguments between the parties, but rather the internal discussion of the Panel with a view to reach its conclusions. We note that our interpretation of the term "deliberation" conforms to the use of that term in the statutes of other international judicial bodies.[350] It is also confirmed by the

---

[348]   WT/DSB/RC/1, 11 December 1996.
[349]   *The New Shorter Oxford English Dictionary* (4th ed., 1993), p. 624.
[350]   Article 46 of the Statute of International Court of Justice provides that "[t]he hearing in Court shall be public, unless the Court decides otherwise, or unless the parties demand that the public be not admitted". Article 54.3 of the Statute provides that "[t]he deliberations of the Court shall take place in private and remain secret ...". Article 26 of the Statute of the International Tribunal for the Law of the Sea provides that" [t]he hearing shall be public, unless the Tribunal decides otherwise, or unless the parties demand that the public be not admitted". Article 42 of the Rules of the Tribunal

context of Article 14.1. Article 14 deals with confidentiality in the work of panels *stricto sensu* (deliberations, drafting of the panel report, opinions of panelists), whereas the provisions dealing with the conduct of the proceedings with the parties are contained in Article 12. The Panel therefore concludes that Article 14.1 of the DSU does not apply to panel hearings and that opening the Panel's substantive meetings with the parties to public observation does not breach that provision.

7.50   Regarding the requirement contained in Article 18.2 of the DSU that "[w]ritten submissions to the panel ... shall be treated as confidential", we note that, by opening its hearings to public observation, the Panel did not disclose to the public the content of the parties' written submissions. By making statements to which the public could listen, the parties themselves exercised their right under Article 18.2 to "disclos[e] statements of [their] own positions to the public". The Panel is mindful that, by asking questions or seeking clarifications during the hearings with respect to written submissions of the parties, it may have itself "disclosed" the content of such submissions. However, the Panel notes that at all times the parties retained the right to request that specific statements of theirs not be broadcasted so as to remain confidential and that, in this case, the parties had made their written submissions public. The Panel notes also that Article 18.2 provides that "Members shall treat as confidential information submitted by another Member to the Panel or the Appellate Body *which that Member has designated as confidential.*"[351] We consider that this sentence clarifies the scope of the confidentiality requirement which applies to the Panel and to Members, and that panels have to keep confidential only the information that has been designated as confidential or which has otherwise not been disclosed to the public. Any other interpretation would imply a double standard, whereby panels would have to treat as confidential information which a WTO Member does not have to treat as confidential. The Panel also notes that, by requesting that the Panel hold hearings open to public observation, the parties to this dispute have implicitly accepted that their arguments be public, with the exception of those they would identify as confidential.

7.51   Finally, the Panel notes that Article VII of the Rules of Conduct for the Understanding on the Rules and Procedures Governing the Settlement of Disputes provides that "[e]ach covered person shall at all times maintain the confi-

---

provides that "[t]he deliberations of the Tribunal shall take place in private and remain secret ..." Article 20 of the Statute of the International Criminal Tribunal for Former Yugoslavia provides that "[t]he hearing in Court shall be public, unless the Trial Chamber decides to close the proceedings in accordance with its rules of procedure and evidence". Rule 78 of its Rules of Procedure and Evidence provides: "[a]ll proceedings before a Trial Chamber, other than deliberations of the Chamber, shall be held in public, unless otherwise provided." Rule 29 provides that "[t]he deliberations of the Chambers shall take place in private and remain secret."
[351]   Emphasis added.

dentiality of dispute settlement deliberations and proceedings together with any information identified by a party as confidential." The Panel notes that such confidentiality obligation on the covered persons during the panel proceedings is applicable to the extent not inconsistent with the DSU provisions.[352] In this case, the parties waived their right to confidentiality and requested open hearings. As demonstrated above, the Panel accordingly adapted its working procedures by departing from Appendix 3 in a manner consistent with the DSU provisions. Therefore, the Rules of Conduct should not be construed in a manner that would restrict the rights of Members under the DSU. The Panel concludes that Article VII does not prevent the Panel from holding hearings open to observation by the public.

7.52   The Panel is mindful that the issue of transparency of panel and Appellate Body proceedings is currently under review as part of the negotiations on improvements and clarifications of the DSU. However, the Panel recalls that the dispute settlement system of the WTO serves to preserve the rights and obligations of Members under the covered agreements, which include the DSU, and to clarify the existing provisions of those agreements in accordance with customary rules of interpretation of public international law. The Panel considers that its role is not to address transparency in general terms, but to determine whether the DSU as it currently stands permits that, under the circumstances of this particular case, the Panel hearing be open to public observation. When called upon to decide on whether to open hearings to public observation, the Panel concluded that this was the case. However, this finding is limited to this particular case and is without prejudice to any approach to the issue of transparency that the Members may negotiate.

7.53   For the reasons set out in the previous paragraphs, the Panel considers that it is entitled, under the particular circumstances of this case and pursuant to Article 12.1 of the DSU, to open its hearings for public observation. This is why the Panel decided to accept the parties' request to open its meetings with the parties for public observation. The third-party session was, however, not open to public observation, due to the absence of consensus among the third parties on this matter.[353]

7.54   The first substantive hearing with the parties was held on 12, 13 and 15 September 2005. The hearing with third parties took place on 14 September 2005. The hearing with the scientific experts was held on 27-28 September

---

[352]   See Rules of Conduct for the Understanding on Rules and Procedures Governing the Settlement of Disputes (WT/DSB/RC/1), Article II.1:
  "These Rules shall in no way modify the rights and obligations of Members under the DSU nor the rules and procedures therein."
[353]   See WT/DS320/8.

2006. The second substantive meeting with the parties was held on 2 and 3 October 2006.

> 2. *Panel's decisions relating to the consultation of individual scientific experts and international organizations*

(a)   Decision to consult scientific experts

7.55   During its first substantive meeting, the **Panel** requested the parties' views as to whether there was a need to consult scientific experts should the Panel deem it necessary to examine the consistency of the EC implementing measure with the *SPS Agreement* as part of its review of this case.[354]

7.56   The **European Communities** replied that it did not believe that it was necessary for this Panel to look into these scientific issues to make findings and rulings within its terms of reference. However, the Panel did not have the expertise to decide on such issues itself, should the Panel decide to review the scientific issues at stake. In such a scenario, the consultation of scientific and technical experts would be absolutely necessary. However, the European Communities considered that this Panel could not consult the experts that were used in the original *EC – Hormones* case. New experts would have to be chosen.[355]

7.57   The **United States** considered that, in view of the clarity of the scientific issues in this dispute, there was technically no need to consult experts in this proceeding. However, the Panel, in a scientific dispute such as this, had discretion to consult with experts on the scientific evidence in developing its analysis and making its findings. This said, a panel could not delegate to experts the panel's central task of interpreting the covered agreements cited in a dispute. Experts may advise only on factual issues, not on the application of the legal standards in the covered agreements to the facts at hand.

7.58   On whether the Panel should consult with the scientific experts from the original *EC – Hormones* proceedings, the United States noted that the process by which the original experts were selected differed from that which had evolved over the course of subsequent disputes and that experts should be selected pursuant to current practice, which would mean that the three experts selected by the original panel should be consulted.[356]

---

[354]   Question 74 of Panel questions after the first substantive meeting.

[355]   EC's reply to Panel questions after the first substantive meeting, question 74, Annex B-1.

[356]   US's reply to Panel questions after the first substantive meeting, question 74, Annex B-3.

7.59   After having considered the parties' replies, the **Panel** noted that, from the parties' replies to its questions, it appeared that no party disagreed that, should the Panel proceed with an assessment of the measure taken by the European Communities to comply with the recommendations and rulings of the DSB in the *EC – Hormones* case, advice from technical or scientific experts would be necessary.

7.60   The Panel noted the views expressed by the European Communities regarding the nature of this case and the order in which its claims should be reviewed by the Panel, but it was of the opinion that, at that stage, it was in its interest, as well as in the interest of the parties, to be fully informed of all relevant aspects of the dispute. The Panel thus decided to initiate a process for consultation with experts in relation to the technical or scientific aspects of the compatibility of the EC implementing measure with the relevant provisions of the *SPS Agreement*, without prejudice to the positions held by any party in this respect and without prejudice to the conclusions that the Panel would ultimately reach on the claims raised by the European Communities. The Panel informed the parties accordingly in a letter dated 20 October 2005.[357]

7.61   The Panel does not deem it necessary to add to its reasoning on this issue except to recall that, as specified by the Appellate Body in *US – Shrimp*:

> "... the DSU accords to a panel established by the DSB, and engaged in a dispute settlement proceeding, ample and extensive authority to undertake and to control the process by which it informs itself ... of the relevant facts of the dispute ... That authority, and the breadth thereof, is indispensably necessary to enable a panel to discharge its duty imposed by Article 11 of the DSU to 'make an objective assessment of the matter before it, including an *objective assessment of the facts of the case*.'"[358]

7.62   In this particular case, as explained further in the subsequent sections of this report and in spite of the approach of the European Communities focusing on the breach of certain provisions of the DSU by the defending party, the Panel deemed it important to consult experts in order to "make an objective assessment of the matter before it, including an objective assessment of the facts of the case." In addition, Article 11.2 of the *SPS Agreement* "explicitly instructs"[359] panels to seek expert advice in disputes under the *SPS Agreement* involving scientific and technical issues:

---

[357]   Annex A-3 to this Report.
[358]   Appellate Body Report on *US – Shrimp*, para. 106 (emphasis original).
[359]   See Appellate Body Report on *Japan – Agricultural Products II*, paras. 127-128.

> "In a dispute under this Agreement involving scientific or technical issues, a panel *should seek advice from experts* chosen by the panel in consultation with the parties to the dispute."[360]

7.63   The Panel is mindful that this case is not exactly a dispute "under [the SPS] Agreement" since its terms of reference do not refer to the *SPS Agreement*. We nonetheless consider that, since we may have to determine whether the European Communities has complied with its obligations under the *SPS Agreement* if we need to determine whether Article 22.8 of the DSU has been breached, this dispute is, at least indirectly, "under [the SPS] Agreement".

7.64   We therefore conclude that our decision to consult scientific experts is consistent with the requirements of the DSU and the *SPS Agreement*.

(b)   EC request for a single expert review group

7.65   Once it decided to consult scientific experts, the **Panel** sought comments from the parties on the proposed Working Procedures for Consultation with Scientific and/or Technical Experts, the technical or scientific aspects on which the Panel should consult experts and on whether the meeting with the experts and parties should be open for observation by the public.

7.66   In a letter dated 3 November 2005, commenting on the draft working procedures for the consultation of experts, the **European Communities** requested that a single expert review group be called upon to assist the Panel, arguing that it was important that the Panel receive consistent advice on the issues and that it would reduce the risk of the Panel having to review and decide between competing scientific views among the experts.

7.67   The **United States** objected to the request of the European Communities in a letter of 8 November 2005, noting that in every sanitary and phytosanitary dispute to date in which experts had been consulted, including the original *EC – Hormones* proceeding, they had been consulted on an individual basis. This method for consultations had proven effective, and there was no reason to depart from this practice in these proceedings.

7.68   The United States was also concerned by the implication of the consultation of the experts as a group instead of on an individual basis. The requirement that a response be coordinated within the group of experts could lead to substantial delays and potentially limit the Panel's ability to hear and weigh the spectrum of opinions as they relate to the hormones at issue in this dispute. Also, given the spectrum of areas of expertise at issue, there would not seem to be much value to

---

[360]   Article 11.2 of the *SPS Agreement*, emphasis added.

a "group" report since each expert was going to be consulted on different areas.[361]

7.69   The **European Communities** commented that its request was based on a desire to ensure the legitimacy of the Panel's findings by providing for a systematic, coherent and non-polarizing approach to complex scientific issues. Conversely, if experts acted as individuals, the Panel ran the risk of having to review and decide between competing scientific views amongst the Panel's experts as well as the experts advising the parties. This would normally be very difficult, if not impossible, to do in a way that would ensure transparency, excellence and credibility in this contested area of scientific research.

7.70   The European Communities also drew the Panel's attention to Article 13.2 and Appendix 4 of the DSU, Article 11.2 of the *SPS Agreement* and Article 14.2 and Annex 2 of the *TBT Agreement* which, most probably for the reasons just mentioned above, all refer to the possibility to establish *expert review groups*. The European Communities did not see any reason to deviate from this normal procedure which the drafters of the WTO Agreements clearly preferred.[362]

7.71   The **Panel** reached its final decision on the working procedures for consultations with scientific and/or technical experts on 25 November 2005.[363] Regarding the form the consultation of the experts should take, the Panel was not persuaded that the EC suggestion to consult an expert review group was the preferable option. Firstly, the fields of competence proposed by the parties were quite varied, rendering it difficult to find individual experts with competence in most or all of these fields to serve in an expert review group. The fact that no expert would have a comprehensive knowledge of all the relevant subjects made it even more important for the Panel to seek advice from the experts on an individual basis on their respective fields of expertise. Secondly, the Panel wished to hear any dissenting or minority views among the experts rather than receiving a consensus text from an expert review group. The Panel did not consider that the risk that experts may have diverging opinions would generate difficulties as serious as those alleged by the European Communities. The Panel rather saw the risk that an expert review group would only agree on a minimum common position, thus depriving the Panel of a full picture of the problems. It was also worth noting that so far, all WTO panels had preferred to consult scientific and/or technical experts on an individual basis.

---

[361]   US's letter to the Panel of 8 November 2005.
[362]   EC's letter to the Panel of 11 November 2005.
[363]   Annex A-5 to this Report. The Panel also decided that the meeting with the experts would be open for observation by the public in the same manner as the meeting with the parties.

7.72   The Panel does not deem it necessary to add to the reasons mentioned above, except to clarify that, in its view, none of the provisions cited by the European Communities sets a preference for expert review groups. On the contrary, the consultation of expert review groups is mentioned only as one option, both in Article 13.2 of the DSU and in Article 11.2 of the *SPS Agreement* and the terms of those provisions suggest that panels enjoy wide discretion in deciding to seek or not the assistance of an expert review group rather than that of individual experts. Indeed, Article 13.2 of the DSU provides that:

> "Panels may seek information from any relevant source and may consult experts to obtain their opinion on certain aspects of the matter. With respect to a factual issue concerning a scientific or other technical matter raised by a party to a dispute, a panel *may* request an advisory report in writing from an expert review group."[364]

7.73   Article 11.2, second sentence, of the *SPS Agreement* provides that:

> "To this end, the panel *may, when it deems it appropriate*, establish an advisory technical experts group, or consult the relevant international organizations, at the request of either party to the dispute or on its own initiative."[365]

7.74   We read these provisions as leaving a wide margin of discretion to the Panel. We find confirmation of this reading in the Appellate Body Report on *EC – Hormones*, where the Appellate Body recalled that:

> "Both Article 11.2 of the *SPS Agreement* and Article 13 of the DSU enable panels to seek information and advice as they deem appropriate in a particular case ...
>
> We find that in disputes involving scientific or technical issues, neither Article 11.2 of the *SPS Agreement*, nor Article 13 of the DSU prevents panels from consulting with individual experts. Rather, both the *SPS Agreement* and the DSU leave to the sound discretion of a panel the determination of whether the establishment of an expert review group is necessary or appropriate."[366]

---

[364]   Emphasis added.
[365]   Emphasis added. *A contrario*, Article 14.2 of the *TBT Agreement* cited by the European Communities expressly limits the choice of the panel to a technical expert group.
[366]   Appellate Body Report on *EC – Hormones*, para. 147.

7.75   We therefore conclude that our decision complies with the DSU, the *SPS Agreement* and the practice of the Appellate Body.

(c)   Experts selection process

7.76   One single expert selection process was carried out for the two cases WT/DS320 and WT/DS321.[367]

7.77   After receiving input from the parties, the Panel, in its letter of 20 January 2006[368], identified the need for expert advice in seven fields, namely:

(a)   risk analysis, in particular, the conduct of a risk assessment as it relates to food safety;

(b)   animal science, including good veterinary practices in relation to the administration of the six hormones[369] to cattle through implants or other means;

---

[367]   In this section, the term "Panel" refers to the Panel in case WT/DS320 and the Panel in case WT/DS321. The same individuals served as panelists in the two cases.

[368]   Letter from the Panel to the parties of 20 January 2006.

[369]   The six hormones can be defined as follows:

Oestradiol-17β

Oestradiol-17β is the most potent mammalian oestrogenic sex hormone, responsible for female characteristics. It is a member of a class of compounds called steroids. In females, it functions in the ovarian cycle and maintains uterine health; in males it inhibits the synthesis of testosterone. It is produced primarily by the ovaries and the placenta. In cattle, it is administered either alone or in combination with testosterone, progesterone and trenbolone by a subcutaneous implant to the base of the ear to improve body weight and feed conversion in cattle. The ear is discarded at slaughter. (Replies of Dr. Boisseau, Dr. Boobis and Dr. Guttenplan to Panel Question 1 to the experts. Annex D, paras. 1; 7-8; 17)

Progesterone

Progesterone is the major mammalian progestational hormone, responsible for maintaining pregnancy. It is a steroid and is secreted primarily by the corpus luteum in the ovary of adult females and in the placenta. Progesterone is used as a contraceptive and to correct abnormalities in the menstrual cycle. In cattle, it is administered to steer, usually in combination with oestradiol-17β or oestradiol benzoate by a subcutaneous implant to the base of the ear to improve body weight and feed conversion in cattle. The ear is discarded at slaughter. (Replies of Dr. Boisseau, Dr. Boobis and Dr. Guttenplan to Panel Question 1 to the experts. Annex D, paras. 2; 9-10; 18)

Testosterone

Testosterone is a mammalian androgenic hormone, responsible for male characteristics. It is a steroid and is produced primarily in the testes of adult males. In cattle, testosterone is administered in combination with oestradiol -17β or oestradiol benzoate by a subcutaneous implant to the base of the ear to improve body weight and feed conversion in cattle. The ear is discarded at slaughter. (Replies of Dr. Boisseau, Dr. Boobis and Dr. Guttenplan to Panel Question 1 to the experts. Annex D, paras. 3; 11; 19)

(c)   toxicology, including genotoxicity[370], and carcinogenicity[371] risks arising from the six hormones in meat;

(d)   inspection, sampling and testing methods, particularly in relation to residue analysis and characterization with respect to the six hormones;

(e)   human endocrinology[372], including endogenous[373] production of hormones by humans, in particular prepubertal children;

(f)   dietary intake studies and epidemiology[374] linked to meat consumption;

Trenbolone acetate
Trenbolone acetate is a synthetic steroid with anabolic (growth-stimulating) properties several fold above that of testosterone. In cattle, it is administered alone or in combination with oestradiol-17β by a subcutaneous implant to the base of the ear to improve body weight and feed conversion in cattle. The ear is discarded at slaughter. (Replies of Dr. Boisseau, Dr. Boobis and Dr. Guttenplan to Panel Question 1 to the experts. Annex D, paras. 5; 12; 20).
Zeranol
Zeranol is an oestrogenic substance produced by certain fungal, or mold, species. It is a non-steroidal anabolic (growth-stimulating) agent and has been used for the management of menopausal and menstrual disorders. Zeranol is administered to cattle either alone, or in combination with trenbolone acetate by a subcutaneous implant to the base of the ear to improve body weight and feed conversion in cattle. The ear is discarded at slaughter (replies of Dr. Boisseau, Dr. Boobis and Dr. Guttenplan to Panel Question 1 to the experts. Annex D, paras. 6; 13-14; 21). Although zeranol occurs naturally, it is sometimes referred to as one of the synthetic hormones, together with trenbolone and melengestrol acetate.
Melengestrol acetate
Melengestrol acetate (MGA) is an orally active synthetic progestogen about 30 times as active as progesterone. It is fed to female cattle to improve body weight and feed conversion (replies of Dr. Boisseau, Dr. Boobis and Dr. Guttenplan to Panel Question 1 to the experts. Annex D, paras. 4; 15-16; 22).

[370] Ability to cause damage to genetic material (DNA). Such damage may be mutagenic and/or carcinogenic (Replies of Dr. Boobis and Dr. Guttenplan to Panel question 2 to the experts. Annex D, paras. 41 and 58. See also Transcript of the Panel meeting with the experts, Annex G, paras. 85-90).

[371] Process of induction of malignant neoplasms (cancer) by chemical, physical or biological agents (Replies of Dr. Boobis and Dr. Guttenplan to Panel question 2 to the experts. Annex D, paras. 44 and 60).

[372] *Endocrinology:* "A subspecialty of internal medicine concerned with the metabolism, physiology, and disorders of the endocrine system." (Webster Online Dictionary) The *endocrine system* is defined by the same dictionary as "The system of glands that release their secretions (hormones) directly into the circulatory system. In addition to the endocrine glands, included are the chromaffin system and the neurosecretory systems."

[373] *Endogenous:* "Produced inside an organism or cell. The opposite is external (exogenous) production." (Webster's Online Dictionary)

[374] "A branch of medical science that deals with the incidence, distribution, and control of disease in a population; the sum of the factors controlling the presence or absence of a disease or pathogen" (Merriam-Webster Online Dictionary (http://www.m-w.com/dictionary/epidemiology)).

(g)   physiology, in particular related to the possible effects of the six hormones when consumed in meat on the immune and nervous systems, and growth and reproduction.

7.78   As stipulated in the Working Procedures for Consultations with Scientific and/or Technical Experts adopted by the Panel on 25 November 2005 after consultation with the parties[375], the Panel sought information not only from selected experts but also from three relevant international entities, the Codex Alimentarius Commission (Codex)[376], the Joint FAO/WHO Expert Committee on Food Additives (JECFA)[377], and the International Agency for Research on Cancer (IARC).[378] While the questions to experts focused on the seven areas identified, the questions to the above-mentioned entities focused on institutional and procedural issues as well as definitions relevant to the case.

7.79   Pursuant to the Working Procedures the Panel, on 29 November 2005, requested the Secretariats of the Codex Alimentarius Commission, JECFA and the IARC to recommend names of candidate experts in the relevant fields. The Panel contacted the 22 experts suggested by those international entities and requested that those experts interested and available to provide advice to the Panel submit their curriculum vitae, including publication lists, and disclose potential

---

[375]   Annex A-4, letter from the Panel to parties on 25 November 2005, Annex A-5, Working Procedures for Consultations with Scientific and/or Technical Experts.

[376]   The Codex Alimentarius Commission was established by FAO and WHO, under the Joint FAO/WHO Food Standards Programme, to develop international food standards, guidelines and other recommendations such as codes of practice; its First Session met in 1963. The main purposes of this Programme are protecting health of the consumers, ensuring fair trade practices in food trade, and promoting coordination of all food standards work undertaken by international governmental and non-governmental organizations. The Codex Alimentarius Commission is one of the three international standard-setting organizations referenced in the *SPS Agreement* (reference: Codex Alimentarius website – www.codexalimentarius.net). Within the framework of the Codex Alimentarius Commission and its procedures, the responsibility for providing advice on risk management lies with the Commission and its subsidiary bodies while the responsibility for risk assessment lies primarily with the joint FAO/WHO expert bodies and consultations.

[377]   The Joint FAO/WHO Expert Committee on Food Additives (JECFA), which has been meeting since 1956, is an international expert scientific committee that is administered jointly by the Food and Agriculture Organization of the United Nations (FAO) and the World Health Organization (WHO). Its work includes the evaluation of food additives, contaminants, naturally occurring toxicants and residues of veterinary drugs in food. JECFA serves as an independent scientific committee which performs risk assessments and provides advice to FAO, WHO and the member countries of both organizations. The requests for scientific advice are in general channelled through the Codex Alimentarius Commission (Codex). Some countries use information from JECFA in the establishment of national food safety control programmes and Codex adopts standards based on evaluations by JECFA (reference: *Fact Sheet – What is JECFA? See* Annex 1 attached to Annex E-2).

[378]   The International Agency for Research on Cancer (IARC), established in 1965, is part of the World Heath Organization. IARC's mission is to coordinate and conduct research on the causes of human cancer, the mechanisms of carcinogenesis, and to develop scientific strategies for cancer control. The Agency is involved in both epidemiological and laboratory research and disseminates scientific information through publications, meetings, courses, and fellowships (reference: IARC website – www.iarc.fr).

conflicts of interests. Eleven experts were interested and available. The Panel provided all the information received from the experts to the European Communities, the United States and Canada, requesting them to indicate any compelling reasons why particular experts should not be chosen to provide advice to the Panel in this dispute. The parties provided their comments on the proposed experts on 16 January 2006. The United States provided comments on one issue in the EC comments on 19 January 2006, i.e. the exclusion of experts who had participated in JECFA's risk assessment work. The European Communities responded to the US comments on 30 January 2006.

7.80   Because the parties' positions with respect to the candidate experts differed significantly, on 20 January 2006, the Panel requested the parties to suggest further names of candidate experts, in application of paragraph 6 of the Working Procedures.

7.81   On 31 January 2006, the Secretary to the Panel sent letters to 49 additional experts suggested by the parties. The Panel Secretary requested that experts interested and available to provide advice to the Panel submit their curriculum vitae including a list of publications and a disclosure of any potential conflicts of interests.

7.82   Of the 71 experts suggested by the international organizations and the parties to the two disputes, 40 experts indicated that they were available and 35 responded to the request for curriculum vitae and information regarding potential conflicts of interests.

7.83   The information provided by the experts was sent to the parties. The parties were once again given the opportunity to comment on each expert and to provide any compelling reasons why particular experts should not be chosen to provide advice to the Panel in these disputes.

7.84   The parties provided their comments on the second set of experts names on 22 February 2006. The European Communities replied to comments from the United States and Canada on certain experts proposed by the European Communities in an additional letter to the Panel of 27 February 2006. The United States and Canada commented on the EC letter of 27 February on 1 and 2 March respectively. One party or another submitted objections with regard to all but one of the experts by arguing either that an expert lacked sufficient expertise in the areas of the dispute identified as needing scientific or technical expertise, or was affiliated with the government of a party to this dispute; or was affiliated with JECFA; or had received funding from the pharmaceutical industry; or had been involved in the regulatory approval of any of the six hormones.

7.85   On 24 March 2006, the Panel informed the parties of the names of the experts that it had selected. The Panel wishes to recall that, in the selection process, it amply consulted the parties and selected the experts in accordance with procedures previously determined by the Panel in consultation with the parties.[379] The Panel excluded experts with close links with governmental authorities directly involved in policy-making regarding the six hormones and experts with close links to pharmaceutical companies or involved in public advocacy activities. The Panel chose not to exclude *a priori* experts who had participated in the preparation and drafting of JECFA's risk assessments because this would deprive the Panel and the parties of the benefit of the contribution of internationally recognized specialists[380] and because the Panel was of the opinion that experts familiar with the JECFA reports would be well-placed to assist the Panel in understanding the work of JECFA extensively referred to by the parties in their submissions, in particular by the European Communities. Moreover, the Panel, who was fully aware of the fields of competence of these experts, considered that they would be competent to answer questions with respect to risk assessment regarding the hormones at issue. The Panel also decided not to exclude *a priori* all experts who were current or past governmental employees unless a potential conflict of interests could reasonably be assumed from their official functions. In selecting the experts, the Panel also had in mind the need to choose experts with expertise to cover all the fields identified as at issue in the dispute.

7.86   The experts selected by the Panel were:

Dr. Jacques Boisseau, Former Director, French Agency for Veterinary Medicinal Products;

Dr. Alan R. Boobis, Director, Experimental Medicine & Toxicology Division of Medicine, Faculty of Medicine, Imperial College London (also Professor of Biochemical Pharmacology at Imperial College London);

Dr. Hubert De Brabander, Professor and Head of Faculty of Veterinary Medicine, Department of Veterinary Public Health & Food Safety, University of Ghent, Belgium;

Dr. Ronald L. Melnick, US National Institute of Environmental Health Sciences;

Dr. Wolfgang G. Sippell, Deputy Director, Department of Pediatrics, University of Kiel; Head of the Division of Pediatric Endocrinology & Diabetology, Children's Hospital, Christian-Albrechts-University of Kiel, Germany;

Dr. Kurt Straif, Scientist, Unit of Carcinogenic Identification and Evaluation, International Agency for Research on Cancer, Lyon, France.

---

[379]   Appellate Body Report on *EC – Hormones*, para. 148.
[380]   See Annex E-2, JECFA's replies to Panel question 14, regarding the selection process of experts involved in JECFA's work.

7.87   On 28 March 2006, the European Communities requested that the Panel reconsider its choice of two of the experts, reiterating concerns already discussed above by the Panel and arguing that these experts had real or perceived conflicts of interests that should disqualify them from assisting the Panel. The Panel carefully considered the European Communities' request, including the information given regarding potential conflicts of interests. The Panel found in particular that the statement that one expert had made before the French Senate in 1996 had not been made in relation to hormones used for growth promotion purposes. Rather, it had been made with respect to hormones used for medical treatment purposes. The Panel also found that the links of another expert with two companies involved in research and counselling were not in the area of veterinary drugs or hormonal substances. The Panel concluded that the EC objections regarding those two experts were not justified. Therefore, on 31 March 2006, the Panel gave notice to the parties that it had found no reason to change its decision concerning the selection of experts.[381] In addition, having considered the information available about the various candidates, the Panel found that these two experts were the best choices among the very few individuals available with expertise in the area of risk assessment and would be able to provide the Panel with insight on international standards on the hormones at issue.[382]

7.88   On 12 April 2006, the Panel gave notice to the parties that Dr. Melnick and Dr. Straif were no longer available to assist the Panel and that the Panel had chosen to replace these experts with:

> Dr. Vincent Cogliano, Head of Programme, IARC Monographs on the Evaluation of Carcinogenic Risks to Humans, International Agency for Research on Cancer, Lyon, France; and
>
> Dr. Joseph Guttenplan, Professor, Department of Basic Science, New York University Dental Center; Research Associate Professor, Department of Environmental Medicine, New York University Medical Center.

7.89   In choosing experts to replace Dr. Melnick and Dr. Straif, the Panel was especially mindful of the need to replace these experts with others who could cover the same fields of expertise. Of the final six experts selected, three were amongst those originally suggested by the European Communities and three were suggested by the international organizations consulted by the Panel.

---

[381]   Letter dated 31 March 2006 from the Panel to parties.

[382]   The Panel wishes to highlight the challenges it encountered in selecting experts There was a limited number of specialists suggested and actually available in each of the fields on which the Panel needed assistance and almost always one or more of the parties objected to that specialist. For example, only six of the identified available experts were deemed to have extensive expertise in risk analysis. All of these experts were objected to by at least one party.

7.90   The United States submitted an objection, on 19 April 2006, to the Panel's selection of an expert originally recommended by the European Communities to replace one of the unavailable experts.

7.91   The United States, in a letter dated 20 April 2006, also requested that the Panel amend its list of experts to include an expert with relevant experience in animal science, including good veterinary practices as they relate to the administration of the six hormones to cattle. In a letter dated 10 May 2006, the European Communities objected to the request for an animal science expert made by Canada and the United States, stating that all relevant questions could already be answered by the six experts.

7.92   In light of the experts' replies as to which questions they would not be in a position to answer, and in light of the parties' comments, the Panel decided that it would first consider the written replies from the experts to the questions and then would determine if it was necessary to seek advice from additional experts. The Panel decided not to amend the list of selected expert unless there was a real need in the future and communicated its decision to the parties in a letter dated 10 May 2006.

7.93   Because the Panel had requested Dr. De Brabander and Dr. Boisseau to answer the questions on good veterinary practices to the extent that they could, and because all questions were ultimately answered by at least one of the selected experts, the Panel did not find a need to consult additional experts.

7.94   In accordance with the Working Procedures for Consultations with Scientific and/or Technical Experts adopted by the Panel in consultation with the parties, the experts were requested to act in their individual capacities and not as representatives of any entity.

7.95   On 24 February 2006, the Panel sent to the parties the draft questions to scientific experts and international organizations for comments. The parties provided the Panel with their comments on 15 March 2006. After considering the parties' comments and after revising the draft questions as necessary, the Panel sent its 62 written questions to the individual scientific experts and its 26 written questions to the three international organizations (namely Codex, JECFA and IARC) on 13 April 2006, together with the parties' submissions and accompanying exhibits.

7.96   The Panel requested that the experts and the international entitities provide their written replies to the scientific and technical questions by 12 June 2006.[383]

7.97   The Panel, after receiving replies from experts and Codex, JECFA, and IARC, forwarded these replies to the parties on 14 June for their comments. The parties provided their comments on these replies on 30 June 2006.[384] Afterwards, parties were given a further opportunity to comment on each other's comments on experts' replies and replies from international organizations. Parties provided these second rounds of comments on 12 July 2006.[385]

7.98   The Panel met with the six experts and four representatives from Codex, JECFA and IARC in the presence of the parties on 27-28 September 2006 in a meeting that was open for public observation through a closed-circuit television broadcast. In this meeting, Dr. Vincent Cogliano, Head of the IARC Monographs Programme, served both as an individual scientific expert and as the representative of the IARC. The other representatives were WHO JECFA Secretary Dr. Angelika Tritscher, FAO JECFA Secretary Dr. Annika Wennberg, and Codex Secretary Dr. Kazuaki Miyagishima. The meeting provided an opportunity for the parties and the Panel to ask questions to the experts and for the experts to clarify points that they had made in their written responses to the questions.[386] This meeting was followed by the Panel's joint second substantive meeting with the parties on 2-3 October 2006.

7.99   The Panel wishes to record its appreciation to the experts and the representatives of the international entities for their contributions. They were provided with large volumes of scientific materials and a limited timeframe to reply to a long set of questions. They were also requested to reply to extensive questions from the parties and the Panel during the two-day meeting in Geneva. They provided detailed and comprehensive responses. They provided the necessary scientific input to assist the Panel in understanding the issues raised by the parties and resolve the trade dispute before it. The clarity of their explanations and their professionalism were particularly appreciated by the Panel.

---

[383]   A compilation of the written replies received from the scientific experts can be found in Annex D. The written replies from the Codex Alimentarius Commission, JECFA and IARC can be found in Annex E-1, Annex E-2, and Annex E-3, respectively.
[384]   See Annexes F-1, F-2, and F-4.
[385]   See Annexes F-3 and F-5.
[386]   A copy of the transcript of the meeting (hereafter the "transcript") can be found in Annex G.

3.   *Other procedural issues*

(a)   Request by the European Communities that relevant scientific evidence and data be provided by the United States

7.100 In a letter dated 21 October 2005, the **European Communities** requested that the United States provide the scientific studies on the basis of which it conducted its risk assessments and approved the six hormones at issue for animal growth promotion so that the Panel, the experts and the European Communities could be given an opportunity to consider them.

7.101 The **United States** objected to this request arguing that a panel was not expected to make a *de novo* review of the safety of the hormones and draw its own scientific decisions on whether a Member should apply a measure. Nor was a panel called upon to conduct its own risk assessment. The US decision to allow the use of the six growth promoting hormones was not within the Panel's terms of reference. Rather, it was the EC import ban, and the purported risk assessments and studies allegedly underpinning that ban, which speak to whether or not the European Communities has complied with the DSB's recommendations and rulings in the *EC – Hormones* dispute.[387]

7.102 In a letter to the Panel dated 8 November 2005, the **European Communities** argued that the scientific basis of the EC measure at issue was being challenged with reference to assessments done by other bodies or institutions, including the defending party's own regulatory bodies. If the Panel and the experts were to assess objectively the relevance and sufficiency of the scientific information on which the European Communities relied in order to ban these substances, they would have to review also the underlying evidence on which JECFA and some WTO Members relied in order to conclude that the hormones at issue were safe. Due process required that the Panel request the defending party to submit its underlying scientific studies.

7.103 In addition, the European Communities requested that the Panel ask Codex to submit to the Panel the underlying scientific evidence and data that served as the basis of the JECFA's assessments, which were invoked by the defending party in these proceedings. In the view of the European Communities, the Panel was competent to request the information at issue both from the defending party and from Codex under Article 13 of the DSU.[388]

7.104 The **United States** replied to the EC comments in a letter of 9 November 2005, that it did not refer to its own risk assessment but to determinations of the

---

[387] US's letter to the Panel of 3 November 2005.
[388] EC's letter to the Panel of 8 November 2005.

relevant international standard setting bodies (Codex and JECFA) regarding the safety of the hormones at issue. At the same time, the United States agreed with the European Communities that an examination of JECFA's and Codex's conclusions regarding the hormones may be useful for an overall review of the EC characterization of its ban as a "provisional measure" for five of the hormones and of the EC purported risk assessment for the sixth hormone.

7.105 The **European Communities** replied to the comments by the United States and Canada in a letter to the Panel dated 11 November 2005. The European Communities observed that a substantial amount of data on which JECFA based its findings came from, and were available only with, the United States' and Canada's authorities since JECFA had to rely exclusively on data provided to it, *inter alia*, by its members and the relevant industry. Thus, in the case of the six hormones in question, JECFA, where it did not base itself on scientific evidence publicly available, examined and relied on evidence that was available only with the United States' and Canada's regulatory authorities. Most of these studies were old and had never been published in peer reviewed scientific journals.

7.106 The European Communities added that, because the Panel had decided to examine the scientific basis of the EC compliance measure, this examination had to be carried out in the light of the assessments on which the responding party explicitly based itself in order to question the European Communities' risk assessment and continue its unilateral suspension of concessions, i.e, its own risk assessments and those of Codex/JECFA.

7.107 On 17 November 2005, the **United States** commented on the EC arguments by mentioning that what was at issue in these proceedings was whether or not the European Communities had, through the studies it had chosen to rely upon and the Opinions it had put forward in support of its bans, based its measures on a risk assessment within the meaning of Article 5.1 of the *SPS Agreement* or imposed a provisional ban within the meaning of Article 5.7 of the *SPS Agreement*. In carrying out its task to examine these issues, the question was whether what the European Communities had produced and put forward as evidence in support of its ongoing ban met the requirements of the *SPS Agreement*.

7.108 Furthermore, according to the United States, detailed summaries of the studies and materials relied upon by JECFA were available for each of the hormones at issue in this proceeding in the WHO Technical Report Series publications.[389]

---

[389]   US's letter to the Panel of 17 November 2005.

7.109 The **European Communities** commented on 21 November 2005 that, because the Panel was to make an objective assessment of the matter before it, it would also have to evaluate the conclusions of JECFA. Since the European Communities and JECFA had come to differing conclusions, the question was whether they had done so on the basis of the same data. In particular, it was not enough to refer to the summaries in the Technical Report Series because they were too concise to allow such an assessment, and they referred to old and unpublished US data from the 1970s.

7.110 The **Panel** considered the parties' arguments in its letter to the parties on the finalized working procedures for consultation with scientific and /or technical experts:

> "With respect to the EC's request that the Panel ask the US and Canada to provide the studies underlying the risk assessments of the US, Canada (and JECFA), the Panel is not in a position to fully assess the necessity for this information at this stage. This said, the Panel notes that its task is not to conduct a comprehensive assessment of the safety of hormones in meat. Rather, should the Panel consider it necessary for the resolution of the present dispute, it would assess the compatibility of the EC's measure with the provisions of the *SPS Agreement*. Nevertheless, to the extent that this information becomes necessary for the Panel to make its determination in this case, the Panel cannot exclude that it may request part or all of the information referred to by the EC. More generally, the Panel expects the Parties' full collaboration in gathering the information necessary for an objective assessment of the matter before it. The Panel also recalls that it is for each party to submit sufficient evidence in support of its assertions."[390]

7.111 In addition, the Panel wishes to recall its comments above on its discretionary power to seek information or not pursuant to Article 13 of the DSU. The Panel also agrees with the parties that, while it has to make an objective assessment of the matter before it, including an objective assessment of the facts, it is not supposed to make a *de novo* review of factual information, including scientific evidence, regarding the six hormones at issue. Thus, the Panel considered primarily in this context the measure taken by the European Communities to comply with the recommendations and rulings of the DSB in the *EC – Hormones* dispute. Having regard to the allocation of the burden of proof, the Panel deemed it appropriate to rely more particularly on the extensive amount of evidence submitted by the European Communities and the United States in their submissions. The Panel also took into account the opinions of the experts and

---

[390] Panel letter to the parties of 25 November 2005.

the inputs from the international entities it consulted under Article 13 of the DSU. To the extent that the parties and the experts discussed the EC implementing measure in the context of the work of JECFA and Codex, the Panel believes that it was sufficiently informed to make an objective assessment of the facts and did not need to ask the United States and Codex to provide the information requested by the European Communities.

(b)   Request by the United States to exclude materials not cited in the EC risk assessment as well as those published after the completion of its risk assessment by the European Communities and the adoption of the ban

7.112 On 14 March 2006, the **United States** sent a letter to the Panel requesting it not to provide to scientific experts materials that had not been cited in the EC risk assessment, nor those published after the completion of the EC risk assessment and the adoption of the ban at issue. The United States also requested the Panel not to consider nor base its findings on these extraneous materials provided by the European Communities.

7.113 The United States recalled that Directive 2003/74/EC[391] which the European Communities claimed complies with the recommendations and rulings of the DSB in the underlying *EC – Hormones* dispute, was based on the results of its 1999, 2000, and 2002 Opinions which, the European Communities contended, demonstrated that the amended ban satisfied the conditions of Articles 5.1 and 5.7 of the *SPS Agreement*.

7.114 Accordingly, materials that had no apparent relationship to the European Communities' alleged risk assessment, including materials published after the completion of the EC risk assessment and the adoption of its ban, were extraneous for purposes of the Panel's examination in this dispute.

7.115 To the extent that the European Communities, by submitting these materials, was inviting the Panel (or the experts) to review them as part of a *de novo* risk assessment, this was not a proper role for either the Panel or the experts. Rather, the question presented was whether the risk assessment identified by the

---

[391]   Directive 2003/74/EC of the European Parliament and of the Council of 22 September 2003 amending Directive 96/22/EC concerning the prohibition on the use in stockfarming of certain substances having hormonal or thyrostatic action and beta-agonists, Official Journal No. L 262, 14 October 2003, p. 178 (hereinafter also "the Directive").

European Communities actually had brought the European Communities into compliance with its WTO obligations.[392]

7.116 The **European Communities** stated that it had fundamental objections to the requests of the defending party. They were contrary to the Appellate Body's interpretation of the requirements of a "risk assessment", as set out in *EC – Hormones*. They were in violation of the Panel's Working Procedures in this case, and they ran diametrically counter to the whole purpose of an expert consultation by the Panel.

7.117 According to the European Communities, the issue of whether a measure could be considered to be based on scientific evidence that was not cited or had not been taken into account in a risk assessment, or both, had already been settled by the Appellate Body in its report on *EC – Hormones*, at paragraphs 188 through 191. There the Appellate Body had dismissed the proposition by the complaining parties and the finding by the panel that scientific evidence had to be cited in the risk assessment, as a "minimum procedural requirement". The European Communities failed to understand why the defending party now reopened an issue that had already been decided.

7.118 The European Communities had submitted new materials as exhibits in its replies to the Panel's questions and as part of its second written submission. They were, therefore, lawfully before the Panel and were directly covered by Paragraph 13 of the Expert Working Procedures.

7.119 In this context, the European Communities also pointed to the fact that the United States itself had submitted materials that had been published after the EC risk assessment (see e.g. US – Exhibits 7, 16, 20; CDA – Exhibits 20, 26, 27, 28, 33). The US request was, therefore, based on a double standard: In case recent evidence served the objectives of the United States it had to be admitted, whereas evidence that was unfavourable to the United States should not be taken into account.

7.120 According to the European Communities, the United States' request had to be dismissed in view of the purpose of the experts' consultation. The principal objective of consulting experts was to provide the Panel with *objective* information and advice on questions related to the scientific basis of Directive 2003/74/EC. In order to fulfil this task, the experts could not ignore the most recent and directly relevant scientific evidence that is publicly available.[393]

---

[392] US's letter to the Panel of 14 March 2006.
[393] EC's letter to the Panel of 23 March 2006.

7.121 On 31 March 2006, the **Panel** addressed this issue in its letter to parties informing the parties that it would not reject *a priori* any piece of evidence at that stage. However, the Panel decided to ask experts to specify whether their reply would have been different at the time of adoption of Directive 2003/74/EC and why. The Panel also requested the parties to identify, among the exhibits submitted, those studies to which they had had access before their publication date.

> "With respect to the issues raised in the letter of the United States on 14 March 2006, in Canada's comments of 15 March 2006, and in the European Communities' letter of 23 March 2006, the Panel is reluctant to reject a priori any piece of evidence at this stage. It will revert to this matter in its findings, as appropriate. In the meantime, and without prejudice to its final decision, the Panel has decided to amend some of its questions to the experts and request them to specify whether their reply would have been different at the time of adoption of the measure at issue (September 2003) and, if not, why.
>
> In this respect, the Panel would be grateful if the parties could specify by Friday, 7 April 2006, among the exhibits they submitted, those studies to which they had access before their official publication dates and, if so, specify the date on which they had access to each of them."[394]

7.122 Also, in its guideline letter sent on 30 March 2006 to the selected scientific and technical experts, the Panel specified that "wherever reference is made to scientific or technical facts, or comment is made on scientific evidence or literature, you are requested to provide references to the relevant studies and publications".[395]

7.123 The Panel considers that its approach allowed it to have a better understanding of the situation at the time of the adoption of Directive 2003/74/EC. However, since nothing has been submitted that became available subsequent to the adoption of the Directive and that differed in any fundamental way from the evidence available at that time[396], the Panel does not deem it necessary to address this issue any further.

---

[394] Panel letter to the parties of 31 March 2006.

[395] Panel guideline letter to selected experts of 30 March 2006.

[396] This was confirmed by the experts when they were requested to specify in their replies to questions of the Panel whether their views would have been different at the time of the adoption of Directive 2003/74/EC.

      (c)   A new version of Exhibit EC-107, submitted by
               the European Communities on 29 May 2006.

7.124 On 29 May 2006, the **European Communities** submitted a new version of its Exhibit EC-107, entitled "The sensitivity of the child to sex steroids: possible impact of exogenous estrogens", a study published on 2 May 2006. The European Communities stated that it would leave it to the Panel to decide whether to forward this version to experts.[397]

7.125 The **Panel** decided on 23 June 2006 not to forward this version of Exhibit EC-107 to the scientific experts for the following reasons:

> "With regard to the EC letter of 29 May and its attachment, the Panel takes note of the fact that the study submitted as Exhibit EC-107 has now been published. However, the Panel notes that the version of the study submitted as Exhibit EC-107 and the version attached to the EC letter of 29 May are somewhat different and that the difference are apparently not merely editorial. In this respect, the Panel recalls that the parties had been given until 21 December 2005 to submit factual evidence to the experts. Therefore, the Panel has decided not to send the published version of the study contained in Exhibit EC-107 to the experts."[398]

7.126 We confirm the position we took in this letter. We note that previous panels dealing with SPS measures have, in the context of proceedings under Article 21.5 of the DSU, considered *measures* adopted after the establishment of the panel.[399] However, as far as *evidence* is concerned, panels have generally refused to accept evidence submitted after a certain date, generally after the first substantive meeting, except for rebuttal purposes or upon a showing of good cause. In this particular case, the parties had been given until 21 December 2005, i.e. several weeks after their second written submissions, to provide factual evidence that they deemed relevant. The Panel considered also that submitting a modified study to experts at a relatively late stage of the expert consultation proceedings could generate confusion.

      (d)   Procedure for allowing the parties to comment on
              each other's replies to questions after the second
              Panel meeting

7.127 On 18 October 2006, the **United States** requested the Panel to provide the parties with the opportunity to comment on each other's replies to questions

---

[397] EC's letter to the Panel of 29 May 2006.
[398] Panel letter to the parties of 23 June 2006.
[399] See *Australia – Salmon (Article 21.5 – Canada)*, *Japan – Apples (Article 21.5 – US)*.

posed to the parties by the Panel and the parties following the second Panel meeting.[400]

7.128 On 20 October 2006, the **Panel** confirmed to the parties that the deadline for such counter comments would be 31 October 2006.[401]

(e) Request by the European Communities to be allowed to correct factual errors allegedly contained in the other party's comments on its replies to questions following the second Panel meeting

7.129 On 13 November 2006, the **European Communities** informed the Panel that it had studied the comments submitted by the United States and Canada on 31 October 2006 and had identified a number of inaccuracies and factual errors in their comments likely to affect the adjudication of the cases.

7.130 The European Communities requested that the Panel allow the parties to submit comments on the factual allegations contained in the comments on the responses. These comments would be restricted to factual matters and would not seek to further discuss any of the legal issues. This would enable the Panel to make an objective assessment of the facts and ensure a high quality panel report.[402]

7.131 According to the **United States**, the European Communities had already had the opportunity to present what it considered to be the facts and there was no reason to give it another opportunity to present its view of the facts. Given the brevity of the US comments and the amount of time that the European Communities had had to study them, the EC request was untimely.

7.132 The United States considered that the Panel was more than capable of performing the task assigned to it by the Dispute Settlement Body and sorting out the various factual elements without the need for additional filings from the parties. Finally, the parties would presumably have an opportunity to point out any factual errors in their comments on the descriptive part and comments on the interim report.[403]

7.133 The **Panel** decided, on 20 November 2006, to reject the EC request:

---

[400] US's cover letter to its replies to the questions of the Panel after the second substantive meeting, dated 18 October 2006.
[401] Panel letter to the parties of 23 October 2006.
[402] EC's letter to the Panel of 13 November 2006.
[403] US's letter to the Panel of 13 November 2006.

"Having carefully reviewed the arguments of the parties, the Panel does not consider it appropriate to offer them another opportunity to comment on alleged factual errors made by the other party. Procedurally, the Panel does not see any difference between comments on factual elements and comments on legal arguments; both can easily lead to endless discussions. The Panel is concerned that giving such an opportunity to parties could open the door to further delays in these proceedings since it would be difficult, once the Panel has allowed comments not foreseen in its timetable, to reject requests for additional comments on the other party's comments. At this juncture, the Panel believes that it has been sufficiently informed by the parties and the experts to be able to make an objective assessment of the case and deems it preferable to continue with the preparation of its report without further exchanges of comments between the parties. The Panel notes in this respect that the DSU provides opportunities for the parties to submit written comments, at a later stage, on the descriptive (factual and arguments) sections of the Panel Report and to request the Panel to review precise aspects of its Interim Report."[404]

7.134 The Panel does not deem it necessary to add anything to the reasoning above.

(f)   Request by the European Communities for tape recordings of the transcript of the Panel meeting with scientific experts

7.135 On 31 January 2007, the **Panel** sent to the parties a draft written transcript of the hearing with the experts, for their review and comments.

7.136 On 14 February 2007, the **European Communities**, in the cover letter accompanying its comments on the transcript, requested the Panel to provide the parties with the tape recordings of the meeting with the experts to check the accuracy of the transcription of the experts' replies. The European Communities argued that the replies of some of the experts were not properly or not fully reflected in the transcript, but did not identify specific parts of the transcript where such errors allegedly occurred.[405]

7.137 The **Panel**, in a letter dated 19 February 2007, requested the European Communities to identify in the draft transcript the places where the European Communities believed the replies of the experts during the meeting had not been

---

[404]   Panel letter to the parties of 20 November 2006.
[405]   EC's letter to the Panel of 14 February 2007.

properly reflected. The Panel added that, once the information had been provided, the Panel itself would further review the draft and make appropriate corrections if necessary. The Panel added that the parties had until 5 April 2007 to submit such information.

7.138 The **European Communities** responded to the Panel on 28 February 2007, confirming that it was not in a position to identify in advance all the places where the transcript may not be entirely accurate, unless it was given copies of the tapes. The European Communities added that some of its doubts had already been pointed out by the United States and some more doubts existed as regards the statements by one expert and by the representatives of the WHO and JECFA. The European Communities also stated that the tapes had been provided to parties in the past in the *EC – Hormones*, the *EC – Asbestos* and the second *EC – Bananas* cases.[406]

7.139 The **Panel** replied that, to its knowledge, in circumstances similar to the present dispute, panels had never provided the tape recordings used in transcripts of meetings with scientific or technical experts to parties for review. As the Panel indicated in its message on 19 February to all parties, parties were welcome to identify any places in the draft transcript where they believed inaccuracies could exist and the Panel would further review the draft and make appropriate corrections if necessary.[407]

7.140 On 28 March, the **European Communities** replied that tapes of recordings had been provided previously upon request. In support of its allegation, it submitted a transmission slip of 21 April 1997 in the *EC – Hormones* panel procedure. The European Communities added that it was entitled to expect that tapes be provided in this case as well.

7.141 The European Communities also pointed out that the written transcript of the meeting of the Panel with the scientific experts had been sent with considerable delay to the parties for verification. In view of the time which had elapsed, it was very difficult to verify the transcript with the required degree of certainty, in the absence of the recordings.

7.142 The **United States** commented on the EC remarks on 5 April 2007, arguing that the experts had reviewed the draft transcript in order to ensure that the transcript accurately reflected their interventions and to make any necessary clarifying changes. Accordingly, in the view of the United States, the only purpose for which the European Communities could be seeking access to the tapes

---

[406] EC's e-mail to the Panel of 28 February 2007.
[407] E-mail of the Panel to the parties of 26 March 2007.

was to verify the transcript with respect to its own interventions. The United States did not see a reason why the tapes would be needed for this purpose.

7.143 In response to the EC argument that it needed the tapes because time had elapsed between the preparation of the transcript and the experts meeting, the United States argued that in every panel proceeding there was significant time between panel meetings and the preparation of the descriptive part of a panel's report. No party in any dispute to which the United States had been a party had ever claimed that it needed access to the tapes of a panel meeting in order to be able to verify that the descriptive part accurately presented the interventions of that party at the panel meeting. Presumably, if there were a particular portion of the transcript of concern to the European Communities, the European Communities could have identified that in its earlier communications and the Panel could have consulted the tapes to confirm that the transcript was accurate with respect to that portion.

7.144 The United States indicated that the transmission slip attached by the European Communities to its communication raised a number of questions while failing to demonstrate the EC claim of "entitlement" to the tape recordings. There was no evidence that copies of the audio tapes from the meeting with the experts in the original proceedings had been provided to the United States for review or that similar tapes of expert meetings were provided to the United States in other dispute settlement proceedings. The European Communities had failed to mention that the transmission slip was not related to the tapes of the experts meeting in the original *EC – Hormones* dispute. The United States noted that the cover slip submitted by the European Communities to the Panel cited a date (7 January 1997) that neither corresponded to the dates of the meeting with the scientific experts in the original dispute (17-18 February 1997), nor did it correspond to any of the meeting dates in the original *EC – Hormones* dispute between the United States and the EC (WT/DS26). Furthermore, that transmission slip involved a separate dispute with different panelists and different terms of reference than the current proceeding. The United States therefore disagreed that the transmission slip in question was relevant to sharing recordings of meetings with scientific experts with the parties to a dispute.[408]

7.145 The **Panel** sent to the parties an additional message on 18 April 2007, rejecting the EC request for tape recordings:

"Since the latest message from the Panel to the parties on 26 March 2007, the Panel has received from the European Communities an additional communication on 28 March, indicating that tape

---

[408] US's letter to the Panel of 5 April 2007.

recordings had been provided to the European Communities in the original *EC – Hormones* panel proceedings.

The Panel subsequently received a letter from the United States indicating that the EC failed to mention that the transmission slip it submitted together with its 28 March letter is not related to the tapes of the expert meeting in the original *EC – Hormones* dispute because the date mentioned on that slip (7 January 1997) does not correspond to the date of the experts meeting (17-18 February 1997) in the original *EC – Hormones* dispute between the United States and the European Communities (WT/DS26).

The Panel found that the meeting date mentioned on the slip provided by the EC was the date of the first substantive meeting of the panel in the original *EC – Hormones* dispute between the European Communities and Canada. The meeting with experts in the two disputes was jointly held on 17-18 February 1997, while the meetings with parties were held separately. After further verification, we can confirm that, to the best of our knowledge, the tape recordings of the experts meeting on 17 and 18 February in the two original *EC – Hormones* panels were never provided to the parties.

The Panel recalls that the European Communities' request is based on its desire to check whether the experts' replies at the experts meeting have been accurately reflected in the transcript. Consistent with the practice of other panels, the Panel has invited the parties and the experts to verify the accuracy of their own interventions during the meetings. In addition, the Panel invited the parties to identify any places in the draft transcript where they believe inaccuracies could exist and the Panel was ready to review those portions of the transcript and make appropriate corrections if necessary.

By 5 April 2007, a deadline date set by the Panel in its communication to the parties on 26 March 2006, none of the parties had identified any such inaccuracies.

Therefore, on the basis of the above, the Panel does not deem it necessary to provide the tape recordings of the meeting with the experts to the parties."[409]

---

[409] Panel letter to the parties of 18 April 2007.

7.146 The **European Communities** sent another message to the Panel on 11 May 2007, commenting on the Panel's decision:

"The European Communities appreciates the e-mail of the Panel of 18 April replying to our additional communication on 28 March, indicating that the tape recordings that had been provided to the European Communities in the original *EC – Hormones* panel proceedings were not from a hearing with scientific experts.

In that case we did indeed receive (and still have in our archives) from the panel five tapes of 90 minutes each of the meeting held on 7 January 1997, which was indeed a meeting not with scientific experts. The point we were making is that since panels have provided the parties in the past tapes of a regular hearing, why is it not possible to provide the tapes of a hearing with scientific experts (where verification of what exactly was said is even more important)?

More generally, panels send to parties the factual part of the draft report for verification (which is essentially done on the basis of the written submissions of the parties). The hearing with scientific experts is also part of the factual part of the report. So, one can expect that the tapes from such a hearing with scientific experts can also be sent for verification. This is all the more important in the case of a hearing with scientific experts, because it is impossible both for the scientific experts and the parties to take verbatim notes of a hearing that lasted two days and with the speed at which the oral exchanges take place in such hearing. Indeed, the scientific experts presumably did not take verbatim notes of what they said during the hearing and so they are in the same difficult position as the parties to remember what exactly they have said several months ago. For example, the European Communities has some doubts whether the following paragraphs of the draft report it has received reflect accurately what exactly has been said by the experts during the hearing on 27-28 September 2006: paragraphs 353, 386, 388, 390, 421-422, 500, 690, 706, 710, 719-720, 734, 779, 785, 891, 994, 1018, 1028. Furthermore, the European Communities considers that something may be wrong or missing between paragraphs 972 and 973 of the draft report.

The European Communities respectfully requests the Panel to reconsider its position. If the Panel still feels unable to provide the European Communities with the tapes, it would ask the Panel to set out its reasons for refusing this request in the Report."

7.147 The **United States** sent a letter to the Panel on 14 May 2007 in response to the EC message of 11 May 2007 stating that:

"As noted by the Panel in its April 18, 2007, communication to the Parties on this issue, '[c]onsistent with the practice of other panels, the Panel has invited the parties and the experts to *verify the accuracy of their own interventions during the meetings*.' (Emphasis added). The United States was therefore surprised to note that all but two of the paragraphs (972-73) cited by the EC in its request relate to interventions of experts (specifically Drs. Boobis and Boisseau):

Paragraphs 353 (Boobis); 386 (Boobis); 388 (Boobis); 390 (Boobis); 421-22 (Boobis); 500 (Boobis); 690 (Boobis); 706 (Boobis); 710 (Boobis); 719-20 (Boisseau); 734 (Boisseau); 779 (Boobis); 785 (Boobis); 891 (Boisseau); 994 (Boobis); 1018 (Boobis); 1028 (Boobis).

It is unclear why it took the EC several months to identify these paragraphs. Indeed, the EC has missed the deadline set by the Panel (April 5, 2007) for identifying specific issues with the transcript by more than a month. It is even more perplexing why the EC, when it finally provided a list of "doubts" regarding the transcript, cited non-EC interventions, ignoring the Panel's clear instructions in its January 31, 2007 communication to the parties. The United States considers that Drs. Boobis and Boisseau, both preeminent experts in their respective fields, are more than capable of confirming that what they said or did not say is accurately reflected in the transcript, without the assistance of the EC or any other party. Were it otherwise, the parties to a dispute would be afforded the opportunity to rewrite expert opinions after the fact and based upon their six-month old recollections, thereby calling into question the purpose of consulting independent experts in the first place.

As for the other two paragraphs cited by the EC (972-73) that actually appear to relate to EC interventions, the United States considers that the Panel, should it decide to set aside its April 5, 2007 deadline for identifying problematic portions of the transcript, is more than capable of double-checking the accuracy of this discrete portion of the transcript without the need to circulate copies of the tapes of the expert meetings to the Parties (see e-mail from the Panel dated March 26, 2007, in which the Panel indicated that, by April 5, 2007, the 'parties are welcome to identify any places in the draft transcript where they believe inaccuracies could exist and the

Panel will further review those portions of the transcript and make appropriate corrections if necessary')."

7.148 On 5 June 2007, the Panel informed the parties that the European Communities had not identified the relevant paragraphs in the draft transcript that it wanted the Panel to review before the deadline of 5 April 2007, as specified by the Panel in its earlier communication to the parties. At such a late stage, the Panel had every reason to disregard the request for review of the paragraphs identified by the European Communities in its letter of 11 May 2007. Nevertheless, as a matter of prudence, the Panel checked the relevant paragraphs in the draft transcript against the original tape recordings and did not find any discrepancy beyond minimal editorial adjustments. Therefore, the Panel saw no reason to reverse its decision not to provide tape recordings of the meeting with scientific experts to the parties for further review.

7.149 The Panel believes that the reasons for its decision not to provide tape recordings of the meeting with scientific experts were sufficiently described in its communications. It does not deem it necessary to elaborate on them any further.

4. Scope of the Panel's mandate

(a) The measure at issue and the claims of the European Communities

7.150 The matter before this Panel is the alleged failure of the United States to comply with the DSU and the GATT 1994 in response to the adoption and notification to the DSB of an alleged compliance measure by the European Communities in the *EC – Hormones* case.[410]

7.151 The measure at issue is the continued application by the United States, after the notification to the DSB of Directive 2003/74/EC by the European Communities, of its decision to apply, as from 29 July 1999, import duties in excess of bound rates by imposing a 100% ad valorem duty on a number of products imported from certain member States of the European Communities[411] without recourse to the procedures under the DSU. This decision had been taken pursuant to an authorization granted by the DSB to the United States to suspend concessions and other obligations on 26 July 1999.[412]

7.152 In its request for establishment of a panel, the European Communities lists Articles I and II of the GATT 1994 and Articles 23.1, 23.2(a) and (c); 3.7,

---

[410] WT/DS26.
[411] US Federal Register, Vol. 64, No. 143 of 27 July 1999, p. 40638.
[412] WT/DSB/M/65, p. 19.

22.8 and 21.5 of the DSU as having been breached by the United States. However, in its first written submission and subsequently, the European Communities elaborates on the scope of those claims. More particularly, it divides its claims between a set of *main* claims and one *conditional* claim.[413]

7.153 The European Communities also specifies how its *main* claims of violation of the DSU should be addressed. The European Communities makes a first series of main claims, alleging a violation of Article 23 of the DSU and, more particularly, Article 23.2(a) read in conjunction with Articles 21.5 and 23.1 of the DSU. The European Communities also makes a second series of main claims, alleging a violation of Article 23.1, read in conjunction with Articles 22.8 and 3.7 of the DSU. In support of the second series of claims, the European Communities alleges that it enjoys a presumption of good faith compliance "which cannot be undermined by a unilateral and unsubstantiated determination by the United States."[414]

7.154 The European Communities also specifies in its first submission that Directive 2003/74/EC, which it claims implemented the recommendations and rulings of the DSB in the *EC – Hormones* case, is compatible with Article 5.1 and 5.7 of the *SPS Agreement*. However, there is no reference to provisions of the *SPS Agreement* in the EC request for establishment of a panel.

7.155 The *conditional* claim, that of a violation of Article 22.8 of the DSU *per se,* is "made in the alternative and only on the condition that the Panel does not establish any violation under Articles 23.1, 23.2(a), 3.7, 22.8 and 21.5 of the DSU".[415]

7.156 This *conditional* claim is, like the second series of main claims raised by the European Communities, based on the EC view that it has complied with the recommendations and rulings of the DSB in the *EC – Hormones* case by adopting Directive 2003/74/EC and properly notifying it to the DSB. The difference is that, under the conditional claim, the European Communities alleges actual compliance, and not that it should be presumed to have complied in good faith.

7.157 The EC implementing measure imposes a definitive import prohibition on meat and meat products from animals treated for growth promotion purposes with oestradiol-17β and a provisional ban on meat and meat products from animals treated for growth promotion purposes with testosterone, progesterone, trenbolone acetate, zeranol and melengestrol acetate. The EC implementing measure is allegedly "based on a comprehensive risk assessment and, thus, is

---

[413]   EC's first written submission, para. 8.
[414]   EC's first written submission, para. 72.
[415]   EC's first written submission, para. 132.

fully compliant with the DSB recommendations and rulings. In particular, [according to the European Communities and] as stipulated by the Appellate Body, the results of the risk assessment 'sufficiently warrant' the definite import prohibition regarding one of the hormones (Article 5.1 of the *SPS Agreement*), [footnote omitted] and provide the 'available pertinent information' on the basis of which the provisional prohibition regarding the five hormones has been enacted (Article 5.7 of the *SPS Agreement*)."[416]

> (b) Are the indications provided by the European Communities on how it wants its claims to be addressed part of the mandate of the Panel?

7.158 As a preliminary remark, the Panel notes that, when dealing with the scope of panel terms of reference, panels and the Appellate Body so far addressed situations where panel requests were alleged to be insufficiently precise. In the present case, the EC request for the establishment of a panel, while not as explicit as the EC first written submission, explains in its section 2 ("The object of the dispute") some of the elements of the approach that the European Communities wants the Panel to follow. Yet, it does not outline its claims as was done in the EC first written submission. For instance, the request for the establishment of a panel lists Article 22.8 but it does not differentiate between the main "systemic" claim relating to Article 22.8 (violation of Article 23.1, read in conjunction with Articles 22.8 and 3.7 of the DSU) and the conditional "direct" claim of violation of Article 22.8. Likewise, in the request for establishment of a panel, each provision is identified separately, without any terms like "read together with" or "read in conjunction with."

7.159 In *Korea – Dairy*, the Appellate Body defined the meaning of *claim* and *arguments* as follows:

> "By *claim*, we mean a claim that the respondent party has violated, or nullified or impaired the benefits arising from, an identified provision of a particular agreement. Such a *claim of violation* must, as we have already noted, be distinguished from the *arguments* adduced by a complaining party to demonstrate that the responding party's measure does indeed infringe upon the identified treaty provision."[417]

7.160 In the opinion of the Panel, the approach of the European Communities as developed in its first written submission does not amount to "arguments" insofar as it does not "demonstrate that the responding party's measure does indeed in-

---

[416] EC's first written submission, para. 17.
[417] Appellate Body Report on *Korea – Dairy*, para. 139

fringe upon the identified treaty provision". In fact, it does not purport to explain to what extent the EC claims are justified, but simply circumscribes their scope.

7.161 We further note that, in *US – Carbon Steel*, the Appellate Body stated that:

> "[I]n considering the sufficiency of a panel request, submissions and statements made during the course of the panel proceedings, in particular the first written submission of the complaining party, may be consulted in order to confirm the meaning of the words used in the panel request and as part of the assessment of whether the ability of the respondent to defend itself was prejudiced. Moreover, compliance with the requirements of Article 6.2 must be determined on the merits of each case, having considered the panel request as a whole, and in the light of attendant circumstances."[418]

7.162 The Panel is mindful that this statement was made in relation to a situation where the terms of reference were alleged not to cover specific claims. On the contrary, in the present case, the European Communities narrows the terms of reference of the Panel insofar as it requires a specific approach to the provisions allegedly breached. However, this statement equally applies in the present circumstances to the extent that the EC first written submission may be consulted in order to confirm the meaning of the words used in the request for establishment of a panel.

7.163 In that context, it can be considered that the approach to this case requested by the European Communities and contained in its first written submission is actually a clarification of the claims listed in its request for establishment of a panel and not arguments, and that it informs those claims.

7.164 We therefore conclude that the EC approach outlined in its first written submission is part of the Panel's terms of reference. One consequence is that since the claim of "direct" violation of Article 22.8 is made *in the alternative*, the Panel cannot and will not address it unless the European Communities fails to establish its main claims. The other consequence is that we should address the main claims as elaborated by the European Communities in its first written submission and subsequently.

---

[418] Appellate Body Report on *US – Carbon Steel*, para. 127.

(c) Meaning of "read together with" and "in conjunction with" in the EC submissions

7.165 The main or principal claims of the European Communities raise an additional question, i.e. whether the European Communities alleges a violation of Article 23 of the DSU alone or of all the provisions cited in its submission in support of its claim of violation of Article 23.

7.166 The Panel notes that in questions put to the European Communities after the first substantive meeting, and in its second written submission, the United States challenges the EC claim of violations of Article 21.5 "together with" Article 23.2(a) and of Article 22.8 "in conjunction with" Article 23.1 on two grounds:

(a) the United States alleges that the European Communities abandoned its claims of specific violations of each of these provisions *per se;*

(b) the United States argues that the EC approach is inconsistent with the customary rules of interpretation of international law by trying to impose obligations that are not supported by the text of the provisions concerned.

7.167 The European Communities replies that the United States is acting contrary to Articles 23.1, 23.2(a) and 21.5 read together and that, as a result, the European Communities maintains its claim under Article 21.5. As far as Article 22.8 is concerned, the European Communities states that the panel request lists all the relevant provisions which the United States is currently violating and, in particular, Article 22.8 and Article 23.1. The European Communities also considers that its approach consisting of citing various provisions to substantiate a claim was approved by the Panel in *US – Certain EC Products*.

7.168 The Panel recalls that the request for establishment of a panel made by the European Communities refers to "Article 23.1; 23.2(a) and (c); 3.7; 22.8 and 21.5 of the DSU". Thus, examining the conformity of the US measures with Articles 3.7, 21.5 and 22.8 of the DSU is part of the Panel mandate.

7.169 The Panel does not believe that the European Communities abandoned its claims under Articles 3.7, 21.5 and 22.8 of the DSU because it alleged a violation of those provisions "read together with" or "in conjunction with" other provisions. This is confirmed by the European Communities itself in its reply to questions of the United States referred to above.

7.170 The Panel notes the argument of the United States that the European Communities is trying to impose obligations that are not supported by the text of the provisions concerned. We recall that paragraph 1 of Article 31 of the Vienna Convention on the Law of Treaties, embodying the customary rules of interpretation of public international law referred to in Article 3.2 of the DSU, provides that:

"A treaty shall be interpreted in good faith in accordance with the ordinary meaning to be given to the terms of the treaty in their context and in the light of its object and purpose."

7.171 The Panel does not exclude that there could be situations where the rights or obligations of Members could vary depending on which other provision a particular article of the DSU is read together with. However, either the terms of the provisions concerned interpreted in their ordinary meaning, in their context and in the light of the object and purpose of the treaty or the provisions support the claim, or they do not. Likewise, it is often the case that the violation of a particular provision will have consequences on the legality of the measure at issue under other provisions of the same or of other covered agreements.

7.172 We note that, in *US – Certain EC Products*, the panel stated that:

"Since we have already concluded that the 3 March Measure constituted a measure taken to redress a WTO violation (covered by Article 23.1), we proceed to examine whether the same 3 March Measure violated the provisions of the sub-paragraph 2(c) of Article 23 of the DSU, as well as Articles 3.7 and 22.6 of the DSU."[419]

7.173 In other words, it would appear that the panel in *US – Certain EC Products*, even though it considered the effects of a finding of violation of one provision on the other – this is probably what it meant by "Article 23.1 together with Articles 23.2(c), 3.7 and 22.6 of the DSU" in the title of the section where the above quotation is found – nevertheless made findings of violation of each provision individually. We note that, likewise, the Appellate Body assessed the panel findings on each provision separately.[420]

7.174 The European Communities states that, if it had not specified Articles 21 and 22 in its request for establishment of a panel, the United States would have probably argued that these provisions were not part of the terms of reference of the Panel. This would suggest that the European Communities is actually requesting findings only in relation to Article 23.1 and 23.2(a), the references to the other provisions being part of the context in which the obligations under Article 23 have to be assessed. This seems to be confirmed by the EC conclusion in its first written submission where the European Communities states that the United States violates Article 23 of the DSU and, more particularly, Arti-

---

[419] Panel Report on *US – Certain EC Products*, para. 6.36.
[420] Appellate Body Report on *US – Certain EC Products*, para.106 *et seq.*

cle 23.2(a) read in conjunction with Articles 21.5 and 23.1 of the DSU and violates Article 23.1, read in conjunction with Articles 22.8 and 3.7 of the DSU.

7.175 We note, however, that the European Communities listed all these provisions in its request for establishment of a panel and confirmed in its reply to the US question referred to above that it "is maintaining its claim under Article 21.5". As far as Article 22.8 is concerned, the European Communities states that the panel request lists all the relevant provisions which the United States is currently violating and, in particular, Article 22.8 and Article 23.1.

7.176 While the European Communities seems to insist on the violations of Article 23, the Panel does not believe that the terms "read together with/read in conjunction with" were meant to limit its findings of violation to Article 23. Rather, the European Communities is seeking findings on all the provisions cited but, because of the broadly cast wording of Article 23, the European Communities seeks to circumscribe the context in which that violation is to be found. In other words, it wants us to articulate any findings of violation of Article 23 with the violations of Articles 21.5, 22.8 and 3.7 of the DSU.

7.177 The Panel concludes that the fact that the European Communities is seeking findings of violation of Article 23 "read together with" or "read in conjunction with" should not be understood as meaning that the European Communities exclusively claims a violation of Article 23. The Panel believes that its mandate includes Articles 21.5, 22.8 and 3.7 of the DSU.

(d) Conclusion

7.178 From the above we conclude that:

(a) the indications given by the European Communities on how it wants this case to be addressed (main claims and alternative claim) are part of the Panel's mandate;

(b) the indication by the European Communities that certain provisions referred to in its request for establishment of the Panel be "read together" or "in conjunction with" does not mean that the Panel is not expected to make findings on each of these provisions.

5. *Approach of the Panel on the basis of its mandate*

7.179 We are mindful of the EC position that this case is primarily about alleged violations of the DSU and, in particular, Article 23 thereof. We note in particular the EC argument that it brought this case because the United States refused to initiate a procedure under Article 21.5 of the DSU and did not agree to any other procedural arrangement.[421] We note that the European Communities also claims that the United States breaches Article 23 of the DSU read together with Article 22.8 because it failed to withdraw its suspension of obligations in spite of the EC removal of the measure found to be inconsistent with a covered agreement.

7.180 We also recall that the United States' defence consists of arguing first that the European Communities has failed to prove that the United States has breached Article 22.8 of the DSU. The position of the United States is that it does not breach Article 22.8 of the DSU because the European Communities has failed to comply with the recommendations and ruling of the DSB in the *EC – Hormones* case. In support, it argues that Directive 2003/74/EC still breaches provisions of the *SPS Agreement*, more particularly Articles 3.3, 5.1 and 5.7 thereof. The other violations of the DSU and GATT 1994 are only addressed by the United States in a second stage.

7.181 In our opinion, the EC claims of violation of Article 23.2(a) read together with Articles 21.5 and 23.1 are not premised on compliance by the European Communities with the DSB recommendations and ruling in the *EC – Hormones* case, whereas the claims of violation of Article 23.1, read together with Articles 22.8 and 3.7 of the DSU, are. Indeed, the EC claims of violation of Article 23.2(a), read together with Articles 21.5 and 23.1 of the DSU are premised on the fact that the respondent would have maintained a measure that could be deemed to be a "determination to the effect that a violation has occurred" without having recourse to dispute settlement in accordance with the DSU. Such a determination could take place whether or not the European Communities has complied with the DSB recommendations and rulings in *EC - Hormones*. Comparatively, the second series of EC claims is, to the extent that it includes Article 22.8, premised on the requirement that the respondent measure can "only be applied until such time as the measure found to be inconsistent with a covered agreement has been removed", as claimed by the European Communities. Thus, addressing the second series of main claims of the European Communities entails that we review the question of the presumed or actual compliance of the EC implementing measure with the DSB recommendations and rulings in the *EC – Hormones* case.

7.182 We believe that these two series of claims, as presented by the European Communities, are independent from each other and can be addressed completely separately. However, while we are free to structure the order of our analysis as we see fit[422], we see no reasons not to review the EC claims in the order fol-

---

[421] EC's first written submission, para. 5.
[422] Appellate Body Report on *Canada – Wheat Export and Grain Imports*, paras. 126-129.

lowed by the European Communities in its submissions. We therefore proceed now with the first series of claims raised by the European Communities.

B.   First Series of EC Claims: Violation of Article 23.2(a) Read Together with Articles 21.5 and 23.1

1.   Summary of the main arguments of the parties[423]

7.183   The **European Communities** argues that by maintaining its suspension of obligations, the United States is seeking redress of a perceived violation of the WTO Agreement. Pursuant to Article 23 of the DSU, any attempt to seek "redress" can take place only pursuant to the rules and procedures of the DSU. The US continued suspension of obligations is contrary to the specific prohibition of unilateral conduct set out in Article 23.2(a) of the DSU. Instead, the United States should have introduced a compliance procedure under Article 21.5 of the DSU. By not doing so, the United States has violated the specific prohibition of unilateral conduct set out in Article 23.2(a) of the DSU. This violation of Articles 23.2(a) and 21.5 constitutes at the same time a violation of Article 23.1 of the DSU.

7.184   The European Communities, referring to the panel report in *US – Section 301 Trade Act,* notes that the following three conditions need to be fulfilled in order to find a violation of Article 23.2(a) of the DSU.

(a)   First, given the "chapeau" of Article 23.2, it needs to be established that a Member is seeking to redress a WTO violation. In the opinion of the European Communities, this is the case here.

(b)   Second, Article 23.2(a) of the DSU requires that a Member has made a "determination to the effect that a WTO violation has occurred." Such a decision need not have a specific form, and can be inferred from action. The suspension of concessions or other obligations is the very means (albeit of last resort) of reacting to a violation and therefore necessarily implies a decision that there is a violation. The multilateral determination at the origin of the current US suspension of concessions was, however, made with respect to the measures previously applied by the European Communities. Logically, it could not and did not apply to the measures subsequently adopted and properly notified to the WTO by the European Communities. If the United States continues to apply the suspension of concessions and related obligations, it necessarily

---

[423]   A more detailed account of the parties' arguments can be found in Section IV of the descriptive part of this Report. The order in which the respective arguments of the parties are presented does not reflect any allocation of the burden of proof by the Panel.

implies that it has unilaterally determined that there continues to be a violation. It has, in addition, explicitly said so.

(c)   Third, Article 23.2(a) of the DSU is violated if the determination is not made in accordance with the rules and procedures of the DSU or is not consistent with the findings of a dispute settlement organ. The DSU provides for a specific procedure, namely Article 21.5 of the DSU, to address the situation that Members disagree over the existence or consistency of measures taken to comply with the recommendations and rulings of the DSB.

7.185 In the view of the European Communities, there exists obviously a disagreement as to whether or not, by adopting Directive 2003/74/EC, the European Communities has implemented the recommendations and rulings from the DSB in the *EC – Hormones* case. Article 21.5 of the DSU requires that that disagreement *shall* be decided through recourse to dispute settlement. To date, the United States has refused to initiate a compliance procedure under Article 21.5 (or, for that matter, any other dispute settlement procedure under the DSU). Instead, it continues to apply the suspension of concessions and other obligations as if no "measure to comply" had been taken or the non-compliance of the new directive of the European Communities had already been multilaterally established.[424]

7.186 The **United States** argues that it does not seek anything within the meaning of Article 23.1 with respect to the EC declaration of compliance. The United States has already sought and obtained redress through the multilateral dispute settlement system for a violation found by the DSB. There is no provision in the WTO Agreement that provides that a single Member can unilaterally invalidate the multilateral decision of the DSB to authorize suspension of concessions. The European Communities has not provided any evidence that it has complied with the conditions of Article 22.8 of the DSU.

7.187 According to the United States, Article 23.2(a), like Article 23.1, applies only in situations where a Member is "seeking redress for a violation" of a WTO obligation. The United States has not, through the continued application of the DSB authorization, sought redress for another Member's violation. Likewise, the United States did not make a "determination" within the meaning of Article 23.2(a). The United States has simply continued to act according to the DSB authorization. The United States did not need to make further determinations to continue to apply the suspension of concessions.

7.188 The United States believes that none of the statements made by the United States and referred to by the European Communities constitute a determination within the meaning of Article 23.2(a). They are simply statements of

---

[424] EC's first written submission, paras. 35-68.

the status of the US evaluation of the EC measure at that point in time based on the information available. The statements referred to by the European Communities make no reference to a WTO violation. The United States remained open to discussing any further information that the European Communities might have developed in support of its declaration of compliance and to this end engaged in informal consultation and technical discussions and made a request under Article 5.8 of the *SPS Agreement* seeking all of the material underpinning the EC import ban.

7.189 For the United States, under the European Communities' reading of Article 23.2(a), a complaining Member need not actually indicate any definitive view on the WTO consistency of an implementing Members' measure to have made a determination. The implementing Member can force a complaining Member into breach of Article 23.2(a) by making a unilateral declaration of compliance that the complaining Member does not immediately agree with or test through the immediate invocation of Article 21.5 proceedings.

7.190 The United States adds that the *US – Section 301 Trade Act* panel report concluded that a "determination" must be sufficiently firm and immutable, in other words "a more or less final decision". The definition of the term "determination" emphasizes not only the finality of the decision, but also its formality. It does not contemplate that a determination can be implicit. The ordinary meaning of the term makes it clear that the opinions and views of the United States cited by the European Communities did not rise to the level of "determinations" within the meaning of Article 23.2(a).

7.191 The United States argues that the EC Article 21.5 claim fails because the European Communities has not established that there is a "disagreement as to the existence or consistency with a covered agreement of measures taken to comply". Article 21.5 sets no deadline by which such a proceeding must be brought and nothing in the text of Article 21.5 places the onus of initiating a compliance proceeding on the original complaining party (in this case, the United States). Finally, the phrase "these dispute settlement proceedings" in Article 21.5 is not restricted to proceedings under Article 21.5, but rather could include proceedings such as arbitration under Article 22.6 of the DSU, proceedings under Article 25 of the DSU, or the proceedings of a *de novo* panel, as the European Communities has sought in this instance.[425]

7.192 Regarding the term "seeking redress" in Article 23.1, the **European Communities** argues that a DSB authorization which has been granted in view of an original WTO-inconsistent measure cannot justify the continued application of sanctions against a different measure which has never been found multi-

---

[425] US's first written submission, paras. 177-202.

laterally to constitute a WTO violation. Any present application of sanctions must be linked to a present measure. The US argument leads to the absurd result that the United States could continue to apply sanctions irrespective of any event occurring after the DSB authorization. The United States fails to acknowledge that the original situation has been altered by the adoption of the EC implementing measure. The United States is under no obligation to continue to suspend obligations. The very fact that it does it in this new situation demonstrates that it indeed considers that there is a causal link between the continuation of the suspension and the determination of inconsistency of the EC compliance measure. If one considers that the United States continues to apply sanctions because of an import ban as such, it would do so against a new measure, since the current import ban is different from the one which the DSB found WTO inconsistent.

7.193 With respect to the term "determination" in Article 23.1(a), the European Communities argues that it is clear from the panel report in *US – Section 301 Trade Act*, that even an implicit determination through the continuation of sanctions would be covered by this requirement. Article 23 aims at preventing that a Member seek the redress of a violation on the basis of a unilateral determination. In light of the overall context and fundamental importance of Article 23, it is justified to look at a Member's behaviour as a whole when confronted with a particular situation. Not every policy statement may be equal to a "determination" or made with the purpose of "seeking a redress of a violation". However, in the present case the United States has clearly stated that it does not consider the EC compliance measure to be sufficient. For instance, the US statement at the DSB meeting of December 2003 is evidence that the United States expressed a definitive judgement about the EC measure. The United States also continues to apply sanctions. There is no way to consider this as "inaction" on the part of the United States, just because stopping the sanctions would require some action. The European Communities also recalls that it notified its implementing measure in 2003, which begs the question when the United States will make a "determination". If the United States truly wanted to reflect further before making any "determination" or initiating any procedure under Article 21.5, it could have suspended the application of sanctions. Article 23 does not prohibit any determination, it prohibits only unilateral determinations of non-compliance.

7.194 The **United States** argues that the Panel findings in *US – Certain EC Products* cited by the European Communities are based on the lack of any DSB recommendations and rulings. The panel found that the United States acted without having yet been authorized to do so by the DSB. The European Communities appears to insinuate that its declaration of compliance has placed the parties back in the position they found themselves in the *US – Certain EC Products* case.

7.195 The United States also argues that, as a procedural matter, the EC interpretation of Article 23.2(a) is complicated by the lack of clarity regarding when a determination on the part of the suspending Member would be inferred. The European Communities argues that there is a reasonable period of time during which the suspending Member may review the measure before a determination is either inferred or due. However, no such reasonable period is set out in the text of Article 23.

7.196 The United States adds that a critical element of the US evaluation is the review of the studies and Opinions underpinning the EC ban. The United States has not had the opportunity to review all of these documents. This is why it has not yet been able to reach a determination on the EC ban. The EC has only recently informed the United States of a number of studies that were not referenced in its response to the US request for information under Article 5.8 of the *SPS Agreement*. Given the difficulty in procuring the material supporting the EC measure, it is perfectly understandable why the United States has not yet made a "determination" as to the WTO-consistency of the EC import ban.[426]

2. *Reasoning of the Panel*

(a) Introduction

7.197 The European Communities claims a violation of Article 23.2(a), read together with Articles 21.5 and 23.1. Article 23.2(a) contains specific obligations compared with Article 23.1. We therefore deem it relevant to address the violation of Article 23.2(a) first.[427]

7.198 Article 23.2(a) reads as follows:

"2. In such cases, Members shall:

(a) not make a determination to the effect that a violation has occurred, that benefits have been nullified or impaired or that the attainment of any objective of the covered agreements has been impeded, except through recourse to dispute settlement in accordance with the rules and procedures of this Understanding, and shall make any such determination consistent with the findings

---

[426] US's second written submission, paras. 15-22.

[427] We note in this respect that, as mentioned by the Appellate Body in *Canada – Wheat Export and Grain Imports*, paras. 126-129:

"As a general principle, panels are free to structure the order of their analysis as they see fit. In so doing panels may find it useful to take account of the manner in which a claim is presented to them by a complaining Member. Furthermore, panels may choose to use assumptions in order to facilitate resolution of a particular issue ..."

contained in the panel or Appellate Body report adopted by the DSB or an arbitration award rendered under this Understanding;"

7.199   In order to decide whether the United States has or has not breached Article 23.2(a) in this case, the Panel must first find whether the determination was made "in such cases", i.e. when the conditions of Article 23.1 are met.

7.200   Article 23.1 reads as follows:

> "When Members seek the redress of a violation of obligations or other nullification or impairment of benefits under the covered agreements or an impediment to the attainment of any objective of the covered agreements, they shall have recourse to, and abide by, the rules and procedures of this Understanding."

7.201   In other words, the Panel must first establish whether the United States, in relation to the facts of this case, has been seeking redress of a violation of obligations or other nullification or impairment of benefits under the covered agreements, within the meaning of Article 23.1 of the DSU.

7.202   Thereafter, the Panel will proceed with determining whether the United States has breached Article 23.2(a). Once this is done, it will review the alleged violation of Articles 21.5 and 23.1, as necessary.

> (b)   "[S]eeking the redress of a violation of obligations or other nullification or impairment of benefits under the covered agreements" (Article 23.1 of the DSU)

7.203   The United States argues that it does not *seek* anything within the meaning of Article 23.1 with respect to the EC declaration of compliance with the WTO Agreement. The United States alleges that it has already sought and obtained redress through the multilateral dispute settlement system for a violation found by the DSB.

7.204   We agree with the United States that Article 23.1 of the DSU is not breached when a Member's suspension of concessions or other obligations has been multilaterally authorized by the DSB, because the Member concerned "ha[d] recourse to, and abide[d] by, the rules and procedures of [the DSU]", within the meaning of Article 23.1. Indeed, the United States already sought redress against the original EC ban under the DSU.

7.205   In the opinion of the Panel, Article 23.1 applies in this case only with respect to a determination against a measure which has not yet been subject to a recourse to the rules and procedures of the DSU. We must therefore determine first whether Directive 2003/74/EC is such a measure.

7.206   We note the arguments of the European Communities that it adopted a new directive which it considers implements the recommendations and rulings of the DSB in the *EC – Hormones* case.[428] We also note that the United States recognized before the DSB that the EC had adopted a "revised ... measure" and a "new directive".[429] We first note that Directive 2003/74/EC has never been as such subject to recourse to the rules and procedures of the DSU by the United States. For instance, no panel has been established at the request of the United States to review the conformity of Directive 2003/74/EC with the covered agreements. Second, the fact that both parties consider that the EC implementing measure is not the same measure as that which was found in breach of the WTO Agreement by the DSB in the *EC – Hormones* case is confirmed by the allegations they made in relation to that implementing measure before this Panel. The European Communities considers that its ban on oestradiol-17β is compatible with Article 5.1 of the *SPS Agreement*, whereas its ban on the other five hormones is justified by Article 5.7. The United States alleges, *inter alia*, the incompatibility of the ban on oestradiol-17β with Article 5.1 and 5.2, and of the provisional ban on the other five hormones with Article 5.7. These are different provisions than those invoked in the *EC – Hormones* case with respect to the same hormones.[430] Thus, the United States acknowledges that the measure is different from the original measure found in breach of the WTO Agreement not only formally but also in substance and legally, even though an import ban on meat treated with hormones for growth promotion purposes is still applied.

7.207   We note that the original ban remains in force. We consider, however, that this is insufficient to conclude that Directive 2003/74/EC is not different from the measure originally found in breach of the WTO Agreement and should be deemed for that reason to have been subject to the rules and procedures of the DSU. We recall that it is not the ban on meat treated with growth promotion hormones as such that was found illegal in the *EC – Hormones* case, but the justification for this ban which was found insufficient. The European Communities is not prevented by the *SPS Agreement* from imposing any ban on import of meat treated with growth promotion hormones. The European Communities can impose such a ban provided it is compatible with the relevant requirements of the *SPS Agreement*. As a result, the Panel does not consider that the fact that the ban remains in place means that no new measure has been adopted.

7.208   The United States argues that its suspension of obligations was, and remains, multilaterally authorized by the DSB. To date, the authorization to suspend concessions and other obligations granted on 26 July 1999 to the United

---

[428]   EC's first written submission, para. 17.
[429]   WT/DSB/M/157, paras. 29-30.
[430]   In the original *EC – Hormones* dispute, the panel noted the EC 's statement that its measures were not provisional measure in the sense of Article 5.7 of the *SPS Agreement*. See Panel Report on *EC – Hormones* (US), para. 8.249.

States by the DSB has not been revoked by the DSB and the United States continues to act pursuant to that authority.[431] The United States also argues that there is no provision in the WTO Agreement that provides that a single Member can unilaterally invalidate the multilateral decision of the DSB to authorize suspension of concessions. According to the United States, the European Communities has not provided any evidence that it has complied with the conditions of Article 22.8 of the DSU.

7.209   We agree with the United States that it was *authorized* to suspend concessions and that this authorization has not been revoked. We note however, that this is only an *authorization*, not an *obligation* imposed by the DSB. The Panel agrees with the European Communities in this respect: "authorization by the DSB" does not mean "obligation to suspend concessions". This is confirmed by the practice under the DSU pursuant to which, in a number of cases where authorizations to suspend concessions have been requested, no suspensions was subsequently applied, in spite of the DSB authorization.[432] In other words, the fact that, after the notification of Directive 2003/74/EC, the United States continues to apply its suspension of concessions even though it has no obligation to do so is evidence that the United States is actively "seek[ing] the redress of a violation of obligations or other nullification or impairment of benefits under the covered agreements".

7.210   We note that the DSU does not provide for any procedure regarding the revocation of an authorization to suspend concessions. The adoption of a decision to revoke such an authorization by the DSB would require consensus[433], which would in turn require an absence of objection from the Member suspending concessions or other obligations, which may be difficult to obtain. We consider that this is not necessary, essentially because the DSB grants an *authorization,* which the Member concerned is free to apply or not. We also note that Article 22.8 of the DSU does not provide for any decision of the DSB for a suspension of concessions or other obligations to cease to apply. The first sentence of Article 22.8 simply provides that:

> "The suspension of concessions or other obligations shall be temporary and *shall only be applied until such time as* the measure found to be inconsistent with a covered agreement has been removed, or the Member that must implement recommendations or

---

[431]   US's first written submission, para. 26.

[432]   In the *Brazil – Aircraft* case and the *Canada – Aircraft Credits and Guarantees* case, the DSB authorized Canada and Brazil respectively to suspend obligations, but neither of them applied the authorization. In the *EC – Bananas III* case, Ecuador was authorized to retaliate but did not exercise its right.

[433]   See Article 2.4 of the DSU.

rulings provides a solution to the nullification or impairment of benefits, or a mutually satisfactory solution is reached." (Emphasis added)

7.211 In none of the circumstances foreseen by Article 22.8 does this provision require a decision of the DSB. In other words, it is for the respondent in this case to take appropriate steps to ensure that the suspension of concessions or other obligations is only applied until such time as foreseen in Article 22.8.

7.212 We also note that, pursuant to Article XVI:4 of the Agreement Establishing the WTO, Members must ensure the conformity of their laws, regulations and administrative procedures with their obligations as provided in the agreements annexed to the Agreement Establishing the WTO, including the DSU.

7.213 We conclude that the United States does not need a multilateral decision in order to terminate the suspension of concessions or other obligations for which it got authorization from the DSB.

7.214 For the reasons stated above, we consider that the EC implementing measure is, compared with the measure for which the United States was granted authorization to suspend concessions and other obligations by the DSB, a measure which has not been subject to a recourse to the rules and procedures of the DSU.

7.215 The United States, by maintaining its suspension of concessions even after the notification of the EC implementing measure, is seeking redress of a violation with respect to the EC implementing measure, within the meaning of Article 23.1 of the DSU. If it were not, as mentioned above, the United States would not have to maintain that suspension.

7.216 We now proceed to assess whether the United States breached Article 23.2(a).

(c)   Violation of Article 23.2(a)

(i)   Introduction

7.217 In order to assess whether the United States breaches Article 23.2(a), we must review the following conditions:[434]

(a)   whether the United States made a determination that the EC implementing measure violates the WTO Agreement;

---

[434] We note that a similar approach was applied by the Panel in *US – Section 301 Trade Act*, footnote 657.

(b) whether the United States failed to make such determination through recourse to dispute settlement in accordance with the rules and procedures of the DSU; and assuming that it did,

(c) whether the United States failed to make any such determination consistent with the findings contained in the panel or Appellate Body report adopted by the DSB or an arbitration award rendered under this Understanding.

7.218 We will review these requirements successively.

(ii) Did the United States make a determination that the EC implementing measure violates the WTO Agreement?

7.219 We note that, in the present case, the European Communities notified its implementing measure on 27 October 2003.[435] At the DSB meeting of 7 November 2003 the United States made the following statement which is worth quoting in full in order to better understand its scope:

> "The representative of the *United States* said that her country had reviewed the communication placed by the EC on the agenda of the present meeting and had listened to the statement that the EC had just made. The United States failed to see how the revised EC measure could be considered to implement the DSB's recommendations and rulings in this matter. For nearly 15 years, the EC had banned the importation of nearly all meat and meat products from the United States. The purported basis of the EC ban was that the consumption of meat from cattle raised in the United States with growth-promoting hormones posed a risk to human health. It was a bedrock principle of the *SPS Agreement*, however, that banning a product for purported health reasons had to be based on science. The EC measure was not based on science. To the contrary, after repeated study, no increased health risk had ever been associated with the consumption of meat from animals treated with growth-promoting hormones. The Joint FAO/WHO Expert Committee on Food Additives had found that there was a wide margin of safety for these products. For example, it had determined that consumption of beef from treated animals resulted in amounts of estradiol that were 300 times lower than the acceptable daily intake level. Moreover, hormones such as estradiol were already produced in abundance by both the human body and cattle, and were naturally present in many everyday foods. For example, each person daily

---

[435] WT/DS26/22.

produced amounts of estradiol ranging from 2,000 to 30,000 times more, or higher, than the amount consumed from eating a 250-gram serving of meat from treated animals. Due to high levels of naturally-occurring hormones in cattle, it was not even possible to distinguish any residues of such hormones administered for purposes of growth promotion. A single chicken egg contained many times more estradiol equivalents than the estradiol contained in a 250 gram serving of meat from a treated animal. A litre of milk from an untreated cow contained approximately 18 times as much estradiol as a 250 gram serving of meat from a treated animal.

In February 1998, the DSB had adopted findings that the EC ban was not based on an appropriate risk assessment, as required by Article 5.1 of the *SPS Agreement*, and had recommended that the EC bring its measure into compliance with its WTO obligations. Near the conclusion of the 15-month compliance period, on 30 April 1999, the EC had issued a report by an EC veterinary committee claiming increased health risks from the use of growth-promoting hormones. However, this claim was not based on science. Just like the reports relied upon by the EC before the panel and the Appellate Body, the April 1999 report consisted of general discussions of types of risks, but had never actually assessed or found any increased risk from the consumption of meat from animals produced with growth-promoting hormones. And, indeed, the EC had never, until now, claimed to the DSB that the April 1999 report was an appropriate basis for adopting a ban on US beef. To the contrary, during the arbitration under Article 22.6 on the level of nullification and impairment suffered by the United States, the EC had acknowledged that – even after the issuance of the April 1999 report – it had not implemented the recommendations and rulings of the DSB. For example, in its opening submission filed on 11 June 1999, the EC had written that it "accepts that it has not taken the required measures to comply with the DSB recommendations". In July 1999, the DSB had authorized the United States and Canada to suspend concessions. Again, the EC had never claimed that its April 1999 report served as an appropriate basis for its ban on meat from treated animals. At the present meeting, the EC had presented Directive 2003/74 to the DSB, and claimed that this directive implemented the DSB's recommendations and rulings. The Directive, however, neither removed the EC's unjustified ban on US beef, nor presented an appropriate risk assessment as a basis for the ban. Further, aside from the ban on estradiol, the directive relabelled its ban on the other five growth-promoting hormones covered in this matter as "provisional measures". A decision by the EC to relabel its measures, however, could not bring it into compliance with its obligations under the

SPS Agreement. Nearly six years had passed since the DSB had recommended that the EC bring its ban on US beef into compliance with its obligations. The United States, however, could not understand how this new directive presented now could amount to implementation of the DSB's recommendation."[436]

7.220 The United States made another statement at the DSB meeting of 1 December 2003:

"The representative of the *United States* said that she would transmit the statement made by the EC at the present meeting to her authorities for their consideration. As had been explained at the 7 November DSB meeting, the United States failed to see how the revised EC measure could be considered to implement the DSB's recommendations and rulings in this matter. The United States had always been ready to discuss with the EC any matters regarding its compliance with the DSB's recommendations and rulings. The United States would be pleased to discuss with EC officials any outstanding issues regarding the EC's ban on certain beef produced in the United States, including their reactions to the detailed points that the United States had raised in its statement at the 7 November DSB meeting. With regard to the suggestion made by the EC at the present meeting that multilateral proceedings be initiated, the United States would be happy to discuss this suggestion with the EC along with other procedural options."[437]

7.221 The European Communities also refers to other statements by the United States.[438]

7.222 We recall that the Panel in *US – Section 301 Trade Act* defined a "determination" as follows:

"[W]e consider that – given its ordinary meaning – a "determination" implies a high degree of firmness or immutability, i.e. a more or less final decision by a Member in respect of the WTO consistency of a measure taken by another Member."[439]

7.223 The two statements quoted above were delivered by an official of the US government at a formal meeting of a WTO body. There is no formal difference

---

[436] WT/DSB/M/157, paras. 29-30.
[437] WT/DSB/M/159, para. 25.
[438] See US press release of 8 November 2003 and 2005 Trade Policy Agenda and 2004 Annual Report of the President of the United States on the Trade Agreements Program, Exhibit EC-5.
[439] Panel Report on *US – Section 301 Trade Act*, footnote 657.

between that statement and any other statement where a formal decision of a Member is conveyed to the DSB.

7.224   We note that the second statement quoted above suggests that the United States was ready to consult with the European Communities, including on procedural issues. The Panel notes that, in response to one of its questions, the parties specified the extent of the consultations that took place after the notification of Directive 2003/74/EC. The Panel notes that they largely related to procedural issues.[440]

7.225   This said, even if the United States showed readiness in its statement to discuss with the European Communities and even if discussions actually took place, the United States position at the time of its statement before the DSB was quite clear, as illustrated by remarks such as: "[t]he United States failed to see how the revised EC measure could be considered to implement the DSB's recommendations and rulings in this matter"; "Directive [2003/74/EC], however, neither removed the EC's unjustified ban on US beef, nor presented an appropriate risk assessment as a basis for the ban"; "[a] decision by the EC to relabel its measures, however, could not bring it into compliance with its obligations under the *SPS Agreement*"; "[t]he United States, however, could not understand how this new directive presented now could amount to implementation of the DSB's recommendation"; or "[as] had been explained at the 7 November DSB meeting, the United States failed to see how the revised EC measure could be considered to implement the DSB's recommendations and rulings in this matter."

7.226   The style and content of the statement are such that they can be reasonably deemed to convey, with a high degree of firmness and immutability, a more or less final decision. Nowhere in that statement is there any indication that the United States was still reviewing the new EC Directive, or that it was expecting more information or planning to seek more information from the European Communities. In this respect, it merely expressed "readiness to discuss". The United States expressed a clear opinion as far as the legality of the EC notified measure was concerned. The United States might have still been in the process of reviewing the EC implementing measure, but this does not show from this statement or from any other statement referred to by the parties. Moreover, the United States had obviously taken the decision to maintain its suspension of concessions, since the latter continued to apply. We therefore consider that the US statement meets all the requirements of the definition in the Panel Report in *US – Section 301 Trade Act* and that the United States made a "determination" within the meaning of Article 23.2(a).

---

[440]   See Annex B-3, US's replies to Panel questions after the first substantive meeting, question 50.

7.227 The United States argues that a critical element of the US evaluation is the review of the studies and Opinions underpinning the EC ban. The United States claims that it has not had the opportunity to review all of these documents. This is why it has not yet been able to reach a determination on the EC ban. The United States notes that the European Communities has only recently informed the United States of a number of studies that were not referenced in its response to the US request for information under Article 5.8 of the *SPS Agreement*. The United States adds that, given the difficulty in procuring the material supporting the EC measure, it is perfectly understandable why the United States has not yet made a "determination" as to the WTO-consistency of the EC import ban.[441]

7.228 We are not convinced by this argument. There is no element in the statements of the United States before the DSB indicating that it was still reviewing the documents or even that it contemplated difficulties in obtaining the studies underpinning the EC new Directive.

7.229 As far as the request under Article 5.8 is concerned, the US letter on this subject was sent on 13 December 2004, more than one year after the notification of the implementing measure by the European Communities and after consultations on the present case were requested by the European Communities. Thus, the Panel finds it difficult to conclude that this request was linked to any review of the EC implementing measure that the United States would have been carrying out since the notification of Directive 2003/74/EC.

7.230 Even if one were to consider that the US statements at the DSB were provisional comments, the subsequent continuation of the suspension of concessions by the United States without alteration and without saying that it was still studying the EC implementing measure is evidence that the statements before the DSB meant that the United States had no intention to remove its retaliatory measure, at least until further notice. We note in this respect that the term "determination" does not necessarily imply a formal decision, all the more so as such a formal decision was not necessary in order to continue the suspension of concessions. The continuation of the suspension of concessions corroborates the fact that the US statements before the DSB constituted "determinations" within the meaning of Article 23.2(a).

7.231 The United States argues that no period of time is provided for in Article 23 within which a Member shall make a determination and that, under the interpretation advocated by the European Communities, the European Communities can force the United States into a violation of Article 23.2(a) by making a unilateral declaration of compliance that the complaining Member does not im-

---

[441] US's second written submission, paras. 19-22.

mediately agree with or test through the immediate invocation of Article 21.5 proceedings.[442]

7.232 We agree with the United States that there is no deadline in Article 23 by which a Member shall have recourse to the DSU. This, however, is not the issue before this Panel. The issue is whether the United States made a determination within the meaning of Article 23.2(a) or not. We have found that the United States has made such determination by making its statements before the DSB on 7 November and 1 December 2003. Even if the determination was not fully made on that date, the continued suspension of concessions by the United States over the period between the EC notification and the date of request of consultations by the European Communities in this case is evidence that the United States made such a determination.

7.233 In this case, the United States could have clearly stated that it was reviewing the EC implementing measure and expressly stated that it needed more time and more information to do so. It did not. On the contrary, it stated before the Dispute Settlement Body that it " failed to see how the revised EC measure could be considered to implement the DSB's recommendations and rulings in this matter" and went on to explain in details why it thought so.

7.234 We note the argument of the United States that the situation in this case is different from that in *US – Certain EC Products*, where no DSB authorization had been granted to the United States at the time of the measure at issue. However, we have concluded above that the authorization to suspend concession or other obligations on the basis of which the United States imposed its sanctions had been granted with respect to the original measure. As far as the implementing measure is concerned, it has not even been subject to a recourse to the rules and procedures of the DSU.

7.235 The United States also argues that the EC interpretation would lead to an endless loop of litigation because any Member could notify a "scam legislation" and force the original complainant to request a panel under Article 21.5 of the DSU.

7.236 We are mindful that this argument was raised by the United States in relation to its alleged violation of Article 21.5 of the DSU. We nonetheless believe that we should address it to the extent that the notification of an implementing measure would be the type of measure which could, according to the United States, start such an "endless loop of litigation".

---

[442] US's second written submission, para. 17.

7.237 First, we believe that not only scam legislation, but also any other imple-menting measures could lead to recurrent litigations. One could envisage that, in a complex case, a Member could notify in good faith an implementing measure which would be subsequently found not to fully comply with the original rec-ommendations and ruling of the DSB. This Member would have to submit a re-vised measure which could, once again, be challenged and found to comply only partly with the covered agreements. Such repeated inconsistencies could have to do with the fact that, pursuant to Article 19.1 of the DSU, panels and the Appel-late Body may only recommend that the Member concerned bring its legislation into conformity with the covered agreement(s) found to be breached, and may only make non-binding suggestions regarding ways in which the Member con-cerned could implement their recommendations. Since Members remain free to implement recommendations and rulings as they deem appropriate, differences in the interpretation of the recommendations of the DSB cannot be excluded, which can result in old inconsistencies remaining in the implementing measure or in new ones creeping into it.

7.238 Second, we recall that our findings are limited to the facts of this particu-lar case. In this case, the European Communities has adopted Directive 2003/74/EC at the outcome of a lengthy and complex internal decision-making process. The Panel notes in this respect that the Commission proposal was sub-mitted in 2000 and 2001 and that the procedure for the adoption of the Directive was the procedure provided for in Article 251 of the Treaty establishing the European Community. This procedure involved a number of steps, including an Opinion of the European Parliament (1 February 2001), a Common Position of the Council of the European Union (20 February 2003) and finally a Decision of the European Parliament (2 July 2003), a Decision of the Council of the Euro-pean Union (22 July 2003) and an adoption by the European Parliament and the Council of the European Union on 22 September 2003.[443] Without prejudice to the question whether Directive 2003/74/EC is actually based on the three opin-ions of the Scientific Committee on Veterinary Measures relating to Public Health (SCVPH) of 1999, 2000 and 2002[444] within the meaning of the *SPS Agreement*, the Panel notes that this Directive expressly refers to those opin-ions[445] and that, as a result, they were part of the process that led to the adoption of the Directive. The Panel also notes the efforts of the European Communities to have the conformity of its measure reviewed under the DSU.[446] Even if the EC implementing legislation were ultimately found not to comply with the *SPS Agreement*, the Panel considers that it shows all the signs of an implement-

---

[443] See Directive 2003/74/EC, Preamble and footnote 3.
[444] Hereafter the "1999 Opinion", the "2000 Opinion" and the "2002 Opinion" or, together, the "Opinions".
[445] See Directive 2003/74/EC, whereas clauses 5 and 8.
[446] See EC's replies to Panel questions after the first substantive meeting, question 50, Annex B-1.

ing measure having gone through all the formal process required for its adoption and showing, on its face, all the signs of a measure adopted in good faith.

7.239 We therefore conclude that the United States made a "determination" within the meaning of Article 23.2(a) in relation to Directive 2003/74/EC.

> (iii) Did the United States fail to make such determination through recourse to dispute settlement in accordance with the rules and procedures of the DSU?

7.240 We note that the United States argues that it has not made any *determination* in respect of the EC implementing measure and therefore did not have to have recourse to the dispute settlement procedures of the DSU. However, we found above that it made a determination within the meaning of Article 23.2(a). Therefore, we conclude that the United States made a determination without having recourse to the DSU, thus breaching Article 23.2(a) of the DSU.

7.241 The United States also argues that it benefits from a multilateral authorization to suspend concessions in relation to the breach by the European Communities of the *SPS Agreement*, as a result of the recommendations and rulings of the DSB in the *EC – Hormones* case.

7.242 This is not the issue, however. The issue is whether the authorization to suspend concessions or other obligations granted to the United States under Article 22 of the DSU amounts to a multilateral determination of inconsistency of the EC *implementing measure* (i.e., Directive 2003/74/EC) with the covered agreements through recourse to the DSU. In our opinion, the answer is no.

7.243 We therefore conclude that the United States has not made any determination *through recourse to dispute settlement* in accordance with the rules and procedures of the DSU.

> (iv) Did the United States fail to make any such determination consistent with the findings contained in the panel or Appellate Body report adopted by the DSB or an arbitration award rendered under the DSU?

7.244 Since the United States has not made any determination through recourse to dispute settlement in accordance with the rules and procedures of the DSU, we conclude *a fortiori* that the United States has failed to make any such determination *consistent with the findings contained in the panel or Appellate Body report adopted by the DSB or an arbitration award rendered under the DSU.*

(v)   Conclusion

7.245 For the reasons stated above, we find that the United States has breached Article 23.2(a) of the DSU.

(d)   Violation of Article 21.5 of the DSU

7.246 We note that the European Communities claims that the United States should have had recourse to Article 21.5 of the DSU. The United States argues that it is not obligated to initiate a compliance procedure under Article 21.5.

7.247 We note that Article 23.2(a) provides that a determination must not be made "except through recourse to dispute settlement in accordance with [the DSU]". It does not specify which procedure under the DSU should be followed. While the procedure under Article 21.5 of the DSU could be one of the mechanisms available, in our view, the term "recourse to dispute settlement in accordance with the rules and procedures of this Understanding" encompasses any of the means of dispute settlement provided in the DSU, including consultation, conciliation, good offices and mediation.

7.248 The last proposition of Article 23.2(a) provides that such determination shall be consistent with the "findings contained in the *panel* or *Appellate Body* report adopted by the DSB or an *arbitration award* rendered under this understanding."[447] We do not consider, however, that that proposition *requires* that Members have recourse to a panel or to arbitration. In the opinion of the Panel, the last proposition of Article 23.2(a) only requires the Member *which decides to have recourse to a panel or to arbitration* to abide by the recommendation of the panel or the Appellate Body or the award of the arbitrator.[448]

7.249 As a result, we do not find it necessary to make a finding on whether the United States breached Article 21.5 by not having recourse to the procedure under that provision. Indeed, the United States did not have recourse to any procedure under the DSU with respect to the EC implementing measure (Directive 2003/74/EC). Under those circumstances, we deem it sufficient to limit our findings to Article 23 and exercise judicial economy with regard to the EC claim under Article 21.5 of the DSU.

---

[447] Emphasis added.

[448] Comparatively, there was no need for the negotiators of the DSU to refer to compliance with the results of consultations, mediation, conciliation or good offices since the results of such means of dispute resolution have, by their very nature, to be accepted by the parties in order to produce effects.

(e)   Violation of Article 23.1 of the DSU

7.250 Since we found that the United States has sought the redress of a violation with respect to the EC implementing measure (Directive 2003/74/EC) and
made a determination without having "recourse to dispute settlement in accordance with the rules and procedures of [the DSU]" within the meaning of Article
23.2(a), we conclude that the United States failed to "have recourse to, and abide
by, the rules and procedures of [the DSU]", in breach of Article 23.1 of the
DSU.

3.   *Conclusion*

7.251 On the basis of the above, the Panel concludes that the United States has
violated Article 23.1 and 23.2(a) of the DSU by seeking redress of a violation of
the WTO Agreement through a determination that the EC implementing measure
did not comply with the DSB recommendations and rulings in the *EC – Hormones* case without having recourse to dispute settlement in accordance with the
rules and procedures of the DSU.

C.   *Second Series of EC Claims: Violation of Article 23.1, Read
       Together with Articles 22.8 and 3.7 of the DSU*

1.   *Summary of the main arguments of the parties*[449]

7.252 The **European Communities** argues that, under Article 23.1 of the DSU,
the United States is obliged to have recourse to, and abide by, the rules and procedures of the DSU, which encompass, *inter alia*, Articles 22.8 and 3.7 of the
DSU.[450] The European Communities argues more particularly that Article 22.8
prohibits the continued unilateral application of the suspension of concessions or
other obligations when the measure which has been found inconsistent is removed.[451]

7.253 The European Communities argues that the suspension of obligations
should only apply where and as long as justified and necessary. This is a practical consequence of the fact that suspension of concessions should only be applied as "a last resort", as specified in Article 3.7 of the DSU.

7.254 According to the European Communities, one objective of the suspension
of concessions is to induce compliance. This entails, however, that once a Mem-

---

[449]   A more detailed account of the parties' arguments can be found in Section IV of the descriptive
part of this Report. The order in which the respective arguments of the parties are presented does not
reflect any allocation of the burden of proof by the Panel.
[450]   EC's first written submission, para. 73.
[451]   EC's first written submission, para. 81.

ber has adopted implementing measures which are not properly challenged by the complaining Member, the suspension of concessions or other obligations can no longer be applied. The objective to induce compliance can only revive after it has been properly established that the implementing measure has been insufficient to remedy a WTO violation.

7.255 In the opinion of the European Communities, Article 22.8 of the DSU prohibits the continued unilateral application of the suspension of concessions or other obligations when the measure which has been found inconsistent is removed. The term "removed" thereby refers to the compliance by a WTO Member because this provision is based on the respect of the WTO obligations by the Member concerned.

7.256 The European Communities argues further that Article 22.8 of the DSU does not specify how the removal of the WTO inconsistency is determined. However, in the light of its context, i.e. Articles 21.5 and 23.2(a) of the DSU, and given the exceptional nature of countermeasures, it is clear that a Member cannot unilaterally determine that the WTO inconsistency persists despite the notification of a compliance measure. Likewise, a Member cannot decide to continue to suspend concessions or other obligations unilaterally. Unless a procedure under Article 21.5 concludes that the compliance measure does not fully implement the DSB recommendations and rulings, it cannot be presumed that this is the case.

7.257 According to the European Communities, this also follows from the general principle of good faith as it applies in international State relations, under which States are normally considered to act in conformity with their obligations. This principle has been widely confirmed in the international jurisprudence and in the WTO dispute settlement system. Therefore, it is clear that the United States could not unilaterally determine that the European Communities implemented the DSB recommendations and rulings in a WTO inconsistent way. To the contrary, the European Communities must be presumed to have complied with its WTO obligations, if the United States refuses to establish the contrary.

7.258 The European Communities adds that once the inconsistency of the measure has been removed, Article 22.8 of the DSU provides that "the suspension of concessions or other obligations shall [not be] applied [any longer]." This provision does not leave any margin of discretion to the retaliating Member. Under the same logic, Article 22.8 of the DSU does not allow for the application of countermeasures on the basis of a *unilateral* determination regarding the WTO inconsistency of the measure. It can be inferred from Article 22.8 read together with Article 23.1 of the DSU that the suspension of obligations should not continue to be applied until the WTO inconsistency of the properly notified measure has been positively determined by the DSB.

7.259 According to the European Communities, the DSB authorization cannot justify the maintenance of suspension of concessions or other obligations if a Member properly complies with its obligations after the imposition of these measures and if its compliance measure is not challenged in an Article 21.5 proceeding. Again, the mere temporal difference of the new implementing measure does not mean that the DSB authorization, once received, serves as a blank authorization for a Member to continue the application of the suspension of concessions or other obligations indefinitely in the future and on the basis of unilateral determinations.

7.260 Furthermore, the European Communities notes that, from a systemic point of view, Article 22.8 of the DSU is subsequent to Article 22.7 of the DSU. This indicates that once the situation under paragraph 8 occurs it overtakes the authorization granted under paragraph 7. Paragraph 8 conditions paragraph 7. As it must be assumed that the DSU negotiators followed a logical sequencing in the way they drafted Article 22, it is clear that Article 22.8 of the DSU was supposed to impact on the authorization under Article 22.7 of the DSU. Indeed, to assume that the removal of the inconsistency of the measure under paragraph 8 has no impact on the DSB authorization under paragraph 7 is not legally coherent or reasonable.

7.261 Finally, following the jurisprudence by the Appellate Body, once a Member violates Article 23.1 read in conjunction with Article 22.8 of the DSU, it necessarily also acts contrary to Article 3.7 of the DSU.

7.262 The **United States** argues that Article 22.8 establishes three conditions under which a DSB-authorized suspension of concessions may no longer be applied: (a) the Member imposing the WTO-inconsistent measure "removes" the measure; (b) that Member "provides a solution to the nullification or impairment of benefits"; or (c) the parties to the dispute reach a "mutually satisfactory solution." In order to prevail in its claim that the United States is breaching Article 22.8, the European Communities must establish that one of these conditions has been met.

7.263 According to the United States, the assertion of the European Communities that it has removed its measure or provided a solution is not supported by any demonstration that it actually has done either. Instead, the European Communities relies on an already rejected legal theory that a Member found to have breached its WTO obligations is to be excused from its burden of proof in dispute settlement if it invokes "good faith." This argument is no more valid today than when a WTO panel last rejected it, and the EC failure to meet its burden on the critical element of its case under Article 22.8 means that the EC claim must likewise fail. The United States continues to apply the suspension of concessions to the European Communities in a WTO-consistent manner, fully in accordance with the authorization of the DSB.

7.264 The United States adds that the European Communities failed to demonstrate that it has in fact removed its WTO-inconsistent measure, the import ban on meat and meat products from cattle treated with hormones for growth promotion purposes or that it has "provide[d] a solution" to the nullification or impairment of benefits to the United States caused by the ban.

7.265 According to the United States, Article 22.8 nowhere provides that the issue of removal of a measure or providing a solution can be decided by a Member's simple assertion that it has developed a new, WTO-consistent measure, or that it alone has deemed that it has provided a "solution" to WTO nullification or impairment, without a DSB determination. Indeed the EC proposed interpretation is directly at odds with the last sentence of Article 22.8 which makes it clear that these are questions for ongoing *DSB* surveillance. Article 22.8 stresses that "the DSB shall continue to keep under surveillance the implementation of adopted recommendations or rulings", in situations where "concessions or other obligations have been suspended but the [DSB] recommendations ... have not been implemented." This statement that the DSB's role is to monitor an implementing Member's compliance with DSB recommendations as well as the complaining Member's suspension of concessions further emphasizes that Article 22.8 is concerned with *multilateral* review of compliance. The European Communities errs in claiming that under Article 22.8, the US authorization to suspend concessions could be withdrawn in the absence of a DSB determination to that effect. Furthermore, the EC approach would fundamentally undermine the operation of several critical DSU provisions, most notably the right of complaining parties to seek authorization to suspend concessions through a DSB decision taken by negative consensus under Article 22.6 or Article 22.7 of the DSU.

7.266 In the view of the United States, the European Communities argues that the Panel should find that it has "removed" its WTO-inconsistent measure within the meaning of Article 22.8 analysis because it "must be presumed to have complied with its WTO obligations, if the United States refuses to establish to the contrary." However, the *EC – Bananas III (Article 21.5 – EC)* panel highlighted that there is no basis in the WTO Agreement for the EC's argument that it is presumed compliant with its obligations absent a finding against its measures. Similarly, there is no presumption of compliance for the EC amended ban in this proceeding. Because compliance of the EC amended ban is a condition precedent to several of the claims raised by the European Communities as a complaining party, the European Communities bears the burden in this proceeding of demonstrating its compliance.

7.267 The **European Communities** argues that, contrary to what the United States asserts, the prohibition to continue the application of sanctions under Article 22.8 does not depend on whether the DSB authorization has been formally removed. Article 22.8 is unequivocal in the sense that the suspension of concessions and related obligations may only be "applied" until the inconsistency of the measure has been removed. In addition, Article 22.8 subjects the application of sanctions to a measure which has been found inconsistent. Article 22.8 is also of self-executing nature and the termination of the application of sanctions under this provision does not depend on a specific finding of the DSB or a withdrawal of the DSB authorization. Rather, once the conditions under Article 22.8 of the DSU are met – including in the presence of an unchallenged compliance measure – the application of suspension "shall" automatically stop.

7.268 Moreover, the European Communities does not agree with the United States that the principle of good faith is not relevant for WTO proceedings in general or only relevant for the issue of burden of proof. This radical position is not supported by general public international law, which also applies to the WTO, as for instance expressed in Article 26 of the Vienna Convention on the Law of Treaties (1969). In this context, the European Communities also considers that due to the specific circumstances for the adoption of its compliance measure as explained in detail in its various submissions and in the absence of a concrete challenge by the United States and in the light of the time that has passed since the measure was prepared and adopted, it is fully entitled to invoke the principle of good faith and the presumption of compliance.

7.269 The **United States** argues that the European Communities has failed to make a prima facie case of a US violation of Article 22.8 of the DSU. Rather than presenting any evidence of how it has satisfied the conditions of Article 22.8 (removal of WTO-inconsistent measure; provision of solution to nullification or impairment of benefits; mutually satisfactory solution), it posits its claim "in conjunction with" Article 23 and asserts that the "presumption of good faith" or compliance satisfies its burden of proof. Even were one to presume that the European Communities implemented its amended bans in good faith, this fact would not in turn demonstrate that the EC bans actually satisfy the elements of Article 22.8, *e.g.*, the European Communities could be acting in good faith, but still be wrong about the WTO-consistency or compliance of its amended measure.

2. *Approach of the Panel*

(a) Duty of the Panel to make an objective assessment of the matter before it

7.270 In light of the EC statement that this case is about procedural violations under the DSU[452], and in view of our findings above, we could normally exercise judicial economy and complete our review of this case at this juncture. Indeed, we found that the United States committed a procedural error under the

---

[452] EC's first written submission, para. 24.

DSU, breached Article 23.1 and 23.2(a) and should have had recourse to dispute settlement in accordance with the rules and procedures of the DSU if it wanted to seek redress of a violation of the WTO Agreement through a determination of violation of the WTO Agreement with respect to Directive 2003/74/EC.

7.271 However, the European Communities claims a separate violation of Article 23.1, read together with Article 22.8 and Article 3.7 of the DSU. Under those claims, the European Communities alleges *inter alia* that the United States breached Article 22.8 because it failed to withdraw its suspension of concessions even though the European Communities removed the measure found to be inconsistent with a covered agreement. We also note the US argument that it did not breach Article 22.8 of the DSU because the EC implementing measure does not *comply* with the *SPS Agreement*.

7.272 We recall that we considered that the two series of main EC claims were such that they could be addressed independently from each other.[453] Our findings of violation of Article 23.1 and 23.2(a) under the first series of main EC claims are completely unrelated to whether the European Communities implemented the DSB recommendations and rulings in the *EC – Hormones* dispute in substance. Indeed, our findings are based on the failure of the United States to have recourse to the procedures under the DSU as a result of the notification of Directive 2003/74/EC – a purely procedural step. In contrast, we note that the second series of main EC claims – and the alternative claim of "direct" violation of Article 22.8 of the DSU for that matter – are not premised on the mere existence of an EC implementing measure, but on its *conformity* (presumed or actual) with the *SPS Agreement*.

7.273 Under those circumstances, one cannot exclude that no violation of Article 23.1 of the DSU may be found under the second series of main EC claims even though a violation of Article 23.1 was found under the first series of main EC claims, if only because they are based on different premises.

7.274 We recall in this regard that Article 11 of the DSU instructs us to assist the DSB in discharging its responsibilities and provides that, accordingly, a panel should make an objective assessment of the matter before it. In this case, the matter raised by the European Communities contains two separate elements: a series of claims related to the procedural obligations of the responding party and a series of claims premised on the violation by the responding party of Article 22.8 of the DSU due to compliance by the European Communities with its obligations under the WTO Agreement. We should therefore address both series of claims.

---

[453] See para. 7.182 above.

7.275 In addition, we also note that, since our report may be appealed and the Appellate Body can only rule on issues of law, we must provide sufficient factual basis to allow the Appellate Body to complete the analysis, if necessary.[454] In that context, in order to ensure in all instances a positive resolution of this dispute, we consider that proceeding with a review of the second series of main claims raised by the European Communities is appropriate.

7.276 Before proceeding with the review of this second series of claims, we want to stress that in reviewing the EC claims of violation of Article 23.1 read together with Article 22.8 and Article 3.7 of the DSU, our intention is not to substitute ourselves for a compliance panel under Article 21.5 of the DSU. We will make findings with respect to the second series of main claims of the European Communities with the only purpose to reach a conclusion on the violation of the provisions referred to in those claims.

(b) Order of review of the second series of main claims by the European Communities

7.277 We recall that the second series of EC claims is that the United States breaches Article 23.1, read together with Articles 22.8 and 3.7 of the DSU. We also note that the European Communities argues more particularly that Article 22.8 prohibits the continued unilateral application of the suspension of concessions or other obligations when the measure which has been found inconsistent is removed. We conclude from this that the EC claim under Article 23.1 is conditioned by the EC claim under Article 22.8 or, more precisely, that the findings that the European Communities wants us to make in relation to Article 23.1 are dependent on the findings that the European Communities wants us to make under Article 22.8. In other words, the second series of claims of the European Communities is premised on a violation by the United States of its obligations under Article 22.8.

7.278 We therefore conclude that we should begin our analysis of the second series of main claims of the European Communities with a review of the compatibility of the US measure at issue with Article 22.8 of the DSU. We consider that:

(a) if we find a breach of Article 22.8 of the DSU, we will proceed with reviewing the EC claims of violation of Articles 23.1 and 3.7 of the DSU, read together with Article 22.8;

---

[454] See, e.g., Appellate Body Reports on *Canada – Periodicals*, DSR 1997:I, p. 449 at 469; *Australia – Salmon*, para. 118; and *Korea – Dairy*, para. 92.

(b)   if we find no violation of Article 22.8, there will be no need for us to proceed any further with the review of these second series of claims by the European Communities.

7.279 We now proceed with our review of the EC claim under Article 22.8 of the DSU.

3.   *Violation of Article 22.8 of the DSU*

(a)   Preliminary remarks

7.280 Article 22.8 reads as follows:

"The suspension of concessions or other obligations shall be temporary and shall only be applied until such time as the measure found to be inconsistent with a covered agreement has been removed, or the Member that must implement recommendations or rulings provides a solution to the nullification or impairment of benefits, or a mutually satisfactory solution is reached. In accordance with paragraph 6 of Article 21, the DSB shall continue to keep under surveillance the implementation of adopted recommendations or rulings, including those cases where compensation has been provided or concessions or other obligations have been suspended but the recommendations to bring a measure into conformity with the covered agreements have not been implemented."

7.281 In light of terms of Article 22.8 and the arguments of the parties, we believe that two preliminary questions have to be addressed with respect to the violation of Article 22.8:

(a)   one is when the suspension of concessions should cease to be applied;

(b)   another one is what is meant by "the measure found to be inconsistent with a covered agreement".

7.282 Regarding the first question, we recall that the terms of Article 22.8 make it clear that countermeasures may remain in place only until such time as the measure found to be inconsistent by the DSB is removed. In other words, the removal of the illegal measure by the losing party must lead, without delay, to the removal of the suspension of obligations by the Member authorized by the DSB to suspend concessions.

7.283 Regarding what is meant by "the measure found to be inconsistent with a covered agreement", one interpretation could be to consider that the measure found to be inconsistent was Directive 96/22/EC.[455] This measure was removed. However, such an interpretation is unsatisfactory, as Directive 96/22/EC was replaced by Directive 2003/74/EC which also imposes an import ban. The Panel notes that the European Communities agrees that the phrase "until such time as the measure found to be inconsistent with a covered agreement has been removed" means that the illegality itself, and not only the measure, has been removed.[456]

7.284 The Panel believes that the term "measure" should not be interpreted narrowly as applying only to the legislation at issue. What the United States challenged as a complainant in the *EC – Hormones* case was an import restriction on meat and products from cattle treated with growth promoting hormones. We consider that this interpretation is confirmed by the second sentence of Article 22.8 which refers to the DSB keeping under surveillance situations where obligations have been suspended "but the recommendations to bring a measure into conformity with the covered agreements have not been implemented". We read this phrase as implying that what is to be achieved is not the removal of the measure but the actual compliance with the recommendations or rulings of the DSB.

7.285 We therefore conclude that Article 22.8 may be breached only if the European Communities has complied with the recommendations and rulings of the DSB and the United States has failed to immediately remove its suspension of concessions or other obligations.

7.286 We recall that the European Communities considers that this case is *not* about its compliance with the recommendations and rulings of the DSB in the *EC – Hormones* case. We nonetheless note that the European Communities requests us to make findings in relation to Article 22.8 under its main claim and that it did not exclude the possibility for the Panel to review the substance of the EC implementation measure in the context of its conditional allegation of "direct" violation of Article 22.8. We note, however, that such claim was made "in the alternative", i.e. if the Panel found no violation of the DSU under the other EC claims. In the context of its second series of main claims, the European Communities alleges that it does not have to demonstrate that it has complied with the recommendations and rulings of the DSB since it should benefit from a presumption of good faith compliance with respect to Directive 2003/74/EC. We note that the United States argues that the European Communities has not removed the measure found to be inconsistent with a covered agreement or provided a solution to the nullification or impairment of benefits. More particularly,

---

[455] Official Journal of the European Communities, No. L 125, 23 May 1996, p. 3

[456] See EC's first written submission, para. 81, EC's replies to Panel questions after the first substantive meeting, question 55, Annex B-1.

the United States argues that the EC implementing measure breaches the *SPS Agreement*.

7.287 Having regard to the arguments of the parties regarding the conformity of the EC implementing measure with the *SPS Agreement*, the Panel believes that it must determine the scope of its jurisdiction in this respect.

(b)   Jurisdiction of the Panel

(i)   Introduction

7.288 This case is not the first one about compliance of a Member with its obligations under the DSU and, in particular, under Article 23.[457] However, because of the claim raised by the European Communities under Article 22.8 of the DSU, the arguments of the United States and the links between this case and the *EC – Hormones* case – in particular through the question of the compliance of the EC implementing measure with the *SPS Agreement* – the second series of main claims by the European Communities raises a number of questions which, to our knowledge, were never directly addressed before by a panel established under Article 6 of the DSU.

7.289 In support of its claim under Article 23.1 read together with Article 22.8 and Article 3.7 of the DSU, the European Communities alleges in substance that it does not have to demonstrate that its implementing measure is compatible with the *SPS Agreement*. Rather, the European Communities argues that it should be presumed to have removed in good faith the measure found inconsistent with the *SPS Agreement* in the *EC – Hormones* dispute and that this presumption could only be rebutted through a recourse to Article 21.5 of the DSU by the responding party.

7.290 The United States disagrees that the European Communities benefits from any presumption of compliance and argues, on the contrary, that the European Communities failed to demonstrate that it has complied with the *SPS Agreement*.

7.291 Therefore, before we proceed any further, we believe that we should answer the two following questions:

(a)   In light of the EC claim that it benefits from a presumption of good faith compliance, do we need to determine whether the EC implementing measure *actually* complies with the *SPS Agreement*

---

[457] In *US – Section 301 Trade Act* case, Article 23.2(a) and (c) of the DSU was at issue, in *US – Certain EC Products*, Article 23.1 and 23.2(c) as well as 23.2(a) of the DSU was addressed by the panel and the Appellate Body.

in order to address the EC claim of violation of Article 23.1 read together with Article 22.8 and Article 3.7 of the DSU?

(b)   if yes, do we have the jurisdiction to address the conformity of the EC implementing measure with the *SPS Agreement*?

        (ii)   Does the Panel need to determine whether the EC implementing measure actually complies with the *SPS Agreement* in order to address the EC claim of violation of Article 23.1 read together with Article 22.8 and Article 3.7 of the DSU?

Summary of the main arguments of the parties[458]

7.292 The **European Communities** considers that, in order to demonstrate that the United States is in violation of Article 23.1, read in conjunction with Articles 22.8 and 3.7 of the DSU, it is not required to explain in full the substance of its compliance measure and why this measure implements the DSB recommendations and rulings. Rather, for the purposes of establishing a violation of DSU rules under these claims, the European Communities considers that it is sufficient to refer to the presumption of good faith which is a cornerstone of the DSU and cannot be undermined by a unilateral and unsubstantiated determination by the United States.[459]

7.293 The European Communities further argues that the WTO inconsistency of the implementing measure can only be determined in accordance with the appropriate procedure, namely Article 21.5 of the DSU. Unless such a procedure concludes that the compliance measure does not fully implement the DSB recommendations and rulings, it cannot be presumed that this is the case. This also follows from the general principle of good faith as it applies in international state relations (Article 26 of the Vienna Convention on the Law of Treaties (1969)), under which States are normally considered to act in conformity with their obligations. This principle has been recurrently recognized in WTO jurisprudence. The presumption of good faith also applies for implementing measures, as has been clearly spelt out in Article 21.5 proceedings.

7.294 For the European Communities, the United States could not unilaterally determine that the European Communities implemented the DSB recommendations and rulings in a WTO inconsistent way. On the contrary, the European

---

[458] A more detailed account of the parties' arguments can be found in Section IV of the descriptive part of this Report. The order in which the respective arguments of the parties are presented does not reflect any allocation of the burden of proof by the Panel.

[459] EC's first written submission, para. 72.

Communities must be presumed to have complied with its WTO obligations, if the United States refuses to establish the contrary. This presumption is even more justified as the EC implementation measure required conducting extensive scientific studies and performing a comprehensive risk assessment over several years in a transparent and objective manner, to which the United States had access and could provide comments on at any time.[460]

7.295 The European Communities understands that the United States is denying the good faith principle in this case because it considers that the European Communities has not correctly implemented its obligations. By doing so, however, the defending party confuses the notion of good faith and a possible violation under a covered agreement. In the present case, the European Communities bases itself on the same *rationale* as the Appellate Body in the *Byrd Amendment* case. Thus, even though the defending party alleges that the European Communities is still in violation of the *SPS agreement*, this does not in any event affect the presumption of good faith.

7.296 The European Communities recalls that in *EC – Bananas III (Article 21.5 – EC)* the panel merely said that a Member should not be presumed to agree that another Member is in compliance. Thus, the decision dealt with what a complaining Member is presumed to believe or not to believe. Yet, the general principle of good faith is an *objective* criterion that applies to compliance measures properly adopted and notified to the WTO. This is even more obvious if the other Members do not challenge the legality of the new implementing measures under Article 21.5 within a reasonable timeframe.

7.297 The **United States** considers that the European Communities relies on an already rejected legal theory that a Member found to have breached its WTO obligations is to be excused from its burden of proof in dispute settlement if it invokes the phrase "good faith."[461] The United States continues to apply the suspension of concessions to the European Communities in a WTO-consistent manner, fully in accordance with the authorization of the DSB.[462]

7.298 The United States first considers that the reports cited by the European Communities do not find a "presumption" but simply highlight the issue of burden of proof for complaining parties in Article 21.5 proceedings, or WTO proceedings generally, rather than setting forth a "presumption of good faith." The United States does not disagree that, in WTO dispute settlement, the initial burden rests with the complaining party alleging a WTO violation. In the view of the United States, the European Communities appears to believe that the concept

---

[460] EC's first written submission, paras. 86-94.
[461] *See* Panel Report on *EC – Bananas III (Article 21.5 – EC)*, para. 4.13.
[462] US's first written submission, para. 106.

of good faith would operate only in favour of the European Communities and either believes no other Member would be able to avail itself of the concept of good faith, or ignores that it would apply with respect to the United States. In this proceeding, the European Communities, as the complaining party, bears the burden of proving its prima facie case against the United States. The European Communities has failed to satisfy this burden because it has not demonstrated removal of its measure or that it has provided a solution to US nullification or impairment within the meaning of Article 22.8.[463]

7.299 The United States recalls that, in the *EC – Bananas III (Article 21.5 – EC)* proceeding already, the European Communities argued that its measures taken to comply were "presumed to conform with WTO rules unless their conformity has been duly challenged under the appropriate DSU procedures." The panel disagreed, highlighting that there is simply no basis in the *WTO Agreement* for the EC argument that it is presumed compliant with its obligations absent a finding against its measures. Similarly, there is no presumption of compliance for the EC amended ban in this proceeding.

7.300 According to the United States, there is no presumption of compliance or good faith in WTO dispute settlement that attaches to measures taken by WTO Members. Such a presumption is not found in the text of the DSU, nor is it found in the covered agreements, in the light of relevant provisions of which panels are charged with examining a matter under DSU Article 7.1. The findings of that evaluation then form the basis of the DSB recommendations and rulings, which "cannot add to or diminish the rights and obligations provided in the covered agreements" pursuant to Article 3.2 of the DSU.

7.301 The United States argues that, while Article 3.10 of the DSU uses the term "good faith", it does not do so in a manner indicating that a presumption of good faith attaches to measures taken by Members. Article 3.10 provides, in relevant part, as follows: "It is understood ... that, if a dispute arises, all Members will engage in these procedures in good faith in an effort to resolve the dispute." Article 3.10 is not a general incorporation of "good faith" principles of public international law. On the one hand, Article 3.10 is an understanding, not an obligation. On the other, Article 3.10 simply notes that, when a dispute has been initiated, Members will make best efforts to resolve it. It makes no reference whatsoever to a presumption of good faith which attaches to Member's measures, making them "presumed compliant" or WTO-consistent.

7.302 The United States adds that presumptions *per se* are not applicable in WTO dispute settlement. The only concept that comes close to resembling a presumption in dispute settlement is that the complaining party bears the burden of

---

[463] US's first written submission, footnote 124.

proof in making its prima facie case of the WTO inconsistency of another Member's measure. Rather than a presumption of good faith in dispute settlement, this instead is testament to the fact that there is *no presumption of bad faith* that attaches to measures taken by a WTO Member.

7.303 The United States considers that the established rules of burden of proof in dispute settlement already ensure that a complaining party establish its prima facie case, thereby obviating any need for such a presumption.

7.304 In the opinion of the United States, the European Communities has failed to demonstrate that such a presumption exists in WTO dispute settlement. When the arbitrator's statement in the *EC – Hormones (Article 22.6)* proceeding is viewed in context, it becomes clear that it was simply discussing relevant burdens of proof in WTO dispute settlement, noting that once a Member has claimed WTO-inconsistency of a measure in a dispute, it must prove that this is indeed the case.

7.305 The United States further notes that two other disputes cited by the European Communities, *Canada – Aircraft (Article 21.5 – Brazil)* and *Chile – Alcoholic Beverages,* do not mention a presumption of good faith whatsoever. Rather, they state that there is *no presumption of bad faith* in WTO dispute settlement. In these proceedings, the European Communities, as the complaining party, bears the burden of proving its prima facie case against the United States. The EC has failed to satisfy this burden because it has not demonstrated removal of its WTO-inconsistent measure or that it has provided a solution to US nullification or impairment within the meaning of Article 22.8.

7.306 The United States recall that the European Communities cites an opinion of the International Court of Justice discussing good faith. However, nowhere in the covered agreements is this presumption or principle discussed. As a panel established under Article 6 of the DSU, this Panel is charged under its terms of reference (DSU Article 7.1) with examining this matter "in light of the relevant provisions in [the covered agreements]". The relevant provisions of the DSU and the *SPS Agreement* do not contain a presumption of good faith in dispute settlement.[464]

7.307 Finally, in the opinion of the United States, even were one to presume that the European Communities implemented its amended bans in good faith, this fact would not in turn demonstrate that the EC's bans actually satisfy the elements of Article 22.8, *e.g.*, the EC could be acting in good faith, but still be wrong about the WTO-consistency or compliance of its amended measure.

---

[464] US's replies to Panel questions after the first substantive meeting, question 61, Annex B-3.

Reasoning of the Panel

Introductory remarks

7.308 Having regard to the arguments of the parties, the Panel considers that it needs to determine:

(a) whether the European Communities can invoke a presumption of good faith compliance; and, if yes,

(b) whether, and how, such a presumption could be rebutted.

7.309 The Panel notes that, generally, when good faith is referred to in a dispute, this is in relation to the measure adopted by the defending party[465], not with respect to a measure adopted by the complaining party – in this case the European Communities. Normally, a complainant does not have to show that it applies a measure in good faith, since this is normally not the measure at issue in the dispute. However, the demonstration by the European Communities of a violation of Article 22.8 by the United States in this case implies that it proves that it has removed the measure found to be inconsistent with a covered agreement in the *EC – Hormones* case. The Panel also recalls that it found above that the United States should have had recourse to the DSU in relation to the EC implementing measure. If the United States had had recourse to the dispute settlement procedures under the DSU – including the procedure provided in Article 21.5 – the European Communities would have been the defending party and its implementing measure would have benefited from a presumption of compatibility with WTO rules.[466] For these reasons, the Panel deems it appropriate not to take position on whether good faith can be invoked only by the defendant. Instead, it will address the issue by disregarding the status of the European Communities as complaining party in this case.

Applicability of the principle of good faith in the WTO and under the DSU

Introduction

7.310 We note that what the European Communities claims in this respect is the existence of a presumption of good faith compliance based on the international law principle of good faith. We are mindful of the position expressed by the United States that the impact of general international law on the DSU is limited to the application of the customary rules of interpretation of public international

---

[465] See, e.g., Appellate Body Report on *US – Carbon Steel*, para. 157.
[466] See, e.g., Appellate Body Report on *Canada – Dairy (Article 21.5 – New Zealand and US II)*, para. 66.

law embodied in the Vienna Convention on the Law of Treaties (cf. Article 3.2 of the DSU). However, we note that Article 31.3(c) provides that

> "[t]here shall be taken into account, together with the context: ...
> (c) any relevant rule of international law applicable to the relations between the parties."

7.311 Having regard to the overarching nature of the principle of good faith in international legal relations, we deem it appropriate to determine first whether there is any basis in public international law for the principle to which the European Communities refers. If this is the case, we will then proceed with determining whether the WTO Agreement in general and the DSU in particular exclude the application of this principle.

General international law

7.312 We note that what the European Communities refers to in its submissions is a presumption that it acted in good faith and thus must be presumed to have complied with the recommendations and rulings of the DSB.

7.313 We are of the view that the principle of good faith could be analysed mainly in respect of the following categories:

(a)   good faith conduct in a dispute settlement procedure;

(b)   substantive good faith, i.e. with respect to the substantive obligations of a State;

(c)   good faith in the interpretation process (Article 31 of the Vienna Convention on the Law of Treaties).

7.314 What the European Communities invokes in this case seems to fall primarily within the category of substantive good faith.

7.315 This allegation of the European Communities raises, in our opinion, two related but distinct issues under general international law:

(a)   the first one is whether a presumption that States act in good faith exists under general international law;

(b)   the second one is whether such presumption of good faith can be assimilated to a presumption of compliance.

7.316 Good faith is one of the basic principles regarding the creation and execution of legal obligations in public international law.[467] This principle is expressed *inter alia* in Article 26 of the Vienna Convention on the Law of Treaties:

> "Every treaty in force is binding upon the parties to it and must be performed by them in good faith."

7.317 It is implicit from the duty to perform treaty obligations in good faith that a party to an international agreement should be deemed to have acted in good faith in the performance of its treaty obligations. More generally, even though Article 26 provides for an obligation and not a presumption, *pacta sunt servanda* is but only one expression of the principle of good faith. Good faith is a general principle of international law that governs all reciprocal actions of States.[468] We are therefore inclined to agree with the European Communities that every party to an international agreement must be presumed to be performing its obligation under that agreement in good faith.

7.318 Having concluded that, under general international law, States enjoy a presumption of good faith, we now proceed to determine whether presumption of good faith can be equated with presumption of compliance with treaty obligations.

7.319 The Panel notes in this respect that good faith has been defined as a:

> "disposition d'esprit de loyauté et d'honnêteté consistant en ce qu'un sujet de droit ne tente pas de minorer ses obligations, quels qu'en soit l'origine et le fondement ..."[469]

7.320 According to this definition, a State acting in good faith should be honestly seeking to comply with its obligations. A presumption of good faith could thus extend to compliance. It is the understanding of the Panel that States benefit in their actions from the principle that a breach of the principle of good faith

---

[467] See, e.g., ICJ, *Nuclear Tests Case*, Judgement of 20 December 1974, ICJ Reports 1974, p. 473, para. 49.

[468] See also UN Charter, Art.2.2; Malcom N. Shaw: International Law (5th edition), p. 811-812: "[Pacta sunt servanda] underlies every international agreement for, in the absence of a certain minimum belief that States will perform their treaties obligations in good faith, there is no reasons for countries to enter into such obligations with each other."

[469] Jean Salmon: *Dictionnaire de droit international public*, p. 134. Black Law Dictionary, 6th ed., para. 693:
> "In common usage the term is ordinarily used to describe that state of mind denoting honesty of purpose, freedom from intention to defraud and, generally speaking, means being faithful to one's duty or obligation."

cannot be presumed and that any State alleging an abuse of right (*abus de droit*) or, more particularly, a breach of the principle of good faith, must prove it.[470]

7.321 As a result, we note that, under general international law, the European Communities would be entitled to claim a presumption of good faith compliance.

7.322 However, that does not mean that the State invoking good faith compliance, while acting in total good faith, actually complied with its treaty obligations. It could make an illegal interpretation of its obligations without breaching the principle of good faith. Thus, if good faith compliance is presumed, it cannot be a non-rebuttable or *juris et de jure* presumption.

7.323 An additional element to consider is that, under general public international law, *every* State benefits from the application of the principle of good faith. We therefore agree with the United States that if the European Communities can claim good faith compliance, the United States too should also benefit from the same presumption. Unlike in "normal" cases where only the measure adopted by one Member is at issue, in this case the legality of the US measure challenged by the European Communities depends on whether the measure taken by the European Communities to comply with DSB recommendations and rulings is WTO consistent. In other words, both parties can invoke the presumption of good faith. However, we do not see the fact that both parties can invoke good faith in relation to diametrically opposed positions as affecting the applicability of this principle in this case. Indeed, we are only dealing with presumptions, not with evidence. As long as these presumptions can be rebutted before a panel, we see no inherent problem to the fact that both parties claim good faith.

The text of the DSU

7.324 The Panel first notes that, with the exception of Articles 3.10 and 4.3, there is no reference to good faith in the DSU. Of those two references, that in Article 4.3 relates specifically to consultations. Only that in Article 3, entitled "General Provisions", could have a relevance in this case. However, Article 3.10 reads as follows:

> "It is understood that requests for conciliation and the use of the dispute settlement procedures should not be intended or considered as contentious acts and that, if a dispute arises, all Members will engage in these procedures in good faith in an effort to resolve the dispute. It is also understood that complaints and

---

[470] PCIJ, *Upper Silesia Case*, Judgement of 25 May 1926, Series A. No. 7, p. 30.

counter-complaints in regard to distinct matters should not be linked."

7.325 The Panel understands the reference to good faith in Article 3.10 of the DSU to relate to the manner in which parties to a dispute should participate in the dispute (i.e., procedural good faith, as described above), not specifically to whether Members should be presumed to be acting in good faith. Indeed, the reference to good faith is made in relation to "engage[ing] in [DSU] procedures in good faith *in an effort to resolve the dispute*" (emphasis added) and the preceding phrase provides that DSU procedures "should not be intended or considered as contentious acts".

7.326 The Panel therefore considers that Article 3.10 is of limited direct relevance to determine whether the European Communities should benefit from a presumption of good faith compliance under the DSU.

7.327 However, the references to good faith in the DSU are evidence that the DSU does not exclude the application of the principle of good faith in the resolution of disputes. The Panel is of the view that, since the application of the principle of good faith is not expressly excluded by the DSU, it is applicable to WTO Members.[471]

The panel and Appellate Body practice

Presumption and burden of proof

7.328 The Panel notes that, in *US – Wool Shirts and Blouses*, the Appellate Body recalled that:

"[W]e find it difficult, indeed, to see how any system of judicial settlement could work if it incorporated the proposition that the mere assertion of a claim might amount to proof."[472]

7.329 However, the Appellate Body also mentioned in *Japan – Apples* that:

---

[471] The Panel is not of the view that the fact that some covered agreements, such as the *SPS Agreement* (see Article 2.4) expressly provide that measures of a Member which conform to a given agreement shall be presumed to be in accordance with the obligations of that Member under another covered agreement would imply that the presumption of good faith does not apply in the WTO Agreements unless expressly referred to. The Panel considers that the reference to presumption in Article 2.4 of the *SPS Agreement* is to a legal presumption and is intended to address potentially conflicting interpretations between two provisions. The reference in Article 3.2 of the *SPS Agreement* can be explained by the fact that the "international standards, guidelines or recommendations" are not part of the WTO Agreement.

[472] Appellate Body Report on *US – Wool Shirts and Blouses*, DSR 1997:I, p. 323 at 335.

"[T]he Appellate Body statement in *EC – Hormones* does not imply that the complaining party is responsible for providing proof of all facts raised in relation to the issue of determining whether a measure is consistent with a given provision of a covered agreement. In other words, although the complaining party bears the burden of proving its case, the responding party must prove the case it seeks to make in response."[473]

7.330 We believe that, in arguing that it enjoys a presumption of good faith compliance, the European Communities is not merely *asserting* its claim of violation of Articles 23.1, 22.8 and 3.7. The EC allegation of existence of a presumption of good faith compliance is only one part – although an essential one – of the EC argumentation supporting its claims. Moreover, the European Communities is not directly asserting that it has complied in relation to the conformity of the US measure with Article 22.8, but that it enjoys, as a matter of principle, a presumption that it complied in good faith with its own obligations.

7.331 On its part, the United States argues as a defence that the European Communities did not comply with the recommendations and rulings of the DSB. One may argue that the parties' respective burdens are unbalanced because the European Communities, if one agrees with its position, does not have to demonstrate prima facie that it has complied with the recommendations and rulings of the DSB. However, it should first be recalled that what is at issue in this case is not directly whether the European Communities has complied with the recommendations and rulings of the DSB, but whether the United States complied with its obligations under Articles 23.1, 22.8 and 3.7 of the DSU. By taking this route, the European Communities takes the risk that its claims may be rejected if the Panel disagrees with the existence of a presumption of good faith compliance.

7.332 We therefore conclude that by invoking a presumption of good faith compliance, the European Communities is not merely asserting its claims under Article 22.8, but rather supporting its claims which are, in essence, claims of violations by the United States, not claims of compliance by the European Communities.

7.333 We therefore find that the European Communities' reliance on a presumption does not amount in this case to merely asserting a claim.

---

[473] Appellate Body Report on *Japan – Apples*, para. 154.

Presumption of good faith

7.334 The Panel notes that the Appellate Body has, on several occasions, re-called that the principle of good faith applies to WTO Members in their relations under the WTO Agreement. The Panel recalls that, in *US – FSC*, the Appellate Body stated that:

> "This *pervasive principle* [of good faith] requires both complain-ing and responding Members to comply with the requirements of the DSU (and related requirements in other covered agreements) in good faith." (emphasis added)[474]

7.335 Furthermore, it seems that the Appellate Body understands the obligation to comply with the requirements of the DSU in good faith as implying that Members are to be presumed to act in good faith. In *EC – Tube or Pipe Fittings*, the Appellate Body found that:

> "This excerpt demonstrates that the Panel took into account the European Communities' responses to its questions before reaching its finding. It also indicates that the Panel did not rely *exclusively on the presumption of good faith*, as Brazil suggests, given that some of the Panel's questions were directed at the *validity* of Ex-hibit EC-12. If the Panel had placed *total reliance on the presump-tion of good faith*, it would have simply accepted the European Communities' assertion that Exhibit EC-12 formed part of the re-cord of the investigation and would not have posed questions to assess the consistency of Exhibit EC-12 with other evidence con-tained in the record. Therefore, we are satisfied that the Panel "took steps to assure [itself] of the validity of [Exhibit EC-12] and of the fact that it forms part of the contemporaneous written record of the EC investigation." (footnotes omitted – emphasis added)[475]

7.336 As mentioned above, there is no express exclusion of the application of the principle of good faith in the DSU or in the WTO Agreement. As noted by the panel on *Korea – Procurement*:

> "Article 3.2 of the DSU requires that we seek within the context of a particular dispute to clarify the existing provisions of the WTO agreements in accordance with customary rules of interpretation of public international law. However, the relationship of the WTO Agreements to customary international law is broader than this.

---

[474] Appellate Body Report on *US – FSC*, para. 166.
[475] Appellate Body Report on *EC – Tube or Pipe Fittings*, para. 127.

Customary international law applies generally to the economic relations between the WTO Members. Such international law applies
to the extent that the WTO agreements do not 'contract out' from
it. To put it another way, to the extent there is no conflict or inconsistency, or an expression in a covered WTO agreement that implies differently, we are of the view that the customary rules of international law apply to the WTO treaties and to the process of
treaty formation under the WTO."[476]

7.337 More precisely, in *US – Section 211 Appropriations Act*, the Appellate
Body recalled that:

"... where discretionary authority is vested in the executive branch
of a WTO Member, *it cannot be assumed that the WTO Member
will fail to implement its obligations under the WTO Agreement in
good faith.* Relying on these rulings, and interpreting them correctly, the Panel concluded that it could not assume that OFAC
would exercise its discretionary executive authority inconsistently
with the obligations of the United States under the *WTO Agreement*. Here, too, we agree." (emphasis added)[477]

7.338 The parties have argued on the relevance of the report in *EC – Bananas
III (Article 21.5 – EC)*. The European Communities notes that this report was
never adopted by the DSB. We nevertheless recall that the Appellate Body, in
Japan – Alcoholic Beverages II, found that panels may seek guidance from unadopted panel reports. In *EC – Bananas III (Article 21.5 – EC)*, the panel rejected the EC assertion of a presumption of consistency. In that case, the EC
requested the panel to find that its implementing measures "must be presumed to
conform to WTO rules unless their conformity has been duly challenged under
the appropriate DSU procedures". This position seems largely similar to the position adopted by the European Communities in the present case, where it claims
that the United States will breach Article 23 even if it rebuts the presumption of
compliance because it failed to use the right forum to contest it (i.e. Article 21.5
of the DSU).

7.339 The panel in *EC – Bananas III (Article 21.5 – EC)*, agreed with the European Communities that there was normally no presumption of inconsistency attached to a Member's measures in the WTO dispute settlement system. This was
subsequently confirmed by the Appellate Body in *Chile – Alcoholic Beverages*[478]and it is now well established that no presumption of bad faith can be

---

[476] Panel Report on *Korea – Procurement*, para. 7.96.
[477] Appellate Body Report on *US – Section 211 Appropriations Act*, para. 259. (original footnote
omitted)
[478] Appellate Body Report on *Chile – Alcoholic Beverages*, para. 74.

applied to a Member's measure. However, the panel in *EC – Bananas III (Article 21.5 – EC)* considered that the failure, as of a given point in time, of one Member to challenge another Member's measures could not be interpreted to create a presumption that the first Member accepts the measures of the other Member as consistent with the WTO Agreement.[479]

7.340 First, we find the above reasoning of the Panel in *EC – Bananas III (Article 21.5 – EC)* convincing.

7.341 Second, in the present case, however, the European Communities does not actually allege that there is a presumption of acceptance by the United States that the measure is consistent with the WTO Agreement because the United States failed to challenge the measure. The European Communities claims that there is a presumption of compliance based on the presumption of good faith and that this presumption can only be rebutted in the appropriate forum, i.e. by invoking Article 21.5 of the DSU.

7.342 The United States argues that the presumption of good faith compliance cannot supersede the multilateral authorization of the DSB to the United States to suspend concessions.

7.343 As already mentioned, we first note that Article 22.2 and 22.7 of the DSU refers to "authorization" of the DSB. The United States has no obligation under the DSU to apply the sanctions authorized by the DSB.[480] Second, we note that Article 22.8 provides that the suspension of obligations "shall only be applied until such time as the measure found to be inconsistent with a covered agreement has been removed, or the Member that must implement recommendations or rulings provides for a solution to the nullification or impairment of benefits". There is no reference to the DSB in that phrase and nothing in this provision suggests that a Member suspending concessions can continue to do so as long as the authorization of the DSB has not been repealed by the DSB. On the contrary, it seems that it is for the Member concerned to draw the consequences of a removal of the violation. In other words, the removal of the measure found to be inconsistent with a covered agreement supersedes the DSB authorization to suspend concessions.

7.344 The United States also argues that, if the presumption of good faith compliance were accepted, nothing would prevent the European Communities from notifying a "scam legislation". The United States argues that this could open an

---

[479] Panel Report on *EC – Bananas III (Article 21.5 – EC)*, para. 4.13.

[480] See, e.g., *Canada – Aircraft Credits and Guarantees* and *Brazil – Aircraft*. In both cases authorization of retaliation has been granted by the DSB but the complaining party has not applied the authorized sanctions.

endless loop of litigation[481], as a mere notification of a compliance measure would force the United States to initiate a dispute settlement procedure under Article 21.5 of the DSU.

7.345 We recall that we are called upon to solve this dispute, not to make generally applicable interpretations of the DSU. We have found above that the EC implementing legislation was not a "scam legislation". Therefore, we do not find it necessary to address the situation that would result from our finding if a Member notified a "scam legislation".

Is the presumption of good faith compliance rebuttable only in a specific forum?

7.346 We note that the European Communities claims that the presumption of good faith compliance is rebuttable, but only in the appropriate forum, i.e. by the complaining party in the original case taking the initiative of having recourse to a dispute settlement procedure under Article 21.5 of the DSU.[482] The European Communities alleges a "jurisprudential" need for an irrebuttable presumption to fill up a gap in the DSU and allow respondents to exit from post-retaliation situations.

7.347 The United States argues, on the contrary, that an Article 21.5 proceeding is not the only avenue available if there is a disagreement as to the adoption of a compliance measure and that, in any event, it is not open exclusively to the United States, but also to the European Communities.

7.348 It is therefore important for the Panel to determine the extent to which the unavailability of any legal recourse for the European Communities in a post retaliation situation may justify that the presumption of good faith compliance be irrebuttable, except through recourse to the procedure provided in Article 21.5 of the DSU.

7.349 We first note that nowhere does the DSU provide that a presumption of good faith compliance should be rebuttable only through recourse to Article 21.5 of the DSU.

7.350 Second, it appears that, even under the current DSU, several means seem *a priori* to be available to the European Communities to obtain termination of the suspension of concessions or other obligations:

---

[481] See, e.g., US's reply to Panel question 40 after the first substantive meeting, Annex B-3, para. 6.
[482] EC's reply to Panel question 4(b) after the first substantive meeting.

(a)   Good offices and consultations;[483]

(b)   Article 21.5 of the DSU;

(c)   Arbitration under Article 25 of the DSU; and

(d)   recourse to a normal panel against the continuation of the retaliations (as in this case).

7.351 The Panel is mindful that the option naturally coming to mind when it comes to reviewing compliance is the procedure provided under Article 21.5 of the DSU. The Panel is aware of the broad language ("such dispute shall be decided through recourse to these dispute settlement procedures") used in Article 21.5 and that such language could be deemed to encompass any procedure available under the DSU for the resolution of disputes. The Panel is, however, of the opinion that other terms in Article 21.5 support the view that the Article 21.5 procedure is actually a panel procedure with a shorter deadline. In this regard, the Panel reads the phrase "including whenever possible resort to the original panel" not as meaning that resort to a panel is generally preferred, but as requesting resort to the panelists that reviewed the original case, rather than to other individuals.

7.352 The Panel also notes that this dispute is evidence that a practicable alternative exists to a recourse to Article 21.5. We recall in this respect that even though the European Communities claims a violation of the DSU by the United States, its claim under Article 22.8 of the DSU is based on the compliance of its implementing measure with the WTO Agreement, whether presumed (as part of the second series of main EC claims under Article 23.1 read together with Article 22.8 and Article 3.7) or demonstrated (as in its alternative "direct" claim of violation of Article 22.8). While Members enjoy complete discretion in the way they bring the measure at issue into conformity with the covered agreements, the findings already made by the Panel with respect to Article 23.2(a) and 23.1 of the DSU and the findings the Panel will make under Article 22.8 will have an impact on whether the United States may maintain, suspend or withdraw the suspension of obligations it currently applies.

7.353 We recall that the European Communities considered that Article 21.5 was not an avenue open to the party claiming compliance, but only to the complainant in the original case.[484] Both parties have discussed the relevance of the only case where a party found in breach of its obligations requested an Article 21.5 panel, i.e. the *EC – Bananas III (Article 21.5 – EC)* panel.

---

[483]   Such a solution seems to be implicitly suggested by the United States when it refers to Article 22.8 which mentioned that "a mutually satisfactory solution is reached".

[484]   EC's reply to Panel question 1 after the first substantive meeting, Annex B-1; EC's second written submission, para. 61.

7.354 We note that, in the *EC – Bananas III (Article 21.5 – EC)* case, the panel did not conclude that it could not perform its duties under Article 21.5. The panel, referring to the comments made by Japan as a third party, noted that allowing the defendant before the original panel to initiate a procedure under Article 21.5 presented certain "practical problems or anomalies". The panel was also sympathetic to the concerns of India as a third party that, in an appropriate case, a respondent-initiated Article 21.5 proceeding should be allowed.[485] The Panel concluded:

> "In our view, we would not rule out the possibility of using Article 21.5 in such a manner, particularly when the purpose of such initiation was clearly the examination of the WTO-consistency of implementing measures."[486]

7.355 We are therefore not convinced that Article 21.5 is the only avenue available to address a claim of compliance by a Member alleging to have complied with recommendations and rulings of the DSB. Neither do we believe that proceedings under Article 21.5 are open only to the original complainant.

7.356 For these reasons, the Panel does not agree that the presumption of good faith compliance which the European Communities enjoys should be rebuttable only through a recourse by the complainants in the original case to Article 21.5 of the DSU.

(iii)   Conclusion

7.357 On the basis of the above:

(a)   We note that, under general international law, the corollary to the obligation to perform treaty obligations in good faith is the presumption that Members act in good faith when performing such obligations.

(b)   We find that the general principle of good faith and the presumption of good faith performance of a Member's obligations apply in relation to Members' obligations under the WTO Agreements, including the DSU, as interpreted in accordance with customary rules of interpretation of public international law.

(c)   We also note that there is no presumption of bad faith under general international law and find that no presumption of bad faith

---

[485] Panel Report on *EC – Bananas III (Article 21.5 – EC)*, para. 4.18.
[486] *Ibid.*

applies under the DSU as interpreted in accordance with customary rules of interpretation of public international law.

(d) We find that the presumption of good faith compliance alleged by the European Communities is at best legally identical to the principle of good faith performance of treaty obligations. We do not find in the DSU as interpreted in accordance with customary rules of interpretation of public international law any ground supporting a specific presumption of compliance for Members having to implement DSB recommendations and rulings.

(e) Moreover, we find no support in the DSU to suggest that this presumption may only apply to the measure taken by the European Communities and not to the measures adopted by the United States.

(f) As a consequence, while we agree with the existence of a presumption of good faith compliance, we do not agree with the European Communities that the presumption of good faith that it enjoys may only be rebutted in an Article 21.5 procedure. We find, on the contrary, that this presumption, because it applies to measures taken by all parties, must be rebuttable before this Panel. Just as the EC allegations are intended to rebut the presumption of good faith conformity of the US retaliatory measures with Article 22.8 of the DSU, the United States should be allowed to rebut the presumption of EC compliance by proving actual non-compliance.

7.358 In reaching these conclusions, we do not consider that we add to or diminish the rights and obligations of WTO Members. We do not apply the presumption of good faith compliance independently from the obligations of the European Communities under the WTO Agreement. The European Communities has an obligation to comply with the WTO Agreement in general[487] and with the recommendations and rulings of the DSB and the general principle of good faith implies that the European Communities do so in good faith. In doing so we apply the principle of good faith consistently with WTO law and general public international law.[488]

7.359 We have also found above that we could not agree with the European Communities and base our findings of violation of Article 23.1 read in conjunction with Article 22.8 and 3.7 of the DSU on an irrebuttable presumption of good faith compliance by the European Communities. Whereas the European Communities enjoys a presumption of good faith compliance, this presumption is rebuttable. We agree that, for all practical purposes, this amounts to address-

---

[487] See Article XVI:4 of the WTO Agreement.
[488] As explicitly expressed in Article 2.2 of the Charter of the United Nations, as well as in Article 26 of Vienna Convention on the Law of Treaties.

ing the EC "alternative" claim of violation of Article 22.8 *per se*. However, this is not the result of us merely disregarding the order in which the European Communities wanted us to review this case. We are still reviewing the EC claim of violation of Article 23.1, read together with Articles 22.8 and 3.7. We are not reviewing a claim of violation of Article 22.8 in isolation.

(iv)   Does the Panel have jurisdiction to address the compliance of the EC implementing measure with the *SPS Agreement*?

7.360   We are mindful that our terms of reference do not include any provision of the *SPS Agreement* referred to by the parties during these proceedings and that "[A] panel cannot assume jurisdiction that it does not have."[489] *Stricto sensu*, the conformity of the EC measure with the provisions of the *SPS Agreement* referred to in this case is not part of our mandate. This means that reviewing alleged violations of the *SPS Agreement* is not part of our mandate either and that we are not expected to make *findings* on those provisions.

7.361   However, this absence of reference to the *SPS Agreement* is understandable since the European Communities is not seeking a finding of violation of the *SPS Agreement* by the responding party.

7.362   Moreover, we note that the European Communities claims in its request for establishment of a panel that the United States breached Article 22.8

> "[b]y failing to apply the suspension of concessions or other obligations only until such time as the measure found to be inconsistent with a covered agreement has been removed, or the implementing Member has provided a solution to the nullification or impairment of benefits previously caused to the United States."[490]

7.363   This statement, which essentially repeats the terms of Article 22.8, must be read in conjunction with other relevant remarks of the European Communities in its request for establishment of a panel. For instance, in the introduction, the European Communities stated that:

> "[t]his request concerns the United States' continued suspension of concessions and other obligations under the covered agreements, without recourse to the procedures established by the DSU, *after the European Communities has removed the measures found to be*

---

[489]   Appellate Body Report on *India – Patents (US)*, para. 92.
[490]   WT/DS320/6.

inconsistent with WTO law in case DS26, European Communities – Measures concerning meat and meat products (Hormones) ('EC – Hormones')."[491]

and subsequently:

"[t]he European Communities subsequently removed the measure found to be inconsistent with a covered agreement. It adopted Directive 2003/74/EC of the European Parliament and of the Council of 22 September 2003 amending Council Directive 96/22/EC concerning the prohibition on the use in stockfarming of certain substances having a hormonal or thyrostatic action and of beta-agonists. The Directive was published and entered into force on 14 October 2003.

In conformity with the recommendations and rulings of the DSB and the covered agreements, the new EC legislation is based on comprehensive risk assessments, in particular on the opinions of the independent Scientific Committee on Veterinary Measures relating to Public Health. The risk assessments focussed on potential risks to human health from hormone residues in bovine meat and meat products, in particular such risks arising from residues of six hormonal substances: oestradiol-17β, testosterone, progesterone, trenbolone acetate, zeranol and melengestrol acetate. In carrying out the risk assessments, the European Communities initiated and funded a number of specific scientific studies and research projects. It addressed specific requests to the United States, Canada and third countries to provide any recent scientific data and information in their possession. It took account of the findings of various independent expert bodies.

In light of the risk analyses carried out, the European Communities concluded that the avoidance of intake of oestradiol-17β is of absolute importance to human health and that, consequently, the placing on the market of meat containing this substance should be prohibited. With respect to testosterone, progesterone, trenbolone acetate, zeranol and melengestrol acetate, and on the basis of the available pertinent scientific information reflected in the above-mentioned risk analyses, the European Communities provisionally prohibited the placing on the market of meat containing these substances because the relevant scientific evidence was insufficient.

---

[491] WT/DS320/6 (emphasis added).

On 27 October 2003, the European Communities notified to the DSB the adoption, publication and entry into force of this Directive as well as the preceding scientific risk assessments. In the same communication, the European Communities explained that it considers itself to have fully implemented the recommendations and rulings of the DSB in the *EC – Hormones* dispute and that, as a consequence, it considers the United States' suspension of concessions vis-à-vis the European Communities to be no longer justified."[492]

7.364 In the Panel's view, one instance of violation of Article 22.8 occurs when the suspension is maintained even though the "measure found to be inconsistent ... has been removed". The lengthy explanation above demonstrates that the claims of the European Communities under Article 22.8 are related to its alleged removal of the "measure found to be inconsistent" with the *SPS Agreement*.

7.365 The Panel notes the arguments of the parties in reply to a question on its jurisdiction to review the compatibility of the EC implementing measure with the *SPS Agreement*. The United States replied that, pursuant to Article 7 of the DSU, a panel's standard terms of reference include the provisions referred to by the responding party.[493] The European Communities replied that, in light of the Appellate Body practice, the Panel has, in the present case, no jurisdiction to address Articles 3.3, 5.1 and 5.7 of the *SPS Agreement*. The European Communities adds that, at best, one could venture to draw an analogy to affirmative defences.[494]

7.366 The Panel is not convinced by any of the views of the parties. Regarding the argument of the United States, the Panel recalls that the matter before the Panel is defined by the request for establishment of the Panel.[495] The matter before this Panel is whether the measure maintained by the United States suspending concessions or other obligations *vis-à-vis* the European Communities has breached, *inter alia*, Article 22.8 of the DSU, not whether the European Communities has complied with the *SPS Agreement*. As a result, the US references to provisions of the *SPS Agreement* are not claims. The Panel may address them, however, to the extent necessary to make an objective assessment of the matter,

---

[492] WT/DS320/6 (original footnotes omitted).
[493] US's reply to Panel question 65 after the first substantive meeting, Annex B-3, para. 64.
[494] EC's reply to Panel question 65 after the first substantive meeting, Annex B-1, paras. 239-241.
[495] See Appellate Body Report in *Brazil – Desiccated Coconut*, DSR 1997:I, p. 186:
       "... the 'matter' referred to a panel for consideration consists of the specific claims stated by the parties to the dispute in the relevant documents specified in the terms of reference. We agree with the approach taken in previous adopted panel reports that a matter, which includes the claims composing that matter, does not fall within a panel's terms of reference unless the claims are identified in the documents referred to or contained in the terms of reference."

including an objective assessment of the EC claims, as part of its findings on Article 22.8 of the DSU.

7.367 Neither does the Panel consider that an analogy could be drawn between the reference by the parties to provisions of the *SPS Agreement* in this case and the notion of "affirmative defence". In the opinion of the Panel, an affirmative defence would imply that the responding party invoke a provision of a covered agreement as a justification for a breach of another provision. This is not the case here. The United States does not argue the incompatibility of the EC implementing measure as a *justification* for a breach of Article 22.8. Nor does it seem to invoke the incompatibility of the EC implementing measure as a justification for a breach of Article 23. The Panel concludes that any jurisdiction it may have to review the compatibility of the EC implementing measure with the *SPS Agreement* cannot result from the fact that the United States would have invoked the *SPS Agreement*, including as an affirmative defence.

7.368 We also note the argument of the European Communities that:

> "[this] issue is a perfect illustration of the problems arising if an implementing member is forced to bring a case alleging compliance, instead of the original complaining party bringing a case alleging non compliance ... The terms of reference become wholly devoid of their meaning and the panel's jurisdiction turns into a moving target depending on whatever allegations of inconsistency the 'defending' parties will come up with. It is clear that the dispute settlement system is not designed to accommodate such a procedural constellation."[496]

7.369 We do not agree that the terms of reference of the Panel become wholly devoid of meaning because of the references made by the parties to provisions of the *SPS Agreement*. Neither do we consider that this modifies our terms of reference. We recall that the European Communities claims a violation by the United States of Article 22.8 of the DSU which is premised on the compliance of the EC implementing measure (Directive 2003/74/EC) with the *SPS Agreement*. A discussion of the compatibility of the measure with provisions of the *SPS Agreement* is, thus, the immediate consequence of the inclusion of Article 22.8 of the DSU in the EC request for establishment of a panel. As such, our mandate remains defined by the EC request for establishment of a panel.

7.370 We are mindful that the responding party could bring several allegations of violations with respect to the EC implementing measure. We note however

---

[496] EC's reply to Panel question 65 after the first substantive meeting, Annex B-1, para. 240. See also EC's reply to Panel question 62 after the first substantive meeting, Annex B-1.

that the European Communities did not exclude the possibility for the Panel to consider the actual compatibility of Directive 2003/74/EC with the *SPS Agreement* as part of its alternative "direct" claim under Article 22.8 of the DSU. Such a review would imply that the Panel address the compatibility of the EC implementing measure with the *SPS Agreement*. While the Panel must comply with its terms of reference, nothing in the DSU prevents the Panel from considering the compatibility of the EC implementing measure with the *SPS Agreement* if this is necessary in order to make the findings required by those terms of reference.

7.371 Moreover, we note that, whereas the European Communities "[did] not believe that it [was] necessary for the Panel to look into any scientific issue to make its necessary findings and rulings within its terms of reference in this particular case", the European Communities did not exclude that the Panel could address the scientific issues at stake since it suggested that, in such a case, the consultation of scientific experts would be absolutely necessary.[497] The parties have extensively discussed the question of the compatibility of the EC implementing measure with certain provisions of the *SPS Agreement*, have agreed to the consultation of experts on the scientific issues relating to the compatibility of the measure with the *SPS Agreement* and have extensively commented on these scientific issues.

7.372 We conclude from this that the Panel should be entitled to determine whether the European Communities has removed the measure found to be inconsistent with a covered agreement in order to establish whether Article 22.8 has been breached by the United States. Indeed, the Panel considers that, since the European Communities made a claim of violation of Article 22.8, the compatibility of its implementing measure becomes *ipso facto* an issue that the Panel will have to address if it reviews any of the EC claim relating to Article 22.8. The fact that the European Communities alleges that it benefits from a presumption of good faith compliance does not affect this conclusion. Under both of its Article 22.8 claims, the European Communities needs to demonstrate that it has removed the measure found to be inconsistent. The presumption of good faith compliance does not affect what needs to be demonstrated. It simply shifts the burden of proof since, in application of the presumption of good faith compliance, the European Communities has, in this dispute, made a prima facie case of violation of Article 22.8 which the United States has to rebut.

---

[497] EC's reply to Panel question 74 after the first substantive meeting, Annex B, para. 275. The Panel notes that the European Communities raised an alternative claim of violation of Article 22.8 of the DSU and Articles I and II of the GATT 1994, based on its alleged actual compliance with the recommendations and rulings of the DSB in the *EC – Hormones* case.

7.373 The Panel notes that, pursuant to its mandate, it is only expected to make findings of violation in relation to Article 22.8 of the DSU, the breach of which is alleged by the complaining party. The Panel nonetheless recalls that, for the reasons mentioned above and irrespective of which one of the two Article 22.8 claims is addressed, it will have to determine whether the European Communities has removed the measure found to be inconsistent. Since what has to be demonstrated is a consistency or inconsistency with provisions of the *SPS Agreement*, this is not really an issue of fact but a legal question, which adds to the complexity of the situation before the Panel.

7.374 The Panel is fully conscious of the challenges attached to assessing whether the EC implementing measure is not inconsistent with the provisions of the *SPS Agreement* referred to by the parties in this case. The Panel also notes that, in a case like this one, it is largely dependent on the responding party, not on the complainant, as far as allegations of incompatibility of the EC implementing measure are concerned. However, we believe that it is in the interest of the responding party to demonstrate the incompatibility of the implementing measure. We can count on its full cooperation in this respect, and we have experienced it in this case. The Panel also agrees that, since the allegations of violation of the *SPS Agreement* were not exhaustively listed in its terms of reference and depended on the parties raising them in the course of the procedure, this could have made it difficult to circumscribe the scope of its review under the *SPS Agreement*. We note, however, that in this particular case the legal arguments regarding the conformity of the EC implementing measure with the *SPS Agreement* were all raised early in the proceedings and that no party complained that it had not been given sufficient opportunity to comment on the other party's allegations.

7.375 We therefore conclude that we should address the compatibility of the EC implementing measure with the provisions of the *SPS Agreement* referred to by the parties to the extent necessary to determine, with respect to the EC claim relating to Article 22.8, whether the EC "measure found to be inconsistent" in the *EC – Hormones* case has been removed. We are mindful of the procedural problems raised by this approach, but we do not consider that, by proceeding in this manner, we are exceeding our jurisdiction to the extent that such a review is necessary in order to address the EC claims under Article 22.8.

7.376 The Panel notes in this respect that it is not the first time that a dispute settlement entity, when confronted with a procedurally a-typical issue, decided to adopt a pragmatic solution and perform functions similar to those of an Article 21.5 panel. In the Article 22.6 arbitration in the *EC – Bananas III* case the arbitrator decided to adopt the most "logical way forward":

> "4.10 ... the European Communities argues that we should not consider the consistency of its new banana regime. First, it argues

that to do so would go beyond our terms of reference, which it suggests are limited to determining the level of suspension and its equivalence to the level of nullification or impairment. As noted above, however, setting the level of nullification or impairment may require consideration of whether there is nullification or impairment flowing from a WTO-inconsistency of the new banana regime."

7.377 We too believe that our approach to consider, to the extent necessary, the compatibility of the EC implementing measure with the *SPS Agreement* is the most logical way forward under the circumstances, having regard to our duty to assist the parties and the DSB in solving this dispute and, in particular, to determine whether, as claimed by the European Communities, there is a violation of Article 23.1 in conjunction with Article 22.8 and Article 3.7 of the DSU. This is consistent with our duty to make an objective assessment of the matter before us pursuant to Article 11 of the DSU.[498]

7.378 We also note that panels have not hesitated in the past to consider other provisions than those on which findings had been requested as part of the context of those provisions.[499]

7.379 Therefore, the Panel believes that these are sufficient reasons for it to conclude that it has jurisdiction to consider the compatibility of the EC implementing measure with the *SPS Agreement* as part of its review of the claim raised by the European Communities with respect to Article 22.8 of the DSU.

(c)   Burden of proof

7.380 We note that the European Communities considers that it has made a prima facie case of violation of the DSU provisions, and that, since it cannot be requested to prove a negative, it is for the United States to prove a violation of the *SPS Agreement* by the EC implementing measure. The European Communities also argues that it enjoys a presumption of good faith compliance with the recommendations and rulings of the DSB in the *EC – Hormones* dispute.[500] The United States considers that it is for the European Communities to show that it has complied with Article 22.8 of the DSU and, thus, to demonstrate that its implementing measure actually complies with the provisions of the *SPS Agreement*.[501]

---

[498]   See Section VII.C.2.(a) above.
[499]   Panel Report on *India – Quantitative Restrictions*, para. 5.26.
[500]   EC's first written submission, paras. 92-94.
[501]   US's first written submission, paras. 102, 103 and 106.

7.381 The principles regarding allocation of burden of proof have been well established since the early days of the WTO dispute settlement system and the Panel did not deem it necessary to repeat them in relation to the other claims of the European Communities. However, having regard to the importance given by the parties to the question of burden of proof in relation to the compatibility of the EC measure with the *SPS Agreement*, the Panel considers that it needs to clarify how it addressed burden of proof in relation to the EC claim under Article 22.8.

7.382 First, we deem it necessary to recall that, in *US – Wool Shirts and Blouses*, the Appellate Body stated that:

> "... various international tribunals, including the International Court of Justice, have generally and consistently accepted and applied the rule that the party who asserts a fact, whether the claimant or the respondent, is responsible for providing proof thereof. Also, it is a generally-accepted canon of evidence in civil law, common law and, in fact, most jurisdictions, that the burden of proof rests upon the party, whether complaining or defending, who asserts the affirmative of a particular claim or defence."[502]

7.383 With respect to the violation of Article 22.8 as such, the Panel considered that it had, in principle, no reason to address burden of proof any differently than any other panel established under Article 6 of the DSU. Indeed, as stated by the Complainant itself, this case is about a measure taken by the United States. The fact that this dispute takes place in the context of the EC alleged compliance with the recommendations and rulings of the DSB in the *EC – Hormones* dispute should have no impact on the question of the burden of proof regarding the actual *claim* before us. This means that the principles identified by the Appellate Body above apply, and that the European Communities must prove its claim that the United States breaches Article 22.8 of the DSU.

7.384 Yet, one of the particularities of this case is that the EC claim of violation of Article 22.8 of the DSU by the United States is premised on the removal of the EC measure found to be inconsistent with the *SPS Agreement*. In other words, in order to demonstrate that the United States has breached Article 22.8, the European Communities also alleges that its implementing measure is itself in conformity with the *SPS Agreement*.

7.385 In theory, this should not raise any difficulty in terms of burden of proof since it is well established that each party has to prove its own allegations. We

---

[502] Appellate Body Report on *US – Wool Shirts and Blouses*, p. 14. See also Appellate Body Report on *Canada – Dairy (Article 21.5 – New Zealand and US II)*, para. 66.

agree, however, with the European Communities that in a case like this one, this could generate for the complainant at the beginning of the proceedings a situation equivalent to having to "prove a negative", since the spectrum of provisions against which the legality of the EC measure may have to be reviewed remains very broad as long as the respondent has not made its own allegations of inconsistency of the implementing measure. However, we recall that we found above that the European Communities enjoyed a presumption of good faith compliance, even though that presumption was rebuttable before this Panel. As soon as the European Communities established a prima facie case[503] thanks to the presumption of good faith compliance, the burden shifted on the United States to rebut that presumption. We recall that "... a prima facie case is one which, in the absence of effective refutation by the defending party, requires a panel, as a matter of law, to rule in favour of the complaining party presenting the prima facie case."[504] We believe that the United States sufficiently refuted the EC allegation of compliance in its first written submission through positive evidence of breach of the *SPS Agreement* by the European Communities. In its subsequent submissions before the Panel, the European Communities responded to the allegations of violation made by the United States. Thus, the European Communities never actually had to "prove a negative" in this case.

7.386 While the presumptions based on good faith enjoyed by each party may have played a role in the burden of proof in the early stage of the Panel proceedings, it is the opinion of the Panel that they eventually "neutralized" each other since each party also submitted evidence in support of its allegations. Ultimately, each party had to prove its specific allegations in response to the evidence submitted by the other party.[505] Thereafter, when considering whether an allegation had been proven or not, the Panel followed the practice of other panels to weigh all the evidence before it.

(d)   Compatibility of the EC implementing measure with the provisions of the *SPS Agreement*

(i)   The EC implementing measure

7.387 As already noted, the European Communities has had a ban on the placing on the market, including a ban on the importation, of beef treated with certain hormones for growth promotion purposes since 1988. The hormones concerned are oestradiol-17β, testosterone, progesterone, trenbolone acetate, zeranol and melengestrol acetate. We note that the European Communities stated in its first submission that the DSB recommendations in the *EC – Hormones* cases had

---

[503] See Appellate Body Report on *EC – Hormones*, para. 98.
[504] Appellate Body Report on *EC – Hormones*, para. 104.
[505] See Appellate Body Report on *Japan – Apples*, para. 154.

been implemented through the adoption, on 22 September 2003, of Directive 2003/74/EC the transposition deadline of which was 14 October 2004.

7.388 The European Communities claims that the Directive is based on a risk assessment the results of which "sufficiently warrant" the definitive import prohibition on meat and meat products treated with oestradiol-17β and "provide the available pertinent information" on the basis of which the provisional prohibition regarding the other five hormones has been enacted.

7.389 The Panel understands that, according to the European Communities, its risk assessment:

(a)   is composed of three opinions issued by the EC Scientific Committee on Veterinary measures relating to Public Health (SCVPH) in 1999, 2000 and 2002, the 2000 and 2002 Opinions constituting reviews of the 1999 Opinion;

(b)   is supported by the 17 studies initiated and funded by the European Communities between 1998 and 2001 in order to obtain as much as possible of the missing scientific information that was identified by the panel and the Appellate Body in the *EC – Hormones* case.

7.390 Specifically, the European Communities argues that the 17 scientific studies it commissioned resulted in numerous publications which, along with the pre-existing scientific data, were examined by the SCVPH. The SCVPH issued its first opinion entitled "Assessment of Potential Risks To Human Health From Hormone Residues in Bovine Meat And Meat Products" on 30 April 1999 (hereafter the "1999 Opinion").

7.391 The 1999 Opinion contained the following major conclusions:

(a)   As concerns excess intake of hormone residues and their metabolites, and in view of the intrinsic properties of hormones and epidemiological findings, a risk to the consumer had been identified with different levels of conclusive evidence for the six hormones in question.

(b)   In the case of oestradiol-17β, there was a substantial body of recent evidence suggesting that it had to be considered as a complete carcinogen, as it exerted both tumour initiating and tumour promoting effects. The data available did not, however, allow a quantitative estimate of the risk.

(c)   For the other five hormones at issue, in spite of the individual toxicological and epidemiological data described in the report, the current state of knowledge did not allow a quantitative estimate of the risk.

(d)   For all six hormones endocrine, developmental, immunological, neurobiological, immunotoxic, genotoxic and carcinogenic effects could be envisaged. Of the various susceptible risk groups, prepubertal children was the group of greatest concern. Again the available data did not enable a quantitative estimate of the risk.

(e)   In view of the intrinsic properties of the hormones and in consideration of epidemiological findings, no threshold levels could be defined for any of the six substances.[506]

7.392 In 2000, the SCVPH reviewed two reports, one from the Committee on Veterinary Medicinal Products and one from the UK Veterinary Products Committee, to determine whether the science contained within warranted altering the findings and conclusions of the 1999 Opinion. In May 2000, the SCVPH concluded the following:

"The reports of the UK's Veterinary Products Committee subgroup and of the Committee on Veterinary Medicinal Products presented for review to the Scientific Committee, as well as recent scientific information, did not provide convincing data and arguments demanding revision of the conclusions drawn in the opinion of the SCVPH of April 30th, 1999, on the potential risks to human health from hormone residues in bovine meat and meat products.

The SCVPH discussed again the obvious gaps in the present knowledge on target animal metabolism and residue disposition of the hormones under consideration, including the synthetic hormones. The SCVPH expects that the ongoing EU research programs will provide additional data on both topics."[507]

7.393 Finally, in 2002, the SCVPH reviewed both the 2000 Opinion and the 1999 Opinion and found that review of the 17 studies launched by the European Commission and recent scientific literature allowed the following conclusions:

(a)   Ultra-sensitive methods to detect residues of hormones in animal tissues had become available, but needed further validation.

(b)   Studies on the metabolism of oestradiol-17β in bovine species indicated the formation of lipoidal esters, disposed particularly in body fat. These lipoidal esters showed a high oral bioavailabil-

---

[506]   1999 Opinion, p. 73 (Exhibit US-4).
[507]   2000 Opinion, p. 4 (Exhibit US-17).

ity[508] in rodent experiments. Thus, the consequence of their consumption needed to be considered in a risk assessment.

(c)   Experiments with heifers, one of the major target animal groups for the use of hormones, indicated a dose-dependent increase in residue levels of all hormones, particularly at the implantation sites. Misplaced implants and repeated implanting, which seemed to occur frequently, represented a considerable risk that highly contaminated meats could enter the food chain. There was also a dose-dependent increase in residue levels following the oral administration of melengestrol acetate at doses exceeding approved levels, with a corresponding increased risk that contaminated meats could enter the food chain.

(d)   Convincing data had been published confirming the mutagenic and genotoxic potential of oestradiol-17β as a consequence of metabolic activation to reactive quinones. *In vitro*[509] experiments indicated that oestrogenic compounds *might* alter the expression of an array of genes. Considering that endogenous oestrogens also exerted these effects, the data highlighted the diverse biological effects of this class of hormones.

(e)   No new data regarding testosterone and progesterone relevant to bovine meat or meat products were available. However, it was emphasized that these natural hormones were used only in combination with oestradiol-17β or other oestrogenic compounds in commercial preparations.

(f)   Experiments with zeranol and trenbolone acetate suggested a more complex oxidative metabolism than previously assumed. These data needed further clarification as they might influence a risk assessment related to tissue residues of these compounds.

(g)   Zeranol and trenbolone acetate had been tested for their mutagenic and genotoxic potential in various systems with different endpoints. Both compounds exhibited only very weak effects.

(h)   Data on the genotoxicity of melengestrol acetate indicated only weak effects. However, pro-apoptotic effects were noted in some cell-based assays, which were attributed to the impurities in commercial formulation. Further experiments should clarify the toxicological significance of these impurities.

---

[508]   Bioavailability is the capacity of a substance to enter the general blood circulation and to diffuse into the whole body of the animal or the human being administered this substance, or the fraction of a dose of a substance that is available for systemic circulation (replies of Dr. Boisseau, Dr. Boobis and Dr. Guttenplan to Panel question 43 to the experts, Annex D, paras. 344-357).

[509]   *In vitro* means outside of the body, usually in a cell-based system in a test tube or culture dish. (Transcript of the Panel meeting with the experts, Annex G, para. 96 (Dr. Boobis)).

(i)   Model experiments with rabbits treated with zeranol, trenbolone actetate or melengestrol acetate, mirroring their use in bovines, were designed to study the consequences of pre- and perinatal exposure to exogenous hormones. All compounds crossed the placental barrier easily and influenced to varying degrees the development of the foetus, at the doses used in the experiments.

(j)   Epidemiological studies with opposite-sexed twins suggested that the exposure of the female co-twin *in utero* to hormones resulted in an increased birth weight and consequently an increased adult breast cancer risk.

(k)   Several studies were devoted to the potential impact of the extensive use of hormones on the environment. Convincing data were presented indicating the high stability of trenbolone acetate and melengestrol acetate in the environment, whereas preliminary data were provided on the potential detrimental effects of hormonal compounds in surface water.

7.394   After re-appraisal of the data from the 17 studies and recent scientific literature, the SCVPH confirmed the validity of its previous Opinions (in 1999 and 2000) on the Assessment of Potential Risks to Human Health from Hormone Residues in Bovine Meat and Meat Products, and that no amendments to those opinions were justified.[510]

7.395   A year and a half later, the European Parliament and the Council of the European Union amended Directive 96/22/EC, which was the subject of the original *EC – Hormones* dispute, by adopting Directive 2003/74/EC. In Directive 2003/74/EC, the European Communities restated the SCVPH assessment that "recent evidence suggests that [oestradiol-17β] has to be considered as a complete carcinogen, as it exerts both tumour-initiating and tumour-promoting effects and that the data currently available do not make it possible to give a quantitative estimate of the risk."[511]

7.396   The European Communities went on to conclude in its amended Directive that oestradiol-17β "can potentially be used in all farm animals and residue intake for all segments of the human population and in particular the susceptible groups at high risk can therefore be especially relevant. The avoidance of such intake is of absolute importance to safeguard human health."[512]

7.397   Finally, the European Communities concluded that in order to achieve its chosen level of protection from the risks posed, in particular to human health, by

---

510   2002 Opinion, pp. 21-22 (Exhibit US-1).
511   EC Directive 2003/74/EC.
512   Directive 2003/74/EC, whereas clause 9.

the routine use of these hormones for growth promotion and the consumption of residues found in meat derived from animals to which these hormones have been administered for growth promotion purposes, it was necessary to maintain the permanent prohibition laid down in Directive 96/22/EC on oestradiol-17β, and provisionally ban the other five hormones at issue.

(ii)   Scope of the Panel review

7.398 Given the particular circumstances under which we engage in a review of the compatibility of the EC implementing measure with the *SPS Agreement*, we deem it necessary to clearly circumscribe the scope of our review under that Agreement.

7.399 Indeed, the EC claim of violation of Article 22.8 of the DSU by the United States is premised on the alleged compatibility of the EC implementing measure with the *SPS Agreement*. We note in this respect that the European Communities itself stated in its first written submission that:

> "The new Directive provides that the use for animal growth pro-motion of one of the six hormones in dispute is permanently pro-hibited while the use of the other five is provisionally forbidden. It is based on a comprehensive risk assessment and, thus, is fully compliant with the DSB recommendations and rulings. In particu-lar, as stipulated by the Appellate Body, the results of the risk as-sessment 'sufficiently warrant' the definite import prohibition re-garding   one   of   the   hormones   (Article 5.1   of   the *SPS Agreement*),[513] and provide the 'available pertinent informa-tion' on the basis of which the provisional prohibition regarding the other five hormones has been enacted (Article 5.7 of the *SPS Agreement*). Consequently, through Directive 2003/74/EC the European Communities has implemented the rulings and recom-mendations in the *Hormones* case."[514]

7.400 In its subsequent submissions, the European Communities has argued the compatibility of its implementing measure with the provisions referred to in the quotation above (i.e. Article 5.1 and 5.7 of the *SPS Agreement*). This is, in our view, indicative of the provisions within the scope of which the European Com-munities considers its implementing measure to fall. Yet, we do not consider that the scope of our review of the *SPS Agreement* can be determined exclusively on the basis of the EC allegations of compatibility.

---

[513] The European Communities refers to the Appellate Body Report on *EC – Hormones*, para. 253 lit. (l).
[514] EC's first written submission, para. 17.

7.401 Indeed, we note the argument of the United States in reply to a question from the Panel that:

> "[T]he EC must demonstrate that it has brought its measure into conformity with the DSB recommendations and rulings in the *Hormones* dispute. Those recommendations and rulings include findings of EC breaches of SPS Articles 5.1 and 3.3. The EC argues that it has satisfied the DSB recommendations and rulings by basing its permanent ban for estradiol on a risk assessment and satisfying the four conditions of SPS Article 5.7 for the other five hormones in lieu of a risk assessment. These arguments call for findings as to whether or not the EC has in fact demonstrated that it has brought itself into conformity with the DSB's recommendations and rulings, as these findings are integral part of the EC's Article 22.8 claim."[515]

7.402 As already mentioned above, we consider that we must determine whether the European Communities has removed the measure found to be inconsistent with the covered agreement or has provided a solution to the nullification or impairment of benefits. Therefore, we agree with the United States that we need to review the EC measure against (a) the recommendations and rulings of the DSB in the *EC – Hormones* case and (b) the provisions which the European Communities claims to comply with as part of its claim of violation of Article 22.8 of the DSU by the United States.

7.403 This said, we also agree with the European Communities that it is difficult for the complainant in a case like this one to identify all potential problems of incompatibility. We see other difficulties if, in cases like this one where a finding of violation by a Member is conditioned by the compliance of a measure of the complainant with the WTO Agreement, the scope of review of that measure is defined only by the complainant. Indeed, the complainant could limit the scope of the panel review to provisions with which it believes that its measure is most likely to be found compatible.

7.404 Under those circumstances, we find it preferable, both from a legal and a practical point of view, to consider *all* the allegations and arguments raised by each party, as long as the other party had the opportunity to comment on those allegations and arguments.[516] We consider that this was the case in these pro-

---

[515] US's replies to Panel questions after the second substantive meeting, Annex C-3, para. 24.
[516] We are aware of the risk that the responding party may make a new allegation of violation at a late stage of the proceedings, thus making it difficult for the complainant to reply to this allegation. We nonetheless consider that such a circumstance will not have any impact on due process as long as the complaining party is given sufficient opportunities to comment.

ceedings, since both parties were granted ample opportunities and time to reply to each other's submissions.

7.405 We note that the United States argues an incompatibility of the EC implementing measure with Article 5.1 with respect to the import ban relating to meat and meat products treated with oestradiol-17β. The United States alleges an incompatibility of the EC implementing measure with Article 5.7 with respect to the provisional import ban on meat and meat products treated with testosterone, progesterone, trenbolone acetate, zeranol and melengestrol acetate. The United States alleges an incompatibility of the EC implementing measure with Article 3.3 of the *SPS Agreement* regarding each of the bans applied under that measure with respect to meat from cattle treated with growth promotion hormones for which international standards exist, i.e. oestradiol-17β, testosterone, progesterone, trenbolone acetate and zeranol.[517]

7.406 We nonetheless note that the United States referred to other provisions of the *SPS Agreement* in its submissions. These are Articles 5.2 and 5.6. The United States also makes a reference to Article 2.2 in its rebuttal.[518]

7.407 At our request, the United States clarified that the reference to Article 2.2 of the *SPS Agreement* "was not intended to elicit a finding of a breach of Article 2.2".

7.408 However, "[t]he United States believes that a finding of compliance or non-compliance with the requirements of Article 5.2 would be appropriate as part of the Panel's analysis of whether the EC has based its measure on a risk assessment within the meaning of Article 5.1". We note that the United States argued a violation of Article 5.2 of the *SPS Agreement* in its second written submission.[519]

7.409 With respect to the allegation of the United States regarding a violation of Article 5.2 of the *SPS Agreement*, we note that the European Communities, in its comments of 31 October 2006 on the US replies to the questions of the Panel after the first meeting, states that:

> "The European Communities takes note of the United States reply
> that the Panel would be required to look only at Articles 3.3, 5.1

---

[517] US's reply to Panel question 20 after the second substantive meeting, Annex C-3. The Panel notes that, as far as melengestrol acetate is concerned, JECFA has conducted a risk assessment, set an ADI, and proposed an MRL. However, Codex has not yet adopted an MRL.
[518] US's second written submission, para. 27.
[519] US's second written submission, paras. 50-65.

(including an examination of Article 5.2) and 5.7 [of the *SPS Agreement*]."

7.410 We consider that the European Communities does not exclude that the Panel may review the compatibility of its implementing measure with Article 5.2 of the *SPS Agreement* as part of its review of the compatibility of the EC implementing measure with Article 5.1. Therefore, we will also review the compatibility of the EC implementing measure with Article 5.2.

7.411 We conclude that we shall review, to the extent necessary, the compatibility of the EC implementing measure with Articles 5.1, 5.2, 5.7 and 3.3 of the *SPS Agreement*. We therefore proceed with a review of the compatibility of the EC implementing measure with those provisions in the following sections, once we have addressed other procedural issues.

(iii) Standard applicable to the review of the compatibility of the EC implementing measure with the *SPS Agreement*

7.412 We believe that, in light of the importance and complexity of the scientific information provided by the parties and the experts, it is necessary to lay down the way we plan to review all this information.

7.413 As recalled by the Appellate Body in *EC – Hormones*, the standard of review applicable to legal and factual issues regarding measures reviewed against the *SPS Agreement* is found in Article 11 of the DSU which reads in relevant part that "...a panel should make an objective assessment of the matter before it, including an objective assessment of the facts of the case".

7.414 In *EC – Hormones*, the Appellate Body recalled that:

"So far as fact-finding by panels is concerned, their activities are always constrained by the mandate of Article 11 of the DSU; the applicable standard is neither *de novo* review as such, nor 'total deference', but rather 'the objective assessment of the facts'."[520]

7.415 The Appellate Body further noted that "under current practice and systems, [panels] are in any case poorly suited to engage in such a [*de novo*] review."[521]

---

[520] Appellate Body Report on *EC – Hormones*, para. 117.
[521] *Ibid.*

7.416 We note that we have a duty to consider the evidence presented to us and to make factual findings on the basis of that evidence. It is also generally within our discretion to decide which evidence we choose to utilise in making findings.[522] Likewise, a panel is not expected to refer to all statements made by the experts advising it and should be allowed a substantial margin of discretion as to which statements are useful to refer to explicitly[523] as long as we do not deliberately disregard or distort evidence.[524]

7.417 We also recall that we consulted six scientific experts individually, and not as an expert review group. This may have some consequences in terms of the sometimes diverging views which they expressed. We note that, in *EC – Hormones*, the Appellate Body considered with respect to divergent views taken into account in risk assessment that:

> "We do not believe that a risk assessment has to come to a monolithic conclusion that coincides with the scientific conclusion or view implicit in the SPS measure. The risk assessment could set out both the prevailing view representing the "mainstream" of scientific opinion, as well as the opinions of scientists taking a divergent view. Article 5.1 does not require that the risk assessment must necessarily embody only the view of a majority of the relevant scientific community ... In most cases, responsible and representative governments tend to base their legislative and administrative measures on "mainstream" scientific opinion. In other cases, equally responsible and representative governments may act in good faith on the basis of what, at a given time, may be a divergent opinion coming from qualified and respected sources. By itself, this does not necessarily signal the absence of a reasonable relationship between the SPS measure and the risk assessment, especially where the risk involved is life-threatening in character and is perceived to constitute a clear and imminent threat to public health and safety. Determination of the presence or absence of that relationship can only be done on a case-to-case basis, after account is taken of all considerations rationally bearing upon the issue of potential adverse health effects."[525]

7.418 Although the Panel is not carrying out its own risk assessment, its situation is similar in that it may benefit from hearing the full spectrum of experts'

---

[522] Appellate Body Report on *EC – Hormones*, para. 135.
[523] Appellate Body Report on *EC – Hormones*, para. 138.
[524] Appellate Body Report on *EC – Hormones*, para. 139.
[525] Appellate Body Report on *EC – Hormones*, para. 194.

views and thus obtain a more complete picture both of the mainstream scientific opinion and of any divergent views.

7.419 Likewise, in *EC – Asbestos,* the Appellate Body stated that:

> "In justifying a measure under Article XX(b) of the GATT 1994, a Member may also rely, in good faith, on scientific sources which, at that time, may represent a divergent, but qualified and respected, opinion. A Member is not obliged, in setting health policy, automatically to follow what, at a given time, may constitute a majority scientific opinion. Therefore, a panel need not, necessarily, reach a decision under Article XX(b) of the GATT 1994 on the basis of the 'preponderant' weight of the evidence."[526]

7.420 We note that, in some circumstances, only one or two experts have expressed their views on an issue. Sometimes these views were similar or complemented each other. In other circumstances, a larger number of experts expressed opinions and, sometimes, they expressed diverging opinions. While, on some occasions, we followed the majority of experts expressing concurrent views, in some others the divergence of views were such that we could not follow that approach and decided to accept the position(s) which appeared, in our view, to be the most specific in relation to the question at issue and to be best supported by arguments and evidence. As we have told the parties and the experts during these proceedings, this Panel is not composed of scientists.[527] The experts were also made fully aware of their role – which was *inter alia* to present scientific issues to the Panel members in a way that could be understood by them – and of the role of the Panel in the WTO dispute settlement system – which is *inter alia* one of trier of fact. In assessing the scientific advice received from the experts, we also fully took into account the comments of the parties, when appropriate. However, as already mentioned, we disregarded those comments that attempted

---

[526] Appellate Body Report on *EC – Asbestos*, para. 178.

[527] In the letter sent to the experts in relation to the preparation of their written replies, the Panel made the following remark:

"In drafting your replies, please remember that the three panelists serving on the case have no scientific background and are trying to digest the extensive scientific material submitted by the parties with your help. Therefore, please provide *concise* answers which clarify the issues at hand and which will eventually assist the Panel in reaching its legal findings." (Emphasis in the original)

Likewise, at the outset of the meeting with the experts, the Chairman mentioned the following:

"Last but not least, I would like to recall that the Panel members do NOT have scientific expertise. Therefore, I would like to ask the experts to bear this in mind in replying to questions and explain issues in layman's terms, providing information on underlying concepts as necessary. In order to get a clearer picture with respect to each of the six hormones at issue, I would also like to invite all those taking the floor to clarify which of the six hormones their question or reply applies to."

to put into question the objectivity of specific experts. We believe that such questions had to be dealt with separately.[528]

7.421 We also recall that we are expected to make findings with respect to each of the hormones concerned. Indeed, in *Japan – Apples*, the Appellate Body recalled that findings should be made for each precise agent that may possibly cause the harm (in this case each of the hormones concerned):

> "Under the *SPS Agreement*, the obligation to conduct an assessment of 'risk' is not satisfied merely by a general discussion of the disease sought to be avoided by the imposition of a phytosanitary measure. The Appellate Body found the risk assessment at issue in *EC — Hormones* not to be 'sufficiently specific' even though the scientific Articles cited by the importing Member had evaluated the 'carcinogenic potential of entire *categories* of hormones, or of the hormones at issue *in general*.' In order to constitute a 'risk assessment' as defined in the *SPS Agreement*, the Appellate Body concluded, the risk assessment should have reviewed the carcinogenic potential, not of the relevant hormones in general, but of 'residues of those hormones found in meat derived from cattle to which the hormones had been administered for growth promotion purposes'. Therefore, when discussing the risk to be specified in the risk assessment in *EC – Hormones*, the Appellate Body referred in general to the harm concerned (cancer or genetic damage) *as well as* to the precise agent that may possibly cause the harm (that is, the specific hormones when used in a specific manner and for specific purposes)."[529]

7.422 We will therefore address the compatibility of the EC implementing measure with respect to each hormone concerned, as appropriate. However, in situations where, for instance, information and evidence are similar for all hormones, or where information was not provided for each hormone in spite of our insistence, specific issues are addressed with respect to the hormones concerned as a whole.

7.423 There is another question raised in these proceedings which the Panel believes it must address at this stage. It is the issue of "old" versus "new" evidence, data or studies. Indeed, the European Communities relied extensively on the date of the evidence relied upon by JECFA to support its view that the risk assessments performed by JECFA are outdated and the ensuing recommendations of Codex unreliable.

---

[528] See Section VII.A.2(c) above.
[529] Appellate Body Report on *Japan – Apples*, para. 202. (original footnotes omitted)

7.424 In its submissions before the Panel and during the hearing with the scientific experts, the European Communities contested the validity of JECFA's findings[530] on the basis that it had relied in its assessments on studies that dated back to the 1960s, 1970s and 1980s. The Panel sought the views of the experts on this point.[531] Dr. Boisseau pointed out that "It is just a banality to say that JECFA is provided with new data when it is requested to assess veterinary drugs recently placed on the market and older data in the case of veterinary drugs already marketed since a long time ago. Anyway, the quality and the number of the available data are more important than the dates at which these data have been produced."[532]

7.425 During the hearing with the experts, the European Communities sought the view of Dr. De Brabander as to whether the validity of "old" data from the 1970s and 1980s should be put in doubt because they are old and they have been measured with measurement methods which, it argues, are by today's standards not credible, or are not accurate, because there are new, more powerful and more accurate analytical methods.[533] Dr. De Babander replied: "[t]hat is my conclusion. I cannot say that the data are bad, I don't say that, I just say you don't know that they are good."[534]

7.426 During the same hearing, Dr. Wennberg specified that: "... even if [the studies used by JECFA] were older [than the 1970s], if the methodology that was used, and if the methods had been validated properly, there is no reason to discredit any studies because they were done a long time ago."[535] Dr. Boisseau added that:

> "What the Commission said is true as regards the results that are at the level of the limits of detection of the methods previously used. But once the results obtained are clearly over the limits of detection, what counts is the precision of the method and its reproducibility. The fact that the method used to provide these results is old is irrelevant to the extent that they have been validated. Indeed, we need only concern ourselves with the uncertainty that we may have regarding the very low values at the level of the limits of detection."[536]

---

[530] For a comprehensive list and explanation of JECFA's risk assessment on the six hormones concerned, *see* Annex E-2, JECFA's reply to Panel question 17.

[531] See questions 34 and 35 of the Panel to the scientific experts, Annex D.

[532] Reply of Dr. Boisseau to question 35 of the Panel, Annex D.

[533] Transcript of the Panel meeting with the experts, Annex G, para. 674.

[534] Transcript of the Panel meeting with the experts, Annex G, para. 675.

[535] Transcript of the Panel meeting with the experts, Annex G, para. 651.

[536] Transcript of the Panel meeting with the experts, Annex G, para. 679.

7.427 The Panel first notes that the experts agree that data do not become invalid only because they are old, but that more recent measurement or analytical methods may be more accurate. The Panel notes, however, that a problem related to accuracy is likely to occur with respect to results at the level of the detection limits of the older methods. Outside this particular situation, what matters is whether the method has been validated. The Panel thus concludes that whether a study is old or not is not *per se* a criterion to put in doubt the validity of this study.

(iv) Whether the EC implementing measure is an SPS measure

7.428 Before the Panel can determine whether the EC ban is consistent with the *SPS Agreement*, we must first determine whether the measure is subject to the disciplines of the *SPS Agreement*, *i.e.*, whether the measure is an SPS measure. In order to determine whether the ban is an SPS measure, the Panel will determine whether the measure fits within the definition of an SPS measure set forth in Annex A(1) of the *SPS Agreement*.[537]

---

[537] Article 1 of the *SPS Agreement* reads as follows:

"General Provisions

1.   This Agreement applies to all sanitary and phytosanitary measures which may, directly or indirectly, affect international trade. Such measures shall be developed and applied in accordance with the provisions of this Agreement.

2.   For the purposes of this Agreement, the definitions provided in Annex A shall apply.

3.   The annexes are an integral part of this Agreement.

4.   Nothing in this Agreement shall affect the rights of Members under the Agreement on Technical Barriers to Trade with respect to measures not within the scope of this Agreement."

Annex A, para. 1, to the *SPS Agreement* reads as follows:

DEFINITIONS [footnote 4]

"1.   Sanitary or phytosanitary measure – Any measure applied:

(a)   to protect animal or plant life or health within the territory of the Member from risks arising from the entry, establishment or spread of pests, diseases, disease-carrying organisms or disease-causing organisms;

(b)   to protect human or animal life or health within the territory of the Member from risks arising from additives, contaminants, toxins or disease-causing organisms in foods, beverages or feedstuffs;

(c)   to protect human life or health within the territory of the Member from risks arising from diseases carried by animals, plants or products thereof, or from the entry, establishment or spread of pests; or

(d)   to prevent or limit other damage within the territory of the Member from the entry, establishment or spread of pests.

Sanitary or phytosanitary measures include all relevant laws, decrees, regulations, requirements and procedures including, inter alia, end product criteria; processes and production methods; testing, inspection, certification and approval procedures;

7.429 As the panel in *EC – Approval and Marketing of Biotech Products* explained, in determining whether a measure is an SPS measure, regard must be had to such elements as the purpose of the measure, its legal form and its nature. The purpose element is addressed in Annex A(1)(a) through (d) ("any measure applied to"). The form element is referred to in the second paragraph of Annex A(1) ("laws, decrees, regulations"). Finally, the nature of measures qualifying as SPS measures is also addressed in the second paragraph of Annex A(1) ("requirements and procedures, including, inter alia, end product criteria; processes and production methods; testing, inspection, certification and approval procedures; [etc.]").

7.430 The European Communities explained in Directive 2003/74/EC that the purpose of the ban on the six hormones at issue is to prevent meat and meat products from cattle treated with such hormones for growth promotion purposes from being placed on the EC market.[538] The Panel notes that Annex A(1)(b) defines an SPS measure as any measure applied "to protect human or animal life or health within the territory of the Member from risks arising from additives, contaminants, toxins or disease-causing organisms in foods, beverages or feedstuffs."

7.431 Consistent with the Panel in *EC – Approval and Marketing of Biotech Products* we consider that a substance which a human being or an animal consumes for nutritional reasons may be classified as a "food".[539] The Panel also takes notice of the footnote to Annex A, which specifically defines "contaminants" as including veterinary drug residues, such as the residues of the hormones which are the subject of the EC measure.

7.432 Comparing the definition of an SPS measure in Annex A(1)(b) to the stated purpose of the EC ban on the hormones at issue, the Panel concludes that the purpose of the EC measure is that of an SPS measure within the meaning of Annex A(1)(b) of the *SPS Agreement*.

7.433 The second paragraph of Annex A states that sanitary or phytosanitary measures include all relevant laws, decrees and regulations as well as require-

---

quarantine treatments including relevant requirements associated with the transport of animals or plants, or with the materials necessary for their survival during transport; provisions on relevant statistical methods, sampling procedures and methods of risk assessment; and packaging and labelling requirements directly related to food safety."

Footnote 4 to Annex A reads as follows:

"For the purpose of these definitions, "animal" includes fish and wild fauna; "plant" includes forests and wild flora; "pests" include weeds; and "contaminants" include pesticide and veterinary drug residues and extraneous matter."

[538] Directive 2003/74/EC, Article 1.

[539] Panel Report on *EC – Approval and Marketing of Biotech Products*, paras. 7.291-7.292.

ments and procedures.[540] In this instance, the EC measure is a directive adopted by the Council of the European Union and the European Parliament which was published in the Official Journal of the European Communities. Therefore, this Panel finds that the measure in question is included within the phrase "all relevant laws, decrees, regulations ..." as used in Annex A of the *SPS Agreement*. This Panel also agrees with the panel in *EC– Approval and Marketing of Biotech Products* that a ban may be considered a "requirement" within the meaning of the second paragraph of Annex A of the *SPS Agreement*.[541] Therefore, this Panel finds that the EC measure constitutes such a "requirement".

7.434 In conclusion, because the EC Directive 2003/74/EC was adopted for the purpose of protecting human life from contaminants in food and takes the form and nature contemplated in the second paragraph of Annex A, this Panel finds that the EC Directive 2003/74/EC is an SPS measure within the meaning of Annex A(1)(b) and the second paragraph of Annex A.

        (e)   Compatibility of the EC implementing measure with Article 5.1 and Article 5.2 of the *SPS Agreement* with respect to oestradiol-17β

        (i)   Introduction

7.435 The Panel notes that the European Communities has asserted that it adopted the Directive banning the placing on the market of meat and meat products from cattle treated with oestradiol-17β for growth promotion purposes based on a risk assessment conducted by the SCVPH consistent with Article 5.1 of the *SPS Agreement*.

7.436 Specifically, the European Communities states that in order to comply with the rulings and recommendations of the DSB in the *EC – Hormones* dispute, it conducted a comprehensive risk assessment, which focused on potential risks to human health from hormone residues in bovine meat and meat products.[542] The European Communities also asserts that Directive 2003/74/EC, which provides for a permanent ban on meat and meat products from animals

---

[540] "Including *inter alia* end product criteria; processes and production methods; testing, inspection, certification and approval procedures; quarantine treatments including relevant requirements associated with the transport of animals or plants, or with the materials necessary for their survival during transport; provisions on relevant statistical methods, sampling procedures and methods of risk assessment; and packaging and labelling requirements directly related to food safety."

[541] Panel Report on *EC – Approval and Marketing of Biotech Products*, para. 7.1334.

[542] EC's first written submission, para. 142.

treated for growth promotion purposes with oestradiol-17β, is based on the above referenced risk assessment.[543]

7.437 The DSB found in the *EC – Hormones* dispute that the ban on meat and meat products from cattle treated with the six hormones for growth promotion purposes, according to good veterinary practice ("GVP"), was inconsistent with Article 5.1 of the *SPS Agreement* because it was not based on a risk assessment within the meaning of that Article. In this case, the European Communities has asserted that it has removed that inconsistency with respect to oestradiol-17β by conducting a comprehensive risk assessment and basing its implementing measure on that risk assessment so that the measure is now consistent with Article 5.1 of the *SPS Agreement*. We also recall that the United States has claimed that the EC definitive ban on oestradiol-17β breaches Article 5.1 and 5.2 of the *SPS Agreement*. Therefore, as mentioned above, the Panel considers that it should address the conformity of the EC implementing measure with Article 5.1 and 5.2 of the *SPS Agreement*.

7.438 Article 5.1 of the *SPS Agreement* reads as follows:

"Members shall ensure that their sanitary or phytosanitary measures are based on an assessment, as appropriate to the circumstances, of the risks to human, animal or plant life or health, taking into account risk assessment techniques developed by the relevant international organizations."

7.439 An analysis under Article 5.1 consists of two fundamental questions. First, was a risk assessment, appropriate to the circumstances and taking into account risk assessment techniques developed by the relevant international organizations conducted? Second, is the sanitary measure based on that risk assessment? The Panel will address each question successively.

7.440 This said, Article 5.2 of the *SPS Agreement* further instructs Members on how to conduct a risk assessment. Specifically, Article 5.2 states that:

"In the assessment of risks, Members shall take into account available scientific evidence; relevant processes and production methods; relevant inspection, sampling and testing methods; prevalence of specific diseases or pests; existence of pest- or disease-free areas; relevant ecological and environmental conditions; and quarantine and other treatment."

---

[543] EC's first written submission, para. 145.

7.441 The Panel agrees with the panel in *Japan – Apples* that Articles 5.1 and 5.2 "directly inform each other, in that paragraph 2 sheds light on the elements that are of relevance in the assessment of risks foreseen in paragraph 1".[544] This is because, in the opinion of the Panel, if it were possible for a risk assessment that did not take into account the factors listed in Article 5.2 to be consistent with Article 5.1, Article 5.2 would have no purpose and we must construe the covered agreements in a way that gives meaning to each provision.[545] Essentially, "Article 5.2 imparts meaning to the general obligation contained in paragraph 1 to base measures on an 'assessment ...of risks'."[546] Therefore, we must also consider whether the European Communities took into account the elements contained in Article 5.2 in the course of our analysis under Article 5.1.

(ii)   Is there a risk assessment within the meaning of Article 5.1 of the *SPS Agreement*?

7.442 In assessing whether a measure is based on a risk assessment within the meaning of Article 5.1 of the *SPS Agreement,* the Panel must first determine whether a risk assessment was conducted at all. The Panel is aware that the Appellate Body in *EC – Hormones* determined that "Article 5.1 does not insist that a Member that adopts a sanitary measure shall have carried out its own risk assessment ... The SPS measure might well find its objective justification in a risk assessment carried out by another Member, or an international organization".[547] In the present case, the European Communities has asserted that the three Opinions produced by the SCVPH, an organ of the European Communities, constitute the required risk assessment. Therefore, the task before the Panel is to determine whether the European Communities conducted a risk assessment within the meaning of Article 5.1 of the *SPS Agreement*.

7.443 To determine whether the Opinions constitute a risk assessment, the Panel must measure the European Communities' actions against the requirements of the *SPS Agreement*. The Panel recalls that it is not the appropriate role of the Panel to conduct its own risk assessment based on scientific evidence gathered

---

[544]   Panel Report on *Japan – Apples*, para. 8.230.
[545]   Article 31.1 of the Vienna Convention on Law of Treaties requires that "[a] treaty shall be interpreted in good faith ..." Article 26 requires that "[e]ach treaty is binding upon the parties to it and must be performed by them in good faith". Given these fundamental principles in the Vienna Convention, it is unreasonable to assume that a provision of a treaty is written without any meaning at all. The Appellate Body also stated in *Japan – Alcoholic Beverages II*, that "a fundamental tenet of treaty interpretation flowing from the general rule of interpretation set out in Article 31 [of the Vienna Convention] is the principle of effectiveness (*ut res magis valeat quam pereat*)", p. 12.
[546]   Panel Report on *Japan – Apples,* para. 8.232.
[547]   Appellate Body Report on *EC – Hormones*, para. 190, followed in the Panel Report on *EC – Approval and Marketing of Biotech Products*, para. 7.3024.

by the Panel or submitted by the parties during the Panel proceedings.[548] Similarly, the Panel believes that it is not its role to impose any scientific opinion on the European Communities. The Panel must objectively measure the Opinions against the relevant standard for whether a risk assessment has been conducted, which can be found in the texts of Articles 5.1 (including an examination of Article 5.2) as well as Annex A(4) of the *SPS Agreement*. Therefore, we examined and evaluated the evidence – including the information received from the experts advising the Panel – and the arguments put before us in light of the relevant WTO provisions and based our conclusions on this evidence and these arguments.[549]

7.444 The text of Article 5.1 requires that in the assessment of risks the Members take into account risk assessment techniques developed by the relevant international organizations. Article 5.2, likewise, prescribes several factors that a Member must take into account when making its assessment of the risks. Additionally, Annex A(4) provides a definition of what constitutes a risk assessment. Finally, as the Panel and Appellate Body explained in *Japan – Apples,* for a risk assessment to be valid the science evaluated must support the conclusions reached in the risk assessment.[550]

7.445 The European Communities asserts that the 1999, 2000, and 2002 Opinions constitute its risk assessment for oestradiol-17β. Therefore, in determining whether these Opinions are indeed a risk assessment as appropriate to the circumstances, within the meaning of Article 5.1 of the *SPS Agreement*, the Panel will examine whether the Opinions (1) took into account risk assessment techniques of the relevant international organizations; (2) took into account the factors listed in Article 5.2; (3) satisfied the definition in Annex A(4) and: (4) whether the conclusions in the Opinions are supported by the scientific evidence evaluated.

---

[548]   Panel Report on *EC – Hormones (Canada)*, para. 8.104; Panel Report on *EC – Hormones (US)*, para. 8.101.

[549]   Panel Report on *Australia – Salmon*, para. 8.41. A similar statement was made by the Panel on *Japan – Agricultural Products II*, in para. 8.42.

[550]   This is not to say, as already recalled above, that a risk assessment cannot be based on a minority opinion of the scientists. A risk assessment can be based on a minority opinion which is supported by sufficient scientific evidence. See Appellate Body Report on *EC– Hormones*, para. 194; and Panel Report on *EC– Approval and Marketing of Biotech Products*, para. 7.3240.

Do the Opinions take into account risk assessment techniques of the relevant international organizations?

Introduction

7.446 Article 5.1 includes the proviso that Members, when developing sanitary and phytosanitary measures based on risk assessments, take into account risk assessment techniques developed by the relevant international organizations. The *SPS Agreement* does not specifically identify the relevant international organizations for purposes of Article 5.1. However, the Preamble of the *SPS Agreement* speaks of harmonizing SPS measures between Members on the basis of international standards, guidelines and recommendations developed by the relevant international organizations, including the Codex Alimentarius Commission (Codex). Additionally, Annex A(3) states that for food safety the standards, guidelines and recommendations established by the Codex Alimentarius Commission (Codex) relating to food additives, veterinary drug and pesticide residues, contaminants, methods of analysis and sampling, and codes and guidelines of hygienic practice will constitute international standards, guidelines, and recommendations within the meaning of the *SPS Agreement*. Article 3.2 states that SPS measures which conform to the above referenced standards are deemed to be necessary to protect human, animal, or plant life or health and are presumed to be consistent with the *SPS Agreement* and *GATT 1994*. Moreover, Article 3.4 of the *SPS Agreement* requires Members to participate fully in Codex work, within the limits of their resources. After an examination of these provisions of the *SPS Agreement* and the context of Article 5.1 as part of the process for adopting SPS measures which are consistent with the *SPS Agreement*, the Panel concludes that the Codex Alimentarius Commission constitutes a "relevant international organization" within the meaning of Article 5.1.

7.447 The parties in this dispute as well as the experts have made significant references to JECFA's work. JECFA, while officially not part of the Codex structure, provides independent scientific expert advice to the Codex Alimentarius Commission and its specialist Committees. JECFA conducts risk assessments on various substances, establishes ADIs[551] where appropriate, and in the

---

[551] The Codex Committee on Residues of Veterinary Drugs in Foods defines an Acceptable Daily Intake (ADI) as "[a]n estimate by JECFA of the amount of a veterinary drug, expressed on a body weight basis, that can be ingested daily over a lifetime without appreciable health risk (standard man = 60 kg)." Glossary of Terms and Definition (CAC/MISC 5-1993). The "Glossary of Terms and Definition" has been elaborated by the Codex Committee on Residues of Veterinary Drugs in Foods (CCRVDF) with a view to providing information and guidance to the committee and is intended for internal Codex use only. (The definition was previously established and adopted by JECFA and modified by the Codex Committee on Veterinary Drugs in Foods). More information on how ADIs are set is contained in Annex E-2, responses by JECFA to questions 9 and 10.

case of residues of veterinary drugs in foods, recommends MRLs[552] for consideration by the Codex Committee on Residues of Veterinary Drugs in Foods (CCRVDF). The MRLs adopted by Codex with respect to oestradiol-17β and four of the other five hormones[553] are based on the recommendations of JECFA. Therefore, this Panel believes that the risk assessment techniques of JECFA are also relevant to an analysis of compliance with Article 5.1.

7.448   Codex and JECFA have developed definitions of the relevant phases of a risk assessment as well as guidelines and practices for conducting a risk assessment. [554] The European Communities indicated in the 1999 Opinion, that the accepted definition of a risk assessment, as used by both Codex and JECFA, is an assessment which is "structured to address independently the intrinsic properties of the compound under consideration (hazard identification), the evaluation of the nature of effects in terms of a dose-response relationship (hazard characterization), the estimate of the dose/concentration of a compound in a daily diet (exposure assessment) resulting in the assessment of the incidence and severity of potential adverse effects".[555] In its Procedural Manual, Codex defines the four phases of risk assessment as follows:

(a)   *hazard identification*: The identification of biological, chemical, and physical agents capable of causing adverse health effects and which may be present in a particular food or group of foods.

---

[552]   Codex defines the maximum limit for residues of veterinary drugs (MRLVD) as the maximum concentration of residue resulting from the use of a veterinary drug (expressed in mg/kg or μg/kg on a fresh weight basis) that is recommended by the Codex Alimentarius Commission to be legally permitted or recognized as acceptable in or on a food.

It is based on the type and amount of residue considered to be without any toxicological hazard for human health as expressed by the Acceptable Daily Intake (ADI), or on the basis of a temporary ADI that utilizes an additional safety factor. It also takes into account other relevant public health risks as well as food technological aspects.

When establishing an MRL, consideration is also given to residues that occur in food of plant origin and/or the environment. Furthermore, the MRL may be reduced to be consistent with good practices in the use of veterinary drugs and to the extent that practical analytical methods are available. From: Definitions for the Purposes of the Codex Alimentarius, Codex Alimentarius Commission Procedural Manual (15th Edition), FAO and WHO, 2006, page 43. More information on how MRLs are set is contained in Annexes E-1 and E-2, responses by Codex and JECFA to questions 9 and 10.

[553]   Progesterone, testosterone, zeranol and trenbolone acetate (http://www.codexalimentarius.net/mrls/vetdrugs/jsp/vetd_q-e.jsp).

[554]   In response to the Panel's questions regarding international guidance documents for conducting a risk assessment, in particular with respect to veterinary drug residues, the representative of Codex and JECFA as well as the experts referred to a variety of documents from the Codex Alimentarius Commission, JECFA, the World Health Organization, the Food and Agriculture Organization, and other scientific bodies, see replies of the Codex Alimentarius Commission and JECFA to Panel questions 3 and 4, Annexes E-1 and E-2 respectively, and replies by the scientific experts to Panel questions, Annex D, paras. 62-71.

[555]   1999 Opinion, page 70.

(b) *hazard characterization*: The qualitative and/or quantitative evaluation of the nature of the adverse health effects associated with biological, chemical, and physical agents which may be present in food. For chemical agents, a dose-response assessment[556] should be performed. For biological or physical agents, a dose-response assessment should be performed if the data are obtainable.

(c) *exposure assessment*: The qualitative and/or quantitative evaluation of the likely intake of biological, chemical, or physical agents via food as well as exposures from other sources if relevant.

(d) *risk characterization*: The qualitative and/or quantitative estimation, including attendant uncertainties, of the probability of occurrence and severity of known potential adverse health effects in a given population based on hazard identification, hazard characterization, and exposure assessment.[557]

7.449 Although Codex and JECFA base their relevant work on some general principles and the definition of risk assessment stated above and JECFA relies on a variety of guidance documents on how to conduct a risk assessment with respect to veterinary drug residues in food, the experts confirmed that no specific "techniques" or guidelines had thus far been formally adopted by Codex for use by national governments in conducting risk assessments of veterinary drug residues.[558]

Summary of the main arguments of the parties[559]

7.450 The **United States** recalls that the *EC – Hormones* panel noted that, "even though no formal decision has as yet been taken by Codex with respect to [sanitary] risk assessment techniques, Codex, and more particularly JECFA, has a long-standing practice with respect to the assessment of risks related to veterinary drug residues (including hormone residues)."[560]

7.451 The United States believes that the Opinions predominantly focus on the first step of risk assessment (*hazard identification*). The United States argues

---

[556] Codex defines a dose-response assessment as the determination of the relationship between the magnitude of exposure (dose) to a chemical, biological, or physical agent and the severity and/or frequency of associated adverse health effects (response). *Codex Alimentarius Commission*, Procedural Manual, Fifteenth Edition (2005), p. 45.

[557] *Ibid.*

[558] At its 30th session in July 2007, the Codex Alimentarius Commission adopted "Working Principles for Risk Analysis for Food Safety for Application by Governments".

[559] A more detailed account of the parties' arguments can be found in Section IV of the descriptive part of this Report. The order in which the respective arguments of the parties are presented does not reflect any allocation of the burden of proof by the Panel.

[560] US's first written submission, para. 139, citing Panel Report on *EC – Hormones*, para. 8.103.

that the potential biological effects of hormones, some of which are adverse, are generally not in dispute in the scientific community. The United States argues that the European Communities failed to engage in adequate *hazard characterization*. Specifically, the United States alleges that the European Communities did not conduct a dose-response assessment.

7.452 The United States argues that the Opinions also fail to complete an exposure assessment in terms useful for estimating risks to consumers. The United States alleges that a risk assessment evaluating the potential risk from hormone residues in meat and meat products to consumers, in the absence of a discussion of actual residues, should include a thorough analysis of the relevant pathway, starting with cattle treated with hormones for growth promotion purposes according to good veterinary practices, processing and shipping meat and meat products from those cattle and ending with the consumption of any residues from that meat by humans (*e.g.*, taking into account how humans process ingested hormones). The United States argues that the European Communities' purported risk assessment fails to evaluate either the available residue data or these steps in the exposure pathway.[561]

7.453 The United States considers that the Opinions evaluate identified sources of high exposure inconsistently by dismissing the introduction of pregnant heifers with high levels of endogenous oestradiol-17β into the food chain in Europe while assuming that misplaced and repeated implanting, as well as the entry of the implants into the food chain, are frequent and represent a considerable risk.[562]

7.454 The United States also argues that the European Communities fails to take into account the relative impact on exposure assessment of the low bioavailability of the six hormones for growth promotion purposes, in light of JECFA's conclusion that oestradiol is generally inactive when given orally because it is transported to the liver where it is rapidly inactivated.[563]

7.455 The **European Communities** agrees that the risk assessment techniques developed by Codex are relevant and contemplated in Article 5.1's requirement to take into account the risk assessment techniques developed by relevant international organizations. However, the European Communities maintains that the risk assessment criteria as developed by the WTO dispute settlement bodies are clearly more relevant to the application of the *SPS Agreement*.[564]

---

[561] US's first written submission, para. 144.
[562] US's first written submission, para. 145.
[563] US's first written submission, para. 146, citing 52nd JECFA Report (2000), p. 58 (Exhibit US-5).
[564] EC's second written submission, para. 192; EC's replies to Panel questions after the first substantive meeting, question 24, Annex B-1.

7.456 The European Communities also points out that there is no Codex standard specifically on the risk assessment of the effect of residues of veterinary drugs and that Codex techniques or standards exclusively apply to risk assessments on food safety and not to other risk assessments such as those for animal health and environmental risks.[565]

7.457 The European Communities maintains that its Opinions take into account the conventional risk assessment techniques in addition to other factors that are expressly permissible under the definition of a risk assessment in Article 5.1.[566] The European Communities argues that it went beyond the international standards for a risk assessment to consider "real life" situations as contemplated by the Appellate Body's ruling in *EC – Hormones*.

7.458 The European Communities argues that the risk assessment at the basis of Directive 2003/74/EC precisely follows the four steps of risk assessment as defined by Codex, enabling it to identify different levels of risks presented by different uses, and that this Directive then adapts the management of these risks accordingly.[567] However, the European Communities also notes that the Codex approach has serious limitations in non-linear situations, such as with regard to these hormones. The European Communities argues that the currently available Codex guidance poorly addresses cases such as this where the risks are embedded in changes in exposure to biologically active molecules which may, with minute differences in their bioavailability, have dramatic effects, such as turning on or off complete developmental programmes of the human genome, or inducing pathological conditions.[568]

7.459 Specifically, the European Communities argued that with hormones that are also produced endogenously when you add more of the same kind of hormone, such as oestrogen, you are just increasing the response that is already taking place, and in that case there cannot be a threshold. The threshold has already been exceeded by the concentration of hormones in circulation. So this specific set of conditions results in dose-response curves that will have no threshold, and if there is no threshold, there is no safe dose, unlike the suggestion that there is an acceptable daily intake.[569]

---

[565] EC's second written submission, para. 192.

[566] 1999 Opinion, p. 2 (citing Appellate Body Report on *EC – Hormones* for the premise that the risk to be evaluated is "not only risk ascertainable in a laboratory operating under strictly controlled conditions, but also risk in human societies as they actually exist, in other words the actual potential for adverse effects in human health in the real world where people live and work and die.")

[567] EC's replies to Panel questions after the first substantive meeting, question 24, Annex B-1, para. 142.

[568] EC's replies to Panel questions after the first substantive meeting, question 24, Annex B-1, para. 140.

[569] Transcript of the Panel meeting with the experts, Annex G, para. 252.

7.460 The European Communities asserts that it is generally recognized that for substances which have genotoxic potential (as is the case with oestradiol-17β) a threshold cannot be identified. This would mean that there is no level below which intakes from residues should be considered to be safe. The fact that the doses used in growth promotion are low is not of relevance.[570] Therefore, the European Communities argues that it was not required to do a quantitative evaluation of the dose-response.[571]

7.461 As regards the level of the risk, the European Communities argues that it has undertaken specific studies to evaluate the exposure resulting from real as well as experimental situations of abuse and/or misuse in the market of the United States. The European Communities notes that it carried out specific veterinary inspections in the United States and argues that it has made a specific calculation of the level of the risk for imports coming from the United States.[572]

Reasoning of the Panel

7.462 In determining whether the European Communities took into account the risk assessment techniques of the relevant international organizations in the Opinions, the Panel requested that the experts evaluate the Opinions in light of the Codex definitions, guidelines, and practices.

7.463 The experts who answered the Panel's question on this issue concluded that the Opinions were not entirely consistent with the Codex guidelines and definitions.

7.464 Dr. Guttenplan pointed out that the European Communities had done a thorough hazard identification, but that its hazard characterization was limited and that the extrapolation of the one animal model study from hamster kidney to humans was uncertain. He noted that the European Communities also relied on older studies with no reports of replication and had no epidemiological studies comparing cancer incidence or prevalence in populations consuming hormone-treated or untreated meat.[573] Dr. Boobis stated that the European Communities had not identified the potential for adverse effects on human health of residues of oestradiol in meat as a result of the cattle being treated with the hormone for growth promotion purposes. This was because the analysis undertaken was focused primarily on hazard identification. There was little in the way of hazard characterization, and no independent exposure assessment was undertaken.

---

[570] EC's second written submission, paras. 201-202.

[571] EC's second written submission, para. 200.

[572] EC's replies to Panel questions after the second substantive meeting, Annex C-1, para. 15, citing Exhibit EC-67 and Exhibit EC-73.

[573] Replies by the scientific experts to Panel question 14, Annex D, para. 149.

Dr. Boobis stated that because no adequate exposure assessment was undertaken it was not possible to complete the risk characterization phase of the assessment.[574] In sum, Dr. Boobis concluded that the European Communities' risk assessment of oestradiol did not follow the four steps of the Codex risk assessment paradigm.[575]

7.465 Dr. Boobis indicates in his written replies that a "hazard-based" approach, which is making recommendations as to potential safety based on intrinsic capacity to cause harm rather than on the probability of harm occurring is most commonly used for substances that are genotoxic or have genotoxic potential, although not all such substances would be treated this way.[576] Dr. Boobis further explained the "hazard-based" approach at the meeting with the Panel where he stated that if, for example, a compound is shown to be a direct-acting genotoxicant, this is considered unacceptable at any level of exposure. As permitting exposure would not be appropriate, one stops the risk assessment at that point. It does not need to take account of exposure, because any level of exposure is deemed to be of concern.[577] Dr. Cogliano agrees that there have been cases where calling something a carcinogenic hazard has led an agency to make a decision just on the qualitative element alone.[578] However, Dr. Tritscher, the representative of JECFA maintains that a hazard identification is not a risk assessment; a risk assessment comprises the four steps.[579]

7.466 Both Drs. Cogliano and Boobis explain that the issue of thresholds and whether an acceptable daily intake can be established and all four steps of a risk assessment as defined by Codex can be conducted has to do with the assumptions and interpretations that the scientists conducting the risk assessment are willing to make.[580]

7.467 Although there was considerable debate among the parties and the experts advising the Panel about whether the European Communities followed all four steps of a risk assessment as defined by Codex or indeed whether it was even necessary to do so in the case of a substance such as oestradiol-17β, the Panel must concur with the reasoning of the panel in *Japan – Apples*, that the requirement to "take into account" the risk assessment techniques of international organizations:

---

[574] Replies by the scientific experts to Panel question 13, Annex D, para. 144.
[575] Replies by the scientific experts to Panel question 14, Annex D, para. 148.
[576] Replies by the scientific experts to Panel question 36, Annex D, paras. 310-311.
[577] Transcript of the Panel meeting with the experts, Annex G, para. 385.
[578] Transcript of the Panel meeting with the experts, Annex G, para. 438.
[579] Transcript of the Panel meeting with the experts, Annex G, para. 453.
[580] Transcript of the Panel meeting with the experts, Annex G, paras. 1021-1027.

"[D]oes not impose that a risk assessment under Article 5.1 be 'based on' or 'in conformity with' such risk assessment techniques. This suggests that such techniques should be considered relevant, but that a failure to respect each and every aspect of them would not necessarily, *per se*, signal that the risk assessment on which the measure is based is not in conformity with the requirements of Article 5.1."[581]

7.468 This means that although the risk assessment techniques of Codex and JECFA are relevant and must be considered by the risk assessor, compliance with Codex or JECFA risk assessment techniques is not required by the *SPS Agreement*. What is required is that the risk assessor take those techniques into account and that it comply with the other requirements of Article 5 and Annex A of the *SPS Agreement* with respect to conducting a risk assessment.

7.469 It is undisputed that the European Communities was aware of the Codex and JECFA guidelines and considered them in the preparation of the Opinions. Therefore, the Panel concludes that although it may not have strictly followed them, the European Communities did take into account the risk assessment techniques of the relevant international organizations in the conduct of the Opinions.

Do the Opinions take into account the factors listed in Article 5.2?

Summary of the main arguments of the parties[582]

7.470 The **United States** argues that whether the European Communities engaged in a proper evaluation of the Article 5.2 factors, in particular relevant inspection, sampling, and testing methods, would inform a decision on whether or not it has indeed properly assessed the risk of failure to satisfy good veterinary practices within the meaning of Article 5.1 and Annex A of the *SPS Agreement*. The United States asserts that the European Communities has not engaged in the necessary evaluation of the factors under Article 5.2.[583]

7.471 The United States reasons that Article 5.2 is not mutually exclusive of Article 5.1 of the *SPS Agreement*; rather, it sets out the specific components of the risk assessment on which Members are required to base their measures for purposes of Article 5.1. The United States argues that if the European Communities has not satisfied the requirements of Article 5.2, it has not conducted a risk assessment, as appropriate to the circumstances and, as such, the permanent ban

---

[581] Panel Report on *Japan – Apples*, para. 8.241.

[582] A more detailed account of the parties' arguments can be found in Section IV of the descriptive part of this Report. The order in which the respective arguments of the parties are presented does not reflect any allocation of the burden of proof by the Panel.

[583] US's second written submission, para. 52.

on oestradiol-17β cannot be based on a risk assessment within the meaning of Article 5.1.[584]

7.472 The United States argues that the Opinions ignore or fail to take into account available scientific evidence with respect to the bioavailability of oestradiol-17β, evidence relating to susceptible populations, and evidence relating to *in vivo*[585] repair mechanisms.[586]

7.473 The United States argues that the Opinions fail to adduce scientific evidence of a risk to consumers posed by meat from cattle treated with oestradiol-17β for growth promotion purposes according to good veterinary practices. Assessments which conclude otherwise (*i.e.,* that such a risk exists), such as the 1999, 2000 and 2002 Opinions, do not "take into account available scientific evidence" as required by Article 5.2 of the *SPS Agreement* and are not risk assessments as appropriate to the circumstances within the meaning of Article 5.1 of the *SPS Agreement*.[587]

7.474 The United States argues that the European Communities fails to assess the specific risks at issue in this dispute because it does not consider the available evidence directly related to the expected doses from dietary exposures to hormones. In particular, the United States contends that the European Communities did not make use of relevant bioavailability data, and used unrealistic scenarios to calculate possible exposure estimates.[588]

7.475 Additionally, the United States argues that the Opinions' study of the potential adverse effects from use of hormones without regard to good veterinary practices does not take into account the actual inspection, sampling, and testing methods of the US regulatory agencies, but is rather based on hypothetical violations of GVP induced in a laboratory.

7.476 The **European Communities** argues that the 1999 Opinion took account of all pertinent scientific information available at the time, including JECFA's revised assessment of the three natural hormones oestradiol-17β, testosterone, and progesterone that had been issued in February 1999.[589] The European Com-

---

[584] US's replies to Panel questions after the second substantive meeting, Annex C-4, para. 26.

[585] *In vivo* means in the whole organism, the intact organism (transcript of the Panel meeting with the experts, Annex G, para. 96 (Dr. Boobis)).

[586] US's second written submission, paras. 41-46.

[587] US's second written submission, para. 47, footnote 89.

[588] US's replies to Panel questions after the first substantive meeting, Annex B-3, para. 72.

[589] EC's second written submission, para. 103.

munities also points out that the Opinions have found that the data on which JECFA based its finding on bioavailability are incorrect or insufficient.[590]

7.477 The European Communities contends that it examined relevant inspection, sampling, and testing methods when it specifically examined the issue of the risks to human health if GVP was not observed in the United States.[591] In the *Working Document on Assessment of Risks of hormonal growth promoters in cattle with respect to risks arising from abusive use and difficulties of control*, the European Communities points to the Appellate Body finding in the *EC – Hormones* case that Article 5.2 in conjunction with Article 8 and Annex C authorizes "the taking into account of risks arising from failure to comply with the requirements of good veterinary practice in the administration of hormones for growth promotion purposes, as well as risks arising from difficulties of control, inspection and enforcement of the requirements of good veterinary practice."[592]

7.478 The European Communities argues that its findings regarding misplaced implants, off-label use, black-market drugs, and secondary risks, are based on realistic conditions of use and the possibilities of abuse or misuse which these hormones offer to farmers and are documented as regards the United States in the *Working Document*.[593]

Reasoning of the Panel

7.479 The United States has specifically alleged that the European Communities, in formulating the Opinions, failed to take into account two of the elements listed in Article 5.2, specifically the available scientific information and the relevant inspection, sampling, and testing methods. Therefore, the Panel must determine first whether the Opinions take into account the available scientific information and, second, whether the Opinions take into account relevant inspection, sampling, and testing methods.

7.480 As noted above in the context of risk assessment techniques, taking available scientific evidence into account does not require that a Member conform its actions to a particular conclusion in a particular scientific study. The available scientific information may contain a multiplicity of views and data on a particular topic. It is the view of the Panel that the requirement in Article 5.2 is to ensure that a Member, when assessing risk with the aim of formulating an appropriate SPS measure, has as wide a range as possible of scientific information

---

[590] EC's second written submission, para. 123.

[591] EC's replies to Panel questions after the first substantive meeting, Annex B-1, para. 83.

[592] Assessment of risks of hormonal growth promoters in cattle with respect to risks arising from abusive use and difficulties of control, Exhibit EC-73, p. 5, citing Appellate Body Report on *EC – Hormones*, para. 205.

[593] EC's second written submission, para. 126, citing Exhibit EC-73.

before it to ensure that its measure will be based on sufficient scientific data and supported by scientific principles.

7.481 The United States' argument can be reduced to the contention that because the conclusions in the Opinions are not supported by the scientific evidence, the European Communities must not have considered the available scientific evidence when it formulated the Opinions. However, whether the conclusions in the Opinions are supported by the scientific evidence considered by the European Communities is a question that is not relevant to the issue of whether the European Communities took the available scientific evidence into account in formulating the Opinions, within the meaning of Article 5.2.

7.482 The Opinions specifically addressed the evidence available with respect to bioavailability, susceptibility of sensitive populations, and DNA adducts and DNA damages. The Opinions even included reference to the very scientific studies the United States is alleging they did not take into account. Therefore, the Panel concludes that the European Communities did take the available scientific information into account as required by Article 5.2.

7.483 The second question before the Panel with respect to whether the European Communities took into account the factors listed in Article 5.2 is whether the Opinions take into account relevant inspection, sampling, and testing methods. The Panel notes that the European Communities has compiled a *Working Document* on the abusive use and difficulties of control in the administration of hormones for growth promotion purposes. The European Communities details visits to US regulatory agencies and on-site inspections as well as a review of data related to failures in the US inspection regime. The SCVPH also dedicated a significant portion of the 1999 Opinion to discussing the issue. Whether the conclusions the European Communities reached regarding the likelihood of abuse or misuse of hormone implants given relevant inspection, sampling, and testing methods in the United States are scientifically supported is of no relevance in an analysis of whether the European Communities fulfilled its obligations pursuant to Article 5.2 to take such methods into account.

7.484 Because the European Communities considered the available scientific information as well as relevant inspection, sampling, and testing methods in the preparation of its Opinions, the Panel concludes that the European Communities took these factors into account as required by Article 5.2 of the *SPS Agreement*.

Do the Opinions satisfy the definition in Annex A(4) of the *SPS Agreement*?

Introduction

7.485 Annex A(4) defines a risk assessment as:

"[t]he evaluation of the likelihood of entry, establishment or spread of a pest or disease within the territory of an importing Member according to the sanitary or phytosanitary measures which might be applied, and of the associated potential biological and economic consequences; *or the evaluation of the potential for adverse effects on human or animal health arising from the presence of additives, contaminants, toxins or disease-causing organisms in food, beverages or feedstuffs.*" (Emphasis added)

7.486   In this dispute, the measure at issue is intended to protect human health as a sanitary measure defined in Annex A(1)(b) and, thus, is to be based on a risk assessment in the sense of the second definition in Annex A(4).[594]

Summary of the main arguments of the parties[595]

7.487   The **United States** argues that the Opinions do not appear to be risk assessments within the meaning of Article 5.1.[596]

7.488   The United States refers to the definition for a risk assessment established by the panel in *EC – Hormones* that a risk assessment must "(i) identify the adverse effects on human health (if any) arising from the presence of the hormones at issue when used as growth promoters in meat or meat products, and (ii) if any such adverse effects exist, evaluate the potential ... occurrence of these effects." In the case of an import ban on meat and meat products such as that maintained by the European Communities, the relevant "evaluation" is that of "the potential for adverse effects arising from the presence in food of the hormones in dispute."[597]

7.489   The United States notes that the European Communities relies on studies that demonstrate adverse effects of hormones at concentrations exponentially greater than would be present in residues of meat from cattle treated with hormones for growth promotion purposes, and discusses the effects of substances, such as diethylstilbestrol ("DES"), that have been banned in the United States for decades in support of the notion that hormones can be harmful.[598] The United States argues that the European Communities fails to hone the general risk, or

---

[594]   Panel Report on *Australia – Salmon*, paras. 8.72 and 8.116 (finding that because the measure at issue was meant to protect animal health as a sanitary measure as defined in Annex A(1)(a), the first definition in Annex A(4) applied).

[595]   A more detailed account of the parties' arguments can be found in Section IV the descriptive part of this Report. The order in which the respective arguments of the parties are presented does not reflect any allocation of the burden of proof by the Panel.

[596]   US's first written submission, para. 137.

[597]   US's first written submission, para. 138 citing Panel Report on *EC – Hormones*, paras. 8.98, 8.127.

[598]   US's first written submission, para. 141.

identified hazards, down through hazard characterization and an exposure assessment in order to demonstrate (*i.e.*, identify and evaluate) a specific risk to consumers.[599]

7.490 The United States argues that the Opinions are not a risk assessment within the meaning of Article 5.1 and Annex A of the *SPS Agreement* because they fail to examine relevant pathways, explore the fate of the relevant risk (that posed by meat products to consumers) or to support their conclusions with scientific evidence. The United States contends that the Opinions neither "identify the adverse effects on human health" arising from the consumption of meat from cattle treated with hormones for growth promotion purposes according to good veterinary practice nor "evaluat[e] the potential for adverse effects on human or animal health" arising from consumption of meat products from cattle treated with hormones for growth promotion purposes.[600]

7.491 The United States faults the European Communities for relying upon statements from the US Department of Health and Human Services that estrogens generally are known to be human carcinogens. The United States argues that the conclusions in the report cited by the European Communities are based upon epidemiological tests focused on women and the use of hormone replacement therapies and oral contraception which contain estrogens and are based upon levels of oestradiol-17β or other estrogens high enough to have a hormonal effect on the consumer, not the levels of oestradiol-17β found in meat from cattle treated with the hormone for growth promotion purposes according to good veterinary practices. Such levels of oestradiol-17β that are found in meat, the United States asserts, are exponentially lower than those causing hormonal effects.[601]

7.492 The United States argues that scientific evidence concerning the need to regulate the use of hormones generally is different from specific evidence concerning the health risk associated with consumption of meat and meat products from cattle treated with hormones for growth promotion purposes.[602] The United States asserts that the European Communities did not consider whether consumer dietary exposure to hormone residues in meat and meat products from cattle is specifically a source of risk.[603]

7.493 The United States argues that the European Communities continues to rely on studies such as the 1999 IARC Monograph, which have already been found by the Appellate Body to "constitute general studies which do indeed

---

[599] US's first written submission, para. 142.
[600] US's first written submission, para. 147.
[601] US's second written submission, para. 38.
[602] US's replies to Panel questions after the first substantive meeting, Annex B-3, para. 70.
[603] US's replies to Panel questions after the first substantive meeting, Annex B-3, para. 72.

show the existence of a general risk of cancer; but they do not focus on and do not address the particular kind of risk here at stake – the carcinogenic or genotoxic potential of the residues of those hormones found in meat derived from cattle to which the hormones had been administered for growth promotion purposes."[604] The United States maintains that although the potential for adverse effects from hormones at these high levels is not in dispute, the materials and findings cited by the European Communities (1999 IARC Monograph; 11th Report on Carcinogens) are not, however, evidence of a risk from meat from cattle treated with oestradiol for growth promotion purposes.[605]

7.494 The **European Communities** argues that the Opinions do constitute a risk assessment within the meaning of Article 5.1 of the *SPS Agreement*. Specifically, the European Communities argues that there is a difference between a scientific risk assessment in the narrow sense referred to by the United States and the risk assessment within the meaning of Article 5.1 and Annex A(4) of the *SPS Agreement*.[606]

7.495 The European Communities argues that the Appellate Body has confirmed that a risk assessment within in the meaning of Article 5.1 includes a risk management stage which is the responsibility of the regulator to carry out and not of the scientific bodies.[607]

7.496 Although the European Communities agrees that in principle the risk resulting from human consumption of meat from cattle treated with oestradiol-17β for growth promotion purposes, according to good veterinary practice is the relevant risk, it argues that the assessment of such a risk is qualified by the difficulty in estimating the intake of such hormones. Specifically, the European Communities argues that human beings, including the populations at risk, are exposed to cumulative and synergistic effects, as they may be exposed to multiple sources of hormones and hormone residues, via several intake routes, as well as from endogenous production of some of these hormones. The European Communities contends that it is extremely difficult or impossible to assess accurately consumer exposure patterns, or other exposures from other environmental or endogenous sources, but it is also virtually impossible to assess all cumulative and synergistic effects that may arise from all potential exposure patterns, including for simultaneous exposure to several of these hormones.[608]

---

[604] US's replies to Panel questions after the second substantive meeting, para. 23 citing Appellate Body Report on *EC – Hormones*, Annex C-4, para. 200.
[605] US's replies to Panel questions after the second substantive meeting, Annex C-4, para. 24.
[606] EC's second written submission, para. 191; EC's replies to Panel questions after the first substantive meeting, Annex B-1, para. 135 *et seq.*
[607] EC's second written submission, para. 191.
[608] EC's replies to Panel questions after the first substantive meeting, Annex B-1, paras. 92-96.

7.497 The European Communities argues that the only rationale that can be inferred from the available scientific data is that the higher the exposure to residues from these hormones, the greater the risk is likely to be.[609] The European Communities points out that the Opinions noted that the DNA-damaging effects of oestrogen indicate that no threshold exists for the risk from oestrogen metabolites. The Opinions concluded that, in light of the recent data on the formation of genotoxic metabolites of oestradiol, suggesting that 17β-oestradiol acts as complete carcinogen by exerting tumour initiating and promoting effects, it has to be concluded that no quantitative estimate of risk related to residues in meat could be presented.[610]

7.498 The European Communities goes on to say that the risk resulting from human consumption of meat from cattle treated with oestradiol-17β for growth promotion purposes, according to good veterinary practice, is "assessed in the real world" where "people live, work and die", or may be suffering from clinical disorders, or may be particularly vulnerable segments of the population (e.g., like prepubertal children), etc.[611] The European Communities asserts that it considered in its assessment the potential risks resulting from the actual residues from non-treated as well as treated animals for growth promotion, and came to the conclusion that under realistic conditions of use such residues from treated animals for growth promotion do pose a higher risk and that it could not achieve the level of protection it has considered appropriate in its territory.[612]

7.499 The European Communities argues that it is not necessary to compare the two situations and then try to quantify how much one is more risky than the other and to what measurable level the risk is likely to occur, but rather to assess a situation of additive risks arising from the cumulative exposures of humans to multiple hazards, in addition to the endogenous production of some of these hormones by animals and human beings.[613]

7.500 The European Communities contends that evidence from both the health risk associated with the use of hormones generally and the administration of hormones in animals for growth promotion purposes, is relevant for the performance of a risk assessment in the sense of the *SPS Agreement*, because both sources of evidence impact upon and inform each other.[614]

7.501 The European Communities notes that it is scientifically undisputed that life-time exposure of humans to the levels of endogenous production of oestro-

---

[609] EC's replies to Panel questions after the first substantive meeting, Annex B-1, para. 94.
[610] EC's replies to Panel questions after the second substantive meeting, Annex C-1, para. 38.
[611] EC's replies to Panel questions after the first substantive meeting, Annex B-1, para. 96.
[612] EC's replies to Panel questions after the first substantive meeting, Annex B-1, para.151.
[613] *Ibid.*
[614] EC's replies to Panel questions after the first substantive meeting, Annex B-1, para. 254.

gen (and in particular to oestradiol-17β and its metabolites) is sufficient to cause and/or promote cancer in some individuals. This is frequently called risk of cancer from background (endogenous) exposure. This kind of exposure (and the attentive risk of cancer) cannot be avoided. The European Communities also notes that humans are exposed daily to variable levels of residues of oestradiol-17β from many exogenous sources where these hormones naturally occur, which likewise cannot be avoided.[615]

7.502 The European Communities argues that "additive risk" refers to exposure which is "further added on humans from the levels of residues in meat from animals treated with these hormones for growth promotion." Such exposure leads to a risk of cancer which is "added" to the cancer risk from the existing endogenous exposure through the background levels of hormones and through the exposure to exogenous sources, such as non-treated natural food. The European Communities cites to the 2002 US Report on Carcinogenesis and argues that it agrees with the conclusions in the SCVPH Opinions that "veterinary use of steroidal estrogens to promote growth and treat illness can increase estrogens in tissues of food-producing animals to above their normal levels", in general substantially higher than the normal (endogenously produced) levels. The European Communities argues that exposure to residues from hormone-treated meat is avoidable because these hormones are chemical substances that are deliberately added to meat.[616]

7.503 The European Communities states in response to the Panel's questions on additive risk:

> "The risk of cancer from the consumption of residues in hormone-treated meat are 'additive' (to risk of cancer from the two other sources of exposure), irrespective of whether these hormones are genotoxic carcinogens or only promote cancer through receptor-mediated mechanisms. Indeed, if they cause cancer by direct genotoxic action, the addition of such exposure increases the likelihood of the adverse effect to occur. If they act only through receptor-mediated mechanism, the risk from such exposure will be again 'additive', when they cause the presumed threshold to be exceeded. The risk assessment of the European Communities has established that oestradiol-17β is a proven genotoxic carcinogen and that the other two natural hormones (testosterone and progesterone) are also suspected to be genotoxic. Moreover, the risk assessment of the European Communities has also demonstrated that

---

[615] EC's replies to Panel questions after the second substantive meeting, Annex C-1, paras. 48-49.
[616] EC's replies to Panel questions after the second substantive meeting, Annex C-1, para. 50.

the ADIs recommended by JECFA for all these hormones will be exceeded under realistic conditions of use of these hormones in the US and Canada. They will also be exceeded in any case if the more recent data on the endogenous production of the natural hormones by pre-pubertal children is taken into account."[617]

Reasoning of the Panel

7.504 In *EC – Hormones*, with respect to the methodology for a risk assessment under the second definition of paragraph 4 of Annex A of the *SPS Agreement*, the panel stated that "in this dispute, a risk assessment carried out in accordance with the *SPS Agreement* should (i) *identify* the *adverse effects* on human health (if any) arising from the presence of the hormones at issue when used as growth promoters *in meat or meat products*, and (ii) if any such adverse effects exist, *evaluate* the *potential* or probability of occurrence of these effects".[618]

7.505 Although the Appellate Body did not disagree with the panel, in its report in *EC – Hormones* it noted "that the Panel's use of 'probability' as an alternative term for 'potential' creates a significant concern. The ordinary meaning of 'potential' relates to 'possibility' and is different from the ordinary meaning of 'probability'. 'Probability' implies a higher degree or a threshold of potentiality or possibility. It thus appears that here the Panel introduces a quantitative dimension to the notion of risk."[619]

7.506 In *Australia – Salmon,* the Appellate Body further elaborated on the distinction between the two standards for risk assessment contained in Annex A(4) and the need for a substantive distinction between the evaluation of "likelihood" in the first sentence and the evaluation of "potential" in the second sentence. Specifically, the Appellate Body stated:

> "[w]e note that the first type of risk assessment in paragraph 4 of Annex A is substantially different from the second type of risk assessment contained in the same paragraph. While the second requires only the evaluation of the potential for adverse effects on human or animal health, the first type of risk assessment demands an evaluation of the likelihood of entry, establishment or spread of a disease, and of the associated potential biological and economic consequences. In view of the very different language used in paragraph 4 of Annex A for the two types of risk assessment, we do

---

[617] EC's replies to Panel questions after the second substantive meeting, Annex C-1, para. 51.
[618] Panel Report on *EC – Hormones (Canada)*, para. 8.101; Panel Report on *EC – Hormones (US)*, para. 8.98.
[619] Appellate Body Report on *EC – Hormones*, para. 184.

not believe that it is correct to diminish the substantial differences between these two types of risk assessments ..."[620]

7.507 Therefore, the Panel considers that it is necessary to clarify what constitutes a risk assessment as defined by Annex A(4), second sentence. The Panel considers that Annex A(4) requires a Member to (a) identify the additives, contaminants, toxins or disease-causing organisms in food, beverages or feedstuffs at issue (if any); (b) identify any possible adverse effect on human or animal health; and (c) evaluate the potential for that adverse effect to arise from the presence of the identified additives, contaminants, toxins or disease-causing organisms in food, beverages or feedstuffs.

7.508 The Panel concludes that the European Communities has satisfied the first requirement of Annex A(4) second sentence, in that it has identified the contaminant and food at issue; namely meat and meat products from cattle treated with oestradiol-17β for growth promotion purposes. The European Communities has also identified the possible adverse effects on human or animal health, namely neurobiological, developmental, reproductive and immunological effects, as well as immunotoxicity, genotoxicity, and carcinogenicity.[621]

7.509 The Panel must now evaluate whether it has satisfied the third requirement of the definition of a risk assessment. To do so, the Panel needs to define the terms "potential" and "arise from." The Oxford English Dictionary defines potential as "[p]ossible as opposed to actual; having or showing the capacity to develop into something in the future; latent; prospective."[622] Additionally, in *EC – Hormones* the Appellate Body observed that the ordinary meaning of 'potential' relates to 'possibility'.[623] The American Heritage Dictionary defines "arise" as to come into being, originate, to result, issue or proceed.[624]

7.510 The Appellate Body's findings in both *EC – Hormones* and *Japan – Apples* inform the definition of risk assessment in Annex A(4) second sentence. The Appellate Body has found that the requirement to conduct a risk assessment is not satisfied merely by a general discussion of the disease sought to be avoided by the imposition of a sanitary of phytosanitary measure.[625]

---

[620] Appellate Body Report on *Australia – Salmon*, footnote 69.

[621] 1999 Opinion, page 72, Exhibit US-4.

[622] *The New Shorter Oxford English Dictionary* (Thumb Index Edition, 1993), p. 2310.

[623] (*footnote original*) The dictionary meaning of "potential" is "that which is possible as opposed to actual; a possibility"; L. Brown (ed.), *The New Shorter Oxford English Dictionary on Historical Principles*, Vol. 2, p. 2310 (Clarendon Press, 1993). In contrast, "probability" refers to "degrees of likelihood; the appearance of truth, or likelihood of being realized", and "a thing judged likely to be true, to exist, or to happen"; *Ibid.*, p. 2362.

[624] *The American Heritage Dictionary of the English Language* (4th ed., 2000).

[625] Appellate Body Report on *Japan – Apples*, para. 202.

7.511 Specifically, in *EC – Hormones* the Appellate Body concluded that a risk assessment in this instance required not a general evaluation of the carcinogenic potential of entire categories of hormones, but rather should include an examination of residues of those hormones found in meat derived from cattle to which the hormones had been administered for growth promotion purposes.[626]

7.512 In *Japan – Apples* the Appellate Body clarified that a risk assessment should refer in general to the harm concerned *as well as* to the precise agent that may possibly cause the harm.[627] In a footnote, the Appellate Body explained

> "Indeed, we are of the view that, as a general matter, 'risk' cannot usually be understood only in terms of the disease or adverse effects that may result. Rather, an evaluation of risk must connect the possibility of adverse effects with an antecedent or cause. For example, the abstract reference to the 'risk of cancer' has no significance, in and of itself, under the *SPS Agreement*, but when one refers to the 'risk of cancer from smoking cigarettes', the particular risk is given content."[628]

7.513 Given the Appellate Body's guidance and the ordinary meaning of the terms "potential" and "arising from", the Panel concludes that the European Communities was required to evaluate the possibility that the identified adverse effect came into being, originated, or resulted from the presence of residues of oestradiol-17β in meat or meat products as a result of the cattle being treated with the hormone for growth promoting purposes.

7.514 The Panel, as noted above, will not conduct its own risk assessment or impose its own scientific opinions on the European Communities.[629] However, the Panel must make an objective assessment of whether the Opinions issued by the SCVPH satisfy the definition contained in Annex A(4) to the *SPS Agreement*.

7.515 As a preliminary matter, the Panel notes that there has been significant debate between the parties about the relevance of the Codex and JECFA definitions of the various phases of a risk assessment as well as about a risk assessment's role in the larger process of risk analysis, which consists of three components: risk assessment, risk management, and risk communication.[630]

---

[626] Appellate Body Report on *EC – Hormones*, para. 200.
[627] Appellate Body Report on *Japan – Apples*, para. 202.
[628] Appellate Body Report on *Japan – Apples*, at footnote 372.
[629] See para. 7.443 above.
[630] Codex Procedural Manual, 15th ed., p. 44.

7.516 The Panel also recalls that the European Communities argues that the broader concept of risk analysis, as defined by Codex, including the risk management phase, must be considered in evaluating whether the European Communities conducted a risk assessment within the meaning of Article 5.1 and Annex A(4).

7.517 Specifically, the European Communities points out that, as defined by Codex, risk assessment is normally considered to be only the first component of a three part process.[631] The European Communities argues that the United States ignores the second component of risk analysis, which has to be completed *after* the completion of the four steps of risk assessment, namely risk management. The European Communities defines risk management as the process of "weighing policy alternatives in the light of the results of risk assessment and, if required, selecting and implementing appropriate control options, including regulatory measures."[632] The European Communities also asserts that the Appellate Body has confirmed that a risk assessment within the meaning of Article 5.1 includes a risk management stage which is the responsibility of the regulator to carry out and not of the scientific bodies.[633]

7.518 The Panel agrees with the European Communities that the relevant definition against which to measure the EC Opinions in order to determine whether they constitute a risk assessment is the one contained in the *SPS Agreement,* namely that set forth in Annex A(4). As noted above, the Panel has found that the text of Annex A(4) second sentence defines a risk assessment as evaluating the possibility that an identified adverse effect came into being, originated, or resulted from the presence of the identified additives, contaminants, toxins or disease-causing organisms in food, beverages or feedstuffs.

7.519 The European Communities argues that the Appellate Body in the original *EC – Hormones* case confirmed that a risk assessment within the meaning of Article 5.1 includes a "risk management" stage which entails weighing policy alternatives in light of the results of risk assessment and, if required, selecting and implementing appropriate control options, including regulatory measures. Although the Appellate Body disapproved of the original panel's distinction between "risk assessment" and "risk management" because it had no textual basis in the Agreement, this Panel can find no statement by the Appellate Body confirming that what the European Communities describes as risk management is included within the definition of a risk assessment as set forth in Annex A(4) of the *SPS Agreement.* In fact, the Appellate Body stressed that Article 5 and An-

---

[631] EC's replies to Panel questions after the first substantive meeting, Annex B-1, para. 135.
[632] EC's replies to Panel questions after the first substantive meeting, Annex B-1, paras. 136-137.
[633] EC's second written submission, para. 191.

nex A speak of *risk assessment* only and that the term *risk management* is not to be found either in Article 5 or in any other provision of the *SPS Agreement*.[634]

7.520 The Panel agrees with the Appellate Body that its role as a treaty interpreter is to "read and interpret the words actually used by the agreement under examination, and not words which the interpreter may feel should have been used."[635] The Panel takes note of the Appellate Body's finding that a risk assessment can take into account "matters not susceptible of quantitative analysis by the empirical or experimental laboratory methods commonly associated with the physical sciences."[636] However, the Panel finds that neither that finding nor the text of the Agreement includes within the definition of a risk assessment the concepts put forward by the European Communities as "risk management." Therefore, the Panel maintains that it must determine whether the European Communities evaluated the possibility that the identified adverse effects came into being, originated, or resulted from the presence of residues of oestradiol-17β in meat or meat products as a result of the cattle being treated with the hormone for growth promotion purposes. To that end, the Panel requested the opinions of the scientific experts on what, exactly, the European Communities evaluated in its Opinions.

7.521 The Panel specifically asked the experts whether the EC Opinions identified the potential for adverse effects on human health, including the carcinogenic or genotoxic potential, of the residues of oestradiol-17β found in meat derived from cattle to which this hormone had been administered for growth promotion purposes in accordance with good veterinary practice and to what extent the Opinions evaluated the potential occurrence of these adverse effects.[637]

7.522 Dr. Boobis concluded that "the EC has not identified the potential for adverse effects on human health of residues of oestradiol found in meat from treated cattle. This is because the analysis undertaken was focused primarily on hazard identification. There was little in the way of hazard characterization, and no independent exposure assessment was undertaken.[638]

7.523 Dr. Guttenplan concluded that the European Communities had done a thorough job in identifying the potential for adverse effects on human health of oestradiol-17β found in meat derived from cattle to which this hormone had been administered. Specifically, Dr. Guttenplan found that the European Communities had identified a number of potential adverse effects, established metabolic pathways relevant to these effects, and examined mechanisms of these ef-

---

[634] Appellate Body Report on *EC – Hormones*, para. 181.
[635] Appellate Body Report on *EC – Hormones*, para. 181.
[636] Appellate Body Report on *EC – Hormones*, para. 187.
[637] Panel question 13 to the scientific experts, Annex D, p. 22.
[638] Replies by the scientific experts to Panel questions, Annex D, para. 144.

fects. In addition it had performed thorough studies of residue levels in cattle, and the environment. Dr. Guttenplan also concluded that the evidence evaluating the occurrence of adverse effects is weak. He found that the animal models were very limited and the target organs do not coincide well with the target organs in humans. He also pointed out that there are "basically no epidemiological studies comparing matched populations consuming meat from untreated and hormone-treated cattle. Thus, little can be inferred about the potential occurrence of the adverse effects, the potential for adverse effects seems reasonable."[639]

7.524 Dr. Boisseau noted that "in the 1999 report, SCVPH concluded also that '... it is clear that exogenous oestrogens, present in oral contraceptives or used in hormonal replacement therapy in women, are responsible for an increase of en-dometrial cancer and, to lesser extent, some increased risk of breast cancer, [but] there is no direct evidence on the consequences of the contribution of exogenous oestradiol-17β originating from the consumption of treated meat'."[640]

7.525 Dr. Cogliano observed that even though the European Communities does demonstrate through scientific evidence that oestradiol-17β is genotoxic, the issue is whether this genotoxicity would occur at levels found in meat. In that respect, Dr. Cogliano concluded that the European Communities has not estab-lished that genotoxicity and cell proliferation would be induced by levels found in treated meat added to the pre-existing levels occurring in exposed humans.[641]

7.526 The Panel specifically asked the experts whether the European Communi-ties had demonstrated that a potential for adverse effects on human health arises from the consumption of meat from cattle treated with any of the six hormones in dispute for growth promotion purposes. Dr. Boisseau concluded that the European Communities did not demonstrate that a potential for adverse effects on human health arises from the consumption of meat from cattle treated with any of the six hormones in dispute for growth promotion purposes. Additionally, Dr. Boisseau stated that the kind of evidence required to demonstrate such po-tential adverse effects should be (a) toxicological data indicating that the values of the ADIs established by JECFA are not conservative enough, and (b) data on residues in treated/non-treated cattle and on daily production of hormones in sensitive individuals[642] indicating that the hormonal residue intake associated with the consumption of meat from treated cattle is such that the established ADIs would be exceeded in the case of use of growth promoters.[643]

---

[639] Replies by the scientific experts to Panel question 13, Annex D, para. 145.
[640] Replies by the scientific experts to Panel questions, Annex D, para. 132.
[641] Replies by the scientific experts to Panel questions, Annex D, para. 180.
[642] Such as prepubertal children.
[643] Replies by the scientific experts to Panel questions, Annex D, para. 406.

7.527 Dr. Boobis stated that, in his view, none of the information provided by the European Communities demonstrates the potential for adverse effects in humans of any of the six hormones in meat from cattle in which they are used for growth promotion purposes at the levels to which those consuming such meat would be exposed. The studies on genotoxicity provide no convincing evidence of potential for harm in consumers. The carcinogenic effects observed are entirely consistent with a hormonal mode of action that exhibits a threshold that would be well above the intake arising from consumption of meat from treated cattle.[644]

7.528 Dr. Guttenplan found that the levels in meat could result in bioavailable oestrogen exceeding the daily production rate of oestradiol in pre-pubertal children. "For pre-pubertal children, even with the low bioavailabilty of estrogen ... and its low levels in meats, it appears possible that intake levels would be within an order of magnitude of those of the daily production rate. This is greater than FDA's ADI and suggests some risk to this population. If there [are] genotoxic effects of estradiol in children, they may be reflected over a lifetime, as mutations arising from DNA damage are permanent. It seems the more accurate methods of analysis could now be used to measure the effect of eating hormone-treated beef on blood levels of estrogen in children and post-menopausal women. If practical, this experiment would be important in establishing or refuting the arguments of the EC."[645]

7.529 To the extent that the European Communities argues that the relevant risk from hormones is an "additive risk" the experts concluded that the European Communities did not assess the extent to which residues of hormones in meat and meat products as a result of the cattle being treated with the hormones for growth promoting purposes contribute to additive risks arising from the cumulative exposures of humans to multiple hazards, in addition to the endogenous production of some of these hormones by animals and human beings.[646]

7.530 Dr. Cogliano explains that even if the fact that a substance is a carcinogenic hazard led an agency to make a decision on the qualitative element alone, many agencies still prefer to examine the exposure in their country to determine what to do.[647] Indeed Dr. Boobis indicates that stopping the risk assessment once it was identified that the hazard was such that the dose response was going to be linear, i.e. there is no threshold, would be an unusual circumstance. He states that in most circumstances one would want to understand the relationship between the hazard and the level of exposure that was occurring. For that reason

---

[644] Replies by the scientific experts to Panel questions, Annex D, para. 408.
[645] Replies by the scientific experts to Panel question 52, Annex D, para. 413.
[646] Replies by the scientific experts to Panel question 56, Annex D, paras. 422-431.
[647] Transcript of the Panel meeting with the experts, Annex G, para. 438.

one would progress at least to a semi-quantitative evaluation of the exposure and risk, rather than just stopping at a simple identification of hazard.[648]

7.531 Finally, the Panel has looked at the Opinions and found statements that indicate that specific studies on the potential for the adverse health effects identified by the European Communities to arise from consumption of meat and meat products from cattle treated with oestradiol-17β for growth promotion purposes were not conducted.

7.532 The 1999 Opinion looked at three main areas of potential adverse effects: developmental effects on different stages of life; the relationship between oestrogens and cancer; and the effect of sex hormones on the immune system. In each of these areas, little or no data was presented directly that any of the potential adverse health effects identified come into being, originate, or result from the consumption of meat and meat products which contain veterinary residues of oestradiol-17β as a result of the cattle being treated with the hormone for growth promoting purposes.

7.533 With respect to the developmental effects of exogenous sex hormones, the 1999 Opinion recites generally the biological functions of sex hormones in the biological development of a human being and cites to studies that involve the application of diethylstilbestrol (DES) in experimental settings, even though, as the United States notes, DES is not one of the possible sources of oestradiol-17β residues in meat from treated cattle.[649] With respect to prepubertal children, the 1999 Opinion again cites studies having to do with DES as well as testosterone and allylestrenol (a steroid used in prevention of spontaneous abortion).[650] Although the developmental effects of oestrogens are discussed generally, including some potential adverse health effects, there is no examination of whether these effects arise from the presence of residues of oestradiol-17β in meat and meat products as a result of the cattle being treated with the hormone for growth promotion purposes. In fact, the 1999 Opinion states that "the information available so far falls short of the ideal, or even the sufficient standard to allow observers a well informed judgment when assessing exposure regarding what is acceptable from what is not."[651]

7.534 Regarding cancer, the 1999 Opinion states that "no study has assessed the effects of hormones as growth promoters in farm animals on cancer occurrence in humans. Arguments to be considered when evaluating the hypothesis of a potential link between the use of food promoters in farm animals and cancer in

---

[648] Transcript of the Panel meeting with the experts, Annex G, para. 442.
[649] 1999 Opinion, pp. 5-16.
[650] 1999 Opinion, p. 13.
[651] 1999 Opinion, p. 6.

humans come both from descriptive epidemiology, including studies in migrants, and etiologic epidemiology on diet and cancer as well as on hormones and cancer."[652] "Currently one cannot confirm nor refute the association between high rates of breast cancer and high hormone-treated meat consumption in North-America. This should be urgently studied."[653] Additionally, the 1999 Opinion noted that:

> "The difficulty of evaluating health effects at low dose is here compounded by the fact that the data on exposures of human populations are exceedingly limited. No large data are available on representative samples of foods collected in countries allowing or banning growth promoters in farm animals. Most often, published levels concern measurements realized by the producers of the substances themselves under experimental conditions. However, data on the concentration of hormones and their metabolites present in edible tissues of treated animals are lacking. In addition, the methods used for measurements require a critical reappraisal. Data on the nature and amount of metabolites produced by the target animal are missing."[654]

7.535   Finally, in examining the effect of sex hormones on the immune system, the 1999 Opinion states that "no sound epidemiological data are currently available to establish a link between nutrition, especially meat consumption, and the occurrence of (and apparent current increase in) autoimmune diseases."[655] Additionally, the 1999 Opinion found that relevant data:

> "[I]ndicate that oestrogens modulate the immune system in many species. Direct human data at near physiological levels of oestradiol are lacking. Vingerhoets et. al., (1998) have conducted a self-reporting questionnaire study of DES daughters. A statistically significant difference in the incidence of infections was identified compared with control. This may be considered to be linked to imprinting by DES in utero.
>
> In conclusion, at relatively high doses oestradiol does produce a number of adverse effects on the immune system in humans, e.g. allergy to topical oestradiol (Boehnke and Gall, 1996). The above findings while indicating a possible concern are insufficient to identify whether immune effects could occur in consumers from

---

[652]   1999 Opinion, p. 16.
[653]   *Ibid.*
[654]   *Ibid.*, p. 20.
[655]   1999 Opinion, pp. 22-23.

the ingestion of meat or meat products containing oestradiol residues."[656]

7.536 The 1999 Opinion cited a new method for determining blood levels of oestradiol which suggested that the levels were 100 fold lower than previously determined and the metabolic clearance rate too high by a factor of 10. The 1999 Opinion concluded that if these methods were correct the acceptable daily intake established by the US Food and Drug Administration for meat and meat products derived from treated cattle would be at least 85 fold and possibly as much as 1,700 fold too high. However, the 1999 Opinion went on to note that "[g]iven all of the uncertainties in these estimates, it appears that the data are insufficient to form the basis of a sound risk assessment."[657]

7.537 All of the statements of the experts, and indeed statements from the Opinions, indicate that the European Communities has evaluated the potential for the identified adverse effects to be associated with oestrogens in general, but has not provided analysis of the potential for these effects to arise from consumption of meat and meat products which contain residues of oestradiol-17β as a result of the cattle they are derived from being treated with the hormone for growth promotion purposes. The Panel, therefore, concludes that although the European Communities has evaluated the association between excess hormones and neurobiological, developmental, reproductive and immunological effects, as well as immunotoxicity, genotoxicity, and carcinogenicity, it has not satisfied the requirements of the definition of a risk assessment contained in Annex A(4) because it has not evaluated specifically the possibility that these adverse effects come into being, originate, or result from the consumption of meat or meat products which contain veterinary residues of oestradiol-17β as a result of the cattle being treated with the hormone for growth promotion purposes.

Does the science support the conclusions of the Opinions?

Introduction

7.538 The Panel agrees with the reasoning of the Panel in *Japan – Apples (Article 21.5 – US)* that "the scientific evidence which is being evaluated must support the conclusions of the [risk assessment]. Therefore, if the conclusions of the risk assessment are not sufficiently supported by the scientific evidence referred to in the [risk assessment], then there cannot be a risk assessment appropriate to the circumstances, within the meaning of Article 5.1".[658] Although the Panel has already found, above, that the Opinions do not satisfy the definition of a risk assessment in Annex A(4) of the *SPS Agreement*, the Panel wishes to ensure that

---

[656] 1999 Opinion, p. 45.
[657] 1999 Opinion, pp. 38-39.
[658] Panel Report on *Japan – Apples (Article 21.5 – US)*, para. 8.136 (original footnote omitted).

it has conducted a complete and objective assessment of the facts. Therefore, in determining whether the European Communities complied with Article 5.1, the Panel will determine whether the scientific evidence referred to in the Opinions supports the conclusions contained therein.

Summary of the main arguments of the parties[659]

7.539   The **United States** points out that the United Kingdom's Sub-Group of the Veterinary Products Committee, a service of the UK's Department for Environment, Food and Rural Affairs, concluded that "none of the publications reviewed in the 1999 Opinion provide any substantive evidence that oestradiol is mutagenic/genotoxic at relevant levels of exposure from residues in meat."[660]

7.540   The United States also refers to the report of the Committee for Veterinary Medicinal Products ("CVMP") (a subcommittee of the European Medicines Agency) on the Safety Evaluation of Steroidal Sex Hormones, also from 1999. The United States notes that the CVMP reaffirmed its conclusions that oestradiol-17β is mainly devoid of genotoxic activity and exerts its carcinogenic action after prolonged exposure and/or at levels considerably higher than those required for a physiological response.[661] Additionally, the CVMP concluded that the previous data as well as the recent EC studies described in the 1999 Opinion, support the notion that oestradiol belongs to the group of non-genotoxic carcinogens. According to the CVMP, the new studies "indicate that the presumed genotoxicity alone would not be sufficient to elicit the carcinogenic effects observed in the target tissues."[662]

7.541   The United States argues that the European Communities relies on studies that demonstrate adverse effects of hormones at concentrations exponentially greater than would be present in residues of meat from cattle treated with hormones for growth promotion purposes, and discusses the effects of substances, such as DES, that have been banned in the United States for decades in support of the notion that hormones can be harmful.[663]

7.542   The United States argues that the European Communities draws conclusions on the effects of oestradiol-17β in concentrations in the normal physiological range (*i.e.,* concentrations equivalent to those found in both treated and untreated meat) based solely on observations of DNA damage from doses greatly

---

[659]   A more detailed account of the parties' arguments can be found in Section IV of the descriptive part of this Report. The order in which the respective arguments of the parties are presented does not reflect any allocation of the burden of proof by the Panel.
[660]   US's first written submission, para. 83, citing the "UK Report" in Exhibit US-12.
[661]   US's first written submission, para. 90, citing the "CVMP Report" in Exhibit US-13.
[662]   US's first written submission, para. 91.
[663]   US's first written submission, para. 141.

exceeding that range. This extrapolation fails to take into account the available data on, *e.g.*, differences between oestradiol metabolism at high compared to low concentrations in tissues, the potential for threshold doses for adverse biological effects and the possibility of different dose-response relationships for high and low doses of the compound.[664]

7.543 The United States notes that a central underpinning of the European Communities' determination to ban the importation of meat or meat products from cattle treated with hormones for growth promotion purposes according to good veterinary practices is that oestradiol-17β is genotoxic.[665] However, the United States argues, the European Communities has not in fact demonstrated through scientific evidence that oestradiol has carcinogenic effects other than through the receptor mediated, cell division stimulating activity of the hormone – in other words, at levels exerting a hormonal effect on consumers, and not at the exponentially smaller levels that would be found in meat residues.[666]

7.544 The United States argues that the European Communities reliance upon the JECFA conclusion that oestradiol has "genotoxic potential" for its conclusion that oestradiol is genotoxic is misplaced, because it fails to take into account JECFA's findings that oestradiol-17β did not cause gene mutations *in vitro*, although in some other assays, sporadic but unconfirmed positive results were obtained.[667]

7.545 The United States also argues that although the European Communities relies on the JECFA report to support its argument that oestradiol-17β is genotoxic, the European Communities ignores the ultimate conclusion of the JECFA report, *i.e.*, that a maximum residue level for oestradiol-17β in meat need not be specified because there is a "wide margin of safety for consumption of residues in food when the drug is administered according to good practice in the use of veterinary drugs."[668]

7.546 The United States argues that the Opinions focus on several hypothetical "failure of control" scenarios that ignore actual regulatory processes in the United States, and for which the European Communities presents no support. The European Communities asserts that these scenarios "clearly identify a risk for excessive exposure of consumer to residues from misplaced or off-label used implants and incorrect dose regimes." Yet, the European Communities, accord-

---

[664] US's first written submission, para. 154.
[665] US's second written submission, para. 35.
[666] US's second written submission, para. 36.
[667] US's second written submission, para. 37, citing the 52nd JECFA Report (2000), p. 58 (Exhibit US-5).
[668] US's second written submission, para. 37, citing the 52nd JECFA Report (2000), p. 74, footnote 1 (Exhibit US-5).

ing to the United States, fails to produce any evidence identifying a real risk of failure of controls or failure to satisfy good veterinary practices in the United States.[669]

7.547 The United States relies upon the conclusions of the panel in *Japan – Apples (Article 21.5 – US)* for the premise that evidence relied upon by a Member must actually support the conclusions reached in that Member's risk assessment. The United States argues, therefore, that the European Communities may not simply set out conclusions in its Opinions that are not actually grounded in the studies or evidence it cites as support.[670]

7.548 The United States argues that the European Communities continues to rely on studies such as the 1999 IARC Monograph, which have already been found by the Appellate Body to "constitute general studies which do indeed show the existence of a general risk of cancer; but they do not focus on and do not address the particular kind of risk here at stake – the carcinogenic or genotoxic potential of the residues of those hormones found in meat derived from cattle to which the hormones had been administered for growth promotion purposes."[671] The United States maintains that although the potential for adverse effects from hormones at these high levels is not in dispute, the materials and findings cited by the European Communities (1999 IARC Monograph; 11th Report on Carcinogens) are not, however, evidence of a risk from meat from cattle treated with oestradiol for growth promotion purposes.[672]

7.549 The **European Communities** argues that it is important to understand that the issue of the dose administered is not relevant for the *in vivo* genotoxicity in the case of oestradiol-17β. The European Communities goes on to note that it appears that the doses used to elicit *in vivo* mutagenicity[673] are not massively high, but rather that they seem to fall within the safety margin established by JECFA, which means that the residues in meat from hormone-treated cattle are also capable of producing this adverse effect.[674]

7.550 The European Communities argues that the only rationale that can be inferred from the available scientific data is that the higher the exposure to resi-

---

[669] US's second written submission, para. 56.

[670] US's second written submission, para. 56, citing the Panel Report on *Japan – Apples (Article 21.5 – US)*, para. 8.145.

[671] US's reply to questions from EC after the second substantive meeting, para. 23, citing Appellate Body Report on *EC – Hormones*, para. 200, Annex C-4.

[672] *Ibid.*, para. 24.

[673] Ability of a physical, chemical, or biological agent to induce heritable changes (mutations) in the genetic material in a cell as a consequence of alterations or loss of genes or chromosomes (or parts thereof) (replies of Dr. Boobis and Dr. Guttenplan to Panel question 2 to the experts. Annex D, paras. 34 and 55).

[674] EC's replies to Panel questions after the second substantive meeting, Annex C-1, para. 23.

dues from these hormones, the greater the risk is likely to be.[675] The European Communities goes on to say that the risk resulting from human consumption of meat from cattle treated with oestradiol-17β for growth promotion purposes, according to good veterinary practice, is "assessed in the real world" where "people live, work and die", or may be suffering from clinical disorders, or may be particularly vulnerable segments of the population (*e.g.*, like prepubertal children), etc.[676]

7.551 The European Communities notes that it is scientifically undisputed that life-time exposure of humans to the levels of endogenous production of oestrogen (and in particular to oestradiol-17β and its metabolites) is sufficient to cause and/or promote cancer in some individuals. This is frequently called risk of cancer from background (endogenous) exposure. This kind of exposure (and the attentive risk of cancer) cannot be avoided. The European Communities also notes that humans are exposed daily to variable levels of residues of oestradiol-17β from many exogenous sources where these hormones naturally occur, which likewise cannot be avoided.[677]

Reasoning of the Panel

7.552 The Panel's task is to determine whether the scientific evidence supports the conclusions in the Opinions. The Panel notes in this respect that the 1999 Opinion concluded that "for oestradiol genotoxicity has already been demonstrated explicitly."[678] The 1999 Opinion also concluded that oestradiol-17β is a complete carcinogen that exhibits tumour initiating and tumour promoting effects.[679] Finally, the 1999 Opinion found that "any excess exposure towards 17β-oestradiol and its metabolites resulting from the consumption of meat and meat products presents a potential risk to public health in particular to those groups of the population which have been identified as particularly sensitive, such as prepubertal children.[680] In the 2000 and 2002 Opinions, the SCVPH concluded that none of the additional science developed in the intervening years justified changing those conclusions.

7.553 The Panel is not in a position to evaluate the scientific data the SCVPH reviewed in drawing its conclusions. For this reason, the Panel consulted a group of scientific experts and asked them to evaluate the EC Opinions as well as the underlying science.

---

[675] EC's replies to Panel questions after the first substantive meeting, Annex B-1, paras. 94 and 96.
[676] *Ibid.*
[677] EC's replies to Panel questions after the second substantive meeting, Annex C-1, paras. 48-49.
[678] 1999 Opinion, p. 75, Exhibit US-4.
[679] 1999 Opinion, p. 73.
[680] 1999 Opinion, p. 71.

7.554 The European Communities urged the Panel to disregard the responses of two particular experts because their positions are "purely theoretical" and for the additional reason that they have "never done any specific research on these hormones nor have they published something on these substances."[681] In that vein, the European Communities cites to the Appellate Body's rejection of an opinion given by a scientist in the original *EC – Hormones* dispute in 1998 because it did not "purport to be the result of scientific studies carried out by him or under his supervision focusing specifically on residues of hormones in meat from cattle fattened with such hormones ..."[682] However, the Panel finds that Appellate Body in its report on *EC – Hormones* spoke to a different issue. In that instance the scientist was making specific estimates about the likelihood of breast cancer being caused by eating meat containing oestrogens, even though the scientist had not studied the matter.

7.555 In this case, the Panel has asked the experts not to make their own scientific conclusions but to evaluate the Opinions as experts in the conducting of risk assessments on food additives and contaminants and to assist the Panel in determining whether the evidence relied upon by the SCVPH supports the conclusions in its Opinions. To that end the Panel found the comments by all the experts helpful in its analysis and none shall be disregarded.

7.556 In response to specific questions from the Panel, the experts provided the following information.

7.557 With respect to the genotoxicity of oestradiol-17β, Dr. Boisseau explained that JECFA's conclusion that oestradiol-17β had genotoxic potential was based on the general agreement that oestradiol-17β is associated with a genotoxic effect, thus

> "... although it recognized that oestradiol-17β does not lead to positive results in all the classical tests which have been used to demonstrate its genotoxicity and its mutagenicity (oestradiol-17β did not cause gene mutations *in vitro* and gives, in some assays, sporadic but unconfirmed positive results), JECFA, in its fifty second session held in 1999 concluded 'that oestradiol-17β has genotoxic potential.' "[683]

7.558 In evaluating the EC assertion that the fact that doses of oestradiol-17β used in growth promotion are low is irrelevant because there is no threshold for

---

[681] EC's comments on experts replies to Panel questions, Annex F-1, pp. 35-36.
[682] EC's comments on experts replies to Panel questions, Annex F-1, p. 14, citing Appellate Body Report on *EC – Hormones*, para. 198.
[683] Replies by the scientific experts to Panel questions, Annex D, paras. 134-135.

substances which have genotoxic potential, Dr. Boisseau stated that the general principle did not apply to naturally occurring hormones, which are produced by both humans and food producing animals. Dr. Boisseau noted that even in the absence of any consumption of food coming from animals treated by growth promoting hormones, humans are naturally and continuously exposed to these natural hormones through, among others, (a) their own production of these hormones which may be very high, for example in the case of pregnant women, (b) the consumption of meat from non treated cattle, (c) the consumption of meat from other food producing animals, (d) the consumption of milk and eggs. There is no epidemiological survey indicating that this continuous exposure of humans to these natural hormones results in any identified risk for health.[684]

7.559 Dr. Cogliano explained that "the EC's statement that a threshold cannot be identified reflects their view of genotoxic mechanisms, just as the contrary statement that there is a threshold and that this threshold is above the levels found in meat residues reflects how Canada and the US view genotoxic mechanisms. Neither statement has been demonstrated by the scientific evidence, rather, they are different assumptions that each party uses in their interpretation of the available evidence."[685]

7.560 Dr. Guttenplan replied that:

"[T]he data referred to by the EC supports a genotoxic mechanism as well as a hormonal mechanism. It is true that there is no reason to expect a threshold to exist for a genotoxic chemical. Although DNA repair can occur, it presumably is occurring at all doses and the fraction of DNA damage repaired probably does not change at physiological levels, because the repair enzymes are unlikely to be saturated. The statement that, 'the fact that doses used in growth promotion are low is not of relevance' is not necessarily true. (para. 118-119 of EC Rebuttal Submission (US case)). For any toxin the dose determines the risk. When exposure is very low risk will be very low. However, one can argue about the definition of 'low'. It should also be noted that at very low levels of genotoxic carcinogens the decrease in risk is more than proportional than the decrease in applied dose."[686]

7.561 Dr. Cogliano stated in his written responses that the identification of oestradiol-17β as a human carcinogen indicates that there are potential adverse effects on human health when oestrodiol-17β is consumed in meat from cattle

---

[684] Replies by the scientific experts to Panel questions, Annex D, para. 182.
[685] Replies by the scientific experts to Panel questions, Annex D, para. 186.
[686] Replies by the scientific experts to Panel questions, Annex D, para. 187.

treated with hormones for growth promotion purposes.[687] At the meeting with the Panel, Dr. Cogliano clarified that the IARC has classified oestradiol-17β as possibly carcinogenic based on sufficient evidence in experimental animals. The agents that are known to be carcinogenic in humans are the steroidal oestrogens, non-steroidal oestrogens, and various oestrogen-progestin combinations as used either as birth-control pills or menopausal therapy.[688]

7.562 Dr. Boobis concluded that there is no good evidence that oestradiol is genotoxic *in vivo* or that it causes cancer by a genotoxic mechanism. Indeed the evidence is against this. Hence, the scientific evidence does not support the European Communities' position that the levels of the hormones in meat from treated cattle are not of relevance.[689]

7.563 In a review of the scientific literature and the 1999 report of the Committee for Veterinary Medicinal Products of the European Medicine Agency, Dr. Boisseau concluded that the demonstration remains to be made that the observed indicator effects are representative of mutagenesis at the gene or chromosome level and also occur in somatic cells *in vivo*. This is not likely in the view of the following: earlier studies had mostly indicated that hormones do not induce micronuclei or other chromosomes aberration types *in vivo*. With the exception of the study reported by Dhillon and Dhillon, the recent data confirm the earlier findings and clearly indicate that hormones and/or their synthetic analogues are not associated with genotoxicity properties in the bone marrow micronucleas assay *in vivo*.[690]

7.564 With respect to the carcinogenic and tumour promoting qualities of oestradiol-17β, Dr. Boisseau noted that if the SCVPH, in the 1999 Opinion, expresses its concern in concluding that "[f]inally, in consideration of the recent data on the formation of genotoxic metabolites of oestradiol suggesting oestradiol-17β acts as complete carcinogen by exerting tumour initiating and promoting effects ... no quantitative estimate of the risk related to residues in meat could be presented," it provides no data indicating that oestradiol-17β is associated with the increase of tumours in tissues or organs which are not hormone dependent.[691] Dr. Boisseau concludes that "the EC risk assessment did not support that residues of oestradiol-17β, despite the genotoxic potential of this hormone, can initiate and promote tumours in humans."[692]

---

[687] Replies by the scientific experts to Panel questions, Annex D, para. 154.
[688] Transcript of the experts meeting with the Panel, Annex G, para. 327.
[689] Replies by the scientific experts to Panel questions, Annex D, para. 184.
[690] Replies by the scientific experts to Panel questions, Annex D, para. 136.
[691] Replies by the scientific experts to Panel questions, Annex D, para. 141.
[692] Replies by the scientific experts to Panel questions, Annex D, para. 142.

7.565 In addition, Dr. Boisseau concluded that the scientific evidence relied upon in the Opinions does not support the conclusion that carcinogenic effects of oestradiol-17β are related to a mechanism other than hormonal activity.[693]

7.566 Dr. Boobis also pointed out that the evidence is against direct modification of DNA *in vivo* by hormones in meat from treated animals, or by their metabolites produced *in vivo*. Indirect modification could conceivably come about by product of reactive oxygen species. The DNA repair[694] processes for this are amongst the most efficient (*Arai et al, 2006; Russo et al, 2004*) and even if such modification did occur, it is anticipated that no heritable change would result, because of DNA repair (*Arai et al, 2006*). This would be true even at the levels of exposure that could arise should GVP not be followed.[695]

7.567 Dr. Boisseau also expressed his opinion that epidemiological studies carried out in humans during long enough to take into account this "long latency period" will not be able to discriminate, in the case of a possible but limited increase of tumours, between the responsibilities of (a) hormone residues resulting from the treatment of food producing animals by growth promoting hormones, (b) hormone residues resulting from the endogenous production of these animals, and (c) other components of the diet including other food additives and contaminants. That is the reason for which, to his knowledge, even though the hormones in dispute have already been used as growth promoters over a significant number of years, the epidemiological studies in humans already carried out in this domain have failed to identify any relation between the occurrence of hormonally dependent tumours and the consumption of meat containing hormonally active residues resulting from the treatment of cattle with growth promoters.[696]

7.568 In response to the citation by the European Communities of data indicating different cancer rates between the United States and Europe, Dr. Boobis stated that there is no scientific evidence demonstrating any association between consumption of meat from animals treated with growth promoting hormones and the risk of cancer in humans. Dr. Boobis acknowledged that an appreciable number of studies show an association between a risk of certain cancer types and the consumption of meat, however he pointed out that the studies show little relationship with whether the meat is from animals treated with growth promoting hormones or not. Dr. Cogliano noted that although it is possible that differences in exposure to exogenous hormones could be one cause of the different

---

[693] Replies by the scientific experts to Panel questions, Annex D, para. 156.
[694] DNA repair mechanisms refer to the ability of an organism to recognize different types of damage to DNA and repair it (replies of Dr. Boobis and Dr. Guttenplan to Panel question 22 to the experts. Annex D, paras. 201 and 204).
[695] Replies by the scientific experts to Panel questions, Annex D, para. 202.
[696] Replies by the scientific experts to Panel questions, Annex D, para. 209.

breast cancer rates in the United States and the European Communities, the data are not sufficiently specific to establish a link. Dr. Guttenplan also concluded that the epidemiological studies do not identify a relationship between cancer and residues of hormonal growth promoters.[697]

7.569 Additionally, in response to direct questioning during the Panel meeting with the experts, Drs. Boobis, Boisseau, and Guttenplan all agreed that there is no appreciable risk of cancer from residues of oestradiol-17β in meat and meat products from cattle treated with the hormone for growth promotion purposes. While all the experts who responded to the question agreed that a zero risk could not be guaranteed, the actual level of risk was in their view so small as to not be calculable.[698]

7.570 Finally, the Opinions themselves contain statements that indicate that the science does not support the conclusions in the Opinions. The 1999 Opinion considered that the link, if any, between cancer and consumption of hormone-treated meat cannot, at present, be confirmed nor refuted.[699] It is also important to note that the only study cited with respect to cancer in susceptible populations, such as foetuses and prepubertal children, has to do with *in utero* exposure to DES, which is banned in the United States and is not the source of the oestra-diol-17β residues in the meat and meat products that are the subject of the European Communities' ban.[700]

7.571 With respect to the other potential adverse effects identified by the European Communities, the 1999 Opinion also concludes that no sound epidemiological data are currently available to establish a link between nutrition, especially meat consumption, and the occurrence of (and apparent current increase in) autoimmune diseases.[701] As to the developmental effects of exogenous sex hormones on puberty in humans, the 1999 Opinion, noted that although precocious puberty is somewhat common in the United States, "the importance of environmental oestrogenic compounds present in plastics, insecticides, and *meat from animals treated with sex hormones*, while suggestive, remains as only a possibility in affecting an early onset of puberty."[702]

7.572 The Panel has evaluated the evidence. The Panel considered the SCVPH's own characterization of the science in the Opinions as well as the replies of the experts to the Panel's questions, the transcript of the experts meeting with the

---

[697] Replies by the scientific experts to Panel questions, Annex D, paras. 224, 230, 231, 238, 239, 241 and 242.
[698] Transcript of the Panel meeting with the experts, Annex G, paras. 707-742.
[699] 1999 Opinion., pp. 17-18.
[700] 1999 Opinion, p. 21.
[701] 1999 Opinion, pp. 22-23.
[702] 1999 Opinion, p. 14. (emphasis added).

Panel, and the submissions of the parties. The Panel found that the views expressed by the experts who answered the questions, provided clear and consistent answers, and who had particular expertise in the relevant areas being discussed, were consistent with the statements in the Opinions cited above. The Panel's evaluation of the expert views and the plain language of the Opinions themselves leads the Panel to conclude that the scientific evidence referred to in the Opinions does not support the European Communities' conclusion that for oestradiol-17β genotoxicity had already been demonstrated explicitly[703], nor does it support the conclusion that the presence of residues of oestradiol-17β in meat and meat products as a result of the cattle being treated with the hormone for growth promotion purposes leads to increased cancer risk. Additionally, the scientific evidence does not support the European Communities' conclusions about the adverse immunological and developmental effects of consuming meat and meat products from cattle treated with oestradiol-17β for growth promotion purposes. Therefore, the Panel is of the view that the scientific evidence referred to in the Opinions does not support the conclusions reached by the European Communities.

Conclusion

7.573 On the basis of the above, the Panel concludes that, in its Opinions, the European Communities took into account risk assessment techniques of the relevant international organizations and took into account the factors listed in Article 5.2 of the *SPS Agreement*. The Panel nonetheless concludes that the European Communities has not satisfied the requirements of the definition of a risk assessment contained in Annex A(4) of the *SPS Agreement* and the scientific evidence evaluated does not support the conclusions in the risk assessment. The Panel concludes that the European Communities has not conducted a risk assessment as appropriate to the circumstances within the meaning of Article 5.1 of the *SPS Agreement*.

(iii)   Is the measure "based on" a risk assessment?

Introduction

7.574 The second question to address when determining whether an SPS measure is consistent with Article 5.1 is whether that measure is "based on" a risk assessment. For an SPS measure to be based on a risk assessment, there must be a rational relationship between the measure and the risk assessment.[704]

---

[703] 1999 Opinion, p. 75.
[704] Appellate Body Report on *EC – Hormones*, para. 193.

7.575 Specifically, the Appellate Body in *EC – Hormones* explained that "Article 5.1, when contextually read as it should be, in conjunction with and as informed by Article 2.2 of the *SPS Agreement*, requires that the results of the risk assessment must sufficiently warrant – that is to say, reasonably support – the SPS measure at stake."[705] The Appellate Body went on to explain that this requirement is a substantive one.[706]

Summary of the main arguments of the parties[707]

7.576 The **United States** argues that the EC failed to demonstrate that its amended ban is "based on" a risk assessment within the meaning of Article 5.1, i.e. that the results of the risk assessment sufficiently warrant – that is to say, reasonably support – the SPS measure at stake.

7.577 The **European Communities** concludes that the United States has failed to demonstrate that the scientific risk assessment carried out by the SCVPH does not reasonably support the measures adopted.[708] The European Communities argues that not only does the SCVPH's assessment support the ban on oestradiol-17β, but more recent research equally confirms and further reinforces its opinion that the measure is warranted.[709]

Reasoning of the Panel

7.578 The Panel has concluded that the Opinions do not constitute a risk assessment because the Opinions do not satisfy the definition of a risk assessment contained in Annex A(4) second sentence and because the scientific evidence referred to in the Opinions does not support the conclusions therein. Because the Opinions are not a risk assessment as appropriate to the circumstances, the measure cannot be based on a risk assessment within the meaning of Article 5.1.[710]

---

[705] Appellate Body Report on *EC – Hormones*, paras. 193-194.
[706] *Ibid.*
[707] A more detailed account of the parties' arguments can be found in Section IV of the descriptive part of this Report. The order in which the respective arguments of the parties are presented does not reflect any allocation of the burden of proof by the Panel.
[708] EC's second written submission, para. 210.
[709] EC's second written submission, para. 211.
[710] Panel Report on *Japan – Apples (Article 21.5 – US)*, para. 8.156 (concluding that because the 2004 pest risk assessment did not amount to a risk assessment as appropriate to the circumstances, Japan's measure was not based on a risk assessment).

(iv)   Conclusion

7.579 In light of the above, the Panel concludes that the EC implementing measure on oestradiol-17β is not compatible with Article 5.1 of the *SPS Agreement*.

(f)   Compatibility of the EC implementing measure with Article 5.7 of the *SPS Agreement*

(i)   Introduction

7.580 We have already concluded that the EC implementing measure does not comply with the provisions of Article 5.1 of the *SPS Agreement*. To the extent that we are not seeking to determine any level of nullification or impairment, but rather whether the European Communities has removed the measure found to be inconsistent with a covered agreement in the *EC – Hormones* dispute, we could conclude at this stage that, by adopting Directive 2003/74/EC, the European Communities has not – fully – removed the measure found to be inconsistent with the *SPS Agreement*. We recall, however, the purpose of our considering the EC claims of violation of Article 23.1 of the DSU, read together with Article 22.8 and Article 3.7 of the DSU. It is to assist the DSB in achieving a satisfactory settlement of the matter in accordance with the rights and obligations under the DSU and under the covered agreements, and to allow the Appellate Body to make findings as may be necessary should it disagree with our findings in relation to Article 23.1 and 23.2(a) of the DSU. We therefore proceed with a review of the conformity of the EC measure with Article 5.7 of the *SPS Agreement*.

(ii)   Summary of the main arguments of the parties[711]

7.581 The **European Communities** argues that Directive 2003/74/EC provides that the use of five of the six hormones at issue is provisionally forbidden. This ban is based on a comprehensive risk assessment and, thus, is fully compliant with the DSB recommendations and rulings. In particular, as stipulated by the Appellate Body, the results of the risk assessment provide the "available pertinent information" on the basis of which the provisional prohibition regarding these five hormones has been enacted. Consequently, the European Communi-

---

[711]   A more detailed account of the parties' arguments can be found in Section IV of the descriptive part of this Report. The order in which the respective arguments of the parties are presented does not reflect any allocation of the burden of proof by the Panel.

ties claims that, through Directive 2003/74/EC, it has implemented the rulings and recommendations in the *EC – Hormones* case.[712]

7.582 The **United States** considers that, because the EC ban fails to meet the requirements of Article 5.7, the European Communities is not provisionally exempted from satisfying the obligations set out, *inter alia*, in Articles 2.2 and 5.1 of the *SPS Agreement*.

7.583 The United States recalls that the Appellate Body in *Japan – Agricultural Products II*, clarified that Article 5.7 sets out four requirements that must be cumulatively satisfied in order to adopt and maintain a provisional measure.

7.584 First the United States argues that the European Communities fails to demonstrate how its provisional ban is imposed in a situation where "relevant scientific evidence is insufficient". The United States adds that Codex has adopted standards based on several JECFA risk assessments of the hormones which determined that they are safe at the levels implicated by residues in meat from cattle treated with the hormones according to good veterinary practice. In light of the quality and quantity of scientific evidence relating to the five hormones, there is simply no need to obtain the additional information necessary for a more objective assessment of risk. According to the United States, studies completed since the *EC – Hormones* case reaffirm earlier conclusions. New safety assessments have been conducted for progesterone and testosterone, reaffirming their safety when used according to good veterinary practices.

7.585 In the opinion of the United States, the European Communities also fails to demonstrate how its provisional ban has been adopted on the basis of available pertinent information. For the United States, the studies relied upon by the European Communities as a basis for its provisional ban do not in fact demonstrate a risk associated with residues in meat and meat products from cattle that have been treated with hormones for growth promotion purposes according to good veterinary practices.

7.586 The United States further argues that the European Communities has not sought to obtain the additional information necessary for a more objective assessment of risk.

7.587 The United States finally argues that the European Communities has not reviewed the measure accordingly within a reasonable period of time. The United States considers that the only apparent change over 15 years of ban is the relabeling of its application from "definitive" to "provisional". The United States is of the view that 15 years is not a reasonable period of time especially given

---

[712] EC's first written submission, para. 17.

the fact that the ban addresses substances as intensively reviewed and studied as the five hormones at issue.

7.588 The **European Communities** argues that, since the *EC – Hormones* case, the body of evidence has developed and, while still not providing enough knowledge to carry out a complete and definitive risk assessment, supports the conclusion that precautionary measures are required in order to achieve its chosen level of protection.

7.589 According to the European Communities, the evidence, while pointing to a number of risks, is full of gaps in pertinent information and important contradictions have developed that render no longer valid the conclusions reached by JECFA in 1988, 1999 and 2000, thus not allowing a quantitative or qualitative risk assessment. According to the European Communities, a number of significant scientific developments, taken together with all other available evidence, indicates that it is not possible to undertake a definitive risk assessment for the five hormones concerned.

(iii)   Approach of the Panel

7.590 As a first remark, the Panel recalls its conclusion that the measure at issue, to the extent that it provisionally bans the import of meat from cattle treated with the hormones progesterone, testosterone, trenbolone acetate, melengestrol acetate and zeranol, is an SPS measure within the meaning of Article 1 of, and paragraph 1 of Annex A to, the *SPS Agreement*.[713]

7.591 Second, both parties address the issue of the compatibility of the provisional ban on the above-mentioned five hormones with the provisions of Article 5.7 of the *SPS Agreement*. None of the parties discussed the compatibility of the ban imposed with respect to these five hormones with Article 5.1.[714] The Panel will therefore limit its review to the conformity of the EC ban on the five hormones with the requirements of Article 5.7.

7.592 Article 5.7 of the *SPS Agreement* provides as follows:

---

[713] See para. 7.434 above.

[714] The Panel asked a question to the parties on a possible "automatic" violation of Articles 2.2 and 5.1 as a result of a violation of Article 5.7 (second series of questions from the Panel to the parties, question 2). The Panel notes, however, that neither the European Communities nor the United States requested the Panel to review the compatibility of the EC implementing measure regarding the five hormones subject to a provisional ban with Article 5.1 or Article 2.2. The Panel also notes that the EC implementing measure is supposed to have removed the violation of Article 5.1 through the adoption of a provisional ban compatible with Article 5.7. In light of our approach to the aspect of this case relating to the compatibility of the EC implementing measure with the *SPS Agreement*, we decided to limit our review to the compatibility of the "provisional ban" with Article 5.7.

"In cases where relevant scientific evidence is insufficient, a Member may provisionally adopt sanitary ... measures on the basis of available pertinent information, including that from the relevant international organizations as well as from sanitary ... measures applied by other Members. In such circumstances, Members shall seek to obtain the additional information necessary for a more objective assessment of risks and review the sanitary ... measure accordingly within a reasonable period of time."

7.593 In *Japan – Agricultural Products II*, the Appellate Body recalled that Article 5.7 "set[s] out four requirements that must be satisfied in order to adopt and maintain a provisional measure." These requirements are:

(a)   the measure is imposed in respect to a situation where "relevant scientific evidence is insufficient";

(b)   the measure is adopted "on the basis of available pertinent information";

(c)   the Member which adopted the measure must "seek to obtain the additional information necessary for a more objective assessment of risk"; and

(d)   the Member which adopted the measure must "review the ... measure accordingly within a reasonable period of time".[715]

7.594 The Appellate Body noted that the four requirements are "clearly cumulative in nature", and that "[w]henever *one* of these four requirements is not met, the measure at issue is inconsistent with Article 5.7."[716]

7.595 The Panel recalls that previous panels have addressed each of these requirements successively. Having regard to our duty to review the situation for each of the five hormones concerned by the provisional ban, we will proceed first with the examination of the requirement under (a) above, i.e. whether the measure is imposed with respect to a situation where "relevant scientific evidence is insufficient".

7.596 Moreover, having regard to the arguments of the parties and in line with our duty not to perform a *de novo* risk assessment, we will limit ourselves to review the issues with respect to which the parties exchanged arguments and provided sufficient evidence.

7.597 We also note that the United States' main line of argumentation is based on the fact that "international standards and a significant body of scientific stud-

---

[715] See Appellate Body Report on *Japan – Apples*, para. 176, citing the Appellate Body Report on *Japan – Agricultural Products II*, para. 89.
[716] Appellate Body Report on *Japan – Agricultural Products II*, para. 89.

ies exist on the risks posed by each hormone. [JECFA] and several national regulatory bodies have determined that the scientific evidence regarding these hormones is adequate or sufficient to conduct a risk assessment."[717] In that context, we deem it appropriate to determine to what extent relevant scientific evidence can become insufficient within the meaning of Article 5.7 in the presence of international standards.

7.598 The Panel does not believe that the issue of the possibility or not to make a *quantitative* estimate of the risk to consumers constitutes a subject on which a discussion of whether "relevant scientific evidence is insufficient" is needed. The Panel recalls in this respect that the standard applied by the Appellate Body to determine whether relevant scientific evidence is insufficient is that:

> "relevant scientific evidence" will be "insufficient" within the meaning of Article 5.7 if the body of available scientific evidence does not allow, *in quantitative or qualitative terms*, the performance of an adequate assessment of risks as required under Article 5.1 and as defined in Annex A to the *SPS Agreement*."[718]

7.599 Moreover, we note that the Appellate Body considered that Article 5.1 does not require that risk assessments be quantitative, but that qualitative risk assessments are also compatible with Article 5.1.[719] We recall in this regard that Codex itself does not necessarily require the performance of quantitative risk assessments.[720]

7.600 We also deem it important to recall that, in *Japan – Agricultural Products II*, the Appellate Body stated that:

> "Article 5.7 allows members to adopt provisional SPS measures '[i]n case where relevant scientific evidence is insufficient' and certain other requirements are fulfilled. Article 5.7 operates as a qualified exemption from the obligation under Article 2.2 not to maintain SPS measures without sufficient scientific evidence. An overly broad and flexible interpretation of that obligation would render Article 5.7 meaningless."[721]

---

[717] US's second written submission, para. 29.
[718] Appellate Body Report on *Japan – Apples*, para. 179 (emphasis added).
[719] Appellate Body Report on *EC – Hormones*, para.187.
[720] Working Principles for Risk Analysis for Application within the Framework of the Codex Alimentarius, para. 20.
[721] Appellate Body Report on *Japan – Agricultural Products II*, para. 80.

7.601 The European Communities also refers to paragraphs 194 (on minority scientific views) and 205 (on Article 5.2 and good veterinary practices) of the report of the Appellate Body in *EC – Hormones*.

7.602 We have already addressed above[722] the question of the treatment of minority views among experts and do not find it necessary to come back on this matter. As far as the second issue is concerned, we note that, as recalled by the Appellate Body in *EC – Hormones*, it is also appropriate for the European Communities to consider situations of misuse:

> "... The *SPS Agreement* requires assessment of the potential for adverse effects on human health arising from the presence of contaminants and toxins in food. We consider that the object and purpose of the *SPS Agreement* justify the examination and evaluation of all such risks for human health whatever their precise and immediate origin may be. We do not mean to suggest that risks arising from potential abuse in the administration of controlled substances and from control problems need to be, or should be, evaluated by risk assessors in each and every case. When and if risks of these types do in fact arise, risk assessors may examine and evaluate them. Clearly, the necessity or propriety of examination and evaluation of such risks would have to be addressed on a case-by-case basis. What, in our view, is a fundamental legal error is to exclude, on an *a priori* basis, any such risks from the scope of application of Articles 5.1 and 5.2 ..."[723]

7.603 The above statement was made in relation to the performance of a risk assessment under Article 5.1 and 5.2 of the *SPS Agreement*. We recall that Article 5.7 is applicable when relevant scientific evidence is not sufficient to undertake a risk assessment in conformity with Article 5.1. Whether instances of misuse or abuse in the administration of hormones exist or not is not as such a scientific issue likely to make a risk assessment within the meaning of Article 5.1 and Annex A(4) of the *SPS Agreement* impossible. In our opinion, the scientific issue is related to the effect of the ingestion of high doses of hormones residues, not to potential or actual misuse or abuse in the administration of hormones. Therefore, we will not address the issue of non compliance with good veterinary practices in our analysis under Article 5.7 of the *SPS Agreement*.

---

[722] See para. 7.420 above.

[723] Appellate Body Report on *EC – Hormones*, para. 206. See also Appellate Body Report on *Japan – Apples*, para. 179.

>   (iv)   When will "relevant scientific evidence" be
>   deemed "insufficient"?

> Effect of the level of protection on the consideration of the insuffi-
> ciency of relevant scientific evidence under Article 5.7

7.604   According to the **European Communities**, whether a risk assessment can reach a definitive conclusion depends not only on the data available but also on how a risk assessment has been framed by the risk manager.[724] The European Communities argues that a Member may disagree with the risk assessment underlying an international standard for scientific reasons and, in particular, on the issue of whether the scientific evidence relied upon is sufficient. Such a disagreement may result from the fact that in order to meet a higher level of protection, a Member may require more information than that provided.[725] The European Communities argues that the evidence which served as the basis for the 1988 and 1999-2000 JECFA evaluations is not sufficient "to perform a definitive risk assessment within the meaning of Article 5.7, in particular by the WTO Members applying a high level of health protection of no risk from exposure to unnecessary additional residues in meat of animals treated with hormones for growth promotion".[726]

7.605   The **Panel** first notes that the European Communities refers to the fact that the evidence is not sufficient to perform a "definitive risk assessment". However, the European Communities nowhere defines what it means by a "definitive risk assessment". The Panel recalls the definition of adequate risk assessment proposed by the European Communities in *EC – Approval and Marketing of Biotech Products*: "one which has been 'delivered by a reputable source, [which] unequivocally informs the legislator about what the risk is with a sufficient degree of precision, and [which] has withstood the passage of time and is unlikely to be revised'."[727] It is unclear to the Panel whether this is what the European Communities refers to in this case as a "definitive risk assessment". The Panel would like to specify that there is no obligation under the *SPS Agreement* to perform a *definitive* risk assessment for that risk assessment to be valid under Article 5.1. Moreover, the Panel doubts that a *definitive* risk assessment can in practice ever be performed, since new evidence becomes available and risk assessments may need to be reviewed and updated accordingly, or else the measure based on these risk assessments will have to be adjusted to the evolution of the scientific evidence.[728] The Panel understands the terms "based

---

[724]   EC's oral statement at the second substantive meeting, para. 22.

[725]   EC's replies to Panel questions after the first substantive meeting, question 72, Annex B-1, para. 266.

[726]   EC's second written submission, para. 149; EC's replies to Panel questions after the first substantive meeting, question 31, Annex B-1, paras. 167-172.

[727]   Panel Report in *EC – Approval and Marketing of Biotech Products*, para. 7.3238.

[728]   See Panel Report in *EC – Approval and Marketing of Biotech Products*, paras. 7.3239-7.3240.

on an assessment, as appropriate to the circumstances" to suggest that the link between the SPS measure adopted by a Member and the risk assessment on which it is based may evolve depending on the circumstances, thus implying that Article 5.1 does not require a definitive risk assessment. This is also confirmed by the fact that risk assessments do not have to be "monolithic" as recalled by the Appellate Body in *EC – Hormones*.[729] In any event, the criterion allowing the adoption of sanitary measures on the basis of available pertinent information under Article 5.7 is that "relevant scientific evidence is insufficient" to permit the performance of a risk assessment as required under Article 5.1 and Annex A(4), not that the risk assessment to be performed pursuant to Article 5.1 be a definitive one.[730] The Panel is of the view that, by suggesting that a risk assessment be definitive, the European Communities actually disregards the Appellate Body interpretation mentioned above and seeks to impose a higher threshold for compliance with Article 5.1, or a lower one to meet the conditions of Article 5.7. However, the Panel does not believe that this approach is supported by Article 5.1, Annex A(4) or Article 5.7.

7.606 The Panel also notes the EC view that, in determining whether the relevant scientific evidence is insufficient, within the meaning of Article 5.7, the Panel should take into account the level of health protection applied by the Member concerned. More particularly, the European Communities argue that, when the level of health protection of a Member is particularly high and the body of evidence is in the process of moving from a state of sufficiency to a state of insufficiency, that Member should not be required to demonstrate positively the existence of a clear harm.

7.607 Regarding the issue of whether the level of health protection of a particular Member should play a role in its assessment of whether the relevant scientific evidence is insufficient, the Panel notes that the EC level of health protection is that of "no (avoidable) risk, that is a level of protection that does not allow any unnecessary addition from exposure to genotoxic chemical substances that are intended to be added deliberately to food."[731]

7.608 We recall that the Appellate Body in *Japan – Apples* stated that relevant scientific evidence will be insufficient within the meaning of Article 5.7 if the

---

[729] Appellate Body Report on *EC – Hormones*, para. 194.
[730] The Panel notes in this respect that in *Australia – Salmon*, the Appellate Body stated that:
"We might add that the existence of unknown and uncertain elements does not justify a departure from the requirements of Articles 5.1, 5.2 and 5.3, read together with paragraph 4 of Annex A, for a risk assessment."(Appellate Body Report on *Australia – Salmon*, para. 130).
The Panel also notes Dr. Boisseau's remark, that "it is always possible to ask for more data in order to clarify more issues so that the will to eliminate any scientific uncertainty could result in an endless assessment process." Replies by the scientific experts to Panel questions, Annex D, para. 452.
[731] EC's replies to Panel questions after the second substantive meeting, Annex C-1, para. 69.

body of available scientific evidence does not allow, in quantitative or qualitative terms, the performance of an adequate assessment of risks as required under Article 5.1 and as defined in Annex A to the *SPS Agreement*.[732]

7.609 The terms of Article 5.1 and Annex A to the *SPS Agreement* and, in particular, the definition of "risk assessment" do not indicate that a Member's level of protection is pertinent to determine whether a risk assessment can be performed or not. We agree with the Panel in *EC – Approval and Marketing of Biotech Products* when it states that:

> "[W]e are not convinced that the protection goals pursued by a legislator are relevant to such a determination. The protection goals of a legislator may have a bearing on the question of which risks a Member decides to assess with a view to taking regulatory action, if necessary. And a legislator protection goals are certainly relevant to the determination of the measure ... to be taken for achieving a Member's level of protection against risk. Yet there is no apparent link between a legislator's protection goals and the task of assessing the existence and magnitude of potential risks."[733]

7.610 We note that sufficient scientific evidence is what is needed to make a risk assessment. The assessment whether there is sufficient scientific evidence or not to perform a risk assessment should be an objective process. The level of protection defined by each Member may be relevant to determine the measure to be selected to address the assessed risk, but it should not influence the performance of the risk assessment as such.

7.611 Indeed, whether a Member considers that its population should be exposed or not to a particular risk, or at what level, is not relevant to determining whether a risk exists and what its magnitude is. *A fortiori*, it should have no effect on whether there is sufficient evidence of the existence and magnitude of this risk.

7.612 A risk-averse Member may be inclined to take a protective position when considering the measure to be adopted. However, the determination of whether scientific evidence is sufficient to assess the existence and magnitude of a risk must be disconnected from the intended level of protection.

7.613 This is not to say, however, that we disagree with the European Communities that when the body of evidence is in the process of moving from a state of

---

[732] Appellate Body Report on *Japan – Apples*, para. 179.
[733] Panel Report on *EC – Approval and Marketing of Biotech Products*, para. 7.3238.

sufficiency to a state of insufficiency a Member should not be required "to demonstrate positively the existence of clear harm."[734] In fact, even when the scientific evidence is sufficient, a Member is not required, under the provisions of the *SPS Agreement*, to "demonstrate positively the existence of a clear harm". Rather, the objective of a risk assessment is to evaluate the potential for harm to occur under certain circumstances (e.g., from the consumption of a foodstuff containing certain contaminants).

Can relevant scientific evidence *become* "insufficient"?

7.614 The **United States** notes, and the European Communities agrees, that the Appellate Body clarified in *Japan – Apples* that relevant scientific evidence will be insufficient within the meaning of Article 5.7 if the body of available scientific evidence does not allow, in quantitative or qualitative terms, the performance of an adequate assessment of risks as required under Article 5.1. According to the United States, there is more than sufficient evidence to allow performance of an adequate risk assessment for the five provisionally banned hormones.[735] The United States argues that the relevant question is not the specificity of the evidence relating to the five hormones, but whether the evidence *in toto* permits the European Communities to conduct a risk assessment for those hormones.[736] The United States recalls that JECFA has performed risk assessments for the hormones at issue and concludes that, in the case at hand, while any new studies could hypothetically affect the conclusion of the risk assessment, their existence would not make the scientific evidence "insufficient" for conducting such an assessment.[737]

7.615 The **European Communities** considers that Article 5.7 of the *SPS Agreement* is applicable not only when no risk assessment can be made at all, but also when the latest scientific evidence from any credible and objective source raises doubts or puts into question the previously held scientific opinion about the safety or dangerous nature of the substance in question.[738] The European Communities adds that the evidence assessed by the SCVPH, while inconclusive in terms of demonstrating a risk, does nonetheless point to the possible occurrence of certain adverse effects, which invalidate or put into serious doubt previously held assumptions about the safety of these hormones by the defending parties and Codex/JECFA.[739] The European Communities concludes that serious doubt may exist when the pertinent available evidence is contradictory,

---

[734] EC's second written submission, para. 149.
[735] US's first written submission, para. 124; US's second written submission, para. 28; EC's second written submission, para. 134.
[736] US's replies to Panel questions after the first substantive meeting, Annex B-3, para. 67.
[737] US's replies to Panel questions after the first substantive meeting, Annex B-3, para. 68.
[738] EC's replies to Panel questions after the first substantive meeting, question 67, Annex B-1.
[739] EC's second written submission, para. 181.

inconclusive or incomplete.[740] To guard against potential abuses, the new evidence should not be arbitrary but credible and should show that there is a genuine scientific disagreement identified in a risk assessment.

7.616 The European Communities further argues that, due to the dynamic nature of scientific knowledge, a risk assessment that may at one point in time have been based on sufficient scientific evidence may need to be reviewed when new scientific evidence becomes available. In addition, new international risk assessment standards may become available that have to be taken into account in new risk assessments.[741]

7.617 The **United States** acknowledges that scientific evidence that at one point in time might be sufficient to conduct a risk assessment could be insufficient at a later point, for example if a new pathway for a risk came to light on which information was insufficient.[742] The United States recalls that in the *EC – Hormones* case, the European Communities argued that its ban on all six hormones was definitive, and that it was based on sufficient scientific evidence. The United States considers that nothing has occurred in the interim to render insufficient the scientific evidence on the safety of residues of the five provisionally banned hormones in meat products as a result of the cattle being treated with these hormones for growth promotion. According to the United States, studies completed since the *EC – Hormones* case, including by JECFA, reaffirm earlier conclusions.[743] The United States indicates that it did not uncover any new evidence of risk when reviewing the European Communities' 17 studies and other materials put forward by the European Communities.[744]

7.618 In response to this argument, the **European Communities** recalls that the Appellate Body had found that what the European Communities had considered sufficient evidence was in fact insufficient, and that this had been confirmed by risk assessment standards developed in the years after the *EC – Hormones* ruling. The European Communities also argues that the body of evidence has developed in the meantime. While the evidence is still insufficient to carry out a "complete and definitive risk assessment", it "supports the conclusion that pre-

---

[740] EC's replies to Panel questions after the second substantive meeting, Annex C-1, para. 43.

[741] EC's replies to Panel questions after the first substantive meeting, Annex B-1, para. 268-273.

[742] US's replies to Panel questions after the first substantive meeting, question 73, Annex B-3, para. 82.

[743] US's first written submission, paras. 125-128.

[744] US's second written submission para. 29; US oral statement at the second substantive meeting, 3 October 2006, para. 20.

cautionary measures are required in order to achieve its chosen level of protection".[745]

7.619 First, the **Panel** notes that parties agree to the fact that scientific evidence which was previously deemed sufficient could subsequently become insufficient. Both parties agree that there could be situations where new studies can affect the conclusion of existing risk assessments. The United States considers, however, that in the case at hand the existence of such new studies would not make the scientific evidence "insufficient" for conducting such an assessment.

7.620 The Panel agrees with the parties that there could be situations where existing scientific evidence can be put in question by new studies and information. There could even be situations where evidence which supported a risk assessment is unsettled by new studies which do not constitute sufficient relevant scientific evidence as such to support a risk assessment but are sufficient to make the existing, previously relevant scientific evidence insufficient.[746]

7.621 Indeed, nothing in Article 5.7 prevents such an interpretation. We also note in this respect that Article 2.2 foresees such a possibility when it mentions that sanitary measures must not be "*maintained* without sufficient scientific evidence except as provided for in paragraph 7 of Article 5."[747] The use of the word "maintained" read together with the reference to Article 5.7 suggests the possibility of an evolution from a situation of sufficient evidence to perform a risk assessment to one where, in substance, a risk assessment can no longer be performed.

7.622 The Panel notes in this respect that a procedure is available for Codex members and observers to request the inclusion of a particular compound for evaluation or re-evaluation on a "priority list" that the Codex Committee on Residues of Veterinary Drugs in Foods (CCRVDF) communicates to JECFA.[748] The European Communities refers to an exchange of letters between the European Commission and Codex and JECFA regarding a postponement of the re-evaluation due to be carried out by JECFA in 1999.[749] The European Communities seems to allege that there was a commitment from Codex and JECFA to re-evaluate the hormones at issue once the studies commissioned by the European

---

[745] EC's second written submission para. 137; EC's replies to Panel questions after the first substantive meeting, question 19, Annex B-1, paras. 108-109.

[746] See also Article 2.2 which provides that a sanitary measure must not be maintained without sufficient scientific evidence except as provided for in paragraph 7 of Article 5. This seems to imply that the information relied upon under Article 5.7 may include evidence, including relevant scientific evidence and not merely information, as long as that evidence remains insufficient.

[747] Emphasis added.

[748] Statement by Dr. Miyagishima, Codex representative, transcript of the Panel meeting with the experts, Annex G, paras. 523-524.

[749] Exhibit EC-63.

Communities would be available.[750] However, this explanation was not confirmed by Codex or JECFA. From the information communicated by the representatives of Codex and JECFA at the meeting of the Panel with scientific experts, it appears on the contrary that the European Communities never actually
requested Codex or JECFA to re-evaluate any of the hormones for which risk
assessments had been carried out by JECFA and standards adopted by Codex.
The representative of Codex stated that there was no record in the reports of the
CCRVDF of proposals, either from the European Communities or from Member
States of the European Communities to include the five substances at issue in the
priority list for re-evaluation by JECFA.[751] The representative of Codex added
that, even at the latest session of the CCRVDF in 2006, no such request had been
made.[752]

7.623 Second, since the present situation is one where it is alleged that existing
relevant scientific evidence has become insufficient, it seems important to determine which circumstances could make such existing evidence insufficient.

7.624 The Panel recalls that, in *Japan – Apples*, the Appellate Body found that:

> " '[R]elevant scientific evidence' will be 'insufficient' within the
> meaning of Article 5.7 if the body of available scientific evidence
> does not allow, in quantitative or qualitative terms, the perform-
> ance of an adequate assessment of risks as required under Arti-
> cle 5.1 and as defined in Annex A to the *SPS Agreement*. Thus, the
> question is not whether there is sufficient evidence of a general na-
> ture or whether there is sufficient evidence related to a specific as-
> pect of a phytosanitary problem, or a specific risk. The question is
> whether the relevant evidence, be it 'general' or 'specific', in the
> Panel's parlance, is sufficient to permit the evaluation of the likeli-
> hood of entry, establishment or spread of, in this case, fire blight
> in Japan."[753]

---

[750] EC statement, Transcript of the Panel meeting with the experts, Annex G, para. 527.
[751] Statement by Dr. Miyagishima, Codex representative, transcript of the Panel meeting with the experts, Annex G, para. 524.
[752] Statement by Dr. Miyagishima, Codex representative, transcript of the Panel meeting with the experts, Annex G, para. 529.
[753] Appellate Body Report on *Japan – Apples*, para. 179.

7.625 We also note that in *EC – Approval and Marketing of Biotech Products*, the panel stated that:

> "[I]t must be determined on a case-by-case basis whether the body of available scientific evidence is insufficient to permit the performance of a risk assessment."

7.626 We agree with the *EC – Approval and Marketing of Biotech Products* panel and we will base our assessment on the evidence submitted by the parties in this case, having regard to the views of the experts on each issue.

7.627 This said, the Panel believes that it needs to determine under which circumstances relevant scientific evidence may more particularly be deemed "insufficient" in this case.

7.628 The Panel first reads the first sentence from the extract of the Appellate Body report in *Japan – Apples* quoted above as meaning that relevant scientific evidence will be deemed insufficient within the meaning of Article 5.7 if the relevant scientific evidence does not make it possible to complete a risk assessment on which a sanitary measure can be based *in substance*. It is always possible to perform the four successive steps of a risk assessment as defined by Codex and ultimately reach the conclusion that relevant scientific evidence is insufficient (as the European Communities did in the case of the five hormones in respect of which it applies a provisional ban). However, the fact that the Codex four steps can be formally completed does not mean that such a process is equated with a risk assessment within the meaning of Article 5.1 and Annex A(4) of the *SPS Agreement*. There will be a risk assessment within the meaning of Article 5.1 and Annex A(4) of the *SPS Agreement* when the assessor has analysed fully the potential for the identified adverse effects to arise from the presence of the substance at issue in food, beverages, or foodstuffs. We believe that this was the intention of the Appellate Body when it used the term *adequate*[754] in "adequate assessment of risks as required under Article 5.1 and as defined in Annex A to the *SPS Agreement*." This is confirmed by the second sentence of Article 5.7 which provides that "Members shall seek to obtain the additional information necessary for a *more objective assessment* of risk."[755] In other words, Article 5.7 will apply in situations where, in substance, the relevant scientific evidence does not allow the completion of an objective evaluation of the potential for adverse effects on human or animal health arising from the presence of additives, contaminants, toxins or disease-causing organisms in food, beverages or feedstuffs.

---

[754] "commensurate in fitness, sufficient, satisfactory" (*The Shorter Oxford English Dictionary*, fifth ed., 2002, p. 26).
[755] Emphasis added.

7.629 While this gives a general idea of the circumstances under which Article 5.7 may be invoked, we should strive to ascertain more precisely the scope of "insufficient", if possible. In doing that, we should keep in mind that Article 5.7 operates as a qualified exemption from the obligation under Article 2.2 not to maintain SPS measures without sufficient scientific evidence and that an overly broad and flexible interpretation of that obligation would render Article 5.7 meaningless.[756]

7.630 As a first step, we note that, in *Japan – Apples*, the Appellate Body seemed to consider that *relevant* scientific evidence is insufficient if, irrespective of the quantity of evidence available, it has not led to *reliable* or *conclusive* results.[757] It also seems that evidence providing unreliable or inconclusive results should not be confused with "scientific uncertainty", as it appears from the following Appellate Body statement in *Japan – Apples*:

> "The application of Article 5.7 is triggered not by the existence of scientific uncertainty, but rather by the insufficiency of scientific evidence. The text of Article 5.7 is clear: it refers to 'cases where relevant scientific evidence is insufficient', not to 'scientific uncertainty'. The two concepts are not interchangeable."[758]

7.631 We understand this statement to mean that the existence of scientific uncertainty does not automatically amount to a situation of insufficiency of relevant scientific evidence. In other words, the fact that a number of aspects of a given scientific issue remain uncertain may not prevent the performance of a risk assessment. First, we should exclude theoretical uncertainty, which is the uncertainty that always remains because science can never provide absolute certainty about the safety of a given substance. In *EC – Hormones*, the panel and the Appellate Body concurred in agreeing that theoretical uncertainty was not the kind of risk to be assessed under Article 5.1.[759] In the Panel's view, theoretical uncertainly therefore should also not determine the applicability of Article 5.7.

7.632 Second, we note that in *EC – Hormones*, the Appellate Body stated that the presence of divergent views on an issue could be a form of scientific uncertainty.[760] We nevertheless note that scientific uncertainty may be factored into

---

[756] Appellate Body Report on *Japan – Agricultural Products II*, para. 80.
[757] Appellate Body Report on *Japan – Apples*, para. 185:
"We do not read the Panel's interpretation as excluding cases where the available evidence is more than minimal in quantity, but has not led to reliable or conclusive results."
[758] Appellate Body Report on *Japan – Apples*, para. 184.
[759] Appellate Body Report on *EC – Hormones*, para. 186.
[760] Appellate Body Report on *EC – Hormones*, para. 194.

the conclusions of the risk assessment. We find support for this conclusion in the following comment of the Appellate Body in *Australia – Salmon*:

> "We might add that the existence of unknown and uncertain elements does not justify a departure from the requirements of Articles 5.1, 5.2 and 5.3, read together with paragraph 4 of Annex A, for a risk assessment."[761]

7.633   This issue was further addressed by the panel in *EC – Approval and Marketing of Biotech Products*, which acknowledged that the conclusions of a risk assessment may not be free from uncertainties or other constraints even though there was sufficient relevant scientific evidence to perform the risk assessment.[762] The panel, in agreement with the Appellate Body in *EC – Hormones*, found "that such uncertainties may be legitimately taken into account by a Member when determining the SPS measure, if any, to be taken" and that the scientific uncertainties present in a risk assessment may support a range of possible measures and within the range of measures reasonably supported by the risk assessment and consistent with other applicable *SPS Agreement* provisions, the Member was entitled to choose one that best protects human health and/or the environment.[763] As recalled by the panel in *EC – Approval and Marketing of Biotech Products*, Members were also justified in taking into account factors like a limited body of relevant scientific evidence, assumptions and other constraints that would affect the level of confidence in the risk assessment:

> "We consider that if there are factors which affect scientists' level of confidence in a risk assessment they have carried out[764], a Member may in principle take this into account in determining the measure to be applied for achieving its appropriate level of protection from risks.[765] Thus, there may conceiva-

---

[761]   Appellate Body Report on *Australia – Salmon*, para. 130.

[762]   Panel Report on *EC – Approval and Marketing of Biotech Products*, para. 7.1525.

[763]   Panel Report on *EC – Approval and Marketing of Biotech Products*, para. 7.1525.

[764]   (*footnote original*) E.g., a limited body of relevant scientific evidence may be such a factor.

[765]   (*footnote original*) This view is consistent with risk assessment techniques established by relevant international organizations. For instance, the *Working Principles for Risk Analysis for Application in the Framework of the Codex Alimentarius* state that "[t]he report of the risk assessment should indicate any constraints, uncertainties, assumptions and their impact on the risk assessment. Minority opinions should also be recorded. The responsibility for resolving the impact of uncertainty on the risk management decision lies with the risk manager, not the risk assessors". Codex Alimentarius Commission, *Working Principles for Risk Analysis for Application in the Framework of the Codex Alimentarius* (adopted in June/July 2003), Section III, Codex Procedural Manual, 14th edition, 2004, para. 25. Along similar lines, the Codex *Principles for the Risk Analysis of Foods Derived from Modern Biotechnology* state that "[r]isk managers should take into account the uncertainties identified in the risk assessment and implement appropriate measures to manage these uncertainties". Codex Alimentarius Commission, *Principles for the Risk Analysis of Foods Derived from Modern Biotechnology* (adopted in June/July 2003), CAC/GL 44-2003, para. 18. Similarly, the IPPC's ISPM #11 (2001)

bly be cases where a Member which follows a precautionary approach, and which confronts a risk assessment that identifies uncertainties[766] or constraints, would be justified in applying (i) an SPS measure even though another Member might not decide to apply any SPS measure on the basis of the same risk assessment, or (ii) an SPS measure which is stricter than the SPS measure applied by another Member to address the same risk".[767]

7.634 The panel explicitly recognized that, even though scientific uncertainty existed, there could still be sufficient scientific evidence to perform a risk assessment.[768]

7.635 We note in this respect the comments of Dr. Boisseau and Dr. Boobis before the Panel on how scientific uncertainty is addressed in risk assessment.[769]

---

states in relevant part that "[t]he uncertainty noted in the assessments of economic consequences and probability of introduction should also be considered and included in the selection of a pest management option". IPPC, ISPM #11: *Pest Risk Analysis for Quarantine Pests*, April 2001, para. 3. The quoted passage stayed the same in the 2004 version of ISPM #11, which applies specifically to living modified organisms.

[766] (*footnote original*) We are not referring here to the theoretical uncertainty which inevitably remains because science can never provide absolute certainty that a product will never have adverse effects on human health or the environment. The Appellate Body has made it clear that this theoretical uncertainty is not the kind of risk which is to be assessed under Article 5.1. Appellate Body Report on *EC – Hormones*, para. 186.

[767] Panel Report on *EC – Approval and Marketing of Biotech Products Products*, para. 7.3065.

[768] Panel Report on *EC – Approval and Marketing of Biotech Products Products*, para. 7.1525.

[769] See replies of Dr. Boisseau and Dr. Boobis to question 12 of the Panel, Annex D, paras. 123-128. Dr. Boisseau expressed the following views:

> "In assessing the risk for human health associated with the exposure to veterinary drug residues, JECFA adresses the scientific uncertainty by using the safety factors listed above in my reply to the question n°8 describing, among others, how JECFA builds a margin of safety into its final recommendations.
>
> For the hormonal growth promoters, JECFA has considered that, given the quality and the quantity of the available data, it was possible to carry out a complete quantitative risk assessment. For establishing ADIs and MRLs for the three synthetic hormones, melengestrol, trenbolone and zeranol, JECFA has implemented the usual procedure regarding the safety factors. For the three natural hormones, oestradiol-17β, progesterone and testosterone, JECFA has decided that the margin of safety deriving from the values of the established ADIs and from a maximum estimated intake of residue was such that it was not necessary to set up MRLs.
>
> For oestradiol-17β, the European Communities did not consider any scientific uncertainty as it decided that it was not possible, for reason of principle, to establish an ADI for a genotoxic compound. For the five other hormones at issue, the European Communities did not really consider any scientific uncertainty as it decided that the available data were too limited to allow a complete quantitative risk assessment to be carried out."

Dr. Boobis mentioned the following:

7.636 We find further support for this position in the view of the Appellate Body as expressed in *Japan – Apples* that whether relevant scientific evidence is insufficient must be assessed "not in the abstract, but in the light of a particular inquiry".[770]

7.637 While we agree that under certain circumstances what was previously sufficient evidence could become insufficient, we do not believe that the existence of scientific uncertainty means that previously sufficient evidence has in

---

"Scientific uncertainty is dealt with in a variety of ways in risk assessment. ...
One way of dealing with uncertainty is to default to the worst case in the absence of evidence to the contrary. Hence, the most sensitive relevant endpoint in the most sensitive species is used as the basis of the risk assessment. In extrapolating to humans a default factor of 10 is used to allow for species differences, which assumes that humans are more sensitive than the experimental species. A further factor of 10 is included for interindividual differences. These differences may be due to gender, genetics, life stage or other factors. However, to some extent such differences have already been taken into account in the choice of endpoint, as this will usually represent the most sensitive lifestage, gender and to some extent genetics by using data from the most sensitive species. Where there are additional uncertainties, such as no NOEAL or the absence of a non-critical study, an additional safety factor will be included, and this is almost always conservative, as when the data gaps have been completed, the appropriate safety factor is almost always less than that used to account for these data gaps. The residue may be assumed to be all as active as the most active moiety, which is almost always a conservative assumption. Dietary intake is based on conservative data for food consumption. It is also assumed that all meat that could contain veterinary drug residue will contain the residue and that this will be present at the high end of the range (MRL or other appropriate level). In respect of the ADI, the assumption is that intake will be at this high level for a lifetime, when in reality there will be occasions when little or no meat is consumed or that which is consumed contains less or even no residue. In their risk assessment of the hormones, JECFA applied all of these approaches to dealing with the uncertainty.
In dealing with scientific uncertainty much depends on the expert judgment of the risk assessor. Issues such as biological coherence, whether effects are considered compound related, relevance to humans, the reliability of model systems at predicting effects in vivo all impact on the interpretation of the data. Within the EU, it is clear that there are also differences in the interpretation of data, as illustrated by the differing conclusions of the CVMP (1999) and the SCVPH (1999). In part, the EC assessment of the hormones did not go as far as including some of the considerations for uncertainty used by JECFA because of the conclusion that there was insufficient information to determine whether there was a threshold for the carcinogenic effects. However, for some of the compounds this was based on the results of a small number of non-standard tests of genotoxicity, with equivocal of very weak responses. It is not clear whether the EC applied a weight of evidence approach to evaluating the genotoxicity of all of the compounds, taking account the totality of the available data, as was the case by JECFA."

[770] Appellate Body Report on *Japan – Apples*, para. 179. See also Panel Report on *EC – Approval and Marketing of Biotech Products*, where the Panel "agree[ed] that it must be determined on a case-by-case basis whether the body of available scientific evidence is insufficient to permit the performance of a risk assessment." (para. 7.3238).

fact become insufficient nor should it *ipso facto* justify the applicability of Article 5.7 of the *SPS Agreement.*

Relationship between insufficiency of the evidence and the existence of an international standard

7.638 The **United States** considers that international standards serve as an indicator that evidence is sufficient to conduct a risk assessment, but since Members may be able to react more quickly to new information than international standard setting bodies, the existence of international standards is not dispositive under Article 5.7.[771] Although there can be situations where there is insufficient scientific information for a Member to perform a risk assessment even when an international standard exists, in this case international standards and a significant body of scientific studies exist on the risks posed by each of the five hormones, including the JECFA reports and the studies cited therein. According to the United States, it would therefore in this case be very difficult to demonstrate that scientific evidence concerning the hormones at issue is insufficient in the context of Article 5.7.[772]

7.639 The United States argues that JECFA and several national regulatory bodies have determined that the scientific evidence regarding the five provisionally banned hormones is sufficient, and have completed risk assessments on this basis. According to the United States, the European Communities fails to support its argument that the evidence is insufficient to complete a risk assessment with scientific evidence demonstrating risks to consumers from the five hormones when used for growth promotion purposes according to good veterinary practices.

7.640 The **European Communities** notes that the United States acknowledges that there can be situations where there is insufficient scientific information even though a relevant international standard exists. Contrary to the United States, the European Communities believes this to be the case for the five provisionally banned hormones.[773] In addition, the European Communities argues that a Member may disagree with the risk assessment underlying an international standard for scientific reasons and, in particular, on the issue of whether the scientific evidence relied upon is sufficient. Such a disagreement may result from the fact that in order to meet a higher level of protection, a Member may require

---

[771] US's replies to Panel questions after the first substantive meeting, Annex B-3, para. 82.
[772] US's replies to Panel questions after the first substantive meeting, Annex B-3, para. 81.
[773] EC's second written submission, paras. 133-136.

more information than that provided for the development of the international standard.[774]

7.641 The European Communities further argues that the relevant Codex standards on four of the five provisionally banned hormones are not capable of achieving the chosen high level of protection of the European Communities. According to the European Communities, the overall evidence and recent scientific developments have now "tipped the balance against the previously held assumption (by the defending parties and Codex/JECFA) that residues of these hormones in meat from animals treated for growth promotion pose no risk to human health". The European Communities argues that the evidence which served as the basis for the 1999-2000 JECFA evaluations is not sufficient "to perform a definitive risk assessment within the meaning of Article 5.7, in particular by the WTO Members applying a high level of health protection of no risk from exposure to unnecessary additional residues in meat of animals treated with hormones for growth promotion".[775]

7.642 Referring to the way in which JECFA addresses scientific uncertainty through safety factors, the European Communities states that there is "almost universal agreement that this approach is not scientifically correct". According to the European Communities, a state of uncertainty may result from a number of factors including lacking, incomplete or contradictory data; the quality of the data is more important than the quantity. An issue thought to be clear can become uncertain as more data become available. The European Communities argues that if uncertainty is understood in this sense, it cannot be addressed through safety factors, especially for countries applying a high level of health protection.[776]

7.643 Having regard to the arguments of the parties, the **Panel** deems it important to recall that international standards, guidelines or recommendations exist with respect to four out of the five hormones at issue in this section.[777] The Panel

---

[774] EC's replies to Panel questions after the first substantive meeting, Annex B-1, para. 266.

[775] EC's second written submission, para. 149; EC's replies to Panel questions after the first substantive meeting, question 31, Annex B-1, paras. 167-172.

[776] EC's comments on experts replies to Panel question 12, Annex F-1.

[777] For melengestrol acetate, the situation is as follows: JECFA concluded its evaluation of MGA at its sixty-sixth meeting in Rome on 22-28 February 2006 and proposed MRLs. These MRLs were considered by CCRVDF in 2006, but because there was no consensus for their adoption, the CCRVDF agreed to consider them again at its session in 2007. (For more detail, including references to relevant Codex and JECFA reports, see Annex E-1, p. 103 and Annex E-2, p. 116). Annex A, paragraph 3 of the *SPS Agreement* defines international standards, guidelines and recommendations for food safety as follows:

"*International standards, guidelines and recommendations*

(a)   for food safety, the standards, guidelines and recommendations established by the Codex Alimentarius Commission relating to food additives, veterinary drug and pesticide residues, contaminants, methods of analysis and sampling, and codes and guidelines of hygienic practice".

notes in this respect the important role given to international standards, guidelines or recommendations by the *SPS Agreement*.[778] We also note that Article 3.2 of the *SPS Agreement* reads as follows:

> "Sanitary or phytosanitary measures which conform to international standards, guidelines or recommendations shall be deemed to be necessary to protect human, animal or plant life or health, and presumed to be consistent with the relevant provisions of this Agreement and of GATT 1994."

7.644 The presumption of consistency of measures conforming to international standards, guidelines and recommendations with the relevant provisions of the *SPS Agreement* implies that these standards, guidelines or recommendations, particularly those referred to in this case, are based on risk assessments that meet the requirements of the *SPS Agreement*. This means, therefore, that there was sufficient evidence for JECFA to undertake the appropriate risk assessments.

7.645 As mentioned above, the Panel is also mindful that science continuously evolves. It cannot be excluded that new scientific evidence or information call into question existing evidence. Likewise, it cannot be excluded that different risk assessments reach different interpretations of the same scientific evidence.

7.646 Yet, some meaning has to be given to the role assigned by the *SPS Agreement* to international standards, guidelines and recommendations, even though the rights of Members under Article 3.3 should be acknowledged[779], and this should not lead to the imposition of a special or generalized burden of proof upon the European Communities.[780]

---

[778] See Article 3.1 of the *SPS Agreement*, which reads as follows:
"To harmonize sanitary and phytosanitary measures on as wide a basis as possible, *Members shall base their sanitary or phytosanitary measures on international standards, guidelines or recommendations, where they exist*, except as otherwise provided for in this Agreement, and in particular in paragraph 3." (Emphasis added)

[779] See Appellate Body Report on *EC – Hormones*, para. 172. Article 3.3 of the *SPS Agreement* reads as follows:
"Members may introduce or maintain sanitary or phytosanitary measures which result in a higher level of sanitary or phytosanitary protection than would be achieved by measures based on the relevant international standards, guidelines or recommendations, if there is a scientific justification, or as a consequence of the level of sanitary or phytosanitary protection a Member determines to be appropriate in accordance with the relevant provisions of paragraphs 1 through 8 of Article 5. Notwithstanding the above, all measures which result in a level of sanitary or phytosanitary protection different from that which would be achieved by measures based on international standards, guidelines or recommendations shall not be inconsistent with any other provision of this Agreement." (original footnote omitted)

[780] Appellate Body Report on *EC – Hormones*, para. 102. Regarding the allocation of burden of proof in relation to the *SPS Agreement* in this case, see paras. 7.380-7.386 above.

7.647   As a result, we consider that, in order to properly take into account the existence of international standards, guidelines and recommendations in this case, our approach should be to assess whether scientific evidence has become insufficient by determining whether the European Communities has produced any evidence of some sufficient change in the scientific knowledge so that what was once sufficient to perform an adequate risk assessment has now become insufficient (i.e., "deficient in force, quality or amount").[781] In this respect, suggesting hypothetical correlations or merely arguing that there could be more evidence on one concern or another should not be deemed sufficient to successfully claim that relevant scientific evidence has become *insufficient*. Indeed, more studies can always be performed and there can always be more evidence. We note in this regard that the European Communities shares our position in its second written submission, where it makes a "brief description of insufficiency of *pertinent* scientific information for all five hormones (except oestradiol-17β)". We interpret the use of the word "pertinent" and not "relevant" as in Article 5.7 as meaning that the European Communities agrees that not any insufficiency of relevant scientific evidence would make the performance of a risk assessment impossible. Indeed, "insufficiencies in the evidence" does not necessarily equal "insufficient evidence" to do a risk assessment, as recalled above. Moreover, as mentioned by the Appellate Body in *EC – Hormones*, risk assessments do not need to be based on "monolithic" evidence.

Conclusion

7.648   We therefore conclude that if relevant evidence already exists, not any degree of insufficiency will satisfy the criterion under Article 5.7 that "relevant scientific evidence is insufficient". Having regard to our reasoning above, particularly with respect to scientific uncertainty and the existence of international standards, we consider that, depending on the existing relevant evidence, there must be a *critical mass* of new evidence and/or information that calls into question the fundamental precepts of previous knowledge and evidence so as to make relevant, previously sufficient, evidence now insufficient.[782] In the present case where risk assessments have been performed and a large body of quality evidence has been accumulated, this would be possible only if it put into question

---

[781]   *The New Shorter Oxford English Dictionary* (1993), p. 1384.

[782]   In its second written submission, at para. 149, the European Communities refers to the long latency period of cancer and the numerous confounding factors to claim that it may not be in a position to demonstrate the existence of a clear harm in case of cancer because of the long latency period and the numerous confounding factors that play a role in the development of cancer. We understand this argument to mean that we should accept the "new scientific reality" referred to by the European Communities as constituting a situation where relevant scientific evidence has become insufficient within the meaning of Article 5.7 of the *SPS Agreement*. We do not consider that our test amounts to requesting that the European Communities demonstrate the existence of a clear harm in order for Article 5.7 to apply to its measure. Under the "critical mass" test, the new scientific information and evidence must be such that they are at the origin of a change in the understanding of a scientific issue.

existing relevant evidence *to the point that* this evidence is no longer sufficient to support the conclusions of existing risks assessments. We therefore need to determine whether this is the case here.

(v)   Alleged insufficiencies which should be addressed by the Panel

7.649 The **European Communities** argues that the most important gaps in the evidence are related to carcinogenicity, genotoxicity, dose-response and lack of safe thresholds, endogenous production of hormones by pre-pubertal children, lack of reliable bioavailability data, possibilities of abuse and lack of control. In addition, the European Communities maintains that since the latest SCVPH assessment, new scientific developments further support SCVPH conclusions.[783]

7.650 According to the **United States**, the experts' responses confirm the following points regarding the scientific evidence relating to the six hormones: (a) each hormone has been used for growth promotion purposes in cattle and evaluated for a sufficient period of time with no evidence of adverse effects to address concerns related to long latency periods of cancer; (b) epidemiological studies cited by the European Communities do not identify a link between cancer and hormone residues in meat; (c) the European Communities has failed to demonstrate a risk to sensitive populations; and (d) the European Communities has failed to demonstrate "other risks" to human health from consumption of hormone residues in meat from cattle treated for growth promotion purposes, such as effects on the immune system.[784]

7.651 At this juncture, the **Panel** deems it appropriate to recall that parties have submitted a large amount of materials which was often very intricate and complex. The Panel believes that, as part of its obligations to make an objective assessment of the matter before it, including an objective assessment of the facts pursuant to Article 11 of the DSU, it had to devise an approach which would allow it to address the issues on which insufficiencies were alleged in a clear and transparent manner.

7.652 Whereas, in application of the burden of proof in relation to Article 5.7 of the *SPS Agreement*, it should be for the party challenging the applicability of Article 5.7 to make a prima facie case that the relevant scientific evidence regarding the five hormones is sufficient[785], it is also for the European Communi-

---

[783]   EC's second written submission, paras. 143-144.

[784]   US's comments on experts' replies to Panel questions, Annex F-4, para. 56 (more detail on each point may be found in paras. 57-87).

[785]   *See* Appellate Body Report in *Japan – Agricultural Products II*, para. 80; Panel Report in *Japan – Agricultural Products II*, para. 8.13; Panel Report in *EC – Approval and Marketing of Biotech Products*, paras. 7.2969-7.2979.

ties, in application of the principle that it is for each party to prove its allegations, to support its own allegations with appropriate evidence. This also has to be considered in the light of the fact that, even though in this case the European Communities is the complainant, it also argues as part of its allegations under Article 22.8 of the DSU that its implementing measure complies with Article 5.7 of the *SPS Agreement*. Moreover, we recall the consequence of the presumption of consistency with the *SPS Agreement* and GATT 1994 of measures which conform to international standards, guidelines and recommendations on the risk assessments on which such measures are based.[786] Since, in that context, the European Communities argues that the relevant scientific evidence is insufficient, we consider that it is for the European Communities to identify the issues for which such evidence is insufficient.

7.653 Therefore, we do not consider that, as Panel, we have any obligation to go beyond the insufficiencies identified by the European Communities. We recall that we are neither equipped, nor supposed to make a *de novo* review of the scientific evidence regarding the hormones at issue. Under the circumstances, we deem it appropriate to limit our review exclusively to the "insufficiencies" expressly identified by the European Communities in its submissions to the Panel.

7.654 We note that, in its second written submission, the European Communities considers that the scientific evidence on which JECFA and Codex relied is insufficient with respect to the following issues: (a) carcinogenicity; (b) hormones daily production rate, in particular in pre-pubertal children; (c) dose response and lack of a safe threshold; (d) bioavailability; and (e) misuse or abuse (misplaced implants, off-label use, black market drugs, etc.)[787]

7.655 The European Communities also inserted in its replies to the first series of questions of the Panel and in its second written submission extensive portions of the 1999 and 2002 Opinions.[788]

7.656 In other words, the European Communities made its own description of the issues with respect to which it believes that evidence is insufficient and added quotations in support of its allegations. These passages also identify insufficiencies.

7.657 A number of issues discussed by the European Communities as part of the arguments contained in its submissions seem to overlap with the issues iden-

---

[786] See paras. 7.643-7.647.
[787] We have already explained in para. 7.603 why we do not believe that abuse or misuse is an issue of insufficiency of relevant evidence. To the extent necessary for our finding, this issue has been addressed in para. 7.483.
[788] See EC's reply to questions 22 and 30 of the questions of the Panel after its first substantive meeting, Annex B-1, and paras. 153-172 of the EC's second written submission.

tified in the portions of the Opinions quoted by the European Communities. However, a number of specific issues identified in the quotations are simply not directly *discussed* by the European Communities in its submissions.

7.658 We believe that it is incumbent upon a party making a particular allegation to identify in its submissions the *relevance* of the evidence on which it relies to support its arguments.[789] We consider that, for some of the issues identified in the Opinions, this was not the case. The Opinions were obviously quoted by the European Communities as evidence of the insufficiencies it has identified in its Opinions. However, the European Communities, while stating that the Opinions identified relevant issues, basically left it to the Panel to find out on its own the relevance of certain issues identified in the quotations for the question whether relevant scientific evidence was insufficient or not.[790]

7.659 The Panel is therefore of the view that, in light of its functions under the DSU, it should limit its review of alleged insufficiencies in the relevant scientific evidence to those specifically discussed by the European Communities in its submissions. It will only address the issues identified in the Opinions to the extent they are sufficiently related to an issue *discussed* by the European Communities.

7.660 A second question relates to the fact that, even when a particular insufficiency was specifically discussed by the European Communities, elements were not always available to address this insufficiency on a hormone-specific basis. The arguments and generally the information presented to the Panel were not always specific enough to permit this. In spite of our repeated requests, several questions were addressed by the parties or the experts in general terms, rather than specifically for each of the five hormones, thus making an assessment of particular issues hormone-by-hormone sometimes impossible.

7.661 Under the circumstances, the Panel decided:

   (a)   first, to address the insufficiencies *as identified and discussed* by the European Communities in its arguments and only to the extent evidence had been submitted by the parties in relation to them. This approach is, in our opinion, consistent with the requirement identified by the Appellate Body in its report on *Japan – Agricultural Products II* that panels refrain from "making a case" for one party in the absence of a prima facie case by that party;[791]

---

[789]   See Appellate Body Report in *Canada – Wheat Exports and Grain Imports*, para. 191.
[790]   See Appellate Body Report on *US – Gambling*, para. 140.
[791]   See Appellate Body Report on *Japan – Agricultural Products II*, para. 129.

(b)   second, to address some concerns aggregately for all of the five hormones at issue, to the extent that information was not submitted on an hormone-specific basis, or to the extent an issue was raised with respect to all hormones, but evidence submitted only for one or two of them; and

(c)   third, to address individually for each hormone the issues for which specific information on that hormone was provided to the Panel.

7.662   For these reasons, we have decided to address first, in a "common issues" section, the insufficiencies which were not addressed by the parties and the experts in a hormone-specific manner (i.e. those for which arguments or evidence were not hormone-specific), or which were not addressed specifically enough to justify a separate analysis for each of the hormones concerned. At a second stage, we address for each hormone the alleged insufficiencies which have been discussed in relation to that hormone and for which arguments and evidence were specifically provided.

>   (vi)   Issues common to all five hormones for which evidence was not provided on a hormone-specific basis

Introduction

7.663   We note that, despite our insistence that information be provided for each of the five hormones at issue, arguments, information and opinions have sometimes addressed all or part of the scientific evidence on these hormones together. As a result, in this section, we will address the issues that were specifically discussed by the European Communities in these proceedings in relation to all five hormones in general regarding their use as growth promoters in cattle. More particularly, we will address:

(a)   the effects of hormones on certain categories of population, such as pre-pubertal children;

(b)   dose response;

(c)   bioavailability;

(d)   the EC claim that the long latency period of cancer makes it more difficult to demonstrate insufficiency of the relevant evidence regarding the carcinogenicity of the hormones at issue;

(e)   the impact of the five hormones at issue on the immune system, and

(f)   the impact of the five hormones at issue on development and reproduction.

Effects of hormones on certain categories of population

7.664 Regarding the effect of the hormones at issue on certain categories of populations, we note that the European Communities refers to the conclusions contained in the Opinions. We recall that the 1999 Opinion mentions that prepubertal and postmenopausal women and prepubertal and adult men have the lowest levels of endogenous oestrogens and progesterone and thus would represent the individuals most likely to be at increased risk for the adverse health effects that might be associated with exposure to exogenous sources of oestrogens. Likewise, the 1999 Opinion provides that all women and prepubertal men represent the individuals at greatest risk for adverse health effects that might be associated with exposure to exogenous sources of testosterone.

7.665 The 1999 Opinion specifies that the hormone levels on which it relies were determined by radio-immunoassays (RIA) and that the use of these assays has frequently been associated with production of variable results, particularly when used to detect low levels of endogenous hormones. The 1999 Opinion notes that Klein et al. (1994) developed an ultrasensitive assay (100-fold more sensitive than RIAs) which identified values of oestradiol considerably lower than the range of oestradiol levels found through RIAs for prepubertal children. The 1999 Opinion concludes that "[a] corollary is that perhaps the hormone residues in beef, which are also low and which have been determined by RIA are equally variable and over representative of the actual hormones concentration." The 1999 Opinion concludes that this is a critical area requiring additional study.[792]

7.666 We recall our test regarding insufficiency of relevant evidence in this case, i.e. that there must be a critical mass of new evidence and/or information that calls into question the fundamental precepts of knowledge and evidence so as to make relevant, previously sufficient, evidence now insufficient. In that context, we believe that the question before us is whether the more sensitive detection methods which identified lower hormonal levels in pre-pubertal children than thought until now are such as to call into question the range of physiological levels of the sex hormones in humans currently believed to exist.

7.667 Dr. Sippell specified that:

---

[792] The 2002 Opinion refers to a new method to detect trace amounts of hormones in meats and to three complementary bioassays involving different recombinant-DNA technology for screening and determination of oestrogenic potency of substances used as growth promoters (2002 Opinion, p. 9). The Panel nonetheless understands that these method and bioassays address a different issue than the identification of endogenous levels of hormones in humans.

"There is no doubt that the development of an ultrasensitive re-combinant cell bioassay (RCBA) of E_2 by Karen Klein, Gordon Cutler and co-workers at the N.I.H. in Bethesda, USA (Klein et al 1994) represented a quantum leap in E_2 assay methodology. It opened a new door on our understanding of basic physiological phenomena, e.g. why normal puberty starts so much earlier in girls than in boys or why bone maturation in children differs so much between the sexes. The validity of the N.I.H.-RCBA has now been confirmed by another RCBA of E_2 which was developed by Charles Sultan's group at the University of Montpellier, France (Paris et al 2002). Unfortunately, the complexity of the RCBA so far prevents its wider use for routine measurements in small serum samples from infants and prepubertal children."[793]

7.668   We also note Dr. Sippell's statement that "[t]he risk to children arising from hormones which are naturally present in meat as compared to that from residues of hormonal growth promoters has, to my knowledge, been estimated for E_2 [i.e., oestradiol-17β] only and only in beef (Daxenberger et al. 2001)."[794]

7.669   We recall the statement of the 2000 Opinion referring to novel techniques in chemical analysis[795] but mentioning that "additional time will be required to validate and apply this methodology in a reliable, accepted fashion before a re-evaluation of this issue can be conducted."[796] This opinion is confirmed by Dr. Boobis.[797] Dr. Boobis expressed additional concerns about the validity of the Klein et al. (1994) study:

"There is certainly some evidence that endogenous levels of hor-mones in children are lower than previously thought. However, the suggestion that this is by orders of magnitude is not substantiated by the data. One group has reported very low levels of oestradiol in male children, 0.08 pg/ml *(Klein et al, 1994),* but in a later study *(Klein et al, 1998),* the same group reported mean levels somewhat higher, at 0.27 pg/ml. The reliability of the Klein et al assay has yet to be determined. The assay is particularly sensitive to oestra-diol, but there is no obvious explanation for this, as it relies upon affinity for the oestrogen receptor. Diethylstilbestrol is a potent oestrogen yet is much less sensitive than oestradiol in the assay.

---

[793]   Reply of Dr. Sippell to question 40 of the Panel, Annex D, para. 328.
[794]   Reply of Dr. Sippell to question 41 of the Panel, Annex D, para. 335.
[795]   Results of "hormone" residue analyses of bovine meat and liver imported into the EU and origi-nating from the USA "Hormone Free Cattle Program" analysis – First Interim Report, May 1999 – R.W. Stephany and F. André (rapporteurs).
[796]   2000 Opinion, p. 3.
[797]   Transcript of the Panel meeting with the experts, Annex G, para. 572.

Klein et al (1994) have reported that there are unidentified factors in plasma and in blood collection tubes that can interfere in the assay. In contrast, using a similar yeast-based assay, *Coldham et al (1997)* found that oestradiol and DES had similar potency, and others have found that, if anything, DES is more potent than oestradiol in such assays *(Folmer et al, 2002).* At the very least, this shows that results with the yeast reporter assay are not consistent, and use of such data in risk assessment requires that the assay be adequately validated.[798]

However, there are studies from two other groups using more specific methods than the original radioimmunoassay, reporting that levels were somewhat higher than this. *Ikegami et al (2001)* used a very sensitive, 2-stage immunoassay technique. This was shown to be specific and sensitive. In this assay, mean levels of oestradiol in prepubertal males were 1.85 pg/ml (6.8 pmol/ml). *Paris et al (2002)* used a recombinant oestrogen receptor assay in a mammalian cell line, a similar principle to the assay of Klein et al. In this study, estogenic levels in prepubertal males were found to be 1.44 pg/ml. There are many issues affecting such measurements. These include the presence of binding proteins, relative specificity and sensitivity. None of the assays is entirely specific for oestradiol. Both the oestrogen receptor and the antibodies used could cross-react with structurally relayed compounds. Depending on how the assay is performed, protein binding could reduce the concentration of hormone detectable in the assay by sequestering hormone from the assay target. However, it should be noted that whilst binding to protein in plasma my reduce clearance it will also reduce the biologically active dose. In general, it is the free concentration that determines biological activity *(Teeguarden and Barton, 2004).* Hence, if SHBG is elevated in children this would tend to reduce

---

[798] Dr. Boobis' reply to question 40 of the Panel, Annex D, para. 324. Dr. Boobis cites to:
  Coldham NG, Dave M, Sivapathasundaram S, McDonnell DP, Connor C and Sauer MJ (1997). Evaluation of a recombinant yeast cell estrogen screening assay. Environ Health Perspect, **105**:734-742
  Folmar LC, Hemmer MJ, Denslow ND, Kroll K, Chen J, Cheek A, Richman H, Meredith H and Grau EG (2002). A comparison of the estrogenic potencies of estradiol, ethynylestradiol, diethylstilbestrol, nonylphenol and methoxychlor in vivo and in vitro. Aquat Toxicol, **60**:101-110
  Klein KO, Baron J, Colli MJ, McDonnell DP and Cutler GB Jr (1994). Estrogen levels in childhood determined by an ultrasensitive recombinant cell bioassay. J Clin Invest, **94**:2475-2480
  Klein KO, Baron J, Barnes KM, Pescovitz OH and Cutler GB Jr (1998). Use of an ultrasensitive recombinant cell bioassay to determine estrogen levels in girls with precocious puberty treated with a luteinizing hormone-releasing hormone agonist. J Clin Endocrinol Metab, **83**:2387-2389

the effect of an equivalent total plasma concentration by reducing the free concentration.

The advantage of the recombinant assays is that they measure biologically active material, whereas the immunoassays may include cross-reacting less or inactive metabolites. Whilst the recombinant assays may include hormonally active material other than the specific analyte, this does provide an indication of to what the body is exposed in vivo. Hence, on balance, the data of *Paris et al (2002)* may be the most meaningful to date. This presumably reflects circulating total active oestrogenic material, but not that bound to proteins."[799]

7.670   We note that the evidence presented relates only to oestradiol, but that the claim we are examining with regard to the insufficiencies of the evidence are with respect to the five other hormones at issue, not oestradiol. We note furthermore that the 2002 Opinion concludes that these more sensitive detection methods have not yet been validated.[800]

7.671   On the basis of the above, we are not convinced that the studies discussed by the experts call into question the fundamental precepts of previous knowledge and evidence so as to make relevant, previously sufficient evidence now insufficient in relation to the effect of the five hormones on pre-pubertal children. Particularly, it has not been established that the data regarding the effects of hormones on which the JECFA assessments are based are insufficient in light of new evidence relating to the other five hormones at issue.

Dose response

7.672   The European Communities, in its reply to a question of the Panel[801], quotes an extract of the 1999 Opinion.[802] Whereas this quotation relates to trenbolone acetate, we decided to address it in this general section to the extent that

---

[799]   Reply of Dr. Boobis to question 40 of the Panel, Annex D, paras.325-326. Dr. Boobis cites to:
Ikegami S, Moriwake T, Tanaka H, Inoue M, Kubo T, Suzuki S, Kanzakili S and Seino Y (2001). An ultrasensitive assay revealed age-related changes in serum oestradiol at low concentrations in both sexes from infancy to puberty. Clin Endocrinol (Oxf), **55**:789-795
Paris F, Servant N, Terouanne B, Balaguer P, Nicolas JC and Sultan C (2002). A new recombinant cell bioassay for ultrasensitive determination of serum estrogenic bioactivity in children. J Clin Endocrinol Metab, **87**:791-797
Teeguarden JG and Barton HA (2004). Computational modeling of serum-binding proteins and clearance in extrapolations across life stages and species for endocrine active compounds. Risk Anal, **24**:751-770.

[800]   2002 Opinion, Section 4.1.1, p. 9.

[801]   EC's replies to Panel questions after the first substantive meeting, question 22, Annex B-1.

[802]   1999 Opinion, para. 4.4.8.

the impossibility to perform a dose-response assessment is referred to by the European Communities with respect to the five hormones at issue.[803]

7.673 The European Communities also questions JECFA's findings on dose response as follows:

"The above findings establish that the levels of endogenous production of these hormones by *pre-pubertal children* is much lower than previously thought and this finding, which is subsequent to the 1999 JECFA report, casts serious doubts about the validity of JECFA's findings on the dose-response relationship, because the data on endogenous production on which JECFA based its findings are also very old (since 1974)."[804]

7.674 The Panel can only conclude from the comments of the European Communities that it considers that a dose response would be required to complete a risk assessment for the five hormones other than oestradiol-17β, but that it disagrees with JECFA's findings on dose response. The Panel notes that JECFA could identify a dose response for the five hormones at issue. Comparatively, the European Communities has not provided convincing elements to support its view that there is insufficient relevant evidence on dose response. The EC position on dose response, at least for the natural hormones other than oestradiol, seems to be based on the belief that levels of endogenous production of hormones are much lower than previously thought. The Panel notes in this regard that it has been demonstrated that the ultrasensitive assay relied upon by the European Communities to conclude that endogenous production is lower than assumed by JECFA has not yet been validated and applies only to oestradiol.

---

[803] See the following paragraphs of the EC's second written submission:
 – para. 155, regarding the effect of progesterone on growth and reproduction: "No assessment of the dose response relationship has been presented yet." Also: " In conclusion, these data indicate that progesterone can cause immuno depression; however, they are insufficient to make any realistic assessment of the dose response relationship." (Both from the 1999 Opinion, pp. 51-55);
 – para. 160, regarding the effect of testosterone on growth and reproduction: "No assessment of the dose response relationship has been presented yet." Also: "There are limited experimental data on the effects of testosterone on immuno response but none on the dose response aspects." (Both from the 1999 Opinion, p. 50);
 – para. 165, regarding the effects of trenbolone on growth and reproduction: "These data do not allow a realistic assessment of a dose response relationship."(1999 Opinion, p. 60);
 – para. 172, regarding melengestrol acetate: "These data do not allow an estimate of the dose response relationship." (1999 Opinion, p. 68);
 – para. 168, on the effects of zeranol on growth and reproduction: "No estimate of the dose-response relationship for these effects can be made."(1999 Opinion, p. 65).
[804] EC's second written submission, para. 122.

7.675 For these reasons, the Panel believes that it has not been established that new evidence was such as to put into question existing data on dose response and prevent the performance of a risk assessment.

Bioavailability

7.676 The European Communities argues that another area where recent developments put in doubt the findings of the 1999 JECFA report concerns the bioavailability of residues of the hormones concerned. According to the European Communities, the 1999 and 2002 Opinions have found that data on which JECFA based its findings are incorrect or insufficient.[805]

7.677 The Panel notes that the studies referred to in the 1999 and 2002 Opinions (one of them being study 3 of the 17 studies commissioned by the European Communities)[806] relate to oestradiol-17β, not to any of the specific hormones with respect to which the European Communities applies a provisional ban under Article 5.7 of the *SPS Agreement*. Moreover, there is no indication that the conclusions can be applied to other hormones than oestrogens.

7.678 The Panel recalls that the European Communities argued that "similar findings [had been] made for all of the other five hormones."[807] However, the European Communities did not specify where such findings had been made. The European Communities also refers to study 10 of the 17 studies, by Dr. Florence Le Gac, but does not clearly explain to what extent the results of this study establish or discuss the bioavailability of the five other hormones. This allegation of the European Communities has to be considered in light of the statements of Dr. Boisseau and Dr. Boobis according to which the bioavailability of melengestrol, trenbolone and zeranol residues has not been determined.[808]

7.679 The Panel considers that bioavailabity would be an issue if the new evidence suggested that bioavailability in the case of ingestion of meat treated for growth promotion purposes is higher than previously thought. However, it appears that, in the absence of data, JECFA assumed 100% bioavailability.

7.680 In this respect, Dr. Boisseau said:

---

[805] EC's second written submission, para. 123.
[806] 2002 Opinion, p.12, point 4.1.5, Exhibit US-1.
[807] EC reply to question 28 of the questions of the Panel after the first substantive meeting, Annex B-1, para. 158.
[808] Dr. Boisseau, Annex D, para. 347.

"The bioavailability of melengestrol, trenbolone and zeranol residues have not been determined. Therefore all their residues have been considered as being totally bioavailable."[809]

7.681 Dr. Boobis stated, with respect to natural hormones, that "change in bioavailability is likely to be a consequence of changes in the enzymes of metabolism in the liver and/or small intestine."[810]

7.682 Dr. Boobis also confirms for the non-natural hormones:

"However, it should be noted that in the risk assessment of these hormones by JECFA, the risk characterization involved comparison of the theoretical maximum daily intake with the ADI. No correction was made for bioavailability. Hence, the situation is likely to be similar to that for the natural hormones, in that changes in bioavailability from the normal value would change the margin of safety."[811]

7.683 These statements were not contradicted by Dr. Guttenplan, the third and last expert who replied to question 43 of the Panel, and who limited his remarks to oestrogens.[812]

7.684 We therefore conclude that it has not been established that any new evidence on bioavailability has been developed regarding specifically the five hormones at issue, which would affect the current knowledge on the subject. More particularly, no new evidence has been submitted regarding the three non-natural hormones which would make it impossible to perform a risk assessment within the meaning of Article 5.1 and Annex A(4) of the *SPS Agreement*.

Long latency period of cancer and confounding factors

7.685 Regarding the long latency of cancer, in its second written submission[813], the European Communities claims that it may not be in a position to demonstrate the existence of a clear harm in case of cancer because of the long latency period and the numerous confounding factors that play a role in the development of cancer.

7.686 We first note the importance of latency period in the assessment of cancer, as confirmed by Dr. Cogliano, Dr. Guttenplan and Dr. Boobis:

---

[809] Annex D, para. 347.
[810] Annex D, para. 350.
[811] Annex D, para. 351.
[812] Annex D, para. 357.
[813] EC's second written submission, para. 149.

7.687 Dr. Cogliano stated that:

"It is definitely necessary to take into account the latency period of cancer in the conduct of a risk assessment. In this regard, the guidelines for developing *IARC Monographs* state, 'Experience with human cancer indicates that the period from first exposure to the development of clinical cancer is sometimes longer than 20 years; latent periods substantially shorter than 30 years cannot provide evidence for lack of carcinogenicity.' [International Agency for Research on Cancer, Preamble to the *IARC Monographs*, http://monographs.iarc.fr]"[814]

7.688 Dr. Guttenplan confirmed that:

"When epidemiological data is used in performing a risk assessment, the latency period is extremely important. Usually a latent period of 20 years is taken for cancer, but this varies with the carcinogen. It is indeed necessary to determine incidence or prevalence at different times after the onset of exposure. Attempting to perform a risk assessment based on epidemiological data obtained too soon after the onset of exposure can seriously underestimate risk. [815]

7.689 Dr. Boobis stated that:

"The latency period is an important consideration in risk assessment, both in the design and in the interpretation of studies. Thus, the duration of exposure, either of experimental animals or in epidemiology studies, should be sufficiently long to permit assessment of effects with a long latency period. Most forms of cancer come into this category."[816]

7.690 Dr. Boobis added that:

"The observational studies of humans (e.g. on HRT or oral contraceptives) and the experimental studies in animals covered a sufficiently long period to encompass the latency period for any carcinogenic effects of the hormones (see *IARC, 1999*).

---

[814] Reply of Dr. Cogliano to question 23 of the Panel, Annex D, para. 213.
[815] Reply of Dr. Guttenplan to question 23 of the Panel, Annex D, para. 214. Dr. Guttenplan cited to Lagiou P. Trichopoulou A. Trichopoulos D. Nutritional epidemiology of cancer: accomplishments and prospects. [Lectures] Proceedings of the Nutrition Society. 61(2):217-22, 2002.
[816] Reply of Dr. Boobis to question 23 of the Panel, Annex D, para. 210.

7.691 Dr. Boisseau highlighted the practical difficulties resulting from confounding factors, arguing that:

"[He did] not think possible/useful to take into account the "long latency period" of cancer in order to assess properly and specifically the carcinogenic effects of residues of natural hormones only resulting from the treatment of food producing animals by growth promoting hormones. ... epidemiological studies carried out in humans during [periods] long enough in order to take into account this "long latency period" will not be able to discriminate, in the case of a possible but limited increase of tumours, between the responsibilities of (1) hormone residues resulting from the treatment of food producing animals by growth promoting hormones, (2) hormone residues resulting from the endogenous production of these animals, (3) other components of the diet including other food additives and contaminants. That is the reason for which, ... the epidemiological studies in humans already carried out in this domain have failed to identify any relation between the occurrence of hormonally dependent tumours and the consumption of meat containing hormonally active residues resulting from the treatment of cattle with growth promoters."[817]

7.692 Dr. Boobis added that:

"The long term studies of the hormones undertaken in experimental animals and in humans, involved much higher doses than would be encountered on consumption of meat from animals treated with growth promoting hormones. The maximum risk from such low levels of exposure, even assuming a linear dose-response relationship for cancer, would be such that it would be necessary to study extremely large populations to detect any increase in cancer incidence, particularly as the most likely cancers are quite common. This is because the lower the risk the greater the number of subjects that are required to detect it, a function of the power of the study which takes account the magnitude of the risk and the difference from the background rate (Hunter, 1997). Hence, in the risk assessment of the hormones used as growth promoters, it is questionable whether an increase in risk, even if it existed, could be detected in exposed populations. However, it is still necessary to protect against such a risk. The risk assessment of the hormones conducted by JECFA suggested that there would be no risk at ex-

---

[817] Reply of Dr. Boisseau to question 23 of the Panel, Annex D, para. 209.

posure levels up to the respective ADI. Even if duration of exposure were for a sufficiently long period (usually 20-25 years for solid tissue tumours), any increase in risk would probably not be detectable. Hence, a negative result from such an observational study would not resolve the issue.

A second issue with respect to the latency is the significance it has for interpretation of the exposure pattern. Where there is a long latency, and regular exposure is necessary before a carcinogenic response is manifest, as appears to be the case for the hormones in question *(Coombs et al, 2005)*, occasional exposures above the ADI will not pose any additional risk *(Larsen and Richold, 1999)*. Hence, latency is of value in assessing the risks from different exposure scenarios."[818]

7.693 The European Communities acknowledges that epidemiological studies will not be able to discriminate (or separate out) the true origin of cancer because of so many confounding factors. In this respect, we note that Dr. Cogliano specified that it was generally possible to identify confounding factors in epidemiological studies. It was often difficult, however, to determine whether the observed tumours can be attributed to the agent under study or to a confounding factor. Dr. Cogliano adds that "[w]hen a causal interpretation is credible but confounding factors cannot be ruled out, IARC considers this to provide *limited evidence of carcinogenicity.*"[819]

7.694 The European Communities insists, however, that this undermines the opinion of the respondent that the hormones at issue have been in use for a sufficiently long time to rule out their carcinogenic effect on humans. The European Communities points at IARC studies showing that the frequency of breast cancer in countries where use of hormones for growth promotion is allowed is higher compared with countries where the hormones have not been used.[820]

---

[818] Dr. Boobis cites to the following studies:

Coombs NJ, Taylor R, Wilcken N, Fiorica J and Boyages J (2005). Hormone replacement therapy and breast cancer risk in California. Breast J, 11:410-415

Hunter DJ (1997). Methodological issues in the use of biological markers in cancer epidemiology: cohort studies. IARC Sci Publ, **142**:39-46

IARC (1999). IARC Monographs on the Evaluation of Carcinogenic Risks to Humans, Vol 72. Hormonal Contraception and Post-menopausal Hormonal Therapy, IARC, Lyon, France

Larsen JC and Richold M (199). Report of workshop on the significance of excursions of intake above the ADI. Regul Toxicol Pharmacol, **30**:S2-12.

See Reply of Dr. Boobis to question 23 of the Panel, Annex D, para. 212.

[819] Reply of Dr. Cogliano to question 24 of the Panel, Annex D, para. 220. See also Dr. Guttenplan, Annex D, para. 221.

[820] EC's comments on experts replies to questions 23 and 24 of the Panel, Annex F-1, pp. 19-20.

7.695 Three experts addressed this issue. Dr. Cogliano mentioned that:

"The difference between the US and the EC in rates of breast cancer and prostate cancer almost certainly has multiple causes. It is
possible that differences in exposure to exogenous hormones can
be one cause, but the data are not sufficiently specific to establish
a link between these observations."[821]

7.696 Dr. Guttenplan confirmed that:

"The epidemiological studies do not identify a relationship between cancer and residues of hormonal growth promoters. The
references to the higher rates of breast and prostate cancer observed in the United States as compared to the European Communities are not very convincing as there is considerable variation in
rates in different geographical locations. Also, the differences in
rates of breast and prostate cancer observed in the United States as
compared to the European Communities are relatively small.
There is no way to definitely establish a link between these statistics and the consumption of meat from animals treated with the
hormones at issue as there are many possible confounders, and the
differences in cancer rates are small. However, the results are at
least consistent with a possible effect of hormones on breast and
prostate cancer."[822]

7.697 In this regard, Dr. Boobis added the following:

"There are an appreciable number of studies showing an association between the risk of certain cancer types, including breast and
prostate and the consumption of meat *(Colli and Colli, 2006;
Norat et al, 2005; see also SCVPH Opinion, 1999)*. For breast, the
incidence is similar in developed countries such as Western
Europe, North America and Australasia. The correlation is strong-
est with meat consumption and shows little relationship with
whether the meat is from animals treated with growth promoting
hormones or not. For example rates in Iceland (87.2 per 100,000),
where such hormones are not used, are not dissimilar to those in
the USA (101.1 per 100,000), where they are used. Prostate cancer
rates are 124.8/100,000 in the USA and 90.9 per 100,000 in Sweden *(IARC, 2002)*. For comparison, average daily consumption of

---

[821] Reply of Dr. Cogliano to question 26 of the Panel, Annex D, para. 241.
[822] Reply of Dr. Guttenplan to question 26 of the Panel, Annex D, para. 242.

meat (as protein) in 2000 was as follows: USA 40.2 g/day; Iceland 29.5 g/day; Sweden 24.8 g/day *(FAO, 2003)*. Hence, there is a much better association with meat consumption and risk of breast or prostate cancer than there is with the use of growth promoting hormones to treat cattle. It is also important not to infer too much from geographical differences in cancer incidence rates with respect to causation. This is because of what is known as the ecological fallacy. This has been defined as the inference that a correlation between variables derived from data grouped in social or other aggregates (ecological units) will hold between persons (individual units) *(Society for Risk Assessment, 2004)*. The difficulty is that many factors will vary between populations, including ethnicity, genetics, health and socioeconomic status, diet, lifestyle and environment. Without considering the possibility of confounding, such ecological data is really only of value in generating hypotheses *(Morgenstern, 1995)*. These would need to be evaluated in more structured investigations, with better control of confounding variables."[823]

7.698 We also note Dr. Boobis statement at the meeting of the Panel with the experts:

"The paradigm we have, and there is some evidence to justify the case that this is a reasonable assumption, is that the effects observed scale to the lifetime of the organism, and so that is one of the reasons we use shorter-lived organisms in our toxicological testing. We use rats and mice which live for a couple of years; otherwise we would have to test for a lifetime in a longer-lived species which might be 40 or 50 years. So we are working on the principle that effects that are not evident within the lifetime of a rodent would not be evident, all other things being equal, within the lifetime of a human being. And there is actually very good evidence that that is the case. For a number of carcinogens that IARC have evaluated it takes approximately a quarter of a lifetime after an initial exposure for those tumours to become apparent, and that is true in rodents, it's true in dogs and it's true in humans. So I think that the paradigm is reasonable that if there is going to be an effect manifest over a lifetime, it will be revealed in those experi-

---

[823] Reply of Dr. Boobis to question 26 of the Panel, Annex D, para. 239. Dr. Boobis cited to the following:

Morgenstern H (1995). Ecologic studies in epidemiology: concepts, principles, and methods. Annu Rev Public Health, 16:61-81

Society for Risk Assessment (2004). Glossary of Risk Analysis Terms.
(http://www.sra.org/resources_glossary.php)

mental systems and therefore be predictive of lifetime effects in humans by and large."[824]

7.699 On the one hand, the comments of the experts suggest that epidemiological studies have not been able to single out residues of hormones in meat treated for growth promotion purposes as a cause of cancer, and that this would be quite difficult. On the other hand, the Panel notes that it is possible to assess long term effects through long term studies of experimental animals, even if they involve much higher doses than would be encountered in consumption of meat from animals treated with growth promoting hormones. It has also been possible to take into account the risk attached to latency through the setting of ADI. The European Communities has not identified any evidence quantitatively and qualitatively sufficient to call into question the fundamental precepts of existing knowledge and evidence and the approach followed so far in order to integrate the long latency of cancer in risk assessment.

7.700 Having regard to the opinions of the experts, the Panel concludes that it has not been established that the difficulties attached to the long latency of cancer make it impossible to perform a risk assessment within the meaning of Article 5.1 and Annex A(4) of the *SPS Agreement*. More particularly, the European Communities did not point at a "critical mass" of new evidence and/or information that would call into question the fundamental precepts of previous knowledge and evidence in relation to the long latency period of cancer and the existence of confounding factors.

Effect of hormones on the immune system

7.701 The 1999 Opinion considers, for each of the five hormones for which a provisional ban is applied, that there is insufficient evidence as to their effect on the immune system.[825] The Panel notes that no arguments have been raised specifically in relation to the effects of hormones on the immune system with respect to each of the five hormones at issue. The Panel noted, however, the contention of the European Communities that new important gaps, insufficiencies and contradictions had been identified in the scientific information and knowledge now available as a result of the 17 studies commissioned by the European Communities. The Panel considered that an appropriate way to address this question with respect, *inter alia*, to the effect of hormones on the immune system was to seek the views of the scientific experts on the factual question whether the new scientific studies initiated since 1997 and relied upon by the European Communities identify any adverse effects on the immune system from the con-

---

[824] Annex G, para. 1031.
[825] There does not seem to be any additional development on this matter in the 2000 and 2002 Opinions.

sumption of meat from cattle treated with the growth promoting hormones at issue.[826]

7.702 Three experts expressed their views on the matter. Dr. Boobis argued that:

"The evidence on immune effects of hormones such as oestradiol referred to by the EC does not identify any adverse effects on the immune system from consumption of meat from treated cattle. In general, clear evidence for immune effects were observed only at high doses. There is no evidence that doses such as those resulting from consumption of meat from treated animals has any effect on the immune system *(JECFA, 2000b; CVMP, 1999)*. It should also be noted, that in the case of immune effects, exposure relative to endogenous levels is a critical issue. Given the large margin of exposure on anticipated intake from residues in meat from treated animals, no effect on the immune system is anticipated, as immune modulation is dependent on dose and there are thresholds for such effects."[827]

7.703 Dr. Guttenplan noted that:

"The relationship between estrogen and autoimmune diseases has received considerable attention (Opinion SCVPH, April 30, 1999, section 2.4). There is evidence that estrogens can be involved in Lupus, rheumatoid arthritis, thyroiditis. In addition the development of allergies is thought to be at least partially related to estrogens. The studies in experimental animals also did not identify any immune-related effects, although it is not certain the types of possible effects in humans would be detected in experimental animals. No definitive studies have related intake of meat from hormone-treated animals to the above disorders."[828]

---

[826] Question 59 of the panel to the experts.

[827] Reply of Dr. Boobis to question 59 of the Panel, Annex D, para. 445. Dr. Boobis cited to:
Barton HA and Clewell HJ 3rd (2000). Evaluating noncancer effects of trichloroethylene: dosimetry, mode of action, and risk assessment. Environ Health Perspect, 108 (Suppl 2):323-334
Kroes R, Renwick AG, Cheeseman M, Kleiner J, Mangelsdorf I, Piersma A, Schilter B, Schlatter J, van Schothorst F, Vos JG and Wurtzen G; European branch of the International Life Sciences Institute (2004). Structure-based thresholds of toxicological concern (TTC): guidance for application to substances present at low levels in the diet.Food Chem Toxicol, **42**:65-83

[828] Reply of Dr. Guttenplan to question 59 of the Panel, Annex D, para. 447.

7.704 We note that the Panel question related to all hormones and the experts gave details in relation to oestrogens in general. We also note that the European Communities, in its comments on the experts' replies, referred to effects identified by Dr. Guttenplan in relation to oestrogens. The European Communities concludes that it has offered serious evidence and pointed to a number of gaps and uncertainties in the knowledge. The European Communities considers that it is for the United States, Canada and JECFA to "ensure the Panel that adverse immune effects are not possible to occur from residues in meat treated with these hormones for animal growth promotion".[829]

7.705 First, the Panel doubts that, in this particular case, the standard of proof is that the United States should prove to the satisfaction of the Panel that "adverse immune effects are not possible to occur from residues in meat treated with these hormones for animal growth promotion" purposes. As already specified, in this case the United States has to prove its allegation that relevant scientific evidence is not insufficient to perform an adequate risk assessment under Article 5.1 and Annex A(4) of the *SPS Agreement*.

7.706 Second, with regard to the evidence and gaps allegedly identified by the European Communities, the Panel notes that the statement of Dr. Guttenplan on which the European Communities relies relates exclusively to oestrogens. The Panel notes in this respect that the other experts' replies to question 59 of the Panel relate to oestradiol or oestrogens. None of those replies related to any of the five hormones at issue. The Panel notes that the 1999 Opinion itself does not provide evidence of impact on the immune system for testosterone.[830] For progesterone, the data were deemed to indicate that progesterone can cause immuno depression. However they were described as insufficient to make a realistic assessment of the dose response relationship.[831] On trenbolone, the information was deemed insufficient to assess the possible impact of low levels of trenbolone in meat and meat products on consumers.[832] For zeranol, the 1999 Opinion states that no relevant data on the effect of zeranol on the immune system were found.[833] Finally, for MGA, the 1999 Opinion concluded that the information was insufficient to make a scientific judgement on whether MGA may cause effects on the immune system at a level which could occur in meat treated with MGA as a growth promoters. The 2000 and 2002 Opinions do not seem to contradict these findings.

7.707 The Panel also notes that the three experts who replied to question 59 addressed the potential effects of hormones on the immune system through a

---

[829] EC's comments to experts replies to Panel questions, Annex F-1, pp. 37-38.
[830] 1999 Opinion, p. 51.
[831] 1999 Opinion, p. 55.
[832] 1999 Opinion, p. 60.
[833] 1999 Opinion, p. 66.

dose-response approach.[834] The Panel has received no evidence suggesting that a dose response would not apply to the effect of the five hormones on the immune system as a result of the consumption of meat treated for growth promotion purposes.

7.708 We therefore conclude that it is not established that there exists a critical mass of new evidence and/or information that calls into question the fundamental precepts of previous knowledge and evidence so as to make relevant, previously sufficient, evidence on hormones effects on the immune system now insufficient.

Effect of hormones on growth and reproduction

7.709 The Panel notes that no arguments have been raised specifically in relation to growth and reproduction with respect to each of the five hormones at issue, except for the EC reference to the 1999 Opinion. The Panel notes, however, the contention of the European Communities that new important gaps, insufficiencies and contradictions had been identified in the scientific information and knowledge now available as a result of the 17 studies commissioned by the European Communities. The Panel considers that an appropriate way to address this question with respect, *inter alia*, to the effect of hormones on growth and reproduction was to seek the views of the scientific experts on the factual question whether the new scientific studies initiated since 1997 and relied upon by the European Communities actually support its contention.[835]

7.710 Three experts commented on our question, Dr. Boisseau, Dr. Boobis and Dr. Guttenplan. Only Dr. Boobis and Dr. Guttenplan discussed matters related to growth and reproduction. Dr. Guttenplan originally identified a number of gaps that could relate to growth and reproduction.[836] However, Dr. Guttenplan subsequently stated that "on subsequent reading, [he] could not find anything to indicate adverse effect", and he considered that it was possible to undertake a risk assessment.[837] He added that "the ability [to make a risk assessment] varies between compounds, but that does not mean you can't make a risk assessment, it just means the accuracy of the risk assessment is different."[838]

7.711 Dr. Boobis considered in general that:

---

[834] See also reply of Dr. Boissau to question 59 of the Panel, Annex D, para. 443.
[835] See question 62 of the Panel to the scientific experts, Annex D.
[836] Reply of Dr. Guttenplan to question 62 of the Panel, Annex D, paras. 497-499.
[837] Transcript of the Panel meeting with the experts, Annex G, para. 981.
[838] Transcript of the Panel meeting with the experts, Annex G, para. 983.

"[T]here is little information in the scientific studies initiated by the EC since 1997 that support the contention that they have identified important new gaps, insufficiencies and contradictions in the scientific information and knowledge on the hormones, and that additional studies are necessary before the risks to health of consumption of meat from treated animals can be assessed. Whilst additional information has been obtained on a number of aspects of the hormones in question, this was often not definitive, sometimes it was not relevant, in some instances it confirmed or expanded on previous knowledge. The evidence obtained did not indicate any additional concern regarding the risk from exposure to residues of the hormones in meat from cattle treated for growth promotion."[839]

7.712 Dr. Boobis also discussed the recent data on endocrine and developmental effects of the hormones at issue. Regarding the experimental studies on the effect of in utero exposure of rabbits to the three exogenous hormones: melengestrol acetate, trenbolone acetate and zeranol, also referred to in the 2002 Opinion (study 11), Dr. Boobis noted that, to date, only information on metabolism and disposition had been published *(Lange et al, 2002)*.[840] According to Dr. Boobis:

"[the Lange et al. paper (2002)][841] demonstrates transplacental transfer of the three hormones. This is not surprising given the physicochemical properties of the compounds (lipid solubility, non-polar, molecular size) *(Syme et al, 2004)*.[842] In addition, endogenous hormones are known to cross the placenta. It is notable that in the study of Lange et al, fetal concentrations of the hormones and their metabolites were similar to or less than, sometimes much less than, those in corresponding maternal tissues, suggesting that there was no net accumulation of the compounds in fetal tissues. It is also noted that the number of animals studied was very small, a point commented on by the authors themselves.

The unpublished component of this study was an investigation of the potential health consequences of in utero exposure of rabbits to

---

[839]   Reply of Dr. Boobis to question 62 of the Panel, Annex D, para. 495.

[840]   Dr. Boobis noted that, given the time that had elapsed since this paper was published (submitted September 2001), it was somewhat surprising the data from the remainder of the study had not been published yet.

[841]   Dr. Boobis cited to Lange IG, Daxenberger A, Meyer HH, Rajpert-De Meyts E, Skakkebaek NE and Veeramachaneni DN (2002). Quantitative assessment of foetal exposure to trenbolone acetate, zeranol and melengestrol acetate, following maternal dosing in rabbits. Xenobiotica, **32**:641-65; see reply of Dr. Boobis to question 63 of the Panel, Annex D, para. 488.

[842]   Dr. Boobis cites to Syme MR, Paxton JW and Keelan JA (2004). Drug transfer and metabolism by the human placenta. Clin Pharmacokinet, 43:487-514.

the three hormones. From the information provided, low dose exposure in utero caused modest changes in some parameters, but
was not associated with wither cancer or adverse effects on reproductive capacity. There were no changes in sperm number. It is
not clear whether the changes observed were consistent and hence
compound-related as a only a single dose was used for each compound. Nor is it apparent whether the magnitude of all of changes
discussed reached statistical significance (often the changes were
described as slight and no measure of variance is provided). The
doses used in this study would have provided much higher levels
of exposure than those predicted to arise from residues in meat. In
the case of trenbolone acetate and zeranol exposure was via the
subcutaneous route, thus bypassing presystemic metabolism in the
intestine and/or the liver. In the case of MGA the oral dose was
over 16,500 times the ADI. Hence, even if the effects observed
were of toxicological significance the ADI would provide a more
than adequate margin of protection.

Overall, this study cannot be said to confirm a risk to human
health from consumption of meat from animals treated with these
hormones."[843]

7.713 While the European Communities commented negatively on other considerations by Dr. Boobis, it does not seem to make any specific comment on the
remarks of Dr. Boobis on study 11.

7.714 Dr. Sippell mentioned that "the synthetic androgen Trenbolone and the
gestagen Melengestrol bind with high affinity to the human androgen and progesterone receptors, respectively (Bauer et al., 2000). Exposure during pregnancy might result in severe transplacental virilisation of a female fetus."[844]

7.715 We note that Dr. Sippell does not indicate at what doses such an effect
might occur. It is also not clear whether the last sentence (about exposure during
pregnancy) refers to one of the studies identified by the European Communities,
or whether it is expressing Dr. Sippell's own opinion. We note, however, that
Dr. Boobis said: "There is no basis to think that the effect of hormone growth

---

[843] Dr. Boobis also discussed the study called "Retrospective study on long-term effects in children
of following suspected exposure to oestrogen-contaminated meat" (study 12) and the study *"In utero
exposure and breast cancer: a study in opposite sexed twins"* (Study 13). However these studies
seemed to relates primarily to oestradiol. See reply of Dr. Boobis to questions from the Panel, Annex D, paras. 493 and 491.
[844] Reply of Dr. Sippell to question 41 of the Panel, Annex D, para. 336.

promoters would be different in any way whatsoever from hormones naturally present in meat, at equivalent internal exposure levels."[845]

7.716 In paragraph 804 of Annex G, Dr. Sippell also states that: "It is, of course, difficult to answer such a question as a clinician, but from the experience we have with the low levels, I mentioned this several times before, with the extremely low levels that have been measured by these new recombinant assays, it is conceivable really that this extra burden of oestradiol poses a risk to very small children and particularly prepubertal boys, and this is in line with the very very high sensitivity of prepubertal children to oestrogens induced for other purposes."[846]

7.717 We consider that, in that paragraph, Dr. Sippell merely argues that it is conceivable that there is a risk, but he is not saying that there is evidence of such a risk. Dr. Sippell also stated: "I think that as much as children are concerned, we know really by no means enough and the data are really insufficient to tell or to be confident that this additional exposure from hormone-treated meat poses no risk."[847] Dr. Sippell's statements focused on oestradiol.

7.718 At the hearing, Dr. Guttenplan also mentioned: "So the potential genotoxic damage that is done in an adult would overwhelm that that could be done in a child. However, in boys the levels are even lower, and there I think we have to worry about developmental effects, and there has been less said on that – Dr. Sippell has been the major proponent of that – and I still think that these could be investigated epidemiologically or in some type of study. We might, as Dr. Boobis suggested, need a surrogate, perhaps saliva or urine, but I think it is perhaps the most important issue to address is the sensitivity of children. I should also mention hormone-sensitive cancers in post-menopausal women, it could be another concern."[848]

7.719 These two statement express doubts but do not constitute evidence of risks. The Panel notes that science does not stop studying a substance just because there is sufficient evidence to conduct a risk assessment, but continuously re-evaluates substances. Nothing in the above cited passages suggests that the existing evidence was insufficient to complete a risk assessment. In fact, the Panel notes that the European Communities has once again pointed the Panel to evidence that deals only with oestradiol, a hormone for which it claims to have completed a risk assessment. The European Communities has not explained how the interventions from the experts support a conclusion that the scientific evi-

---

[845] Reply of Dr. Boobis to question 41 of the Panel, Annex D, para. 333.
[846] Annex G, para. 804.
[847] Annex G, para. 1063.
[848] Annex G, para. 1061.

dence was insufficient to conduct a risk assessment with respect to the other five hormones.

7.720 The European Communities does not provide additional evidence in its comments regarding other hormones than oestradiol.[849]

7.721 Having regard to the opinions of the experts, the Panel is of the view that it has not been established that there is a critical mass of new evidence and/or information that calls into question the fundamental precepts of previous knowledge and evidence so as to make relevant, previously sufficient evidence now insufficient in relation to the growth and reproduction effects of the hormones at issue.

(vii)   Is relevant scientific evidence insufficient in the case of progesterone?

Summary of the main arguments of the parties[850]

7.722 The **United States** argues in general that the hormones at the centre of these proceedings have been intensively studied over the last twenty-five years and nothing has occurred since the *EC – Hormones* case, except that the five hormones have been studied in greater details, including by JECFA. New safety assessments were conducted for progesterone in 1999, reaffirming its safety when used according to good veterinary practices. Included in these safety assessments were new, detailed epidemiological studies on the effect of the hormones on post-menopausal women, marking some of the most relevant studies of the effect of hormones on human beings to date.[851] [852]

7.723 The United States adds that the European Communities' CVMP recently re-evaluated the scientific evidence relating to the hormones and reaffirmed its earlier conclusions on the safety of progesterone.

7.724 The United States concludes that there is more than sufficient scientific evidence to permit an adequate assessment of any potential risk.

7.725 The **European Communities** argues that the body of evidence has developed since the *EC – Hormones* case and, while still not providing enough

---

[849]   EC's comments on replies from experts, question 41, Annex F-1, p. 29.
[850]   A more detailed account of the parties' arguments can be found in Section IV of the descriptive part of this Report. The order in which the respective arguments of the parties are presented does not reflect any allocation of the burden of proof by the Panel.
[851]   The United States refers to the 52nd JECFA report (2000), pp. 59-60.
[852]   US's first written submission, paras. 125-128.

knowledge to carry out a complete and definitive risk assessment, supports the conclusion that precautionary measures are required in order to achieve its chosen level of protection.

7.726 The European Communities, quoting the 1999 Opinion, identifies the following insufficiencies in the evidence:[853]

(a)   little knowledge about the specific enzymes in cattle that metabolize progesterone;

(b)   considerable uncertainty associated with the validity of daily production rate data used by the US Food and Drug Administration;

(c)   no information available on mutagenicity and genotoxicity;

(d)   no information available on DNA adducts and DNA damage;

(e)   inadequate evidence for carcinogenicity in humans;

(f)   regarding effects of progesterone on growth and reproduction, alterations of spermatogenesis can be induced by progesterone treatments, but no assessment of the dose-response relationship is available;

(g)   regarding effects on the immune system, there are data indicating that progesterone can cause immuno depression, but they are insufficient to make a realistic assessment of the dose-response relationship.

7.727 In response to the US reference to the 1999 JECFA assessment, the European Communities notes that the 1999 Opinion took JECFA's assessment into account, expressing concern regarding the determination of the ADI since neither the actual data nor a reference to a peer-reviewed publication were provided, and since the dose-response was limited to two doses and the ADI was estimated from just a single dose rather than a curve derived from all the data available.[854]

7.728 In addition, the European Communities indicates that the Opinions, in particular the 2002 Opinion, have taken the 1999 CVMP assessment into account. The European Communities argues that the CVMP opinion was not used as the only basis of the EC measure for progesterone as a growth promoter because new scientific evidence had appeared since and the SCVPH assessment had identified risks that were incompatible with the level of health protection applied by the European Communities to these hormones when used for animal growth promotion purposes. Secondly, the European Communities argues that

---

[853]   EC's second written submission, para. 155.
[854]   EC's second written submission, para. 157-158; EC's replies to Panel questions after the first substantive meeting, question 22, Annex B-1, para. 126.

the CVMP conclusion applies only when progesterone is used in veterinary *medicinal* products authorized in accordance with relevant EC legislation, which would exclude over the counter products freely available to laypeople.[855]

Reasoning of the Panel

7.729 In light of the arguments of the parties, and having regard to the 1999 and 2002 Opinions[856] and to the fact that some of the insufficiencies identified by the European Communities have been addressed in the common section above or were simply not discussed by the European Communities in its submissions, the Panel will limit its analysis to determining whether relevant scientific evidence is insufficient concerning progesterone with regard to evidence of carcinogenicity in humans.

7.730 We note that the European Communities, referring to the 1999 Opinion, argues that there is no information available on the mutagenicity and genotoxicity of progesterone.[857]

7.731 We recall, however, that with respect to genotoxicity, the 2002 Opinion concludes that "[t]here is no evidence that progesterone or testosterone have genotoxic potential."[858]

7.732 Regarding this aspect, we note that Dr. Boisseau quoted the report of JECFA in its thirty-second session (1999), where it concludes that "[a]lthough equivocal results have been reported for the induction of single-strand DNA breaks and DNA adducts have been seen in vivo and in vitro in some studies, progesterone was not mutagenic ... progesterone has no genotoxic potential ". Dr. Boisseau also quotes JECFA's conclusion that "these effects on tumour production occurred only with doses of progesterone causing obvious hormonal effects ... the effect of progesterone on tumour production was directly related to its hormonal activity".[859]

---

[855] EC's second written submission, para. 159; EC's replies to Panel questions after the first substantive meeting, Annex B-1, paras. 130-133, Exhibit US-13, p. 12.

[856] The 2000 Opinion did not identify essentially new toxicological information concerning progesterone and testosterone in the data presented in the toxicological evaluation of the natural hormones oestradiol-17β, progesterone and testosterone in animal production by JECFA (2000 Opinion, section 2.2, p. 4).

[857] EC's second written submission, quoting 1999 Opinion, paras. 155-156.

[858] 2000 Opinion, section 4.3, p. 15.

[859] Reply of Dr. Boisseau to question 16 of the Panel, Annex D, para. 157.

7.733 Dr. Boobis concurred with the above by saying that:

"there is no evidence that the hormones testosterone or progesterone have genotoxic potential. ... Micronuclei can arise via a non-
genotoxic mechanism, particularly at concentrations that may have
caused some toxicity. In addition, the 32P-post-labelling assay is
not specific, and data cited above suggest that DNA adduction can
arise by mechanisms other than direct interaction with DNA. In no
case did any of the compounds produce a mutagenic response.
These data are insufficient to support the conclusion that these
hormones have genotoxic potential in vivo. Thus, there is no evidence that any of the hormones are genotoxic in vivo at the levels
found in meat from treated animals. Even if GVP were not followed, the levels of exposure to the hormones would be such that
no genotoxicity would be anticipated in vivo."[860]

7.734 Dr. Guttenplan added that "there is no conclusive evidence presented by
the European Communities that the five hormones other than oestradiol-17β,
when consumed as residues in meat have genotoxic potential. There is some
evidence that certain of the hormones have genotoxic potential, but generally the
potential is weak. ... progesterone [is] negative in genotoxic assays. ... Any
genotoxic effects of the five hormones are likely to be minimized by good veterinary practice."[861]

7.735 The European Communities considers that JECFA was more prudent than
the experts when rejecting the genotoxicity of progesterone in 1999. The European Communities argues that the 1999, 2000 and 2002 risk assessments by the
SCVPH provide enough evidence to demonstrate that genotoxicity from these
hormones is possible.[862]

7.736 We note that, on the one hand, the SCVPH in its 2002 Opinion concluded
"[t]here is no evidence that progesterone or testosterone have genotoxic potential". We note, on the other hand, that the European Communities did not point
to any study subsequent to the 2002 Opinion which would contradict this conclusion.

7.737 Regarding evidence of carcinogenicity in humans, we note that IARC has
evaluated progestins as *possibly carcinogenic to humans* (Group 2B)[863] based on

---

[860] Reply of Dr. Boobis to question 21 of the Panel, Annex D, para. 198.

[861] Reply of Dr. Guttenplan to question 21 of the Panel, Annex D, para. 200.

[862] EC's comments on experts replies to question 21 of the Panel, Annex F-1, pp. 17-18.

[863] In its reply to question 24 of the Panel, Annex E-3, p. 128, IARC mentioned that it uses the following groupings to characterize potential carcinogenic agents:

sufficient evidence of carcinogenicity in experimental animals.[864] We note, however, that IARC's evaluation relates to the carcinogenicity of hormones in general, not to the carcinogenicity due to exposure to hormone residues in meat as a result of the cattle being treated with growth promoting hormones.

7.738 Dr. Boisseau mentioned that "[i]n its 1999 report, SCVPH concluded, about the carcinogenicity of progesterone, that 'At present, the data are insufficient to make any quantitative estimate of the risk arising from the exposure to residues in meat.' Therefore, the scientific evidence relied upon in the SCVPH Opinions does not support the conclusion that the carcinogenic effects of progesterone are related to a mechanism other than hormonal activity."[865]

7.739 On the basis of the arguments of the parties and of the experts' opinions, we conclude that there is no new evidence and/or information that calls into question the fundamental precepts of previous knowledge and evidence so as to make relevant, previously sufficient evidence, now insufficient. We therefore conclude that the elements before us do not support the conclusion that the relevant scientific evidence has become insufficient, within the meaning of Article 5.7 of the *SPS Agreement*, regarding the genotoxicity, mutagenicity and carcinogenicity of progesterone.

Conclusion

7.740 Having regard to our specific conclusions above, we recall that the Appellate Body clarified in *Japan – Apples* that relevant scientific evidence will be insufficient within the meaning of Article 5.7 if the body of available scientific evidence does not allow, in quantitative or qualitative terms, the performance of an adequate assessment of risks as required under Article 5.1. In this respect, we note that, at our request, the experts also expressed their

---

"*Carcinogenic to humans* (Group 1). This category is used when there is *sufficient evidence of carcinogenicity* in humans.
Probably carcinogenic to humans (Group 2A). This category is generally used when there is *limited evidence* in humans and *sufficient evidence* in experimental animals.
Possibly carcinogenic to humans (Group 2B). This category is generally used when there is *limited evidence* in humans or *sufficient evidence* in experimental animals, but not both.
Not classifiable as to its carcinogenicity to humans (Group 3). This category is generally used when there is *inadequate evidence* in humans and *inadequate* or *limited evidence* in experimental animals. Agents that do not fall into any other group are also placed in this category.
Probably not carcinogenic to humans (Group 4). This category is generally used when there is *evidence suggesting lack of carcinogenicity* in humans and in experimental animals.
Mechanistic and other relevant data also contribute to the grouping. Further details can be found in the Preamble to the *IARC Monographs* (http://monographs.iarc.fr)."

[864] IARC written replies to question 25 of the Panel, Annex E-3, p. 129.
[865] Reply of Dr. Boisseau to question 16 of the Panel, Annex D, para. 158.

views on the more general question whether the scientific evidence available at the time of the adoption of Directive 2003/74/EC and subsequently allowed the conduct of a risk assessment, in relation to meat from cattle treated, *inter alia,* with progesterone. Dr. Boobis replied that:

> "[T]here was sufficient information available to the EC to have enabled it to have conducted an assessment of the risks to human health arising from consumption of meat from cattle treated with any of the six hormones at issue."

7.741 We also note Dr. Guttenplan's comment that:

> "Progesterone, testosterone have been extensively investigated and the assessment seems sound and is based on the no effect level and a safety factor. (JECFA meeting 52, report-WHA TRS 893)."

7.742 These general remarks support our conclusions on the specific elements discussed above. We therefore conclude that it is not established that the relevant scientific evidence is insufficient with respect to progesterone, within the meaning of Article 5.7 of the *SPS Agreement.*

(viii) Is relevant scientific evidence insufficient in the case of testosterone?

Summary of the main arguments of the parties[866]

7.743 As described above, the **United States** argues that JECFA assessments have shown that hormone residues in meat from animals treated for growth promotion are safe and that evidence is sufficient for a risk assessment. The United States also states that new safety assessments have been conducted for progesterone and testosterone, reaffirming their safety when used according to good veterinary practices.

7.744 The **European Communities**, quoting the 1999 Opinion, identifies the following insufficiencies in the evidence regarding testosterone:[867]

(a)   the mechanism of androgen activity is only partially understood, including the role of androgen receptors in ovarian tumorigenesis;

---

[866]   A more detailed account of the parties' arguments can be found in Section IV of the descriptive part of this Report. The order in which the respective arguments of the parties are presented does not reflect any allocation of the burden of proof by the Panel.
[867]   EC's second written submission, paras. 160-161.

(b)   little information is available about the specific metabolic routes and elimination rates for testosterone in cattle;

(c)   there is uncertainty regarding daily production rate data;

(d)   genotoxicity of testosterone has not been demonstrated with the limited testing done to date;

(e)   no information is available on DNA damage induced by testosterone or its metabolites;

(f)   data on carcinogenicity in humans are limited;[868]

(g)   no dose-response estimate can be given for effects on growth and reproduction;

(h)   there is limited experimental data on the effects of testosterone on the immune system and none on dose-response aspects.

7.745 In response to the US reference to the 1999 JECFA assessment, the European Communities notes that the 1999 Opinion questions the quality of the study that provided the data for JECFA's determination of the ADI. According to the European Communities, neither the actual data nor reference to a peer-reviewed publication were provided, the dose-response was limited to two doses and the ADI was estimated from just a single dose where no effect was observed rather than a curve derived from all the data available.[869]

Reasoning of the Panel

7.746 In light of the arguments of the parties, and having regard to the 1999 and 2002 Opinions[870] and to the fact that some of the insufficiencies identified by the European Communities have been addressed in the common section above, or were simply not discussed by the European Communities in its submissions, the Panel does not deem it necessary to address the mechanism of androgen activity, the metabolic routes and elimination rates for testosterone in cattle or the daily production rate data since these issues have either not been discussed specifically by the parties, or were addressed above.

---

[868] In its conclusion on carcinogenicity, the SCVPH notes that evidence about the role of endogenous testosterone in the occurrence of prostate cancer is weak, that there is limited data on genotoxicity but that testosterone might be aromatized to oestradiol, which had been found to be genotoxic, and that no conclusive quantitative estimate of the risk arising from the excess intake with meat and meat products from treated animals can be made.

[869] EC's second written submission, para. 162; EC's replies to Panel questions after the first substantive meeting, question 22, Annex B-1, para. 124.

[870] The 2000 Opinion did not identify essentially new toxicological information concerning progesterone and testosterone in the data presented in the toxicological evaluation of the natural hormones oestradiol-17β, progesterone and testosterone in animal production by the JECFA (2000 Opinion, section 2.2, p. 4).

7.747 We also note that the 1999 Opinion found that genotoxicity of testosterone has not been demonstrated with the limited testing done to date.[871] The 2002 Opinion adds that "[t]here is no evidence that progesterone or testosterone have genotoxic potential."[872]

7.748 Likewise, the 1999 Opinion states that no information is available on DNA damage induced by testosterone or its metabolites.[873] This said, it states that "testosterone is ... aromatized to oestradiol, which is metabolized to reactive forms that damage DNA and induce mutation." The 1999 Opinion then refers to its section on oestradiol-17β.

7.749 The 1999 Opinion also reports that "[w]hereas the evidence in favour of carcinogenicity was considered sufficient for testosterone in experimental animals, data in humans are limited."[874] This reference has to be read in conjunction with the following paragraph of the 1999 Opinion, which states that the evidence regarding the role of testosterone in prostate cancer is currently weak. In addition, it seems to relate to endogenous testosterone. The 1999 Opinion adds that no conclusive quantitative estimate of the risk arising from the excess intake with meat and meat products from treated animals can be made.

7.750 These comments do not, in our opinion, meet our test that there be a critical mass of new evidence and/or information that calls into question the fundamental precepts of previous knowledge and evidence to make relevant, previously sufficient, evidence now insufficient and would lead us to consider that no risk assessment could be performed. We note in this respect that the 1999 Opinion notes that testosterone is "considered as probable carcinogenic to humans (IARC group 2A)".[875] IARC specified that "this category is generally used when there is limited evidence in humans and sufficient evidence in experimental animals."[876] We also note that IARC assessments are made in general terms, not specifically in relation to consumption of meat treated with hormones for growth promotion purposes.

7.751 Regarding carcinogenicity of testosterone, Dr. Boisseau mentioned that IARC confirms the 1999 Opinion to the extent that it has determined that there is *sufficient evidence of carcinogenicity* in experimental animals and advised, "In

---

[871]   1999 Opinion, section 4.2.5.
[872]   2000 Opinion, section 4.3, p. 15. This was confirmed by the experts who expressed views on this question. For instance, Dr. Guttenplan mentioned that: "there is no conclusive evidence presented by the EC that the five hormones other than oestradiol-17β, when consumed as residues in meat have genotoxic potential." Reply of Dr. Guttenplan to question 21 of the Panel, Annex D, para. 200.
[873]   EC's second written submission, para. 160, quoting 1999 Opinion, p. 49.
[874]   *Ibid.*
[875]   1999 Opinion, section 4.2.7.
[876]   See IARC reply to question 24 of the Panel, Annex E-3, p. 128.

the absence of adequate data in humans, it is reasonable, for practical purposes, to regard testosterone as if it presented a carcinogenic risk to humans".[877]

7.752 Dr. Boisseau also stated that "the scientific evidence relied upon in the SCVPH Opinions does not support the conclusion that the carcinogenic effects of testosterone are related to a mechanism other than hormonal activity."[878]

7.753 Having regard to the positions taken by the SCVPH in its 1999 and 2002 Opinions and the views expressed by the experts, we do not find it necessary to address any further the questions of the genotoxicity and carcinogencity of testosterone in our attempt at determining whether relevant scientific evidence is insufficient with respect to this hormone, within the meaning of Article 5.7 of the *SPS Agreement*.

Conclusion

7.754 Having regard to our specific conclusions above, we recall that the Appellate Body clarified in *Japan – Apples* that relevant scientific evidence will be insufficient within the meaning of Article 5.7 if the body of available scientific evidence does not allow, in quantitative or qualitative terms, the performance of an adequate assessment of risks as required under Article 5.1. In this respect, we note that, at our request, the experts also expressed their views on the more general question whether the scientific evidence available at the time of the adoption of Directive 2003/74/EC and subsequently allowed the conduct of a risk assessment, in relation to meat from cattle treated, *inter alia,* with testosterone. Dr. Boobis replied that:

> "[T]here was sufficient information available to the EC to have enabled it to have conducted an assessment of the risks to human health arising from consumption of meat from cattle treated with any of the six hormones at issue."

7.755 We also note Dr. Guttenplan's comment that:

> "Progesterone, testosterone have been extensively investigated and the assessment seems sound and is based on the no effect level and a safety factor. (JECFA meeting 52, report-WHA TRS 893)."

7.756 These general remarks support our conclusions on the specific elements discussed above. We therefore conclude that it is not established that the relevant

---

[877] IARC reply to question 25 of the Panel, Annex E-3, p. 129.
[878] Reply of Dr. Boisseau to question 16 of the Panel, Annex D, para. 160.

scientific evidence is insufficient with respect to testosterone, within the meaning of Article 5.7 of the *SPS Agreement*.

(ix)   Is relevant scientific evidence insufficient in the case of trenbolone acetate?

Summary of the main arguments of the parties[879]

7.757   As described above, the **United States** argues that JECFA assessments have shown that hormone residues in meat from animals treated for growth promotion are safe and that evidence is sufficient for a risk assessment. The United States also notes that the authors of one of the 17 studies relied upon by the European Communities later concluded that none of the three synthetic growth promoters tested demonstrated evidence of genotoxicity.[880]

7.758   The **European Communities**, quoting the 1999 Opinion, identifies the following insufficiencies in the scientific evidence:[881]

(a)   the need to further investigate the metabolic fate and chemical nature of covalently bound residues of trenbolone acetate;

(b)   in humans, no data are currently available to assess the carcinogenicity of trenbolone acetate;[882]

(c)   regarding effects on reproduction, the available data do not allow a realistic assessment of a dose-response relationship;

(d)   investigations of the effects of trenbolone acetate on the immune system are very limited.

7.759   The European Communities adds that the SCVPH concluded that the information is insufficient to assess the possible impacts of low levels of trenbolone acetate in meat on consumers.

7.760   The European Communities indicates that, in its 2002 Opinion, the SCVPH found these conclusions to be compounded by data obtained in certain of the 17 studies and more recent research, none of which was considered by the 1988 JECFA report. The European Communities argues that the only assessment

---

[879]   A more detailed account of the parties' arguments can be found in Section IV of the descriptive part of this Report. The order in which the respective arguments of the parties are presented does not reflect any allocation of the burden of proof by the Panel.

[880]   US's second written submission, footnote 41.

[881]   EC's second written submission, para. 165.

[882]   In its conclusion on carcinogenicity, the SCVPH notes that in consideration of the lack of *in vitro* short-term assays on mutagenicity and genotoxicity of certain TBOH metabolites and in consideration of the equivocal results of cell transformation assays and the *in vivo* studies, the available information is insufficient to complete a quantitative risk assessment. 1999 Opinion, section 4.4.7, p 59.

on trenbolone acetate publicly available is that of JECFA, and that the SCVPH took this assessment into account, but disagreed with a number of its basic findings on the basis of more recent scientific research.[883]

Reasoning of the Panel

7.761 In light of the arguments of the parties and of the fact that some of the insufficiencies identified by the European Communities have been addressed in the common section above, or were simply not discussed by the European Communities in its submissions, the Panel will limit its analysis to determining whether relevant scientific evidence is insufficient concerning trenbolone acetate with regard to the following aspects:

(a)   metabolism of trenbolone acetate;[884]

(b)   inadequate evidence of carcinogenicity in humans.

Metabolism of trenbolone acetate

7.762 The European Communities refers to the 2002 Opinion which states that "experiments with zeranol and trenbolone acetate suggested a more complex oxidative metabolism than previously assumed. These data need further clarification as they might influence a risk assessment related to tissue residues of these compounds."[885]

7.763 We note that Dr. Boobis discussed study 4 of the 17 studies:

> "The metabolism of zeranol and trenbolone had been further investigated (study 4). These data do not appear to have been published in the peer reviewed literature to date.
>
> The data on trenbolone show that the alpha enantiomer in liver slices from bovine is extensively conjugated and hence inactivated. There is some conversion of the alpha to the active β isomer by human liver microsomes, but the kinetics of the reaction and the extent of conjugation have not been determined. No data were presented on levels of the alpha enantiomer in meat from treated cattle. However, these data do not affect the risk assessment of trenbolone acetate. This is because a) the toxicological studies were conducted in animals that would have been exposed to the

---

[883]   EC's second written submission, paras 166-167; EC's replies to Panel questions after the first substantive meeting, question 22, Annex B-1, para. 126.
[884]   EC's second written submission, para. 165, quoting 1999 Opinion at pp. 55-60.
[885]   2002 Opinion, section 7, p. 21.

metabolites of concern, b) JECFA considered residues of both the alpha and the β enantiomers in recommending MRLs for tren-bolone acetate."[886]

7.764   No other expert expressed views on the subject.

7.765   The Panel is cognizant that the European Communities argues that Dr. Boobis' comments on a number of the studies generated by the European Communities are flawed and has given examples of those alleged flaws.[887] How-ever, it does not expressly address Dr. Boobis' comments on the study discussed above. As a result, the Panel sees no reason not to take the comments of Dr. Boobis fully into account in its assessment of the sufficiency of existing relevant scientific evidence.

Inadequate evidence of carcinogenicity in humans

7.766   The European Communities refers to the 1999 Opinion which recalls that trenbolone acetate is a synthetic androgen and that both the parent compound and its metabolite have been extensively tested for their mutagenic/genotoxic potential. The 1999 Opinion notes that it might be concluded that the genotoxic effects of trenbolone acetate are not related to their hormonal activity. It notes that "[f]ormation of DNA adducts has been observed in rat hepatocytes ... (Metzler, 1999)." On carcinogenicity, the 1999 Opinion mentions *inter alia* that a two-year carcinogenesis[888] bioassay in rats and mice did not provide definitive results. In humans, no data are currently available to assess the carcinogenicity of trenbolone acetate. The 1999 Opinion concludes that the available informa-tion is insufficient to complete a quantitative risk assessment.[889]

7.767   Regarding this aspect, Dr. Boisseau mentioned the following:

"In its thirty second session held in 1987, JECFA concluded from carcinogenic studies in animals that "the liver hyperplasia and tu-

---

[886]   Reply of Dr. Boobis to question 62 of the Panel, Annex D, paras. 479-480.

[887]   EC's comments on the replies of the experts, Annex F-1, p. 40.

[888]   *Mechanism (or mode of action) of carcinogenesis:* a mode of action is series of key events which are necessary to lead to the formation of a tumour. These key events comprise the biological changes induced by the chemical and subsequent events which then lead to the development of cancer. A mechanism refers to the molecular events that are responsible for those changes. A hormonal mecha-nism means that it is the endocrine or hormonal effect of a compound that leads to growth or prolif-eration of certain cells that are responsive to the hormone, resulting in the development of a tumour. A genotoxic mechanism means that there is a mechanism independent of the hormonal action result-ing in direct damage to the DNA that leads to a tumour. There are situations where elements of more than one mechanism could apply (Transcript of the Panel meeting with the experts, Annex G, paras. 103-109 (Dr. Boobis, Dr. Cogliano and Dr. Guttenplan)).

[889]   1999 Opinion, pp. 57-59.

mours in mice ... and the slight increase in the incidence of islet-cell of the pancreas of rats arose as a consequence of the hormonal activity of trenbolone". In its thirty fourth session held in 1989, JECFA, having reviewed a comprehensive battery of short term tests, concluded that 'it was unlikely that trenbolone acetate was genotoxic' and decided to confirm its previous conclusion to base the evaluation of trenbolone acetate and its metabolites on their no-hormonal-effect."[890]

7.768   The 2002 Opinion refers to the results of study 2 of the 17 studies with respect to mutagenicity and genotoxicity (Metzler and Pfeiffer, 2001).[891]

7.769   Three experts expressed their views in relation to the subject of this study. Dr. Boobis mentions the following:

"There is no convincing evidence that trenbolone acetate, MGA and zeranol are genotoxic. They were negative in a range of tests for genotoxicity. They were very weakly positive in a micronu-cleus test, at high (potentially cytotoxic) concentrations. Tren-bolone also produced a low level of DNA adducts measured by 32P-post-labelling *(Metzler and Pfeiffer, 2001)*.[892] As indicated above, micronuclei can arise via a non-genotoxic mechanism, par-ticularly at concentrations that may have caused some toxicity. In addition, the 32P-post-labelling assay is not specific, and data cited above suggest that DNA adduction can arise by mechanisms other than direct interaction with DNA. In no case did any of the compounds produce a mutagenic response. These data are insuffi-cient to support the conclusion that these hormones have genotoxic potential in vivo. Thus, there is no evidence that any of the hormones are genotoxic in vivo at the levels found in meat from treated animals. Even if GVP were not followed, the levels of exposure to the hormones would be such that no genotoxicity would be anticipated in vivo."[893]

7.770   Dr. Boobis added that:

"Study 4 reports recent observations on the genotoxicity and mutagenicity of zeranol and trenbolone. Both compounds were negative for tests of mutagenicity, i.e. induction of *lac*I mutations

---

[890]   Reply of Dr. Boisseau to question 16 of the Panel, Annex D, para. 163.
[891]   2002 Opinion, section 4.4.3.
[892]   Dr. Boobis cited to *Metzler M and Pfeiffer E (2001). Genotoxic potential of xenobiotic growth promoters and their metabolites. APMIS, **109**:89-95*
[893]   Reply of Dr. Boobis to question 21of the Panel, Annex D, para. 198.

in *E coli* and induction of *hprt* mutations inV79 cells. Zeranol did not produce DNA adducts in rat hepatocytes whilst a low level of DNA adducts was observed with trenbolone. Both were very weakly positive in a micronucleus test, at high (potentially cytotoxic) concentrations. As indicated above ..., micronuclei can arise via a non-genotoxic mechanism, particularly at concentrations that may have caused some toxicity. In addition, the 32P-post-labelling assay is not specific, and data cited above suggest that DNA adduction can arise by mechanisms other than direct interaction with DNA. These data are insufficient, given the number of well conducted studies in which the compounds were negative, to alter the conclusion that neither zeranol nor trenbolone acetate has genotoxic potential in vivo. Indeed, the *SVCPH (2002)* concluded that "both compounds exhibited only very weak effects" in those in vitro tests in which positive effects were observed."[894]

7.771 Dr. Guttenplan confirmed the conclusions of the two other experts:

"[t]here is no conclusive evidence presented by the EC that the five hormones other than oestradiol-17β, when consumed as residues in meat have genotoxic potential. There is some evidence that certain of the hormones have genotoxic potential, but generally the potential is weak. ... Trenbolone is either negative or marginally active in *in vitro* genotoxic assays. ... Any genotoxic effects of the five hormones are likely to be minimized by good veterinary practice. My reply for the hormones would not have been different in September 2003 (SCVPH 2002 Opinion)."[895]

7.772 The European Communities argues essentially that the 1999, 2000 and 2002 Opinions provide enough evidence to demonstrate that genotoxicity and other adverse effects from these hormones are possible and that there are a number of uncertainties surrounding their mechanism of action to warrant further investigations. The European Communities refers to Dr. Guttenplan's statement.[896]

7.773 We do not read the statement above as the European Communities does. Rather we understand Dr. Guttenplan to say that the genotoxic potential of trenbolone acetate is weak.

---

[894] Reply of Dr. Boobis to question 62 of the Panel, Annex D, para. 483.
[895] Reply of Dr. Guttenplan to question 21 of the Panel, Annex D, para. 200.
[896] EC's comments on expert replies to question 21 of the Panel, Annex F-1, pp. 17-18.

7.774 Regarding carcinogenicity, we first note that trenbolone acetate has not been evaluated by IARC, nor have the specific risks from the consumption of meat from cattle treated with this growth promotion hormone.[897]

7.775 Dr. Boisseau made the following comments:

"In its 1999 report, SCVPH concluded, about the carcinogenicity of trenbolone, that 'in consideration of the lack of in vitro short term assays on mutagenicity and genotoxicity of other trenbolone metabolites other than α-trenbolone and in consideration of the equivocal results of the transformation assays and the in vivo studies, the available information is insufficient to complete a quantitative risk assessment'. Therefore, the scientific evidence relied upon in the SCVPH Opinions does not support the conclusion that the carcinogenic effects of trenbolone are related to a mechanism other than hormonal activity."[898]

7.776 The European Communities seeks to refute Dr. Boisseau's comments on the basis that he refers only to the JECFA's reports, which are outdated and based on old data, and that he interprets lack of data as lack of adverse effects.

7.777 We recall our test in order to assess whether relevant scientific evidence is insufficient is that there should be new evidence and/or information that calls into question the fundamental precepts of previous knowledge and evidence so as to make relevant, previously sufficient evidence, now insufficient. We note that the European Communities points at possibilities which are not confirmed by the experts who expressed their views. We therefore conclude that the elements before us do not support the conclusion that the relevant scientific evidence has become insufficient, within the meaning of Article 5.7 of the *SPS Agreement*, regarding the carcinogenicity of trenbolone acetate.

Conclusion

7.778 Having regard to our specific conclusions above, we recall that the Appellate Body clarified in *Japan – Apples* that relevant scientific evidence will be insufficient within the meaning of Article 5.7 if the body of available scientific evidence does not allow, in quantitative or qualitative terms, the performance of an adequate assessment of risks as required under Article 5.1. In this respect, we note that, at our request, the experts also expressed their views on the more general question whether the scientific evidence available at the time of the adoption of Directive 2003/74/EC and subsequently allowed the

---

[897] IARC reply to question 25 of the Panel, Annex E-3, p. 129.
[898] Reply of Dr. Boisseau to question 16 of the Panel, Annex D, para. 164.

conduct of a risk assessment, in relation to meat from cattle treated, *inter alia,* with trenbolone acetate. Dr. Boobis replied that:

> "[T]here was sufficient information available to the EC to have enabled it to have conducted an assessment of the risks to human health arising from consumption of meat from cattle treated with any of the six hormones at issue."

7.779 We also note Dr. Guttenplan's comment that:

> "There is more limited evidence available for Trenbolone and Zeranol and most of it is *in vitro (SCVPH 2002 Opinion)* or not recent (e.g., JECFA meeting 34th report, 1989 and 32nd report, 1988). However, both appear to be potentially significantly estrogenic. Experimental and analytical methods have improved but it does not appear that accurate ADI's can be established at this point. Studies in experimental animals and studies on levels in beef are still needed. However, from the data available at the time of the Directive, the potential for adverse effects could not be ruled out."[899]

7.780 We note, however, that during our meeting with the experts, Dr. Guttenplan clarified, at the EC request, that "the ability [to make a risk assessment] varies between compounds, but that does not mean that you can't make a risk assessment, it just means that the accuracy of the risk assessment is different."[900] Regarding the establishment of accurate ADIs, Dr. Guttenplan clarified that "accurate means – if it's not accurate, there is just a larger range, but you can still do a risk assessment."[901]

7.781 These general remarks support our conclusions on the specific elements discussed above. We therefore conclude that it is not established that the relevant scientific evidence is insufficient with respect to trenbolone acetate, within the meaning of Article 5.7 of the *SPS Agreement.*

---

[899] Reply of Dr. Guttenplan to question 61 of the Panel, Annex D, para. 457.
[900] Transcript of the Panel meeting with the experts, Annex G, para. 983.
[901] Transcript of the Panel meeting with the experts, Annex G, para. 985.

(x)   Is relevant scientific evidence insufficient
        in the case of zeranol?

Summary of the main arguments of the parties[902]

7.782 As described above, the **United States** argues that JECFA assessments
have shown that hormone residues in meat from animals treated for growth promotion are safe and that evidence is sufficient for a risk assessment. The United
States also notes that the authors of one of the 17 studies relied upon by the
European Communities later concluded that none of the three synthetic growth
promoters tested demonstrated evidence of genotoxicity.[903]

7.783 The **European Communities**, quoting the 1999 Opinion, identifies the
following insufficiencies in the evidence:[904]

(a)   there are only few tests with equivocal results on the genotoxic
        properties of zeranol, which are insufficient for an evaluation of its
        mutagenic/genotoxic properties;

(b)   no data are available on cancer risk for humans linked to meat
        with zeranol residues;[905]

(c)   no dose-response relationship for effects of zeranol on growth and
        reproduction can be made;

(d)   no relevant data on effects on the immune system were found.

7.784 The European Communities notes that, in conclusion, the 1999 Opinion
finds that the available data do not allow a quantitative estimate of the risk arising from exposure to zeranol residues, and that further data are needed on the
nature of the metabolites formed in bovines. The European Communities indicates that in its 2002 Opinion, the SCVPH found these conclusions to be compounded by data obtained in certain of the 17 studies and more recent research.[906]

7.785 The European Communities cites a study by US scientists according to
which meat and serum from zeranol-implanted cattle possess "heat-stable mito-
genicity for cultured breast cells, and that both normal and cancerous human

---

[902] A more detailed account of the parties' arguments can be found in Section IV of the descriptive
part of this Report. The order in which the respective arguments of the parties are presented does not
reflect any allocation of the burden of proof by the Panel.
[903] US's second written submission, footnote 41.
[904] EC's second written submission, para. 168.
[905] In its conclusion on carcinogenicity, the SCVPH states that considering the limited data on
mutagenicity/genotoxicity and the clear evidence for an induction of liver adenomas and carcinomas
in hamsters, no assessment of the possible carcinogenicity of zeranol can be made. See 1999 Opinion,
section 4.5.7, p. 65.
[906] EC's second written submission, paras. 168-169.

breast cells exhibit estrogenic responses to zeranol".[907] These scientists then point to potential tumorigenic effects for oestrogen, including direct genotoxic effects of oestrogen metabolites. They point out that the mechanisms responsible for oestrogen stimulated carcinogenesis remain undefined. The European Communities argues that these studies clearly invalidate the findings of the 1988 JECFA opinion.[908]

7.786 The European Communities also argues that the only assessment on zeranol publicly available is that performed by JECFA in 1988. The European Communities indicates that the SCVPH took this assessment into account, but disagreed with a number of its basic findings on the basis of more recent scientific research, some of which was generated by the 17 studies[909] (studies Nos. 2, 4 and 10) and more recent research.

Reasoning of the Panel

7.787 In light of the arguments of the parties and of the fact that some of the insufficiencies identified by the European Communities have been addressed in the common section above, or were simply not discussed by the European Communities in its submissions, the Panel will limit its analysis to determining whether relevant scientific evidence is insufficient concerning zeranol with regard to the alleged inadequate evidence of carcinogenicity in humans, such as lack of information available on mutagenicity and genotoxicity and lack of information on DNA adducts and DNA damages.

7.788 The 1999 Opinion referred to by the European Communities states that the mutagenicity and genotoxicity of zeranol was investigated only in a few tests which gave equivocal results insufficient for an evaluation of the mutagenic/genotoxic properties of zeranol. As far as carcinogenicity is concerned, the 1999 Opinion concludes that there is clear evidence for the induction of liver adenomas and carcinomas in one animal species, but no assessment of the possible carcinogenicity of zeranol can be made.[910]

7.789 Five experts provided views on this matter. Dr. Cogliano limited his comments to the study by Norat et al. (2005)[911], one of the three recently published studies on which the Panel sought the views of the experts, which addresses the association between consumption of red meat and colorectal cancer.

---

[907] EC's second written submission, paras. 145-146, citing a study by Suling Liu and Young C. Lin, Exhibit EC-8.
[908] EC's second written submission, para. 170.
[909] EC's second written submission, para. 168; EC's replies to Panel questions after the first substantive meeting, question 22, Annex B-1, para. 126.
[910] 1999 Opinion, sections 4.5.5 to 4.5.7.
[911] Exhibit EC-71.

The comments by Dr. Cogliano are not specific with respect to the question of the potential carcinogenicity of zeranol.

7.790 Dr. Boisseau expressed the following opinion:

"In its thirty second session held in 1987, JECFA concluded that zeranol and its metabolites, zearalanone and taleranol, were not mutagenic in a number of tests in bacterial and mammalian systems even if it has noted that zeranol gives a positive result in the Rec-assay and taleranol gives a positive result in the test with Chinese hamster ovary cells in the absence of activation but a negative result with activation. After having reviewed the carcinogenicity studies in animals, JECFA concluded that 'the tumorigenic effect of zeranol was associated with its oestrogenic properties'."[912]

7.791 The 2002 Opinion refers to a comparative study (study 4 of the 17 studies) designed to determine the potential of zeranol, trenbolone and melengestrol acetate to cause genetic damages in various *in vitro* systems. The 2002 Opinion states that "[i]n this study zeranol did not induce genotoxicity or mutagenicity."[913]

7.792 Dr. Sippell mentioned that "[S]ynthetic hormone growth promoters such as Zeranol and its metabolites have been shown to be as potent as [estradiol] and diethylstilbestrol (DES) in increasing the expression of estrogen-related genes in human breast cancer cells (*Leffers et al 2001* – study 17)."[914] However, Dr. Boobis specified that:

"The study referred to (study 17), reported in *Leffers et al (2001)*, showed that a number of oestogenic compounds affected the expression of several genes in the ER positive breast cancer cell line, MCF7. The responsiveness of this cell line to oestrogens is well established. It was of interest that all of the changes reported by *Leffers et al (2001)* were blocked by the selective ERantagonist ICI82.780. The relevance of effects observed in a cultured cell line to the situation *in vivo*, where kinetic and metabolic factors will influence the magnitude of the response is not known, nor is the significance of changes in gene expression to the toxicity of the hormones known. Many of the changes will reflect the proliferative response to an oestrogenic stimulus. However, in general toxicogenomic data, in the absence on any information on the functional

---

[912] Reply of Dr. Boisseau to question 16 of the Panel, Annex D, para. 165.
[913] 2002 Opinion, section 4.4.3, p. 16.
[914] Reply of Dr. Sippell to question 41 of the Panel, Annex D, para. 336.

consequences, is not considered a sound basis for use in risk assessment *(IPCS, 2003)*."[915]

7.793   Dr. Boobis added that:

"There is no evidence that the hormones testosterone or progesterone have genotoxic potential. There is no convincing evidence that trenbolone acetate, MGA and zeranol are genotoxic. They were negative in a range of tests for genotoxicity. They were very weakly positive in a micronucleus test, at high (potentially cytotoxic) concentrations. Trenbolone also produced a low level of DNA adducts measured by 32P-post-labelling *(Metzler and Pfeiffer, 2001)*.[916] As indicated above, micronuclei can arise via a nongenotoxic mechanism, particularly at concentrations that may have caused some toxicity. In addition, the 32P-post-labelling assay is not specific, and data cited above suggest that DNA adduction can arise by mechanisms other than direct interaction with DNA. In no case did any of the compounds produce a mutagenic response. These data are insufficient to support the conclusion that these hormones have genotoxic potential in vivo. Thus, there is no evidence that any of the hormones are genotoxic in vivo at the levels found in meat from treated animals. Even if GVP were not followed, the levels of exposure to the hormones would be such that no genotoxicity would be anticipated in vivo."

7.794   Dr. Boobis, commenting on study 4, added the following:

"Study 4 reports recent observations on the genotoxicity and mutagenicity of zeranol and trenbolone. Both compounds were negative for tests of mutagenicity, i.e. induction of *lac*I mutations in *E coli* and induction of *hprt* mutations inV79 cells. Zeranol did not produce DNA adducts in rat hepatocytes whilst a low level of DNA adducts was observed with trenbolone. Both were very weakly positive in a micronucleus test, at high (potentially cyto-

---

[915]   Reply of Dr. Boobis to question 62 of the Panel, Annex D, para. 475. Dr. Boobis cites to:
IPCS (2003). Toxicogenomics and the Risk Assessment of Chemicals for the Protection of Human Health
(http://www.who.int/entity/ipcs/methods/en/toxicogenomicssummaryreport.pdf)
Leffers H, Naesby M, Vendelbo B, Skakkebaek NE and Jorgensen M (2001). Oestrogenic potencies of Zeranol, oestradiol, diethylstilboestrol, Bisphenol-A and genistein: implications for exposure assessment of potential endocrine disrupters. Hum Reprod, **16**:1037-1045.

[916]   Dr. Boobis cited to Metzler M and Pfeiffer E (2001). Genotoxic potential of xenobiotic growth promoters and their metabolites. APMIS, **109**:89-95; see Reply of Dr. Boobis to question 21 of the Panel, Annex D, para. 198.

toxic) concentrations. As indicated above ..., micronuclei can arise via a non-genotoxic mechanism, particularly at concentrations that may have caused some toxicity. In addition, the 32P-post-labelling assay is not specific, and data cited above suggest that DNA adduction can arise by mechanisms other than direct interaction with DNA. These data are insufficient, given the number of well conducted studies in which the compounds were negative, to alter the conclusion that neither zeranol nor trenbolone acetate has genotoxic potential in vivo. Indeed, the *SVCPH (2002)* concluded that 'both compounds exhibited only very weak effects' in those in vitro tests in which positive effects were observed."[917]

7.795 Dr. Guttenplan commented in more general terms that:

"There is no conclusive evidence presented by the EC that the five hormones other than oestradiol-17β, when consumed as residues in meat have genotoxic potential. There is some evidence that certain of the hormones have genotoxic potential, but generally the potential is weak. .... Zeranol can induce transformation of breast epithelial cells in culture with efficiency similar to that of estradiol, but the mechanism is not known, and it is negative or marginally active in other assays. ... Any genotoxic effects of the five hormones are likely to be minimized by good veterinary practice. My reply for the hormones would not have been different in September 2003 (*SCVPH 2002 Opinion*)."[918]

7.796 Regarding carcinogenicity of zeranol, Dr. Boisseau mentioned that:

"In its 1999 report, SCVPH concluded, about the carcinogenicity of zeranol, that "in consideration of the lack of data on mutagenicity/genotoxicity and the clear evidence for an induction of liver adenomas and carcinomas in one animal species, no assessment of the possible carcinogenicity of zeranol can be made". Therefore, the scientific evidence relied upon in the SCVPH Opinions does not support the conclusion that the carcinogenic effects of zeranol are related to a mechanism other than hormonal activity."[919]

---

[917] Reply of Dr. Boobis to question 62 of the Panel, Annex D, para. 483.
[918] Reply of Dr. Guttenplan to question 21 of the Panel, Annex D, para. 200.
[919] Reply of Dr. Boisseau to question 16 of the Panel, Annex D, para. 166.

7.797 Referring to the study by Liu S and Lin YC (2002)[920], Dr. Guttenplan stated that:

> "The first of the studies suggests a risk from zeranol. That observation was not previously reported. However, the results were obtained in cultured cells and the relevance to human exposure to hormone-treated cannot be extrapolated from this study because of a myriad of uncertainties in such extrapolation. The study does suggest that additional tests of zeranol should be carried out. There is also some evidence that a metabolite of zeranol (zearalenone) induces oxidative damage in cultured cells. This is a possible genotoxic effect, but again it cannot be extrapolated to meat consumption."[921]

7.798 Zeranol has not been evaluated by IARC, nor have the specific risks from the consumption of meat from cattle treated with this growth promotion hormone.[922]

7.799 The European Communities argues that Dr. Guttenplan made a "careful and scientifically sound statement".[923] We note, however, that Dr. Guttenplan concluded that a genotoxic effect cannot be extrapolated to meat consumption, because of the "myriad of uncertainties" that such extrapolation would entail.

7.800 On the basis of the arguments of the parties and of the experts' opinions, we conclude that it is not established that relevant scientific evidence is insufficient in relation to the carcinogenicity of zeranol, within the meaning of Article 5.7 of the *SPS Agreement*.

Conclusion

7.801 Having regard to our specific conclusions above, we recall that the Appellate Body clarified in *Japan – Apples* that relevant scientific evidence will be insufficient within the meaning of Article 5.7 if the body of available scientific evidence does not allow, in quantitative or qualitative terms, the performance of an adequate assessment of risks as required under Article 5.1. In this respect, we note that, at our request, the experts also expressed their views on the more general question whether the scientific evidence available at the time of the adoption of Directive 2003/74/EC and subsequently allowed the con-

---

[920] Liu S and Lin YC (2004). Transformation of MCF-10A human breast epithelial cells by zeranol and oestradiol-17.β Breast J, 10:514-521, Exhibit EC-62.
[921] Reply of Dr. Guttenplan to question 25 of the Panel, Annex D, para. 234.
[922] IARC reply to question 25 of the Panel, Annex E-3, p. 129.
[923] EC's comments on experts replies to question 25 of the Panel, Annex F-1, p. 21.

duct of a risk assessment, in relation to meat from cattle treated, *inter alia,* with zeranol. Dr. Boobis replied that:

"[T]here was sufficient information available to the EC to have enabled it to have conducted an assessment of the risks to human health arising from consumption of meat from cattle treated with any of the six hormones at issue."

7.802 We also note Dr. Guttenplan's comment that:

"There is more limited evidence available for Trenbolone and Zeranol and most of it is *in vitro (SCVPH 2002 Opinion)* or not recent (e.g., JECFA meeting 34th report, 1989 and 32nd report, 1988). However, both appear to be potentially significantly estrogenic. Experimental and analytical methods have improved but it does not appear that accurate ADI's can be established at this point. Studies in experimental animals and studies on levels in beef are still needed. However, from the data available at the time of the Directive, the potential for adverse effects could not be ruled out."[924]

7.803 We note, however, that during our meeting with the experts, Dr. Guttenplan clarified, at the EC request, that "the ability [to make a risk assessment] varies between compounds, but that does not mean that you can't make a risk assessment, it just means that the accuracy of the risk assessment is different."[925] Regarding the establishment of accurate ADIs, Dr. Guttenplan clarified that "accurate means – if it's not accurate, there is just a larger range, but you can still do a risk assessment."[926]

7.804 These general remarks support our conclusions on the specific elements discussed above. We therefore conclude that it is not established that the relevant scientific evidence is insufficient with respect to zeranol, within the meaning of Article 5.7 of the *SPS Agreement.*

---

[924] Reply of Dr. Guttenplan to question 61 of the Panel, Annex D, para. 457.
[925] Transcript of the Panel meeting with the experts, Annex G, para. 983.
[926] Transcript of the Panel meeting with the experts, Annex G, para. 985.

(xi)   Is relevant scientific evidence insufficient
in the case of melengestrol acetate (MGA)?

Summary of the main arguments of the parties[927]

7.805 The **United States** considers that there is sufficient evidence for a risk assessment on melengestrol acetate and argues that JECFA has carried out a risk assessment. The United States also notes that the authors of one of the 17 studies relied upon by the European Communities later concluded that none of the three synthetic growth promoters tested demonstrated evidence of genotoxicity.[928]

7.806 The **European Communities**, quoting passages the 1999 Opinion, identified the following insufficiencies in the evidence:[929]

(a)   only limited data are available concerning residues of melengestrol acetate in treated cattle;

(b)   no information is available on mutagenicity and genotoxicity;

(c)   no information is available on DNA adducts and DNA damage.;

(d)   carcinogenicity studies have been conducted in only one animal species, which is inadequate to assess the carcinogenic potential of melengestrol acetate;[930]

(e)   available data on effects of melengestrol acetate on growth and reproduction do not allow an estimate of the dose-response relationship;

(f)   data on the effect of melengestrol acetate on the immune system are also very limited.

7.807 The European Communities adds that the SCVPH concluded that the available information is insufficient for a quantitative estimate of the risk to the consumer of meat from treated animals. The European Communities indicates that in its 2002 Opinion, the SCVPH found these conclusions compounded by data obtained in certain of the 17 studies.

7.808 The European Communities recalls the finding of the Appellate Body in *EC – Hormones* that no risk assessment had been performed and notes that Co-

---

[927] A more detailed account of the parties' arguments can be found in Section IV of the descriptive part of this Report. The order in which the respective arguments of the parties are presented does not reflect any allocation of the burden of proof by the Panel.

[928] US's second written submission, footnote 41.

[929] EC's second written submission, paras. 172-173.

[930] In its conclusion on carcinogenicity, the SCVPH notes that in view of the lack of data on mutagenicity/carcinogenicity and on DNA interaction, and in consideration of carcinogenicity studies conducted only in one animal species, the data are inadequate to assess the carcinogenetic potential of melengestrol acetate.

dex has not adopted an international standard on melengestrol acetate, although JECFA assessed melengestrol acetate in 2000 (and in 2004 as regards calculation of the MRL). The European Communities argues that in the absence of a Codex standard, the opinion of JECFA becomes irrelevant. In addition, the European Communities indicates that JECFA failed to take into account the more recent data generated by its 17 studies and the 2002 Opinion.[931]

7.809 The European Communities argues that the SCVPH took into account the JECFA assessment and noted that no original data had been presented in the JECFA report and that the majority of references were to reports that had not been published in the peer-reviewed scientific literature.[932]

7.810 The European Communities notes that the United States refers to a draft 2005 report from the UK Committee on Veterinary Practices. According to the European Communities, this report notes that there are important gaps in the evidence base for oestradiol-17β and the other five hormonally-active substances, as acknowledged in the Opinions. The cited passage then states a need for certain information, including a number of issues where more information is needed to improve future risk assessments.[933]

7.811 The European Communities concludes that there is no doubt that the 1999-2002 Opinions constitute the only currently available risk assessment on melengestrol acetate, based on the most recent, peer-reviewed, pertinent information available publicly from the European Communities. The European Communities notes that these Opinions reached the conclusion that the current state of scientific knowledge does not permit a more definitive risk assessment to be carried out.[934]

Reasoning of the Panel

7.812 In light of the arguments of the parties and of the fact that some of the insufficiencies identified by the European Communities have been addressed in the common section above, or were simply not discussed by the European Communities in its submissions, the Panel will limit its analysis to determining whether relevant scientific evidence is insufficient concerning melengestrol acetate with regard to the following aspects:

---

[931] EC's second written submission, para. 171.
[932] EC's second written submission, para. 174; EC's replies to Panel questions after the first substantive meeting, question 22, Annex B-1, paras. 126-127.
[933] EC's second written submission, para. 175.
[934] EC's second written submission, para. 176.

(a)   only limited data are available concerning residues of melengestrol
        acetate in treated cattle;

(b)   inadequate evidence for carcinogenicity in humans, such as no in-
        formation available on mutagenicity and genotoxicity and no in-
        formation available on DNA adducts and DNA damage. [935]

7.813 As a preliminary remark, the Panel notes that Codex did not adopt any
standard with respect to melengestrol acetate. The Panel recalls, however, that
while there is no international standard as such, intensive work has been performed at the international level. JECFA made two assessments of melengestrol
acetate in 2000 and 2004 (the second time in order to propose a MRL). It was
included in the priority list for recalculation of MRLs and TMDI by the fifteenth
session of CCRVDF that met in 2005.[936] The Panel notes in this respect that for
melengestrol acetate, the draft MRL is currently at Step 7 of the Codex elaboration procedure.[937] Moreover, the role of JECFA in the international risk assessment process is such that some degree of relevance should be given to that work.
The Panel also notes that at no time did the European Communities request that
melengestrol acetate be considered by Codex.[938]

Data on residues of melengestrol acetate

7.814 The two main criticisms of the European Communities regarding JECFA'
s assessments are that the residue data used by JECFA on melengestrol acetate
are outdated and that JECFA did not take into account the more recent studies
commissioned by the European Communities. In the 2002 Opinion, the SCVPH
noted that in the JECFA report no original data had been presented and that the
majority of references were to reports that had not been published in the peer-
reviewed scientific literature.[939]

7.815 We sought the views of the experts on this matter and two of them gave
an opinion (Dr. Boisseau, Dr. De Brabander). Both concurred in saying that
nearly all the studies used by JECFA dated back to the 1960s and 1970s. However, neither of the two experts stated that these studies were no longer valid.[940]

7.816 The Panel first recalls its position on so-called "old" data in paragraph
7.423 *et seq.* above.

---

[935] EC's second written submission, para. 172, quoting 1999 Opinion, p. 77.

[936] Dr. Miyagishima, Codex representative, transcript of the Panel meeting with the experts, Annex G, para. 524.

[937] As explained by Dr. Miyagishima, transcript of the Panel meeting with the experts, Annex G,
para. 896.

[938] Dr. Miyagishima, transcript of the Panel meeting with the experts, Annex G, para. 524.

[939] 2002 Opinion, p. 16.

[940] Reply of Dr. De Brabander to question 35 of the Panel, Annex D, paras. 304-305.

7.817 Second, the Panel notes the opinion of Dr. Boisseau: "It is correct to say that nearly all the studies referred to in the 2000 JECFA report on melengestrol acetate date from the 1960s and 1970s. The comment to be made on this issue is [that] JECFA considered a wide series of toxicological studies in its assessment, used as an end point a non hormonal effect dose by far more conservative than a NOAEL based on tumorigenic effect and adopted a 200 safety factor to derive an ADI from this NOAEL."[941]

7.818 Dr. Boobis also expressed his views on the more recent studies commissioned by the European Communities. With respect to the findings of study 4 referred to by the European Communities regarding residues of melengestrol acetate, Dr. Boobis mentioned the following:

"In study 4, unpublished preliminary findings on the in vitro metabolism of MGA were reported. This study provided some evidence for the formation of multiple metabolites of MGA by liver from human, rat and bovine. However, these findings do not affect the risk assessment of MGA because a) the toxicological studies were conducted in animals that would have been exposed to all of the metabolites of concern, b) JECFA assumed that all of the residues in meat from animals treated with MGA were as hormonally active as MGA when it proposed MRLs in 2002 (JECFA, 2002b). It was subsequently shown that this was a conservative decision, as not all of the residues were as active as MGA itself (JECFA, 2006c)."[942]

7.819 Although the European Communities criticized Dr. Boobis' analysis of some of the 17 studies in its comments on the replies of the experts[943], it did not specifically address Dr. Boobis's comments on study 4.

Inadequate evidence for carcinogenicity in humans, such as no information available on mutagenicity and genotoxicity and no information available on DNA adducts and DNA damage

7.820 We note that the 2002 Opinion mentions that the genotoxicity of melengestrol acetate was investigated (study 4) and that "[t]he results were negative in several experiments using concentrations in either 15-125 uM for HPRT

---

[941] Reply of Dr. Boisseau to question 35, Annex D, para. 303.
[942] Reply of Dr. Boobis to question 62 of the Panel, Annex D, para. 484. Dr. Boobis cites to:
  – JECFA (2002b). Residues of some veterinary drugs in animals and foods. FAO Food and Nutrition Paper 41/14, Rome, Italy; and
  – JECFA (2006c). Residues of some veterinary drugs in animals and foods. FAO, Rome, Italy (in press).
[943] EC's comments on the replies of the experts, Annex F-1, p. 40.

mutations, 20-100 uM for micronuclei induction, and 400uM for LacI mutations."[944]

7.821 This statement seems to confirm JECFA's conclusions, as recalled by Dr. Boisseau:

"[I]n its fifty fourth session, JECFA concluded from the review of a range of assays in vitro and in vivo that melengestrol acetate is not genotoxic. It also agreed upon the fact that 'no firm conclusion could be drawn about the carcinogenic potential of melengestrol acetate in ICR mice ... the increased incidence of malignant tumors in the highest-dose group of prepubertal C3Han/f mice was assumed to be due not to a direct carcinogenic effect of melengestrol acetate but to the promoting effect of increased prolactin concentrations'."[945]

7.822 Dr. Boisseau's comment is confirmed by Dr. Boobis, referring *inter alia* to study 4 of the 17 studies commissioned by the European Communities:

"There is no convincing evidence that trenbolone acetate, MGA and zeranol are genotoxic. They were negative in a range of tests for genotoxicity. They were very weakly positive in a micronucleus test, at high (potentially cytotoxic) concentrations. Trenbolone also produced a low level of DNA adducts measured by 32P-post-labelling *(Metzler and Pfeiffer, 2001)*.[946] As indicated above, micronuclei can arise via a non-genotoxic mechanism, particularly at concentrations that may have caused some toxicity. In addition, the 32P-post-labelling assay is not specific, and data cited above suggest that DNA adduction can arise by mechanisms other than direct interaction with DNA. In no case did any of the compounds produce a mutagenic response. These data are insufficient to support the conclusion that these hormones have genotoxic potential in vivo. Thus, there is no evidence that any of the hormones are genotoxic in vivo at the levels found in meat from treated animals. Even if GVP were not followed, the levels of exposure to the hormones would be such that no genotoxicity would be anticipated in vivo."

7.823 Dr. Guttenplan also agreed that:

---

[944] 2002 Opinion, section 4.5.3, p. 18,"The general conclusions", states that "[d]ata on the genotoxicity of melengestrol acetate indicate only weak effects", p. 22.

[945] Reply of Dr. Boisseau to question 16 of the Panel, Annex D, para. 161.

[946] Dr. Boobis cited to Metzler M and Pfeiffer E (2001). Genotoxic potential of xenobiotic growth promoters and their metabolites. APMIS, **109**:89-95, see Annex D, para. 198.

"[T]here is no conclusive evidence presented by the EC that the five hormones other than oestradiol-17β, when consumed as residues in meat have genotoxic potential. There is some evidence that certain of the hormones have genotoxic potential, but generally the potential is weak. ... MGA is negative in genotoxicity assays. Any genotoxic effects of the five hormones are likely to be minimized by good veterinary practice."[947]

7.824 We note that the European Communities argues that new studies have brought fresh evidence which depart from the majority view. At our request, the experts commented on the 17 studies commissioned by the European Communities. Regarding study 4, which is referred to in the 2002 Opinion, Dr. Boobis confirmed the negative results concerning mutagenicity and genotoxicity of melengestrol acetate:

"[i]n study 4 (mutagenicity and genotoxicity of MGA), MGA was negative in studies of the induction of *hprt* mutations in V79 cells, the induction of micronuclei in V79 cells and the induction of *lac*I mutations in *E coli*. Pure MGA had no effect on apoptosis, which could potentially confound interpretation of studies using V79 cells."[948]

7.825 Dr. Boobis adds, with respect to DNA adducts, that:

"[P]reliminary studies with rat liver slices, reported in an abstract but not yet published in the peer reviewed literature, suggested that MGA could produce unidentified adducts with DNA. As indicated above, there are mechanisms of adduct formation that do not involve direct interaction of the inducing compound with DNA. Overall, a report of putative covalent binding to DNA observed using 32P-post-labelling is not sufficient to over-ride the consistently negative results of MGA in a range of tests for mutagenicity. Hence, on the basis of the findings in study 5, there is no reasons to change the risk assessment or MGA."[949]

7.826 Regarding carcinogenicity of melengestrol acetate, we note that melengestrol acetate has not been evaluated by IARC, nor have the specific risks from the consumption of meat from cattle treated with this growth promotion

---

[947] Reply of Dr. Guttenplan to question 21 of the Panel, Annex D, para. 200. Dr. Guttenplan, referring to the 2002 Opinion, mentioned that his reply for the hormones at issue would not have been different in September 2003.

[948] Reply of Dr. Boobis to question 62 of the Panel, Annex D, para. 486.

[949] Reply of Dr. Boobis to question 62 of the Panel, Annex D, para. 486.

hormone.[950] In reply to a question from the Panel on whether the carcinogenic effects of the hormones at issue were related to a mechanism other than hormonal activity, Dr. Boisseau replied that:

"[i]n its 1999 report, SCVPH concluded, about the carcinogenicity of melengestrol, that: 'in view of the lack of data on mutagenicity/carcinogenicity and on DNA interactions and in consideration of carcinogenicity studies conducted only in one animal species, these data are inadequate to assess the carcinogenic potential of melengestrol.' Therefore, the scientific evidence relied upon in the SCVPH Opinions does not support the conclusion that the carcinogenic effects of melengestrol are related to a mechanism other than hormonal activity."[951]

7.827 The European Communities contests these comments, arguing that Dr. Boisseau interprets lack of data as lack of adverse effect.[952] We do not agree with the European Communities. The test to be met under Article 5.7 is that relevant scientific evidence be insufficient, and we have considered that, in this case, this implied that there be a critical mass of new evidence and/or information that calls into question the fundamental precepts of previous knowledge and evidence so as to make relevant, previously sufficient, evidence now insufficient. This is also the case for melengestrol acetate. We recall that JECFA evaluated this hormone on two occasions. This suggests that evidence has been at one point sufficient. Having regard to this context, we do not read the EC comment, nor any evidence presented in the course of these proceedings, as meeting the above-mentioned test.

Conclusion

7.828 Having regard to our specific conclusions above, we recall that the Appellate Body clarified in *Japan – Apples* that relevant scientific evidence will be insufficient within the meaning of Article 5.7 if the body of available scientific evidence does not allow, in quantitative or qualitative terms, the performance of an adequate assessment of risks as required under Article 5.1. In this respect, we note that, at our request, the experts also expressed their views on the more general question whether the scientific evidence available at the time of the adoption of Directive 2003/74/EC and subsequently allowed the conduct of a risk assessment, in relation to meat from cattle treated, *inter alia,* with melengestrol acetate. Dr. Boobis replied that:

---

[950] IARC reply to question 25 of the Panel, Annex E-3, p. 129.
[951] Reply of Dr. Boisseau to question 16 of the Panel, Annex D, para. 162.
[952] EC's comments on the experts replies, question 16, Annex F-1, p. 13.

"[T]here was sufficient information available to the EC to have enabled it to have conducted an assessment of the risks to human health arising from consumption of meat from cattle treated with any of the six hormones at issue."

7.829 We also note Dr. Guttenplan's comment with respect to JECFA's risk assessment that:

"The assessment for melengestrol acetate seems sound. Thorough metabolic and estrogenic studies have been carried out."[953]

7.830 These general remarks support our conclusions on the specific elements discussed above. We therefore conclude that it is not established that the relevant scientific evidence is insufficient with respect to melengestrol acetate, within the meaning of Article 5.7 of the *SPS Agreement*.

(xii)   Conclusion

7.831 We recall that we asked the scientific experts whether the scientific evidence relied upon by the European Communities supports the EC contention that the new scientific studies that have been initiated since 1997 have identified new important gaps, insufficiencies and contradictions in the scientific information and knowledge now available on these hormones such that more scientific studies are necessary before the risk to human health from the consumption of meat from cattle treated with these hormones for growth promotion purposes can be assessed.[954]

7.832 Three experts replied. In his written reply, Dr. Guttenplan saw several important gaps and gave examples. However, at the meeting with the Panel, he specified that, "on subsequent reading, [he] could not find anything to indicate adverse effect, and [he] now think[s] that risk assessment is alright."[955] He added that "the ability [to make a risk assessment] varies between compounds, but that does not mean you can't make a risk assessment, it just means the accuracy of the risk assessment is different."[956] The other two experts considered that "these new data [provided by the European Communities] [did] not demonstrate any important gaps, insufficiencies or contradictions in the scientific information used by JECFA for conducting its risk assessments" (Dr. Boisseau)[957], or that "[t]here was little information in the scientific studies initiated by the EC since 1997 that support the contention that they have identified important new gaps,

---

[953] Reply of Dr. Guttenplan to question 61 of the Panel, Annex D, para. 458.
[954] Panel question 62.
[955] Transcript of the Panel meeting with the experts, Annex G, para. 981.
[956] Transcript of the Panel meeting with the experts, Annex G, para. 983.
[957] Reply of Dr. Boisseau to question 62 of the Panel, Annex D, para. 460.

insufficiencies and contradictions in the scientific information and knowledge on the hormones, and that additional studies are necessary before the risks to health of consumption of meat from treated animals can be assessed" (Dr. Boobis).[958] Dr. Boobis elaborated as follows:

> "Whilst additional information has been obtained on a number of aspects of the hormones in question, this was often not definitive, sometimes it was not relevant, in some instances it confirmed or expanded on previous knowledge. The evidence obtained did not indicate any additional concern regarding the risk from exposure to residues of the hormones in meat from cattle treated for growth promotion."

7.833 We also note that, at our meeting with experts, Dr. Cogliano and Dr. Boobis confirmed, in response to a question from the Panel, that the data were sufficient to perform a risk assessment based on ADI, as done by JECFA.[959]

7.834 We recall that the test we applied in this case was that there must be a critical mass of new evidence and/or information that calls into question the fundamental precepts of previous knowledge and evidence so as to make relevant, previously sufficient evidence now insufficient. We note that the experts who expressed themselves in detail on this matter have confirmed, both in general and for each of the five hormones subject to a provisional ban, that such critical mass had not been reached.

7.835 For all these reasons, we conclude that it has not been demonstrated that relevant scientific evidence was insufficient, within the meaning of Article 5.7 of the *SPS Agreement*, in relation to any of the five hormones with respect to which the European Communities applies a provisional ban.

7.836 We recall that all four of the requirements identified by the Appellate Body in *Japan – Agricultural Products II* with regard to the application of Article 5.7 of the *SPS Agreement* must be satisfied in order to adopt and maintain a provisional measure. The Appellate Body noted that the four requirements are "clearly cumulative in nature". Since we found that the first requirement (the measure is imposed in respect to a situation where "relevant scientific evidence is insufficient") has not been satisfied, we do not find it necessary to address any of the three other requirements. We therefore conclude that the EC compliance measure does not meet the requirements of Article 5.7 of the *SPS Agreement* as

---

[958] Reply of Dr. Boobis to question 62 of the Panel, Annex D, para. 495.
[959] Transcript of the Panel meeting with the experts, Annex G, Dr. Cogliano, para. 871; Dr. Boobis, para. 873.

far as the provisional ban on progesterone, testosterone, zeranol, trenbolone acetate and melengestrol acetate is concerned.

7.837 Having reached that conclusion, we want to make clear that we only determined that it had not been established that the existing relevant scientific evidence was insufficient. This does not mean that no measure can be imposed by
the European Communities under the *SPS Agreement* in relation to the five hormones at issue. Indeed, our determinations are without prejudice to the legality
of any EC measure regarding these hormones, should the European Communities decide to complete its risk assessments pursuant to Article 5.1 of the
SPS Agreement.

(g)   Compatibility of the EC implementing measure
with Article 3.3 of the *SPS Agreement* with
respect to all hormones at issue with the exception
of melengestrol acetate

Summary of the main arguments of the parties[960]

7.838 The **United States** argues that the European Communities' import ban is
not "based on" international standards within the meaning of Article 3.3 as the
relevant standards adopted by Codex permit trade in meat and meat products
from cattle treated with hormones for growth promotion purposes by setting
MRLs, as necessary, for residues of the hormones.[961]

7.839 The United States argues that, although Members may introduce or maintain sanitary measures which result in a higher level of sanitary protection than
would be achieved by measures based on the relevant international standards,
guidelines or recommendations, the European Communities is not permitted to
do so because it does not satisfy the requirement in Article 3.3 that such stricter
measures be in accordance with paragraphs 1 through 8 of Article 5. Specifically, the United States argues that because the European Communities measure
is not based on a risk assessment within the meaning of Article 5.1, or otherwise
satisfies the conditions for maintaining a provisional measure within the meaning of Article 5.7, the European Communities is acting contrary to Article 3.3.[962]

7.840 The United States contends that Article 3.3 of the *SPS Agreement* requires that Members base their measures on international standards where they

---

[960] A more detailed account of the parties' arguments can be found in Section IV of the descriptive
part of this Report. The order in which the respective arguments of the parties are presented does not
reflect any allocation of the burden of proof by the Panel.
[961] US's first written submission, para. 163.
[962] US's first written submission, para. 164.

exist and only permits Members to diverge from such standards if there is a scientific justification for doing so. For purposes of this dispute, the United States contends that such scientific justification could have taken the form of a properly conducted risk assessment for oestradiol. However, the United States believes it has demonstrated that the European Communities has failed to provide such a justification.[963]

7.841 The **European Communities** does not dispute that its ban on oestradiol-17β is not based on international standards, namely the Codex standard which requires no average daily intake or maximum residue levels for oestradiol-17β. Instead, the European Communities argues that it is permitted instead to prohibit the placing on the market, including a ban on imports, of meat and meat products treated with oestradiol-17β for growth promotion purposes because its decision is based on a comprehensive risk assessment, which is not in violation of Article 5.1 of the *SPS Agreement.*[964]

7.842 Additionally, the European Communities argues that it decided not to use the Codex standard on oestradiol-17β, because the Codex recommendations are not only old but also do not allow the European Communities to achieve the level of protection it considers appropriate in its territory.[965]

7.843 With respect to the other five hormones, the European Communities considers that it is possible, in the presence of an international standard, guideline or recommendation that is based on a risk assessment, to adopt a provisional sanitary measure on the grounds that the relevant scientific evidence is insufficient. A Member may disagree with the risk assessment for scientific reasons and, in particular, on the issue of whether the scientific evidence relied upon is sufficient. Such disagreement may stem from differences of views on scientific questions such as methodology, data interpretation etc. It may also result from the fact that in order to meet a higher level of protection, the Member concerned may require more information than what is provided in the risk assessment in question. As a concrete example, the JECFA study referred to by the defending parties did not take into account the data obtained in the seventeen studies which had been performed upon the initiative and with the funding of the European Communities.[966]

---

[963] US's replies to Panel questions after the second substantive meeting, Annex C-3, para. 27.

[964] EC's second written submission, paras. 213-214.

[965] EC's second written submission, para. 119; EC's replies to Panel questions after the first substantive meeting, Annex B-1, para. 129.

[966] EC's replies to Panel questions after the first substantive meeting, question 72, Annex B-1.

Reasoning of the Panel

7.844 Article 3.3 reads as follows:

"Members may introduce or maintain sanitary ... measures which result in a higher level of sanitary ... protection than would be achieved by measures based on the relevant international standards, guidelines or recommendations, if there is a scientific justification, or as a consequence of the level of sanitary ... protection a Member determines to be appropriate in accordance with the relevant provisions of paragraphs 1 through 8 of Article 5.[967] Notwithstanding the above, all measures which result in a level of sanitary ... protection different from that which would be achieved by measures based on international standards, guidelines or recommendations shall not be inconsistent with any other provision of this agreement."

7.845 We concluded above that the European Communities did not comply with Article 5.1 and with Article 5.7 of the *SPS Agreement*. In light of our mandate and of our objectives in engaging in a review of the conformity of the EC implementing measure with the *SPS Agreement*, we see no reason to reach a conclusion on Article 3.3 of the *SPS Agreement*, to the extent that this conclusion depends on a violation of Article 5.

7.846 We therefore refrain from drawing any conclusion with respect to Article 3.3 of the *SPS Agreement*.

(h)   Conclusion on Article 22.8 of the DSU

7.847 For the reasons stated above, we conclude that it has not been established that the European Communities has removed the measure found to be inconsistent with a covered agreement.

7.848 We also note that the European Communities does not claim that it has provided a solution to the nullification or impairment of benefits suffered by the United States within the meaning of Article 22.8 of the DSU.

7.849 None of the parties has claimed that a mutually satisfactory solution had been found in the context of the *EC – Hormones* case.

---

[967] (*footnote original*) For the purpose of paragraph 3 of Article 3, there is a scientific justification if, on the basis of an examination and evaluation of available scientific information in conformity with the relevant provisions of this agreement, a Member determines that the relevant international standards, guidelines or recommendations are not sufficient to achieve its appropriate level of sanitary ... protection.

7.850 For these reasons and those developed above, we find that the European Communities did not demonstrate a breach of Article 22.8 of the DSU by the United States.

4. Violation of Articles 23.1 and 3.7 of the DSU

7.851 The Panel recalls its understanding that violations of Articles 23.1 and 3.7 were only claimed in relation to the violation of Article 22.8 of the DSU. To the extent that Article 22.8 has not been breached, the European Communities has not established a violation of Articles 23.1 and 3.7 of the DSU. The Panel concludes that there is no violation of Articles 23.1 and 3.7 of the DSU by the United States as a result of a breach of Article 22.8.

D. Violation of Article I.1 and Article II of the GATT 1994

7.852 The European Communities has claimed that there is a violation of Articles I:1 and II of the GATT 1994 because the US continued suspension of obligations could not be justified anymore under Article 22 of the DSU.

7.853 In light of our conclusions above, we see no basis to make findings in relation to these claims.

E. Conditional Claim of Violation of Article 22.8 of the DSU Made in the Alternative

7.854 We recall that the European Communities also raised a *conditional* claim of violation of Article 22.8 of the DSU *per se*. The European Communities specified in its first written submission that this claim was "made in the alternative and only on the condition that the Panel does not establish any violation under Articles 23.1, 23.2(a), 3.7, 22.8 and 21.5 of the DSU".[968]

7.855 We note that we have established a violation of Article 23.1 and 23.2(a). We also recall that we have already addressed the alleged violation of Article 22.8 of the DSU as part of our review of the EC claim of violation of Article 23.1 read together with Article 22.8 and Article 3.7 of the DSU. Under those circumstances, it is not necessary for the Panel to address the conditional claim of violation 22.8 of the DSU *per se* in the alternative.

---

[968] EC's first written submission, para. 132.

F. Conclusion

7.856 For the reasons set forth in this report, the Panel concludes that, with respect to the claims of the European Communities concerning the violation of Article 23.2(a) read together with Articles 21.5 and 23.1 of the DSU, the United States made the following procedural violations:

(a) by seeking, through the measure at issue – that is the suspension of concessions or other obligations subsequent to the notification of the EC implementing measure (Directive 2003/74/EC) – the redress of a violation of obligations under a covered agreement without having recourse to, and abiding by, the rules and procedures of the DSU, the United States has breached Article 23.1 of the DSU;

(b) by making a determination within the meaning of Article 23.2(a) of the DSU to the effect that a violation had occurred without having recourse to dispute settlement in accordance with the rules and procedures of the DSU, the United States has breached Article 23.2(a) of the DSU.

7.857 In addition, having addressed the claims raised by the European Communities concerning Article 23.1 read together with Articles 22.8 and 3.7 of the DSU based on the considerations mentioned above[969], the Panel concludes that:

(a) to the extent that the measure found to be inconsistent with the *SPS Agreement* in the *EC – Hormones* dispute (WT/DS26) has not been removed by the European Communities, the United States has not breached Article 22.8 of the DSU;

(b) to the extent that Article 22.8 has not been breached, the European Communities has not established a violation of Articles 23.1 and 3.7 of the DSU *as a result of a breach of Article 22.8.*

VIII. RECOMMENDATIONS

8.1 Article 3.8 of the DSU provides that "[i]n cases where there is an infringement of the obligations assumed under a covered agreement, the action is considered prima facie to constitute a case of nullification or impairment". The United States failed to rebut this presumption. Therefore, to the extent the United States has acted inconsistently with its obligations under the DSU, it must be presumed to have nullified or impaired benefits accruing to the European Communities under that Agreement.

---

[969] See Section VII.C.2 and Section VII.C.3(a), (b) and (c) above.

8.2   In the light of these conclusions, the Panel recommends that the Dispute Settlement Body request the United States to bring its measure into conformity with its obligations under the DSU.

8.3   Whereas it is for the Members to decide on the appropriate steps needed to bring measures found in breach of their WTO obligations into conformity, the Panel deems it important to recall its conclusion in paragraph 7.251 as the parties have apparently diverging opinions as to how this report should be implemented by the respondent. As already mentioned, while the Panel performed functions similar to that of an Article 21.5 panel, this was done only in order to determine whether Article 22.8 of the DSU had been breached. This Panel was not called upon, nor does it have jurisdiction, to determine the compatibility of Directive 2003/74/EC with the covered agreements. In that context, the Panel suggests that, in order to implement its findings under Article 23 and in order to ensure the prompt settlement of this dispute, the United States should have recourse to the rules and procedures of the DSU without delay.

Cumulative List of Published Disputes

Australia - Subsidies Provided to Producers and Exporters of Automotive Leather

Complaint by the United States (WT/DS126)

Report of the Panel	DSR 1999:III, 951
Report of the Panel - Recourse to Article 21.5 of the DSU	DSR 2000:III, 1189

Brazil - Export Financing Programme for Aircraft

Complaint by Canada (WT/DS46)

Report of the Appellate Body	DSR 1999:III, 1161
Report of the Panel DSR 1999:III, 1221	
Report of the Appellate Body - Recourse to Article 21.5 of the DSU	DSR 2000:VIII, 4067
Report of the Panel - Recourse to Article 21.5 of the DSU	DSR 2000:IX, 4093
Report of the Panel - Second Recourse to Article 21.5 of the DSU	DSR 2001:XI, 5481
Decision by the Arbitrators - Recourse to Arbitration by Brazil under Article 22.6 of the DSU and Article 4.11 of the *SCM Agreement*	DSR 2002:I, 19

Brazil - Measures Affecting Desiccated Coconut

Complaint by the Philippines (WT/DS22)

Report of the Appellate Body	DSR 1997:I, 167
Report of the Panel	DSR 1997:I, 189

Brazil - Measures Affecting Import of Retreaded Tyres

Complaint by the European Communities (WT/DS332)

Report of the Appellate Body	DSR 2007:IV, 1527
Report of the Panel	DSR 2007:V, 1649

Canada - Certain Measures Affecting the Automotive Industry

Complaint by the European Communities (WT/DS142);
Complaint by Japan (WT/DS139)

Report of the Appellate Body	DSR 2000:VI, 2985
Report of the Panel	DSR 2000:VII, 3043
Award of the Arbitrator under Article 21.3(c) of the DSU	DSR 2000:X, 5079

Canada - Certain Measures Concerning Periodicals

Complaint by the United States (WT/DS31)

Report of the Appellate Body	DSR 1997:I, 449
Report of the Panel	DSR 1997:I, 481

Canada - Term of Patent Protection

Complaint by the United States (WT/DS170)

Report of the Appellate Body	DSR 2000:X, 5093
Report of the Panel	DSR 2000:XI, 5121
Award of the Arbitrator under Article 21.3(c) of the DSU	DSR 2000:IX, 4537

Chile - Price Band System and Safeguard Measures Relating to Certain Agricultural Products

Complaint by Argentina (WT/DS207)

Report of the Appellate Body	DSR 2002:VIII, 3045
Report of the Panel	DSR 2002:VIII, 30127
Award of the Arbitrator under Article 21.3(c) of the DSU	DSR 2003:III, 1237
Report of the Appellate Body - Corrigendum	DSR 2006:XII, 5473

Recourse to Article 21.5 of the DSU by Argentina

Report of the Appellate Body	DSR 2007:II, 513
Report of the Panel	DSR 2007:II, III, 613

Chile - Taxes on Alcoholic Beverages

Complaint by the European Communities (WT/DS87), (WT/DS110)

Report of the Appellate Body	DSR 2000:I, 281
Report of the Panel	DSR 2000:I, 303
Award of the Arbitrator under Article 21.3(c) of the DSU	DSR 2000:V, 2583

Dominican Republic - Measures Affecting the Importation and Internal Sale of Cigarettes

Complaint by Honduras (WT/DS302)

Report of the Appellate Body	DSR 2005:XV, 7367
Report of the Panel	DSR 2005:XV, 7425

Arbitration under Article 21.3(c) of the DSU (WT/DS302/17)

Report of the Arbitrator	DSR 2005:XXIII, 11663

Egypt - Definitive Anti-Dumping Measures on Steel Rebar from Turkey

Complaint by Turkey (WT/DS211)

Report of the Panel	DSR 2002:VII, 2667

European Communities - Anti-Dumping Duties on Imports of Cotton-Type Bed Linen from India

Complaint by India (WT/DS141)

Report of the Appellate Body	DSR 2001:V, 2049

Report of the Appellate Body (Recourse to Article 21.5
of the DSU by India)   DSR 2003:III, 965

Report of the Panel   DSR 2001:VI, 2077

Report of the Panel - Recourse to Article 21.5
of the DSU   DSR 2003:IV, 1269

**European Communities - Anti-Dumping Duties on Malleable
Cast Iron Tube or Pipe Fittings from Brazil**
Complaint by Brazil (WT/DS219)

Report of the Appellate Body   DSR 2003:VI, 2613

Report of the Panel   DSR 2003:VII, 2701

**European Communities - Anti-Dumping Measure on Farmed
Salmon from Norway**
Complaint by Norway (WT/DS337)

Report of the Panel   DSR 2008:I, 3

**European Communities – Conditions for the Granting of
Tariff Preferences to Developing Countries**
Complaint by India (WT/DS246)

Report of the Appellate Body   DSR 2004:III, 951

Report of the Panel   DSR 2004:III, 1037

Award of the Arbitrator under Article 21.3 (c)
of the DSU   DSR 2004:IX, 4313

**European Communities – Countervailing Measures on
Dynamic Random Access Memory Chips
from Korea**
Complaint by Korea (WT/DS299)

Report of the Panel   DSR 2005:XVIII, 8671

**European Communities - Customs Classification of Certain
Computer Equipment**
Complaint by the United States (WT/DS62, WT/DS67,
WT/DS68)

Complaint by the United States - Ireland

Complaint by the United States - United Kingdom

Report of the Appellate Body   DSR 1998:V, 1851

Report of the Panel   DSR 1998:V, 1891

**European Communities - Customs Classification of Frozen
Boneless Chicken Cuts**
Complaint by Brazil and Thailand (WT/DS269,
WT/DS286)

Report of the Appellate Body   DSR 2005:XIX, 9157

Complaint by Brazil (WT/DS269)

Report of the Panel DSR 2005:XIX, 9295

Complaint by Thailand (WT/DS286)

Report of the Panel DSR 2005:XX, 9721

Arbitration under Article 21.3(c) of the
Understanding on Rules and Procedures Governing
the Settlement of Disputes DSR 2006:XII, 5441

European Communities - Export Subsidies on Sugar

Complaint by Australia, Brazil, Thailand
(WT/DS265, WT/DS266, WT/DS283)

Report of the Appellate Body DSR 2005:XIII, 6365

Complaint by Australia (WT/DS265)

Report of the Panel DSR 2005:XIII, 6499

Complaint by Brazil (WT/DS266) DSR 2005:XIV, 6793

Report of the Panel

Complaint by Thailand (WT/DS283)

Report of the Panel DSR 2005:XIV, 7071

Arbitration under Article 21.3(c) of the Understanding
on Rules and Procedures Governing the Settlement
of Disputes (WT/DS265/33, WT/DS266/33,
WT/DS283/14)

Award of the Arbitrator DSR 2005:XXIII, 11579

**European Communities - Measures Affecting Asbestos and
Asbestos-Containing Products**

Complaint by Canada (WT/DS135)

Report of the Appellate Body DSR 2001:VII, 3243

Report of the Panel DSR 2001:VIII, 3305

**European Communities - Measures Affecting the Approval
and Marketing of Biotech Products**

Complaint by United States, Canada, Argentina
(WT/DS291, WT/DS292, WT/DS293)

Report of the Panel DSR 2006:III, 847

**European Communities - Measures Affecting the Importation
of Certain Poultry Products**

Complaint by Brazil (WT/DS69)

Report of the Appellate Body DSR 1998:V, 2031

Report of the Panel DSR 1998:V, 2089

**European Communities – Measures Affecting Trade in
Commercial Vessels**

Complaint by Korea (WT/DS301)

Report of the Panel DSR 2005:XV, 7733

European Communities - Measures Concerning Meat and Meat Products (Hormones)

Complaint by Canada (WT/DS48);
Complaint by the United States (WT/DS26)

Report of the Appellate Body	DSR 1998:I, 135
Report of the Panel (Canada)	DSR 1998:II, 235
Report of the Panel (United States)	DSR 1998:III, 699
Award of the Arbitrator under Article 21.3(c) of the DSU	DSR 1998:V, 1833
Decision by the Arbitrators under Article 22.6 of the DSU (Canada)	DSR 1999:III, 1135
Decision by the Arbitrators under Article 22.6 of the DSU (United States)	DSR 1999:III, 1105

European Communities – Protection of Trademarks and Geographical Indications for Agricultural Products and Foodstuffs

Complaint by the United States (WT/DS174)

Report of the Panel	DSR 2005:VIII-IX, 3499,4083

Complaint by Australia (WT/DS290)

Report of the Panel	DSR 2005:X-XI, 4603,5121

European Communities - Regime for the Importation, Sale and Distribution of Bananas

Complaint by Ecuador; Guatemala; Honduras; Mexico; and the United States (WT/DS27)

Report of the Appellate Body	DSR 1997:II, 589
Report of the Panel (Ecuador)	DSR 1997:III, 3
Report of the Panel (Guatemala, Honduras)	DSR 1997:II, 695
Report of the Panel (Mexico)	DSR 1997:II, 803
Report of the Panel (United States)	DSR 1997:II, 943
Award of the Arbitrator under Article 21.3(c) of the DSU	DSR 1998:I, 3
Decision by the Arbitrators under Article 22.6 of the DSU (US)	DSR 1999:II, 725
Report of the Panel - Recourse to Article 21.5 of the DSU (European Communities)	DSR 1999:II, 783
Report of the Panel - Recourse to Article 21.5 of the DSU (Ecuador)	DSR 1999:II, 803
Decision by the Arbitrators under Article 22.6 of the DSU (Ecuador)	DSR 2000:V, 2237

European Communities - Selected Customs Matters

Complaint by United States (WT/DS315)

Report of the Appellate Body	DSR 2006:IX, 3791
Report of the Panel	DSR 2006:IX, 3915

**European Communities - The ACP-EC Partnership
Agreement - Recourse to Arbitration Pursuant to the
Decision of 14 November 2001 (WT/L/616)**

Award of the Arbitrator	DSR 2005:XXIII, 11667

**European Communities - The ACP-EC Partnership
Agreement - Second Recourse to Arbitration Pursuant to
the Decision of 14 November 2001 (WT/L/625)**

Award of the Arbitrator	DSR 2005:XXIII, 11701

European Communities - Trade Description of Sardines

Complaint by Peru (WT/DS231/R)

Report of the Appellate Body	DSR 2002:VIII, 3359
Report of the Panel	DSR 2002:VIII, 3451

European Communities - Trade Description of Scallops

Complaint by Canada (WT/DS7);
Complaint by Chile (WT/DS14);
Complaint by Peru (WT/DS12)

Report of the Panel (Canada)	DSR 1996:I, 89
Report of the Panel (Chile, Peru)	DSR 1996:I, 93

**Guatemala - Anti-Dumping Investigation Regarding Portland
Cement From Mexico**

Complaint by Mexico (WT/DS60)

Report of the Appellate Body	DSR 1998:IX, 3767
Report of the Panel	DSR 1998:IX, 3797

**Guatemala - Definitive Anti-Dumping Measures on Grey
Portland Cement from Mexico**

Complaint by Mexico (WT/DS156)

Report of the Panel	DSR 2000:XI, 5295

India - Measures Affecting the Automotive Sector

Complaint by European Communities (WT/DS146)
Complaint by the United States (WT/DS175)

Report of the Appellate Body	DSR 2002:V, 1821
Report of the Panel	DSR 2002:V, 1827

**India - Patent Protection for Pharmaceutical and Agricultural
Chemical Products**

Complaint by European Communities (WT/DS79);
Complaint by the United States (WT/DS50)

Report of the Appellate Body (United States)	DSR 1998:I, 9
Report of the Panel (European Communities)	DSR 1998:VI, 2661

United States - Countervailing Duty Investigation on Dynamic Random Access Memory Semiconductors (DRAMS) from Korea

Complaint by Korea (WT/DS296)

Report of the Appellate Body	DSR 2005:XVI, 8131
Report of the Panel	DSR 2005:XVII, 8243

United States - Countervailing Measures Concerning Certain Products from the European Communities

Complaint by European Communities (WT/DS212)

Report of the Appellate Body	DSR 2003:I, 5
Report of the Panel	DSR 2003:I, 73

Recourse to Article 21.5 of the DSU by the European Communities

Report of the Panel	DSR 2005:XVIII, 8950

United States - Customs Bond Directive for Merchandise Subject to Anti-Dumping/Countervailing Duties

Complaint by Thailand, India and United States (WT/DS343, WT/DS345)

Report of the Appellate Body	DSR 2008:VIII, 2773
Report of the Panel	DSR 2008:VIII, 2925

United States - Definitive Safeguard Measures on Imports of Certain Steel Products

Complaint by Brazil (WT/DS259);
Complaint by China (WT/DS252);
Complaint by European Communities (WT/DS248);
Complaint by Japan (WT/DS249);
Complaint by Korea (WT/DS251);
Complaint by New Zealand (WT/DS258);
Complaint by Norway (WT/DS254);
Complaint by Switzerland (WT/DS253)

Report of the Appellate Body	DSR 2003:VII, 3117
Report of the Panel	DSR 2003:VIII, 3273

United States - Definitive Safeguard Measures on Imports of Circular Welded Carbon Quality Line Pipe from Korea

Complaint by Korea (WT/DS202)

Report of the Appellate Body	DSR 2002:IV, 1403
Report of the Panel	DSR 2002:IV, 1473
Award of the Arbitrator under Article 21.3(c) of the DSU	DSR 2002:V, 2061

United States - Definitive Safeguard Measures on Imports of Wheat Gluten from the European Communities

Complaint by the European Communities (WT/DS166)

Report of the Appellate Body	DSR 2001:II, 717
Report of the Panel	DSR 2001:III, 779

United States - Final Anti-Dumping Measures on Stainless Steel from Mexico

Complaint by Mexico (WT/DS344)

Report of the Appellate Body	DSR 2008:II, 513
Report of the Panel	DSR 2008:II, 599

United States - Final Countervailing Duty Determination with Respect to Certain Softwood Lumber from Canada

Complaint by Canada (WT/DS257)

Report of the Appellate Body	DSR 2004:II, 587
Report of the Panel	DSR 2004:II, 659
Recourse by Canada to Article 21.5 of the DSU	
Report of the Appellate Body	DSR 2005:XXIII, 11355
Report of the Panel	DSR 2005:XXIII, 11399

United States - Final Dumping Determination on Softwood Lumber from Canada

Complaint by Canada (WT/DS264)

Report of the Appellate Body	DSR 2004:V, 1917
Report of the Panel	DSR 2004:V, 1981
Arbitration under Article 21.3(c) of the DSU (WT/DS264)	
Report of the Arbitrator	DSR 2004:X, 5011
Report of the Appellate Body - Recourse to Article 21.5 of the DSU by Canada	DSR 2006:XII, 5087
Report of the Panel - Recourse to Article 21.5 of the DSU by Canada	DSR 2006:XII, 5147

United States - Import Measures on Certain Products from the European Communities

Complaint by the European Communities (WT/DS165)

Report of the Appellate Body	DSR 2001:I, 373
Report of the Panel	DSR 2001:II, 413

United States - Imposition of Countervailing Duties on Certain Hot-Rolled Lead and Bismuth Carbon Steel Products Originating in the United Kingdom

Complaint by the European Communities (WT/DS138)

Report of the Appellate Body	DSR 2000:V, 2595
Report of the Panel	DSR 2000:VI, 2623

United States - Import Prohibition of Certain Shrimp and Shrimp Products

Complaint by India (WT/DS58);
Complaint by Malaysia (WT/DS58);
Complaint by Pakistan (WT/DS58);
Complaint by Thailand (WT/DS58)

Report of the Appellate Body	DSR 1998:VII, 2755
Report of the Panel	DSR 1998:VII, 2821
Report of the Appellate Body - Recourse to Article 21.5 of the DSU (Malaysia)	DSR 2001:XIII, 6481
Report of the Panel - Recourse to Article 21.5 of the DSU (Malaysia)	DSR 2001:XIII, 6529

United States – Investigation of the International Trade Commission in Softwood Lumber from Canada

Complaint by Canada (WT/DS277)

Report of the Panel	DSR 2004:VI, 2543
Report of the Appellate Body - Recourse to Article 21.5 of the DSU by Canada	DSR 2006:XI, 4865
Report of the Panel - Recourse to Article 21.5 of the DSU by Canada	DSR 2006:XI, 4935

United States - Laws, Regulations and Methodology for Calculating Dumping Margins ("Zeroing")

Complaint by European Communities and the United States (WT/DS294)

Report of the Appellate Body	DSR 2006:II, 417
Report of the Panel	DSR 2006:II, 521

United States - Measure Affecting Imports of Woven Wool Shirts and Blouses from India

Complaint by India (WT/DS33)

Report of the Appellate Body	DSR 1997:I, 323
Report of the Panel	DSR 1997:I, 343

United States - Measures Affecting the Cross-Border Supply of Gambling and Betting Services

Complaint by Antigua (WT/DS285)

Report of the Appellate Body	DSR 2005:XII, 5663

United States - Safeguard Measures on Imports of Fresh, Chilled or Frozen Lamb Meat from New Zealand and Australia

Complaint by Australia (WT/DS178);
Complaint by new Zealand (WT/DS177)

Report of the Appellate Body	DSR 2001:IX, 4051
Report of the Panel	DSR 2001:IX, 4107

United States - Section 110(5) of the US Copyright Act

Complaint by the European Communities (WT/DS160)

Report of the Panel	DSR 2000:VIII, 3769
Award of the Arbitrator under Article 21.3(c) of the DSU	DSR 2001:II, 657
Award of the Arbitrator under Article 25 of the DSU	DSR 2001:II, 667

United States - Sections 301-310 of the Trade Act of 1974

Complaint by the European Communities (WT/DS152)

Report of the Panel	DSR 2000:II, 815

United States - Section 211 Omnibus Appropriations Act of 1998

Complaint by the European Communities (WT/DS176)

Report of the Appellate Body	DSR 2002:II, 589
Report of the Panel	DSR 2002:II, 683

United States- Section 129(c)(1) of the Uruguay Round Agreements Act

Complaint by Canada (WT/DS221)

Report of the Panel	DSR 2002:VII, 2581

United States - Standards for Reformulated and Conventional Gasoline

Complaint by Brazil (WT/DS4);
Complaint by Venezuela (WT/DS2)

Report of the Appellate Body	DSR 1996:I, 3
Report of the Panel	DSR 1996:I, 29

United States – Subsidies on Upland Cotton

Complaint by Brazil (WT/DS267)

Report of the Appellate Body	DSR 2005:I, 3
Report of the Panell	DSR 2005:II- III- IV- V- VI, 297
Recourse by Brazil to Article 21.5 of the Understanding on Rules and Procedures Governing the Settlement of Disputes	
Report of the Appellate Body	DSR 2008:III, 809
Report of the Panel	DSR 2008:III, 997

United States - Sunset Review of Anti-Dumping Duties on Corrosion-Resistant Carbon Steel Flat Products from Japan

Complaint by Japan (WT/DS244)

Report of the Appellate Body	DSR 2004:I, 3
Report of the Panel	DSR 2004:I, 87

United States – Sunset Reviews of Anti-Dumping Measures on Oil Country Tubular Goods from Argentina

Complaint by Argentina (WT/DS268)

Report of the Appellate Body	DSR 2004:VII, 3341
Report of the Panel	DSR:2004:VIII, 3421

Arbitration under Article 21.3(c) of the DSU (WT/DS268/12)

Award of the Arbitrator	DSR:2005:XXIII, 11617

Recourse by Argentina to Article 21.5 of the Understanding on Rules and Procedures Governing the Settlement of Disputes (WT/DS268)

Report of the Appellate Body	DSR 2007:IX, 3529
Report of the Panel	DSR 2007:IX, 3615
	DSR 2007:X, 3829

United States - Tax Treatment for "Foreign Sales Corporations"

Complaint by the European Communities (WT/DS108)

Report of the Appellate Body	DSR 2000:III, 1619
Report of the Panel	DSR 2000:IV, 1675
Report of the Appellate Body - Recourse to Article 21.5 of the DSU	DSR 2002:I, 55
Report of the Panel - Recourse to Article 21.5 of the DSU	DSR 2002:I, 119
Decision by the Arbitrator under Article 22.6 of the DSU and Article 4.11 of the *SCM Agreement*	DSR 2002:VI, 2517
Report of the Appellate Body - Second Recourse to Article 21.5 of the DSU by the European Communities	DSR 2006:XI, 4721
Report of the Panel - Second Recourse to Article 21.5 of the DSU by the European Communities	DSR 2006:XI, 4761